SOCIOLOGY, STUDENTS, AND SOCIETY

JEROME RABOW

University of California at Los Angeles

with the assistance of
Ellen Neiman and Roberta Lee Stern

GOODYEAR PUBLISHING COMPANY, INC.
Pacific Palisades, California

© 1972 by GOODYEAR PUBLISHING COMPANY, INC.
Pacific Palisades, California

Current printing (last digit) :

10   9   8   7   6   5   4   3   2   1

ISBN : 0-87620-870-7

Library of Congress Catalog Card Number : 77-181344

Y-8707-5

Printed in the United States of America

This book is dedicated to
Joshua Mark
and
David Michael

Contents

Preface   xi

PART 1 Introduction: Basic Concepts and
Perspective   **3**

Chapter 1: *Sociology, Students and Social Scientists*   4

Uses and Purposes of Sociology   4

The Role of the Social Scientist   5

Social Science in Crisis   *Robert S. Lynd*   7

Science in Human Relations   *George A. Lundberg*   13

". . . Who Shall Prepare Himself to the Battle?"
Thomas Ford Hoult   23

Chapter 2: *The Perspective of Sociology*   36

Levels of Analysis   36

The Study of Group Properties   37

Some Effects of Certain Communication Patterns
on Group Performance   *Harold J. Leavitt*   39

Group Leadership and Institutionalization
Ferenc Merei   46

Chapter 3: *The Setting of Social Organization*   62

Population   62

Environment   64

Technology   65

v

vi

Famine 1975: Fact or Fallacy   *Paul R. Ehrlich*   66

The Search for Environmental Quality: The Role
  of the Courts   *Joseph L. Sax*   79

Technology and Social Change: Choosing a Near Future
  Kent D. Shinbach   90

PART 2 The Image of Man in Society   **99**

Chapter 4: *The Image of Man in Society: Culture*   102

The Essence of Culture   102
Culture as a Group Property   104
Values and Norms   104

The Diversity of Culture   *Ruth Benedict*   106
Things in Common   *Ulf Hannerz*   113
Body Ritual Among the Nacirema   *Horace Miner*   124

Chapter 5: *The Image of Man in Society: Interaction*   132

The Intertwining of Social Interaction,
  Relationship and Organization   132
Elements and Parts   133
Interaction Contingencies   134

Negotiating Reality: Notes on Power in the Assessment
  of Responsibility   *Thomas J. Scheff*   136
I Never Promised You a Rose Garden
  Hannah Green   153
The Routinization of Love: Structure and Process in
  Primary Relations   *Guy E. Swanson*   159

Chapter 6: *The Image of Man in Society:
  Socialization*   188

Societal and Individual Views of Socialization   188
Internalization   189
Position and Role   190

Cultural Contradictions and Sex Roles
  Mirra Komarovsky   195
The Married Professional Woman: A Study in the
  Tolerance of Domestication   *Margaret M. Poloma* and
  T. Neal Garland   201
The Irwins   *R. D. Laing* and *Aaron Esterson*   212

PART 3 Patterns of Social Organization **225**

Chapter 7: *Definition and Criteria of Social
    Organization* 228

Generic Concept of Social Organization 228
Patterns of Social Organization 228
Criteria for Evaluating Social Organizations 229

Death by Dieselization. A Case Study in the Reaction to
    Technological Change *W. F. Cottrell* 233
Commitment and Social Organization: A Study of
    Commitment Mechanisms in Utopian Communities
    Rosabeth Moss Kanter 243

The Cincinnati Social Unit Experiment:
    1917-19 *Anatole Shaffer* 269

The Death and Ressurection of
    the Rural Village *Stan Steiner* 284

Chapter 8: *Patterns of Loyalty* 296

Attraction 296
Cohesion 297
Primary Groups 297
Problems of Multiple Membership 298
Conflict 298

Lysistrata *Aristophanes* 301
The Significance of Multiple-Group Membership in
    Disaster *Lewis Killian* 318
Secrecy and the Police *William A. Westley* 326

Chapter 9: *Patterns of Exchange* 334

Interdependence 335
Functional Differentiation 335
Functional Integration 335
Specialization and Alienation 336

The Mature Society: Personal Autonomy and Social
    Responsibility *Marvin E. Olsen* 338
The American Student Movement: Causes and Implications
    Samuel R. Friedman 351
On Face Work: An Analysis of Ritual Elements in
    Social Interaction *Erving Goffman* 358

viii

Chapter 10: *Patterns of Control*   386

Imperative Order and Social Control   386
Definition of Power   387
Sources of Power   387
Resistance to Power   388
Legitimacy, Deviance, and the Labelling Theory   389

Some Conditions of Obedience and Disobedience to
   Authority   *Stanley Milgram*   391
Liberating Effects of Group Pressure
   Stanley Milgram   405
The Wartime Evacuation   *Harry H. Kitano*   413
The Defects of Total Power   *Gresham M. Sykes*   427

Chapter 11: *The Establishment of a Normative Order*   438

The Importance of Normative Order   438
Types of Norms   439

The Provo Experiment in Delinquency Rehabilitation
   La Mar T. Empey and *Jerome Rabow*   441
What the First "Teach-In" Taught Us
   Kenneth E. Boulding   463

PART 4 The Background of Contemporary
      Society   **471**

Chapter 12: *Folk, Feudal, Preindustrial and Urban-
      Agrarian Societies*   474
Some Views of the Shift   474
The Social Organization of Folk Society   475
Folk Urban Continuum   476
Preindustrial City   476
Urban-Agrarian Society   477
Transformation of the Feudal Order   478

The Folk Society   *Robert Redfield*   480
The Preindustrial City   *Gideon Sjoberg*   500
The Communist Manifesto   *Karl Marx* and
   Friedrich Engels   510

PART 5 Modern Society   **521**

Chapter 13: *Bureaucracy*   524

Legitimation and Authority   524

Weber's Typology of Authority   525

Weber's Criteria for Bureaucracy   525

Critique of Weber's Views   526

Bureaucratic Pathologies   527

Bureaucracy and Metaphysical Pathos   527

Co-operation and Competition in a Bureaucracy
   Peter M. Blau   529

The "Liberation" of Gary, Indiana   *Edward Greer*   536

Chapter 14: *Mass and Totalitarian Society*   556

Modern Society as Mass Society   556

Kornhauser's Typology   556

Accessible Elites   558

Pluralism   559

The Garrison State   *Harold D. Lasswell*   559

Mass Society and Extremist Politics
   Joseph R. Gusfield   570

The Theme of Contemporary Social Movements
   Ralph H. Turner   586

Chapter 15: *Social Mobility, Pluralism, and the
   Quality of Life*   602

Social Mobility   602

Mobility in the United States   602

Structural Factors Affecting Mobility   603

Review and Reconciliation: Pluralism and Mobility   604

Social Organization and the Quality of Life   606

Indians and Modern Society   *Vine Deloria, Jr.*   608

The Making of a Counter Culture   *Theodore Roszak*   620

The Search for New Forms   *Stokely Carmichael* and
   Charles V. Hamilton   633

A Case Study of Innovation   *Elting E. Morison*   641

How to Commit Revolution in Corporate America
   G. William Domhoff   655

Appendix: Bringing It All Back Home   *Ellen Neiman*
   and *Patricia Strauss*   680

Preface

The fact that there has been great movement and flux in American sociology over the past ten years indicates that there is no one way to introduce students to the field. Students today are calling for relevance and honesty in learning about their social world. These students with their own unique interests, values, and personal concerns have done much to bring about new and different approaches to the teaching of sociology and have helped to initiate a new direction in the kinds of texts used in introductory courses.

There are also other reasons for the proliferation of introductory sociology books in the past few years. The number of trained sociologists has increased and the theoretical and empirical work that they have produced has provided new challenge and vigor to the field. Also, the number of students who enroll and major in sociology continues to spiral. As a discipline, sociology attracts students because it focuses on social life as a whole. In an age when social life seems to be fragmented, incomplete, and somewhat devoid of meaning, the attempts of sociologists to account for the total patterns within societies or other social units is especially compelling.

This book attempts to bring the view of sociology as social organization to bear upon the crucial problems of our time. Studying sociology can help to clarify and refocus student concerns and values. My participation in the discipline as a student and as a teacher has required that I try to make sense out of the fragmentation and multiple perspectives in the field in order for sociology to serve this purpose. Sociologists are not merely concerned with describing, analyzing, and understanding the means and processes by which social life, or an organization develops; how social arrangements change; how units break down, become disorganized, evolve or dissolve. Although, in reality, a great deal of contemporary sociological work is involved with the study of interpersonal phenomena. These phenomena are an important *part* of the study of social organization, but cannot be equated with it. I have tried to clarify the distinction between the study of the

xii

individual and the study of social organization by using illustrative material, and by showing how a generic concept—social organization —can be useful in analyzing and understanding social life.

My viewpoint that sociology is the study of social organization is certainly not a radical departure from traditional sociological thought, but I have tried to be more conscious about this perspective in my choice of readings as well as with the chapter introductions. Rather than using essays on poverty, the family, and ethnic groups as separate chapter units, I have tried to develop the concept of social organization as a tool to bring insight and coherence to sociology. The attempts by sociologists to discover principles and to explain some of the processes about total social units was my major guide in the selection of readings.

The book is organized into chapters consisting of introductory sections and then articles which illustrate, elaborate, and clarify some of the concepts that were discussed. In each chapter introduction, I refer to the specific articles in order to provide a link between theory and illustrative material. I have used both well known, established readings and contemporary materials in order to provide students with a sense of balance and historical perspective in the discipline of sociology and the study of society. In addition, one of my special interests is the methods of discussion learning. While this book was compiled for use in any introductory class, the readings were selected with an eye towards their use in discussions. The appendix, "How to Bring It Back Home," grew experientially from courses taught by two different discussion methods. It was written to provide instructors and students with suggestions for the implementation of discussion learning techniques.

I hope that my professional colleagues will recognize the Michigan orientation in this text. My graduate education at the University of Michigan, in a program of sociology and psychology headed by Theodore Newcomb, was a rare experience. Students had the opportunity to work closely with professors with a wide variety of interests and to study with a cohort of students who were seriously concerned with each other as well as the state of the field. This program encouraged teaching and research by graduate students and many did give seminars and did teach classes. My experiences in teaching an honors section of introductory sociology contributed greatly to my interest in this project. In addition to supportive arrangements, I had invaluable encouragement from Guy E. Swanson, Albert J. Reiss, Jr., and Leon Mayhew. The latter was especially helpful, as I had an opportunity to work as a teaching assistant in his introductory sociology course. The students who helped produce an intellectual community at Michigan included Dodd Bogart, Dave Bradford, Mark Chesler, Jack Fowler, Ernie Harburg, Peggy Hofeller, Allen Kraut, Ron Lambert, Judy Long, Dave Lundgren, and Shalom Schwartz.

Roberta L. Stern did a major job in criticizing and editing first and second drafts of these chapters, and helped to select and review articles from a student's perspective. David Fein, Marta Greenwald, and Patricia Strauss also helped judge articles and materials for their relevance. Ellen Neiman did a final review of articles and helped with

the last revision. Much of the clarity of the text is due to her effort and **xiii**
energy, and her insistence that students need to be listened to and
challenged. The typing chores fell to Barbara Lieberman and Aban
Commissariat, who accepted my ultimatums graciously and responsibly. Barbara Bain, Mary Takami, and Adele Fishgold helped me
meet my deadlines.

It is traditional for authors to express their appreciation to
individuals and groups who facilitated their intellectual development
and academic careers. I would like to go a step further. A portion of
the royalties from the sale of this book will be given to my department to provide funds for both graduate and undergraduate students
in financial need, especially those from minority groups. In a small
way, this is an attempt to attack the cycle of poverty, inequality, and
discrimination often perpetuated by our university system. I hope that
this act will be emulated by others, so that in time a considerable
impact can be achieved.

Alfred W. Goodyear and David Grady of Goodyear Publishing
have been patient, generous, and helpful. Al Goodyear has my special
thanks for his longstanding encouragement.

Finally, there are Joshua and David, my children, to whom this
book is dedicated, who have little to do with the text but much to
do with me.

Introduction:
Basic Concepts
and Perspective

PART **1**

This section introduces some of the issues involved in social research and discusses goals, purposes, and uses of sociology. The sociological levels of analysis and the external factors that influence and bound groups are presented and examined.

AWARENESS

Dilemma

REASON

MORTIFICATION

Passion

RATIONALITY

CHOICE

CHANGE

MANKIND

CONSCIOUSNESS

RELEVANCE

KNOWLEDGE

Crisis

JUDGMENT

Human Nature

Personal Freedom

CONCERN

Study Questions

1. What should be the goals of undergraduate education?
2. What does academic freedom mean?
3. Should social scientists take an active role in politics?
4. Should social scientists work for change?
5. How can sociology be useful to you?

Sociology, Students, and Social Scientists

1 This chapter examines the uses and purposes of sociology, the role of the social scientist, and his relationship to society.

USES AND PURPOSES OF SOCIOLOGY

Studying sociology is exciting primarily because it involves you in the process of discovery. Sometimes it can be the discovery and exploration of unfamiliar worlds—the occult world, the world of crime, the world of the military leader or of the industrialist. However important and exciting such experiences might be, the process of discovery becomes even more impressive when the sociologist perceives worlds that are familiar but whose meanings have been transformed. Sociology, as a distinctive way of viewing our everyday surroundings, becomes exciting when we can look anew and see afresh. The process of transforming understanding into a higher form of awareness and consciousness can lead to greater personal freedom. How does this movement from knowledge to enhanced freedom occur?

Imagine that you have just finished reading an article in your local newspaper about student protest at a school's employment office, in which the demonstrators are expelled from school. On the same page you read about welfare mothers who have successfully won an increase in their weekly welfare payments. You might ask yourself which group was more successful and why. An easy response would be that the difference in the degree of success attained in each case was due to the number of people, the amount of power, or the kinds of influence. But it would be difficult to assess the importance of each factor without a systematic analysis of the events. A more general question, which involves not only students and welfare mothers but rich and poor, men and women, blacks and whites, asks: What are the conditions under which an act of apparent rebellion might be seen as protest which can successfully lead to change? Knowledge based on well-documented and systematically gathered evidence assists us in interpreting and understanding events, and can aid us in answering

4

that general question. It can help students take rational, conscious, meaningful positions on important issues.

The point is that greater awareness means enlarged choice and therefore greater freedom. At the same time, the study of sociology is not inevitably linked to social adjustment or change. The knowledge and understanding of a community, of an ethnic group, of a university classroom or of a commune, does not necessarily lead the student to conform or adjust to the system, or to initiate change in the environment. Knowledge sustained by a sociological perspective provides tools which the student or the citizen can use to uphold, confirm, or modify his surroundings, if he so chooses.

The learning of sociology, then, should introduce students to the diverse ways in which man carries on his collective social life. Sociology's attempt to discover and develop principles about total social systems is both attractive and difficult for the beginning student. I hope this book will help develop students' awareness of the diversity of social life, and in so doing provide them with a vantage point from which to judge and evaluate their own society in a more objective, systematic manner. As the student comes to understand why and how societies and organized social life flourish, he may be able to exercise greater judgment and control over his own environment.

You may still wonder about the practical uses of sociology. It would be fair to say that sociologists have been concerned with the description and, wherever possible, the explanation of how social events have taken place. They have not, for the most part, been engaged in trying to change the course of events. But by focusing on the arrangement of social life, on the structure of social events, sociology provides a framework from which meaningful change-oriented activity may spring. More fundamentally, sociological thought conveys the potentiality of human nature and the opportunities, the failures, and the achievements which flow from man's collective efforts.

Whatever their own views, most of the instructors or students using this book will agree that the study of mankind, the attempt to regard a society or a group as a whole and to compare it with other forms of social life, is valuable in undergraduate education, because sociology broadens understanding and increases sympathy and empathy with one's fellow men. The study of sociology may develop in the student a greater sense of his relationship to others.

The articles and excerpts for this reader have been chosen for the most part because they indicate the way in which sociologists have attempted to develop principles about organized social life, and because they speak to student concerns and, hopefully, contribute to knowledge and freedom. The issues that I have introduced above—the uses of sociology and the role of sociologists in society—are the background to the more detailed arguments by the authors in this chapter.

THE ROLE OF THE SOCIAL SCIENTIST

Robert S. Lynd's provocative and still-relevant book, *Knowledge for What?* was written in 1939, and the excerpt from it pleads for attention to the world crisis which the author witnessed at that time.

6 Lynd quotes W. H. Auden, who suggested that the scientist may continue to lecture on navigation "while the ship is going down." He calls for the social scientist to work in areas relevant to the concerns of civilization and mankind. He notes that man's mastery of his physical environment stands in sharp contrast to the floundering of his social institutions. He asserts that if the questions being asked of social scientists are not answered by them, they will be answered by "practical" men such as the "hard-headed politician," who is pressured by interest blocks and concerned with votes. There is, of course, another side to this. Robert K. Merton, a colleague of Lynds at Columbia, expressed this alternative view in the following way:

It's not the sociologist's fault that society is in bad need of his help today, when his science is still immature. Suppose that three centuries ago, Harvey had been told to limit himself to the problem of coronary thrombosis just when he was trying to establish the fact of the circulation of the blood? If sociology in its present state were to address itself only to practical problems, it would never become the science you yourself want it to be—a science whose benefits will be as wonderful as they are unpredictable.[1]

The position taken by Lynd is challenged by George A. Lundberg in the second selection included in this chapter. In an excerpt taken from his book *Can Science Save Us,* written in 1947, Lundberg deprecates those who would not continue to search for and study the basic principles of their subject matter. He discusses the accomplishments of social science, the cost of the establishment of society based upon scientific management, and the neutrality of social science. Lundberg argues that social science can and should thrive in a totalitarian regime as well as in a democratic country. You will have to answer for yourself whether Lundberg's or Lynd's position is more acceptable.

The final selection in this chapter, written 30 years after Lynd's by Thomas Ford Hoult, takes a slightly different and more complex stance than either Lynd's or Lundberg's. Hoult argues that the very qualities of the social scientist—his interest in free inquiry and his willingness to follow any leads—are essential to the development of a "good" society. Hoult argues that it is important for sociologists to disengage from the "ethical neutrality" tradition of sociology.

While Lynd and Lundberg assume that social scientists could influence man's progress, Hoult notes that scientists may be so provincial and narrow-minded as to function as an elite—an elite which may be estranged from large numbers of its fellow citizens. Lynd and Lundberg do not talk to that issue. One may also bring into question the general issue of reason in human affairs. Lundberg recognizes that the advancement of science does not lead to an increase in the reasoning ability of the general population, and he assumes that the scientific elite will work for the general interest of the people. Hoult is much more pessimistic. I shall return to the issue of science in human affairs in our final chapter.

These three authors pose the following questions: What is the role of the social scientist as a public person? Should the social scientist

make value judgments and work for social change? How can we ensure
that freedom of inquiry is maintained for social scientists? Is there
a way for men to be concerned with the major social issues of the day
and still be committed to science and reason as methods attacking social
problems? Should undergraduate education be concerned with the
training of students in technical or professional terms or with increasing general reasoning abilities, social awareness, and, hence, freedom?
The fact that debate has raged over these questions for so long means
that answers must come from each generation, each student, each
citizen.

NOTES

1. Morton M. Hunt. "Profiles: How Does It Come to Be So?" *New Yorker*,
Jan. 28, 1961, p. 63.

ROBERT S. LYND

Social Science in Crisis

Contemporary social science contains within itself two types of orientation that divide it into two blocs of workers: the scholars and the
technicians. Both work within the protective tradition of free intellectual inquiry; and both assume continuity and relevance between their
respective realms in the common task of exploring the unknown. Actually they tend to pull apart, the scholar becoming remote from and even
disregarding immediate relevancies, and the technician too often accepting the definition of his problems too narrowly in terms of the
emphases of the institutional environment of the moment. The gap
between the two, while not sharp or even commonly recognized, is
significant for two reasons: important problems tend to fall into oblivion between the two groups of workers; and the strains generated by
current institutional breakdowns are prompting sharp and peremptory
scrutiny of the roles and adequacy of the social sciences. Nazi power-
politics has stripped the social sciences in Germany of their intellectual
freedom, while professors-in-uniform in Italy have been forced to
betray their heritage by solemnly declaring the Italian population to be
of Aryan origin. This is a critical time for social science.

The scholarly bloc among social scientists is placed in jeopardy
precisely by that leisurely urbanity upon which it prides itself as it
looks out upon the confusions in the midst of which we live. The time

Knowledge for What? by Robert S. Lynd (Copyright 1939 © 1967 by
Princeton University Press), pp. 1–10. Reprinted by permission of Princeton University Press and Robert S. Lynd.

8 outlooks of the scholar-scientist and of the practical men of affairs who surround the world of science tend to be different. The former works in a long, leisurely world in which the hands of the clock crawl slowly over a vast dial; to him, the precise penetration of the unknown seems too grand an enterprise to be hurried, and one simply works ahead within study walls relatively sound-proofed against the clamorous urgencies of the world outside. In this time-universe of the scholar-scientist certain supporting assumptions have grown up, such as "im-person objectivity," "aloofness from the strife of rival values," and the self-justifying goodness of "new knowledge" about anything, big or little. Such a setting has tended to impart a quality of independent validity and self-sufficiency to the scholar-scientist's work. The practical man of affairs, on the other hand, works by a small time-dial over which the second-hand of immediacy hurries incessantly. "Never mind the long past and the infinite future," insists the clattering little monitor, "but do this, fix this—now, before tomorrow morning." It has been taken for granted, in general, that there is no need to synchronize the two time-worlds of the scholar-scientist and of the practical man. Immediate relevance has not been regarded as so importanat as ulti-mate relevance; and, in the burgeoning nineteenth century world which viewed all time as moving within the Master System of Progress, there was seemingly large justification for this optimistic tolerance.

Our contemporary world is losing its confidence in the inevita-bility of Progress. Men's ways of ordering their common lives have broken down so disastrously as to make hope precarious. So headlong and pervasive is change today that the scholar's historical parallels are decreasingly relevant as present guides, because so many of the varia-bles in the situation have altered radically. The scholar-scientist is in acute danger of being caught, in the words of one of Auden's poems,

> Lecturing on navigation while the ship is going down.

Both scholar and technician are placed in a new and exposed position by the recent sharp shift in the relative importance of the so-cial sciences. Until the great depression that began in 1929, they were poor relations of the natural sciences. In a world whose "progress" and "manifest destiny" were so generally accepted as dependent upon the production of goods, natural science and its technologies seemed to be the primary antecedents to general welfare. Edison, Ford, the Wright brothers—men like these, aided of course by American business enter-prise, were the great creators, and American boys have placed such men with the traditional political giants, Washington and Lincoln, as the "great Americans." An increasing stream of able young scientists flowed into the private laboratories of General Electric, United States Steel, Du Pont, and other corporations, there to develop new alloys and plastics. A world of enterprising businessmen which bought inven-tion and efficiency by giving subsidies to science appeared to be the latest and happiest formula in that succession of lucky circumstances known as "the American way."

In this world, which had hitched its dreams to material progress, the social sciences moved less confidently. They were newer, afraid of being thought unscientific by their rich relations, and generally less venturesome. Dealing as they do with the familiar fabric of institution-alized behavior, they were especially exposed when they ventured upon novel hypothesis or prediction. If they erred, popular familiarity with their subject-matters, and their consequent lack of mystery, brought swifter ridicule from the man on the street than is generally meted out to the worker within the sheltered walls of a natural-science laboratory. Then, too, the monistic theory of progress through business prosperity rendered divergence from the customary suspect and extra-hazardous *ab initio.* "Radical" means one thing in a natural-science laboratory and something vastly different in the social sciences. So the social sciences were prone to content themselves with the retrospective look, or with describing and analyzing current trends, like a retailer taking inventory of the stock on his shelves. Such an astute critic as Parring-ton pointed out near the close of the 1920s that political science and economies have "largely joined the Swiss guards" protecting the inner sanctuary of the vested system.[1] This over-ready acceptance of the main assumptions of the going system has been a source of confusion and embarrassment to the social sciences as that system has become highly unmanageable since the World War, and particularly since 1929.

The depression has reversed the relative emphases upon the nat-ural and the social sciences. The poor relation finds itself wealthy and important—or at least supposed to act as if it were—while the former rich relative finds itself in the unaccustomed position of being less im-portant. For it is the intractability of the human factor, and not our technologies, that has spoiled the American dream; and the social sci-ences deal with that human factor. The depression has made us acutely aware of the fact that our brilliant technological skills are shackled to the shambling gait of an institutional Caliban. As a result—

... While man's effort to control the forces of Nature is ac-companied by increasing success and mounting optimism, his efforts to regenerate society lead only to confusion and despair.
... We see no lack of fertile farms, of elaborate and fully equipped factories, no lack of engineers and technicians and mechanics to operate the factories and cultivate the farms. ... Yet we note that the factories are running intermittently or not at all, that the farms are cultivated only in part. It is not that all have enough; for we see millions of men and women, lacking the necessities of life. ... We see ... other men, in obedience to governmental decree, refrain from plant-ing wheat and plow growing cotton under ground. A survey of human history will often enough disclose millions of men starving in time of famine: what we see now is something unprecedented—millions of men destitute in the midst of potential abundance....
... Mankind has entered a new phase of human progress—a time in which the acquisition of new implements of power too swiftly outruns the necessary adjustment of habits and ideas to the novel conditions created by their use.[2]

Some people have even clamored for a moratorium on inven-tions until the rest of our living can catch up; while NRA codes have

10 struggled to slow down the introduction of more efficient machinery, and relief work has been done in many cases by hand in order to thwart the labor-efficiency of the machine. Were Thorstein Veblen alive, he would smile sardonically at this evidence that our institutional sabotaging of machine-efficiency has at last come of age as an officially sanctioned public practice.

The spotlight has turned with painful directness upon the social sciences. And it has found them, in the main, unprepared to assume the required responsibility. We social scientists have great arrays of data:

> data on production and distribution, but not the data that will enable us to say with assurance, as the experts dealing with such matters, how our economy can get into use all of the needed goods we are physically capable of producing;
>
> data on past business cycles, but not data that enabled us to foresee the great depression of 1929 even six months before it occured;[3]
>
> data on labor problems, but not the data to provide an effective program for solving the central problems of unemployment and of the widening class-cleavage between capital and labor;
>
> legal data, but not the data to implement us to curb admittedly increasing lawlessness;
>
> data on public administration, non-voting, and politics, but not data for a well-coordinated program with which to attack such central problems of American democracy as the fading meaning of "citizenship" to the urban dweller and what Secretary Wallace has called the "private ownership of government" by business;[4]
>
> data on the irrationality of human behavior and on the wide inequalities in intelligence, but not the data on how a culture can be made to operate democratically by and for such human components.

Is the difficulty, as the social sciences maintain, that they do not have "enough data"? Or do we have data on the wrong problems? Or are too many of our data simply descriptive and too infrequently projective and predictive in the sense of being aimed at deliberate planning and control? Or are they too atomistic, reyling upon the "unseen hand" of circumstances and upon common sense to tie bits of knowledge together and to make them work? All of these are involved. The net result is none the less decidedly uncomfortable—for the social sciences and for our American culture which supports them.

A world floundering disastrously because of its inability to make its institutions work is asking the social sciences: "What do you know? What do you propose?" And, unfortunately for the peace of mind of the social scientist, these questions are not asked with complete dispassion; not infrequently they are loaded in the sense of, "Tell us what we want to hear, or else—!" For the social sciences are parts of culture, and it so happens that they are carried forward predominantly by college and university professors, who in turn are hired by business-men trustees. The stake of these last in the status quo is great. That is why they are trustees. The social scientist finds himself caught, there-fore, between the rival demands for straight, incisive, and, if need be, radically divergent thinking, and the growing insistent demand that his thinking shall not be subversive. The solution of problems that beset the culture requires the utmost use of intelligence. And, as P. W. Bridgeman of Harvard University has remarked,[5] "The *utmost* exercise of intelligence means the *free* use of intelligence; [the scientist] must be willing to follow *any* lead that he can see, undeterred by any inhibi-tion, whether it arises from laziness or other unfortunate personal characteristics, or intellectual tradition or the social conventions of his epoch. In fact, intelligence and *free* intelligence come to be synony-mous to him. It becomes inconceivable that anyone should consent to conduct his thinking under demonstrable restrictions, once these re-strictions had been recognized, any more than as an experimenter he would consent to use only a restricted experimental technique." But in a world rapidly being forced to abandon the sunny tolerance of individ-ual trial and error under *laissez-faire*, "the utmost exercise of free intelligence" will be continually in jeopardy. And nowhere will the strain be so great as in the social sciences, for they deal with the white-hot core of current controversy, where passions are most aggravated and counsel most darkened.

Under these circumstances our university administrators—those who control fates of working social-scientists—are in some important cases wavering. They are concerned in their enforced daily decisions with the short-run "welfare of an institution," and this may be viewed as not synonymous with the long-run welfare of our American culture. To go ahead frankly into the enlarged opportunity confronting the so-cial sciences invites trouble. Putting one's head into the lion's mouth to operate on a sore tooth has its manifest disadvantages. So we are wit-nessing today an active administrative espousal of the humanities, and controversies over the wisdom of the "liberal arts" emphasis as over against the "over-practical" emphasis of the social sciences. "After all," runs the administrator's comment, in effect, "education should make rounded men. The university's job is not to solve problems but to turn out men with a liberal education, possessed of the great wisdoms of the past, ripe in judgment, and having the ability to meet the varied problems of life."

And so it is. It is not the intention in the pages which follow to deprecate the humanities or education in the liberal arts. The fact that most social science research must go forward in our culture within colleges and universities, however, makes the policies of educational administrators of direct relevance to the problems on which this re-search engages. Insistent public dilemmas clamor for solution. Deci-sions will be made and public policies established—because no delaying or turning back is possible in this hurrying climactic era. If the social scientist is too bent upon "waiting until all the data are in," or if uni-versity policies warn him off controversial issues, the decisions will be made anyway—without him. They will be made by the "practical" man

12

and by the "hard-headed" politician chivvied by interested pressure-blocs.

* * *

A final word as to the social researcher as teacher: Most social science research is done by men who gain their main livelihood as teachers. The problems they select for research determine to a considerable extent what they teach. And what they teach determines to an important degree the outlook of their students upon technical problems and related policies; and, in the case of those students who will go on to make a career of research, the teaching they receive will influence heavily the kind and acuteness of the problems they will eventually elect to investigate. Like everyone else, the teacher has given heavy hostages to fortune: he has a family to rear, usually on a not too ample salary; his income depends upon the academic advancements he can win, and these in turn depend upon "productive research"; he has been sensitized to research by his training, his head is full of projects he wants to get at, and yet research increasingly demands in these days that the golden sun of outside funds shine upon the would-be investigator. He lives in a world which, by and large, is not asking, "Is Smith trying to get at the facts? Is he trying to be fair and constructive at the same time that he is unwilling to pull his punch?" but which asks, "Are you for us, or against us?" Just because the need for acute, candid, fearless thinking is so great, the teacher-researcher of our generation carries perforce a heavy, inescapable responsibility. If he fails this oncoming generation at this critical moment—for reasons other than his sheer inability to comprehend, even as a so-called expert, the rush and complexity of the problems our culture confronts—his will be a desperate betrayal indeed. Upon those teachers who are on what is called, probably increasingly optimistically, "permanent tenure," there would appear to rest special obligation to carry for their less-secure junior colleagues the main brunt of hard-hitting, constructive thought that spares no one, least of all themselves.

NOTES

1. "In the welter that is present-day America militant philosophies with their clear-cut programs and assured faiths are wanting, and many feel, as Matthew Arnold felt fourscore years ago, that they are dwelling between worlds, one dead, the other powerless to be born. The old buoyant psychology is gone and in the breakdown and disintegration of the traditional individualism no new philosophies are rising. Builders of Utopias are out of a job. Political and economic theory is in charge of paymasters and is content with the drab rim of the familiar landscape. Retainer-fees have blotted out for it the lovelier horizons that earlier thinkers contemplated. Academic political scientists and economists have largely joined the Swiss guards, and abdicated the high prerogative of speculative thought. It is the men of letters—poets and essayists and novelists and dramatists, the eager young intellectuals of a drab generation—who embody the mind of present-day America; not the professional custodians of official views." (V. L. Parrington, *Main Currents in American Thought* (New York: Harcourt Brace Jovanovich, 1930), vol. 3, p. xxvii.)

2. Carl Becker, *Progress and Power* (Palo Alto: Stanford University Press, 1936), pp. 88–91.

3. The final summary chapter of the authoritative cooperative study of *Recent Economic Changes*, written as late as the spring of 1929, shares, though guardedly, the general optimism of that period regarding the future of American business. There were a few single economists, like B. M. Anderson of the Chase National Bank and H. Parker Willis of Columbia University, who viewed the prospect in the late 1920s with apprehension, but these Jeremiahs were but a minor note in the general chorus of bold or cautious optimism.

4. *New Frontiers* (New York: Reynal and Hitchcock, 1934), chap. iv.

5. "Society and the Intelligent Physicist," address before the annual meeting of the American Association of Physics Teachers in 1938, scheduled for publication in *American Physics Teacher* for March 25, 1939.

GEORGE A. LUNDBERG

Science in Human Relations

What are some examples of types of work by social scientists that are of vast importance in managing human relations?

The work of such agencies as the Census Bureau is known to all and is taken more or less for granted. Without the data and and the analyses which it provides, the administration of public affairs would certainly dissolve in choas and perhaps civil war. It is equally certain that no international organization can function without an elaborate organization of this kind to provide the essential facts regarding people and their characteristics and activities. Perhaps the most permanent contribution of the ill-fated League of Nations was the establishment of an international statistical bureau which still continues to function at Princeton University. The Office of Population Research of the same university is engaged in detailed studies of local population trends in Europe and elsewhere, including predictions of future areas of population pressure. This work would be of the utmost practical importance to the administration of any world organization. The Scripps Foundation, the Milbank Memorial Fund, and many others are engaged in similar or related work of a character that measures up very well to the standards of the physical sciences.

In the meantime anthropologists and sociologists have greatly extended our scientific knowledge of other peoples and cultures. This knowledge has in turn thrown a flood of light on our own civilization and permits the formulation at least of hypotheses regarding human behavior in general. The importance of this kind of knowledge in facilitating our contacts with other cultures during the recent war is too well known to require review. Is it not generally agreed that increasing

14

contacts make the accumulation of such knowledge imperative in peace as well as in war?

We mentioned in the preceding chapter the importance of instruments and methods of observation and measurements in the social as well as in the physical sciences. Hundreds of such instruments have already been invented by means of which vocational aptitudes, success in college and other undertakings, and social behavior of great variety can be accurately measured and predicted. Perhaps the best known, but by no means the only one, of these devices is the public opinion poll. We have in this technique an illustration of how the development of the social sciences may be significant for the future of social organization as many physical inventions have been in our industrial development.

The degree to which the public will make itself reliably felt in government and in community action has always been in the foreground of political discussion. With the expansion of the areas within which public opinion must operate, many students of the problem have despaired of the capacity of the town meeting technique adequately to make operative the public will. In the face of this situation, social scientists have developed in recent years an instrument which cheaply and accurately permits us to learn the beliefs, the attitudes, and the wishes of the rank and file of the population. To be sure, the public opinion polls are at present thought of as interesting devices mainly for predicting the outcome of elections. But this is a very minor aspect of their full possible importance. These techniques also have been extensively used in the army and as a guide to the administration of liberated areas in Europe and elsewhere. Under the auspices of allied Force Headquarters, Stuart C. Dodd developed a polling organization for determining in the invaded areas facts regarding the behavior and conditions of life as well as opinion regarding such subjects as public security, crime and the mores governing its control, the people's satisfaction with governing officials, attitudes toward co-belligerency, status of shelter and clothing, food supply and distribution, etc.

For example, complaints reached Allied authorities in Sicily regarding the malfunctioning of the rationing system. The local officials denied it and pointed to long lines of people ostensibly being served. A survey indicated that very few people had received their sugar ration for five months. Thereupon the local officials were confronted with these facts and were told to get busy. A follow-up survey in a week showed the situation greatly improved, and in two weeks practically corrected. Here we have a public which for the first time in years finds itself consulted on such matters and then observes that its complaints actually bring results. Experience of this kind probably goes farther than any propaganda for democracy that could be invented.

It may well be that in the perspective of history we have here a social invention—a technological device based on social science and on social research—which may rank in importance with gunpowder, telephone, or radio. It may be a device through which can be resolved the principal impasse of our age, namely, the apparent irreconcilability of authoritarian control on one hand and the public will on the other. It may be that through properly administered public opinion polls professionalized public officials can give us all the efficiency now claimed for authoritarian, centralized administration, and yet have that administration at all times subject to the dictates of a more delicate barometer of the people's will than is provided by all the technologically obsolete paraphernalia of traditional democratic processes. In short, it is impossible that as advancing technology in one department of our lives leads to a threatened breakdown of democracy, so an improved social technology may restore and even increase the dominance of the people's voice in the control of human society.

I envision a time when the science of public opinion will be a science comparable to meteorology; when charts of all kinds of social weather, its movements and trends, whether it be anti-Semitism, anti-Negro sentiment, or mob-mindedness, will be at the disposal of the administrators of the people's will in every land. Dodd formulated and proposed to the United Nations plans for the establishment of a Barometer of International Security[1] designed to detect authoritatively and early the tensions that lead to war. It is true that mere knowledge of these tensions does not automatically operate to alleviate them. But it is also true that a reliable diagnosis of the tension and an understanding of the sentiments that underlie it is essential for an intelligent approach to the problem. Right now it would be helpful to know exactly where are the pressure areas against Negroes and American-born Japanese. Is it not vitally important in postwar Europe to know where high and low pressure areas are in respect to the scores of minorities that must find their place in European society? We shall probably not hear anything more about the Barometer of International Security for the time being. The powers that be are obviously not interested in the wishes of the people who are being mercilessly bartered and moved about like so many pawns. But that does not affect the importance of the instrument as a technological achievement.

It would be easy to continue this recital of how developments in the social sciences already have ameliorated many social problems and have greatly facilitated public administration and policy. But the achievements are not merely in such obvious and practical fields as I have mentioned. The underlying theoretical and scientific knowledge upon which such practical devices rest must also be developed. As only one example of scientific work aiming directly at the construction and verification of scientific theory, I might call attention to Stouffer's study of the mobility habits of an urban population.[2] Stouffer observed the apparently chaotic movements of the people of Cleveland in their frequent change of apartments. But isn't this much too complex for scientific study? Well, he considered various hypotheses which might constitute a generalized description of this behavior. He finally arrived at one hypothesis, which he states in rigorous mathematical terms. He then shows that a comprehensive study of the actual behavior of the people corresponds with remarkable accuracy to this hypothesis. The resulting generalization may be stated as follows: "The number of persons going a given distance is directly proportional to the number of opportunities at that distance and inversely proportional to the number of intervening opportunities." This law has subsequently been tested for

16   other cities and large areas, and for at least one foreign country. It has already been found to hold with certain modifications and under stated conditions for the movements of the people of the United States as a whole and for Sweden.

We are not here interested primarily in the possible practical uses of these findings. I cite the case rather as an illustration of the possibility of arriving at scientific generalizations of social behavior essentially of the same sort as those that, in their full development, have proved so valuable in the physical sciences.

To those who constantly have their minds on quick and dramatic solutions to the world's troubles this type of research is likely to seem offensively trivial—a kind of fiddling while Rome burns. "Writers" are fond of referring contemptuously to basic scientific work as an "ivory tower" and as "lecturing on navigation while the ship sinks." Navigation today is what it is because some people were willing to study the *principles* of their subject while their individual ships went down, instead of rushing about with half-baked advice as how to save ships that could not be saved, or were not worth saving anyway. As A. J. Carlson has recently said: "The failure of bacteria to survive in close proximity to certain moulds looked trivial at first, but few informed people would label the discovery of that initial fact *trivial* today."

So much, then, for a few illustrations, rather than a summary, of the type of work that is being done and that needs to be done in the social sciences. Is there enough of it being done? Clearly not, or we would not need to flounder as we are in national and international affairs, pursuing diametrically opposite courses within the same decade. Can the social sciences ever hope to catch up with the other sciences, the increasingly rapid advance of which constantly creates new social problems? Certainly we can, if we devote ourselves to the business with something like the seriousness, the money, and the equipment that we have devoted to physical research. Consider how the physical scientists are today given vast resources to concentrate on the invention of a new submarine detector or a new bomb, not to mention the peacetime occupations of these scientists with penicillin and sulpha drugs. Obviously, I am not criticizing this action. On the contrary, it is the way to proceed if you want results. Is there anything like that going on regarding the world organization and its numerous subsidiary problems, all of them important to peace and prosperity?

Comparatively speaking, there is almost nothing that could be called fundamental research into the basic nature of human relations. To be sure, there are endless petty projects, surveys, conferences, oratory, and arguments by representatives of pressure groups, as if argument ever settled any scientific questions. Of basic social research there is hardly anything. Why? As we pointed out in the first chapter, it is not yet realized that scientific knowledge is relevant to a successful world organization. We still think that common sense, good will, eloquent leaders, and pious hopes are sufficient when it comes to management of social relations.

This brings us to our second question. What price must we probably pay for a social science of a comprehensiveness and reliability comparable to some of the better developed physical sciences? The costs are undoubtedly considerable, and it remains to be seen to what extent men are willing to pay them. What are some of the principal items both as regards material and psychological costs.

The mention of costs suggests that I am about to digress into the subject of research finance. The advancement of science undoubtedly does involve costs of this type. I shall not go into them here, because I am at present more concerned with other types of costs which have nothing to do with money or budgets. Let me therefore dismiss the question of monetary costs with a brief estimate by Huxley: "Before humanity can obtain," he says, "on the collective level that degree of foresight, control and flexibility which on the biological level is at the disposal of human individuals, it must multiply at least ten-fold, perhaps fifty-fold, the proportion of individuals and organizations devoted to obtaining information, to planning, to correlation and the flexible control of execution." This may seem staggering to educators who are wondering how to maintain merely their present activities. But how does the entire expenditure for scientific research compare with the price of a single battleship? The total annual prewar expenditure for scientific research of all kinds averaged, according to the recent Bush report, less than five dollars per $1,000 of national income. Consider what we have spent and are spending on war. Perhaps it will occur to the postwar generation to try a reallocation of public funds. If so, adequate research and training in social science can be readily financed.

But are we or is some future generation likely to change so radically our notions of what is worth spending money for? This brings us face to face with those costs of science which perhaps come higher, and touch us more deeply, than any of its financial costs.

First of all, the advancement of the social sciences would probably deprive us in a large measure of the luxury of indignation in which we now indulge ourselves as regards social events. This country, for example, has recently enjoyed a great emotional vapor-bath directed at certain European movements and leaders. Such indignation ministers to deep-seated, jungle-fed sentiments of justice, virtue, and a general feeling of the fitness of things, as compared with what a scientific diagnosis of the situation evokes. In short, one of the principal costs of the advancement of the social sciences would be the abandonment of the personalistic and moralistic interpretation of social events, just as we had to abandon this type of explanation of physical phenomena when we went over to the scientific orientation.

Closely related and indeed inseparably connected with the necessary abandonment, in science, of personalistic and moralistic types of explanation is the necessity of abandoning or redefining a large vocabulary to which we are deeply and emotionally attached. Concepts like freedom, democracy, liberty, independence, aggression, discrimination, free speech, self–determination, and a multitude of others have never been realistically analyzed by most people as to their actual content under changing conditions. Any such analyses, furthermore, are sure to seem like an attack upon these cherished symbols and the romantic

18   state of affairs for which they stand. As every social scientist knows, these are subjects that had better be handled with care.

*   *   *

Social sciences worthy of the name will have to examine realistically all the pious shibboleths which are not only frequently the last refuge of scoundrels and bigots, but also serve as shelters behind which we today seek to hide the facts we are reluctant to face. The question is, how much pain in the way of disillusionment about fairy tails, disturbed habits of thought, and disrupted traditional ways of behavior will the patient be willing to put up with in order to be cured of his disease? He will probably have to become a lot sicker than he is before he will consent to take the medicine which alone can save him.

Finally, the advancement of the social sciences will cost the abandonment not only of *individual concepts* carried with us from prescientific times, it will require us to abandon deeply cherished *ideologies*, resembling in form, if not in content, their theological predecessors. The notion of some final solution, preferably in our own generation, of the major social problems that agitate us is a mirage which even scientists have great difficulty in abandoning. Many of them still confuse the social sciences with various cults, religions, and political dogmas, from Marxism to astrology. Scientists must recognize that democracy, for all its virtues, is only one of the possible types of organization under which man have lived and achieved civilization.

It is a disservice to democracy as well as to science to make preposterous claims that science can prosper only under some particular form of government, that only under our particular form of political organization do minorities have rights, etc. The favorite cliche is that "science can flourish only in freedom." It is a beautiful phrase, but unfortunately it flagrantly begs the question. The question is, under what conditions will the kind of freedom science needs be provided? The historical fact is that science has gone forward under a great variety of forms of government, and conversely, at other times, has been suppressed and frustrated by each of the same types including democracy. The first truly popular democratic government in Europe, namely, the French Revolution, declared itself to have "no use for scientists" and proceeded to behead Lavoisier, the father of modern chemistry. Only a few years ago, several states, under the leadership of American "statesmen," passed laws against the teaching of evolution. American citizens of Japanese ancestry have even more recently discovered precisely what the Bill of Rights amounts to in a pinch, especially under an administration and a Supreme Court eloquent in their verbalizations about the rights of minorities. In short, the great democratic "gains" in this department appear to consist, in the opinion of qualified legal analysts,[3] of creating a legal status for minorities in the United States somewhat comparable to that which they had in Nazi Germany.

In short, attacks both on science and on "freedom" *do occur* also in democracies. I would condemn them *wherever* they occur. The attempt to make science the tail of *any* political kite whatsoever must be vigorously opposed by all scientists as well as by others who believe in uncorrupted science. Political systems have changed, and they will change. Science has survived them all as an instrument which man may use under any organization for whatever ends he seeks.

The mere fact that I, personally, happen to like the democratic way of life with all its absurdities, that I would find some current alternatives quite intolerable, and that I may even find it worth-while to go to any length in defense of democracy of the type to which I am accustomed are matters of little or no importance as touching the scientific question at issue. My attachment to democracy may be, in fact, of *scientific* significance chiefly as indicating my unfitness to live in a changing world. To accept this simple notion is perhaps a cost of social science that few are prepared to pay.

. . . What does the future promise for social scientists in the way of freedom to perform the tasks which I have outlined as their proper business?

Social scientists need not expect to escape the troubles which other scientists have encountered throught history. Chemists and physicists from time to time have suffered persecutions because of the conflict of their findings with more generally accepted views. They have continued to hew to the line, however, until today they enjoy a certain immunity and freedom of investigation which social scientists do not share. Why do physical scientists enjoy this relative security in the face of changing political regimes, and how may social scientists attain a corresponding immunity?

The answer is popularly assumed to lie in the peculiar subject matter with which social scientists deal. I doubt if this is the principal reason. I think a far more fundamental reason for the relative precariousness of the social sciences lies in their comparative incompetence.

Social scientists, unfortunately, have failed as yet to convince any considerable number of persons that they are engaged in a pursuit of knowledge of a kind which is demonstrably true, regardless of the private preferences, hopes, and likes of the scientist himself. *All* sciences have gone through this stage. Physical scientists are, as a class, less likely to be disturbed than social scientists when a political upheaval comes along, because the work of the former is recognized as of equal consequence under any regime. Social science should strive for a similar position. Individual physicists may suffer persecution, but their successors carry on their work in much the same way. If social scientists possessed an equally demonstrably relevant body of knowledge and technique of finding answers to questions, that knowledge would be equally above the reach of political upheaval. The services of *real* social scientists would be as indispensable to Fascists as to the Communists and Democrats, just as are the services of physicists and physicians. The findings of physical scientists at times also have been ignored by political regimes, but when that *has* occurred, it has been the *regime* and not the *science* that yielded in the end.

* * *

I have emphasized that physical scientists are indispensable to any political regime. Social scientists might well work toward a corresponding status. Already some of them have achieved it to a degree. Qualified social statisticians have not been and will not be disturbed greatly in their function by any political party as long as they confine themselves to their speciality. Their skill consists in the ability to draw relatively valid, unbiased, and demonstrable conclusions from societal data. *That* technique is the same, regardless of social objectives. No regime can get along without this technology. It is the possession and exercise of such skills alone that justifies the claim of academic immunity. To claim it for those who insist on taking for granted that which needs to be demonstrated can only result in the repudiation for everybody of the whole principle of academic freedom. For the same reason, we had better not become so devoted to blatant crusades for academic freedom that we forget to bolster the only foundation upon which academic freedom can ever be maintained in the long run, namely, the demonstrated capacity of its possessors to make valid and impersonal analyses and predictions of social events.

The temptation is admittedly considerable to bolster one's favorite "movement" by posing as a disinterested appraiser of the truth while actually engaging in special pleading. It is also tempting in this way to seek the right of sanctuary in the form of academic freedom to escape the ordinary consequences of pressure group activity as visited on less clever and less privileged people. Special pleading must be recognized for what it is whether it serves the CIO or the NAM. I have no objection to universities maintaining forums for special pleading nor do I object to scientists taking part in such discussion as long as no attempt is made to pass the whole thing off as "science." Too frequently scientists forget this distinction and put forward absurd scientific claims for what they personally happen to prefer.

The form of social organization which will yield to men the satisfaction they desire obviously depends upon a great number and variety of factors, including traditions, resources, technology, scientific development, and education. Scientists would do better to make it perfectly clear that their personal preferences in these matters are merely their own current preferences and not scientific conclusions valid for all times and places or conditions of people.

My conclusion, then, is that the best hope for the social sciences lies in following broadly in the paths of the other sciences. I have not tried to minimize the difficulties that beset these paths. I have merely argued that they are not insurmountable, and that in any case we really have no choice but to pursue this one hope. For we are already so heavily committed to the thoughtways and the material results of science in so large a part of our lives that we are likely to go farther in the same direction. In short, the trends that have been strikingly evident in the social sciences in recent decades will, I believe, continue at an ever more rapid rate. Social scientists will talk less and say more. They will rely ever more heavily on a more economical type of discourse, namely, the statistical and mathematical. Much of what now passes for social science will be properly relegated to other equally honorable departments, such as journalism, drama, or general literature. As such, this material will have its uses as propaganda, news, art, and a legitimate outlet for the emotions of men. Indeed, nothing I have said regarding the possibilities of scientific study of human affairs should be interpreted as in any way contemplating an abandonment or a restriction upon the artistic, religious, literary, or recreational arts which also minister to the cravings of men. I have on the contrary rather advocated that the social sciences should not handicap themselves by aggrandizing to themselves roles which they cannot fulfill.

Social scientists, as scientists, had better confine themselves to three tasks: First and foremost, they should devote themselves to developing reliable knowledge of what alternatives of action exist under given conditions and the probable consequences of each. Secondly, social scientists should, as a legitimate part of their technology as well as for its practical uses, be able to gauge reliably what the masses of men want under given circumstances. Finally, they should, in the applied aspects of their science, develop the administrative or engineering techniques of satisfying most efficiently and economically these wants, regardless of what they may be at any given time, regardless of how they may change from time to time, and regardless of the scientists' own preferences.

. . . What further consequences might we expect in a transition to a scientific view of human relations? The question has been raised as to whether the above proposal contemplates that every citizen should become a social scientist. On the contrary, the proposal is rather to relieve the ordinary citizen of many impossible duties with which he is now saddled and which, because they are impossible, he refuses to perform. The development of the physical sciences did not require every person to become skilled in every science. We do not try to teach every person that there *is* such a thing as science, and that it is better for him to consult its duly licensed practitioners rather than to doctor himself. To be sure, this is not an infallible system, but it works pretty well. I contemplate a similar relation with respect to social science.

Will the citizen, then, be expected to lean more heavily than at present on the conclusions of social scientists? Well, he can do as he pleases, but I notice that he pleases to accept rather blindly the authority of physical scientists.

A similar attitude toward the conclusions of social scientists is suspected of being authoritarian, as indeed it probably is. A lot of nonsense has been spoken and written about authority in recent years. We need to recognize that it is not authority as such that we need fear but incompetent and unwisely constituted authority. When we undertake to insist on the same criteria of authority in the social as in the physical sciences, no one will worry about the delegation of that authority, any more than he worries about the physician's authority. All persons who presume to speak with authority will be expected to submit credentials of training and character of the type that physicians and other professsionals now submit, and *to the state*, at that. This will hold for all would-be authorities whatsoever, whether they purport to speak for God

22

or for nature. The state may in turn *delegate* the function of formulating and administering these requirements back into the hands of members of the profession concerned. This does not alter the importance of retraining the ultimate authority in the hands of the community's accredited governmental agency.

Those who are more interested in labeling an idea with an epithet than in examining its validity or in refuting it, will doubtless find this idea authoritarian, fascist, and what not. That will soon become tiresome. Name-calling is quite generally recognized for what it is, namely, an attempt to distract attention from something one is afraid to examine. In any event, I am here engaged in making an analysis, and its validity is in no way affected by whether anyone likes it or not.

* * *

Scientists in general are finally awakening to the fact that unless the social sciences are developed our net reward for the development of the other sciences may be destruction. When that is fully realized, we may expect the same kind of support for the social services as the physical sciences have received and from the same sources and for the same reasons. Corporations have for some time been adding sociologists to their staffs, because what they want from business and from life is to be secured only through an adjustment of human relations in the factory as well as in the community, the nation, and between nations. Social scientists do not compete with physical scientists, but complement them. The further development of mechanical technology is of doubtful interest if the net result is to lay waste the countryside with bombs. When that fact is realized, institutes of social research will rise in every university and in every large industrial establishment.

NOTES

1. S. C. Dodd, "A Barometer of International Security," *Public Opinion Quarterly*, Summer 1945.

2. S. A. Stouffer, "Intervening Opportunities: A Theory Relating Mobility to Distance," *American Sociological Review* (1940) : 845–67.

3. *See* E. V. Rostow, "Our Worst Wartime Mistake," *Harper's*, September 1945.

THOMAS FORD HOULT

". . . Who Shall Prepare Himself to the Battle?"

The central purpose of this paper is to demonstrate that it is both logical and necessary for sociologists to become involved in at least certain aspects of building "the good society." To accomplish this purpose, the paper has three sections. the first section presents arguments to support the proposition that—

It is appropriate for sociologists, *acting as such*, to "take sides" relative to those controversial social issues which are functionally related to conditions that seem likely to enhance or undermine the development of social science.

—hence the section is concerned with providing empirically minded and discipline-oriented sociologists a logical basis for declaring themselves on selected public issues and policies; the second section is a plea to American sociologists to face up to the implications of the fact that they are, at least theoretically, the best qualified people available to lead others in building the kind of society where there would be optimum opportunity for the greatest numbers to achieve happiness; and in the final section, the various, illegitimate uses of the "ethical neutrality" position are illustrated and commented on. Underlying the discussion at every point is the writer's conviction that the future welfare of society and of sociology are interlocked—that the special knowledge and empirical methods of modern sociologists are two of the most crucial tools needed for development of the "good society," and that sociology's very existence is dependent upon preservation of those aspects of the good society that we symbolize by the term "liberalism."

SOCIOLOGY, SOCIAL ACTION, AND THE LIBERAL SOCIETY

It is a hopeless task, some assert, to attempt to rally any significant number of today's sociologists to the cause of the general welfare. Such a cause is too reminiscent of our ministerial past; it smacks of dogooderness. "The dominant drift in American sociology is toward professionalization, the growth of technical specialists toward the diffusion of the value-free outlook. . .," Alvin Gouldner has observed.[1] I agree. It is true, I believe, that most modern sociologists are profession-orientated. But, this fact does not *automatically* mean that the majority of sociologists will not contribute their services to any cause; it means—to put the

Thomas Ford Hoult, ". . . Who Shall Prepare Himself to the Battle?" Reprinted with permission of the author and the publisher from *American Sociologist*, February 1968, pp. 3–7.

24

best face on it—that he who wishes to obtain the help of sociologists in general must show that the help sought is fairly directly related to the good of the discipline. It was with this point in mind that the introductory proposition was phrased in such a way as to put total stress on sociology's development—however, it will be seen from subsequent discussion that, in large part, the same social conditions which contribute to sociology also contribute to the general welfare, hence the proposition's focus is not nearly as narrow as it may seem.

The introductory proposition will, it is hoped, appeal to the many sociologists who do not "take a stand" on controversial public issues primarily because, being profession-, not cause-, oriented—and being aware of the long-standing disagreement among honorable men about the implications of ethical neutrality—they have not been conscious of any discipline-related logical reasons for taking such stands. But there *are* such reasons, the proposition asserts—there are social conditions which enhance the development of sociology, and there are others which undermine it, and it is a perfectly proper aspect of the professional role of the sociologist to contribute to the former and work against the latter.

In effect, thus, the proposition recommends two things: 1) that in some respects it is not only *logically* necessary to dispense with the Lundbergian idea of differentiating between citizen role and scientist role—it is *wise* to dispense with the idea; and, 2) that we view the status "sociologist" as calling for a dual role involving interdependent a) research-reaching activity, and b) selected action activity.[2] Such a view of the sociologist role is simply an assertion that particular types of social action, in addition to other kinds of action, are as proper for the sociologist as is laboratory building for the chemist; neither activity is "pure science," but each is essential to its respective profession.

There may be those who will accept the idea of the dual role outlined, but who will object to the implication that *all sociologists* should engage in both of the role activities described. "What is the objection to specialization?" it might be asked. "Why would it be improper for a sociologist to specialize in either 'a' (research-teaching) *or* 'b' (social action)?" The answer to the second part of the query (dealing with the proposed social action specialty) may be phrased in the form of a question: Is there anyone in sociology today who would seriously contend that an individual engaging in social action only, and doing no research-teaching, is—on the basis of his activity—qualified for the title "sociologist"? I doubt it. On the other hand, with regard to the proposed research-teaching specialty, it is logically impossible to take a "non-position" relative to social issues. As will be indicated in the third section of this paper, the man who attempts to stay "above or beside" the battle by not taking sides on social issues, actually, by the consequences of such "non-choice," becomes an ally of the existing power structure—and has, thus, taken sides after all. In other words, there is no alternative to playing *both* parts of the dual role—which is not to say that all sociologists must become soap box orators (effective tactics may more often call for quiet analysis rather than flamboyant preaching) ; nor does it deny that some individuals may be more interested in the researching-teaching aspects of the role while others may be more aroused by the role's social action aspects. But the important point is that it is illogical to speak of a *sociologist* who does research-teaching only or who participates in social action only—if an individual confines his activities to the former, then it is more to the point to title him "apologist for the status quo" or "non-rocker of boats"; and if he does only the latter, then he is appropriately termed a politician or administrator.

Among the sociologists who would agree with the foregoing, there may be a sizeable number who would still feel concern for one or both of two reasons—namely, that if we follow the recommendation to support particular social conditions, we: 1) thereby reject Max Weber's logically sound observation that "... it can never be the task of an empirical science to provide binding norms and ideals from which directives for immediate activity can be derived"[3]; and/or, 2) sociology might degenerate into a plethora of competing sectarian movements led by a never-ending series of prophets and messiahs who will cry, "Follow *me*—I *alone* have the truth, the light, the way to the peace that passeth understanding."

In answer to those who may feel concern for the first reason I believe I am on defensible logical grounds in saying that there is no necessary contradiction between Weber's observation, on the one hand, and the recommendation, on the other hand, that we support particular social conditions. While engaging in the latter activity we would *not* be saying, "Sociology indicates we 'should' hold to these ideals"—that *would* be a rejection of Weber. We would just be saying, "We adopt these (given) ideals because they appear to promise the most for our discipline"

For those who are concerned that sociology might break down into sectarian movements, the answer lies in several aspects of the nature of the discipline and in one of its prime needs. Its "nature" includes a strong emphasis on cultural relativity, on the importance of adequate empirical data, and on the value of dispassionate, objective examination of evidence and alternatives: when people are trained in terms of such emphasis, they generally become particularly resistant to would-be charismatic leaders. As for the relevant prime need of the discipline, Professor Parsons has pointed out that we "... have a vested interest in what is in some cases a 'liberal' society"[4]—that is, we can function effectively, as sociologists, only in a society where equalitarianism and social justice are basic values, and where democratic controls, due process, free inquiry, and free speech and press are meaningfully supported. Such social conditions are not only needed by sociology—they are ideals toward which American sociologists—despite their general inaction—have a strong positive orientation. This is the well-known "liberal bias" of sociology; it is a bias which is common among social scientists because such people, in the course of their training, almost uniformly learn that in Western countries, at least, there is a strong historical and current association between a liberal society (as defined by implication above) and the type of society where there are optimum chances

26

for the greatest number to achieve happiness (i.e., the "good society"). This type of learning, and the resulting liberal bias—along with the scientific training of sociologists—suggests that, no matter how politically active sociologists may become, it is most unlikely that a multitude of sectarian ideological movements will develop in American sociology.

If the question arises as to *how* the needed and desired goal of creating and supporting a liberal society can best be achieved, Weber—our man for all seasons—supplies a handy answer.

The question of the appropriateness of the means for achieving a given end is undoubtedly accessible to scientific analysis. Inasmuch as we are able to determine (within the present limits of our knowledge) which means for the achievement of a proposed end are appropriate or inappropriate, we can in this way estimate the chances of attaining a certain end by certain available means. In this way we can indirectly criticize the setting of the end itself as practically meaningful (on the basis of the existing historical situation) or as meaningless with reference to existing conditions. Furthermore, when the possibility of attaining a proposed end appears to exist, we can determine (naturally within the limits of our existing knowledge) the consequences which the application of the means to be used will produce in addition to the eventual attainment of the proposed end, as a result of the interdependence of all events.[5]

To those who would argue that social science's need for a liberal society is not an established fact, I would call attention to the state of social "science" in authoritarian environments. Anyone who has read the "sociological" literature produced in Stalinist Russia knows what a travesty social science becomes when its practitioners are forced to cleave to sectarian dogma.[6] Under such conditions, even purely physical science can suffer, as indicated by Lysenkoism in Russia and by the Hitlerian dichotomy of "Aryan science" as opposed to "Jewish science." It was chilling to read, in the *American Sociological Review*, about the fate of one of mainland China's greatest sociologists:

In reply to a letter to Dr. Sun Pen-wen asking for a set of his works, he wrote, "I have come to understand that all my books are only good for burning and hence I have none to send you. I have also learned that I formerly neglected to study the works of Karl Marx which I am now doing many hours a day. Please don't write again.[7]

KNOWLEDGE FOR MAN

If I could be granted a wish, I would wish that a sizeable number of sociologists would go much further than suggested in the opening proposition. I fully accept Robert S. Lynd's thesis[8] that social and psychological scientists are, by far, the theoretically best qualified people in the land to sketch the dimensions of, and to lead others toward, the "good society" (as defined above). *We* are the specialists in the principles of human behavior; *we*, better than anyone else, can properly assess previous faltering attempts to improve the general welfare; *we*, above all—as put so forcefully in *Can Science Save Us?* [9]—know how to create and apply the measuring techniques and devices which can pinpoint the real sources of social discord and dissatisfaction and thus reduce to a minimum the supposed need for "educated guesswork" on the part of leaders of vital human affairs.

"But," some will object, "the 'new sociologist' merely measures, counts, observes—he does not judge." This has been our own popular stereotype, but it is now appropriate to ask: Is the supposedly non-judging type of "new sociologist" truly up-to-date? Or is he so "out of it" he does not realize that, in terms of knowledge and status, we have passed beyond the era of the thirties and forties when sociologists in general were so insecure about their standing as scientists that many of them, trying to play-it-safe, concentrated on developing a "science of that which is not worth knowing"?[10] We're big boys now! And, like other "real scientists" such as physicists and biologists, we're qualified to make judgments about what apparently will and what won't con-tribute—given particular sociocultural conditions—to the betterment of man.

And what are we doing, we "naturals" for leaders of the age? As a group, we are spending a good share of our time and energies making out grant applications and collecting and analyzing mountains of trivial data on superficial subjects. We also play a mean game of fac-ulty politics, and we party well, especially when publishers pay the li-quor bill. Meanwhile, the planet teeters on the brink of Word War III. It is enough to make one weep to think that almost three decades after Lynd published his indictment we are still hawking status quo sociol-ogy. *Knowledge for What?* Lynd asked, and, clinging to the line fol-lowed by Nazi medical experimenters—and by developers of atomic, chemical, and bacteriological weapons—we quote Aristotle as our au-thority that knowledge is a good in itself and cannot be judged on external grounds:

All knowledge is obviously good because the good of any thing is that which belongs to the fullness of being which all things seek after and desire . . .[11]

It is perhaps monstrously presumptuous of me to do so, but I am here asking others who are concerned to join me in building, at long last, a *meaningfully* new sociology. (I say "presumptuous" and "at long last" because I too am guilty of having been apathetic—if not coward-ly.)[12]
Such a sociology would begin and end with the advice of Francis Bacon:

I would address one general admonition to all: that they consider what are the true ends of knowledge, and that they seek it not either for pleas-ure of the mind, or for contention, or for superiority to others . . . but for the benefit and use of life, and that they perfect and govern it in charity . . . [13]

The meaningfully new sociology would teach its recruits that it is not an indication of scholarly detachment for a sociologist to refuse to indicate which of a variety of alternatives seems most likely, on the

28   basis of available evidence, to contribute to the good of society (as defined); it is a cheap avoidance of responsibility. The recruits would also be taught that the so-called apolitical scientist is not *just* irresponsible; he is always a Frankenstein who can quite easily engage in activities that threaten to destroy man himself. As Tom Lehrer puts it with bitter humor, the politically non-committed scientist, having no significant group loyalties, is motivated by expedience only and can therefore be *expected* to choose the side of the highest bidder regardless of the nature of the job requirements:

"Don't ask me where the bombs come down"—says the ex-Nazi missile expert, now working for the United States—
"That's not my department . . ."

The logical opposite of the apolitical scientist described is not—at least for present purposes—the "political man" who is almost totally lacking in objectivity. Neither is he the teacher who carelessly, and without labeling, presents *evaluations* of facts as if they were *empirical* observations. The politically-responsible sociologist I envisage would cling tenaciously to the generally accepted canons of science. He therefore would not think of supporting or opposing given issues, controversial or not, without having a defensible (i.e., "scientific") basis for his stand. He would, whenever possible—in line with his training and responsibility—insist upon having adequate empirical, and even experimental, knowledge before drawing conclusions. Where such knowledge is lacking—because of the pressure of time or because of the inherent complexities of any given case, as in international affairs—then he would feel that the *minimum* requirement is to be as certain as possible that sources of information are reliable (in accordance with *generally* accepted standards, not Pentagon, pacifist, or other specialist point of view) and that judgments which appear tentatively justified are properly qualified and labeled.

THE USES OF ETHICAL NEUTRALITY

The philosophical position which is usually termed "ethical neutrality" may seem to some to be a major obstacle to this paper's "call to commitment." However, the *legitimate* use of ethical neutrality constitutes no such obstacle; it is only when it appears in what may be called its "illegitimate" forms that it is a block to decision and action. It is a perfectly legitimate application of the ethical neutrality principle when an investigator, while gathering and analyzing data, temporarily suspends his culture- and time-bound values for the purpose of doing his work as objectively as possible. But it is clearly an illegitimate application of the principle when an individual, strictly for personal reasons, cites it as a rationalization for inaction, as a cover, a disguise.

Since arguments for the illegitimate uses of ethical neutrality often have a certain surface plausibility, it is wise to become familiar with the relevant characteristics and tactics of those who use the arguments. One such tactic is illustrated by the individual who says "Sociologists should not take sides on controversial issues because they are scientists and scientists should not draw conclusions until they are "absolutely sure' "—an interpretation which amounts to a permanent abrogation of responsibility because, of course, in the complex affairs of mankind we can be *absolutely* sure of nothing of importance. Another approach is that of the individual who says "I believe in taking a stand *as a man*; but it is not appropriate to take a stand *as a sociologist* a differentiation which is illogical but which, if acted on, might yield defensible practical results. But it is notable that people who say "I only take a stand as a man, not as a social scientist," are almost always the very same people who take no stands at all. Hence, in such cases, it appears that the careful differentiation between "men" and "sociologists" has, at best, an unintended ironic meaning.

Those who use ethical neutrality or similar arguments as an excuse for inaction, for not "choosing sides," are, it should be remarked, adopting a philosophical stance that was undermined decades ago. It is *impossible*, as it has been shown repeatedly, to take a "non-position" relative to social issues. Even Max Weber, often cited—in a kind of "If it was good enough for old Max, it's good anough for me" spirit— as the granddaddy of the ethical neutrality approach to data, clearly saw the logical fallacy of the "non-choice" position.

> ... all action and naturally, according to circumstances, inaction imply
> in their consequences the espousal of certain values—and herewith—
> what is today so willingly overlooked—the rejection of certain others.[14]

Then almost thirty years ago, Lynd wrote his "portrait in acids" of American social science in general and of sociology in particular.[15] Said one reviewer:

> His colleagues won't like what he bids them see. They will refuse to face
> the fairly patent fact that the 'detachment' and 'objectivity' that they
> have exacted of themselves have been excuses for keeping quiet, dodges
> to avoid thinking, devices for saving their skins.[16]

Much more recently, Alvin Gouldner gave us "Anti-Minotaur: The Myth of a Value-Free Sociology". [17] As Gouldner and a host of others have made clear, value neutrality is a myth because the man who does not self-consciously take a "side" on any given issue has—whether he means to or not—declared for entrenched forces. Politics enmesh us nowadays, said Mahatma Gandhi, ". . . as with serpent's coils from which there is no escape however hard one may try." [18] In the words of Karl Popper:

> ... anti-interventionism is untenable—even on purely logical grounds,
> since its supporters are bound to recommend political intervention aimed
> at preventing intervention.[19]

There are a variety of reasons which may be cited to account for the "no stand as a sociologist" position. One of the more obvious is ava-

30   rice; this would appear to be the motive of those who have sold out—to industry, to the military, or to the hope for the next grant—and who make use of the seasoned bureaucrat's stock answer, "That's not my department." In addition, there are the many who are just plain lazy—the ones who, for example, say the only reason they haven't made up their minds about the Vietnam war is because they haven't taken the time to do any systematic reading on the subject: "I feel sort of guilty," they say, "but with term papers to grade, and all—you know— I just don't seem to get around to it. And anyway, the situation is so confused that a really *objective* person can't make any firm decisions. So why bother to try?"

Although greed and sloth may account for a significant number of those who choose to remain on what they *think* is dead center so far as controversial social issues are concerned, I am personally convinced that *cowardice* is the most important single explanation. That is, I hypothesize that among the sociologists who refuse to declare themselves pro or con on such questions as nuclear weapons, civil liberties, racial discrimination, etc., the majority are motivated by fear—they are, I hypothesize, consumed with fear of those who hold power and/or fear that they may commit the supposedly cardinal sin of the academic (i.e., doing or saying something that may turn out to be wrong or foolish).[20]

There are, so far as I am now aware, no "hard" data to support the proffered hypothesis—it remains to be tested. But its plausibility is suggested by a multiplicity of small signs and events; the sociologists who refuse to sign a petition until they see who else is signing; the ones among us who say they are "above the battle," but who eagerly lead the charge when they are personally touched by some safe issue such as the allocation of faculty parking space; the seeming correlation between taking a stand and having tenure; the apparent readiness with which so many of our "greats"—excepting the rare George Lundbergs among us—openly, and frequently as *sociologists*, espouse a variety of causes, while those of us who have not "arrived" are so often the ones to shout about making sociology a "pure" science.

In conjunction with the foregoing, it is intriguing to speculate on *why* sociology, in comparison with the other behavioral disciplines, is seemingly so overloaded with "scientismists—many of whom, I have asserted, are sheep in scientists' clothing. The American Anthropological Association has gone on record in opposition to the Vietnam war on the grounds that "genocide is not in the interests of the AAA." It seems doubtful that enough support could be mustered to pass such a resolution in the ASA. Why? Is it, perhaps, because so many of us, in our classes and elsewhere, stress scientism to such a degree that we tend to "pull' a superfluity of the frightened and the unsure who find our ranks attractive *because* being a sociologist means (they think) that one is safe from the world's controversies—means, indeed, that one can, with in-group approval, spend one's life fiddling with trivia, while Hanoi burns? [21] And on the other hand, do students who have some faith in themselves, and therefore the courage of their convictions, leave us in disgust and go into other fields? I don't know—but I see here the makings of some provocative dissertations in the general field of the sociology of sociology.

* * *

Those who agree with the foregoing points—that it is logically impossible to be neutral about values; that the very existence of our discipline is dependent upon "liberalizing" social conditions; that the so-called apolitical scientist is likely to be a cad or a coward; and that we sociologists are, at least theoretically, particularly well qualified to point the way to the good society—will see the logic of the proposition with which this paper begins. They may also wish to play a part in building a meaningfully new sociology, one of the norms of which would be that practitioners must, relative to significant political and ideological issues, speak out fearlessly—

For if the trumpet give an uncertain sound, who shall prepare himself to the battle? [22]

NOTES

1. Alvin W. Gouldner, "Anti-Minotaur: The Myth of a Value-Free Sociology," *Social Problems* 9, no. 3:199–213, Winter 1962; *see* p. 210.

2. A suggestion that is mildly reminiscent of Lester F. Ward's "pure" and "applied" sociology.

3. Max Weber, *The Mythology of the Social Sciences*, ed. and trans., Edward A. Shills and Henry A. Finch (Chicago: Free Press of Glencoe, Illinois, 1919), p. 52.

4. Talcott Parsons, "The Editor's Column," *American Sociologist* 2, no. 2 (May 1967), 62–64 *see* p. 64.

5. Weber, op cit., pp. 52–53; but note that the passage quoted is taken from a section of Weber wherein he is stressing his belief that scientists, while acting as such, should not recommend courses of action *except* in terms of efficiency for reaching defined ends.

6. *See*, for example, M. Baskin, "Soviet Evaluation of American Sociology," translated by John K. Musgrave, *American Sociological Review* 14, no. 1 (February 1949) : 137–43.

7. Albert R. O'Hara, "The Recent Development of Sociology in China," *American Sociological Review* 26, no. 6 (December 1961) : 928–29. See fn. 2, p. 928.

8. Robert S. Lynd, *Knowledge for What?* The Place of Social Science in American Culture (Princeton: Princeton University Press, 1939).

9. George A. Lundberg, *Can Science Save Us?* 2d. ed. (New York: David McKay Co., 1961).

10. Quoted by Karl Mannheim in his review of *Methods in Social Science*, edited by Stuart A. Rice (Chicago: University of Chicago Press), 1931; review reprinted in Karl Mannheim, *Essays on Sociology and Social Psychology* (New York: Oxford University Press, 1953), pp. 185–94; the fragment quoted appears in Mannheim's volume, p. 192, in the following context:

> In the introduction to the volume under discussion (p. 10), the question is asked whether Marx and Carlyle would have been unable to envisage their problems had they known the statistical method. If the answer is in the affirmative, then we do not hesitate to confess that we would rather renounce statistical exactness than forego seeking answers to those questions which seem important to us. Should it not be possible to save these questions, then the

32

cruel name of a 'science of that which is not worth knowing', which was originally applied to academic, dry classical philology, would befit our science.

11. Aristotle, interpreted by Thomas Aquinas, in Hans Jonas, "The Practical Uses of Theory," as reprinted in *Philosophy of the Social Sciences*, edited by Maurice Natanson (New York: Random House, 1963), pp. 119–42; *see* p. 119.

12. Although I finally decided to include this and one other note of self-denigration, I remain unsure about the wisdom of making such observations. I would agree with N. J. Demerath III, who wrote (*see* p. 77 of his "In a Sow's Ear: A Reply to Goode," *Journal for the Scientific Study of Religion* 6, no. 1 (Spring 1967): 77–84 "There is a certain arrogance in pointing at the weaknesses of one's own work since modesty is easily labelled false, and nothing is hollower than the implied promise of greater works to come."

13. Natanson op. cit. p. 120.

14. Weber, op. cit. p. 53.

15. Lynd loc. cit.

16. Max Lerner, "The Revolt Against Quietism," *New Republic*, July 1939, pp. 257–58; *see* p. 257.

17. Gouldner, loc. cit.

18. Paraphrased by Martin Buber in "Letter to Mahatma Gandhi," as reprinted in *The Pacifist Conscience*, edited by Peter Mayer (New York: Holt, Rinehart and Winston, 1965), pp. 269–283; *see* p. 279.

19. Karl R. Popper, *The Poverty of Historicism* (Boston: Beacon Press, 1957), pp. 60–61.

20. The poor souls who are being taught that "if it can't be said in numbers, it's not worth saying" should be exempted; to the degree that they are well integrated into their academic sub-culture, they are just plain uninformed about what is of permanent importance in human affairs—therefore, they cannot logically be held accountable for their actions or the lack thereof.

21. Having published my own share of frivolous nothings, I do not exempt myself from the implied accusation; but note footnote 12.

22. 1 Corinthians XIV, 8.

Autonomy
Authority
SATISFACTION
Aggressiveness
Group
Leadership
UNIQUENESS
EMERGENCE
BEHAVIOR
CLOSENESS
RECOGNITION

Study Questions

1. Are groups real?
2. Does a group as a unit, have qualities which transcend those of each individual member?
3. What are levels of analysis?
4. What are group properties?
5. What are the additive and relational group properties in your classroom?
6. Do the Leavitt results make sense to you? How might they be modified?

The Perspective of Sociology

2

When I was an undergraduate major in sociology at Brooklyn College in the early 1950s, the standard definition of sociology that I repeated to professors was that "sociology is the study of human group life." I then elaborated on the meaning of "groups" to demonstrate that I attended lectures and had learned the required material. Later, in graduate school, I became aware of this overly simple definition of sociology and began to understand that it did not lead one to an analytical or distinctive description of the discipline. One can study human beings as they participate in group situations and not necessarily view the subject matter from a sociological perspective. Other social sciences also study man and his actions. Psychology, anthropology, economics, and political science are other disciplines in which we read about man's behavior. What is unique about the perspective of sociology? What can a student hope to gain by an introduction to sociology? The answers to these questions involve the notion of levels of analysis.

LEVELS OF ANALYSIS

In order to understand the sociological perspective, we must consider related disciplines and must differentiate the conceptual approaches to man which flow from each. Four levels of analysis (perspectives) have been developed to analyze man's behavior: Each of these levels applies to a number of disciplines, *organic, psychological, social,* and *cultural*.[1] The organic perspective includes the academic disciplines of biology and medicine. This perspective views man *as an organism.*" Studies about man's physical problems in interplanetary travel, or about heredity, employ this *organic* view. A second perspective, the psychological one, views *man as a personality.*" Psychology and psychoanalysis are disciplines which approach the individual in this way. The third level of analysis, the social level, views *man as a member of a social relationship.* The disciplines of sociology, social anthropology, and political science share this view of man. Finally, the cultural level includes subjects such as philosophy, law, literature, and linguistics.

These disciplines all view *man as a carrier of shared cultural ideas.* The analysis of these transmitted and modified materials form the subject matters of this perspective.

Each of these levels of analysis attempts to empirically describe and theoretically explain different aspects of man. As such, the analysis of man as an organism cannot help us to understand or predict man's behavior at a social level or at a cultural level. Some disciplines cross levels and study relationships between them. Thus, psychosomatic studies of illness and social psychology both view man as being influenced by two levels. The levels of analysis are even more fundamentally interrelated. First, each level develops or *emerges* out of the level preceding it. The emergence of a new level means that any one level is dependent upon all lower levels. Thus, organic life is necessary for the development of a personality. A personality, in turn, is required for participation in social interaction. In the course of social interaction, personalities produce and develop ideas, values, or conventions of acting. While each level is interdependent with the prior level, each achieves a degree of independence. Each level has certain exclusive, defining characteristics. A personality is something separate and beyond the level of biological functions. In the same way, a group cannot be explained merely by consideration of the organic structures or personality profiles of each of the group members. Therefore, while the levels are emergent and interpenetrating, they are also autonomous. This idea is critical for understanding the perspective of sociology.

Sociology, then, is a discipline that studies man by trying to understand the laws and principles that govern group life. What distinguishes it from other social sciences, such as political science or economics, is that sociology is larger in its focus. For example, it is not concerned only with political behavior, but with all organized group life.

The introductory student is likely to see people in groups as clusters of individual personalities. The perspective of sociology is that groups are units of analysis that exist independently of the member's organic or personality dispositions. They are:

1. Units of analysis that can be studied;
2. Units of analysis that have distinctive group properties;
3. Units of analysis whose group properties are related systematically to other group properties; and
4. Units of analysis whose group properties influence individuals' feelings, attitudes, beliefs, and knowledge.

THE STUDY OF GROUP PROPERTIES

Group properties are variables that are used to describe a group. Sometimes these variables are based upon counting or evaluating the individuals in the group. Thus, groups can be compared with reference to size, rates of behavior (such as cheating or suicide), or other compositional properties (such as the proportion of males, Catholics, or blacks). In each case the individuals in the group are used as the basis

38   for determining the group properties. When we describe the group by counting its members we are referring to the *additive* properties of the group. The other type of group property is called *relational*. Relational properties cannot be determined by counting individuals. They are described by referring to the relationship between the units or individuals. Thus, the same number of houses may exist on a rural and city street, but when we compare the position of the houses relative to each other, we discover that the streets differ in dispersion or density. Relational properties refer to the way units are related to each other.

The first selection in this chapter, written by Harold Leavitt, is on its face an article about communication networks and group performance in problem-solving. A superficial survey of the article might conclude that certain communication networks are more efficient than others, and that certain types of communication patterns lead to more or less satisfaction. The article, however, can be described in more depth in terms which relate to group properties. In Leavitt's experiment, the additive properties of group size and intelligence are the same in each group. Because he held constant the size of each group (5 members), and because the students were distributed randomly into the different types of networks, we cannot explain the differences in accuracy or speed of problem-solving in terms of individual characteristics of the students. However, the one condition that was varied in each group was the communication pattern. Students were seated in the pattern of a circle, a chain, a Y, and a spoked wheel. Leavitt found that changes in the communication network—in the relational properties of the group—affected its efficiency, accuracy, and satisfaction. Moreover, group properties systematically affected each individual's perceptions of the leader, enthusiasm for the task, and attractiveness of the group itself. Before you read the article, you might want to make some predictions about the way in which these different communication networks affected problem-solving. Note that the "S's" in the article refer to the "subjects" involved in the study. After reading about Leavitt's findings, you may want to speculate on the kinds of networks that exist in your family, classroom, or college.

The second article, by Ferenc Merei, attempts to demonstrate that groups have a uniqueness that cannot be accounted for by merely assessing members' characteristics. Merei conducted his research among school children between 4 and 11 years of age. He began his experiment by observing children's behavior for several hours over a two-week period. He was able to identify as leaders those boys and girls who were more dominant, tended to initiate activities, and were often imitated by other children. Merei pulled out these leaders and kept them separate from the other children. He then assigned the remaining children to 12 groups, each homogeneous with respect to age and sex. The group members spent time together until habits and traditions were well formed. Using our earlier language, the personalities, through interaction, developed rules about the uses of materials and the maintenance of relationships. These were the "habits" and "traditions" of the newly formed groups. One of the leaders was then added to each group. From observations, Merei attempted to determine if the leader was able to influence and change the group's customary way of doing things, or if the group forced its traditions on the leader.

The two articles in this chapter, taken from a laboratory setting and a field experiment, illustrate and document the conceptual independence of a group, the relationship of group properties to each other, and the influence of group properties upon individual behavior and feelings. Later readings will demonstrate these principles in "real-life" groups.

NOTES

1. Marvin E. Olsen, *The Process of Social Organization* (New York: Holt, Rinehart and Winston, 1968), pp. 4–5.

HAROLD J. LEAVITT

Some Effects of Certain Communication Patterns on Group Performance

It was the purpose of this investigation to explore experimentally the relationship between the behavior of small groups and the patterns of communication in which the groups operate. It was our further purpose to consider the psychological conditions that are imposed on group members by various communication patterns, and the effects of these conditions on the organization and the behavior of its members. We tried to do this for small groups of a constant size, using two-way written communication and a task that required the simple collection of information.

SOME CHARACTERISTICS OF COMMUNICATION STRUCTURES

The stimulus for this research lies primarily in the work of Bavelas (1), who considered the problem of defining some of the dimensions of group structures. In his study, the structures analyzed consist of cells connected to one another. If we make persons analogous to "cells" and communication channels analogous to "connections," we find that some of the dimensions that Bavelas defines are directly applicable to the description of communication patterns. Thus, one way in which com-

Harold J. Leavitt, "Some Effects of Certain Communication Patterns on Group Performance," *Journal of Abnormal and Social Psychology* 46 (1951): 38–50. Copyright © 1951 by the American Psychological Association and reproduced by permission.

40

munications patterns vary can be described by the sum of the neighbors that each individual member has, neighbors being defined as individuals to whom a member has communicative access. So, too, the concept of *centrality*, as defined by Bavelas, is of value in describing differences within and between structures. The most central position in a pattern is the position closest to all other positions. Distance is measured by number of communicative links which must be utilized to get, by the shortest route, from one position to another.

* * *

Unfortunately, these dimensions we have mentioned do not in themselves uniquely define a pattern of communication. What defines a pattern is the *way* the cells are connected, regardless of how they are represented on paper. In essence, our criterion is this: if two patterns cannot be "bent" into the same shape without breaking a link, they are different patterns.

* * *

METHOD

The Problem to Be Solved

We have already described the task to be given our *Ss*—a task of discovering the single common symbol from among several symbols. When *all five* men indicated that they knew the common symbol, a trial was ended. Another set of cards, with another common symbol, was then given to the *Ss*. and another trial was begun. Each group of *Ss* was given 15 consecutive trials....

The Apparatus

The *Ss* were seated around a circular table (Fig. 1) so that each was separated from the next by a vertical partition from the center to six inches beyond the table's edge. The partitions had slots permitting subjects to push written message cards to the men on either side of them.

To allow for communication to the other men in the group, a five-layered pentagonal box was built and placed at the center of the table. The box was placed so that the partitions just touched each of the five points of the pentagon. Each of the five resulting wedge-shaped work-spaces was then painted a different color. The *Ss* were supplied with blank message cards whose colors matched that of their work spaces. Any message sent from a booth had to be on a card of the booth's color. On the left wall of each partition, 16 large symbol cards, representing 16 trials, were hung in loose-leaf fashion. The cards were placed in order with numbered backs to *S*. At the starting signal, *S* could pull down the first card and go to work.

In addition, each work space was provided with a board on which were mounted six switches. Above each switch appeared one of the six symbols. When S got an answer to the problem, he was to throw the proper switch, which would turn on an appropriate light on a master board of 30 lights in the observer's room. When five lights (whether or not they were under the correct symbol), representing five different Ss, were lit, the observer called a halt to the trial. The observer could tell by a glance at the light panel whether (a) five different Ss had thrown their switches, (b) whether all five had decided on the same answer, and (c) whether the answer decided on was right or wrong. The same detailed instructions were given to all Ss.

Figure 1. Apparatus

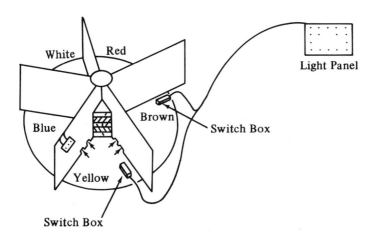

A preliminary series of four problems, in which each S was given all the information required for solution, was used. This was done to note the extent of differences among Ss in the time required to solve such problems.

The Procedure

One hundred male undergraduates of M.I.T.[1] drawn from various classes at the Institute, served as Ss for these experiments. These 100 were split up into 20 groups of five men each. These 20 groups were then further subdivided so that five groups could be tested on each of four experimental patterns.

Each group was given 15 consecutive trials on *one* pattern, a process which required one session of about fifty minutes. These Ss were *not used again*. The order in which we used our patterns was also randomized. Just in case the color or geographical position of one's workspace might affect one's behavior, we shifted position for each new group. After a group had completed its 15 trials, and before members were permitted to talk with one another, each member was asked to fill out a questionnaire.

The Patterns Selected

The four five-man patterns selected for this research are shown in Figure 2.

Figure 2. The Experimental Patterns

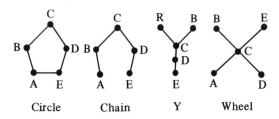

Circle   Chain   Y   Wheel

These four patterns represented extremes in centrality (as in the circle vs. the wheel), as well as considerable differences in other characteristics.

RESULTS

The data which have been accumulated are broken down in the pages that follow into (a) a comparison of total patterns and (b) a comparison of positions within patterns.

A. Differences among Patterns

It was possible to reconstruct a picture of the operational methods actually used by means of: (a) direct observations, (b) post-experimental analysis of messages, and (c) post-experimental talks with *Ss*.

The *wheel* operated in the same way in all five cases. The peripheral men funnelled information to the center where an answer decision was made and the answer sent out. This organization had usually evolved by the fourth or fifth trial and remained in use throughout.

The *Y* operated so as to give the most central position, C . . . complete decision-making authority. The next-most-central position, D . . . served only as a transmitter of information and of answers. In at least one case, C transmitted answers first to A and B and only then to D. Organization for the Y evolved a little more slowly than for the wheel, but, once achieved, it was just as stable.

In the *chain* information was usually funelled in from both ends to C, whence the answer was sent out in both directions. There were several cases, however, in which B or D reached an answer decision and passed it to C. The organization was slower in emerging than the Y's or the wheels, but consistent once reached.

The *circle* showed no consistent operational organization. Most commonly messages were just sent in both directions until any *S* received an answer or worked one out. In every case, all available links were used at some time during the course of each trial.

Direct Measures of Differences among Patterns

* * *

One measure of speed did give statistically significant differences. A measure of the *fastest single trial* of each group indicates that the wheel was considerably faster (at its fastest) than the circle. . . . It seems clear that the circle pattern used more messages to solve the problem than the others.

Errors. An error was defined as the throwing of any incorrect switch by an *S* during a trial. Errors that were *not* corrected before the end of a trial are labelled "final errors"; the others are referred to as "corrected errors."

Although more errors were made in the circle pattern than any other, a greater proportion of them (61 percent) were corrected than in any other pattern. Too, the frequency of unanimous five-man final errors is lower, both absolutely and percentage-wise, for the circle than for the chain.

Questionnaire Results

1. *"Did your group have a leader? If so, who?"*

Only 13 of 25 people who worked in the circle named a leader, and those named were scattered among all the positions in the circle. For all patterns, the total frequency of people named increased in the order *circle, chain, Y, wheel*. Similarly, the unanimity of opinion increased in the same order so that, for the wheel pattern, all 23 members who recognized any leader agreed that position C was that leader.

2. *"Describe briefly the organization of your group."*

The word "organization" in this question was ambiguous. Some of the *Ss* understood the word to mean pattern of communication, while others equated it with their own duties or with status difference.

These differences in interpretation were not random, however. Sixteen people in the wheel groups fully reproduced the wheel structure in answer to this question, while only one circle member reproduced the circle pattern.

3. *"How did you like your job in the group?"*

In this question *Ss* were asked to place a check on a rating scale marked "disliked it" at one end and "liked it" at the other. For purposes of analysis, the scale was translated into numerical scores from 0 at the dislike end to 100. Each rating was estimated only to the closest decile.

Again, we find the order circle, chain, Y, wheel, with circle members enjoying their jobs significantly more than the wheel members.

4. *"See if you can recall how you felt about the job as you went along. Draw the curve below."*

The *Ss* were asked to sketch a curve into a space provided for it. We measured the height of these curves on a six-point scale at trials 1, 5, 10, and 15. These heights were averaged for each group, and the averages were plotted.

Although the differences between groups are not statistically significant, trends of increasing satisfaction in the circle and decreasing satisfaction in the wheel seemed to corroborate the findings in the question on satisfaction with one's job. Except for a modst Y-chain reversal, the order is, as usual, from circle to wheel.

5. *"Was there anything, at any time, that kept your group from performing at its best? If so, what?"*

The answers to this question were categorized as fas as possible into several classes.

None of the circle members feels that "nothing" was wrong with his group; a fact that is suggestive of an attitude different from that held by members of the other patterns. So, too, is the finding that insufficient knowledge of the pattern does not appear as an obstacle to the circle member but is mentioned at least five times in each of the other patterns.

6. *"Do you think your group could improve its efficiency? If so, how?"*

Circle members place great emphasis on *organizing* their groups, on working out a "system" (mentioned 17 times). Members of the other patterns, if they felt that any improvement at all was possible, emphasized a great variety of possibilities.

7. *"Rate your group on the scale below."*

For purposes of analysis, these ratings (along a straight line) were transposed into numbers from 0, for "poor," to 100.

The same progression of differences that we have already encountered, the progression *circle, chain, Y, wheel,* holds for this question. Once again the circle group thinks less well of iteslf (Mean=56) than do the other patterns (M_{ch}=60; M_y=70; M_w=71).

Message Analysis

The messages sent by all *Ss* were collected at the end of each experimental run and their contents coded and categorized. Some of these categories overlapped with others, and hence some messages were counted in more than one category.

The now familiar progression, *circle, chain, Y, wheel,* continues into this area. Circle members send many more informational messages than members of the other patterns M_{ci}=283; M_w=101). Circle members also send more answers (M_{ci}=91; M_w=65).

The same tendency remains in proportion to total errors as well as absolutely. The circle has a mean of 4.8 recognition-of-error messages for a mean of 16.6 errors; the chain has a mean of 1 recognition-of-error messages for a mean of 9.8 errors.

*   *   *

B. A Positional Analysis of the Data

Observation of the experimental patterns indicates that every position in the circle is indistinguishable from every other one. No one has more neighbors, is more central, or is closer to anyone than anyone else. In the wheel, the four peripheral positions are alike, and so on.

2. *"See if you can recall how you felt about the job as you went along. Draw the curve below."*

The data for this question are gathered after all most-peripheral and all most-central positions are combined. Peripheral positions were: positions A and E, in the chain; position E in the Y; and positions A, B, D, and E in the wheel. Central positions were all C positions with the exception of C in the circle. The data thus combined highlight the trend toward higher satisfaction with increasing centrality. The central positions progress from a mean of 2.1 at trial 1 to a mean of 3.9 at trial 15. Peripheral positions decline from 3.9 to 2.3.

Message Analysis by Position

One of the things that immediately stands out from an examination of the messages is an apparent peculiarity in the *informational message* category. Although the most central man in the chain sends more informational messages (52) than the other positions in that pattern, the same is not true of the most central men in the Y and the wheel. In the Y, it is position D, the next-most-central position, that sends most; while in the wheel all positions are about equal. This peculiarity becomes quite understandable if we take into account (a) the kind of organization used in each pattern and (b) the fact that these figures represent the entire 15 trials, some of which occurred before the group got itself stably organized. In the wheel, the Y, and the chain, the center man really needed to send *no* informational messages, only answers; but in the *early* trials, before his role was clarified, he apparently sent enough to bring his total up to or higher than the level of the rest.

It can also be noted that the number of *organizational messages* (messages which seek to establish some plan of action for future trials) is negatively correlated with positional centrality. The most peripheral men send the greatest numbers of organizational messages, the most central men least.

DISCUSSION

Patternwise, the picture formed by the results is of differences almost always in the order *circle, chain, Y, wheel.*

We may grossly characterize the kinds of differences that occur in this way: the circle, one extreme, is active, leaderless, unorganized, erratic, and yet is enjoyed by its members. The wheel, at the other extreme, is less active, has a distinct leader, is well and stably organized, is less erratic, and yet is unsatisfying to most of its members.

* * *

SUMMARY AND CONCLUSIONS

Within the limits set by the experimental conditions—group size, type of problem, source of S_s—these conclusions seem warranted:

46

1. The communication patterns within which our groups worked affected their behavior. The major behavioral differences attributable to communication patterns were differences in accuracy, total activity, satisfaction of group members, emergence of a leader, and organization of the group. There may also be differences among patterns in speed of problem solving, self-correcting tendencies, and durability of the group as a group.

2. The positions which individuals occupied in a communication pattern affected their behavior while occupying those positions. One's position in the group affected the chances of becoming a leader of the group, one's satisfaction with one's job and with the group, the quantity of one's activity, and the extent to which one contributed to the group's functional organization.

* * *

REFERENCES

1. Bavelas, A. "A Mathematical Model for Group Structures, *Appl. Anthrop.* 7 (1948) : 16–30.
2. Freeman, H. *Industrial Statistics.* New York: Wiley, 1942.

NOTES

1. Data on female graduate students are being gathered at M.I.T. by Smith and Bavelas, and the indications are that their behavior differs in some ways from the behavior of our male *Ss*.

FERENC MEREI

Group Leadership and Institutionalization

PRELIMINARIES TO THE EXPERIMENT

The problem we set ourselves concerns the relationship between leader and group. To tackle it, we took the following steps.

Children suitable to form a group were selected. Previous observation showed that from the age of 5 upward, in spontaneously formed groups the sexes as a rule do not mix. Hence, the groups had to

Ferenc Merei, "Group Leadership and Institutionalization." Reprinted from *Human Relations* 2:1 (1949) : 23–39 with permission of Plenum Publishing Company and *Human Relations*.

be homogeneous as to sex. They had to be homogeneous as to age, too, because, as our observations showed, in spontaneous groupings the age differences seldom exceed two years. Homogeneity was desirable also regarding the ties between members, e.g., children had to be chosen who had no strong likes or dislikes for one another. Finally, for the most pertinent purpose of our experiment, we tried to select children with an average capacity for leadership and social influence.

To rate the individual on these scores, we made some preliminary observations. We saw the children of two day nurseries for 35 to 40 minutes each day for a period of two weeks. Two people worked simultaneously and afterward unified their notes. The observations were not selective: everything that occurred in the nursery during that period was chronologically and fully recorded. On the basis of these observations we picked out those children whose social qualities were an average for that nursery group and who were *not* leaders. Children were selected in whom the frequency of: (1) "following orders" greatly outnumbered "giving orders"; (2) imitation outnumbered being imitated; (3) participation in group play was an average in number as well as in degree of cooperation; and (4) acts of attacking, crying, telling on each other, were about the average of the group. Furthermore, their ties to one another had to be no more solid or lasting than to other members of the nursery.

The children were formed into a group. An assembly was considered a group when it developed a relatedness, with permanent rules, habits, traditions, entirely of its own.

The children chosen were put in a separate room. Their field was permanent: the same set of furniture, toys, and tools every day. In this room they spent 30 to 40 minutes each day. Their actions were fully recorded by two observers who later synchronized and combined their notes. The observers were completely passive.

The group thus met until a tendency to "institutionalization" became noticeable, and their habits and traditions appeared to become lasting. Only such habits were considered traditions as were not found in the day nurseries, but had developed during the experimental period. This gave us an objective criterion of the point at which an assembly constituted a group. To form a tradition from three to six meetings were needed.

The children formed traditions such as permanent seating order (who should sit where); permanent division of objects (who plays with what); group ownership of certain objects, ceremonies connected with their use, expressions of belonging together; returning to certain activities; rituals; sequence of games; forming a group jargon out of expressions accidentally uttered, etc.

A leader was placed in the group so formed. The leader was chosen from the same day nursery. He was a child who the nursery-school teachers—they had spent many days with him—considered to have initiative and directing power, who was older than the members of the group, and who, during the preliminary observation, more often gave than followed orders, more often was imitated than imitating, and more often was the attacker than the attacked.

48

Thus the leader was chosen because he was older, domineering, imitated, aggressive rather than submissive, and because he had initiative.

After the group had formed fixed traditions we added such a leader. The place, the objects remained the same. Recording went on as before.

What did we expect to learn from the experiment thus set up? Our question was: Do group habits and traditions change with the appearance of a leader? Does the leader introduce new habits, and does the group accept them? Does the group follow the leader, or does it force its traditions upon him? We see the group through its traditions—the objective expressions of the existing relationship. Hence, the vector of forces between the stronger leader and the group of weaker individuals is determined not by *who* gives the orders but by *what* the orders are. The question is not whether they accept leadership, but whether they give up their traditions by accepting what the leader initiates, whether they form new habits, rules, traditions, under his influence.

By carrying out this experiment we hoped to get the answer to our question.

THE EXPERIMENTAL PLAN

The experimental plan used the method of *varying the situation*. Individuals who scored high on leadership were observed in three situations: (1) in a larger group, where the members had no particular relationship with each other and where the leader's influence was felt by the group as a whole; (2) in a more closely knit group of the presocial stage formed through evolving group traditions; and (3) in a group with strong traditions of its own, facing a leader stronger than any one group member.

To record the entire process, we needed an adequate technique. We evolved a system of 76 symbols, each representing one complex act. The five people taking the notes synchronized them at 5-minute intervals.

Further variation was afforded through the objects in the room. By giving as many toys as there were children, we weakened group activity, since each could find something to do. By giving one object only we strengthened group activity, since all had to congregate around it. Setting a concrete task also strengthened the group. If an object familiar only to the leader was given, he was strengthened and the group weakened.

The choice of objects offers further possible variations which we have not sufficiently explored as yet.

We tried out many objects. Finally, the younger children (4 to 7 years) were given a tin toy house and a box of building blocks, the older ones (8 to 11 years) cardboard, picture magazines, scissors, crayons, paste, and paint brushes, and the instruction, "We want to make an exhibition." Of the latter objects there were fewer than there were children in the group, so that some manner of collaboration was required.

Most groups consisted of three children plus the leader, with some groups of four and six as well. The number chosen was determined by previous observations which showed that spontaneously formed groups, up to the age of 7, lasted longer when consisting of three to four children, and, between the ages of 7 and 10, of three to six children. Larger groups easily disintegrated.

We worked with twelve groups. In them we tried out the power of penetration of twenty-six children capable of leadership. The ages of all children ranged from 4 to 11 years. The difference within a group never exceeded two years. In every case but one the leader was older than any group member.

THE CONQUERED CONQUEROR

Let us now see the results of this experiment.

To summarize schematically, the same definite tendencies could be observed in all the experimental units: the group absorbed the leader, forcing its traditions on him. The leader takes over the habits and traditions of children who are younger than himself and who in the day nursery had been his underlings following his guidance. Now he engages in those activities which the group had developed before he entered it. His own undertakings either remain unsuccessful or gain acceptance only in a modified form suiting the traditions of that group.

Examples from our material demonstrate the point.

Table 1. Modeling: Being Modeled

Subject no.	In day nursery	In the experimental situation	
		Without leader	With leader
13	3:4	17:5	10:5
15	1:4	3:8	1:2
25	1:5	1:11	3:4
10	2:8	0:2	0:3
20 (leader)	6:3		5:11

Table 1 will be understood from the following definitions:

Modeling is one of the most important types of social behavior. When a child's act or behavior is spontaneously imitated by some others, the child, we say, is *modeling*. When a child, even if unintentionally, imitates another—as members of a group do to take over each other's mode of behavior and thereby form common habits—we say that he is *being modeled*. We avoid the word "imitation" because it has a connotation of intention.

The ratio of *modeling* to *be modeled* is a measure of the social penetrating power of a person.

Table 1 shows the ratio *modeling/being modeled* of four children (Nos. 13, 15, 25, 10). In the day nursery all four tended to

50 follow some model, rather than to serve as a model to others. It was for just this behavior that we selected them.

When they became members of a separate group forming its own traditions, a change occurred: one of the four children (No. 13) took on the modeling role, while the others went on being modeled.

It was after this change had taken place that the leader (No. 20) joined the group. In the day nursery he did the modeling: he served as a model six times, but followed another model only three times, making this ratio of social penetration 6:3. (Column 2 "In day nursery" shows an inverse ratio for all the others in this group.)

In the experimental situation—when the leader was confronted with a developed group—his ratio changed: his power of social penetration diminished. Formerly he was *modeling* (6.3), but now he was *being modeled* (5:11)—that is, the others did not take over his mode of action, but he took over the habits developed by the group. In other words, he followed those who in the day nursery had followed him.

In other groups and with other leaders a similar tendency was observed. The ratio *modeling/being modeled* of an extremely influential and willful leader in the day nursery changed from 9:5 to 0:8. For another such child the ratio changed from 6:2 to 1:6.

This portion of our results shows that, in a group possessing traditions, the leader introduced does not become the source of new habits and rules; rather, he will be the one to take over existing group traditions and thus to follow a model. This happens in spite of the fact that in the larger social formation (day nursery) he had served as a model to every member of the group.

Since "forming traditions" was our criterion of social influence, we came to the conclusion that, *confronted by a group having its own traditions, the leader proves weak; this in spite of the fact that when confronting them singly he is stronger than any one member of the group—stronger precisely as to his social penetrating power.*

PLAY OF FORCES

The last paragraph is only a schematic summary of our results. Reality is richer and more varied; what we see in reality is a wide variety of *tendencies*—a pull of the group force facing other pulls in other directions.

What does this mean? Though the group generally assimilates the leader, we find that it does so only on certain conditions and within certain limits. We find that the leading personality, while accepting the traditions and habits of the group, also influences and changes them. Let us then inquire into the modes of this influence, into the conditions which allow the assimilated leader to become that group's leader.

On the twenty-six leaders of the experiment the group force acted in varied ways.

At one extreme is the case where the group entirely assimilated the child who previously showed definite capacity to lead. This occurred in a group that possessed particularly strict traditions, and had well established and meticulously carried out rituals of activity. One such group played with a doll house and two dolls. In the course of three play periods they worked out a ritual of activity of playing around the house and of taking the dolls for a walk. The leader, one and a half years their senior, joining the group at its fourth meeting, tried to introduce something new (fourth and fifth play periods). He suggested a circle game and group singing. He was not followed. When he started singing alone they followed him for a few moments, then returned to their old game. The third time he came (sixth play period), the leader joined in the group's original game. Only for a few moments, here and there, did he start new activities, but he was followed by no one. At the seventh and eighth play periods no sign was left that this child had once (before these same children had developed a group habit) been a leader among them

At the other extreme is the case of the child who proved to be stronger than the group: he broke its traditions. There was one such case. The leader, a little girl (a year and a half older than the members) completely reorganized the group. She gave orders, she modeled, she decided what to do and how to play. The rules she introduced took the place of those the group had had.

This group's history is important: it was subjected to increasing difficulties, while the leader was given virtual training in leadership. After the group had formed its habits, each day a different leader was introduced. In three days three different leaders tried to foist their initiative upon it and to change its rituals. Against these three leaders the group was able to preserve its customs, rejecting their suggestions, in the face of all the enticing and aggression these leaders tried out on it. However, the struggle exhausted the group and it began to weaken. This weakening showed itself in that the children more often played by themselves, less often played their old organized games, playing instead merely side by side. The traditions were still formally there, but the members of the group tended to observe them singly, by themselves. The group lost much of its coherence.

These are borderline cases. *In the overwhelming majority of our cases the leader was forced to accept the group's traditions—that is, he proved weaker than the group but still managed to play the role of leader.* We observed each leader's ways of doing this.

1. *The Order-giver.* The group whose data on "modeling" and "being modeled" were given above had fully developed customs when the leader was introduced. The new boy, older, more experienced, and more of a leader than any member of the group, attempted to take over. He gave orders, made suggestions, bossed everybody. The children carefully avoided him, ignored his orders, and carried on in their traditions.

Soon the leader found himself alone. Suddenly his behavior changed, he joined the group in its activities and quickly learned its rituals. He learned their expressions, their habits, their games. During his second play period with them, he again gave orders. Though keeping within the frame of activities he had just learned from them, and according to their rules, he told the children what to do—that is, he ordered them to do exactly what they would have done anyway. He appropriated the leadership without being able to change the group's traditions. The members accepted this situation by following his orders, since this did not change their habitual activities.

The data on the frequency of group activity shows this. Table 2 contains the proportion of *order-giving* to *order-following*.

Table 2.   Order-Giving: Order-Following

Experimental subject no.	In day nursery	In the experimental situation	
		Without leader	*With leader*
13	3:5	3:6	1:4
15	1:2	8:1	0:2
25	1:4	0:2	2:5
10	2:3	0:3	0:3
20	12:2		11:3

Four members of the group (Nos. 13, 15, 25, 10) were *order-followers* in the day nursery. After they had formed a separate homogeneous group, one of them (No. 15) became an *order-giver*. When group habits were developed and a leader (No. 20) was added, all followed the leader's orders, as in the day nursery. In the group with a tradition, the leader became just as much of an order-giver (11:3) as he was in the day nursery (12:2). Regarding order-giving, then, the leader was stronger than the group (he gave orders—they accepted them). At the same time, however, he was the one to copy the others, he took over their ways (his modeling proportion changed from 6:3 to 5:11).

If a person should observe the group for only a short period of time, for example by the Goodenough 1-minute or 5-minute method, he would see a leader giving orders and a group obeying. A prolonged observation of the group plus its history would, however, soon disclose the inner workings of this *order-giving*: the leader gives such orders as have reference to the group's traditional activities; he expropriates the leadership without changing the group's traditional modes of activity.

The leader is weaker than the group because he takes over its traditions and because his own suggestions do not take root. At the same time he is also stronger because everyone follows his orders.

The gist of the phenomenon lies just in this dichotomy.

The leader is stronger than any one group member. (He gives orders—they obey.) He is weaker than *group traditions* and is forced to accept them. He is stronger than the individual member, weaker than the "plus" which a group is over and above the sum of the individuals in it. He is stronger than the members, weaker than the formation.

In the relationship between group and leader, two factors stand out: (1) the group as a particular order of quality, whose strength is expressed by the change of the leader's modeling proportion (from 6:3 to 5:11); and (2) the members, whose *weakness* is expressed by the constancy (12:2 to 11:3) of the leader's ratio of *order-giving/order following.*

Thus the curious situation obtains where the order-giver imitates, while the models follow the orders of their imitator.

What appears here is the "group plus"—the unique reality of a group—experimentally verified.

2. *The Proprietor.* A second way in which leadership may express itself is ownership: the leader joining the developed group takes possession of all the objects in the room. They continue being used according to group tradition; the games played with them remain the same. The leader joins in these games, but all the objects "belong" to him. Table 3 presents the data on this phenomenon, concerning the group discussed before.

Table 3. Frequency of Object Appropriation
(borrows or takes away from another child)

		In the experimental situation	
Experimental subject no.		Without leader	With leader
13		21	1
15		9	0
25		7	1
10		3	1
20			12

The frequency of taking possession of objects sharply falls for group members, and rises for the leader.

Into some groups, after traditions had been formed, outstanding leading personalities were placed—leaders obeyed in the day nursery by everyone, virtual dictators to more than thirty children. Let us follow one of them. If a child's behavior displeased him, he beat up that child; he allowed no opposition, and always had to have his way. The group into which he was put consisted of children younger than himself, children who in the day nursery always obeyed him. The result was unexpected: this structured group virtually swallowed him. (His proportion of modeling changed from 9:5 to 0:8.) He followed the group's every activity, accepted its every custom, while his own suggestions were *never* followed.

However, his exceptional personality still asserted itself with the group. The children gave him every object without his asking, and with that acknowledged his authority. The group had two traditional activities: using blocks they built a train, and using chairs they built a bridge. The leader soon learned these constructions and used the objects acquired to build just these. From time to time the group gathered around him, eloquently praising whatever he did. They praised his beautiful creation, his skill, the wonderful things he made

54

(which he had learned from them), as if to placate some dangerous genie. At the same time they followed him in nothing; on the contrary they drew him into their own activities and caused him to accept their habits. Their play remained unchanged; the same game with the same toys. They talked of the toys as they did before—Johnny's blocks, Tom's box—but occasionally they said: "The blocks belong to Andrew" (Andrew was the leader), or: "Tom's box belongs to Andrew." The owners of the objects became their users, while the right of ownership was given over, voluntarily or otherwise, to the new leader.

Observation over only a short period would lead to mistaken conclusions. One might see only that one child has all the toys, while the others surround and admire him. Only prolonged observation would show that those are but scenes of ceremonial offerings with which the children purchase, as it were, the leader's continued trust, with which they protect their traditions.

Again we see that apparently the leader is stronger than *the members* of the group (he appropriates their belongings), but weaker than *the group* because he is forced to accept its customs, traditions, and forms of activity.

3. *The Diplomat.* The third way of asserting leadership, as observed in our experimental situation, is quite devious. The cases belonging here are peculiar. The leader, having a greater force of social penetration than the group members, attempts to force upon them a new mode of activity. He fails. However, the leader, for reasons as yet unclear to us—perhaps because of the tense situation—does not get lost in the group, nor take over its habits, as did those leaders who complied in order to rule or in order to take possession of the toys.

This type of leader takes a roundabout course: he accepts the traditions of the group in order to change them.

Into old forms he pours new contents. What takes place here is a veritably dramatic struggle. We had one group with particularly strong traditions and institutionalization. This group rose to the highest level of spontaneous organization of games: to the level of division of roles.

One of the children, who in the day nursery showed no leadership, in this narrower group developed into a leader: games he suggested were followed, and their various parts become traditional with the group. It was at this point that a new leader was added. He tried to suggest new games but was not accepted. Then he joined their traditional game and slowly took over the leadership. The first day there were only two instances in which he led, the second day there were already nine. However, he was the one being modeled, taking over the group's habits. He accepted those habits but introduced minute changes. For example, he joined in the block game traditional with the group, but he demanded that always the red side of a block be on top. He was being modeled, he imitated, but he also introduced changes; then he became the leader of the traditional activities thus changed.

The third time he was with the group he again suggested new

activities. One was "hide and seek." (They had a game involving hiding, and this feature attracted the leader.) The group did not accept the suggestion and played instead another traditional game they called "acting with hats."

The leader yielded, joined the "hat game" and instantly began to organize it, in the course of which he made changes so as to combine with it the hide-and-seek game he had suggested. He was *being modeled* to the group, but he also *modeled* the group; he accepted their traditions but changed them.

His roundabout road to leadership is clear here:

1. He tries to do away with the group traditions and lead it on to new ones.
2. He is rejected.
3. He accepts the traditions and quickly learns them.
4. Within the frame of those traditions he soon assumes leadership, and, though reluctantly, the group follows him because he does a good job.
5. He introduces insignificant variations, loosening the tradition.
6. He then introduces new elements into the ritual already weakened by variation.

In this case accepting the traditions is a roundabout way to introducing new ones. This is a very active process in which the leader plays an important role. Only children with exceptional social influence and a great deal of initiative could act this way.

Thus, between the extremes of total assimilation and total conquest, we find three types of behavior. In the experimental situation the leader either (1) is being modeled—but gives orders; or (2) is being modeled—but obtains possession of the toys; or again (3) is being modeled—but he also models the others.

It has to be emphasized that in all these cases the leader must accept the traditions and can give orders only within their framework. The following is a nice example: into a well-developed group of children, 4 to 5 years old, a leader of 6½ with a strong personality was introduced. The group had traditional ways of using the toys. It was exactly determined who would play with what. Each toy, though they might exchange them for a while, traditionally constituted the possession of a certain child.

The leader was unable to change this rule of ownership. Yet he found himself a place in the system. At the beginning of the play period he distributed the objects, giving each child the one that "belonged to him." The children continued to ask the "owners" for the blocks or boxes when they wanted to play with them; they continued to exchange toys as before. Only now the blocks, house, or boxes were distributed by the leader at the beginning of the period. Thus he found himself a role in an order which was there when he first arrived, though unable essentially to change the existing traditions.

56 THE FORMING OF TRADITION

We have examined the influence of the group on a new leader. We have seen that the group forces its traditions on the leader; and that with varying circumstances the process involves changes while the basic tendency remains the same. We have seen that the capitulating leader still makes his superior personality felt. Even though he accepts the group's traditions, he exerts an influence. Even in the case of total assimilation of the leader we find changes in the group's life which can be ascribed to his influence.

For example, one group always built trains out of blocks. The leader followed this activity. He too built trains, only he put a chimney on his locomotive. The others followed suit.

Another group's traditional game was to climb up and hang on to the top edge of a wardrobe and to swing there. The leader—of the type that gives orders but is being modeled—soon joined the game. Only one child at a time could swing on the wardrobe. On each side stood a chair to climb up on. Shortly after the leader joined the group he introduced a "one-way traffic." Everything went on as before with the execption that the children had to climb up one side and down the other. This innovation added color to the game without changing its structure. Such phenomena occurred often. Almost every leader, just as soon as he met the group, reorganized it, introducing direction and order.

In other cases this coloring lent by the leader pertained rather to the contents, as when a fitting little story was introduced. One group that played with a small house said: "This is the mailman's house—in the evening he comes home—in the morning he leaves." In the game itself there was no mailman. The children put nothing into the house. The mailman was not even symbolically represented. The words were merely additional coloring. On this the leader elaborated: "The mailman brings coal—they put it on wagons and trucks, etc." The others took over these little themes and their activity, though undamaged, became more colorful.

Often the leader would step up the pace of activity. This is another way to impose his will on the group. He would dictate a very fast tempo, driving them. A certain type of leader needed to create this acceleration of pace: a child who is very active, who has many interests, whose attention is divided, and who has a stormy temperament. Such leaders busy themselves with several things at once, join several games at once, and with their "swing" accelerate the group's life.

An interesting influence of the leader is the *widening of the terrain*. The group's accustomed space becomes larger: a group that has worked in one portion of the room will, after the leader appears, expand into the entire room. The way this occurs clearly shows the relationship between a developed group and a new leader.

One group would play around a table in the middle of the room. From time to time they would go to the wardrobe in one corner of the room and try to climb up. Then the new leader appropriated the table, whereupon a migration to the wardrobe took place where they started the game of climbing up. The leader followed them and started organizing that game. Slowly the children shifted back to the table, but the leader was on their trail. The result was a pendulum-like movement between table and wardrobe. Then one child went to a new place and started doing something there. At once the leader extended his pendulum motion to that place. A veritable pilgrimage began. Everywhere the leader was being modeled: he was the one who adjusted to the others' mode of activity.

Another frequent influence of the leader is that he changes the degree of concerted action. The degree of group action is not to be confused with the degree of creative activity of a person. When a presocial formation of four people sit together, one reading a philosophical treatise, the other solving a mathematical problem, the third writing an ode, etc., without having anything in common with each other, the group is of a lower social level than a foursome playing bridge.

During our investigations we observed that in some cases the leader brings a presocial group to a higher degree of concerted action, in other cases to a lower one. If, for example, a group that has merely congregated around a set of toys is organized into one with a division of roles, the group level has been raised. It will be lowered if group activity is reduced to mere side-by-side play. Such raising or lowering of group level depends mostly on the personal qualities of the leader, especially on his capacity to organize. The capacity consists of the bent to remember every custom, to see to it that objects are returned where they belong and that the rituals are observed, even if these were learned from the group. The leader who has this quality raises the group level even if he totally submits to the group's traditions.

THE POWER OF THE GROUP

Our question was: Which is stronger, the group made up of individuals of average social penetration, or the individual of high degree of social penetration but alien to the group?

Our criterion was, not the relationship between the new leader and the individual group members, but that "plus" arising from "groupness" which raises the power of the group above the aggregate strength of its members. This "plus" shows in the habits, customs, rules, and relationships making for institutionalization. Accordingly, the individual is the stronger of the two if he can change those traditions; but the group is the stronger if it assimilates the leader.

Couching our inquiry in these terms lent decisive importance to the ratio *modeling/being modeled.*

Our investigations have shown that the group with a tradition is stronger than the leader (though he is stronger than any one group member).

The play of forces between leader and group resulted in the following graduations:

1. The leader is totally assimilated;
2. The leader is being modeled but gives orders;
3. The leader is being modeled but gains possession of the toys;

58

4. The leader is being modeled but modifies the traditions;
5. The leader destroys the group's traditions and introduces new ones. It is rare that the leader should become not only the center of the group but also the maker of its rules.

Which of these five situations will obtain depends on:

1. The degree of crystallization of traditions;
2. The extent of collaborative play;
3. The degree of group cohesion (the marginal child included).

These conditions issue from the nature of the group. It is no doubt important what kind of person, what character type the new leader is. It may be that in the child who expropriates the toys in order to set himself up as leader a desire for acquisition asserts itself; it may be that the child who gives orders is driven by narcissism and aggression. However, our investigation did not extend to these motivations.

Even the leader who is forced to accept existing traditions makes his superiority felt: he may lend color to activities, step up the pace, widen the field, or change the group level by influencing cohesion.

In our experiment, individuals of strong social penetrating power seldom became changers of traditions; however, being modeled to the existing traditions, they influenced them.

We were thus able to experience that "plus" which makes the group more than and different from the aggregate of its members: as in cases where the new leader conquered everyone, where each child followed his orders—as long as *what* he ordered was in agreement with the group's traditions.

It is in this peculiar strength of tradition that this group "plus" appears. Its carriers are the individuals constituting the group. By belonging to the group each is "more" and stronger. This became clear when children who in the day nursery were *being modeled* by leaders there, became the models of these leaders in the organized group.

Thus the group "plus" is not some substance hovering above the group; it is the hold their customs and habits have on the members; it is tradition, the carrier of which is the individual, who, in turn, is strengthened by it. Conceivably, the feeling of heightened intensity always evoked by group experience is the experiencing of just this "plus."

Why does the leader accept the group's traditions? Is it because he is weaker than its members, or more suggestible? No. We have seen him in the day nursery, modeling the others. Is it because he is in a new situation where the group members have the advantage of being familiar with the situation? This is contraindicated by the behavior of leaders who give orders quite without inhibition. The dichotomy is clear: the leader is supraordinated since he gives orders; but he is also subordinated since he is being modeled. He has the upper hand vis-a-vis the members but has to bow to group tradition.

Thus the reaction of the group to the new leader clearly brings into view the power of the group "plus." It is this "plus" that is stronger than the leader who is stronger than any one group member.

With this we can discard all hypotheses which deny the uniqueness of the group, and which attempt fully to account for the group by assessing its members.

Our experiment refutes the prejudice of metaphysical social psychology that the group, through an evening effect, lowers the level of the individual. We observed exactly the opposite: the strength of the group strengthens its members. Group experience not only pleases, it also strengthens.

Study Questions

1. Assuming that the experts are correct and that our population is growing faster than we can feed it, how would you propose to control the worldwide birth rate?
2. Do you feel that litigation is the answer to the environmental crises? Explain.
3. What would you do to make antipollution laws effective, if you had the authority to do so?
4. If, when you leave college, you have a 2 or 3 day work week, how do you think you might use your leisure time? Consider the fact that running your car helps to pollute the environment. Consider also that little wilderness remains for recreation, and that it is overcrowded.

The Setting of
Social Organization

3

The second chapter discussed the group as a unit of analysis which cannot be explained simply by describing and analyzing its individual members. The personalities of individuals are greatly deemphasized when a group perspective is established and maintained. It is also important to remember that groups and social organizations do not operate in a vacuum. All organizations exist in time and space and are influenced in important ways by factors that are neither group nor individual properties. All organizations, from tribes to universities, exist in a setting, are bounded by it. The factors which provide the background to social organizations are population, environment, and technology. In this chapter, I have selected one article to illustrate each of these three areas which influence social organization.

POPULATION

A population is the raw material for the creation of social organization. Population characteristics are important, for they affect the social organization of all groups. Emile Durkheim, one of the founding fathers of European sociology, argued that the study of the size and density of a society was critical for gaining understanding of the society itself. The study of society with reference to its size and density and the heterogeneity of its population is known as social morphology. The study of the characteristics of human population (such as growth, distribution, and migration as well as size and density,) and the effect of all of these on social and economic conditions is called demography. Sociologists trained in these areas are involved in the testing of hypotheses regarding the changing size and composition of social units and the ways in which population affects social processes. Let me provide an example that may be helpful in illustrating the importance of social morphology and demography. Table 1 indicates the age at marriage of American males and females for two time periods, and provides us with the median age of parents at the birth of their last child for the same time periods.

Table I.

Median age at first marriage by sex for two time periods.

Sex	Median Age	
	1890*	1966**
Male	26.1	22.8
Female	22.0	20.5

Median age of parents by sex at birth of their last child for two time periods.

Sex	Median Age	
	1890*	1966**
Male	36.0	27.9
Female	31.9	25.8

*U. S. Bureau of Census, *Historical Statistics of the United States: Colonial Times to 1957*, Washington, D. C., 1960, p. 15.

**U. S. Bureau of Census, *Statistical Abstracts of the U. S. 88th Ed.,* Washington, D. C., 1967, p. 64.

An examination of the tables indicates that the age of marriage for men and women dropped in the 75-year period. The drop in age has been about three years for men and about one and one-half years for women. The median age of parents at the time their last child is born has also declined. Here the decrease is much larger, with almost a nine-year decrease for men and a six-year decrease for women. A major implication of these facts is that in 1966 the last child born into a family will be getting married when the mother is approximately 45 to 47 years old. In the 1960s and 1970s, then, there is an increasingly larger pool of married women whose maternal career is ended at a relatively early age. A woman's children may be married before she is 50. Some women with this newly found time on their hands are interested in returning to school. Colleges have been pushed to develop special programs at special hours for these returning women. Other women, who may have finished their undergraduate education, are interested in working directly in their communities on various kinds of projects. Many women are being trained as sub-professionals to work in schools and private and public agencies. The tables show how certain morphological changes modify and influence the organization of social life.

While few of us can experience these changes, many of us experience the consequences of them. We hear, "I shouldn't have gotten married when I was 18," or, "I wish I hadn't stopped my education when I got married." These are personal statements, but at the same

64   time they reflect basic changes in the social morphology of the population.

Population is, of course, absolutely necessary for social organization. Today we have, at best, an ironic situation enveloping the world where population is concerned. That which is necessary also poses a threat to our very existence.

I have included in this chapter an article by Paul R. Ehrlich that deals with the crisis in population. Ehrlich, a biologist, predicts that world-wide famine will occur at the time you are graduating from college.

ENVIRONMENT

Environment is probably the most basic of the background conditions affecting the organized group. As we begin the 1970's, geographical determinism—the view that the physical environment determines the quality and nature of social life—no longer finds acceptance by most social scientists. More and more, man is able to control his external environment. However, as we learn about the continual pollution of our air and waters and the decimation of our land with pesticides, we are reminded of the dependency of all populations and all organized groups upon the environment.

The kinds of orientations that groups might have to the environment depend on the relationships that exist between man and nature. Man can be seen as one with, as subordinate to, or as opposed to nature. These views can be illustrated by the difference between industrial society and that of the Navajo in the choice of words used to describe man's relationship to his environment. In English we blast and build, we tunnel and bridge. We say, "I plowed the field." The Navajo, on the other hand, says, "There was a plow of the field to which I was related as to the following of the plow." Many Eastern societies stress the fact that man is at one with nature and therefore ought not to disrupt the harmony of that whole. Western societies tend to stress man's domination over nature.[1]

The prevalent mode of domination and control of the environment in Western societies has led to a needless wastefulness and destruction of our natural surroundings. In the past few years, tremendous momentum has developed to sensitize the public to the need for careful consideration of our environment. There are now a variety of old and newly developed social organizations that are attempting to change our ways of dealing with our natural resources. Whether these organizations will have any major impact on the way we use and abuse the air, water, forests, and land is problematic.

The second article in this chapter, by Joseph L. Sax, a law professor, highlights the interrelationship between social organizations and environment. Sax is concerned with the problem of making the courts into an effective instrument for change in dealing with the crisis in the environment. His article points to the difficulty, challenge and possible success of working within existing social organizations to solve environmental problems.

TECHNOLOGY

Technology is often considered to be an aspect of culture. Some scholars regard technology as the cultural feature responsible for causing changes in social organizations. The view taken here is that while technology is fundamentally important to the development of social organizations and especially to their increasing complexity, change within a social unit may occur through many other sources as well as through technological innovations. Technology, however, is important as it relates to potential and real levels of development. The names of the great ages of man, such as the Stone and the Bronze Ages, reveal the importance of technology in societal organization.

Technology also has tremendous importance in our modern industrial societies. Technology is a major factor in social change and in the quality of collective life that develops. One of the main themes of Karl Marx's early writings was that the kind of technology he witnessed affected the content of the human relations in industry.[2] Marx noted how the new factory technology with its highly mechanized system had replaced the craft type of production. In the craft type organization of work, the worker or artisan is the master over his tools and his materials. In the industrial organization, the worker is at the mercy of machines that control the pace and rhythm of his work. Marx felt that this loss of freedom, this inability to control work, this subordination of the worker to the machine, turned the worker from a person into a thing. The worker no longer had a feeling of potency or worth; instead, feelings of powerlessness grew. The fact that the jobs and tasks were simpler meant that the worker was only involved in simple hand, foot, or other bodily movements that did not require thought or decision making. This robbed the worker of his sense of purpose. The loss of meaning or purpose and the feeling of powerlessness are some aspects of the concept of alienation, a phenomenon that I shall return to in a later chapter.

Marx's consideration of alienation as an inexorable consequence for all workers has been examined in a study by Robert Blauner. Blauner found that alienation is distributed unevenly throughout the labor force. He differentiated three types of technology: (1) craft technology, found in the printing industry, in which the worker is not dominated by technology as much as he is diminished as an important variable in the work; (2) assembly-line technology, found in the automobile industry, which is characterized by an extreme subdivision of work and a set speed and method for completing the task determined by a conveyor belt; and (3) continuous-process technology, found in certain chemical and oil plants, in which the worker does not deal with the product directly but must utilize his judgment in monitoring and controlling the equipment. He reads instruments at his own pace and has a certain freedom of movement. Blauner discovered different types of social relations and different amounts of alienation in these varying work situations.[3]

Technology continues to be a source of great change and hence great challenge for mankind. The possibilities of having ma-

66

chines make machines and of creating man anew through molecular biological transformations are real issues for contemporary societies.

The third article in this chapter is by Kent D. Shinbach, a psychiatrist. Shinbach describes the impact of technology on social organization. Specifically, he touches on the organization of leisure, education, and on the possible changes in sexual identity and social structure wrought by automation and molecular biology. Shinbach's article raises a number of questions that he does not answer, but poses for us to reflect on our future together on this earth.

NOTES

1. Florence Rockwood Kluckhohn, "Dominant and Variant Value Orientations," *Personality in Nature, Society and Culture* (New York: Alfred A. Knopf, Co., 1956), pp. 342–57.

2. T. B. Bottomore and Maximilien Rubel, *Karl Marx: Selected Writings in Sociology and Social Philosophy* (London: C. A. Watts and Co., 1956). *See also* C. Wright Mills, *The Marxists* (New York: Dell Publishing Co., 1962).

3. Robert Blauner, *Alienation and Freedom: The Manual Worker in Industry* (Chicago: University of Chicago Press, 1963).

PAUL R. EHRLICH

Famine 1975: Fact or Fallacy

The population problem has already been solved. It took a person willing to step outside the narrow bounds of a discipline, to look at the whole paradigm, to come up with an answer which was both simple and yet unthought of by people working under the strictures of their narrow interests. Dr. Sripati Chandrasekhar, the head of Family Planning in India, came up with the final answer. It will clearly work for India, and it could also work very well in other parts of the world. His proposed solution: at least a one-year moratorium on sexual intercourse in India. However, just in case that does not solve our population and environmental problems, perhaps we should look at them once again so that we will have some background to judge what to do next.

Where did this current crisis come from? Probably, the place to date it is about 8,000 years ago when mankind in small groups first gave up a hunting and food-gathering existence and began the practice of agriculture. Two very important things started at that time. First, life became a little more secure. Man was able to pro-

Paul R. Ehrlich, "Famine 1975: Fact or Fallacy?" from Harold W. Helfrich, Jr., ed., *The Environmental Crisis*, pp. 46–63. Copyright © 1970 by Yale University. Reprinted by permission of Yale University Press.

duce a more secure food supply and so, slowly but surely, the human death rate (the number of people dying per thousand annually) started to drop. Second, man began to create ecologically unstable situations. He began to arrest succession in early stages to take advantage of the high productivity, and started a process which has continued to this day.

The growth of the human population was slow at first. With a Ouija board, one of the main tools of a demographer, we could guess that there were about 5 million people alive around 6000 B.C., and it took until approximately A.D. 1650 to increase that to 500 million. This means that during that 7,650-year period the population doubled about every 1,000 years. The next doubling required just 200 years; so we had roughly a billion inhabitants of earth around A.D. 1850. In only 80 years, by 1930, mankind numbered 2 billion. Less than 40 years later we are nearing the next doubling; the figure stands at about 3.5 billion. The gap between the death and birth rates is widening so fast that the population of our planet will double in a brief 35 years.

The basic reason for this speed-up is improved socioeconomic conditions which have depressed the death rate. The agricultural revolution came first. Then—particularly between 1500 and 1700 in Europe—improvements in agriculture further lowered the death rate. The succeeding Industrial Revolution did two things: it again bettered people's living conditions and so depressed the death rate, and it started a trend in industrialized countries to lower birth rates slightly.

The medical revolution at the dawn of this century pushed down the death rate even farther, but birth rates in industrial countries were also declining rather rapidly as a result of changed conditions. People no longer looked upon children as a source of farm labor. They could see the possibility of affluence, and children were expensive to educate. So, in the industrialized countries, the birth rate started to follow the death rate down.

With World War II the ultimate catastrophe was upon us in the sense that we took our tremendous medical technology for death control and suddenly disseminated it all over the world. The result: throughout what the euphemists like to call the "undeveloped world" (or, as others more correctly label it, the "hungry world") we had a disastrous decline in the death rate. At the same time there were slight rises in the birth rate, thanks to the eradication of such diseases as gonorrhea in areas where it causes a certain amount of sterility. Thus, by disseminating death control at the end of World War II, we put the finishing touches on our problem so far as the demography goes, and some population growth rates have moved up to degrees which we would have thought theoretically impossible 10 or 15 years ago. What we have done is to alter half of the demographic equation, the death rate, without intervening to lower the birth rate.

You can always recognize that someone is kidding you about demography when he talks only in terms of birth rates. You can have a lot of fun saying, "Gee, India has a great program. We are going to reduce the birth rate from 45 to 35 per thousand over the next ten

68   years." This sounds like a big move, because demographers talk classically in terms of numbers per thousand per year instead of percentages. What they do not tell you is that the death rate will simultaneously drop from 14 to 9 per thousand. Therefore, the growth rate, which is the difference between the death and birth rates expressed as a percentage, will remain virtually the same. The clue for discovering whether somebody is pulling your leg when he talks about demography is to find out whether he includes the death rate or talks only about goals in terms of the birth rate.

Our population now is doubling roughly every 35 years. A lot of people ask, "Why can't population grow forever?" The old statistics are still valid for a reply. At the current rate, in 900 years there will be a billion billion people on the face of the earth or 1,700 for every square mile. Projecting this farther into the future, in about 2,000 or 3,000 years people would weigh more than the earth; in 3,000 to 4,000 years, the mass of humans would equal the size of a sphere with the same diameter as the earth's orbit around the sun; in 5,000 years everything in the visible universe would be converted into people, and their expansion would be at the speed of light. All of those mathematically foreseeable results are far enough in the future to relieve us of any necessity for worry.

Occasionally, someone can be convinced that population growth will end sooner or later. Unfortunately for us, it is going to be sooner, because like other organisms with a very rapid population increase, we tend to press on our resources, and the second part of the population-food environment crisis is that we are running out of food. Out of the 3.5 billion humans on earth today, between 1 and 2 billion are malnourished or undernourished.

The number who are actually starving is a matter for some debate, since we have the problem of how to define starvation. It is very difficult to starve someone to death. He has to live in an abiotic environment with a slow deprivation of food. Otherwise, he will be carried away by pneumonia, the flu, or something else before he even technically gets a chance to starve to death.

Demographic statistics produced by most countries arise from imagination. The Indians, for instance, just make up their figures. The ones that might be valid are created in curious ways. In the *New York Times Magazine* of October 13, 1968, correspondent Joseph Lelyveld in India had the following commentary which sums it up very well: "The Indian government does not like to concede that there is starvation in the country and so splits hairs by insisting that all grossly undernourished persons who die are actually carried off by identifiable diseases, thereby side-stepping the fact that it is precisely the lack of food that makes killers of what would otherwise be curable ailments."

If we take the only intelligent definition of starvation—that a person is starved to death if an adquate diet would have assured survival—then the level of deaths due to starvation in the world today is truly colossal, somewhere between 5 million and 20 million people a year. Again, we have this definition problem. The statistics are worse where the problem is worse, but there is a tremendous amount of death from starvation. It is estimated that of 530 million Indians, only 10 million have an adequate diet. This reveals a lot, also, about the sluggishness, the laziness, of tropical peoples; a great many characteristics that we regard as natural sloth result from combined malnutrition and high levels of parasite infection. A recent series of studies has shown, for instance, that a person with a low protein diet early in life finds it virtually impossible ever to catch up, so far as IQ or brain volume is concerned, to say nothing of physical size.

Evolutionarily, from an anthropomorphic view, we faced a little problem a good number of millions of years ago: How do you have a child with a very big head and, at the same time, women who are not shaped entirely like bells? Somehow, you must get that head out through the mother's pelvis at birth. Evolution solved it by providing for the majority of brain growth immediately after birth. Of course, brain growth involves protein synthesis; you synthesize proteins from components of other proteins that you have digested. If either the mother in the late stages of pregnancy or the child early in life does not have an adequate diet, the youngster never catches up and becomes a mentally retarded individual.

Many of the reasons for our own starvation and poverty problems in this country can be traced to the Department of Agriculture's running of our food programs and feeding white flour and lard to people who are on relief, rather than having the Department of Health, Education, and Welfare do it and feed adequate protein-rich food to the disadvantaged.

An extremely serious starvation problem exists on earth at this moment. In 1965 and 1966 a tremendous crisis in world agriculture was blamed on "bad weather." It was a "good" year in 1967; there was a 3 percent worldwide rise in agricultural productivity. However, it was an increase from the low 1965-1966 base, and in 1967 per capita food production (which is the critical thing) had not caught up to 1964. So things were very bad. They continue to be very bad.

Summing up so far, we have too many people and a ridiculously high growth rate, and we are running out of food.

Several other things have not been pointed out often in the area of population growth. First, all demographic projections are linear. This does not mean they are necessarily straight lines. They may be curvilinear, but when you hear a prediction that we are going to have 7 billion or 7.5 billion people in the year 2,000, it is based on the assumption that you can continue the curve.

However, there are some very fancy possibilities for discontinuities caused by increasing death rates. Famine is only one possible death-rate solution if we are not careful. Thermonuclear war is rather obvious to everybody. Interestingly enough, a top science adviser of the British government quite willingly has acknowledged to me that population pressures are, and will continue to be, adding to political tension and instability; but he was not willing to admit that population pressures would therefore add to the possibility of thermonuclear war. I leave the question open for evaluation; I am no expert in this field.

70

The potential for worldwide pestilence has been neglected by people interested in the population-food crisis. At this moment we have the largest population of human beings that has ever lived on the Earth. There are now more hungry and weakened people on this planet than there were human beings in 1850. We have jet airplanes capable of carrying sick people around the globe in about 24 hours. We know that viruses have a tendency to do crazy things when they circulate in large populations, so there is always a possibility of a virus giving us a super influenza. This could end the population explosion abruptly.

We know, too, that biological warfare laboratories are cooking up all sorts of nightmarish "weapons." (I am told that it is theoretically possible to develop a virus against which there is absolutely no resistance.) They are trying to breed drug-resistant strains of anthrax, and I am sure that they are having quite a lot of success. There have been rumblings about rabies in a pneumonic form. Rabies can be transmitted as an aerosol under very special conditions—in bat caves, for instance—and it is not a tremendous stretch of the imagination to think that a pneumonic rabies could be created. We have been assured that biological laboratories are escape-proof, that nothing will ever get out, any more than nerve gas would ever get loose because conditions there are absolutely safe, or than an underground atomic test would ever vent because the Atomic Energy Commission assures us of its impossibility. Curiously enough, though, men like Joshua Lederberg and Sir Macfarlane Burnet (both Nobel laureates in medicine and physiology) are a bit nervous about how escape-proof biological warfare labs are. Apparently here is another possibility for a discontinuity to end the population explosion by sharply bringing up the death rate again.

The third part of the equation is environmental deterioration. Anybody who has eyes or a nose should be well aware of it. There are several points to be made about environmental deterioration: we are changing the climate of the earth in various ways, by the pollutants we put into the atmosphere, by deforestation, and so on. Changing the climate cuts down agricultural productivity because people are extremely conservative in their agricultural practices. Once we have modified the weather, we have to plant different crops; a transition to a new kind of crop culture means a depression in the amount of food, so that kind of environmental deterioration plays directly back on our food supply. A very serious and desperate moral problem follows as a result of our frantic attempts to create more and more food.

A politically active petrochemical industry has created in this country preposterous pesticide procedures in which everybody is persuaded to spray on schedule whether there are pests present or not. K.E.F. Watt of the University of California (Davis) has done a lot of systems analyses on this problem; his general conclusion seems to be that pesticide usage in the United States is a losing game financially for everyone except the petrochemical industry.

Biologists have long been able to tell people that broadcast usage of pesticides is ecologically ignorant. Thanks to the second law of thermodynamics and other considerations, herbivore populations are virtually always larger than predator populations; they automatically contain a greater degree of genetic variability, and therefore they are most likely to become genetically resistant. I would also point out something of which most people in the pesticide business do not seem to be aware: plants have been in the pesticide business longer than industrialists; virtually all plant biochemicals are antibiotic agents of one kind or another, mostly aimed at insects. The insects have been evolving in this system for a long time; they have already prepared themselves to be poisoned and are quite capable of developing resistance. Despite many professional conversations, I have yet to hear of a single case where a pest insect has been eradicated through pesticide usage, although there are many cases of nonpest insects winning promotion to pest status by ridiculous pesticide usage. So the whole thing—how pesticides are applied, how extremely resistant pests are to change, and how ignorant people are of this entire problem—really beggars the imagination.

Pesticides recently have been shown to reduce photosynthesis in marine phytoplankton. We know there is plenty of DDT in the ocean because it shows up in rather high quantities in Antarctic seals, Antarctic penguins, and other organisms not subjected to daily spraying. There is now rather strong evidence that chlorinated hydrocarbon poisoning may already be a major cause of human mortality, and that the worst is yet to come.

We have an extremely serious problem in the way agriculturists think about agricultural revolution. Producing more food almost always involves dramatic deterioration of the environment. In fact, it usually involves the worst possible consequence: simplifying the ecosystem.

Basically then, we have a tripartite problem. We have too many people and an incredible growth rate, and we are just about out of food. And we have this fantastically difficult and important problem of environmental deterioration; this scares me much more than being almost out of food, because we are quite capable of turning off the life-support systems on which we absolutely depend.

Why isn't something being done? One of the best reasons is that there are a great many people, narrowly trained technologists, who can see only their own little areas. They keep publishing absolutely absurd things about how we are going to save the world with this, that, or the other simple solution.

At a population meeting in Princeton some time ago, a suggestive cure was to look into ways of shipping our surplus population to the other planets. The person who proposed this is a typical technological optimist; he can do anything but count. Let me make a few optimistic assumptions. Let's suppose that an Apollo spacecraft could carry 100 people. That would require some modifications; it would be a bit crowded, but let's do it—100 colonists. Let's assume that it could not just put people into orbit but could carry them to any planet. Let's assume that the uninhabitable planets of our solar system were really inhabitable. And let's assume that you could send off these rocket ships for exactly the same cost as an Apollo craft, even though they would have to be much larger, more complex, and there would be the extra cost of rounding up and training all the colonists.

We *could* keep the population of the earth constant in number by exporting surplus humans. All we would have to do is send off 2,000 of our normal-sized Apollo space vessels every day. The daily cost would be $300 billion. That is the equivalent of our Gross National Product in less than three days, so we really would have to pay hefty taxes to get such a job done.

If we could get Congress to repeal the laws of thermodynamics and a few other things, it would take only 250 years at the present growth rate for humans to occupy the entire solar system to exactly the present population density of the earth. If we then wanted to move on to the stars, which involves some slightly bigger logistical problems (we do not want to get into them because we are being optimists) we would face the fact that the nearest stars with possible habitable planets are a long way off. They would take generations to reach. We would have to export people willing to practice strict birth control, and leave the technological optimists and other people back here to breed. That would be quite a program!

Actually, such thinking does a lot of damage. We all can laugh at it because *we* presumably know that doing something with 70 million more people a year—and that is the yearly increment (more than the population of the United States every three years)—is not so easily solved. But every time someone appropriately "reputable" says, "When it gets really tough here, we will send our surplus to the stars," he gets newspaper headlines; and everyone says, "Well, that is a solution to the problem. We can forget about it. Turn on the pollution, George. They are going to take care of everything, and there is no problem."

The AEC has been in this game recently. It did a huge feasibility study for feeding the underdeveloped world. (Let's hope that part of the globe stays underdeveloped, because if we ever tried to develop it, the world would end for reasons I will explain later.)

The AEC came up with a few simple technological assumptions. For instance, it is going to be able to develop functional breeder reactors. That is not too bad an idea, although it may overestimate the speed at which we will get them. After a lot of figuring it found that it could build nuclear agro-industrial complexes on the seashore in which nuclear power could desalt water. It reached more optimistic assumptions about the cost of desalted water than any expert in desalinization would make, but we will give it that; we are going to give it all its assumptions. Then, it would create fertilizer and make a wonderful complex capable of feeding 3 million people.

This can be done for a mere $1.5 billion per complex. So far as I can find out, that estimate does not include the cost of buying the land, or shipping people to the food or food to the people if the complex is put in an uninhabited area, or training the technicians, or maintenance, or anything like that. But let's just use the $1.5 billion figure as the total cost. If the AEC began this project tomorrow and could finish it within a decade, we would have to put in $400 billion (a very large sum when you recall that our annual foreign aid is $2 billion) simply to feed the 770 million people who will be added to the population during those ten years. Assuming all the AEC assumptions are correct, the 1978-1988 decade would cost about $500 billion and the 1988-1998 decade about $600 billion, which means that we would have spent somewhere around $1,500 billion by 1998.

At that point, we would be worse off than today. All the people who are hungry today still would be hungry then. We would not have fed any of them, just the increase.

We would have all the environmental deterioration associated with this fantastic complex: all the pesticides that would have been dumped, all the salt which nobody would know what to do with. If you dump the salt back into the ocean as brine, you kill off the inshore richness of the sea, which is one of the places where you can get some food; if you leave it lying out in huge pans, it blows into the sky and changes the weather.

Here are serious people who have put together this absolutely preposterous scheme. The way they set it up, we could not even start to build one of these nuclear agro-industrial complexes with the equivalent of our present foreign aid funds—not one. Yet we would need hundreds of them just to cope with the population increase alone. Let's suppose that people were willing to spend just the first ten years' $400 billion. With that much money we could offer $650 bounties for vasectomies to 500 million young men. We even could set aside $100 for the medical costs of doing each vasectomy. That is a tremendous input of money, but let me point out that $650 equals eight years' income for the average Indian. They are trying to sell vasectomies in India for a couple of dollars apiece or a cheap transistor radio. The difference of scale is tremendous, and if we could get even a sizable portion of the males to accept such a tremendous bounty, we would instantly solve a very large part of the essential population problem. This, of course, hinges on whether or not we want to spend that kind of money.

Technological optimists have other schemes for feeding the world that are not quite so far out. They include the "unmeasurable" resources of the sea which have really been measured very accurately and found to be wanting. By now it is quite commonly recognized that most of the sea is a biological desert, very unproductive. Most of the productivity is inshore where we are now facing colossal pollution problems around the globe. Thermodynamically, what we do at sea anyway is equivalent to harvesting lions on land, using only the top of the food chain.

Besides the tremendous problem of ocean pollution, we can see now the beginning of what is probably world history's biggest race. That is the race to loot the sea of what protein it still contains. The Japanese, the Russians, the Chileans, the Americans, the Norwegians, and many others are building huge, more efficient fleets to sail out and get what there is while the getting is good. For instance, an undeclared shooting war exists between Mexico and Japan off Baja California because of Japanese fishing-fleet activities. The northern coun-

74   tries are moving into southern waters because their own seas have become depleted. A single Rumanian ship with "space-age" equipment recently outfished all 1,500 ships of the New Zealand fleet.

The oceans will never be a tremendously important source of calories, although they might continue to supply a significant amount of animal protein. If we have the agricultural revolution in the tropics with pesticides, as some undeveloped countries now plan, very soon they will not be any source of food at all.

Another scheme involves growing microorganisms on algae or the fecal slime of sewage treatment plants. It is not clear to me who is going to eat this stuff, but that is one of the proposals I have recently picked up in a newspaper story. It is of some consequence to note that the hungry people in the world are much more conservative about their food habits than we are. Why? Because to them food is a very limited number of items. We have trouble, for instance, convincing some people to eat IR-8 rice (this is the new high-yield rice grain developed in the Philippines at the International Rice Research Institute); they balk if it is too starchy and sticks together, since they are used to eating rice that falls apart. People will starve to death in rice areas rather than eat wheat, which they do not recognize as food. And yet somebody suggests taking algae from the sewage treatment plants and shipping it overseas to feed the hungry! Imagine the propaganda asspects of this particular plan. Fortunately, nobody is really trying to push it. We can grow microorganisms on petroleum and get protein, quite true. Nobody has tried to market it. Attempts have been made to market food additives such as Incaparina (corn combined with high-protein cotton-seed meal, Vitamin A, and yeast, developed by the Nutrition Institute of Central America and Panama), which is quite close to what we regard as food. But in Latin America for about the last 15 years efforts to get people to use this as a food supplement have been a total failure.

Recently I saw in a popular periodical a plan for farming blue whales in coral atolls; it was a real beauty, and I will not bother to describe it. The direct synthesis of food is put forth as a possible solution by people who do not understand thermodynamics. One little old lady asked me, "Can't we all eat dehydrated food like the astronauts?"

All of the technological panaceas for increasing food production are either impractical, impossible, ludicrous, or worse. One that is highly touted by our Department of Agrobusiness in Washington is known in the trade as the "Green Revolution." I believe the "Revolution" is to be created in the bankrolls of certain businesses in the United States, because it certainly is not being created anywhere else. The reversal of stories from the U.S. Department of Agriculture is something magnificent to behold. In the 1965-1966 "bad weather" time, everybody was filled with pessimism. Then, in 1967, the weather improved in India and the other key regions. All of a sudden agriculture was doing a great job; all the high-yield wheat, sorghum, and rice varieties were going to save the world. This is still the current story.

If we are going to increase food production, the most intelligent way is to get higher yields from land already in cultivation. There is nothing wrong with that idea if it is done with great care for the ecological consequences—which, of course, it is not. But there are all kinds of problems in the new high-yield grains; they are high-yield only with proper cultivation, including a great input of fertilizer, and in most of the areas where they are being planted, there are serious problems of fertilizer distribution. Raymond H. Ewell at the State University of New York (Buffalo) has been India's chief fertilizer consultant for the last dozen years; he says quite frankly that he does not think that India has a hope of producing enough. It is certainly impossible for the United States to produce enough fertilizer for India, in addition to meeting our domestic needs, to get the maximum yield out of these grains; it also seems unlikely that the world will donate enough fertilizer to India. So there is a very big fertilizer problem. You have to grow crops exactly right to get successful harvests. From what other people and I have seen personally in India, the chance of their doing things exactly right seems to be about zero. An even more serious problem arises in planting grains which have been inadequately field tested against pest and blight resistance because this project is rush-rush. Already IR-8 rices have had a lot of trouble from this problem (recently "miracle rats" have invaded "miracle rice" fields in the Philippines), but even bigger monocultures are being created. A complete switch to the new high-yield grain varieties would leave India with only about half of the possible diversity of wheat strains. This means that, instead of a Bihar or a Pakistan famine, when a virus gets in and wipes out the crops, it will cover a much larger area. These are dangers of increased monoculture.

Another problem which seems to be endemic to agriculturists is that almost all of their projections are based on optimism—that good years are normal years. When I visited Australia, that country was having a colossal drought, and the agriculturists were saying in the press: "This is once in a million years; we have got to build, we have got to get relief; everything is going to be all right when the rains come." However, Australian weather records indicate that similar droughts occur with monotonous regularity every ten years or so. It is the same story in India, the same in China. They have deforested most of their land; among other things, this helps to create unstable weather. We know very well that you cannot expect long stretches of good years. There are good years interspersed with doses of bad years. For instance, last July the Indian government—which was churning out all kinds of propaganda about how it is going to become self-sufficient in agriculture by 1971—was so pleased with the year's crops that it created a special commemorative postage stamp about the great agricultural breakthrough. If India, which now can feed adequately only 10 million out of 530 million inhabitants, is to gain self-sufficiency in food by 1971, it will mean feeding 530 million people—plus an increment of 50 to 60 million. I have yet to meet any person who has been there who thinks that India could possibly be close to self-

76 sufficiency in food by 1971. Indeed, I am willing to predict that India will never be self-sufficient in food unless it succeeds in cutting its population far back.

The headlines of the "Green Revolution" have been seen all over India. The Indian government is afraid that we will not send them any more food if it does not make progress in agriculture, so it makes unwarranted claims. However, if you look in the *New York Times*, you will find the following pieces of information: on September 24, 1968, six of 17 Indian states were drought-stricken, with uncertain crop outlooks; the Indian government was looking around for additional food; on October 13, a cholera epidemic hit other states of India which were flooded.

Still, agriculturists have a general feeling that somehow these new crops will solve the world's food problem. This feeling resulted primarily from a square yard of corn planted in Iowa. Five agronomists crouched over it constantly, gave it absolutely perfect everything, and got a yield from it. Then they ran inside, took out an atlas, and figured how many square yards there are in the Amazon basin. By multiplication they determined the amount of food that could be provided in the Amazon basin—and everything is going to be all right.

Unfortunately, that just is not the way the game is played. We do not know how to farm the tropics. We do know that most tropical soils are abysmal. We are not really making substantial progress with farming anywhere in the tropics, and it seems highly unlikely that we are going to. In other words, we will score some little gains with these high-yield crops, but they will be made at great ecological risk.

Here is another quotation, this one from a *Time* book review:

The neo-Malthusians want to warn man of danger, but their alarm
is so loud that it may have the effect of deafening the world to its opportunities. To the real agricultural scientists close to the soil and its sciences,
such pessimism sounds silly or worse. They are sure that the modern
world has both soil and the scientific knowledge to feed, and feed well,
twice as many people as are living today. By the time the population has
increased that much man may, and probably will have, discovered new
ways of increasing his food supply.

The article describes the optimism of a Dr. R. Salter of—guess what!—the U.S. Department of Agrobusiness about how we can feed the 2.25 billion humans who the Food and Agriculture Organization (FAO) of the United Nations predicted would be living in 1960. The quotation is from *Time* of November 8, 1948. Actually, when 1960 arrived, there were 3 billion people living, not the 2.25 billion estimated by the FAO. (*Time*, by the way, thought the 2.25 billion was probably a high estimate.) It is also a fact that in 1960 those agriculture experts were not adequately feeding even 2 billion of the 3 billion.

I wish I could avoid taking some of the blame for the agricultural experts, but academic biologists have a large share here. In my generation we were trained to think that anything pertaining to agriculture or applied or technical study was dirty, not to be mentioned, and we had to go into esoteric research. As a result we have produced a generation of agriculturists who can farm Iowa beautifully; they can get out press releases beautifully, but they cannot count and do not realize what the world situation is. We have a generation of agriculturists who, I am afraid, do not realize what really dreadful results their propaganda is having. My story for them still must be the same; I have told it to a good number of them. They stand up in meetings and say, "But, you know we can do high-yield this and high-yield that." I reply, "When you can feed the 3.5 billion people living today, come around again, and we will talk about going on to 7 billion. Until then, sit down and shut up, because you are not doing any good.

The summary is very simple. We have dramatically outstripped our food supply with our population growth, and we are destroying our planet. The title of my discussion here is supposed to be "Famine 1975: Fact of Fallacy?" I do not know whether we are going to have famine in 1975 in the context it is usually put. We have famine right now over most of the earth, if you want to define famine as people being hungry. We have famine right now over most of the earth, if you want to define it as people starving to death. You might want to define it as that level of famine at which every American will become aware of it, because there will be almost nothing else in the newspapers. The timing of such a massive famine will depend on just a couple of things. (This is, of course, skipping the possible discontinuity—a thermonuclear war or a massive plague—either or both of which could help us avoid famine.) It will depend slightly on how successful the agriculturists are in increasing food yields, because that will put the famine off in time to make the crash bigger when it comes. And it will depend very largely on the weather. I think an estimate of 1975 is still as good as we can make, but it could be anywhere from 1972 to 1985, depending primarily on luck. I think the actual date is a quibble.

What can we do about all this? Do we just sit back and let the whole food supply system go down the drain as it is now, or do we try to do something? Those are difficult questions. If we are going to do something, we must first get the situation in the United States under some kind of control. This country needs fewer inhabitants. We must stop our population growth; we must get our population down to a size which we can properly maintain, and we have to do all kinds of dramatic things to save what is left of our environment.

In this country the rich are getting richer, the poor are getting poorer; among the nations of the earth the same situation holds true. Nobody trusts our motives. The white majority in our country must convince Black Power advocates that there is no effective conspiracy to wipe out the blacks through population control. It is quite clear that a lot of people who advocate population control really mean to stop the blacks from breeding, but that is a typically inept viewpoint that you would expect of a racist. Actually, nothing could be better for the black community than to avoid the problem of black mothers with eight or nine children who do not get proper care and who do not have proper fatherly guidance. It is quite clear that in the world today group numbers mean nothing. It is the *quality* of people that matters. So if the racists are really trying to get to the blacks by promoting population control among them, then the racists are working to defeat their own end.

We have similar problems in other countries. Former President Arthur da Costa e Silva of Brazil recently said that population control is decadent and that more people are needed to develop South America. He governed one of the few countries in South America that has a prayer of hope for bettering the lives of its people. But if his successors retain such opinions and act on them, they will guarantee that the prayer is unanswered.

First we must get things under control in the United States, and this involves some complicated maneuvering to overcome a great many difficulties. It will involve governmental intervention, changes in tax structure, and formidable changes in attitude. I believe we can get the job done in this country without real governmental coercion. However, when you start looking at other nations, the problems escalate monstrously because they do not have equivalent communications systems and we do not understand enough about their cultural fabric. We understand enough to know that family planning does not work, that just making available condom, intrauterine devices (IUDs) and contraceptive pills does not work. The basic problem lies in the people's attitudes, particularly toward family size. We must find a much greater variety of approaches—economic and governmental—which probably will be different in every country and require colossal, simultaneous campaigns. We hope each will work, and we will have to find out quickly why they do not work if they show signs of failure. It is going to be fantastically difficult. We will need worldwide and governmental policy planning of an unfamiliar type. We will have to figure out where our aid can be spent best, rather than scatter it indiscriminately. We will have to recognize the fact that most countries can never industrialize and that giving them industrialization aid is wasteful. We will have to accept the fact (already shown by theory, computer simulation, and practice) that it is pointless to help any country with a rapidly growing population unless the aid is very largely for population control, or at least unless such population control aid is included.

We are going to have to make so many changes in our behavior pattern and in the minds of men that I frankly tend toward tremendous pessimism. People say to me, "What do you think our chances are?" I answer that our chances for success may be 2 percent now, and that if we work really hard, we might move them up to 3 percent.

A great deal of political action is needed first and foremost in this country. If you do not want to be bothered with this sort of thing, perhaps you can adopt a philosophy which I find rather appealing: if you book passage on the *Titanic*, there is no point in going steerage.

JOSEPH L. SAX

The Search for Environmental Quality:
The Role of the Courts

We have an enormous quantity of rhetoric about environmental quality, and all too little talk about immediate, effective, and direct action programs. If tomorrow we amended the federal Constitution and declared that the earth was a spaceship, it would not stop a single marsh from being filled.

While we sit around at conferences and university seminars talking about the ecological conscience, dredging and filling, excavating and spraying and bulldozing go relentlessly forward. If those of us who are concerned about the degradation of the environment have something to assert, we had better plug into the mundane world of construction and condemnation, of builders and engineers, and begin to say some specific things about specific operative programs.

One very good way to achieve results when someone is doing something of dubious propriety or legality is to ask a judge to order that conduct to cease, under penalty of law. That is action of a kind which has been too rarely considered in our often grandiose plans to deal with environmental quality problems. It is action which centers on the courtroom.

Lawsuits are certainly not going to solve all our problems, but the judicial forum has been seriously underrated and too often ignored as a management institution both by those who are professionally concerned with resource problems and by the courts themselves. A particular case study may promote some understanding, if only impressionistically, of the range of potentials and limitations of the courtroom in dealing effectively and directly with environmental quality problems.

Anyone who enters a courtroom with a conservation case can first expect resistance from the court itself. The judge's principal thoughts are almost sure to be, "Why did you come to me? Why don't you take your troubles to the legislature? What do I know about all this? This is not a matter for judicial consideration. What reasons can you possibly give for suggesting that I—a judge—should substitute my judgment for the expertise of an agency or enterprise whose business it is to make the kinds of decisions you are challenging? Aren't you asking me to serve as a super-planning agency? And, in any event, what law was broken by the defendants?

"I am not here to enforce the good, the true, and the beautiful; to be the fount of ultimate wisdom and social conscience. I am here

Joseph L. Sax, "The Search for Environmental Quality: The Role of the Courts," from Harold W. Helfrich, Jr., ed., *The Environmental Crisis*, pp. 99–114. Copyright © 1970 by Yale University. Reprinted by permission of Yale University Press.

80   to enforce the law. What rule is violated by this highway plan, this dam project, or this proposal to spray elm trees with DDT?"

Finally, the judge will ask, "What damage do you charge has been done to you? Where is the broken arm or the broken contract? I am not a prophet who can speculate upon the ultimate fate of gulls and terns. I redress loss; I do not paint the future rosy."

This may appear a formidable prospect for the conservation lawyer and his client. Be assured that it *is* quite as formidable as it seems. Any forecasts of a revolution in conservation litigation are composed largely of hope and will power.

The fact is that, after six years of litigation, the famous Consolidated Edison—Storm King case involving questions of environmental damage by a proposed power plant along the Hudson River has again been decided for the utility by the presiding examiner.[1] The court which sent the case down for a second trial held only that the previous hearings had been procedurally inadequate and did not really come to grips with the specific issues.[2]

Every highway location case of which I know has been lost, or at the very most has been won on a procedural ground—such as notice or hearing irregularities—rather than on the merits of the case.[3] The pesticide litigations thus far have been largely unsuccessful in the courtroom.[4] A good many cases have been summarily dismissed on the simple ground that there was no right to sue, or that some unavailable and indispensable party was not present.[5]

Why do I think the courts have an important role to play? Why does it seem to me that the general unresponsiveness of the courts to conservation litigation is misguided? How do I think a more appropriate judicial response can be elicited?

The case which I have chosen for an illustration is by no means a typical one. Nonetheless it has several quite special virtues: it was appealed twice to the state Supreme Court, thus providing a variety of judicial reactions to conservation litigation. It involved in this process a complete trial on merits of the conservation resource issue, which is extremely rare. And it was tried by competent lawyers and a judge who was open-minded, candid, and nontechnical in his approach—not rare, but not universal either. The issue in the case was clear-cut enough to disclose how and why the court responded as it did.

The case is *Texas Eastern Transmission Company* v. *Wildlife Preserves.*[6] It involved Texas Eastern's efforts to condemn a right of way across Troy Meadows—a tract of land owned by Wildlife Preserves in New Jersey—to install one segment of a natural-gas pipeline. Wildlife Preserves is a private, nonprofit organization devoted to acquiring important natural habitats and maintaining them in that condition for such purposes as wildlife preservation, scientific study, and esthetic enjoyment. Troy Meadows, which was conceded in this case to be one of the finest inland, fresh-water marshes in the northeastern United States, is such a habitat.

Composed principally of marshland with a smaller wooded upland area on its western side, the Wildlife Preserves tract contained two significant developments when Texas Eastern instituted its suit to condemn a right of way. Running essentially north and south in the wooded area was a 50-foot-wide cleared area under which lay another company's gas pipeline, the so-called Algonquin route. In the marsh area to the east was an electric power right of way, where overhead transmission lines were strung on high towers.

Texas Eastern originally sought to condemn another 50-foot right of way in the wooded area, directly west of the Algonquin route. It wanted to clear this area, bring in its heavy equipment to dig a trench, lay its pipe, and then cover the pipe with the previously excavated earth.

Wildlife Preserves objected to this proposed condemnation, but it took neither the position that the pipeline should not be laid at all nor that it should not be laid across Wildlife Preserves land (although it had originally so claimed). If it had asserted such broad defenses, it would probably have lost the case before it even went to trial. Rather, Wildlife Preserves posed a specific and, according to them, ecologically superior alternative. It suggested that the pipe should be laid in the preserve's marsh area along the existing power-line route, and not along the upland, forested route requested by Texas Eastern. In support of this declaration—before the case went to trial—and in support of its claim that there should be a trial on the routing question, Wildlife Preserves filed affidavits which briefly sought to explain why the marsh route was more desirable. The affidavits maintained that a route through the marsh would produce less erosion and, thus, less stream pollution than a route through an upland excavation; less disturbance of the vegetative cover and a more rapid recovery of that which would be disturbed; and less adverse impact on limited and needed woodland area. It asserted that the marsh route was feasible as both an engineering and an economic matter, and that it was available.

As the case took legal form, the question was not whether Wildlife Preserves was correct in the claim that its proposed route was superior, but whether it had a legal right to litigate that issue.

Under traditional doctrine the answer has usually been a simple "no." The rule has been that when an agency with authority to condemn land (public utilities, like governments, commonly have that prerogative) exercises its condemnation power for a legitimate purpose—such as a pipeline right of way—the only question open to litigation is the amount of monetary compensation to which the condemnee is entitled. Although this is not an absolutely unqualified rule, the courts are exceedingly reluctant to permit litigation over a condemnation's necessity or wisdom, or over the manner in which the condemnation power is exercised.

Such reluctance is easily understandable. Condemnees are not frequently eager to exchange their property for cash. It would always be possible to argue interminably over the merits of taking tract A, rather than tract B, as a site for a school or fire station, or for putting a highway interchange up or down the roadway, on a neighbor's land rather than on one's own.

Therefore, at the outset, counsel for the condemnee, Wildlife

82   Preserves, was faced with a formidable legal obstacle. He wanted to litigate an issue which—for quite good reason—the courts had ruled nonlitigable.

The response of the Wildlife Preserves' counsel was one of those happy marriages of doctrine and policy which distinguishes the good lawyer from the mediocre. In it lies an essential message for all who want to get the courts to respond to conservation cases.

Courts will generally permit litigation on the merits of a condemnation in one situation: where an agency with the power of eminent domain tries to condemn property held by another agency with the same power. This is not an uncommon situation. Cities, states, highway departments, public utilities, and many other entities possess such power, and they often covet each other's land. In such cases courts may permit a trial on the question of which carries the predominant public interest, the existing or the proposed use. Obviously, without a judicial decision, the two agencies might perpetually condemn and reclaim a particular parcel of land.

Because the power of eminent domain is bestowed only on those bodies supposedly engaged in serving the public interest, it is the issue of greatest public interest which determines judicial conflicts between such agencies.

Counsel for Wildlife Preserves seized upon this doctrine. He declared that the function of his client was also public service, the maintenance of a natural area and its availability to the general public. Therefore, he said, Wildlife Preserves should be treated in the same light as a possessor of the power of eminent domain, and should be permitted to litigate the question of predominant public interest with Texas Eastern.

The idea was particularly felicitous for several reasons. To a court accustomed to thinking, "Our job is to interpret and enforce the law, and not to generate social policies," the defendant Wildlife Preserves said, "Yes, and we are asking you to apply a very conventional sort of law to a slightly unconventional situation which does not change your function. If my client were a public agency—a state park department, for example, engaged as it often is in just such disputes as this—precedent would compel you to do exactly what we are asking you to do here."

To a court which is all too ready to say that it is not equipped to indulge in this second-guessing of technical experts, or to be a super-planner, or believing that it is not competent to choose between birds and people (as many judges think of these problems), this traditional format says unanswerably: "You have engaged in such decision-making for decades, and have done it acceptably; only you never thought of it that way. So, you have nothing to fear in terms of your competence."

Moreover, by claiming that operation of a wildlife preserve is an activity invested with a public interest—as a power company or a railroad is—and entitled to the same consideration at law, counsel indirectly and cleverly moves the court toward that very radical-seeming change which is so often discussed in the abstract and so little made a part of the operative world: putting the concern with preservation of the environment on a footing with the interest in exploitation of the environment.

I have detailed this development in order to contrast it with those arguments which urge the development of an ecological conscience by judges or the recognition of a conservation bill of rights. I am by no means opposed to legislative reform or reformed attitudes—quite the contrary. However, I am dubious that such changes are going to be brought about either by statutory fiat or by a brilliant lawyer's argument. Those who say that we cannot legislate social attitudes—odious as is the context in which such views are often expressed—have a point.

Experience suggests to me that courts will not jump into the environmental quality arena with do-good zeal. They will have to be led gradually, via traditional routes (artificial as they may seem to the layman). They are not only professionally conservative, but they are genuinely and correctly concerned about their competence and their proper role in such disputes.

If judicial attitudes are to change, it will have to be an evolution arising out of accumulated experience—first with easier and more traditional-seeming cases. As the courts recognize both the potentials and the limitations of their competence, and as they educate themselves to feel more comfortable with the substantive problems, I believe they will move on to seek to deal with the problems they perceive to exist.

I do not want to appear to advocate glacial change, because I personally would like to see some needed jobs get done soon. But I believe lawyers must work carefully and cautiously in this field, lest they bring discredit on the cause they want to advance, and destroy that which they seek to create.

The process thus far described in the Wildlife Preserves case illustrates the cautious creativity which I believe is needed in this field. Counsel for Wildlife Preserves extracted from the New Jersey Supreme Court an extremely significant legal precedent with good language, with a doctrinal advance, and, most important, with a belief in his client's right to a trial on the merits of the condemnation issue.

In its opinion the New Jersey Supreme Court reasoned as follows: A public agency subject to condemnation would be entitled to a trial on whether its existing use is paramount to the condemnor's proposed use. Wildlife Preserves does not quite rise to this status, since it is not a public agency with the right of eminent domain itself. Conversely, even a private person could raise a claim of arbitrariness, and Wildlife Preserves ought to be viewed as on a somewhat higher legal plane than that. So, said the court, inventing a doctrinal middle ground to fit the case:

[Wildlife Preserve's] voluntary consecration of its lands as a wildlife preserve, while not giving it the cloak of a public utility, does invest it with a special and unique status. Qualitatively, for purposes of the present type of proceeding, the status might be described as lower than that of

84   a public utility but higher than that of an ordinary owner who puts his land to conventional use. Unquestionably, conservation of natural resources would become a legitimate public purpose if engaged in by the federal or state government or an authorized agency thereof. . . .

Under the circumstances and though [Texas Eastern's] right to condemn land in this area for the pipeline is clear, we believe . . . that Wildlife Preserves is entitled to have a plenary trial of its claim that a satisfactory alternate route is available to plaintiff which will not result in such irreparable damage to the preserve.

We conclude, [that Wildlife Preserves] should have the opportunity to present its proof as to available alternate routes for plaintiff's pipeline, which defendant claims would better serve the over-all public interest and convenience.

This was a considerable victory. It rested upon two critical factors: the court's ability to satisfy itself that it was performing a more or less conventional function; and the assurance that the case would not be merely a vague debate over vague values, but rather a rigorous comparison between two precise and available alternatives with specific evidence of specific damage to be used to compare them.

It should be noted that it was not necessary for counsel to imbue the court with an ecological conscience. Significantly—and this is a factor which is distinctly underestimated in most discussions of conservation cases—the court was perfectly ready to accept the importance of conservation, as have a number of other courts. That job of public education has already progressed surprisingly far. The problem is to put one's case in a context where a court feels that it is capable of giving recognition to those values within a familiar legal framework. That is the job which was so successfully undertaken in the first phase of the Wildlife Preserves case.

Within a month the case was back in the Superior Court of New Jersey and ready to go to trial.[7] At that point, a whole new set of questions arose: Would Wildlife Preserves really have a chance to establish the relative merit of its proposal, or would it in fact be put to the traditional and virtually impossible burden of establishing conventional arbitrariness? Would the judge be responsive? Would he be able to respond intelligently to the scientific testimony, or would he nervously tap his fingers all the while, feeling that he had a birds versus people case before him? Even with an open-minded judge, could the issues be put into a format which would make possible an intelligent decision by a nonexpert?

Even in so relatively simple a case as this there are a multitude of issues which could make a rational decision almost impossible by their incomparability. For instance, if it were found that the defendant was right about the loss of tree cover but wrong about the impact of laying the pipe in the marsh, right about the impact on streams but wrong about siltation, it is not at all clear that a rational decision would be advanced.

A principal virtue of the litigation process is its special sensitivity to the problem of defining issues. It is not simply a forum for the accumulation of information; it is also a mechanism for making decisions. Therefore, it puts a high premium on sorting and sifting **85** a controversy until it settles on the critical facts, so it can appraise the evidence and decide whether the necessary burden of proof has been carried. This is what lawyers call "joining the issue."

As one reads the trial transcript, one can almost see and feel Judge Joseph H. Stamler in the early part of the Wildlife Preserves case struggling to determine for himself not only what the facts are, but what the decisive issues are. He is trying to get the issue joined, to get the case down to a set of facts which are specific and concrete enough for the mind to assimilate and compare, and come to grips with some manageable questions. This is what is unique about the litigation process. If you have ever seen or taken part in congressional or administrative hearings, or in the processes of planning-type commissions, you know how much hot air, unproven assertion, vague denials, and plain obfuscation usually attend the resource decision-making process. In the well-run courtroom, there is no place for such nonsense. If you have an assertion to make, you had better stand ready to prove it; if you have exaggerated, you will pay for it on cross-examination; if your perspective is limited, the court will be apprised of the fact through the adversary process.

The judge in this case was not an expert on the technical questions being debated by the experts. Indeed, at one point in the trial he said, "Before this case started I looked up the meaning of ecology in the dictionary because I noted it in the Supreme Court's opinion. I was not aware of that before." But he *is* an expert in decision-making, and for this reason he was able to make sense out of the controversy. That, after all, is what was required.

For nearly 500 pages of testimony—more than a third of the trial—the judge said little. He listened and he absorbed. He wanted to know the bases of the objections by the Wildlife Preserves people. Finally, he made a tentative decision on that question: they were fundamentally concerned about all the digging up involved in the trench-laying, the erosion and siltation, the loss of vegetative cover.

If the transmission company's activities would truly have an adverse effect on the marsh and the alternate route was feasible and less destructive, Wildlife Preserves probably ought to win. While there had been some testimony about the need for continued wooded habitat for wildlife and about such things as wind-shielding trees, the defendants seemed not to have emphasized those factors and appeared to be unable to adduce any solid evidence in relation to them. Their emphasis was on the excavation problem and its aftereffects.

Now the judge had a manageable problem before him. He was hearing Wildlife Preserves' testimony on the excavation problem, and he would hear Texas Eastern testify on the same issue. He could weigh the two, and he could discover if they conflicted or were compatible. If there was conflict, possibly something could be done to make the damage less serious and reduce the conflict.

The case was not yet over, but at least the judge knew what he wanted to learn. He had plenty of witnesses left on whom to try this preliminary hypothesis about what the case involved. If it did not

86 seem to be working out—if other issues intruded, or if the testimony was excessively inconclusive, he would have to go back and work out another decisional hypothesis.

All that I have just said, of course, is my exercise in mind reading Judge Stamler. But I think that anyone who examines the stenographic transcript of the trial will find it a credible theory.

By the third day of the trial, the judge was ready to test his hypothesis. He jumped in with a question, both to educate himself and to signal the lawyers about molding the balance of the case.

Texas Eastern's lawyer had just finished cross-examining one of the Wildlife Preserves' principal witnesses; the witness was about to leave the stand. The judge interposed:

"I have one question. Stay there for a moment, please. You testified, if I understood you correctly . . . as recently as 1964, 1965, or 1966 you observed some siltation downstream that you could attribute as coming from the [Algonquin] pipeline right of way?"

A. I saw siltation leaving the pipeline in 1964.

Q. Now, you as one of the trustees of Wildlife Preserves and an expert in the field of recovery and stabilization, what steps did you take between 1953 and 1964-65 to stop that siltation from the Algonquin pipeline right of way?

A. To answer your question, we took none, sir.

Q. Steps could have been taken though, couldn't they? . . . Technology would have permitted steps to be taken to preclude the excessive or increased siltation in the lower area of the stream where it became shallow.

A. Yes.

Q. [To the lawyers] Do you have any questions?

Lawyer for Texas Eastern: No, Your Honor.

The Court. I don't know whether my questions generated anything.

Lawyer for Wildlife Preserves. I am pondering, if Your Honor please.

The Court. Take your time.

From this point on the case began to take shape. Wildlife Preserves' next witness was their most impressive, and he brought a new and critical factor into the case. When asked to state his choices on location of the pipeline, he enlarged the original two alternatives to three by saying his first choice would be the use of the old Algonquin right of way, under circumstances where great effort would be made to protect against erosion and to promote revegetation. This was a turning point because it suggested that use of the upland area for excavation was not irrevocably undesirable but seemed to depend upon the conditions of excavation and subsequent maintenance.

Again the judge intervened with a series of questions, among them the following:

"Do you feel that specific conditions can be laid down by a qualified person which would insure an equitable relationship between the ability to construct the line according to your first choice and do the least disturbance to the Algonquin line?"

The judge was now opening the way to consideration of a

new alternative, suggesting to the lawyers that they had best pursue this line of thought.

From this point on, it was Texas Eastern's case without doubt. Their lawyer first brought into the case the promise that if an upland route were allowed a number of protective measures would be taken: safeguards against erosion and to promote revegetation, to protect older trees, and to refrain from spraying the excavation area. He narrowed the easement from 50 to 30 feet, agreed that the trench would be open not more than five days, that the soil would be double ditched, aerated to prevent compaction, reseeded and mulched; that no trees exceeding 12 inches would be cut, stream banks would be protected during construction, that there would be no spraying, and that shrubs and other herbaceous growth would be permitted to grow upon the right of way.

Then the transmission company put on its own case, and that clinched its victory. Its prestigious witnesses testified that such protections would be adequate to minimize the harm. Uncontroverted engineering testimony was submitted to the effect that building too close to the existing pipeline was unsafe, so that the desired 30-foot right of way was needed. It was claimed without contradiction that to lay the pipeline in the marsh would require building a large dike for equipment to use as a roadway, which itself would create both siltation problems and the prospect of regrowth of undesired plant life.

Everything was fitting together, and as the case progressed it became inevitable that the judge would decide to grant Texas Eastern its desired right of way with the proviso that the extensive protective promises be kept.

I do not know as a technical matter whether the right decision was made in this case, but on the basis of the record, I feel confident in asserting these things:

1. I know of no nonjudicial conservation controversy in which, after having examined the record, I had so positive a feeling that every party had a fair and forthright chance to present his story to a decision-maker.

2. I know of no other controversy in which the diverse issues were so skillfully shaped and tested to bring the prospect for an orderly and comprehensible decision out of the potential chaos of multiple facts.

3. I am aware of no similar controversy in which the decision-maker—whatever his expertise—had so firm a grip on the relevant facts or was so confidently able to make a knowledgeable decision.

4. I know of no other forum in which assertion has been so skillfully tested by precise examination and cross-examination, with greatly enhanced understanding as a result. There was none of the did-you-stop-beating-your-wife business; cross-examination was used only for honorable purposes.

88

We all have heard a great deal about the job of resource managers and decision-makers in promoting what Wilbert White calls a "broader basis for choice," a wider range of alternatives. We have heard a lot of such theorizing, but I know of few instances in which resource managing and planning institutions have made alternatives emerge so effectively as in this case.

This Superior Court judge in Morristown, New Jersey, listened and learned. With his decision-making power he stimulated a large utility company into a set of specific and exact promises to conduct its business with substantially more concern for the protection of the conservation resources with which it intended to deal. I would trade his exaction of those conditions for a good many statutes with high-flown rhetoric about public hearings, local participation, concern for resource preservation, and conservation bills of rights.

The Wildlife Preserves case suggests the unique usefulness of the courts as participants in conservation resource controversies. It casts serious doubt on those decisions, particularly in highway location cases, which blithely declare that courts cannot undertake to decide the merits of such disputes. It also suggests that, while not every case is likely to be amenable to judicial resolution, a good many seemingly broad controversies can be made justiciable if they are properly prepared and shaped before the plaintiff rushes into court with complaint flying, and if he learns the lesson of joining issue, presenting alternatives, and preparing scientific witnesses to give testimony a court can understand.

I am sorry to have seen this potentially great case lost. Rarely has an appellate court so nicely set the stage for conservation litigation as did this New Jersey court. Rarely has so open a trial judge sat on such a case. It was a perfect opportunity to prove the litigability of such disputes (and it did, of course, to a substantial degree). But it would have been a much more significant precedent if Wildlife Preserves had prevailed on the merits.

I do not know whether the case was lost because the defendant's lawyer did not do his homework sufficiently well or because his clients did not know their own case as thoroughly as they should have. But coming at the case, as I did, with considerable sympathy for Wildlife Preserves, I left it persuaded that in the trial judge's place, I too would have entered judgment for Texas Eastern.

As one who is eager to promote the sensible use of the courts—not as a panacea for every resource problem, but as an extremely useful and largely disregarded instrumentality for rational management—I am deeply troubled by careless, ill-prepared, and premature litigation which can destroy the credibility of the effort to promote intelligent use of the courts. It is lamentable that Judge Stamler had to end his opinion by saying:

"I must comment that in the testimony here before me I was concerned when Mr. Perkins [President of Wildlife Preserves] stated that the Texas Eastern route would destroy valuable springs but having accepted the alternative of . . . the Algonquin right of way, I cannot see why this would not equally jeopardize the springs except that one of the expert witnesses precisely measured the springs and found them 700 feet away from the proposed right of way. I don't want to comment here upon the refutation by witnesses in open court of almost everything that Mr. Perkins averred would be the devastating damage to Wildlife Preserves property. The record is clear."

Unless I have read the record very badly, I find Judge Stamler's statement—though harsh—justifiable. He spent a week trying this case; the Supreme Court and the Appellate Division of the court twice considered the case. They made novel law for the benefit of this trial. Yet, once the way was opened, nothing solid was ready to stand the test of proof.

Similar cases exist of legal hyperbole by some of our conservation-minded brethren. They are defeating themselves by such tactics.

The critical time has arrived to take a reflective step backway to caution and responsibility, if there is to be a successful step forward to a legal strategy for environmental quality control.

NOTES

1. Consolidated Edison Company of New York, Inc., Docket No. P-2338, Presiding Examiner's Initial Decision, Federal Power Commission (Aug. 6, 1968).

2. Scenic Hudson Preservation Conference v. Federal Power Commission, 354 F. 2d 608 (2d Cir. 1965), cert. denied 384 U.S. 941 (1966).

3. E.g. Road Review League v. Boyd, 270 F. Supp. 650 (D.C., S.D.N.Y., 1967); Nashville I-40 Steering Committee v. Ellington, 387 F. 2d 179 (6th Cir. 1967), cert. denied 390 U.S. 921 (1968); D.C. Federation of Civic Associations v. Airis, 391 F. 2d 478 (D.C. Cir. 1968).

4. E.g., Murphy v. Benson, 270 F. 2d 419 (2d Cir. 1959), cert. denied 362 U.S. 929 (1960); Yannacone v. Dennison, 55 Misc. 2d 468, 285 N.Y.S. 2d 476 (1967); Environmental Defense Fund v. Ball, Supreme Court of Michigan No. 51900 (Nov. 22, 1967), and Court of Appeals of Michigan, File No. 4594 (Nov. 13, 1967).

5. E.g. Comment, Standing to Sue and Conservation Values, 38 U. Colo. L. Rev. 391 (1966); though it must be noted that standing to sue is becoming less and less a problem.

6. 48 N.J. 261, 225 A.2d 130 (1966); 49 N.J. 403, 230 A.2d 505 (1967); see McCarter, "The Case That Almost Was," 54 *American Bar Association Journal* 1076 (1968).

7. The remanded cases are Texas Eastern Transmission Corp. v. Wildlife Preserves, Inc. et al, Superior Court of New Jersey, Law Division—Morris County, Morristown, New Jersey, Docket Nos. L-8612-64, L-13678-64; L-13784-64; L-5853-65; L-5856-65; L-5860-65 (January 1967).

90 KENT D. SHINBACH

Technology and Social Change: Choosing a Near Future

For just a moment imagine a young man, somewhere in Africa, who stands wide-eyed and transfixed before the miraculous phenomenon of a ringing telephone. Only a few months ago he decided to leave his nomadic tribe and take a job as houseboy with a modern urban family. Confronting him is not merely a telephone, but the arduous process of somehow adjusting to the more than ten thousand years of cultural evolution that separate his own essentially neolithic ways from those of our world.

Or consider the members of a Puerto Rican family who, until last month, had lived on a small, remote farm which was almost unchanged from the mid-1800's. They had received an invitation from their uncle on East 110th Street in Manhattan. Last week they stepped cautiously from a jet at Kennedy Airport, and yesterday the mother and her oldest daughter found jobs before electric sewing machines in a garment district factory. This family and many others have become immersed in one of the most ambitious and unpredictable adventures of man today—the poorly understood process of cultural evolution, which anthropologists call *"acculturation."* Under this name are included not only the process of contact between different cultures, but also the infinite range of social results, such as assimilation, adaptation, rejection, and disorganization.

Malinowski[1] was among the first to emphasize acculturation; he referred to it as "the anthropology of the changing native." Today we, the most modern of us in the world's most modern cities, can and should consider ourselves changing natives. Like the tribesman, we now stand on the threshold of a new culture; before us an unfamiliar, new device is ringing, but we have hardly the faintest idea of how to respond. This device is the incredible promise that science and technology are likely to realize within decades. Our own acculturation to technical advances is therefore among the most meaningful and personally vital tasks of our time. For acculturation will occur. The question is whether it will be planned and consonant with man's interests, or haphazard and capricious.

NON-SPECIFIC EFFECTS OF TECHNOLOGY

Any new invention has at least three effects on us. First, there is the task it was designed to perform, its expected result. Second, there are the unexpected results it will have. These are often in a totally un-

Kent D. Shinbach, "Technology and Social Change: Choosing a Near Future," *Mental Hygiene* 52:2 (April 1968): 276–83. Reprinted by permission of the author and the publisher.

anticipated sphere. Our communications satellite, Telstar, was first planned to by-pass costly land-based relay stations. But certainly its greatest impact is in capturing all of us as eyewitnesses of events everywhere. Wars are seen in terms of men in deadly action, rather than as delayed, impersonal statistics and images compiled by a distant secretary. But, tragically, not all unexpected results are even this "beneficial." In this category we have the relationship between the industrial revolution and environmental pollution, or between advanced medical techniques and the population explosion. The third effect I shall term the "aura of introduction." By this I mean the remarkable extent to which a new device can evoke our involvement. Certainly the attraction of the new has often fostered invaluable results; however, the involvement has sometimes seemed to inspire a particular momentum of its own that excludes less dramatic but more human needs. Many argue, for example, that more highways cannot aid efficient transportation, but only replace the cities they were meant to serve. In a similar vein, disposable beer cans often litter picnic grounds as well as facilitate picnics. It may be the same with modern weaponry.

AUTOMATION

Today computers keep exotic company. Without them there would be no nuclear power plants, no space program, and probably no commercial jet airline service. At this moment, computers are simulating molecular motion, rocket trips, and the thinking process. Their greatest impact, though, will result from their partnership with men in everyday life.

Computers are capable of wide application because they use the same simple logic for all problems. It is called "binary logic" because it has only two states, usually writen as 1 and 0, but capable of signifying yes/no, true/false, hot/cold, or any other alternatives, which makes it uniquely suited for communication between different systems.[2] Unlike proposed international languages, which failed because they required all users to be uniform, the computer will, in the future, be able to accept any number of different languages, or different systems, process them in its own binary logic, and respond in the user's idiom. Computers offer an electronic Esperanto immediately comprehensible to each person. Significantly, among the first messages that men received from space were digital signals sent from Mariner IV near Mars; they were converted on earth by a data-processing system into the international language of pictures. How will the first beings from another world communicate with us? Whatever mode they use, if man can discern it, the likelihood is that standard data-processing techniques will be able to translate it. Another important aspect of what we could term the impending conversation among all men is the development of input devices that will allow us to address the computer in everyday English. It is already possible to do this by drawing a picture on a monitor with a light pencil; but still greater accessibility (e.g., with handwritten and verbal instructions) will lead to unparalleled application, so that the ability to program will be as widespread as literacy is today.

92

Two more characteristics of computers figure importantly in our future. One remote access, allows the use of the same computer by persons anywhere in the world, often by means of ordinary telephone equipment. The second is time sharing which depends on the computers' high speed of calculation and enables them to give each one of several users the machine's entire attention for the few microseconds required by his particular program.

These features make it reasonable and likely that there will be a computer console in each home to distribute information and to be paid for much as any other public utility.[3] In his own home, everyone would then have better access to any public library than the librarians therein now have; not only will overdue fines be obviated, but also the same page of the same book will be available to many people at any hour of the day or night. A daily, home computer, mental status examination could be automatically taken by each member of a large, at risk, psychiatric, outpatient population, all pathologic findings being immediately reported to any local clinic. If a student wanted a job, a college, or an apartment, he could ask for immediate data on availability, location, size, and cost. Anyone could rent space on such a computer and offer information to the entire country. On industrial channels, production programs could be put into the computer for sale and, once bought, the program could be used to direct standardized, but highly versatile, automated factories capable of producing any item from a teaspoon to a tractor. In this example, no human would need be involved except in the creation of the program and, possibly, in the decision to buy it. For housewife and industrialist alike, information would be the most important commodity. We may even anticipate data bargain basements: hours when everything from cake recipes to illustrated home courses in astrology would be offered at discount prices.

We have now wandered into the financial province, but it is just as well, for here, too, little will remain the same. The most momentous change is promised by the realization of worldwide abundance, which is already possible and could appear in our lifetime. The contribution of automation to the solution of the problem of want will be so thorough as to alter wholly any economy traditionally based on buying, selling, debt, credit, supply, and demand.[4] With the passing of scarcity, these concepts will become archaic, even quaint. We can anticipate that money will be eliminated and financial transactions conducted electronically—aided, perhaps, by a device that will identify an individual by his voice. History may teach that, like cattle in Kenya or gold ingots, paper money was found clumsy and wasteful. A future King Midas may need only to produce a stream of electric impulses by his touch. The results of all this will greatly alter our lives. Consider the effects on banks and on bank robbers, or on the major cities, which today function largely as financial centers. In these cities, the entire financial district may be encompassed in several floors of computer equipment, operated by a relatively small staff, in a few buildings.

A large number of today's most knotty problems in the sociopolitical realm should be wholly eliminated by the instant pervasiveness of electronic technology. For instance, when votes are cast via home computer consoles on election day, equal voting opportunities throughout America can be greatly improved. Congressmen and others will quickly be able to poll all of their constituents on any issue as it arises. One writer has suggested that "town meetings of the world" will be quite feasible by combining worldwide television, home consoles, and routine data-processing techniques.[4] This possibility for feedback will create an accessible pool of public particpation and consciousness. If this existed today, we can be certain that the community of Watts would not have required a week of violence to enlist this country's attention and aid. Political scientists of the future may conceive of electronic data-processing as so essential to the nature of democracy that they will marvel that we survived at all without it.

MOLECULAR BIOLOGY

Molecular biology promises a degree of change rivaling that brought about by automation. By the study of normal and disease processes at the molecular level, we will develop whole disciplines in which our values, concepts, and emotions will at first be stunned. Let us consider, for example, warfare and embryology.

Warfare may soon be revolutionized by new drugs that will drastically disorganize the mood or thinking of the enemy and produce instantaneous incapacitation.[5] This weapon might prove more effective than our present instruments of death, and would be reversible and more humane. Since nuclear weapons are capable of destroying everything immediately, we may hope that they have made themselves useless; indeed, from a technologic point of view, war itself is now outmoded.

In embryology, advances may be applied not just to persons bearing obvious chromosomal aberrations, but to the entire public. Thus, the selection of ideal genetic sperm and egg cells will be possible; parents will predetermine the sex of their children; intelligence and creativity may be selectively enhanced; and the human embryo may be developed outside the womb, allowing for wide manipulation of its growth and perhaps leading to the development of qualitatively different human beings. These advances would, of course, be welcome to parents with genetic abnormalities such as Mongolism or hemophilia; but I think we could anticipate other applications as varied as humans are curious.

In the area of treatment, doctors will manipulate cellular genetics by performing a sort of microsurgery on chromosomes. They will then be in a position to stimulate the natural regeneration of lost limbs and organs in adults. Doctors will also replace many complex organs by transplantation. Until now, this has been impossible because of the barrier of immunity. But research now indicates that cellular antigens will soon be identifiable for each individual; and exact matching with other persons will be possible, just as it is with blood transfusions today. This would be called "histocompatibility";

94   and, by genetic control, animal breeds histocompatible with man can be developed to provide an unlimited reservoir of organs for replacement in humans.[5]

The discovery of a new drug today requires the blind, random screening of thousands of compounds. The molecular biologist of the future will produce drugs tailor made for the precise sites that influence specific biochemical events. Control over the structure of DNA will first be used to develop multivalent vaccines that confer immunity against a large number of viral diseases at once. Leukemia, if it is a viral disease—as now appears possible—would be readily susceptible to such a vaccine. Genetic deficiency diseases in which essential DNA is lacking could be cured by a harmless virus carrying a man-made gene; this cure would be similar to catching a cold.

Aging will also be fair game for this approach. The most cogent current theory on aging cites gradually increasing chromosomal abnormalities as the likely cause. With more knowledge we may expect that a way will be found to stabilize chromosomal structure in man and thereby add years, and youthful years, to the human life span.

Meaning as well as length will be added to man's life by molecular biology. Recent studies have closely related RNA synthesis to learning. It is conservative to predict merely that drugs are on the way that will selectively enhance learning, memory, creativity, and mood, as well as control neurotic and psychotic symptoms. There is a clear inference here that drugs will be even more widely used in conditions we now tolerate as health than in those known as illness.

But nothing changes human life or knowledge like collaboration between two diverse fields. The intersection of electronics and molecular biology is destined to offered extraordinary proof of this principle. For one example, genes are composed of DNA, which can be considered a message spelled in amino acids to form a sequence of words without spaces. Though the genetic code is long and complex, the spelling of each of our chromosomes will be known and recorded like any other fixed pattern. This code could be radioed over long distances and, where it is received, either a primal human cell or, ultimately, a complete human being could be recreated or reorganized, given an ample pool of chemicals in a supportive environment.[6] This realization, that life may be "sent on," has already prompted novel questions and solutions for problems we haven't yet encountered. For instance, although the rocket ship will be a relatively sluggish, mechanical device that may not be able to get from this galaxy to the next in one man's lifetime, electronic transmission or teleportation could offer a solution to the vastness of space. Or, if we call this process telecreation, it is clear that one human could be exactly replicated again and archeologists, in contrast, are left with the question of whether man himself was not sent to earth in this very manner. Indeed, a number of them have long called attention to the remarkable similarity among myths of man's origin, in widely scattered cultures, that describe a race of gods from whom we have descended and then lost again. This possibility would also answer the mystery of man's apparent multi-focal appearance on earth and his debut as a quite fully organized being.

One contemporary effect of these eventualities is already clear. Consciousness can no longer be understood as a metaphysical entity, but rather as a purely physical property that can be created wherever certain conditions exist.[7] Among the many results of this formulation we may expect a new approach to the restoration of consciousness in the brain-damaged patient and the development of computers that are fully "conscious."

The outlook, therefore, is for radical changes in traditional arenas of function for both man and machine. Minsky,[8] a pioneer in studies of artificial intelligence, reflected this view in a recent article:

It is reasonable, I suppose, to be unconvinced by our examples and to be skeptical about whether machines will ever be intelligent. It is unreasonable to think machines could become *nearly* as intelligent as we are and then stop, or to suppose we will always be able to compete with them in wit or wisdom. Whether or not we could retain some sort of control of the machines, assuming that we would want to, the nature of our activities and aspirations would be changed utterly by the presence on earth of intellectually superior beings.

SOME PROBLEMS OF A SOCIETY IN TRANSITION

Our society has become legendary for boldness in abandoning the old and seizing the new. Change is our banner. Unfortunately, our mercurial acceptance of change has not conferred notable wisdom regarding its use. As a result, we have often been endangered not by astounding new machines, but by the use to which men put them. Ignorance of our own best interests will continue to plague us in the future, but the stakes will be much greater than in the past.

For instance, we can single out leisure education, and social structure as three already obvious dance-floors on which the behavioral scientist must learn in advance to waltz with particular grace and perseverance despite a curtailed and awkward adolescence.

Concerning leisure and its partner, work, there seems to be some agreement that within 40 years only one-fourth of the population will be involved in what we now call work. And this involvement will usually amount to a 24-hour work week. Consider, then, the statement of Dr. P. A. Martin, who heads the American Psychiatric Association Committee on Leisure Time and Its Uses: "We must face the fact that a great majority of our people are not emotionally and psychologically ready for free time. This results in unhealthy adaptations which find expression in a wide range of . . . psychopathologic states,"[9] The importance of work for psychic functioning was emphasized by Freud. It is implicit in our legislation, our calendar, and our childhood. But jobs and workers will eventually be known as outmoded concepts from our mechanical heritage. Yet, is there a viable psychic alternative to work? What forms can leisure take? What of Michael Harrington's warning that we may merely replace today's degrading work with degrading leisure? Or could our need to work be artifactual?

96   Whatever answers evolve, all of us who anticipate, cherish, and celebrate the weekend are probably among the last adherents to a fading
cult.

Perhaps only education will compete with leisure for human involvement. Learning is destined to become the major kind of production and consumption. Paid learning, which has flourished in recent
decades, is nonetheless in its infancy. Of all the current professions,
teaching alone may continue into the twenty-first century in recogniz-
able form. But even here behavioral scientists face innumerable questions. How can we best utilize Benjamin Bloom's conclusion that fully
half of our total growth in basic intelligence occurs between birth and
age four? If a computer can teach hundreds of children simultaneously, each at his own speed, with full knowledge of individual capabilities, interests, and past performances, and to different depths in
pertinent side issues, what unique contribution can the teacher make?
To what extent should a computer program encourage differences in
learning style between, for instance, the impulsive student and the
methodical one? Certainly the outlook is encouraging; for, when
most rote learning can be done on home computer consoles and when
learning time becomes reduced by drugs and better programs, there
will be time to spare. But for what?

Another field the behavorial scientist must develop is that
of adult education. A fixed body of knowledge throughout life will be
inadequate for the business man or the Ph.D. since this knowledge
may become outmoded within ten years. In the future, many people
will be in school throughout their lifetime; and education will be
perceived as experience rather than preparation, as it is now. There
will be a need to alter today's mechanical model of education, which
is piecemeal, sequential, and departmentalized in its approach; the
arbitary gerrymandering by which academic subjects are separated
will have little ability to cope with electronic comprehensiveness.

But perhaps the most baffling questions to be asked of the behavioral scientist will arise from the very fabric of society. For
example, sexual identity cannot survive on its contemporary cues,
which, for the male, dictate that he will usually leave his home from
nine to five and then return victorious from the business world, sometimes with a paycheck slung over his shoulder. Certainly sexual
identity will survive, but we must ask how. The disappearance of childhood is another prospect as children gain access to, and involvement
in, whole areas of knowledge today known only to adults. There will
still be a child in the future, but he will be qualitatively different
from the child of today. This can also be said of his family.

Still another likelihood is a total alteration of our social class
structure, perhaps eventuating in a classless society. But we must
first know what important functions are served by these classes. Have
they perhaps been so widely sanctioned in the world's societies for
reasons deeply intrinsic to human life? What anxieties would arise
without them? If they do prove indispensable, is there a class structure less injurious than our present one that would suffice?

What will supplant our needs for human associations when

we live in a mobile society without the friends formerly supplied by neighborhoods and work? Considerable insecurity will be generated by these changes, and enormous pressures will be expressed through the social system by those who find adaptation most difficult. Today we cannot distinguish between social change and criminality. Experts disagree on whether the man should be punished or his society should be treated.

But there can be no disagreement on the importance of a new body of social knowledge as technology elaborates a wholly different environment, in which we will recognize few landmarks. Even though we are told that the earth is round, we can hardly conceive of it by merely taking a walk, especially a walk among the skyscrapers of civilization. We are in the same predicament when we try to gauge the shape of the social planet. Both physicists and behavioral scientists must use distant reference points. Certainly, in our field, we can't afford not to use the future as one such point.

THE ALTERNATIVES FOR A FUTURE SOCIETY

In a number of primitive tribes, medicine men used discarded scraps of Western printing and long-empty tin cans to heighten their magic powers. These people have literally understood an influence in our technology that we often denied until we were faced with its eruption as a social pressure. But is there a special variety of influence that we can anticipate for ourselves in the technology of the future? The over-all theme is one of transformation and, most importantly, it will be of a psychic order.

Electronics will reverse the trend to specialization in which one man's ideas have been inaccessible to another because of different professional languages and insufficient time. Compartmentalization will no longer be the rule. Automation can permit persons widely separated in interests and experience to work together with the entire supply of available knowledge; and, unlike in the mechanical age, they need not gather in uniform small groups to do it. This sort of small groupings, which require both geographic and ideologic uniformity will be unnecessary when a computer can link a forest cabin and a city apartment to each other through a large, rich, data bank. Although automation will foster total interdependence, the range of personal alternatives will be broader than ever. Individuality can, if we choose, be maximized. Automation reformulates the world as a single room richly furnished with information. The effect can be human diversity to a degree unmatched in the world's history.

Clearly, the technology of the future can be extraordinarily valuable to man. By the same token, it exposes our society to a process that has caused the disorganization of many other cultures. Anthropologists have often described primitive groups that suffered sociocultural disintegration when they were introduced to our contemporary technology. The stressful evolution thrust upon them may be quite comparable to the task of cultural transformation now confronting us. Acculturation is today widely recognized as the major challenge to under developed countries. But the modern countries of the world are now

98   engaged in exactly the same process. In our favor is the notion of effective social sciences; in question is their imaginative application to the problems of the near future. Sociocultural disintegration is not likely to be our fate, but we can seriously question whether we will emerge into the future problem-ridden and disabled or expansive and free.

Most of this paper has dealt with developments that, if not true in detail, are at least accurate in direction. We can be sure that machines will continue to develop. But there is a highly unpredictable element in the future: man himself. The problem is whether he will carefully prescribe for his society, as he does for his punch cards, "Do not fold, spindle, or mutilate."

NOTES

1. R. Beals, Acculturation in: A. L. Kroeber, ed.; *Anthropology Today* (Chicago: University of Chicago Press, 1953), p. 624.

2. D. C. Evans, *Scientific American*, September 1966, p. 74.

3. J. McCarthy, *Scientific American*, September 1966, p. 64.

4. H. F. W. Perk, *American Scholar* 35 (Spring 1966): 358.

5. A. J. Schwarz, *Bioscience* 16 (October 1966): 730.

6. B. Fuller, *Saturday Review*, 12 Nobember 1966, p. 29.

7. D. E. Wooldridge, *The Machinery of the Brain* (New York: McGraw-Hill Book Co., 1963), chapt. 12.

8. M. Minsky, *Scientific American*, September 1966, pp 46.

9. H. Rome, et al, *American Journal of Psychiatry* 123 (November 1966): 5.

The Image of Man in Society

PART **2**

The first three chapters concerned themselves with a very general introduction to the perspective of sociology, the role of the social scientist and the matrix within which social organizations operate.

This second section approaches man as he is influenced by and participates in culture, interaction and socialization.

Art
Polygamy
CULTURE
VALUES
Oppression
Institution
CUSTOMS
DIVERSITY
Tradition
Variation
TABOO
Pugnacity
INCEST
RITUAL
LAWS
RIGHTEOUSNESS
MYTHS
HERITAGE
MORALS
MONOGAMY
MATERIALISM
GESTURE
RIGHTEOUSNESS
JUSTICE
DIVERSITY
SOUL
PROTEST
Puberty

Study Questions

1. Can you think of any taboos, values or norms that are universal for all societies?
2. How do the concepts of ethnocentrism and cultural relativity apply to the three articles included in the chapter?
3. What are some of the values and norms that have helped guide and shape your life? Your participation in sociology? Your participation in your family?
4. You are going to help organize a new society. What would be some cultural patterns and traits, values and norms that you would like to build into your community or tribe? How can you insure that those are dominant? Maintained?
5. Do you feel that a white European can make a valid study of black American ghetto residents? Why or why not?
6. Does the description of ghetto culture by Hannerz contribute to a stereotyping of blacks? Why or why not?

The Image of Man in Society: Culture

4

THE ESSENCE OF CULTURE

Technology, described as one of the important background variables influencing social organization, is part of a larger phenomenon called culture. Culture was defined by E. B. Tylor in 1871 as ". . . that complex whole which includes knowledge, belief, art, morals, laws, customs, and any other capabilities and habits acquired by man as a member of society."[1] This is a very broad definition and may not help differentiate culture from other concepts, such as civilization or historical heritage. Some 80 years later, Alfred Kroeber and Clyde Kluckhohn, two anthropologists, attempted to refine this wide–ranging concept by examining all the definitions of culture they could find. They discovered 164 definitions, synthesized them, and concluded that culture is a product; is historical: includes ideas, patterns, and values: is selective: is learned: is based upon symbols: and is an abstraction from behavior and the products of behavior.[2] Several aspects of this definition deserve further exploration. However, the most basic point to be made is that *all* men have culture. Culture is learned or acquired by members of the society at large, and inculcated by membership in various groups within society. Culture builds on the biological foundations of man, actualizing his tremendous capacity to learn. Because man is not controlled exclusively by inflexible or instinctual responses, he lacks built-in response patterns and has no normal or natural way of behaving. Thus, there can be and is a tremendous variation in human affairs. There are polygamous and monogamous societies. Some people eat seal udders and white ants. Even the seemingly universal taboo of incest assumes various forms in different societies. Despite this variability, many people insist that their way of life is best, is the most natural and is based on human nature. This view, called *ethnocentrism*, is illustrated by the following excerpt:

100 PERCENT AMERICAN, by Ralph Linton

Our solid American citizen awakens in a bed built on a pattern which originated in the Near East but which was modified in Northern Europe before it was transmitted to America. He throws back covers made from cotton, domesticated in India, or linen, domesticated in the Near East, or wool from sheep, also domesticated in the Near East, or silk, the use of which was discovered in China. All of these materials have been spun and woven by processes invented in the Near East. He slips into his moccasins, invented by the Indians of the Eastern woodlands, and goes to the bathroom, whose fixtures are a mixture of European and American inventions, both of recent date. He takes off his pajamas, a garment invented in India, and washes with soap invented by the Ancient Gauls. He then shaves, a masochistic rite which seems to have been derived from either Sumer or ancient Egypt.

Returning to the bedroom, he removes his clothes from a chair of southern European type and proceeds to dress. He puts on garments whose form originally derived from the skin clothing of the nomads of the Asiatic steppes, puts on shoes made from skins tanned by a process invented in ancient Egypt and cut to a pattern derived from the classical civilizations of the Mediterranean, and ties around his neck a strip of bright-colored cloth which is a vestigial survival of the shoulder shawls worn by the seventeenth-century Croatians. Before going out for breakfast he glances through the window, made of glass invented in Egypt, and if it is raining puts on overshoes made of rubber discovered by the Central American Indians and takes an umbrella, invented in southeastern Asia. Upon his head he puts a hat made of felt, a material invented in the Asiatic steppes.

On his way to breakfast he stops to buy a paper, paying for it with coins, an ancient Lydian invention. At the restaurant a whole new series of borrowed elements confronts him. His plate is made of a form of pottery invented in China. His knife is of steel, an alloy first made in southern India, his fork a medieval Italian invention, and his spoon a derivative of a Roman original. He begins breakfast with an orange, from the eastern Mediterranean, a cantaloupe from Persia, or perhaps a piece of African watermelon. With this he has coffee, an Abyssinian plant, with cream and sugar. Both the domestication of cows and the idea of milking them originated in the Near East, while sugar was first made in India. After his fruit and first coffee he goes to waffles, cakes made by a Scandinavian technique from wheat domesticated in Asia Minor. Over these he pours maple syrup, invented by the Indians of the Eastern woodlands. As a side dish he may have the egg of a species of bird domesticated in Indo-China, or thin strips of the flesh of an animal domesticated in Eastern Asia which have been salted and smoked by a process developed in Northern Europe.

When our friend has finished eating he settles back to smoke, an American Indian habit, consuming a plant domesticated in Brazil in either a pipe, derived from the Indians of Virginia, or a cigarette, derived from Mexico. If he is hardy enough he may even attempt a cigar, transmitted to us from the Antilles by way of Spain. While smoking he reads the news of the day, imprinted in characters invented by the ancient Semites upon a material invented in China by a process invented in Germany. As he absorbs the accounts of foreign troubles he will, if he is a good conservative citizen, thank a Hebrew deity in an Indo–European language that he is 100 percent American.[3]

104   A different approach to the phenomenon of culture is *cultural relativity*. This view states that various cultures cannot be judged as superior or inferior to each other. The differences and varieties of cultural forms attest to the facts that human nature is plastic and pliable. The concept of cultural relativity maintains that no group possesses fundamentally true, valid beliefs in religious, sexual, or other matters. The culturally relativistic view requires one to suspend judgment about what is good, true, vulgar, obscene, or pure.

The variability in cultural affairs is discussed by anthropologist Margaret Mead in her book, *Sex and Temperament in Three Primitive Societies*.[4] Mead went to New Guinea in 1931 and did research on three different tribes. She describes three kinds of relationships that exist between males and females in these different societies. Among the Arapesh tribe, for instance, there are no differences in temperament between males and females. Both men and women are described as gentle and cooperative. Sexual aggressiveness is attributed to neither sex. In this tribe, a man is not considered wiser than his wife by virtue of his maleness. Among the Mundugamor, both men and women are aggressive toward each other. Pregnancy is not welcomed by either parent. A new-born baby is barely cared for. Among the Tchambuli the situation is still different. The women are dominant. They do the fishing, and produce trade items. Here, the women are the instigators of sexual encounters. The men are emotionally dependent and are generally subservient. Thus, the three groups have differing cultural patterns which affect basic sex roles and sexual behavior. If culture is so specific to its people and milieu, what general model can we develop?

A study of culture, as stated earlier, exemplifies the plasticity of human nature and human forms. However, the study of culture also relates to the symbolic nature of man's responses. That is, men respond to meanings, not to physical objects. If I showed you a chair and asked you what use it had, most of you would say it is something to sit on. To the people of a different culture, our chair might be perceived as a shield or a weapon. There is no inherent quality of "chairness" which makes its definition final. Thus, we respond to a symbol which mediates between us and the physical object. The cultural phenomenon rests on just such symbolic interactions. It is neither the act nor artifact but the inferred meaning which shapes symbolic associations.

CULTURE AS A GROUP PROPERTY

You may ask, "How does culture fit in with regard to the social organization or sociological study groups? Why do sociologists concern themselves with culture?" To answer these questions, I return to my earlier comments about the levels of analysis. There are four such levels, with the cultural level the highest. I noted how each level evolves from the prior level and how each level, while interpenetrating, achieves some degree of autonomy and independence. The cultural level of analysis, being the highest, grows out of the social or organizational level and influences the organizational level by providing general values. Culture, then, is developed by a group, but becomes independent of individual members and of the group itself. By its interpenetration with the social level, culture, as a dynamic process, shapes the activities of group members. Social organizations cannot develop and continue to exist without culture.

VALUES AND NORMS

In the process of developing organizations, members are guided by broad cultural expectations which determine the general trends and tendencies of the group. The distinction between culture and organization can be made clearer by reference to values and norms.

Values are general principles which influence desired ends. They are not specific operational guides to action or behavior; they are the broad orientations. Norms, on the other hand, are the specific, sanctioned ground rules for behavior. While materialism and justice may be said to be part of the American value system, a highly developed market system and the right to a fair trial are norms which operationalize those values. The values-to-norms transaction is realized and legitimized at the organizational level by actors in social organizations. Thus culture—that whole which includes knowledge, beliefs, art, morals, laws and customs—becomes infused with social organization by providing meaning for the individuals' acts and deeds. Culture might be conceived as the socially shared and transmitted knowledge which is considered necessary for membership in the group. This will have more meaning in chapter 6, in the discussion of socialization.

Three readings have been selected for this chapter. The first is an excerpt from *Patterns of Culture*, written by anthropologist Ruth Benedict early in the 1930s. Her thesis, supported by observations of the traditions and customs of many tribal groups, is that human cultures vary widely. Benedict supports the concept of cultural relativity. She states that each society selects the traits it will live by, depending for its choices on its needs and the wide range of human imagination. She stresses the point that one group's cultural norms may be another's cultural deviation, and that cultures cannot be compared as right or wrong, good or bad, but simply as different and equally valid patterns of life.

The second selection was written in 1969 by Ulf Hannerz, a Swedish social anthropologist who lived in Washington, D.C.'s black ghetto for two years. It is part of a chapter from *Soulside: Inquiries Into Ghetto Culture & Community*, called "Things in Common." Dr. Hannerz perceives ghetto culture as distinct and significant, but greatly influenced by the mainstream of American life. While Benedict wrote of *selection* of traits as the most important aspect of cultural differences, Hannerz wrote of external forces: the South, poverty, oppression, suffering, and lack of control by the individual over his future. Both of these social scientists, however, are clear about the sharing of experiences and beliefs which shape and sustain the culture along the continuum of time.

The third article, by Horace Miner, a sociologist, deals with another North American group of people who at first may seem very strange. Indeed, you may wonder why the members of this group continue to torture themselves. They seem to be a very unhappy collectivity. A reading of the article, "Body Ritual Among the Nacirema," however, might help illustrate how a seemingly bizarre society takes on familiar qualities. The Nacirema is one of the most fascinating tribes I have ever encountered.

NOTES

1. E. B. Tylor, *Primitive Culture* (New York: Henry Holt and Co., 1871), p. 81.

2. Alfred L. Kroeber and Clyde Kluckhohn, *Culture* (New York: Vintage Books, 1963), p. 308.

3. Ralph Linton in Terrance A. Almquist and Gary R. Glodick, *Readings in Contemporary American Society* (Englewood Cliffs, N.J.: Prentice-Hall, 1968), p. 22.

4. Margaret Mead, *Sex and Temperament in Three Primitive Societies,* (New York: North American Library, Mentor Paperbacks, 1950).

RUTH BENEDICT

The Diversity of Cultures

A chief of the Digger Indians, as the Californians call them, talked to me a great deal about the ways of his people in the old days. He was a Christian and a leader among his people in the planting of peaches and apricots on irrigated land, but when he talked of the shamans who had transformed themselves into bears before his eyes in the bear dance, his hands trembled and his voice broke with excitement. It was an incomparable thing, the power his people had had in the old days. He liked best to talk of the desert foods they had eaten. He brought each uprooted plant lovingly and with an unfailing sense of its importance. In those days his people had eaten the health of the desert, he said, and knew nothing of the insides of tin cans and the things for sale at butcher shops. It was such innovations that had degraded them in these latter days.

One day, without transition, Ramon broke in upon his descriptions of grinding mesquite and preparing acorn soup. 'In the beginning,' he said, 'God gave to every people a cup, a cup of clay, and from this cup they drank their life. I do not know whether the figure occurred in some traditional ritual of his people that I never found, or whether it was his own imagery.

* * *

Our cup is broken. These things that had given significance to the life of his people, the domestic rituals of eating, the obligations of the economic system, the succession of ceremonials in the villages, possession in the bear dance, their standards of right and wrong—these were gone, and with them the shape and meaning of their life. The old man was still vigorous and a leader in relationships with the whites. He did not mean that there was any question of the extinction of his people. But he had in mind the loss of something that had value equal to that of life itself, the whole fabric of his people's standards and beliefs. There were other cups of living left, and they held perhaps the same water, but the loss was irreparable. It was no matter of tinkering with an addition here, lopping off something there. The modelling had been fundamental, it was somehow all of a piece. It had been their own.

Ramon had had personal experience of the matter of which he spoke. He straddled two cultures whose values and ways of thought were incommensurable. It is a hard fate. In Western civilization our experiences have been different. We are bred to one cosmopolitan culture, and our social sciences, our psychology, and our theology persistently ignore the truth expressed in Ramon's figure.

The course of life and the pressure of environment, not to speak of the fertility of human imagination, provide an incredible number of possible leads, all of which, it appears, may serve a society to live by. There are the schemes of ownership, with the social hierarchy that may be associated with possessions; there are material things and their elaborate technology; there are all the facets of sex life, parenthood and post-parenthood; there are the guilds or cults which may give structure to the society; there is economic exchange; there are the gods and supernatural sanctions. Each one of these and many more may be followed out with a cultural and ceremonial elaboration which monopolizes the cultural energy and leaves small surplus for the building of other traits. Aspects of life that seem to us most important have been passed over with small regard by peoples whose culture, oriented in another direction, has been far from poor. Or the same trait may be so greatly elaborated that we reckon it as fantastic.

It is in cultural life as it is in speech; selection is the prime necessity. The numbers of sounds that can be produced by our vocal cords and our oral and nasal cavities are practically unlimited. The three or four dozen of the English language are a selection which coincides not even with those of such closely related dialects as German and French. The total that are used in different languages of the world no one has ever dared to estimate. But each language must make its selection and abide by it on pain of not being intelligible at all. A language that used even a few hundreds of the possible—and actually recorded—phonetic elements could not be used for communication. On the other hand a great deal of our misunderstanding of languages unrelated to our own has arisen from our attempts to refer alien phonetic systems back to ours as a point of reference.

* * *

108

In culture too we must imagine a great arc on which are ranged the possible interests provided either by the human age-cycle or by the environment or by man's various activities. A culture that capitalized even a considerable proportion of these would be unintelligible as a language that used all the clicks, all the glottal stops, all the labials, dentals, sibilants and the gutturals from voiceless to voiced and from oral to nasal. Its identity as a culture depends upon the selection of some segments of this arc. Every human society everywhere has made such selection in its cultural institutions. Each from the point of view of another ignores fundamentals and exploits irrelevancies.

*　*　*

The case of adolescence is particularly interesting, because it is in the limelight in our own civilization and because we have plentiful information from other cultures. In our own civilization a whole library of psychological studies has emphasized the inevitable unrest of the period of puberty. It is in our tradition a physiological state as definitely characterized by domestic explosions and rebellion as typhoid is marked by fever. There is no question of the facts. They are common in America. The question is rather of their inevitability.

The most casual survey of the ways in which different societies have handled adolescence makes one fact inescapable: even in those cultures which have made most of the trait, the age upon which they focus their attention varies over a great range of years. At the outset, therefore, it is clear that the so-called puberty institutions are a misnomer if we continue to think of biological puberty. The puberty they recognize is social, and the ceremonies are a recognition in some fashion or other of the child's new status of adulthood. This investiture with new occupations and obligations is in consequence as various and as culturally conditioned as the occupations and obligations themselves. If the sole honourable duty of manhood is conceived to be deeds of war, the investiture of the warrior is later and of a different sort from that in a society where adulthood gives chiefly the privilege of dancing in a representation of masked gods.

*　*　*

In Australia, on the other hand, adulthood means participation in an exclusively male cult whose fundamental trait is the exclusion of women. Any woman is put to death if she so much as hears the sound of the bull-roarer at the ceremonies, and she must never know of the rites. Puberty ceremonies are elaborate and symbolic repudiations of the bonds with the female sex; the men are symbolically made self-sufficient and the wholly responsible element of the community. To attain this end they use drastic sexual rites and bestow supernatural guaranties.

The clear physiological facts of adolescence, therefore, are first socially interpreted even where they are stressed. But a survey of puberty institutions make clear a further fact: puberty is physiologically a different matter in the life-cycle of the male and the female. If cultural emphasis followed the physiological emphasis, girls' ceremonies would be more marked than boys'; but it is not so. The ceremonies emphasize a social fact: the adult prerogatives of men are more far-reaching in every culture than women's, and consequently, as in the above instances, it is more common for societies to take note of this period in boys than in girls.

Girls' and boys' puberty, however, may be socially celebrated in the same tribe in identical ways. Where, as in the interior of British Columbia, adolescent rites are a magical training for all occupations, girls are included on the same terms as boys. Boys roll stones down mountains and beat them to the bottom to be swift of foot, or throw gambling-sticks to be lucky in gambling; girls carry water from distant springs, or drop stones down inside their dresses that their children may be born as easily as the pebble drops to the ground.

*   *   *

The usual ideas around which girls' puberty institutions are centered, and which are not readily extended to boys', are those concerned with menstruation. The uncleanness of the menstruating woman is a very widespread idea, and in a few regions first menstruation has been made the focus of all the associated attitudes. Puberty rites in these cases are of a thoroughly different character from any of which we have spoken. Among the Carrier Indians of British Columbia, the fear and horror of a girl's puberty was at its height. Her three or four years of seclusion was called 'the burying alive,' and she lived for all that time alone in the wilderness, in a hut of branches far from all beaten trails. She was a threat to any person who might so much as catch a glimpse of her, and her mere footstep defiled a path or a river. She was covered with a great headdress of tanned skin that shrouded her face and breasts and fell to the ground behind. Her arms and legs were loaded with sinew bands to protect her from the evil spirit with which she was filled. She was herself in danger and she was a source of danger to everybody else.

Girls' puberty ceremonies built upon ideas associated with the menses are readily convertible into what is, from the point of view of the individual concerned, exactly opposite behaviour. There are always two possible aspects to the sacred: it may be a source of peril or it may be a source of blessing.

*   *   *

The adolescent behaviour, therefore, even of girls was not dictated by some physiological characteristic of the period itself, but rather by marital or magic requirements socially connected with it. These beliefs made adolescence in one tribe serenely religious and beneficent, and in another so dangerously unclean that the child had to cry out a warning that others might avoid her in the woods. The adolescence of girls may equally, as we have seen, be a theme which

110   a culture does not institutionalize. Even where, as in most of Australia, boys' adolescence is given elaborate treatment, it may be that the rites are an induction into the status of manhood and male participation in tribal matters, and female adolescence passes without any kind of formal recognition.

These facts, however, still leave the fundamental question unanswered. Do not all cultures have to cope with the natural turbulence of this period, even though it may not be given institutional expression? Dr. Mead has studied this question in Samoa. There the girl's life passes through well-marked periods. Her first years out of babyhood are passed in small neighbourhood gangs of age mates from which little boys are strictly excluded. The corner of the village to which she belongs is all-important, and the little boys are traditional enemies. She has one duty, that of baby-tending, but she takes the baby with her rather than stays home to mind it, and her play is not seriously hampered. A couple of years before puberty, when she grows strong enough to have more difficult tasks required of her and old enough to learn more skilled techniques, the little girls' play group in which she grew up ceases to exist. She assumes woman's dress and must contribute to the work of the household. It is an uninteresting period of life to her and quite without turmoil. Puberty brings no change at all.

*　*　*

Warfare is another social theme that may or may not be used in any culture. Where war is made much of, it may be with contrasting objectives, with contrasting organization in relation to the state, and with contrasting sanctions. War may be, as it was among the Aztecs, a way of getting captives for the religious sacrifices. Since the Spaniards fought to kill, according to Aztec standards they broke the rules of the game. The Aztecs fell back in dismay and Cortez walked as victor into the capital.

There are even quainter notions, from our standpoint, associated with warfare in different parts of the world. For our purposes it is sufficient to notice those regions where organized resort to mutual slaughter never occurs between social groups. Only our familiarity with war makes it intelligible that a state of warfare should alternate with a state of peace in one tribe's dealings with another. The idea is quite common over the world, of course. But on the one hand it is impossible for certain peoples to conceive the possibility of a state of peace, which in their notion would be equivalent to admitting enemy tribes to the category of human beings, which by definition they are not even though the excluded tribe may be of their own race and culture.

On the other hand, it may be just as impossible for a people to conceive of the possibility of a state of war.

*　*　*

I myself tried to talk of warfare to the Mission Indians of California, but it was impossible. Their misunderstanding of warfare was abysmal. They did not have the basis in their own culture upon which the idea could exist, and their attempts to reason it out reduced the great wars to which we are able to dedicate ourselves with moral fervour to the level of alley brawls. They did not happen to have a cultural pattern that distinguished between them.

War is, we have been forced to admit even in the face of its huge place in our own civilization, an asocial trait. In the chaos following the World War all the wartime arguments that expounded its fostering of courage, of altruism, of spiritual values, gave out a false and offensive ring. War in our own civilization is as good an illustration as one can take of the destructive lengths to which the development of a culturally selected trait may go. If we justify war, it is because all peoples always justify the traits of which they find themselves possessed, not because war will bear an objective examination of its merits.

Warfare is not an isolated case. From every part of the world and from all levels of cultural complexity it is possible to illustrate the overweening and finally often the asocial elaboration of a cultural trait. Those cases are clearest where, as in dietary or mating regulations, for example, traditional usage runs counter to biological drives. Social organization, in anthropology, has a quite specialized meaning owing to the unanimity of all human societies in stressing relationship groups within which marriage is forbidden. No known people regard all women as possible mates. This is not in an effort, as is so often supposed, to prevent inbreeding in our sense, for over great parts of the world it is an own cousin, often the daughter of one's mother's brother, who is the predestined spouse. The relatives to whom the prohibition refers differ utterly among different peoples, but all human societies are alike in placing a restriction. No human idea has received more constant and complex elaboration in culture than this of incest.

*   *   *

. . . Australia has in addition an unparalleled horror of sister marriage and an unparalleled development of exogamous restrictions. So the Kurnai, with their extreme classificatory relationship system, feel the Australian horror of sex relationship with all their 'sisters,' that is, women of their own generation who are in any way related to them. Besides this, the Kurnai have strict locality rules in the choice of a mate. Sometimes two localities, out of the fifteen or sixteen of which the tribe is composed, must exchange women, and can have no mates in any other group. Sometimes there is a group of two or three localities that may exchange with two or three others. Still further, as in all Australia, the old men are a privileged group, and their prerogatives extend to marrying the young and attractive girls. The consequence of these rules is, of course, that in all the local group which must by absolute prescription furnish a young man with his wife, there is no girl who is not touched by one of these tabus. Either she is one of those who through relationship with his mother is his "sister," or she is already bargained for by an old man, or for some lesser reason she is forbidden to him.

That does not bring the Kurnai to reformulate their exogamous rules. They insist upon them with every show of violence. Therefore, the only way they are usually able to marry is by flying violently in the face of the regulations. They elope. As soon as the village knows that an elopement has occurred, it sets out in pursuit, and if the couple are caught the two are killed. It does not matter that possibly all the pursuers were married by elopement in the same fashion. Moral indignation runs high. There is, however, an island traditionally recognized as a safe haven, and if the couple can reach it and remain away till the birth of a child, they are received again with blows, it is true, but they may defend themselves. After they have run the gauntlet and been given their drubbing, they take up the status of married people in the tribe.

The Kurnai meet their cultural dilemma typically enough. They have extended and complicated a particular aspect of behaviour until it is a social liability. They must either modify it, or get by with a subterfuge. And they use the subterfuge. They avoid extinction, and they maintain their ethics without acknowledged revision. This manner of dealing with the *mores* has lost nothing in the progress of civilization. The older generation of our own civilization similarly maintained monogamy and supported prostitution, and the panegyrics of monogamy were never so fervent as in the great days of the red-light districts. Societies have always justified favourite traditional forms. When these traits get out of hand and some form of supplementary behaviour is called in, lip service is given as readily to the traditional form as if the supplementary behaviour did not exist.

* * *

Such a view of cultural processes calls for a recasting of many of our current arguments upholding our traditional institutions. These arguments are usually based on the impossibility of man's functioning without these particular traditional forms. Even very special traits come in for this kind of validation, such as the particular form of economic drive that arises under our particular system of property ownership. This is a remarkably special motivation and there are evidences that even in our generation it is being strongly modified. At any rate, we do not have to confuse the issue by discussing it as if it were a matter of biological survival values. Self-support is a motive our civilization has capitalized. If our economic structure changes so that this motive is no longer so potent a drive as it was in the era of the great frontier and expanding industrialism, there are many other motives that would be appropriate to a changed economic organization. Every culture, every era, exploits some few out of a great number of possibilities. Changes may be very disquieting, and involve great losses, but this is due to the difficulty of change itself, not to the fact that our age and country has hit upon the one possible motivation under which human life can be conducted. Change, we must remember, with all its difficulties, is inescapable. Our fears over even very minor shifts in custom are usually quite beside the point. Civilizations might change far more radically than any human authority has ever had the will or the imagination to change them, and still be completely workable. The minor changes that occasion so much denunciation today, such as the increase of divorce, the growing secularization in our cities, the prevalence of the petting party, and many more, could be taken up quite readily into a slightly different pattern of culture. Becoming traditional, they would be given the same richness of content, the same importance and value, that the older patterns had in other generations.

The truth of the matter is rather that the possible human institutions and motives are legion, on every plane of cultural simplicity or complexity, and that wisdom consists in a greatly increased tolerance toward their divergencies. No man can thoroughly participate in any culture unless he has been brought up and has lived according to its forms, but he can grant to other cultures the same significance to their participants which he recognizes in his own.

ULF HANNERZ

Things in Common

*   *   *

Here we are concerned specifically with the kinds of understandings of life which ghetto dwellers communicate about and which they formulate more or less explicitly into a notion of soul. There is no reason to believe that even within this community an absolute consensus could easily be reached about what to include and what to emphasize. Essentially, the ghetto concept of soul involves an affirmation of the black experience: One should "tell it like it is" instead of making pretenses of being different from others; one should value earthiness, the "nitty gritty" of black life. Soul is not only acceptance but an assertion of empathy with the typical experiences and actions of ghetto dwellers—even when it is only a gently mocking empathy with human weakness. But these are general and abstract terms. To become more specific and concrete, one must turn to contexts where the understandings of soul may be affirmed.

There is the rather recent history of most ghetto dwellers as Southern country people. Many are certainly of two minds about this;

Ulf Hannerz, "Things in Common" from *Soulside: Inquiries into Ghetto Culture and Community* (New York: Columbia University Press, 1969), pp. 145–58. Reprinted by permission of the publisher.

114 as we have noted before, recent arrivals from down South are typed as simpletons, "bamas". Yet it cannot be denied that this is part of the common ghetto identity. As the comedienne Moms Mabley put it in front of a black audience in Washington, D.C.:

> ... I said to my old man, "I'm going to the country for the weekend. Do you know anything about the country?" He says, "Sure, I know all about the country. I used to live in the country when I was a boy." I says, "When you was a boy everybody lived in the country."

Thus there is a "home country" not too many generations back, and ghetto dwellers recognize that they are still marked by it in many ways. They know that they are not only black people surrounded by whites but also Southerners in a Northern city. The ghetto dialect may be referred to as "big feet talk"—poor people down South got big feet because they could not afford shoes. From a Southern background the ghetto dwellers have also derived one of the domains of most intense soul symbolism. The things poor Southern country folk ate, most of the time or as circumstances sometimes permitted, have been transplanted into ghetto kitchens: greens of various kinds—collard, mustard, turnips, and kale—blackeyed peas, chitterlings, ham hocks, neck bones, hog maw, barbecued ribs, pork chops, fried chicken, fried pig skins, grits, corn bread, sweet potato pies, water melon, and so forth. These are the things redefined as soul food. Although many groceries and carry-outs still advertise them as "Southern", more and more of these businesses turn to the soul vocabulary. And so do the storefront churches when advertising take-away meals, prepared and sold by members to earn money for church activities. Thus a very tangible component of the Southern heritage has become understood as a part of what it means to be black.

Soul also means perseverance. To be black is to be poor and oppressed and to suffer, and most likely to be marked by this, but to keep on struggling, successfully or not. Having to cope with adverse conditions is generally recognized as a common ghetto experience; in one way or another, it is a part of most ghetto dwellers' definitions of soul. It also has correlates. One of them is the feeling of lack of control over the circumstances which influence one's life. A lot of things can happen both within the ghetto milieu and in the wider environment to give one's life a new and unexpected turn, often for the worse. Since one's possibilities to protect oneself are limited, a ghetto dweller can only try to keep on his toes to be aware of what is going on. One understanding involved in this centers on the possibility that things are not what they seem to be. Life is a game, and a lot of people are working their personal games in situations where this is not readily apparent; they are corrupting contexts and relationships which should not ordinarily be looked at in terms of profit. Sonny summed up the ghetto perspective toward gaming, the concern with "figuring out an angle", with an irony well appreciated by his listeners as he commented on the amount of drinking at a recent funeral reception in the neighborhood:

Some of the greatest throats in town were there. Ooh! I wish I had had
the ice cube concession.

On the night of Halloween, as the children had been going trick-or-
treating up and down Winston Street, one of the men in the neighborhood had a similar idea:

Why don't we go trick-or-treating now, to all them bootleggers? And we
tell them we don't want no candy either.

Another facet of the common ghetto perspective often mentioned in the
soul context is the experience of the ambivalent relationship between
the sexes. We have already noted that there is a shared public imagery
concerning male and female characteristics and the problems men and
women have with one another. What is covered by the imagery is also
held to be common personal experience; ghetto dwellers may vary in
the intensity of this experience, but they assume that they share the
knowledge of what it means to be "hurt" by the opposite sex. However, this is not all that has to do with soul as far as sex is concerned.
Soul also involves the open expression of appreciation of sex; this is
one of the points where one should "tell it like it is" rather than feign
a lack of interest. One man makes the point this way:

When white people see a good-looking chick go by, you know, they pretend they ain't interested, almost like they were looking the other way.
They don't think it's *nice* to look. Did you ever see any of the brothers
up here pretend they didn't see nothing? Did you? They're looking them
all over, and then they tell them what they look like. That's soul
brothers.

The term soul itself points to another ingredient in the ghetto perspective. Soul, the essence of a human being, is a religious term, and fundamentalist religion continues to be an influence on the ghetto dwellers
even as the institutional grip of black churches on them is loosening.
There are still lots of churches in the community, and a great many
people have had some kind of religious education, if not in Sunday
school perhaps in a less organized and conscious way by female kin—
mothers, grandmothers, or aunts. Phrases such as "a soul-stirring revival meeting" are still common in the public relations sheets distributed by ghetto churches, and the vocabulary of even quite secularized ghetto dwellers contain such exclamations as "God, have
mercy!" or "God almighty!" Freddy, a streetcorner man, reminisces
about a chance encounter:

I was downtown about 2 a.m. one night, and a girl, really wild one, you
know, comes up to me. So she says, 'Don't you recognize me, Freddy?'
Last time I'd seen her she'd been going to church and everything. The
devil had certainly got hold of her.

Jimmy, another streetcorner man whom we have already encountered
as one who often gets into fights, says about his life:

But I don't worry, you know, 'cause I know He's up there taking care of us all.

Such unsolicited remarks show that religion is still a part of the ghetto perspective, even for those whom the regular church goers consider most obviously lost to the flock; it is something ghetto dwellers can more or less count on having in common. But many have skeptical words to say about God's representatives on earth, and in particular about those in the ghetto. The unofficial image of the ghetto preacher borrows much from the notion that some people always turn human affairs into a game. For all his pious words on Sunday and in quite a few weeknight meetings, the preacher is seen by many ghetto dwellers as a con man in a silk suit and with a long white Cadillac, forever fooling around with the sisters in his congregation, and every preacher risks having his own actions interpreted in this ready-made fashion. There were those in the Winston Street neighborhood who suspected a preacher in a nearby storefront church of being both a moonshiner and a slumlord, although there was actually nothing to substantiate this. One of the preachers who hold forth on black radio stations on Sundays made a point in one of his broadcasts of denying the rumor that he had lost his ghetto church because he had used the rent money of his congregation to buy a new car. But even though ghetto dwellers may at times exaggerate the shady sides of the persons who are supposed to be their spiritual leaders, there are certainly examples among the preachers of people with conspicuously worldly interests.

* * *

In any case, it may contribute to our understanding of the cynicism with which some ghetto dwellers regard the hold of religion on some of their compatriots.

The blessing service is well under way; it is held at WUST Radio Music Hall at 9th and V Streets, at the heart of the ghetto. Tickets are $2.00 in advance, $2.25 at the door, and some 170 persons have paid their way in. As you came into the hall you passed a large waterfilled plastic bowl into which the persons entering dropped coins, nothing less than dimes. You could also buy a record by one of the gospel groups to appear during the service (at a price higher than that of the record stores). The service started at about 8:30, about a half-hour after the time advertised, but people continued to enter even later. There has been an opening prayer by a visiting minister, the congregation has done some half-hearted singing, and the minister has asked its members to return to the plastic bowl at the entrance to put a silver coin in it, "and I don't want no nickels now". They should do this "'cause this will do something for you, and you'll feel better when you get back to your seats." Visiting ministers have stood up to present themselves—about five or ten of them—and about thirty visitors from Baltimore have been introduced; there has been a charter bus tour arranged. After testifying service two gospel groups have made short appearances, and now the emcee, the man who presents station

WUST's religious broadcasts, introduces Prophet Isaiah Jones, "a man who has done *so* much for *so* many here in Washington". Prophet Isaiah seems to be between thirty-five and forty years old and claims to have been a prophet for some twenty years. He hails from Birmingham, Alabama, and now has his church in a basement on S Street. Tonight he is dressed in a blue flowing brocade gown. He takes up a hymn and gets the congregation to join in. Then he starts talking about his blessing—"Yeah, I'm still in the blessing business." Will everybody please line up in the right aisle to receive a candle and a piece of paper, in order to receive a large sum of money before Wednesday? About half the people in the congregation, most of them women, do and step forward to the prophet one by one to receive the blessed candle and the paper at a price of $2.00. As the line has passed him Prophet Isaiah affirms that by Wednesday night when people begin to receive all the money, he will be the talk of the town. He points out that those who did not get his blessing are foolish, but he will give them another chance. However, nobody else stands up. Prophet Isaiah's style of speech is typical of storefront and travelling preachers, a constant alternation between aggressiveness toward the congregation and assurance of future successes.

*　　*　　*

The South, poverty, oppression, suffering, and lack of control over one's destiny are thus part of the ghetto dwellers' shared perspective, as are the battle of the sexes, the old-time religion, and a certain irreverence toward man's motives. Last but not least, soul is in black music. If a belief that all black people have a good sense of rhythm is a part of the stereotype white people believe in, it is also a part of the ghetto dwellers' collective self-conception. "Clap your hands and show you got soul", the emcee at the Howard Theatre tells his audience. Soul music is the area where the current concept of soul may have its strongest roots. James Brown is "soul brother number one", Aretha Franklin "soul sister number one", according to record liners, black disc jockeys, and the emcees of black stage shows. Although jazz has had its own soul tradition, soul music is now above all the term for what has otherwise been known as rhythm and blues or the black variety of rock and roll, the popular music of the ghetto.

*　　*　　*

We see that soul music is not only one of the parts of the soul perspective. By serving also as a running commentary on the other parts, it serves to integrate this thing of shreds and patches into a whole. It gives expression to a great many of the shared understandings of the ghetto, and by giving them an impersonal form—while yet involving intensely personal concerns—soul music also gives them a more official standing as community ideology, above the level of particular personal relationships. But in so stabilizing the ghetto perspective, soul music does not work alone.

118   THE SOULFUL APPARATUS

What we have just said is that music is not only an ingredient of the shared perspective but also a vehicle of it. It objectivates the public imagery which we have otherwise found expressed only in the every-day face-to-face interaction of ghetto dwellers. It is also distributed through channels of a more institutional character than personal rela-tionships. We will now turn to these community institutions which pro-mote the ghetto understandings discussed above: church, radio, enter-tainment business. While these institutions have no authority over the community as such, they engage in symbolic action aimed at the entire ghetto, and in this sense they come as close to overarching institutions as anything in the community. Ghetto dwellers can expose themselves to the institutions at will, but most people tend to be reached by their messages in one way or other. Thus they form a kind of ghetto-specific cultural apparatus which is at work beside the mainstream apparatus of school, TV, newspapers, and so forth. . . .

Like soul music, ghetto churches are not only involved as a part of the shared understandings but also in spreading the word about them. Particularly the smaller and more independent churches are ac-tive in this way. While their theology may be derived to a great extent from outside sources, their anthropology is soul. Storefront church preachers dwell on the evils of drinking and gambling, on the dangers of the streets, on the hardships of poverty, and the road to salvation from all this—"Hallelujah Avenue", as one travelling preacher called it. Since these churches have a considerable female predominance in the congregation, both male and female ministers tend to emphasize the trouble no-good men cause for their women, thus adopting a woman's perspective toward trouble between the sexes. Even so, the conflict is acknowledged as a commonplace occurrence, and so is the fact that there are strong women. A female preacher made this anec-dote a part of her sermon, showing one of the advantages of being a good church member:

I want to make you feel so good you can go home tonight and take just anything. I'll tell you about this woman, she was married and she had a mean left, so she used to knock her old man to the floor every time. And he didn't dare do nothing, he wouldn't even cash his own check. So she came to church once, and she was taken by the Holy Spirit, and when she came home that night she was just like a lamb, and she said to her old man, 'Look, there will be no more fighting in this house.' And all week she kept her peace, so her husband started to shape up. And next Friday when he got his check he went out and cashed it, and then he had a taste, he had many, and then he went on home and said to the woman, 'Look, I cashed my check, and I've been drinking, and don't you say nothing about it.' And she just stood there real sweet and said, 'Darling, I have your dinner ready, will you eat now please so I can get down to the church in time for the service tonight.' So the man said, 'Something must have happened to her. I'd better get down to that church and see what's going on down there.' And you see, if she hadn't been so holy after she'd been to church, if she'd gone right on beating him up, ain't nobody seen him in church.

Ghetto preachers thus work with the collection of motifs which they expect to be familiar to the members of their congregations, as a way of establishing a relationship to them. The more secular components of the ghetto cultural apparatus work in the same way. The black radio stations—three in Washington, D.C., WOL, WOOK, and WUST—have hit music, almost all soul, on their programs more or less around the clock, interspersed with newscasts; Sunday programming is largely occupied by religious broadcasts (mostly services from ghetto churches) and community service programs. The radio stations are thus the major channels of soul music into the community and thereby contribute to strengthening the shared perspective of the ghetto dwellers. But beyond this, the disc jockeys—who are the leading radio personalities of the community—have their commentaries revolving around soulful motifs. The WOL disc jockeys have the collective label "the Soul Brothers", and WOOK and WUST have followed suit with "the Soul Men" and "the Soul Bandits". WOL, the leading station in recent years, has had a superman parody serial named "Captain Soul", and one of the disc jockeys had a white friend of his elected "honorary Negro", with the privilege of burning water melons on white people's front lawns—an inversion of Ku Klux Klan cross-burning which a ghetto dweller hardly fails to appreciate. The disc jockeys express their soulful enjoyment of music in cries, shouts, and comments interjected into it, they address themselves to the subject of women, and they make references to soul food in their running commentaries. After one record during which he had loudly proclaimed his appreciation, a disc jockey commented, "Whoo-ee, I ain't had this much fun since Lurleen Wallace got sick," Lurleen Wallace being the then governor of Alabama. While the comment might seem in bad taste and would probably strike most ghetto dwellers as a little risque, there can be no doubt that it could strike a black refugee from the South as rather funny.

Stage entertainment in the ghetto is strongly linked to radio programming. The soul artists and groups in strongest demand for appearances at the Howard Theatre or other places such as the occasional shows at the Washington Coliseum are those with frequent or at least recent recordings on the hit list of black radio stations. While stage shows may be emceed by such travelling celebrities as King Coleman or Gorgeous George, nationally known in America's black ghettos, or by a freelancing local talent such as Petey Green, most often the master of ceremonies is a local disc jockey. Thus what occurs on stage has some similarity to what black radio stations broadcast, with the same emphasis on what ghetto dwellers have in common. In the old days the performers at the Howard Theatre sometimes announced the winning number of the day on the late afternoon show, as they could find out about it in the alley next to the theater before going on stage. Perhaps they do not do so anymore because with the current style of shows the audience at that time of day tends to be too young to be numbers enthusiasts. But the emcees continue to ask now and then if there is anybody from Alabama or from Georgia or from South Carolina in the audience, getting more and more response as they name states close to Washington. Of course, many are too shy to stand up, for no particular

120   reason or because it is a little awkward to admit to being "from the country". King Coleman comments on this as he makes his entry on the Howard stage to emcee the Wilson Pickett Show:

It's good to see the same old faces I've been seeing here the last thirty years . . . Yeah, I see some are making their first visit to the Howard. Some of them come from down home, you see. They won't say so, though, 'cause they think there's something wrong about being from down home. Folks, there ain't nothing wrong about that. It's being down home that's bad.

Soul music, of course, is the major ingredient of a Howard Theatre show. A ghetto hero like James Brown has no problem packing the house for two shows a night for a week as he brings his show to Washington; at other times the quality of the performers is more varied and the reception considerably cooler. As a supplement to the music there is sometimes a black comedian. Someone with the reputation of a Moms Mabley may well headline a show; Moms Mabley is a versatile woman in her upper middle age who typifies the lowly, bitchy old lady who after all has a lot of common sense and a good heart. Dressed in a flowerpot-model hat, clothes with bright flower patterns carefully chosen to clash wildly, and gym shoes, she speaks her mind in her husky voice while continuously chewing gum, commenting on poverty, crime, the South, and the state of the nation. Other comedians usually get less prominent positions in a show. Some of them, like Pigmeat Markham, are masters of the old-fashioned vaudeville, others like Clay Tyson and Irwin C. Watson are standup comedians, while some such as Slappy White are somewhere between such categories or move over a wider field of expression. A great deal of what most of them do, however, involves the shared understandings of the ghetto which we have discussed above. Sex and food are topics they share with soul music; poverty and the South are subjects which are more often dealt with by the comedians. The jokes about the South often involve the Ku Klux Klan:

There was a real nice story in the paper this morning. Two hundred Klansmen were choked to death 'cause somebody had sold them plastic sheets.

Down where I'm from the Klan is so bad they put a cross on your front yard and then they come and ask you for a match.

My old lady is running around with a member of the Ku Klux Klan. She says he's a wizard under the sheet.

The poverty jokes often take the form of reminiscences from childhood:

Remember how you felt when your mama greeted you with a Western sandwich—two slices of bread with wide open space in between? Or when the rats came in and looked around and said, 'Ain't no use staying here, we'll starve to death.' Or the running water—from the front door to the back door when it rained?

We were so poor our daddy couldn't afford even the thinnest slice of cheese for the mouse trap, so he put a picture of a cheese in it. Next morning there was a picture of a mouse in the trap.

We were so poor our daddy invented the limbo when he tried to enter a pay toilet.

A short skit may be a final example of joking about poverty:

This new place of mine is a boss place. You really got to come and see it some time. It's ninety by fifteen by thirty.
Uhuh . . . Hey, what does that mean—ninety by fifteen by thirty?
It means if I don't pay ninety by the fifteenth, I'm out by the thirtieth.

* * *

Preachers, disc jockeys, soul singers, emcees, and comedians all celebrate the cultural integration of the ghetto community. In the introductory chapter of this book, we noted that this community is only loosely structured; its population constitutes a pool from which a ghetto dweller draws the participants in his personal network, but with most of the constituents he never interacts directly. As partners they remain potentialities. However, the persons who enact the roles of the ghetto cultural apparatus show that this pool of people is indeed a collectivity set apart from the rest of the society, not only because it is excluded from effective mainstream participation but because shared understandings form a basis for communication within the collectivity. Ghetto preachers, disc jockeys, and stage personalities are not engaging in anything resembling symmetrical relationships with their audiences, even if there is a perceptible response from these. They are not familiar with the personal characteristics of audience members but establish the same simple categorical relationship to each one of them, ignoring individual variation. As expert communicators within the ghetto perspective, they can assume that the cultural homogeneity of their audiences is great enough for them to enter into a kind of we-relationship on the basis of understandings they all have in common. Functioning in such a way, the ghetto cultural apparatus also assures the members of the audience that their personal troubles are only reflections of the public issues of the community. It gives the conventional understandings a more enduring public standing in the community than they would have if their relevance to the individual ghetto dweller depended only on the personal experiences of his immediate social circle.

On the whole the ghetto community obviously responds rather favorably to the dramatization of its concerns by the cultural apparatus, and it seems to have a certain effect in strengthening community integration not only in asserting the common ghetto perspective but also in serving as a set of institutional foci of attention for the community. These institutions are not under community control, however, but privately managed and responsible only to themselves or outside

122 interests for their exploitation of their ghetto niches. They must rely on the purely voluntary support of the ghetto dwellers in order to gain for themselves a sufficient piece of the action. Thus preachers must constantly try to win over new members to their congregations and keep the old ones active and in line; collections and offerings of various kinds take up much time during services, and the ministers complain about those unsatisfactory Christians who stay home and watch TV instead of coming to weeknight meetings. And, one of them wonders out aloud in her sermon, why do so few people think of bringing the preacher a gift basket some time? There can be little doubt that the precarious economy of many storefront church leaders forces them to pursue financial questions so openly as to make other ghetto dwellers wonder if they have any other motives at all. The black radio stations, too, are in competition with each other to guarantee potential advertisers as large a slice as possible of the ghetto market as listeners to their commercials. In a situation like that of Washington, D.C., with three ghetto-oriented stations as well as a host of others which ghetto dwellers may also choose from, a successful station may need to engage in some vigorous self-promotion.

* * *

THE CORNERSTONES OF SOUL

The shared perspective contains the ghetto dweller's reflections on the condition of his community. As we have seen, it is consciously held to be a cultural complex known only to him, and in this sense it helps draw the demarcation line between the ghetto and the outside world. Yet if we go beyond this we see how unseparable mainstream culture and society remain from the social reality of the ghetto dwellers. They feel mainstream power impinging on their lives, they see the ghetto through a mainstream screen and the mainstream through a ghetto screen. Varied as the soulful understandings may be, three themes seem to return again and again—the struggle for solidarity, the bittersweet mood, and the impiety toward society. These cornerstones of the ghetto-specific outlook all have a great deal to do with the mainstream.

Soul as solidarity is a reaction to the threat of a split in the community. Its internal differentiation is tied to mainstream society and culture so that individual striving for improved standing ultimately leads out of the community. Furthermore, we have noted (in chapter 2) how some "respectable" ghetto dwellers refer to others as "no good"; they are judging their compatriots on the basis of mainstream standards and disregarding that human equality which as ghetto dwellers they should understand. Some of them go to the big Baptist churches which are almost like white churches and thus deny the traditional black religious experience. Storefront church preachers keep complaining about this conceit. It looks as if these people were bent on *not* telling it like it is, on disavowing that they have much in common with the rest of the black community. "These people", of course, are not always the same; a lot of people turn renegade at one time or other by espousing mainstream culture in some way that is detrimental to ghetto cohesion. The vocabulary of soul—soul brother, soul sister, soul food, and so forth—is used with all its implications of shared understandings to regain their loyalty to the community, and it is also used as a reaffirmation of their allegiance by those very persons whose ghetto loyalty may be in doubt. James Brown, after recounting his successes from the time he shined shoes in Augusta, Georgia, until the present when he owns a plane and shakes hand with the president, says, "A soul brother made it, now ain't that a groove?" But in order to make this solidarity encompass even the least privileged, it must be symbolized by those most undiluted forms of black proletarian experience which everybody can claim as his heritage, and to give it a positive valence weakness must be turned into strength. Thus poverty, oppression, and troubled relationships are interpreted as the foundation of an endurance which can only be truly appreciated by others who have passed the same way. There may be no better example of this than the ghetto use of the term "nigger". It is a repulsive term of abuse when used by white people, and ghetto dwellers themselves certainly often use it in a similar way. But many times they also use it in affectionate mockery. By using it they signalize the understanding that they are separate from the outside world. They intimate that they know all the mainstream prejudices toward the ghetto but themselves have a better understanding, since they, too, know what it means to be a "nigger". This is why black people may say "nigger", but nobody else.

In calling for solidarity on the basis of a shared perspective no outsider is expected to understand, the ghetto dwellers are also expressing their bittersweet view of their condition; it is a part of their understandings that life has been less than fair to them. Man is not supposed to be poor and oppressed, nor should he be hurt by the people closest to him. The comedians' jokes about poverty and the old theme of lost love in black music are assertions that what goes on is not what should go on. The ghetto dwellers have not adjusted their perspective so as to take the ghetto condition for granted as a satisfactory state of affairs. Their understanding of its human consequences differs from that of outsiders, but the standards of what life ought to be like which they apply to such problems are mainstream standards. This is how ghetto dwellers see their own community through a mainstream screen.

The impious view of the working of society is also based on the disjunction between mainstream doctrine and ghetto reality which the ghetto dweller experiences. The representatives of what should be good, right, and just in society are too often seen as corrupt, brutal cops or preachers who are actually con-men. In comparison with such examples of what happens behind the façade of the official moral order, the ghetto dwellers find rather little wrong with such community institutions as bootlegging and the numbers game—which the guardians of the outside world do not accept. So the ghetto dwellers become used to suspecting that things are not necessarily what they seem to be or what they are supposed to be; there is also the understanding that in those innocent relationships within the ghetto community which should be characterized by friendship and cooperation, there may be someone working his own game for profit and thus corrupting the situation. Piety is the sense of what properly goes with what, according to Kenneth Burke (1965:74); ghetto dwellers share their ideas of what moral arrangements ought to be with mainstream society, but their understanding of what really goes on is more likely to be impious, as they have their doubts about the efficient functioning of righteousness in their world. Here again, they apply mainstream standards to ghetto reality. But they are also bringing their knowledge of ghetto reality to bear on their judgment of the mainstream execution of morality, as they find the representatives of mainstream society certainly no less hypocritical than anyone else.

*   *   *

The shared perspective of the ghetto community is a complex phenomenon with a changing structure and composition. Attempting to analyze it we are constantly faced with the danger that we depict it too statically and in terms too intellectually clearcut to represent well the vague moods of an entire community. In the summary we have tried to give in this chapter, we have particularly emphasized the significance of a ghetto-specific culture to community integration; we have also dwelt on the relationship of this culture to the influences of the outside world.

*   *   *

HORACE MINER

Body Ritual among the Nacirema

The anthropologist has become so familiar with the diversity of ways in which different peoples behave in similar situations that he is not apt to be surprised by even the most exotic customs. In fact, if all of the logically possible combinations of behavior have not been found somewhere in the world, he is apt to suspect that they must be present in some yet undescribed tribe. This point has, in fact, been expressed with respect to clan organization by Murdock (1949:71). In this light, the magical beliefs and practices of the Nacirema present such un-

Horace Miner, "Body Ritual among the Nacirema." Reproduced by permission of the American Anthropological Association from *American Anthropologist* 58 (1956): 503–7.

usual aspects that it seems desirable to describe them as an example of the extremes to which human behavior can go.

Professor Linton first brought the ritual of the Nacirema to the attention of anthropologists twenty years ago (1936:326), but the culture of this people is still very poorly understood. They are a North American group living in the territory between the Canadian Cree, the Yaqui and Tarahumare of Mexico, and the Carib and Arawak of the Antilles. Little is known of their origin, although tradition states that they came from the east. According to Nacirema mythology, their nation was originated by a culture hero, Notgnihsaw, who is otherwise known for two great feats of strength—the throwing of a piece of wampum across the river Pa-To-Mac and the chopping down of a cherry tree in which the Spirit of Truth resided.

Nacirema culture is characterized by a highly developed market economy which has evolved in a rich natural habitat. While much of the people's time is devoted to economic pursuits, a large part of the fruits of these labors and a considerable portion of the day are spent in ritual activity. The focus of this activity is the human body, the appearance and health of which loom as a dominant concern in the ethos of the people. While such a concern is certainly not unusual, its ceremonial aspects and associated philosophy are unique.

The fundamental belief underlying the whole system appears to be that the human body is ugly and that its natural tendency is to debility and disease. Incarcerated in such a body, man's only hope is to avert these characteristics through the use of the powerful influences of ritual and ceremony. Every household has one or more shrines devoted to this purpose. The more powerful individuals in the society have several shrines in their houses and, in fact, the opulence of a house is often referred to in terms of the number of such ritual centers it possesses. Most houses are of wattle and daub construction, but the shrine rooms of the more wealthy are walled with stone. Poorer families imitate the rich by applying pottery plaques to their shrine walls.

While each family has at least one such shrine, the rituals associated with it are not family ceremonies but are private and secret. The rites are normally only discussed with children, and then only during the period when they are being initiated into these mysteries. I was able, however, to establish sufficient rapport with the natives to examine these shrines and to have the rituals described to me.

The focal point of the shrine is a box or chest which is built into the wall. In this chest are kept the many charms and magical potions without which no native believes he could live. These preparations are secured from a variety of specialized practitioners. The most powerful of these are the medicine men, whose assistance must be rewarded with substantial gifts. However, the medicine men do not provide the curative potions for their clients, but decide what the ingredients should be and then write them down in an ancient and secret language. This writing is understood only by the medicine men and by the herbalists who, for another gift, provide the required charm.

The charm is not disposed of after it has served its purpose, but is placed in the charm-box of the household shrine. As these magical

126 materials are specific for certain ills, and the real or imagined maladies of the people are many, the charm-box is usually full to overflowing. The magical packets are so numerous that people forget what their purposes were and fear to use them again. While the natives are very vague on this point, we can only assume that the idea in retaining all the old magical materials is that their presence in the charm-box, before which the body rituals are conducted, will in some way protect the worshipper.

Beneath the charm-box is a small font. Each day every member of the family, in succession, enters the shrine room, bows his head before the charm-box, mingles different sorts of holy water in the font, and proceeds with a brief rite of ablution. The holy waters are secured from the Water Temple of the community, where the priests conduct elaborate ceremonies to make the liquid ritually pure.

In the hierarchy of magical practitioners, and below the medicine men in prestige, are specialists whose designation is best translated "holy-mouth-men." The Nacirema have an almost pathological horror of and fascination with the mouth, the condition of which is believed to have a supernatural influence on all social relationships. Were it not for the rituals of the mouth, they believe that their teeth would fall out, their gums bleed, their jaws shrink, their friends desert them, and their lovers reject them. They also believe that a strong relationship exists between oral and moral characteristics. For example, there is a ritual ablution of the mouth for children which is supposed to improve their moral fiber.

The daily body ritual performed by everyone includes a mouth-rite. Despite the fact that these people are so punctilious about care of the mouth, this rite involves a practice which strikes the uninitiated stranger as revolting. It was reported to me that the ritual consists of inserting a small bundle of hog hairs into the mouth, along with certain magical powders, and then moving the bundle in a highly formalized series of gestures.

In addition to the private mouth-rite, the people seek out a holy-mouth-man once or twice a year. These practitioners have an impressive set of paraphernalia, consisting of a variety of augers, awls, probes, and prods. The use of these objects in the exorcism of the evils of the mouth involves almost unbelievable ritual torture of the client. The holy-mouth-man opens the client's mouth and, using the above mentioned tools, enlarges any holes which decay may have created in the teeth. Magical materials are put into these holes. If there are no naturally occurring holes in the teeth, large sections of one or more teeth are gouged out so that the supernatural substance can be applied. In the client's view, the purpose of these ministrations is to arrest decay and to draw friends. The extremely sacred and traditional character of the rite is evident in the fact that the natives return to the holy-mouth-men year after year, despite the fact that their teeth continue to decay.

It is to be hoped that, when a thorough study of the Nacirema is made, there will be careful inquiry into the personality structure of these people. One has but to watch the gleam in the eye of a holy-mouth-man, as he jabs an awl into an exposed nerve, to suspect that a certain amount of sadism is involved. If this can be established, a very interesting pattern emerges, for most of the population shows definite masochistic tendencies. It was to these that Professor Linton referred in discussing a distinctive part of the daily body ritual which is performed only by men. This part of the rite involves scraping and lacerating the surface of the face with a sharp instrument. Special women's rites are performed only four times during each lunar month, but what they lack in frequency is made up in barbarity. As part of this ceremony, women bake their heads in small ovens for about an hour. The theoretically interesting point is that what seems to be a preponderantly masochistic people have developed sadistic specialists.

The medicine men have an imposing temple, or *latipso*, in every community of any size. The more elaborate ceremonies required to treat very sick patients can only be performed at this temple. These ceremonies involve not only the thaumaturge but a permanent group of vestal maidens who move sedately about the temple chambers in distinctive costume and headdress.

The *latipso* ceremonies are so harsh that it is phenomenal that a fair proportion of the really sick natives who enter the temple ever recover. Small children whose indoctrination is still incomplete have been known to resist attempts to take them to the temple because "that is where you go to die." Despite this fact, sick adults are not only willing but eager to undergo the protracted ritual purification, if they can afford to do so. No matter how ill the supplicant or how grave the emergency, the guardians of many temples will not admit a client if he cannot give a rich gift to the custodian. Even after one has gained admission and survived the ceremonies, the guardians will not permit the neophyte to leave until he makes still another gift.

The supplicant entering the temple is first stripped of all his or her clothes. In every-day life the Nacirema avoids exposure of his body and its natural functions. Bathing and excretory acts are performed only in the secrecy of the household shrine, where they are ritualized as part of the body-rites. Psychological shock results from the fact that body secrecy is suddenly lost upon entry into the *latipso*. A man, whose own wife has never seen him in an excretory act, suddenly finds himself naked and assisted by a vestal maiden while he performs his natural functions into a sacred vessel. This sort of ceremonial treatment is necessitated by the fact that the excreta are used by a diviner to ascertain the course and nature of the client's sickness. Female clients, on the other hand, find their naked bodies are subjected to the scrutiny, manipulation and prodding of the medicine men.

Few supplicants in the temple are well enough to do anything but lie on their hard beds. The daily ceremonies, like the rites of the holy-mouth-men, involve discomfort and torture. With ritual precision, the vestals awaken their miserable charges each dawn and roll them about on their beds of pain while performing ablutions, in the formal movements of which the maidens are highly trained. At other times they insert magic wands in the supplicant's mouth or force him to eat substances which are supposed to be healing. From time to time the medicine men come to their clients and jab magically treated needles into their flesh. The fact that these temple ceremonies may not cure, and may even kill the neophyte, in no way decreases the people's faith in the medicine men.

There remains one other kind of practitioner, known as a "listener." This witch-doctor has the power to exorcise the devils that lodge in the heads of people who have been bewitched. The Nacirema believe that parents bewitch their own children. Mothers are particularly suspected of putting a curse on children while teaching them the secret body rituals. The counter-magic of the witch-doctor is unusual in its lack of ritual. The patient simply tells the "listener" all his troubles and fears, beginning with the earliest difficulties he can remember. The memory displayed by the Nacirema in these exorcism sessions is truly remarkable. It is not uncommon for the patient to bemoan the rejection he felt upon being weaned as a babe, and a few individuals even see their troubles going back to the traumatic efforts of their own birth.

In conclusion, mention must be made of certain practices which have their base in native esthetics but which depend upon the pervasive aversion to the natural body and its functions. There are ritual fasts to make fat people thin and ceremonial feasts to make thin people fat. Still other rites are used to make women's breasts larger if they are small, and smaller if they are large. General dissatisfaction with breast shape is symbolized in the fact that the ideal form is virtually outside the range of human variation. A few women afflicted with almost inhuman hypermammary development are so idolized that they make a handsome living by simply going from village to village and permitting the natives to stare at them for a fee.

Reference has already been made to the fact that excretory functions are ritualized, routinized, and relegated to secrecy. Natural reproductive functions are similarly distorted. Intercourse is taboo as a topic and scheduled as an act. Efforts are made to avoid pregnancy by the use of magical materials or by limiting intercourse to certain phases of the moon. Conception is actually very infrequent. When pregnant, women dress so as to hide their condition. Parturition takes place in secret, without friends or relatives to assist, and the majority of women do not nurse their infants.

Our review of the ritual life of the Nacirema has certainly shown them to be a magic-ridden people. It is hard to understand how they have managed to exist so long under the burdens which they have imposed upon themselves. But even such exotic customs as these take on real meaning when they are viewed with the insight provided by Malinowski when he wrote (1948:70):

Looking from far and above, from our high places of safety in the developed civilization, it is easy to see all the crudity and irrelevance of magic. But without its power and guidance early man could not have mastered his practical difficulties as he has done, nor could man have advanced to the higher stages of civilization.

REFERENCES 129

Linton, Ralph. *The Study of Man*. New York: D. Appleton-Century Co., 1936.

Malinowski, Bronislaw. *Magic, Science, and Religion*. Glencoe: The Free Press, 1948.

Murdock, George P. *Social Structure*. New York: Macmillan Co., 1949.

CONVERSION Honor

FRIENDS ACTIONS

Insanity COOPERATION

Dignity FEELINGS

TACT Parents Enhancement

RELATIONSHIP
WILLINGNESS CONTINGENCY

Interaction Human Nature

MUTUALITY Influence

Love Poise

Honor LAWYERS

Study Questions

1. Do "elements" and "parts," "self" and "collective" behavior exist in any of the readings for this chapter? In your sociology class? If so, where and how are they originated and maintained?
2. Apply the different kinds of contingencies to the chapter readings and to the interactions of student with student and student with professor. What is the value of analyzing social interaction in this way?
3. Can you indicate some area where you have attempted to negotiate reality? Are all areas of human behavior negotiable?
4. What is love? How is it imitated? Can it be negotiated?

The Image of Man in Society: Interaction

5 While culture provides the general expectations and values of groups, it is interaction that more directly shapes individual choices, acts, and behavior. "Interaction" refers to the process of mutual influence between social actors. Interaction cannot be understood by referring merely to the qualities of individuals, but must be more fundamentally perceived as the *process* by which individuals, in their actions, take account of others' minds, intentions, and deeds.

THE INTERTWINING OF SOCIAL INTERACTION, RELATIONSHIP, AND ORGANIZATION

An interaction between social actors may occur once, (an isolated event), or may be repeated in such a way that a stable form of interrelating occurs and a social relationship develops. Social relationships always involve interaction, and can evolve when two or more individuals or groups, or an individual and a group, interact with one another. Social interaction, then, may be the genesis of a relationship, and social relationships are essential for the development of social organization. Social interaction is also an ongoing process, occurring wherever relationships and groups already exist. The process of interaction, with its intricacies and stages of involvement, has been dramatically described by Albert Cohen:

Human action, deviant or otherwise, is something that typically develops and grows in a tentative, groping, advancing, backtracking, sounding-out process. People taste and feel their way along. They begin in an act and do not complete it. They start doing one thing and end up by doing another. They extricate themselves from progressive involvement or become further involved to the point of commitment. These processes of progressive involvement and disinvolvement are important enough to deserve explicit recognition and treatment in their own right.[1]

The ways in which a person or actor relates to, deals with, and

132

responds to others—the process of social interaction—has traditionally been the domain of social psychologists such as Guy E. Swanson, who has even argued that the study of social interaction, the means by which men come to take account of each other's "minded" process, is the *only* proper study for social psychologists.[2] Other social psychologists, who hold a contrasting view, consider that the main concern of their discipline should be with the impact of group properties on the individual. Leavitt's experiment with communication networks and their impact on individual satisfaction (excerpted in chapter 2) is an example of this approach. Swanson's social interaction perspective, however, helps us focus on the more fundamental process of mutual influence.

People, of course, need not influence each other at all when they meet. They can come together in a number of ways. They may literally bump into each other, in which case they meet as biological organisms. There is no "minded" influence at work. They may meet at a party and carry on a conversation without either individual paying much attention to the other's remarks. Here, there is minimal influence. Mutual influence occurs when both actors' ideas, goals, and wishes are expressed, heard, and taken into account. Personalities, in interacting with each other, may or may not develop social relationships, may or may not develop an organization. Earlier comments on the levels of analysis (in chapter 2) help clarify the concepts of interaction, relationship, and organization as they affect each other. When influence and mutual adaptation, implicit in social relationships, become infused with cultural meanings, we have social organization. A group or social organization is distinguished from a relationship by the degree of cooperation among members, the sense of belonging that the members have, and their capacity to maintain and defend the group against the external environment.

ELEMENTS AND PARTS

Another way of examining the phenomenon of influence is to differentiate between *elements* and *parts*. The transition from element to part can be perceived as a factor in the growth of a social relationship from an initial interaction. Before coming together with another social actor, a person can be viewed as independent and autonomous. We say that in that condition, he is acting as an element. Once social interaction begins, however, a relationship may develop. With the advent of a social relationship and with it a mutual influence, the actions of the actor are altered. The moment a relationship is established, whether out of personal satisfaction or common interests and goals, whether out of expectations or obligations or because of mutual interdependence, the actors in that relationship act not as elements but as parts.[3] Membership and participation in an established social relationship influence the behavior of the participants. The salient features of our actions may be as elements or parts, dependent on the situation, but it is probably most accurate to say that social actors are always acting simultaneously as both elements *and* parts. The analogy that can clarify the elements and parts distinction can be taken from chemistry. Hydro-

134 gen and oxygen are elements. They have their own unique characteristics, weights, and densities. When joined in the proper quantities, however, they develop into a new substance, the compound H_2O. Each of the elements has, to some extent, lost its identity in the process of being transformed into something different. Thus it is with social relationships. A social relationship may be described by the extent to which the actors are oriented toward element (self) versus part (collective).[4]

INTERACTION CONTINGENCIES

Richard Jones and Harold Gerard, two social psychologists, provide a useful scheme for examining social interaction in terms of mutual influence. They make a number of distinctions which help us to understand more precisely the relationship between elements and parts. Jones and Gerard suggest that it is important to determine the following:

1. The degree of importance of the person's plans—the goals, motives, and values of the actor entering the interaction
2. The degree of importance of the actions of others toward him
3. The degree to which the actor's reaction to others is independent of his own plans
4. The degree of influence of the combination of points 1 and 2 above.

The degree to which these variables become implicated in an interaction determines the amount and kind of influence and helps classify the types of interactions. The first type that Jones and Gerard describe is *pseudo-contingency*. Here, each actor pays attention almost exclusively to his own plans. The actors may be in close physical proximity, but there is no connection between them. They speak but do not respond to each other. The actions and expressed thoughts and feelings of one person do not influence those of the other. Pseudo-contingency involves ritualistic elements such as those which occur in weddings and inaugurals. It also involves patterned interactions between people where little meaning is involved for the participants. Few of us take seriously the question, "How are you?" or the response, "Fine." Statements like "I'll call you," help to facilitate departure, but these routinized forms of exchange add little to a relationship between two people. Although the potential always exists for moving into an exchange involving something deeper, these amenities tend to be used as ritualized ways of interacting.

In *assymetrical contingency* there is influence and response, but it is not in balance. One person dominates the interaction in plans and intentions. A job interview is a good example. The applicant tries to make sense of the questions, to pick up cues, and to present the kind of face he believes the interviewer wants to see. The interviewer has his own plan. He has a set number of questions and a program of information to obtain; the bulk of influence emanates from him. Interviewer and applicant respond to each other, but in a one-sided way; the behavior and responses of the applicant are affected to a greater degree by the questions and status of the interviewer than the converse.

Reactive contingency occurs when an actor has no particular plans, but responds impulsively to the action of others. Much panic behavior is like this. Finally, in the *mutual contingency* type of interaction, each actor responds both in terms of his own plans and the plans of others. There is a joint emphasis upon each other's goals, skills, and talents. Mutual contingency can occur not only between lovers or friends, but also, for example, between parent and child, when the parent tries to take account of the individuality of his child while setting limits for him and helping him learn to get along with others.[5] The concept of contingencies is a formal way of analyzing interaction. It is interesting to try to identify and compare the types of contingencies at work in various groups, organizations and social relationships.

In this section, I have included three articles related to interaction, to which the concepts introduced in this chapter can be applied. The first article, by Thomas J. Scheff, a sociologist, focuses on the process of interaction. Scheff is interested in the problem of "negotiated reality." He concerns himself with conditions which determine a social actor's sense of what is true and real. He compares the transactions in a psychiatric and a legal interview (examples of asymmetric contingency) in order to develop his argument that much, if not all, of "social reality" is part of the socially shared definition of truth. You can analyze the shifting and changing contingencies in the two interviews as the lawyer and the psychiatrist attempt to influence their clients.

The second selection is an excerpt from a poignant autobiographical novel, *I Never Promised You a Rose Garden*. It is the story of a young, sensitive, schizophrenic girl, and describes the interactions and relationships between her and her family, her therapist, other patients, and staff during three long, difficult years of hospitalization, of groping toward emotional health and strength. The excerpt helps us to further understand some of Scheff's points. Because the line between sanity and insanity is not well defined, the grey area of judgment permits persons with legitimacy, in their capacities as agents of social control, to determine the sanity or insanity of another human being. In this excerpt you will also read about the way in which legitimate authority, in this case the government, allows one of its citizens to make a choice against participating in action which is morally and ethically unthinkable for him. In making this choice the person places himself in a situation that is very painful in its impact on his being. Finally, this excerpt shows how the barriers of "appropriate" social behavior between patient and attendant are broken in such a way that the line between sanity and insanity is at least temporarily erased. Two people face a task, with each person taking responsibility not only for his own behavior but for their joint effort as well. We have, then, the beginning of a social relationship.

The final reading in this chapter is by Guy E. Swanson, a social psychologist, who writes about the most complex of all human relationships, that of love. In "The Routinization of Love," Swanson tries to give scientific meaning to the nature and process of loving. He notes that love is the most complete form of social interaction between human beings. The loving relationship is challenging and sustaining, demanding and nurturing. Because love is such a thoroughly complex phenomenon, it has many imitations. Many relationships that are mutually contingent do not fully capture the definition of love that Swanson offers us.

I think it is important for students to struggle with this article, for it is an excellent example of how systematic analysis can permit them to understand an elusive phenomenon. You may find it tedious or pretentious that a social scientist has tried to objectify so fluid and elusive a concept as love. I would venture to guess that all of you have thought of love in some of the ways that Swanson describes. He takes these varied conceptions of love, synthesizes them, and brings them together in an analytical framework that is rich in feeling.

NOTES

1. Albert K. Cohen, "The Sociology of the Deviant Act: Anomie Theory and Beyond," *American Sociological Review* 30, no. 1 (February 1965): 8–9.

2. Guy E. Swanson, "On Explanations of Social Interaction," *Sociometry* 28, no. 2 (June 1965): 101–23.

3. Ibid.

4. Talcott Parsons, and Robert F. Bales, *Family Socialization and Interaction Process* (Glencoe, Ill.: Free Press), pp. 142–44.

5. Richard Jones, and Harold Gerard, *Foundations of Social Psychology*, (New York: John Wiley & Sons, 1967), pp. 506–12.

THOMAS J. SCHEFF

Negotiating Reality: Notes on Power in the Assessment of Responsibility

This paper illustrates the difference between absolute and social conceptions of responsibility, by employing the perspective of the sociology of knowledge. Comparing the degree of shared awareness and the organization of the format of the transaction in initial psychiatric and legal interviews,

Thomas J. Scheff, "Negotiating Reality: Notes on Power in the Assessment of Responsibilty;" *Social Problems* 16:1 (Summer 1968): 3–17. Reprinted by permission of the author and The Society for the Study of Social Problems.

propositions showing the relationship between the power and authority of the interactants, and the resultant shared definition of the client's responsibility, are suggested. The implications of these points for psychiatric and legal policy, and for social science research are discussed in the conclusion.

The use of interrogation to reconstruct parts of an individual's past history is a common occurrence in human affairs. Reporters, jealous lovers, and policemen on the beat are often faced with the task of determining events in another person's life, and the extent to which he was responsible for those events. The most dramatic use of interrogation to determine responsibility is in criminal trials. As in everyday life, criminal trials are concerned with both act and intent. Courts, in most cases, first determine whether the defendant performed a legally forbidden act. If it is found that he did so, the court then must decide whether he was "responsible" for the act. Reconstructive work of this type goes on less dramatically in a wide variety of other settings, as well. The social worker determining a client's eligibility for unemployment compensation, for example, seeks not only to establish that the client actually is unemployed, but that he has actively sought employment, i.e., that he himself is not responsible for being out of work.

This paper will contrast two perspectives on the process of reconstructing past events for the purpose of fixing responsibility. The first perspective stems from the common sense notion that interrogation, when it is sufficiently skillful, is essentially neutral. Responsibility for past actions can be fixed absolutely and independently of the method of reconstruction. This perspective is held by the typical member of society, engaged in his day-to-day tasks. It is also held, in varying degrees, by most professional interrogators. The basic working doctrine is one of *absolute* responsibility. This point of view actually entails the comparison of two different kinds of items: first, the fixing of actions and intentions, and secondly, comparing these actions and intentions to some predetermined criteria of responsibility. The basic premise of the doctrine of absolute responsibility is that both actions and intentions, on the one hand, and the criteria of responsibility, on the other, are absolute, in that they can be assessed independently of social context.[1]

An alternative approach follows from the sociology of knowledge. From this point of view, the reality within which members of society conduct their lives is largely of their own construction.[2] Since much of reality is a construction, there may be multiple realities, existing side by side, in harmony or in competition. It follows, if one maintains this stance, that the assessment of responsibility involves the construction of reality by members' construction both of actions and intentions, on the one hand, and of criteria of responsibility, on the other. The former process, the continuous reconstruction of the normative order, has long been the focus of sociological concern.[3] The discussion in this paper will be limited, for the most part, to the former process, the way in which actions and intentions are constructed in the act of assessing responsibility.

138

My purpose is to argue that responsibility is at least partly a product of social structure. The alternative to the doctrine of absolute responsibility is that of relative responsibility: the assessment of responsibility always includes a process of negotiation. In this process, responsibility is in part constructed by the negotiating parties. To illustrate this thesis, excerpts from two dialogues of negotiation will be discussed: a real psychotherapeutic interview, and an interview between a defense attorney and his client, taken from a work of fiction. Before presenting these excerpts it will be useful to review some prior discussions of negotiation, the first in courts of law, the second in medical diagnosis.[4]

The negotiation of pleas in criminal courts, sometimes referred to as "bargain justice," has been frequently noted by observers of legal processes.[5] The defense attorney, or (in many cases, apparently) the defendant himself, strikes a bargain with the prosecutor—a plea of guilty will be made, provided that the prosecutor will reduce the charge. For example, a defendant arrested on suspicion of armed robbery may arrange to plead guilty to the charge of unarmed robbery. The prosecutor obtains ease of conviction from the bargain, the defendant, leniency.

Although no explicit estimates are given, it appears from observers' reports that the great majority of criminal convictions are negotiated. Newman states:

A major characteristic of criminal justice administration, particularly in jurisdictions characterized by legislatively fixed sentences, is charge reduction to elicit pleas of guilty. Not only does the efficient functioning of criminal justice rest upon a high proportion of guilty pleas, but plea bargaining is closely linked with attempts to individualize justice, to obtain certain desirable conviction consequences, and to avoid undesirable ones such as "undeserved" mandatory sentences.[6]

It would appear that the bargaining process is accepted as routine. In the three jurisdictions Newman studied, there were certain meeting places where the defendant, his client, and a representative of the prosecutor's office routinely met to negotiate the plea. It seems clear that in virtually all but the most unusual cases, the interested parties expected to, and actually did, negotiate the plea.

From these comments on the routine acceptance of plea bargaining in the courts, one might expect that this process would be relatively open and unambiguous. Apparently, however, there is some tension between the fact of bargaining and moral expectations concerning justice. Newman refers to this tension by citing two contradictory statements: an actual judicial opinion, "Justice and liberty are not the subjects of bargaining and barter;" and an off-the-cuff statement by another judge, "All law is compromise." A clear example of this tension is provided by an excerpt from a trial and Newman's comments on it.

The following questions were asked of a defendant after he had pleaded guilty to unarmed robbery when the original charge was armed robbery.

This reduction is common, and the judge was fully aware that the plea was negotiated:

> Judge: You want to plead guilty to robbery unarmed?
> Defendant: Yes, Sir.
> Judge: Your plea of guilty is free and voluntary?
> Defendant: Yes, Sir.
> Judge: No one has promised you anything?
> Defendant: No.
> Judge: No one has induced you to plead guilty?
> Defendant: No.
> Judge: You're pleading guilty because you are guilty?
> Defendant: Yes.
> Judge: I'll accept your plea of guilty to robbery unarmed and refer it
> to the probation department for a report and for sentencing Dec. 28.[7]

The delicacy of the relationship between appearance and reality is apparently confusing, even for the sociologist-observer. Newman's comment on this exchange has an Alice-in-Wonderland quality:

This is a routine procedure designed to satisfy the statutory requirement and is not intended to disguise the process of charge reduction.[8]

If we put the tensions between the different realities aside for the moment, we can say that there is an explicit process of negotiation between the defendant and the prosecution which is a part of the legal determination of guilt or innocence, or in the terms used above, the assessment of responsibility.

In medical diagnosis, a similar process of negotiation occurs, but is much less self-conscious than plea bargaining. The English psychoanalyst Michael Balint refers to this process as one of "offers and responses":

Some of the people who, for some reason or other, find it difficult to cope with problems of their lives resort to becoming ill. If the doctor has the opportunity of seeing them in the first phases of their being ill, i.e. before they settle down to a definite "organized" illness, he may observe that the patients, so to speak, offer or propose various illnesses, and that they have to go on offering new illnesses until between doctor and patient an agreement can be reached resulting in the acceptance by both of them of one of the illnesses as justified.[9]

Balint gives numerous examples indicating that patients propose reasons for their coming to the doctor which are rejected, one by one, by the physician, who makes counter-proposals until an "illness' acceptable to both parties is found. If "definition of the situation" is substituted for "illness," Balint's observations become relevant to a wide variety of transactions, including the kind of interrogation discussed above. The fixing of responsibility is a process in which the client offers definitions of the situation, to which the interrogator responds. After a series of offers and responses, a definition of the situation acceptable to both the client and the interrogator is reached.

140

Balint has observed that the negotiation process leads physicians to influence the outcome of medical examinations, independently of the patient's condition. He refers to this process as the "apostolic function" of the doctor, arguing that the physician induces patients to have the kind of illness that the physician thinks is proper:

> Apostolic mission or function means in the first place that every doctor has a vague, but almost unshakably firm, idea of how a patient ought to behave when ill. Although this idea is anything but explicit and concrete, it is immensely powerful, and influences, as we have found, practically every detail of the doctor's work with his patients. It was almost as if every doctor had revealed knowledge of what was right and what was wrong for patients to expect and to endure, and further, as if he had a sacred duty to convert to his faith all the ignorant and unbelieving among his patients.[10]

Implicit in this statement is the notion that interrogator and client have unequal power in determining the resultant definition of the situation. The interrogator's definition of the situation plays an important part in the joint definition of the situation which is finally negotiated. Moreover, his definition is more important than the client's in determining the final outcome of the negotiation, principally because he is well trained, secure, and self-confident in his role in the transaction, whereas the client is untutored, anxious, and uncertain about his role. Stated simply, the subject, because of these conditions, is likely to be susceptible to the influence of the interrogator.

Note that plea bargaining and the process of "offers and responses" in diagnosis differ in the degree of self-consciousness of the participants. In plea bargaining the process is at least partly visible to the participants themselves. There appears to be some ambiguity about the extent to which the negotiation is morally acceptable to some of the commentators, but the parties to the negotiations appear to be aware that bargaining is going on, and accept the process as such. The bargaining process in diagnosis, however, is much more subterranean. Certainly neither physicians nor patients recognize the offers and responses process as being bargaining. There is no commonly accepted vocabulary for describing diagnostic bargaining, such as there is in the legal analogy, e.g. "copping out" or "copping a plea." It may be that in legal processes there is some appreciation of the different kinds of reality, i.e. the difference between the public (official, legal) reality and private reality, whereas in medicine this difference is not recognized.

The discussion so far has suggested that much of reality is arrived at by negotiation. This thesis was illustrated by materials presented on legal processes by Newman, and medical processes by Balint. These processes are similar in that they appear to represent clear instances of the negotiation of reality. The instances are different in that the legal bargaining processes appear to be more open and accepted than the diagnostic process. In order to outline some of the dimensions of the negotiation process, and to establish some of the limitations of the analyses by Newman and Balint, two excerpts of cases of bargaining will be discussed: the first taken from an actual psychiatric "intake" interview, the second from a fictional account of a defense lawyer's first interview with his client.

THE PROCESS OF NEGOTIATION

The psychiatric interview to be discussed is from the first interview in *The Initial Interview in Psychiatric Practice.*[11] The patient is a thirty-four year old nurse, who feels, as she says, "irritable, tense, depressed." She appears to be saying from the very beginning of the interview that the external situation in which she lives is the cause of her troubles. She focuses particularly on her husband's behavior. She says he is an alcoholic, is verbally abusive, and won't let her work. She feels that she is cooped up in the house all day with her two small children, but that when he is home at night (on the nights when he *is* at home) he will have nothing to do with her and the children. She intimates, in several ways, that he does not serve as a sexual companion. She has thought of divorce, but has rejected it for various reasons (for example, she is afraid she couldn't take proper care of the children, finance the baby sitters, etc.). She feels trapped.[12]

In the concluding paragraph of their description of this interview, Gill, Newman, and Redlich give this summary:

> The patient, pushed by we know not what or why at the time (the children—somebody to talk to) comes for help apparently for what she thinks of as help with her external situation (her husband's behavior as she sees it). The therapist does not respond to this but seeks her role and how it is that she plays such a role. Listening to the recording it sounds as if the therapist is at first bored and disinterested and the patient defensive. He gets down to work and keeps asking, "What is it all about?" Then he becomes more interested and sympathetic and at the same time very active (participating) and demanding. *It sounds as if she keeps saying "This is the trouble." He says, "No! Tell me the trouble." She says, "This is it!" He says, "No, tell me," until the patient finally says, "Well I'll tell you." Then the therapist says, "Good! I'll help you."*[13]

From this summary it is apparent that there is a close fit between Balint's idea of the negotiation of diagnosis through offers and responses, and what took place in this psychiatric interview. It is difficult, however, to document the details. Most of the psychiatrist's responses, rejecting the patient's offers, do not appear in the written transcript, but they are fairly obvious as one listens to the recording. Two particular features of the psychiatrist's responses especially stand out: (1) the flatness of intonation in his responses to the patient's complaints about her external circumstances; and (2) the rapidity with which he introduces new topics, through questioning, when she is talking about her husband.

Some features of the psychiatrist's coaching are verbal, however:

T. 95: Has anything happened recently that makes it . . . you feel that . . . ah . . . you're sort of coming to the end of your rope?

I mean I wondered what led you . . .

P. 95: (Interrupting.) It's nothing special. It's just everything in general.

T. 96: What led you to come to a . . .

P. 96: (Interrupting.) It's just that I . . .

T. 97: . . . a psychiatrist just now? (1)

P. 97: Because I felt that the older girl was getting tense as a result of . . . of my being stewed up all the time.

T. 98: Mmmhnn.

P. 98: Not having much patience with her.

T. 99: Mmmhnn. (Short Pause.) Mmm. And how had you imagined that a psychiatrist could help with this? (Short pause.) (2)

P. 99: Mmm . . . maybe I could sort of get straightened out . . . straighten things out in my own mind. I'm confused. Sometimes I can't remember things that I've done, whether I've done 'em or not or whether they happened.

T. 100: What is it that you want to straighten out? (Pause.)

P. 100: I think I seem mixed up.

T. 101: Yeah? You see that, it seems to me, is something that we really should talk about because . . . ah . . . from a certain point of view somebody might say, "Well now, it's all very simple. She's unhappy and disturbed because her husband is behaving this way, and unless something can be done about that how could she expect to feel any other way." But, instead of that, you come to the psychiatrist, and you say that you think there's something about you that needs straightening out. (3) I don't quite get it. Can you explain that to me? (Short pause.)

P. 101: I sometimes wonder if I'm emotionally grown up.

T. 102: By which you mean what?

P. 102: When you're married you should have one mate. You shouldn't go around and look at other men.

T. 103: You've been looking at other men?

P. 103: I look at them, but that's all.

T. 104: Mmmhnn. What you mean . . . you mean a grown-up person should accept the marital situation whatever it happens to be?

P. 104: That was the way I was brought up. Yes. (Sighs).

T. 105: You think that would be a sign of emotional maturity?

P. 105: No.

T. 106: No. So?

P. 106: Well, if you rebel against the laws of society you have to take the consequences.

T. 107: Yes?

P. 107: And it's just that I . . . I'm not willing to take the consequences. I . . . I don't think it's worth it.

T. 108: Mmhnn. So in the meantime then while you're in this very difficult situation, you find yourself reacting in a way that you don't like and that you think is . . . ah . . . damaging to your children and yourself? Now what can be done about that?

P. 108: (Sniffs; sighs.) I dunno. That's why I came to see you.

T. 109: Yes. I was just wondering what you had in mind. Did you think a psychiatrist could . . . ah . . . help you face this kind of a situation calmly and easily and maturely? (4) Is that it?

P. 109: More or less. I need somebody to talk to who isn't emotionally involved with the family. I have a few friends, but I don't like to bore them. I don't think they should know . . . ah . . . all the intimate details of what goes on.

T. 110: Yeah?

P. 110: It becomes food for gossip.

T. 111: Mmmhnn.

P. 111: Besides they're in . . . they're emotionally involved because they're my friends. They tell me not to stand for it, but they don't understand that if I put my foot down it'll only get stepped on.

T. 112: Yeah.

P. 112: That he can make it miserable for me in other ways. . . .

T. 113: Mmm.

P. 113: . . . which he does.

T. 114: Mmmhnn. In other words, you find yourself in a situation and don't know how to cope with it really.

P. 114: I don't.

T. 115: You'd like to be able to talk that through and come to understand it better and learn how to cope with it or deal with it in some way. Is that right?

P. 115: I'd like to know how to deal with it more effectively.

T. 116: Yeah. Does that mean you feel convinced that the way you're dealing with it now. . . .

P. 116: There's something wrong of course.

T. 117: . . . something wrong with that. Mmmhnn.

P. 117: There's something wrong with it.[14]

Note that the therapist reminds her *four times* in this short sequence that she has come to see a *psychiatrist*. Since the context of these reminders is one in which the patient is attributing her difficulties to an external situation, particularly her husband, it seems plausible to hear these reminders as subtle requests for analysis of her own contribution to her difficulties. This interpretation is supported by the therapist's subsequent remarks. When the patient once again describes external problems, the therapist tries the following tack:

T. 125: I notice that you've used a number of psychiatric terms here and there. Were you specially interested in that in your training, or what?

P. 125: Well, my great love is psychology.

T. 126: Psychology?

P. 126: Mmmhnn.

T. 127: How much have you studied?

P. 127: Oh (Sighs.) what you have in your nurse's training, and I've had general psych, child and adolescent psych, and the abnormal psych.

T. 128: Mmmhnn. Well, tell me . . . ah . . . what would you say if you had to explain yourself what is the problem?

P. 128: You don't diagnose yourself very well, at least I don't.

T. 129: Well you can make a stab at it. (Pause.)[15]

This therapeutic thrust is rewarded: the patient gives a long account of her early life which indicates a belief that she was not "adjusted" in the past. The interview continues:

T. 135: And what conclusions do you draw from all this about why you're not adjusting now the way you think you should?

    P. 135: Well, I wasn't adjusted then. I feel that I've come a long way, but I don't think I'm still . . . I still don't feel that I'm adjusted.

T. 136: And you don't regard your husband as being the difficulty? You think it lies within yourself?

    P. 136: Oh he's a difficulty all right, but I figure that even . . . ah . . . had . . . if it had been other things that . . . that this probably—this state—would've come on me.

T. 137: Oh you do think so?

    P. 137: (Sighs.) I don't think he's the sole factor. No.

T. 138: And what are the factors within. . . .

    P. 138: I mean. . . .

T. 139: . . . yourself?

    P. 139: Oh it's probably remorse for the past, things I did.

T. 140: Like what? (Pause.) It's sumping' hard to tell, hunh? (Short pause.) [16]

After some parrying, the patient tells the therapist what he wants to hear. She feels guilty because she was pregnant by another man when her present husband proposed. She cries. The therapist tells the patient she needs, and will get psychiatric help, and the interview ends, the patient still crying. The negotiational aspects of the process are clear: After the patient has spent most of the interview blaming her current difficulties on external circumstances, she tells the therapist a deep secret about which she feels intensely guilty. The patient, and not the husband, is at fault. The therapist's tone and manner change abruptly. From being bored, distant, and rejecting, he becomes warm and solicitous. Through a process of offers and responses, the therapist and patient have, by implication, negotiated a shared definition of the situation—the patient, not the husband, is responsible.

A CONTRASTING CASE

The negotiation process can, of course, proceed on the opposite premise, namely that the client is not responsible. An ideal example would be an interrogation of a client by a skilled defense lawyer. Unfortunately, we have been unable to locate a verbatim transcript of a defense lawyer's initial interview with his client. There is available, however, a fictional portrayal of such an interview, written by a man with extensive experience as defense lawyer, prosecutor, and judge. The excerpt to follow is taken from the novel, *Anatomy of a Murder*.[17]

    The defense lawyer, in his initial contact with his client, briefly questions him regarding his actions on the night of the killing. The client states that he discovered that the deceased, Barney Quill, had raped his wife; he then goes on to state that he then left his wife, found Quill and shot him.

". . . How long did you remain with your wife before you went to the hotel bar?"

"I don't remember."

"I think it is important, and I suggest you try."

After a pause. "Maybe an hour."

"Maybe more?"

"Maybe."

"Maybe less?"

"Maybe."

I paused and lit a cigar. I took my time. I had reached a point where a few wrong answers to a few right questions would leave me with a client—if I took his case—whose cause was legally defenseless. Either I stopped now and begged off and let some other lawyer worry over it or I asked him the few fatal questions and let him hang himself. Or else, like any smart lawyer, I went into the Lecture. I studied my man, who sat as inscrutable as an Arab, delicately fingering his Ming holder, daintily sipping his dark mustache. He apparently did not realize how close I had him to admitting that he was guilty of first degree murder, that is, that he "feloniously, wilfully and of his malice afore-thought did kill and murder one Barney Quill." The man was a sitting duck.[18]

The lawyer here realizes that his line of questioning has come close to fixing the responsibility for the killing on his client. He therefore shifts his ground by beginning "the lecture":

The Lecture is an ancient device that lawyers use to coach their clients so that the client won't quite know he has been coached and his lawyer can still preserve the face-saving illusion that he hasn't done any coaching. For coaching clients, like robbing them, is not only frowned upon, it is downright unethical and bad, very bad. Hence the Lecture, an artful device as old as the law itself, and one used constantly by some of the nicest and most ethical lawyers in the land. "Who, me" I didn't tell him what to say," the lawyer can later comfort himself. "I merely explained the law, see." It is a good practice to scowl and shrug here and add virtuously: "That's my duty, isn't it?"

. . . "We will now explore the absorbing subject of legal justification or excuse," I said.

. . . "Well, take self-defense," I began. "That's the classic example of justifiable homicide. On the basis of what I've so far heard and read about your case I do not think we need pause too long over that. Do you?"

"Perhaps not," Lieutenant Manion conceded. "We'll pass it for now."

"Let's," I said dryly. "Then there's the defense of habitation, defense of property, and the defense of relatives or friends. Now there are more ramifications to these defenses than a dog has fleas, but we won't explore them now. I've already told you at length why I don't think you can invoke the possible defense of your wife. When you shot Quill her need for defense had passed. It's as simple as that."

"Go on," Lieutenant Manion said, frowning.

"Then there's the defense of a homicide committed to prevent a felony —say you're being robbed—; to prevent the escape of the felon—suppose he's getting away with your wallet—; or to arrest a felon—you've caught up with him and he's either trying to get away or has actually escaped." . . .

... "Go on, then; what are some of the other legal justifications or excuses?"

"Then there's the tricky and dubious defense of intoxication. Personally I've never seen it succeed. But since you were not drunk when you shot Quill we shall mercifully not dwell on that. Or were you?"

"I was cold sober. Please go on."

"Then finally there's the defense of insanity." I paused and spoke abruptly, airily: "Well, that just about winds it up." I arose as though making ready to leave.

"Tell me more."

"There is no more." I slowly paced up and down the room.

"I mean about this insanity."

"Oh, insanity," I said, elaborately surprised. It was like luring a trained seal with a herring. "Well, insanity, where proven, is a complete defense to murder. It does not legally justify the killing, like self-defense, say, but rather excuses it." The lecturer was hitting his stride. He was also on the home stretch. "Our law requires that a punishable killing— in fact, any crime—must be committed by a sapient human being, one capable, as the law insists, of distinguishing between right and wrong. If a man is insane, legally insane, the act of homicide may still be murder but the law excuses the perpetrator."

Lieutenant Manion was sitting erect now, very still and erect. "I see— and this—this perpetrator, what happens to him if he should—should be excused?"

"Under Michigan law—like that of many other states—if he is acquitted of murder on the grounds of insanity it is provided that he must be sent to a hospital for the criminally insane until he is pronounced sane." ...

... Then he looked at me. "Maybe," he said, "maybe I was insane."

... Thoughtfully: "Hm. ... Why do you say that?"

"Well, I can't really say," he went on slowly. "I—I guess I blacked out. I can't remember a thing after I saw him standing behind the bar that night until I got back to my trailer."

"You mean—you mean you don't remember shooting him?" I shook my head in wonderment.

"Yes, that's what I mean."

"You don't even remember driving home?"

"No."

"You don't remember threatening Barney's bartender when he followed you outside after the shooting—as the newspaper says you did?" I paused and held my breath. "You don't remember telling him, 'Do you want some, too, Buster?' ?"

The smoldering dark eyes flickered ever so little. "No, not a thing."

"My, my," I said blinking my eyes, contemplating the wonder of it all. "Maybe you've got something there."

The Lecture was over; I had told my man the law; and now he had told me things that might possibly invoke the defense of insanity. ... .[19]

The negotiation is complete. The ostensibly shared definition of the situation established by the negotiation process is that the defendant was probably not responsible for his actions.

Let us now compare the two interviews. The major similarity between them is their negotiated character: they both take the form of a series of offers and responses that continue until an offer (a definition of the situation) is reached that is acceptable to both parties. The major difference between the transactions is that one, the psychotherapeutic interview, arrives at an assessment that the client is responsible; the other, the defense attorney's interview, reaches an assessment that the client was not at fault, i.e., not responsible. How can we account for this difference in outcome?

DISCUSSION

Obviously, given any two real cases of negotiation which have different outcomes, one might construct a reasonable argument that the difference is due to the differences between the cases—the finding of responsibility in one case and lack of responsibility in the other, the only outcomes which are reasonably consonant with the facts of the respective cases. Without rejecting this argument, for the sake of discussion only, and without claiming any kind of proof or demonstration, I wish to present an alternative argument; that the difference in outcome is largely due to the differences in technique used by the interrogators. This argument will allow us to suggest some crucial dimensions of negotiation processes.

The first dimension, consciousness of the bargaining aspects of the transaction, has already been mentioned. In the psychotherapeutic interview, the negotiational nature of the transaction seems not to be articulated by either party. In the legal interview, however, certainly the lawyer, and perhaps to some extent the client as well, is aware of, and accepts the situation as one of striking a bargain, rather than as a relentless pursuit of the absolute facts of the matter.

The dimension of shared awareness that the definition of the situation is negotiable seems particularly crucial for assessments of responsibility. In both interviews, there is an agenda hidden from the client. In the psychotherapeutic interview, it is probably the psychiatric criteria for acceptance into treatment, the criterion of "insight." The psychotherapist has probably been trained to view patients with "insight into their illness" as favorable candidates for psychotherapy, i.e., patients who accept, or can be led to accept, the problems as internal, as part of their personality, rather than seeing them as caused by external conditions.

In the legal interview, the agenda that is unknown to the client is the legal structure of defenses or justifications for killing. In both the legal and psychiatric cases, the hidden agenda is not a simple one. Both involve fitting abstract and ambiguous criteria (insight, on the one hand, legal justification, on the other) to a richly specific, concrete case. In the legal interview, the lawyer almost immediately broaches this hidden agenda; he states clearly and concisely the major legal justifications for killing. In the psychiatric interview, the hidden agenda is never revealed. The patient's offers during most of the interview are rejected or ignored. In the last part of the interview, her last offer is accepted and she is told that she will be given treatment. In no case are the reasons for these actions articulated by either party.

148   The degree of shared awareness is related to a second dimension which concerns the format of the conversation. The legal interview began as an interrogation, but was quickly shifted away from that format when the defense lawyer realized the direction in which the questioning was leading the client, i.e., toward a legally unambiguous admission of guilt. On the very brink of such an admission, the defense lawyer stopped asking questions and started, instead, to make statements. He listed the principle legal justifications for killing, and, in response to the *client's* questions, gave an explanation of each of the justifications. This shift in format put the client, rather than the lawyer, in control of the crucial aspects of the negotiation. It is the client, not the lawyer, who is allowed to pose the questions, assess the answers for their relevance to his case, and most crucially, to determine himself the most advantageous tack to take. Control of the definition of the situation, the evocation of the events and intentions relevant to the assessment of the client's responsibility for the killing, was given to the client by the lawyer. The resulting client-controlled format of negotiation gives the client a double advantage. It not only allows the client the benefit of formulating his account of actions and intentions in their most favorable light, it also allows him to select, out of a diverse and ambiguous set of normative criteria concerning killing, that criteria which is most favorable to his own case.

Contrast the format of negotiation used by the psychotherapist. The form is consistently that of interrogation. The psychotherapist poses the questions; the patient answers. The psychotherapist then has the answers at his disposal. He may approve or disapprove, accept or reject, or merely ignore them. Throughout the entire interview, the psychotherapist is in complete control of the situation. Within this framework, the tactic that the psychotherapist uses is to reject the patient's "offers" that her husband is at fault, first by ignoring them, later, and ever more insistently, by leading her to define the situation as one in which she is at fault. In effect, what the therapist does is to reject her offers, and to make his own counteroffers.

These remarks concerning the relationship between technique of interrogation and outcome suggest an approach to assessment of responsibility somewhat different than that usually followed. The common sense approach to interrogation is to ask how accurate and fair is the outcome. Both Newman's and Balint's analyses of negotiation raise this question. Both presuppose that there is an objective state of affairs that is independent of the technique of assessment. This is quite clear in Newman's discussion, as he continually refers to defendants who are "really" or "actually" guilty or innocent.[20] The situation is less clear in Balint's discussion, although occasionally he implies that certain patients are really physically healthy, but psychologically distressed.

The type of analysis suggested by this paper seeks to avoid such presuppositions. It can be argued that *independently* of the facts of the case, the technique of assessment plays a part in determining the outcome. In particular, one can avoid making assumptions about actual responsibility by utilizing a technique of textual criticism of a trans-

149

action. The key dimension in such work would be the relative power and authority of the participants in the situation.[21]

As an introduction to the way in which power differences between interactants shape the outcome of negotiations, let us take as an example an attorney in a trial dealing with "friendly" and "unfriendly" witnesses. A friendly witness is a person whose testimony will support the definition of the situation the attorney seeks to convey to the jury. With such a witness the attorney does not employ power, but treats him as an equal. His questions to such a witness are open, and allow the witness considerable freedom. The attorney might frame a question such as "Could you tell us about your actions on the night of ———?"

The opposing attorney, however, interested in establishing his own version of the witness' behavior on the same night, would probably approach the task quite differently. He might say: "You felt angry and offended on the night of ———, didn't you?" The witness frequently will try to evade so direct a question with an answer like: "Actually, I had started to . . . ." The attorney quickly interrupts, addressing the judge: "Will the court order the witness to respond to the question, yes or no?" That is to say, the question posed by the opposing attorney is abrupt and direct. When the witness attempts to answer indirectly, and at length, the attorney quickly invokes the power of the court to coerce the witness to answer as he wishes, directly. The witness and the attorney are not equals in power; the attorney used the coercive power of the court to force the witness to answer in the manner desired.

The attorney confronted by an "unfriendly" witness wishes to control the format of the interaction, so that he can retain control of the definition of the situation that is conveyed to the jury. It is much easier for him to neutralize an opposing definition of the situation if he retains control of the interrogation format in this manner. By allowing the unfriendly witness to respond only by yes or no to his own verbally conveyed account, he can suppress the ambient details of the opposing view that might sway the jury, and thus maintain an advantage for his definition over that of the witness.

In the psychiatric interview discussed above, the psychiatrist obviously does not invoke a third party to enforce his control of the interview. But he does use a device to impress the patient that she is not to be his equal in the interview, that is reminiscent of the attorney with an unfriendly witness. The device is to pose abrupt and direct questions to the patient's open-ended accounts, implying that the patient should answer briefly and directly; and, through that implication, the psychiatrist controls the whole transaction. Throughout most of the interview the patient seeks to give detailed accounts of her behavior and her husband's, but the psychiatrist almost invariably counters with a direct and, to the patient, seemingly unrelated question.

The first instance of this procedure occurs at T6, the psychiatrist asking the patient, "what do you do?" She replies "I'm a nurse, but my husband won't let me work." Rather than responding to the last part of her answer, which would be expected in conversation between equals, the psychiatrist asks another question, changing the subject: "How old are you?" This pattern continues throughout most

150

of the interview. The psychiatrist appears to be trying to teach the patient to follow his lead. After some thirty or forty exchanges of this kind, the patient apparently learns her lesson; she cedes control of the transaction completely to the therapist, answering briefly and directly to direct questions, and elaborating only on cue from the therapist. The therapist thus implements his control of the interview not by direct coercion, but by subtle manipulation.

All of the discussion above, concerning shared awareness and the format of the negotiation, suggests several propositions concerning control over the definition of the situation. The professional interrogator, whether lawyer or psychotherapist, can maintain control if the client cedes control to him because of his authority as an expert, because of his manipulative skill in the transaction, or merely because the interrogator controls access to something the client wants, e.g., treatment, or a legal excuse. The propositions are:

> 1a. Shared awareness of the participants that the situation is one of negotiation. (The greater the shared awareness the more control the client gets over the resultant definition of the situation.)
>
> b. Explicitness of the agenda. (The more explicit the agenda of the transaction, the more control the client gets over the resulting definition of the situation.)
>
> 2a. Organization of the format of the transaction, offers and responses. (The party to a negotiation who responds, rather than the party who makes the offers, has relatively more power in controlling the resultant shared definition of the situation.)
>
> b. Counter-offers. (The responding party who makes counter-offers has relatively more power than the responding party who limits his response to merely accepting or rejecting the offers of the other party.)
>
> c. Directness of questions and answers. (The more direct the questions of the interrogator, and the more direct the answers he demands and receives, the more control he has over the resultant definition of the situation.)

These concepts and hypotheses are only suggestive until such times as operational definitions can be developed. Although such terms as offers and responses seem to have an immediate applicability to most conversation, it is likely that a thorough and systematic analysis of any given conversation would show the need for clearly stated criteria of class inclusion and exclusion. Perhaps a good place for such research would be in the transactions for assessing responsibility discussed above. Since some 90 percent of all criminal convictions in the United states are based on guilty pleas, the extent to which techniques of interrogation subtly influence outcomes would have immediate policy implication. There is considerable evidence that interrogation techniques influence the outcome of psychotherapeutic interviews also.[22] Research in both of these areas would probably have implications for both the theory and practice of assessing responsibility.

CONCLUSION: NEGOTIATION IN SOCIAL SCIENCE RESEARCH

More broadly the application of the sociology of knowledge to the negotiation of reality has ramifications which may apply to all of social science. The interviewer in a survey, or the experimenter in a social psychological experiment, is also involved in a transaction with a client—the respondent or subject. Recent studies by Rosenthal and others strongly suggest that the findings in such studies are negotiated, and influenced by the format of the study.[23] Rosenthal's review of bias in research suggests that such bias is produced by a pervasive and subtle process of interaction between the investigator and his source of data. Those errors which arise because of the investigator's influence over the subject (the kind of influence discussed in this paper as arising out of power disparities in the process of negotiation), Rosenthal calls "expectancy effects." In order for these errors to occur, there must be direct contact between the investigator and the subject.

A second kind of bias Rosenthal refers to as "observer effects." These are errors of perception or reporting which do not require that the subject be influenced by investigation. Rosenthal's review leads one to surmise that even with techniques that are completely nonobtrusive, observer error could be quite large.[24]

The occurence of these two kinds of bias poses an interesting dilemma for the lawyer, psychiatrist, and social scientist. The investigator of human phenomena is usually interested in more than a sequence of events, he wants to know why the events occurred. Usually this quest for an explanation leads him to deal with the motivation of the persons involved. The lawyer, clinician, social psychologist, or survey researcher try to elicit motives directly, by questioning the participants. But in the process of questioning, as suggested above, he himself becomes involved in a process of negotiation, perhaps subtly influencing the informants through expectancy effects. A historian, on the other hand, might try to use documents and records to determine motives. He would certainly avoid expectancy effects in this way, but since he would not elicit motives directly, he might find it necessary to collect and interpret various kinds of evidence which are only indirectly related, at best, to determine motives of the participants. Thus through his choice in the selection and interpretation of the indirect evidence, he may be as susceptible to error as the interrogator, survey researcher, or experimentalist—his error being due to observer effects, however, rather than expectancy effects.

The application of the ideas outlined here to social and psychological research need to be developed. The five propositions suggested above might be used, for example, to estimate the validity of surveys using varying degrees of open-endedness in their interview format. If some technique could be developed which would yield an independent assessment of validity, it might be possible to demonstrate, as Aaron Cicourel has suggested, the more reliable the technique, the less valid the results.

The influence of the assessment itself on the phenomena to be assessed appears to be an ubiquitous process in human affairs, whether in ordinary daily life, the determination of responsibility in legal or clinical interrogation, or in most types of social science research. The sociology of knowledge perspective, which suggests that people go through their lives constructing reality, offers a framework within which the negotiation of reality can be seriously and constructively studied. This paper has suggested some of the avenues of the problem that might require further study. The prevalence of the problem in most areas of human concern recommends it to our attention as a substantial field of study, rather than as an issue that can be ignored or, alternatively, be taken as the proof that rigorous knowledge of social affairs is impossible.

NOTES

1. The doctrine of absolute responsibility is clearly illustrated in psychiatric and legal discussions of the issue of "criminal responsibility," i.e., the use of mental illness as an excuse from criminal conviction. An example of the assumption of absolute criteria of responsibility is found in the following quotation. "The finding that someone is criminally responsible means to the psychiatrist that the criminal must change his behavior before he can resume his position in society. *This injunction is dictated not by morality, but, so to speak, by reality.*" See Edward J. Sachar, "Behavioral Science and Criminal Law." *Scientific American*, 209 (1963), pp. 39–45, (emphasis added).

2. Peter L. Berger and Thomas Luckmann, *The Social Construction of Reality: A Treatise in the Sociology of Knowledge* (New York: Doubleday 1966).

3. The classic treatment of this issue is found in E. Durkheim, *The Elementary Forms of the Religious Life.*

4. A sociological application of the concept of negotiation, in a different context, is found in Anselm Strauss, *et al.*, "The Hospital and its Negotiated Order," in Eliot Freidson, ed., *The Hospital in Modern Society* (New York: Free Press, 1963), pp. 147-69.

5. Newman reports a study in this area, together with a review of earlier work, in "The Negotiated Plea," Part III of Donald J. Newman, *Conviction: The Determination of Guilt or Innocence Without Trial* (Boston: Little, Brown, 1966), pp. 76–130.

6. Ibid, p. 76.

7. Ibid, p. 83.

8. Idem.

9. Michael Balint, *The Doctor, His Patient, and The Illness*, New York: International Universities Press, 1957, p. 18. A description of the negotiations between patients in a tuberculosis sanitarium and their physicians is found in Julius A. Roth, *Timetables: Structuring the Passage of Time in Hospital Treatment and Other Careers.* Indianapolis: Bobbs-Merrill, 1963, pp. 48–59. Obviously, some cases are more susceptible to negotiation than others. Balint implies that the great majority of cases in medical practice are negotiated.

10. Balint, op. cit., p. 216.

11. Merton Gill, Richard Newman, and Frederick C. Redlich, *The Initial Interview in Psychiatric Practice*, (New York: International Universities Press, 1954).

12. Since this interview is complex and subtle, the reader is invited to listen to it himself, and compare his conclusions with those discussed here. The

recorded interview is available on the first L.P. record that accompanies Gill, Newman, and Redlich, op. cit.

13. Ibid., p. 133. (Italics added.)

14. Ibid., pp. 176–82. (Numbers in parenthesis added.)

15. Ibid., pp. 186–87.

16. Ibid., pp. 192–94.

17. Robert Traver, *Anatomy of a Murder* (New York: Dell, 1959).

18. Ibid., p. 43.

19. Ibid., pp. 46–47, 57, 58–59, and 60.

20. In his Foreword the editor of the series, Frank J. Remington, comments on one of the slips that occurs frequently, the "acquittal of the guilty," noting that this phrase is contradictory from the legal point of view. He goes on to say that Newman is well aware of this, but uses the phrase as a convenience. Needless to say, both Remington's comments and mine can both be correct: the phrase is used as a convenience, but it also reveals the author's presuppositions.

21. Berger and Luckman op. cit., p. 100, also emphasize the role of power, but at the societal level. "The success of particular conceptual machineries is related to the power possessed by those who operate them. The confrontation of alternative symbolic universes implies a problem of power—which of the conflicting definitions of reality will be "made to stick" in the society." Haley's discussions of control in psychotherapy are also relevant. See Jay Haley, "Control in Psychoanalytic Psychotherapy," *Progress in Psychotherapy* 4 (New York: Grune and Stratton, 1959), pp 48–65; see also by the same author, "The Power Tactics of Jesus Christ" (in press).

22. Thomas J. Scheff, *Being Mentally Ill* (Chicago: Aldine, 1966).

23. Robert Rosenthal, *Experimenter Effects in Behavorial Research* (New York: Appleton-Century Crofts, 1966), Friedman, reporting a series of studies of expectancy effects, seeks to put the results within a broad sociological framework; Neil Friedman, *The Social Nature of Psychological Research: The Psychological Experiment as Social Interaction* (New York: Basic Books, 1967).

24. Critics of "reactive techniques" often disregard the problem of observer effects. See, for example, Eugene J. Webb, Donald T. Campbell, Richard D. Schwartz, and Lee Seechrest, *Unobtrusive Measures: Nonreactive Research in Social Science* (Chicago: Rand-McNally, 1966).

HANNAH GREEN

I Never Promised You a Rose Garden

When the evening shift came on, Helene placed herself in front of the nursing station and began stamping her feet heavily. The noise soon brought an attendant out.

"What's the matter now, Helene?"

From *I Never Promised You a Rose Garden* by Hannah Green. Copyright © 1964 by Hannah Green. Reprinted by permission of Holt, Rinehart and Winston, Inc.

"Case closed," Helene said. "I'm stamping Mr. Hobbs's case closed."

She was smiling archly, so that the attendant's face tightenend. It was supposed to be a big secret that the night before Mr. Hobbs had gone home after his shift, closed his doors and windows, turned on the gas, and died. In the nun-prisoner-pigmy confinement of Ward D everyone knew, even the unknowing.

As lunatics, crazies, screwballs, nuts, the patients felt no responsibility to be decent and desist from speaking ill of the dead. Where deformity of the body was regarded with a certain mercy, death and its conventions were heaped with scorn. Helene had once said, "A nut is someone whose noose broke," for they all had wanted to kill themselves, they had all tried suicide more or less diligently, and they all envied the dead. Part of their illness was that they saw the whole world revolving around themselves, and so what Hobbs had done was to stick out his tongue at them from a place where they could not get at him to slap his face for it.

The evening shift was here, and the patients were all waiting to see who would be taking Hobbs's place. When those at the head of the hall saw, they carried the news back.

"It's a Nose—a new one—a new Nose," and there was an almost palpable groan. Noses were Conscientious Objectors who had selected to work in mental hospitals as an alternative to prison. Lee Miller had originated the name "Nose" a long time ago by saying, "Oh, those conchies; I hate them. They won't fight, so the government says 'We'll rub your noses in it for you! It's either prison or the nuthouse!'" Helene had laughed and someone else had said, "Well, they're the noses and we're *it.*"

Now Carla only murmured, "I like being somebody's punishment; it makes me feel needed," and she laughed, but with a bitterness that was rare for her.

The Noses usually came in pairs. "I suppose we should call one of them a Nostril," precise Mary said, rubbing the blood from invisible stigmata. The patients laughed.

"Maybe he'll be all right," Carla said. "Anything's better than Hobbs."

They watched the new staff member go his first long and hard walk down the hall. He was terrified. They saw his terror with feelings caught between amusement and anger. Constantia, in the seclusion section, began to scream when she saw him, and Mary, hearing it, said, "Oh, my God, he's going to faint!" laughing and then hurt: "She's only a *person,* you know."

"He's afraid he'll catch what we have," Deborah said, and they all laughed, because Hobbs had caught it, and died from it too.

The expedition neared them.

"Get up off the floor, will you please?" the head ward nurse said to the group of patients sitting against the walls of the hall and corridor.

Deborah looked at the Nose. "Obstacle," she said.

She meant that she and the other patients with feet stuck out before the terrified man were like the contrivances in the obstacle courses that men must run through in their military training; that she and they understood their substitution as "the horrors of war," and that they would try to fulfill the Army's desire that this man's training be rigorous. But the nurses neither laughed nor understood, and passed by with another admonition about getting off the floor. The patients all knew that it was merely form. Everybody always sat on the floor and it was only when guests came that the nurses, like suburban wives, clucked at the dust and wished that "things were neater."

Constantia was beginning to work herself up into an all-night howl, when the ward door opened and McPherson let himself in. Deborah looked hard at him, saw everyone suddenly go easier, and said meaningfully, "They should have changed the lock."

She was thinking that McPherson's key-turn and incoming was a completely different order from the one which had preceded it —as different as if there had been different doors and different locks. She felt obscurely that the words had somehow done her injury, and so she went over them, seeking the culprit.

"They . . . should . . . have . . . changed . . . the . . . lock."

McPherson said, "I don't like this key business anyway." Carla looked around, as Deborah had just before, knowing that no one understood, but with McPherson, not understanding carried no penalty of scorn or hatred. She sat back quietly.

They were all glad that McPherson was there, and because feeling this meant that they were vulnerable, they had to try to hide it. "Without those keys you wouldn't know yourself from us!"

But McPherson only laughed—a laughter at himself; not at them. "We're not so different," he said, and went into the nursing station.

"Who is he kidding!" Helene said. There was no malice in her statement; she was merely hurrying to rebuild the wall that he had breached. She turned and disappeared into her limbo, and because McPherson's afterimage still hung in the air there were no catty remarks about her fadeout. But when the procession of magi passed by once more, bearing with them the Nose, rigid and clamp-jawed with fear, no one could withhold the cruelty which seemed to each her true and natural self. Helene shuddered as he passed; Carla looked blank; Mary, always inappropriately gay, trilled laughter, saying, "Well, Hobbs's bodkins, here comes another gas customer!"

"Let's call him Hobbs's Leviathan, because he may be a whale of a lot worse!"

"Their religion doesn't permit them to commit suicide," Sylvia said from her place against the wall.

The ward was suddenly silent. Sylvia had not said anything at all for over a year and her voice was so toneless that the sound almost seemed to come from the wall itself. The silence hung in the ward as everyone sought to make sure that there had really been words and that they had come from the frozen and mute piece of ward furniture that was Sylvia. They could all see each other checking for

156 symptoms—did she say it or did I only hear it? Then Lee Miller broke from inaction and went to the closed door of the nursing station. She pounded on it until the nurse opened the door and looked out in annoyance, as if confronted by an unfamiliar salesman.

"Call the doctor," Lee said tersely. "Sylvia talked."

"The ward report is not finished," the nurse said and closed the door. Lee pounded again. After awhile the door opened. "Well . . .?"

"You'd better get that doctor, because if you don't, it will be your fault and not mine. Adams will come—she always does. She came last time at three in the morning when Sylvia talked!'

"What are you all excited about, Miller?" the nurse said. "What did she say?"

"It doesn't matter and it wouldn't make sense to you because it was part of the conversation."

"About what?"

"Oh, Christ. *Please.*"

Standing between Sylvia and the excited Lee Miller, Deborah saw how stupid any fragment of the conversation would sound. Sylvia had extinguished her brief, faint light.

*   *   *

She had to do something. Lee was all alone in that hideous place called "Involvement" or "Reality" and no one could help her. Locked in a motionless body—as motionless now as Sylvia's—mute in English. Deborah began to tremble.

*   *   *

The struggle between the new Nose, Hobbs's Leviathan, and the patients went on. His rigid fundamentalist beliefs made him see insanity as a just desert for its victims, as God's vengeance, or as the devil's work, and sometimes as all three at once. As the days passed, his fear waned and the time of his righteous wrath was at hand. He saw that he was suffering persecution for his faith.

Against his loathing, the sick fought in their sick way. The literate rewrote the Bible or ridiculed its passages to make him horrified. Constantia made flagrant sexual advances to him. Helene took the towel he brought her with a little curtsey, saying, "From Paraclete to Paranoid. Amen, amen." And Deborah made a few pointed observations about the similarity between psychotics and religious fanatics. McPherson sensed the anger and violence blowing like a wind over the ward and wondered what he could do about it. There was not enough staff anyway. The two other new conscientious objectors were doing well on different wards, and one of them was showing signs of ability at working with mental patients. He didn't like the new man on ward D, Ellis, much himself, but he was sympathetic toward him. Ellis was not suited for the work at all; he feared and hated the patients, and looked upon the government which had

punished him as the early Christian martyrs must have looked upon
the Roman procurators. Because of this, Ellis had to drag the dead
Hobbs after him in the nickname the patients had given him. The
worst of it was that Ellis' religion could not see suicide as anything
but a sinful horror, monstrous in nature.

So, Ellis dragged a dead and stinking whale, and McPherson
mused that there was no hunter in the world as clever or merciless in
placing barbs in a weak place as these sick people. Sometimes he
wondered why Hobbs had been attacked and never he; why Ellis,
now, and not he. Never was Helene's tremendous store of knowledge
used to damn him; never did the hard-faced Deborah Blau set her
knife-edged tongue against him. He felt somehow that it might just
be more than luck, but he did not truly know how or why he escaped
the bitterness and unhappiness that vented itself all around him.

Now he watched the patients as they stood, waiting for dinner, waiting for darkness, waiting for sedatives, waiting for sleep.
Blau was standing near the barred and screened radiator, staring
out at something beyond the wall. He had once asked her what she
was looking at and she had answered him from her otherness, "I'm
the dead, reckoning."

Constantia was out of her seclusion room, but in seclusion
still, muttering quietly in a corner. Lee Miller was clenching and un-
clenching her teeth; Miss Cabot from the dormitory, insisting, "I'm
the Wife of an Assassinated Ex-President of the United States!" Linda,
Marion, and Sue Jepson, and all the rest were doing what they usually
did. Yet there was a lingering sense of dangerous unrest—more than the
sum of the parts of unrest. Ellis came out of the nursing station where
he had been writing up the medication reports. The badgering began.

"Thar he blows—it's Hobbs's Leviathan!"

"Get thee behind me, Satan!"

"Hobbs committed suicide and the army committed him!"

"He got a commission, but not the kind that gives you eagles
on the shoulder."

"With his commission they give bats in the belfry!"

"What's the latest from Hell today, preacher?"

"Don't ask him now. Let him look over his holdings first."

There was a radio built in behind a heavy mesh screen in the
wall. It was supposed to be on only during certain hours of the day
and tuned only to certain innocuous semi-light music, but now Mc-
Pherson went to the screen, unlocked it, and turned the radio on
good and loud. Into the ward poured the tinny sounds of romantic-
love dance music, pathetically, even hilariously, incongruous in the
heavy urine-and-disinfectant atmosphere that permeated the ward.
When the announcer's moist voice bade them "Good night from the
Starlight Roof," Carla replied in a parody of romantic wistfulness. "A
farewell flutter of my restraints, delicately, good night . . . good
night . . ."

The whole ward erupted into laughter and relaxed, although
the mind-scent of tension still hung in the air like the ozone smell
after a lightning bolt. Something had been narrowly averted.

158

After Deborah had been given her sedative, she got into her bed, waiting the familiar wait, the gods and the Collect reduced to a somnolent undertone. McPherson came into the dormitory and stopped by her bed.

"Deb," he said gently, "lay off on Mr. Ellis, will you?"

"Why me?" she said.

"I want all of you to let him alone. No more jokes. No more references to Hobbs."

"Are you going to tell everybody?" (The guarded vying-for-favor and the guarded suspicion of all the world's motives and representatives overcame prudence and forced the question.)

"Yup," he said. "Everybody on the ward."

"Even Marie and Lena?" (They were acknowledged to be the sickest on the ward, even by the patients.)

"Deb . . . just lay off."

For a moment she felt that he was using her. He was the only one who could get away with calling the patients by nicknames without sounding strained, but it sounded strained now.

"Why me? I thought you normal ones had agreed that we were out of it—your conventions and routines. I'm not nice and I'm not polite and I know more about Hobbs than you do. He was one of *us!* The only thing that separated him from us was three inches of metal key he used to fondle for assurance. Ellis is another one. I know about him and his hate."

McPherson's voice was low, but his anger was real, and Deborah felt it coming from a place in him that he had never shown before.

"Do you thing the sick people are all in hospitals? Do you girls think you have a corner on suffering? I don't want to bring up the money business—it's been overdone—but I want to tell you right now that lots of people on the outside would *like* to get help and can't. You ought to know mental trouble when you see it. You don't bait other patients. I've never heard you say anything against one of them." (She remembered what she had said to Carla and the stroke of guilt fell again for it.) "Lay off Ellis, Deb—you'll be glad for it later."

"I'll try."

He looked down hard at her. She could not see his face in the shadow, but she sensed that it was in repose. Then he turned and walked out of the dormitory. Deborah fought the sedative for a while, thinking about what he had said and how. It was tough but true, and under the anger of it ran the tone—the tone rare anywhere, but in a mental ward like a priceless jewel—the tone of a simple respect between equals. The terror she felt at the responsibility it bore was mingled with a new feeling. It was joy.

The Routinization of Love:
Structure and Process
in Primary Relations

Whenever we search for the roots of human fulfillment or courage or creativity, we soon confront the fact of love. To be sure, the word itself appears but rarely in scientific reports; but those reports are filled with terms which catch some aspect, phase, or variety of love. We are told, for example, that the parents of psychiatrically healthy children are "nurturant" or "permissive" or "supportive" and make only "reasonable" demands of youngsters (136). Soldiers "integrated into" or "solidary with" their officers, units, or comrades display higher morale in battle (132). "Cooperation" sometimes enhances productivity (41, 78, 96). Intellectually creative adults are "secure" in their relations with others and "dedicated" to the realization of long-range objectives (103, 104). Men who withstand the rigors of imprisonment in concentration camps have a comparable dedication (20, 21) as do families which thrive despite an abrupt loss of income (4, 29, 87).

These discoveries concern only some bits and facets of love. Observations which capture more of its features relate with even greater precision to particular variations in behavior and experience. To illustrate, it has been shown that parental supportiveness is associated with the mental health of children only when the support is dependable and is directed toward promoting the child's growing independence (79). This reveals something that most people understand; that overprotection is not love, and altruism without justice may signify masochism or dominance rather than mature concern and respect.

* * *

Why is it that love, loving, and being loved help us explain so much of importance in human conduct? If love enhances a man's satisfaction, personal force and social responsibility and underlies the flowering of his capacities, what are its sources and how can it be encouraged? Can one routinize the presence and potency of so subtle a relationship as love? Are the tensions and problems which often accompany love inherently uncontrollable or can they, like love's presence, be directed and modified? We must say what love means before these questions can be understood or answered.

THE MEANING OF LOVE

The objects of love are many. The occasions for love are various. The means by which love is shown are great in number. But, within these

160

variations, there is a common theme, an essential meaning (21, 39, 65, 67, 85, 94, 103, 104, 141, 142). At least within societies of the modern West there is general agreement about the meaning of love, and people commonly feel they can identify the genuine article from the counterfeit.

In common usage, love stands for that relationship in which people are committed knowingly, willingly, freely and responsibly to enhance the lives and growth of others in whatever ways they can. Loving is behavior which implements these commitments. If any one of the ingredients in this definition is found missing, the genuineness of the love is suspect. Thus if a person initiates this sort of association but is not committed to it, he is condemned as arousing false expectations, as "trifling with" the other's life, as being insincere and, if only by implication, committing a breach of promise (17). Again, if love is genuine it involves a somewhat conscious choice. People try to learn whether persons seeming to extend love do so knowingly, or whether they will withdraw from the relationship when they see its implications. Further, enhancement is not to be called love if it is extended unwillingly or if the enhancer's will is not free—is coerced by forces and interests he does not consider consistent with his personal desires (27, 33, 75). In addition, as Fromm (67) says, attempts at enhancement unrestrained by responsibility, by efforts to do only that for which one is competent, contain great hazards (60). They can easily become negligent, inconsiderate or thoughtless.

Genuine love is also defined as a diffuse relationship. The individual does not elect to perform one or more particular acts, but to assist, by whatever means he can, in bringing about a certain state of affairs. His commitment is fulfilled only when that state is achieved. For some commitments, such as those to promote the welfare of one's family or friends or country, no final achievement is possible.

Genuine love does not require that people be committed to enhance all aspects of each others' lives. It does require that they stand ready to do what they can with respect to those aspects of the other's concerns for which they accept responsibility. This may, for example, be the nurturance by colleagues of each other's professional growth, or the teacher's devotion to his student as student, or the support any men give each other as fellow citizens or as co-workers or as comrades in a common enterprise.

Finally, in authentic love, this generalized commitment is guided by the concern to nourish the powers, independence, and integration of the other—to promote not just that which is presently in his interest but to assist a partner in developing interests that he will find of even greater worth (59). Ideal friends wish not only that one will be what one is, but that one will become the more enriched person that one is capable of being.

The notion that partners in love must be equals has its great relevance at this point. As many successful marriages and friendships demonstrate, the participants may be quite unequal in the nature or absolute amount of their contributions to one another (76, 155). There is, however, one respect in which equality is required for the success of their relationship as love. They must be similar in the *proportion* of their requirements which are satisfied through this relationship. One of them may get far more than the other if enhancement is measured in absolute amount, but they must be equal in the *importance* for each of whatever he receives. This equivalence of *relative* reward and cost is the ultimate guarantee that each will take the relationship with equal seriousness and ensures that each will respect the independence and integrity of his partners (82).

The problem of distinguishing genuine love from its counterfeits is especially difficult because some of love's several ingredients can be present without the others, and because the mixture of those which are available at a particular time is subject to great and unanticipated modifications. Farber (55) documents the independence among three of love's facets in a study of the relations of 495 husbands with their wives. He measured the extent to which each man: (*1*) sought to enhance his wife's experience) e.g., was cooperative and supportive toward her), (*2*) took account of her needs and potentialities (e.g., correctly interpreted her attitudes, intentions, and behavior), and (*3*) contributed responsibility to their relations with each other (e.g., was resourceful in devising new and effective solutions to problematic interpersonal situations; was skillful in handling interpersonal tensions where self-esteem was threatened or challenged). There is no relationship between a man's rating on any of these measures and his scores on the others.

The difficulties of evaluating professed love are further increased by the subtlety of the judgments required. Reasonable accuracy in these matters reflects extensive training and high skill. By some means, much of the population acquires facility in making such judgments.

THE RELEVANCE OF LOVE

Why is love important for so many aspects of human life and experience? Having said what love means, one can answer this further question. We must consider love's significance for the lover as well as for one who is loved.

Love's most obvious importance is for the person who receives it. It nutures to a degree and in a fashion unique in human experience. This unusual nurturance flows from love's properties as perhaps the most elaborated instance of social interaction. By calling it "the most elaborated instance," I mean that, in love, one finds employed in consummate measure the ingredients and processes which characterize all instances of social interaction [Interestingly, the more exquisite forms of sadism seem to be among love's closer competitors for this distinction (15, 21, 58, pp. 354–358, 67, pp. 18–20 and 30–31, 69, pp. 12–48, 72, chapters 3, 4, 7, 8, and 9).]

Men can relate to each other in several ways. They can interact, for example, as do physical bodies, exerting blind force on one another. Social interaction refers to situations in which people take into account each other's knowledge, intentions, preferences, hopes, beliefs

162

and the like. It refers, in short, to men relating to each other's minds. Social interaction can occur if people learn that they depend on one another, if they come to appreciate the essential requirements for their continued association, if they have some experiences in common which they can share, if they possess standardized symbols to serve as a medium for the expressing and sharing of experience in a form that will be understood, if they have become aware of the existence and importance of their own and each other's mental life and the conditions under which it can be influenced. These are the understandings and skills in which parents first train their children and easy competence in their use—competence employed despite great obstacles and in a wide variety of situations—is customarily taken as the mark of an individual's maturity (90). A life-time of exploration and experience seems not to exhaust the potentiality for further significant growth in such competence.

The special nurturance which love provides is its support for the individual's mental life. Loving means close attention by others to an individual's problems and potentialities. It means efforts to enhance his behavior and his powers for behaving. Loving is thus directed toward discerning and influencing his mental life as, for example, the wisdom with which he formulates objectives, the appropriateness of his choices from among alternatives, the security with which he can venture and take risks, the effectiveness of his efforts to make restitution for errors and to find and accept forgiveness, the justness with which he evaluates failures, and the gaiety or contentment with which he celebrates a success. A loving relationship provides not just particular deeds that lead to such benefits, but whatever acts will have these results. So generalized or diffuse a commitment, requires that the person who offers love relate not merely to another's immediate behavior, but to his long-term purposes and potentialities and to changes that will occur in them. Within this generalized relationship more specialized forms of interaction can grow as the occasion may demand. They will be particular applications of love to given situations, but love is their general form and their source. In return, a loving relationship costs the loved individual the commitment to employ these resources for the maintenance and development of himself as a person—as a minded individual who interacts with the minds of others. Because love, or an association bordering on it, so often provides the infant's first social experience and because it affords general principles to be employed in developing more specialized forms of social interaction. Cooley spoke of love as the socially "primary" relation and of the groups most distinguished by it as "primary groups" (13, 25, 36, 37, 57, 119, 124).

Thinking only of receiving love, men commonly make this relationship the foundation for their pictures of utopia. But the cost of being loved can be substantial. Stagnation may prove easier than growth, wisdom may appear less desirable than immediate action, and forgiveness may prove harder to bear than the absence of love. A man may prefer to receive fear or blind admiration from others because these require no changes in him. Love, as psychotherapists and theologians insist, is work for him who receives it as well as he who provides it. Willingness to perform such work is founded on a sense of its necessity.

Although it is sensible to speak of the members of a formally organized group as loving each other, such love will not be as diffuse as that possible between particular individuals (1). This is so because the leaders or members of such a group define their responsibilities toward each other in terms of the joint enterprise in which they are engaged, not toward all enterprises in which any of them may engage as individuals. Love between individuals, interpersonal love, has the possibility of this widest of references. This may be why many writers treat it as the standard for all expressions of love.

Greater scope is not the only benefit which interpersonal love may provide. Because it can be directed to all of an individual's interests, it is of unusual importance in assisting his personal integration. Each individual is at once a particular organism, the bearer of a distinctive history from previous experiences, and the center of a unique set of present conditions. In most of his relations with other people he is expected to employ some of his skills and tastes and inhibit others. What he is obliged to do or to forego varies from one group to another and often is the subject of conflicting instructions. But the individual as a sentient being is not divisible. Organism, mind, and relations with others, even with diverse or conflicting others, are co-essential in his existence. His ability to achieve fulfillment as a single, total being requires that all his several aspects with their differing, competing requirements become organized.

The love of another person can nurture him as a distinctive individual. It can, for example, help him interpret the application of general social rules to his particular situation, needs, and deeds. This is possible not only because interpersonal love can relate to the whole of a given individual's situation, but because love is, as we have seen, the most elaborated form of the principles general to social interaction itself. The more general the principles, the greater is the range of special situations to which they may be applied and for which they may supply guidance. The most generalized principles of a fully developed social relationship are thus the ground for the integration of particular individuals with themselves and with the social order. To be fulfilled most completely as a distinctive individual in all one's particularity one must enter into the most profoundly social of relationships.

We have found that love's special importance for the person who receives it is its nurture of some large range of his interests as a minded individual, that this is perhaps true in greatest degree of interpersonal love, and that some people consider the costs of receiving love to outweigh its benefits. But what of the person who gives love? What is its importance for him? If one views man as living only for rewards, then getting love is the chief thing. It is in studies that treat man as being most fulfilled when expanding or exercising his powers that we obtain a picture of love's significance for the lover (2, 67).

Loving, say these accounts, is the expression of the highest social skill. It is the sign of real maturity, full membership in humanity. It employs most completely those talents which seem to distinguish men from all other animals and in which they most resemble God.

Loving, these writers say, deals with difficult and challenging problems forever leading men to new, stimulating experiences. For a mature person, loving is the embodiment of his essential self and he delights in both the exercise of his potency and the evidence for it. To live is to act. To act as other than what one is is frustrating. Therefore, the argument goes, mature people get their greatest fulfillment in loving. As Fromm (67) writes, the theme of maturity is "I need you because I love you," not "I love you because I need you."

To be sure, gains from auto-fulfillment are not the only importance love is said to have for lovers. He who loves is often applauded by others and this may be sufficient reward. Loving another is often the requisite for obtaining another's love, and, if so, he who wants to be loved must first love others. Finally, one may love another to end an intolerable separation or estrangement, not so much because one wants the other's love but because one wants to be with him or at peace with him and there is no relationship short of love that will bridge the gap.

However important love may be in human affairs, it certainly is not enough for man's survival or accomplishment. Health, rationality, self-government, competence in modifying the environment to serve human needs, skill in framing symbols to represent, objectify, and bring order into experience—these capacities and abilities and many others are among the essentials (60, 85). Most of them are required for love to arise and many seem to require love in order to increase their fruition.

* * *

Establishment

Where will loving appear? How do its scope and form get established? By what means is its genuineness determined? The very definition of love suggests a part of the answers to these questions.

THE OCCURRENCE OF LOVE: It seems plausible to think that loving is likely to occur when people find that they are similar in their relative need for one another to be what each potentially is, providing that this need is satisfied not by a few readily specified acts to be performed at certain times but by the performance of whatever acts may be appropriate to meet changing conditions. To forecast the occurrence of love we should know the degree to which all these conditions are met.

a. DIFFUSE DEPENDENCY: Adequate evidence is lacking on all these matters, but a considerable body of observations supports the notion that a diffuse dependency is one requisite for love.

* * *

It is impossible to examine each familiar setting in which love flourishes to see whether a diffuse dependency preceded the occurrence of devotion and affection, but a few additional illustrations may indicate the range of affairs over which such dependency seems to be a precondition for love: the responsibility of professional men for their clients, the devotion of a family's members for each other's concerns, the affectionate care of a citizen for his country. Illustrations like these which suggest that love grows where people are broadly dependent on each other also remind one that such dependency is, at best, a necessary, not a sufficient, requisite for love.

b. FACILITATIVE ROLE INTERDEPENDENCE: There have been systematic studies of five conditions which, in addition to diffuse dependency, might relate to the appearance of love. These are: facilitative role interdependence, trust and trustworthiness, approachability, similarity or interpersonal characteristics, and the willingness with which people engage in a relationship. These certainly are not independent phenomena, but an approach through each reveals distinctive preconditions for love.

c. TRUST AND TRUSTWORTHINESS: Deutsch and his collaborators (43, 44, 45, 100, 128) have sought to define a task and other conditions that lead persons to trust one another when there are dangers of exploitation or injury from collaboration. They assume that people will trust each other if they: 1) are committed to reach some goal and failure will cost more than they want to risk in an uncertain venture, 2) need each other's help and perceive one another as able to help, 3) perceive one another as similarly dependent, and 4) are each . . .

*   *   *

In a second experimental manipulation, Deutsch showed that individuals are more likely to trust one another if they believe the other person has nothing to gain from untrustworthy behavior and if they perceive themselves as able to exert some control over the other person's outcomes.

*   *   *

d. APPROACHABILITY: There is evidence that people who want and seek intimate relations with others tend to have them (73, 93, 153). They approach others and are approachable.

*   *   *

e. SIMILARITY OF PERSONAL CHARACTERISTICS: It has often been argued that love is most likely to arise in a population with homogeneous characteristics. The rationales to support this position are two: 1) people can relate in a diffuse and intimate manner only if they share many understandings in common and 2) people with common tastes and objectives are more likely to find one another attractive. The counter argument is that to love one another, people must find in their fellows qualities or services they themselves lack and want and which can be acquired by association.

*　　*　　*

There seems, however, no gain in continuing to treat these issues in the simple terms conventionally employed. It is evident from every-day experience that "birds of a feather flock together" and that "op-posites attract." ...

f. WILLINGNESS: At the beginning of our survey, we found that a criterion of genuine love was the willingness of participants to undertake it.

*　　*　　*

SEARCH AND SELECTION: If people happen to be thrown to-gether with others who are attractive and approachable, or engaged with them in facilitative interaction so safeguarded that trustfulness is justified and willingness evident, love may flourish without much further effort. It often happens, however, that individuals must seek out the love or the beloved they need. This may entail a long search and difficult choices, depending on the alternatives available and the character of a person's desires.

A search of this kind by a thoughtful girl, hiding with her family and some neighbors from German persecution, is the prin-cipal theme of Anne Frank's diary (61). Her experience is especially revealing, not because her hopes or desires were unusual, but because the persons who might have helped with them were drastically limited in number and, for various reasons, unsuited to the task.

Anne was on the verge of adolescence. She also was unusually perceptive of meanings in human relations. She wanted to explore the values around which a worthy adult life might be organized. She wanted to evaluate and control her own selfishness, her dis-gust with the compromised standards of adults, her ambivalence toward her mother, and her varied feelings about sexuality. She wanted to express and clarify sentiments that were variously bizarre, grandiose, highly idealistic, superficial, earthy, or harsh. Trying to establish an appropriate friendship with each of the others in hiding with her, she slowly came to realize that each had interests or responsibilities that made him unsuitable. Anne was already at odds with her mother. The adults in neighboring families were insensitive and egocentric. Margot, her older sister, proved helpful for a time, but, as their relation deepened, broke it off to protect her specially favored place in their mother's esteem. Peter, the adolescent son of a neighbor's family, was more concerned with endearments and sexual explorations than serious discussions of Anne's inner self. Finally there was her perceptive and loving father. It seemed for a long time that here was the friend she sought. Then Albert Frank's responsibilities to his wife and older daughter (and his duty as a parent who corrected, disciplined, and taught Anne) precluded his becoming her intimate friend, her co-conspirator, and someone who could freely exchange fantasies, ambitions, and dislikes.

Everyone around Anne was capable of love and was, in fact, giving it, seeking it, and receiving it. But none of them could provide love for the purposes Anne required, legitimate though those objectives were, without seriously compromising other important obligations.

The friend Anne sought, and might well have found in some other girl of her age had she lived under normal conditions, would have been a person highly gratified by Anne's being all her many selves, a person without conflicting commitments. This friend would almost certainly have been somewhat removed from Anne's ordinary round of life; not her superior or subordinate, her competitor or someone mutually responsible with her for some common enterprise. That friend would be a person whom she could neither threaten nor fail by being herself.

A search for someone who can give the love one needs is a part of dating and courtship of the choice of an advisor, counselor, clergyman, therapist, or faith, of affiliation with voluntary associations, an employing company, and with political figures and parties. Aristotle's (6) judgment that persons capable of skillful, complete love are rare, corresponds to what is known concerning the distribution of such component skills as empathy, ego-strength, insight, self-discipline, and devotion to the welfare of others. It is not the whole story.

To nourish a man adequately in one respect commonly prevents our aiding him in others. To support his most penetrating explorations of self requires a suitable social role as well as interpersonal competence, and this role may prevent the offering of other kinds of love. For example, Albert Frank could not have supported Anne in such a venture and also provided her with the fatherly care she required. There is, in short, no perfect lover, no complete friend, and persons who supply a man with one kind of love should often be socially removed from those who supply other kinds.

As a consequence, most people obtain love from a variety of sources for a variety of purposes. This means that, other things being equal, the number and diversity of a man's social contacts increase the likelihood of his getting the love he desires.

*   *   *

Whether needs for love are differently satisfied as a consequence of this uneven distribution of certain potential sources, we do not know. (We also do not know the distribution within any substantial population of needs for various degrees and types of love.) If, however, one is right in thinking that the loves men need must come from specialized and separated sources, each person is left with the difficult task of integrating all these experiences into a coherent style of life. (Indeed, the specialized loves he receives may only nourish expectations and potencies that the individual cannot bring together in a mutually compatible whole. To take one ex-

168   ample, the nurturance by colleagues of one another's professional skills and tastes may exacerbate the conflict between their careers and their roles as husbands and fathers.)

Involvement in a social order whose norms embrace the whole of the individual's life career and which provide him with criteria for the evaluation and reconciliation of his specialized experiences seems to be a precondition for his development of personal coherence (48). If no embracive normative or institutional framework is experienced as real or valid or worthy, all the specialized loves lose their meaning and worth (48, 141). Then, in Sartre's words, man's condition is one of anguish. There is no information about the frequency with which given induviduals experience this kind of despair during their careers or its incidence or intensity in any society. Some psychotherapists and social observers believe it is on the rise in post-industrial societies and efforts to cope with its presence are the great objective of a new school of practitioners, the existential psychotherapists (105).

As the person in need seeks love, many people, often the same ones, search for someone they may love. The task is to establish the relevance of others' needs for one's love and their capacity to accept and use it.

It is frequent in such assessments that love must be given before its relevance can be fully judged. If the subjects have little present capacity to use it, they must be able at least to receive it, and every assurance must be provided that it is given freely and for the recipients' sake to be what they are and what, in freedom and integrity, they may become. Thus it is standard practice in therapeutic institutions for badly traumatized children to provide a full larder, its contents available whenever the child wants to eat; unlocked doors that permit him to explore or withdraw as he will; extremely considerate handling of wakening and going to sleep; a tolerance for his display of symptoms limited only by the requirement that he not destroy essential propertly nor make physical attacks on the staff (19, 114, 115). If the child becomes incapable of handling even these limits, he is removed gently from the situation, accompanied by an adult who waits with him until he becomes calm. Simultaneously, his ability for action and decision is encouraged through enterprises such as team games and free art in which he can take some initiative without being threatened by pressures to compete or choose as an individual.

*   *   *

In varying degree, as fits particular situations, these four considerations—the granting of love, the acceptance of the person for what he is including his unloveable characteristics, the setting of limits within which love is exercised, and the determination of probable capacity to receive and use love for his enhancement—are employed in establishing a loving relationship. Friendships and courtships, for example, often have their rudimentary beginnings in some special kindness beyond the requirements of formal social obligation, progressing, perhaps to the sharing of small confidences and to the acceptance of joking and teasing which indicate that the other person is desired even when he proves prickly. Occasions may be created in which each can move toward greater intimacy or, gracefully, keep the relation as it is (146). All these initial steps must be taken with delicacy or too much may seem promised and graceful withdrawal made impossible.

Judgments of the quantity of love that can be accepted, even by one who needs it, pose subtle problems. An offer of great love may frighten or may raise intolerable guilt. Similarly, the support offered must be useable for the beloved's particular enterprises or it may be seen as competitive with them or as exploitative. Thus Litwak, Count, and Hayden (99) present findings which suggest that the exercise by a wife of creative social sensitivity in areas where her husband feels he should excell is associated with less satisfaction in marriage for both of them.

THE SCOPE OF LOVE: The forms of love vary in their scope from the almost limitless obligations entailed in love for God or a close friend to the circumscribed commitments of a physician or attorney to his client. Wherever something of love appears, there are delicate problems of setting its scope. These problems arise because, in love, the extent of responsibility is inherently vague, and because the genuineness of professed love is so difficult to determine.

The work of love cannot go on within clearly defined boundaries. Even in the relatively limited relationship between professional and client the obligation is one of creating a general state of affairs in which growth can occur.

*   *   *

What then if the friend or client seeks to define certain vital matters as off limits or if either makes demands that go beyond the relationship's boundaries? How, short of terminating the relationship, may its necessary indeterminateness be preserved while suggesting the presence of limits?

Perhaps the most common strategy employed in our society to counter excessive expectations is tactful but persistent refusal to deal directly with those demands, not defining them as unrealistic or an imposition and not acceding to them. This appears most likely of success if accompanied by unobtrusive but clear evidence of making some special effort in matters that come legitimately within the relationship's scope.

Clark (34) describes this procedure, developed to a self-conscious technique, in the junior colleges, the so-called "open door" colleges, where many students ill equipped for advanced studies must be given the opportunity to develop their intellectual skills at their own pace and as fully as they can in the hope of eventual success, a task in which large numbers will fail. The college counselor must keep open the door to further attempts, seeking always for some legitimate means by which the student may achieve his goals, yet must keep him aware of the real state of his present achievements. To this end, the counselor devotes endless time, effort, and ingenuity in helping a failing student overcome personal difficulties that impede his progress. The counselor always confronts him with the continuous measures of his performance, but never says directly either that the cause is hopeless or that success is likely. By thus giving of himself beyond what seem to be in the formal requirements of his office, the counselor testifies to the depth and sincerity of his commitments while defining, indirectly, the limits to their scope.

We should notice that the counselor's approach succeeds because it employs yet another criterion of love and because the environing society defines that criterion as a limit to the demands men may make on one another. Genuine love, as we saw earlier, is a commitment to nourish the powers, independence, and integration of another; to enrich another in these respects, not just to maintain him as he is. To fulfill this objective, the one who receives love must show greater potency in dealing with the environment and with himself; increased powers in defining objectives and obtaining and utilizing resources from that environment. Movement toward these accomplishments provides a standard governing lover and loved alike, limiting as well as describing their mutual responsibilities. Under this standard, the friend or parent or spouse is, like the professional, limited to practicing within his competence and governing his conduct by its relevance for enhancing the person he loves. Under the same standard, the person loved is obligated to use the support received for growth and to respect the integrity and independence of the person or institution that nourishes him (21, 112).

Because those who give love and those who receive it often violate this standard and are, themselves, unwilling or unable to implement it, or are ignorant of the consequences of its violation, a variety of sanctions are routinely employed in its support. There is always the threat, inherent in the situation, that the relationship will be broken off, or, if continued, that it will fail of its purpose and make pressing needs go unsatisfied. There are the continued costs of attending college or paying the professional or spending time with the friend which go for nothing if the relationship is unproductive. There are evaluations by supervisors, kinsmen, acquaintances, teachers, and other friends.

* * *

Maintenance and Development

Once begun, love may or may not be sustained. It will not persist or grow without special effort. There are at least four activities concerning which some difficulties are likely to appear. These are: 1) efforts to differentiate this socially "primary" association from other relations in which people engage, 2) efforts to conduct necessary relations with the environment outside the primary relationship, 3) efforts to manage the internal routines of giving love and receiving it, and 4) efforts to guide individual participants' careers in love.

DIFFERENTIATING A PRIMARY RELATIONSHIP FROM OTHER ASSO-
CIATIONS: In comradeship men are beside each other, jointly confronting their common task. In love, men are face to face, their relationship itself the focus of attention. The outer world is a source
of support or interference, but not the occasion for their union. Each
person attracts the other to himself, not merely to his works. The
more diffuse their obligations for one another, the more are they
oriented inward toward their own interaction.

All human organizations requiring large commitments from
their participants try to encapsulate their members' lives, eliminating
potential sources of seduction and subversion. The more intense forms
of love are among these.

* * *

There are, however, special reasons why love is a relationship
closed to influences from without. The first is that, in love, the
focus of attention is on developing a relationship with one's fellow
participants. This distinguishes it from any enterprise in which the
objective is to modify the outer world and in which the social relationship, as such, is only a means to this external end, evaluated by
its efficiency for that purpose.

Second, if love is authentic, it is aimed at the enhancement
of participants relative to their own needs and potentialities. The
standard of enhancement or growth is not what someone else has accomplished. The nature of the participants' needs and possibilities
define the relation's productivity and their advance. To judge their
growth by some other standards may be necessary, but it is not love.
As a consequence, it becomes necessary to avoid situations and contacts with the outer world that might involve such judgments. . . .

Again, the work of love deals with people as they really are
and, to proceed, they must be free to be what they are. By definition,
this means that many of the parts they play in life must be dropped
(68) revealing private and central aspects of their selves. The deeper
the love given and accepted, the more are people vulnerable to one
another. It is inescapable that, as the popular song has it, "you always hurt the one you love." Because heightened vulnerability makes
traumatic incidents inevitable, even though quite unintended, forbearance, patience, contrition, and forgiveness are a required part
of successful loving. The working through of all these relations require somewhat private surroundings.

Complementing these needs for privacy is the seemingly universal social norm that any legitimate instance of love has the right
to privacy (106, 125). The state may define conversations between
a professional man and his client as privileged. Spouses cannot be
called to testify against each other in court. The house of a blood
brother is a legitimate sanctuary for a man fleeing from tribal justice,
however heinous his crime. Relatives are discouraged from prying
into the affairs of a married couple; outsiders from disturbing the

172 communion of friends. Friends and monks are forbidden to tattle about each other (31, 131, 133, 143, 149).

A peculiar feature of the economics of love also militates against its ready accessibility to outside influences. The source of gain in love is from a relation to someone else as a person. Other things equal, the degree of such intimacy between an original pair declines in the presence of a third person. The former members come under constraints to compete with each other for the newcomer's devotion and with him for each other (24). Impersonality grows.

* * *

MANAGING INTERNAL ROUTINES: The origin and conduct of all human associations require that men be somewhat different from one another. People come together because they need each other to provide what none can supply for himself. They may have different kinds or amounts of skill or resources, but they must differ at least in that one has what the other needs and lacks.

Once together, participants must become different in certain additional respects in order to share their respective resources. As Bales (11) points out, there is some measure of specialization among men in every conversation, for, in the nature of the case, they do not repeat each other's words, but elaborate, evaluate, question, or otherwise respond to what was said. They also divide up the use of such facilities as time and space, each becoming different from the others with respect to the particular share available to him.

It is a long distance, but one without discontinuity, from these microscopic forms of social differentiation to the massive, clearly marked division of labor in complex societies. In groups of all sizes we find differentiation in its two forms—in "specialization" which refers to the *nature* or *source* of the influence that men exert, and in "stratification" comprised by variations in the *amount* of social influence.

Whether in the form of specialization or stratification, differences among men are as necessary a means for the conduct of love as for *any* other instance of social interaction. Such differences are also potentially subversive of the *particular kind* of social interaction that love represents. We have seen that loving involves a considerable equality among participants. Differentiation is a condition which commonly represents inequality. Loving is directed toward the enhancement of others. The coordination of differentiated activites may be so time-consuming that it becomes an end in itself rather than a means to love. Loving requires intimacy. Specialization and stratification generate differences in interest and commitment within a group and embody a degree of social distance among members.

* * *

GUIDING THE CAREERS OF INDIVIDUALS: All these efforts to preserve equality do not mean that there are no careers in loving, no socially acknowledged stages in an individual's developing skill, no routinized measures of his progress. Without such measures it would be difficult for him to guide his conduct, to judge his competence, and to formulate plans for future development.

* * *

I have sketched four special considerations that operate to shield a primary relationship from the influence of its environing world: the focus on the development of the relationship itself, the avoidance of standards of accomplishment unrelated to the needs and potentialities of its own members, the provision of privacy in which participants need not fear to be themselves, and the protection of deep itimacy against dilution from impersonality. A fifth should be added: A primary relationship requires considerable "local autonomy" because it embodies responsible action.

Loving nurturance, we found, must be responsible. Responsible action, in turn, is impossible without the freedom to allocate resources and make choices which one is committed to pursue. Successful love is impossible without responsibility and responsibility is impossible without considerable autonomy of action.

CONDUCTING NECESSARY RELATIONS WITH THE OUTER ENVIRONMENT: "Love," says Bettelheim's memorable title, "is not enough (19). It supplies some, not all, of man's needs. Its actualization and maintenance require that skills, standards, and resources be brought from without into the loving relationship.

There is no way for lovers to avoid immersion in the world beyond their circle, no way even for their love to flourish apart from that wider environment. Love is not the whole of human life. As people devote more and more of their relationship to loving, they are ever less capable of employing it to provide other requirements for life and must obtain them elsewhere. In sum, loving is not self supporting.

As we have seen, the objective of genuine love is to increase the participants' powers of self-conscious, discriminating beings. Those powers are exercised in many enterprises in addition to love and, at least in Western thought, a primary relationship's relevance for the problems posed by that outer world is one essential test of its worth. It is, we say, unhealthy to continue a love which fails this test. Love means greater, more effective involvement in the world, not less.

Requirements for love's fruition through performance in the world outside, have long been recognized as important safeguards against certain pathologies which otherwise would go uncorrected. It is, to take an instance, all too easy for the members of a group to fall in love with loving, making of their mutual devotion an ultimate goal and fearing to disrupt their beatific relationship by solving problems. When this occurs, difficulties and deficiencies are papered over for the sake of harmony until the point is reached at which they cannot be ignored and the group's integration cannot bear their cummulative weight.

174

Again, love is a diffuse relationship. Without the criteria provided by particular tasks which need attention, objective, rational standards to govern the relationship would be difficult to define and maintain, including those which test love's genuineness and appropriateness.

Then there is the dilemma that the tendencies toward privacy in any living relationship make it suspect in the larger society (70). Are the lovers developing standards that subvert other groups? Service in the outer world prevents the rise of such interpretations and affords a test, for lovers, of the likely viability of any novel standards emerging among them.

*　　*　　*

Because the objective of loving is the enhancement of another and not personal aggrandizement, the appropriate measure of success must be a man's contribution, not his own gains. One does not set out to be a saint or a great benefactor of mankind or a superb patriot and to do so would preclude achieving one's end. One would be exploiting the needs of others for personal benefit and so precluding the growth of love. One can succeed only by setting out to serve, not to gain for oneself. It would, consequently, be grossly inappropriate to recognize growth in love by a gift that would benefit the lover in particular apart from the causes to which he is devoted. The most appropriate gift will be one that furthers those causes or allows him to contribute to them more fully and effectively or that displays, by some special growth of the beloved, the efficacy of his efforts in the past. The retiring professor is suitably honored by a *festschrift* displaying his students' best talents or an endowment to support his favorite scholarly programs. The parent is honored appropriately by mementos of his children's growing competence.

Although a career in love occurs through time, the main course of that career has a markedly cyclical character. One changes by becoming more fully what one has been but never completely what one might be. The career is the elaboration and perfection of a single style of life, not the exploration of various styles. One's skills and outlook may be applied to many diverse tasks, but the general character of their objective is the same in each and the mechanisms by which their work is accomplished are essentially constant. It could scarcely be otherwise. Here, comprising this most elaborated form of social interaction, are the relationships on which all special forms of human association depend. As with any highly general principles, however varied their applications, the possibilities for employing these foundational skills are never fully exhausted, their meaning is never completely grasped, nor is the need for their exercise outgrown. There is a constant venturing forth from these principles, a continuous reference back to them for guidance, and, when one enterprise is finished, a return to them as preparation for tasks to come (11, pp. 30–84).

There are, however, other aspects of an individual's career in loving. He becomes irritated. He wants to withdraw and pursue other

activities. He finds increasing involvement frightening as well as fulfilling. Social arrangements must be provided if these periods of stress
are to remain within bounds.

* * *

Essayists on love often remark that, among the symptoms of
growing devotion, is satisfaction with silence, with merely being together though "doing nothing." They are less likely to note something that seems typical of all situations in which people are to love
one another over many areas of their lives and for long periods of
time. An initial period of goodwill is followed by a time of great
coolness or hostility. In these periods of stress, people may hold together in stark dependency, no graces lightening the burden of their
need for each other, no respite at hand in which to enjoy such fruit
as their relation bears. Yet this may be as much a part of loving as
the moments of gaiety or consummation. Moreover, this cycle will be
repeated should they be called upon to make some further, significant
increase in their commitments to each other. The sequence is familiar
in the "sunshine to storm" cycle as the child moves from infancy to
early childhood or from late childhood to adolescence. It is often
noted in observations of courtship and marriage, of psychotherapy and
of friendships. Students of occupational careers have noted it in
schoolteachers and in managers of large concerns. Directors of institutions which provide long term care for children expect it of many
youngsters during the first year or two under their roof.

Two interpretations of the cycle are common. First, the individual can test the trustworthiness and depth of the affection proferred
him only by becoming a major liability. If that behavior is accepted,
he is probably desired for what he is, not for some particular service
he performs. Second, love will require him to give up behaviors he
may enjoy even though they appreciably weaken his potentialities. He
may need to withdraw from a relationship to assess his own willingness to make a still greater commitment to it. In this sense, a withdrawal from intimacy or even open hostility may be a necessary
preparation of the ground for deeper love.

* * *

Thus, throughout the child's socialization, the healing of sick
minds, the growth of friendships and marital love, and the reaching
of souls toward a divine love, problems are raised for which many
lovers are unprepared. Assuming devotion to be unalloyed beatitude,
they are dismayed or crushed by the obligation of the loved to grow,
or, as lovers, are overwhelmed by the effort, skill, and commitment
required to deal creatively with the developments they have nourished.
They cannot accept dissent from their present views, even when the
disagreement is directed toward helping them. They find it hard to
see a conflict of responsible opinions as creative and lack skills to
resolve such issues fruitfully.

Nothing is more fatal than to love or accept love beyond one's competence, yet nothing more likely than the flourishing of love beyond those bounds. Even when loved and lover can name what they are doing, when they understand enough to seek for those hindrances to the growth that alone can relieve the tension and can take comfort in knowledge that it is love, not madness, with which they wrestle, there is no certainty that they will have the strength or competence or opportunity to realize a fortunate conclusion.

Where love is wise, informed by experience and training, it moves, but moves gradually. Where love is institutionalized, there are methods for controlling as for promoting its growth. There is a routine of work, wakening, relaxation, bathing, and sleep, there is care for diet and health, and there are opportunities for privacy, withdrawal, deviance, candor, intimate interaction, and separation (19, 31, pp. 30–43, 206).

Routine and care sustain with a minimum of novel decisions. They underscore elemental dependencies and realities, provide time and opportunities for assimilating past experiences and the testing of new approaches. If directed only to preserving relations as they are, they generate conflicting feelings of obligation and rebellion (14, 95). If directed to providing for future growth, they encourage development by affording participants with the experience of larger continuities and the fresh opportunities that a new day brings.

But routines have another, greater, significance. As we have seen, routinized, unrewarded, steady care and sacrifice characterize authentic love. They are not the only authentication of love, but they are necessary and the persistence of such care in spite of adversities can take on a heroic quality rarely matched by more spectacular sacrifices, its very cumulativeness being sufficient to provide the energies needed for fresh advances. Perhaps such care is additionally important because it affords evidence that the lover's need is also great, thus making it respectable for the beloved to accept his gifts (110, pp. 125–213).

Finally, routines require continued effort from the person seeking love. Submission to them indicates sufficiency of need and continued willingness to bear the costs of growth. It is evidence of strength to meet these requirements. Without this evidence, there is reason to doubt that love, as such, can be accepted. What is sought is, perhaps, hospitalization without therapy or, perhaps, resources to use, not for growth, but for whatever one pleases.

*　　*　　*

AN INTEGRATION OF THESE OBSERVATIONS

Love, we said as our study began, is the commitment, knowingly, willingly, and responsibly to do whatever one can toward enhancing the powers, independence, and integration of another in some area of his conduct. Each of the many social arrangements we subsequently reviewed serves as a means for routinizing love—for establishing it, implementing it, or protecting it.

"Love is the commitment. . . ." We have seen that the strength of this commitment and its constancy are tested. In this survey, we found that the requirements for continuous interaction, steady support, and the passing of an initiation provided such tests. The requirement for equality of need among the participants provided a guarantee of their faithfulness.

"Love is the commitment . . . to do whatever one can. . . ." The diffuseness of love must also be established and repeatedly evaluated. Requirements for informality, personalization, and intimacy serve this purpose.

"Love is the commitment . . . to do whatever one can . . . in some area of his conduct." We found that alternating periods of harmony and conflict test the scope of love and that a variety of methods are employed to perpetuate the relationship despite these shifts in affective climate. We found also that loving cannot escape the world in which it occurs and certain devices have been found especially suited for preserving love's character even while the participants relate to the outer world as well as to each other.

Love occurs "knowingly, willingly, and responsibly." The autonomy of the lover, whether it be an individual or an organization, seems to be one guarantee that the relationship is a matter of conscious choice and is entered willingly. Autonomy is likewise necessary for that freedom to allocate resources and commit oneself to choices which distinguish responsible action. Of equal importance in promoting responsible behavior—the practice of love within one's competence—are the presence of objective norms, binding upon lover and loved alike, and the tests of love's strength and scope, each requiring a decision about competence and willingness to enlarge the relationship. Again, the demand for continuous participation insures opportunities to expend the necessary effort.

Finally, love is directed toward "enhancing the powers, independence, and integration" of another. Some of our observations have shown how this objective is kept in view; others indicate devices by which one measures or guides movement toward such a goal. In keeping this objective in focus, equality of need among the participants is once again important, in this case to prevent dominance and exploitation. So is the requirement that the quality of the beloved's performance in the outer world be employed as an objective measure of the fruitfulness of the loving relationship. The several procedures for testing the existence of interests that conflict with love's goal and for judging the ability to receive love are also relevant here.

Movement toward the goals of love is measured by the stages of loving and being loved. Many techniques discovered in our survey have arisen to promote one or more of these stages, to manage the strains they engender, and to break up resistance to further growth.

* * *

The organizational pathologies to which particular approximations of love seem unusually susceptible should be understood as consequences of the special difficulty inherent in each of routinizing some aspect of love (39, 67, 94, 142). Take, for example, what C. S. Lewis calls "affection"—the loving association characterized by easy familiarity, warm comfortableness, and mutual acceptance of participants for what they are. Founded on an appreciation of people as they are at present, this relationship is threatened if they begin to change. Because affection typically appears without a very searching exploration of the equality of the participants' needs, or the responsibility of their commitment, persons become diffusely open to one another without strong safeguards against exploitation and other injury. In friendship, by contrast, equality, responsibility, and many other criteria of love are usually well-established. Typical problems here, however, are the growth of mutual enjoyment at the expense of pressing commitments in the outer world and the loss of objectivity of judgment about the relationship and each other.

REFERENCES

1. Alderidge, G. J. "Informal Social Relationships in a Retirement Community." *Marriage Fam. Living* 21 (1959) : 70–72.
2. Allport, G. W. *Becoming*. New Haven: Yale University, 1955.
3. Almond, G. A. *The Appeals of Communism*. Princeton: Princeton University, 1954.
4. Angell, R. C. *The Family Encounters the Depression*. New York: Scribner, 1936.
5. Angell, R. C. "The Moral Integration of American Cities." *Amer. J. Sociol.*, 1951, 57 (2), 1–140.
6. Aristotle, *The Nichomachean Ethics*.
7. Aronfreed, J. *The Nature, Variety, and Social Patterning of Moral Responses*. (Mimeographed) Dept. of Psychology, University of Pennsylvania, 1961.
8. Aronson, E. and Mills, J. "The Effect of Severity of Initiation on Liking for a Group." *J. Abnorm. Soc. Psychol.* 56 (1959) : 177–81.
9. Axelrod, M. "Urban Structure and Social Participation." *Amer. Sociol. Rev.* 21 (1956) : 13–18.
10. Baldwin, M. *I Leap over the Wall, a Return to the World after Twenty-eight Years in a Convent*. London: Hamish Hamilton, 1949.
11. Bales, R. F. *Interaction Process Analysis*. Cambridge: Addison-Wesley, 1950.
12. Banfield, E. C. *The Moral Basis of a Backward Society*. Glencoe, Ill.: Free Press, 1958.
13. Bates, A. P. and Babchuk, N. "The Primary Group: A Reappraisal. *Sociol.*" *Quart.* 2 (1961) : 181–91.
14. de Beauvoir, S. *Memoirs of a Dutiful Daughter*. (J. Kirkup, Trans.) Cleveland: World Publ. Co., 1959.
15. de Beauvoir, S. "Must We Burn de Sade?" In P. Dinnage (ed. and trans.), *The Marquis de Sade*. New York: Grove Press, 1953. Pp. 11–82.
16. Becker, H. *German Youth, Bond or Free*. London: K. Paul, Trench, Trubner, 1946.
17. Becker, H. S. Notes on the Concept of Commitment. *Amer. J. Sociol.* 66 (1960) : 32–40.

18. Bell, W. and Boat, M. D. "Urban Neighborhoods and Informal Social Relations." *Amer. J. Sociol.* 62 (1957) : 391–98.
19. Bettelheim, B. *Love is Not Enough: The Treatment of Emotionally Disturbed Children.* Glencoe, Ill.: The Free Press, 1950.
20. Bettelheim, B. "Individual and Mass Behavior in Extreme Situations." In G. E. Swanson, T. M. Newcomb, and E. L. Hartley, eds. *Readings in Social Psychology.* New York: Henry Holt, 1952. Pp. 33–43.
21. Bettelheim, B. *The Informed Heart, Autonomy in a Mass Age.* Glencoe, Ill.: Free Press, 1960.
22. Bion, W. R. *Experiences in Groups.* New York: Basic Books, 1961.
23. Blau, P. M. "Structural Effects." *Amer. Sociol. Rev.* 25 (1960) : 178–93.
24. Blau, P. M. "A Theory of Social Integration." *Amer. J. Sociol.* 65 (1960) : 545–56.
25. Blumer, H. G. "Social Psychology." In E. P. Schmidt, ed. *Man and Society.* New York: Prentice-Hall, 1938. Pp. 144–98.
26. Brandt, R. B. *Hopi Ethics, a Theoretical Analysis.* Chicago: University of Chicago Press, 1954.
27. Brandt, R. B. *Ethical Theory, the Problems of Normative and Critical Ethics.* Englewood Cliffs, N.J.: Prentice-Hall, 1959.
28. Bronfenbrenner, U. *The Role of Age, Sex, Class, and Culture in Studies of Moral Development.* (Mimeographed) Dept. of Psychology, Cornell University, 1961.
29. Burgess, E. W. and Locke, H. J. *The Family, from Institution to Companionship.* New York: American Book Co., 1945.
30. Burns, T. "Friends, Enemies, and the Polite Fiction." *Amer. Sociol. Rev.* 18 (1953) : 654–62.
31. Butler, E. C. *Benedictine Monachism: Studies in Benedictine Life and Rule.* London: Longmans, Green and Co., 1924.
32. Butler, E. C. *Western Mysticism.* London: Constable, 1927.
33. Campbell, C. A. "Is "Freewill" a Pseudo-problem." *Mind.* 60 (1951) : 441–65.
34. Clark, B. R. " 'The Cooling-out' Function in Higher Education." *Amer. J. Sociol.* 65 (1960) : 569–76.
35. Cohen, Y. A. "Some Aspects of Ritualized Behavior in Interpersonal Relationships." *Hum. Relat.* 11 (1958) : 195–215.
36. Cooley, C. H. *Social Organization.* New York: Scribners, 1909.
37. Cooley, C. H. "A Primary Culture for Democracy." *Publications of the American Sociological Society* 13 (1918) : 1–10.
38. Crossman, R. H. S., (ed.) *The God that Failed.* New York: Harper, 1950.
39. D'Arcy, M. C. *The Mind and Heart of Love.* New York: Henry Holt, 1947.
40. Davis, F. "The Cabdriver and his Fare: Facets of a Fleeting Relationship." *Amer. J. Sociol.* 65 (1959) : 158–65.
41. Deutsch, M. "An Experimental Study of the Effects of Cooperation and Competition upon Group Processes." *Hum. Relat.* 2 (1949) : 199–232.
42. Deutsch, M. "A Theory of Cooperation and Competition." *Hum. Relat.* 2 (1949) : 129–52.
43. Deutsch, M. "Trust and Suspicion." *J. Conflict Resolution* 2 (1958) : 265–79.
44. Deutsch, M. "Trust, Trustworthiness, and the F Scale." *J. Abnorm. Soc. Psychol.* 61 (1960) : 138–40.

180

45. Deutsch, M. "The Effect of Threat upon Interpersonal Bargaining." *J. Abnorm. Soc. Psychol.* 61 (1960) : 181–89.

46. Drucker, P. F. *The Practice of Management.* New York: Harpers, 1954.

47. Du Bois, C. A. *Studies of Friendship.* (Mimeographed) Dept. of Social Relations, Harvard University, 1955.

48. Durkheim, E. *Suicide.* (J. A. Spaulding and G. Simpson, Trans.) Glencoe, Ill.: Free Press, 1951.

49. Dynes, R. R. "The Consequences of Sectarianism for Social Participation." *Soc. Forces* 35 (1957) : 331–34.

50. Edwards, P. *The Logic of Moral Discourse.* Glencoe, Ill.: Free Press, 1955.

51. Eisenstadt, S. N. African Age Groups, a Comparative Study. *Africa* 24 (1954) : 100–13.

52. Eisenstadt, S. N. *From Generation to Generation.* Glencoe, Ill.: Free Press, 1956.

53. Etzioni, A. "The Functional Differentiation of Elites in the Kibbutz." *Amer. J. Sociol.* 64 (1959) : 476–87.

54. Fanelli, A. A. "Extensiveness of Communication Contacts and Perceptions of the Community." *Amer. Sociol. Rev.* 21 (1956) : 439–45.

55. Farber, B. "Elements of Competence in Interpersonal Relations: A Factor Analysis." *Sociometry* 25 (1962) : 30–47.

56. Farber, S. M. and Wilson, R. H. L., (eds.) *Control of the Mind.* New York: McGraw-Hill, 1961.

57. Faris, E. "The Primary Group: Essence and Accident." *Amer. J. Sociol.* 38 (1932) : 41–50.

58. Fenichel, O. *The Psycho-analytic Theory of Neurosis.* New York: Norton, 1945.

59. Foote, N. Love. *Psychiat.* 16 (1953) : 245–51.

60. Foote, N., and Cottrell, L. C. *Identity and Interpersonal Competence.* Chicago: University of Chicago, 1955.

61. Frank, A. *The Diary of a Young Girl.* New York: Doubleday, 1952.

62. Freeman, H. E., Novak, E., and Reeder, L. G. "Correlates of Membership in Voluntary Associations." *Amer. Sociol. Rev.* 22 (1957) : 528–33.

63. French, J. R. P. "Organized and Unorganized Groups Under Fear and Frustration." In K. Lewin et al., *Authority and Frustration.* Iowa City, Iowa: University of Iowa, 1944. Pp. 299–308.

64. Freud, S. *Group Psychology and the Analysis of the Ego.* (J. Strachey, trans.) London: Hogarth, 1922.

65. Friedman, M. S. *Martin Buber: The Life of Dialogue.* Chicago: University of Chicago, 1955.

66. Friedrichs, R. W. "Alter *Versus* Ego: An Exploratory Assessment of Altruism." *Amer. Sociol. Rev.* 25 (1960) : 496–508.

67. Fromm, E. *The Art of Loving.* New York: Harpers, 1956.

68. Goffman, E. *The Presentation of Self in Everyday Life.* Edinburgh: University of Edinburgh, 1956.

69. Goffman, E. *Asylums: Essays on the Social Situation of Mental Patients and other Inmates.* Garden City, N.Y.: Doubleday, 1961.

70. Goode, W. J. "The Theoretical Importance of Love." *Amer. Sociol. Rev.* 24 (1959) : 38–47.

71. Goode, W. J. "Illegitimacy, Anomie, and Cultural Penetration." *Amer. Sociol. Rev.* 26 (1961) : 910–25.

72. Gorer, G. *The Life and Ideas of the Marquis de Sade.* London: Peter Owen, 1953.

73. Gough, H. G. "Predicting Social Participation." *J. Soc. Psychol.* 35 (1952) : 227–33.
74. Gouldner, A. W. "The Norm of Reciprocity: A Preliminary Statement." *Amer. Sociol. Rev.* 26 (1960) : 161–78.
75. Grant, C. K. "Freewill: A Reply to Professor Campbell." *Mind* 61 (1952) : 381–85.
76. Gross, E. "Symbiosis and Consensus as Integrative Factors in Small Groups." *Amer. Sociol. Rev.* 21 (1956) : 174–79.
77. Gross, E. "Social Integration and the Control of Competition." *Amer. J. Sociol.* 67 (1961) : 270–77.
78. Hammond, L. K. and Goldman, M. "Competition and Noncompetition and its Relationship to Individual and Group Productivity." *Sociometry* 24 (1961) : 46–60.
79. Harris, I. D. *Normal Children and Mothers.* Glencoe, Ill.: The Free Press, 1959.
80. Helfgott, M. J. *The Effect of Variations in Mobility Norms upon the Legitimation of the Personnel Distribution by Subordinate Populations.* (Unpublished dissertation,) Doctoral Program in Social Psychology, The University of Michigan, 1954.
81. Hollander, E. P. and Webb, W. B. "Leadership, Followership, and Friendship: An Analysis of Peer Nominations." *J. Abnorm. Soc. Psychol.* 50 (1955) : 163–67.
82. Homans, G. C. *Social Behavior: Its Elementary Forms.* New York: Harcourt, Brace, World, 1961.
83. Hulme, K. *The Nun's Story.* Boston: Little, Brown, 1956.
84. Hyma, A. *The Brethren of the Common Life.* Grand Rapids, Mich.: Eerdmans, 1950.
85. Jahoda, M. *Current Concepts of Positive Mental Health.* New York: Basic Books, 1958.
86. Jandy, E. C. *Charles Horton Cooley: His Life and His Social Theory.* New York: Dryden, 1942.
87. Komarovsky, M. *The Unemployed Man and His Family.* New York: Dryden, 1940.
88. Kornhauser, W. *The Politics of Mass Society.* Glencoe, Ill.: Free Press, 1959.
89. Ladd, J. *The Sructure of a Moral Code: a Philosophical Analysis of Ethical Discourse Applied to the Ethics of the Navaho Indians.* Cambridge: Harvard University Press, 1959.
90. Lantz, H. R. "Number of Childhood Friends as Reported in the Life Histories of a Psychiatrically Diagnosed Group of 1,000." *Marriage Fam. Living* 18 (1956) : 107–13.
91. Lazarsfeld, P. F. and Merton R. K. Friendship as a Social Process." In M. Berger, (ed.) *Freedom and Control in Modern Society.* New York: D. Van Nostrand, 1954. Pp. 18–66.
92. Lenski, G. E. Social Participation and Status Crystallization." *Amer. Social. Rev.* 21 (1956) : 458–64.
93. Levine, G. N. and Sussmann, L. A. "Social Class and Sociability in Fraternity Pledging." *Amer. J. of Sociol.* 65 (1960) : 391–99.
94. Lewis, O. S. *The Four Loves.* London: G. Bles, 1960.
95. Lewis, O. *Children of Sanchez.* New York: Random House, 1961.
96. Likert, R. *New Patterns of Management.* New York: McGraw-Hill, 1961.
97. Lippitt, R. *Training in Community Relations.* New York: Harper, 1949.
98. Lipset, S. M. *Political Man.* Garden City, N. Y.: Doubleday, 1960.

182

99. Litwak, E., Count, G., and Hayden, E. M. "Group Structure and Interpersonal Creativity as Factors Which Reduce Errors in the Prediction of Marital Adjustment." *Soc. Forces* 38 (1960): 308–15.

100. Loomis, J. L. "Communication, the Development of Trust, and Cooperative Behavior." *Hum. Relat.* 12 (1959): 305–15.

101. "Love in a Marxist Climate." *New Statesman*, Sept. 1, 1960, p. 326.

102. Mann, P. H. "The Concept of Neighborliness." *Amer. J. Sociol.* 60 (1954): 163–68.

103. Maslow, A. H. "Self-actualizing People: A Study in Psychological Health." *Personality* 1 (1950): 11–34.

104. Maslow, A. H. "Love in Healthy People." In A. Montagu, ed. *The Meaning of Love.* New York: Julian Press, 1953. Pp. 57–93.

105. May, R., ed. *Existence; a New Dimension in Psychiatry and Psychology.* New York: Basic Books, 1958.

106. Mayer, J. E. "The Self-Restraint of Friends: A Mechanism in Family Transition." *Soc. Forces* 35 (1957): 230–38.

107. Merriam, A. P. and Mack R. W. "The Jazz Community." *Soc. Forces* 38 (1960): 211–22.

108. Miller, D. R. and Swanson, G. E. *The Changing American Parent.* New York: Wiley, 1958.

109. Munson, B. E. "Attitudes Toward Urban and Suburban Residence in Indianapolis." *Soc. Forces*, 35 (1956): 76–80.

110. Orwell, G. *Down and Out in Paris and London.* New York: Harcourt, Brace, 1950.

111. Otto, R. *Mysticism East and West.* New York: Macmillan, 1932.

112. Parsons, T. "Illness and the Role of the Physician: A Sociological Perspective." *Amer. J. Orthopsychiat.* 21 (1951): 452–60.

113. Pepitone, A. and Sherberg, J. "Intentionality, Responsibility, and Interpersonal Attraction." *J. Pers.* 25 (1957): 757–66.

114. Redl, F. and Wineman, D. *Children Who Hate.* Glencoe, Ill.: Free-Press, 1951.

115. Redl, F. and Wineman, D. *Controls from Within.* Glencoe, Ill.: Free Press, 1952.

116. Reiss, A. J., Jr. "Rural-urban and Status Differences in Inter-Personal Contacts." *Amer. J. Sociol.* 15 (1959): 182–95.

117. Reiss, I. L. "Toward a Sociology of the Heterosexual Love Relationship." *Marriage Fam. Living.* 22 (1960): 139–45.

118. Reissman, L. Class, Leisure, and Social Participation." *Amer. Sociol. Rev.* 19 (1954): 17–84.

119. Rosenberg, B. and Humphrey, N. D. "The Secondary Nature of the Primary Group." *Social Research* 22 (1955): 25–38.

120. Sarma, J. *The Social Categories of Friendship.* Unpublished doctoral dissertation. Department of Sociology, University of Chicago, 1964.

121. Schein, E. W., Schneier, I. and Barker, C. H. *Coercive Persuasion: A Socio-Psychological Analysis of the "Brainwashing" of American Civilian Prisoners by the Chinese Communists.* New York: Norton, 1961.

122. Schwartz, R. D. "Functional Alternatives to Inequality." *Amer. Sociol. Rev.* 20 (1955): 424–30.

123. Scott, J. C., Jr. "Membership and Participation in Voluntary Associations." *Amer. Sociol. Rev.* 22 (1957): 315–26.

124. Shils, E. A. "The Study of the Primary Group." In D. Lerner and

H. D. Lasswell, eds. *The Policy Sciences.* Stanford: Stanford University, 1951. Pp. 44–69.

125. Shils, E. A. *The Torment of Secrecy, the Background and Consequences of American Security Policies.* Glencoe, Ill.: Free Press 1956.
126. Shuval, J. T. "Class and Ethic Correlates of Casual Neighboring." *Amer. Sociol. Rev.* 21 (1956) : 453–58.
127. Smith, J., Form, W. H., and Stone, G. P. "Local Intimacy in a Middle-sized City." *Amer. J. Sociol.* 60 (1954) : 276–84.
128. Solomon, L. "The Influence of Some Types of Power Relationships and Game Strategies Upon the Development of Interpersonal Trust." *J. Abnorm. Soc. Psychol.* 61 (1960) : 223–30.
129. Spiro, M. E. *Kibbutz: Venture in Utopia,* Cambridge: Harvard, 1956.
130. Stevenson, C. L. *Ethics and Language.* New Haven: Yale University, 1944.
131. Stouffer, S. A. "An Analysis of Conflicting Social Norms." *Amer. Sociol. Rev.* 14 (1949) : 707–17.
132. Stouffer, S. A., et al., eds. *The American Soldier,* vols. I & II. Princeton: Princeton University, 1950.
133. Stouffer, S. A. and Toby, J. "Role Conflict and Personality." *Amer. J. Sociol.* 56 (1951) : 395–406.
134. Swanson, G. E. "The Effectiveness of Decision-making Groups, Effects of Constitutional Arrangements on Group Efficiency." *Adult Leadership* 8 (1959) : 48–52.
135. Swanson, G. E. *The Birth of the Gods, Origins of Primitive Beliefs.* Ann Arbor, Mich.: University of Michigan, 1960.
136. Swanson, G. E. "Determinants of the Individual's Defenses Against Inner Conflict: Review and Reformulation." In J. C. Glidewell, ed. *Parental Attitudes and Child Behavior.* Springfield, Ill.: Charles C. Thomas, 1961. Pp. 5–41.
137. Tagiuri, R. and Petrullo, L., eds. *Person Perception and Interpersonal Behavior.* Stanford: Stanford University, 1958.
138. Tettmer, J. *I Was a Monk.* New York: Knopf, 1951.
139. Thibaut, J. W. and Riecken, H. W. "Some Determinants and Consequences of the Perception of Social Causality." *J. Pers.* 24 (1955) : 113–33.
140. Thomas, E. J. "Effects of Facilitative Role Interdependence on Group Functioning." *Hum. Relat.* 10 (1957) : 347–66.
141. Tillich, P. *The Courage to Be.* New Haven: Yale University, 1952.
142. Tillich, P. *Love, Power, and Justice.* Gloucester, Mass.: Peter Smith, 1960.
143. Turner, R. H. "Self and Other in Moral Judgment." *Amer. Sociol. Rev.* 19 (1954) : 249–59.
144. Underhill, E. *Mysticism.* New York: Meridian Books, 1955.
145. Wallin, P. A. "Guttman Scale for Measuring Women's Neighborliness." *Amer. J. Sociol.* 59 (1953) : 243–46.
146. Watson, J. "A Formal Analysis of Sociable Interaction." *Sociometry* 21 (1958) : 269–80.
147. Weeks, H. A. *Youthful Offenders at Highfields.* Ann Arbor, Mich.: University of Michigan, 1958.
148. Weinberg, S. K. *Incest Behavior.* New York: Citadel Press, 1955.
149. Westley, W. A. "Secrecy and the Police." *Soc. Forces* 34 (1956) : 254–57.
150. Whiting, J. W. M., Kluckhohn, R. and Anthony, A. The Function

184

of Male Initiation Ceremonies at Puberty. In E. E. Maccoby, T. M. Newcomb, and E. L. Hartley, eds. *Readings in Social Psychology*. New York: Henry Holt, 1958, Pp. 359–70.

151. Wilensky, H. L. "Orderly Careers and Social Participation: The Impact of Work History on Social Integration in the Middle Mass." *Amer. Sociol. Rev.* 26 (1961) : 521–39.

152. Williams, J. H. "Close Friendship Relations of Housewives Residing in an Urban Community." *Soc. Forces* 36 (1958) : 358–62.

153. Williams, R. M., Jr. "Friendship and Social Values in a Suburban Community: An Exploratory Study." *Pacific Sociol. Rev.* 2 (1959) : 3–10.

154. Wilson, A. T. M., Trist, E. L., and Curle, A. "Transitional Communities and Social Reconnection: A Study of the Civil Resettlement of British Prisoners of War. In G. E. Swanson, T. M. Newcomb, and E. L. Hartley, eds. *Readings in Social Psychology*. New York: Henry Holt, 1952. Pp. 561–79.

155. Winch, R. F. "Mate-selection, a Study of Complementary Needs." New York: Harper, 1958.

156. Workman, H. B. *The Evolution of the Monastic Ideal from the Earliest Times to the Coming of the Friars*. London: Epworth Press, 1927.

157. Wright, C. R. and Hyman, H. H. "Voluntary Memberships of American Adults: Evidence from National Sample Surveys." *Amer. Sociol. Rev.* 23 (1958) : 284–94.

158. Zborowski, M. and Herzog, E. *Life is with People*. New York: International Universities Press, 1952.

159. Zimmer, B. G. and Hawley, A. H. "The Significance of Membership in Associations." *Amer. J. Sociol.* 65 (1959) : 196–201.

PRIDE
RULE
Independence
MORTIFICATION
Expectation
Attitude
Position
Object
FEMALE
INSTRUCTION
MALE
ROLE
MOTIVE
OTHERS
SELF
MARRIAGE
HABIT
Symbolization
Internalization
SANCTION
RIGHT
Attitude
LANGUAGE
NORM

Study Questions

1. Do Komarovsky's findings apply to your own socialization? Describe the similarities and differences.
2. Have you ever met a liberated male or female? What special qualities did they have? What does it mean to be liberated?
3. Is Deborah in **I Never Promised You a Rose Garden** much like Mary in **The Irwins?**
4. Can you demonstrate how your conceptions of yourself are intimately tied to the reflection of others?
5. Describe two groups that differ in their emphasis upon socialization as conformity rather than socialization as the enhancing of growth and skills.

The Image of Man in Society: Socialization

6 While culture provides the general framework for learning and interaction within which influence occurs, the actual process of learning to
be a member of a group—of learning the group's rules and beliefs—
is known as socialization. In an operational sense, socialization is the
means by which the newcomer, new arrival, or newborn is inculcated
with the elements of culture. It is the process whereby the expectations
of the group are conveyed, via language, writing, instruction, or gesture. In chapter 4, the Naciremian was depicted as an unusually ec-
centric person. You may have perceived him in this way until you
realized that you were observing him as an outsider looking in, and
that the author did not interpret the natives' acts to make them logical
for you. When you adopt the position of a native, the strange rituals
begin to make sense. You come to perceive the Naciremian cultural
system and way of life as plausible and coherent. Within organized
social units, socialization makes possible this transition between object and symbol. Through interaction, socialization teaches the secrets
and habits of the group and makes intelligible that which at first
seems random, chaotic, and meaningless. Socialization is the process
by which the human animal (organic level) is transformed into a
personality, and the personality into a social individual—an individual
who is capable of guiding his own conduct according to his own expectations or those of others.

SOCIETAL AND INDIVIDUAL VIEWS OF SOCIALIZATION

One can approach the phenomenon of socialization from the *societal*
or the *individual* view. From the societal point of view, socialization
can be seen as the process by which culture is transmitted, ensuring
that the individual becomes aware of the sanctioned way of life. From
the individual point of view, socialization can be seen as the mechanism for fulfillment of human potentialities, for personal growth and
development. Instead of viewing the means by which man is made to

188

fit into the ongoing patterns of social life, we concern ourselves with **189** the way socialization transforms the individual from an organic into a social being. In this context, social does not mean sociable, but refers to an independent person who can participate in organized social life. Socialization helps create enduring competencies, standards, judgment, attitudes, and motives which together form a personality.

INTERNALIZATION

Socialization need not mean unquestioning conformity or adherence to the rules of society or to the group way of life, although it is often understood to be simply the control of impulses, conformity to norms, or internalization of the parental conscience. One can be socialized into a group which itself is organized around values of independence, autonomy, and freedom. The rigidly traditional conception of socialization neglects the active, creative role of the child or adult. In actuality, the process of integrating new experiences and their meanings is constant and ongoing throughout life. Whenever an individual moves into a new school, job, or neighborhood, when one in any way enters a new phase of life, different expectations are introduced. Getting married or divorced, becoming a Californian or a member of Women's Liberation—all these acts and their implications must be newly processed and absorbed. The mechanism of internalization—the taking in of group values and rules and making them our own without the necessity of external control—allows for the transmission of these new expectations and obligations. However, internalization does not mean a mere ingestion of culture and standards, for that which is taken in by child or adult is processed by intelligence, and intelligence changes with age and experience. To quote Roger Brown, a social psychologist:

> Conformity to the norms is sometimes said to be the end result of a positive or successful socialization. This is much too narrow a conception. The norms of a language are rules of pronunciation, spelling, semantics, and grammar. Some who have learned these rules very well —children, poets, the Beatles—elect on occasion to violate them. Others who know them well undertake to reform them: to make spelling consistent or to strip certain words of ambiguity. Similarly the moral theory an individual forms by working over his moral experience can lead him to reject some part of the conventional morality. He is likely to argue, in support of his position, that the change he favors will make the total morality more consistent or that the substitution he offers will more truly realize the basic values of the culture than does the rejected part. Saints and revolutionaries and reactionaries all take some such position. It does not seem socialization. They have successfully internalized the norms but they have made a novel system of them and novel systems sometimes displace established ones.[1]

Socialization, as the ongoing process of transmitting culture, involves an important integration of the self with others. We internalize conceptions of objects and situations and also of ourselves. Writing in 1890, psychologist William James described the self as an object of knowledge.[2] Through early socialization, the child comes to

190   define himself in ways which greatly influence his later achievements and growth. At the turn of the century, Charles Horton Cooley, one of the central figures of American sociology, emphasized the social nature of the self. He described the self as an entity derived from the responses of others. According to Cooley, the behavior of others is the mirror in which the individual sees himself.[3] He defines himself as good, bright, lovely, unsuccessful, or dumb because others define him in these ways. Cooley states, that self-idea has three principal elements: the imagination of our appearance to the other person; the imagination of his judgment of that appearance; and some sort of self-feeling, such as pride or mortification.

Via interaction, socialization helps produce different kinds of selves. George Herbert Mead, a social philosopher, also argued that the self is derived from social interaction. The human organism is able to conceive of its "self" through participating in the minds of others. We see ourselves as human organisms with abilities, motives, and attitudes because that is how others see us. Mead felt that man can only know his own personality through reflection in the eyes of another. Furthermore, the child does not acquire a conception only of himself from others' responses: he also acquires a concept of others' roles.[4]

POSITION AND ROLE

Socialization does more than help the child and adult internalize conceptions of themselves and others. It has important consequences for the organization and operation of social units. Individuals who hold important positions in social units—mothers, nursery school teachers, probation officers, or sergeants, to name a few—are all guided in their reactions by expectations of what they believe to be their responsibilities or obligations and rights. Behavior in a social unit is differentiated by the position that a person holds in the organized group; members are not all expected to behave in the same way. Whether a rule or norm applies to a particular person depends on his position in the group. Having a position in a social group implies, then, that a person has both obligations and rights in that social unit. These aspects of the position, the expected and associated rights and obligations, are often referred to as the person's role. Some sociologists may refer to the actual behavior associated with the position as the role. Some view the role as the culturally prescribed performance of an occupant of a given position in the group. In any case, the individual does not act randomly, but responds according to the position he holds in the organized social system. The importance of play in helping the child to internalize concepts of roles and positions was stressed by George Herbert Mead. In a game of tag, or of baseball, the players are not merely viewed as Johnny or Roberta but as occupants of certain positions with rights and obligations applicable to those positions. The players come to see that the rules of the game help define the roles and guarantee equality for all players. The child first sees rules emanating from adults, comes to see that the rules are associated with

positions in social units, and, recognizing this, can begin to develop **191**
his own standards and his own social units.

In growing up, then, the child internalizes concepts of roles. Mead, in his work on socialization, stressed the importance of play in the learning of roles. He saw games as helpful tools for preparing the child to participate in organized social groups. According to Mead, socialization proceeds through three stages. The first stage is one of haphazard and random emulation which occurs among children under the age of two or three years. Here, the child reads the newspaper upside down, and in general copies the behavior of others without understanding the meaning of activities. In the second stage, or play stage, the child begins to take on different roles in a meaningful fashion. He now plays father or big brother and acts back toward his "self" as an object. The third stage, known as the game stage, is marked by the child's ability to have a fairly consistent conception of self. Instead of taking on the role of a specific person, the child reconciles diverse expectations and takes on the role of the "generalized other." In a given situation, our baseball game for example, all shortstops are expected to act alike when a ground ball is hit to them with one out and a man on first.[5]

Presented below are a series of propositions which integrate the work of Cooley and Mead and link the ideas of the organization of groups, the role behavior of members in groups, and the personality of the child:

1. Self image is derived from the response of others to the self.
2. Others, in responding to the self, are guided by norms that govern people's behavior in various roles.
3. The self reflects roles in which people are engaged.
4. Socialization creates motivation for appropriate role behavior.

The readings in this chapter focus primarily on the socialization of women. I have chosen to illustrate the several facets of socialization in this manner because all students are involved with or related to women in some way, and because widespread discrimination against women in our society needs examination and understanding. Socialization is especially important for the enhancement or suppression of the person. Women's Liberation has tremendous potential for the increased freedom of both males and females. For the most part, the readings will focus on the socialization of women from the societal view rather than from the individual view. The first selection was written over 25 years ago by a sociologist. In her article, Mirra Komarovsky sketched the dilemma that many college women faced in 1941. She showed how broad and contradictory cultural expectations guided the interaction and socialization of female children. College women felt a conflict about the extent to which they could express their independence and sense of self. They were, for the most part, frightened of openly expressing their ideas and opinions. Komarovsky

192   showed how the conceptions of the self that women developed were intimately tied to others' conceptions of them. Women who expressed some degree of individuality by selecting a job or career that was not sex-linked (teaching, nursing, social work) experienced either the disdain of their families or the rejection of men. The fact that this article was written before most of you were born should not hinder your interest in discussing its issues, for I think you will find them relevant in the 1970s. To what extent are Komarovsky's findings applicable to your own expectations regarding women? How do men feel about women lawyers, doctors, and journalists, about sharing domestic chores and child care? What will men and women have to give up if they are involved in a loving relationship with each other?

The question of the feasibility of a relationship of equality between men and women is examined in the second selection. Two sociologists, Margaret Paloma and Neal Garland, examine marital relationships among professional men and women. In "The Married Professional Woman: A Study in the Tolerance of Domestication," the authors provide more ammunition for the Women's Liberation Movement, for they discovered that the professional men in their study merely tolerate the careers of their wives. The basic finding of their research is that professional men approve their wives' careers as long as the career does not interfere with the man's career or the domestic side of the relationship. The authors also demonstrate the impact of early socialization upon these professional women, who feel guilty about neglecting their homes and have doubts about the advisability of leaving their children. This article, written in 1971, raises some basic issues about the effect of marriage upon both women and men.

Marriage in America in the 1970s seems to involve a division of labor based not upon the unique qualities of the participants but upon sex and the broad cultural patterns described in Komarovsky's study. Garland and Paloma found only one couple who had an egalitarian relationship, where husband and wife shared child care and domestic chores and supported each other in their careers.

What type of socialization and what type of expectations would men and women have if they were committed to a union of persons? Allice Rossi, a sociologist, writes poignantly about how it would be if men and women were socialized to the quality of being human, rather than to positions of superiority or inferiority based on sex:

*   *   *

She will be reared, as her brother will be reared, with a combination of loving warmth, firm discipline, household responsibility and encouragement of independence and self reliance. She will not be pampered and indulged, subtly taught to achieve her ends through coquetry and tears, as so many girls are taught today. She will view domestic skills as useful tools to acquire, some of which, like fine cooking or needlework, having their own intrinsic pleasures but most of which are necessary repetitive work best gotten done as quickly and efficiently as possible.

She will be able to handle minor mechanical breakdowns in the home a swell as her brother can, and he will be able to tend a child, press, sew and cook with the same easy skills and comfortable feeling his sister has.

During their school years, both sister and brother will increasingly assume responsibility for their own decisions, freely experiment with numerous possible fields of study, gradually narrowing to a choice that best suits their interests and abilities rather than what is considered appropriate or prestigeful work for men and women. They will be encouraged by parents and teachers alike to think ahead to a whole life span, viewing marriage and parenthood as one strand among many which will constitute their lives. The girl will not feel the pressure to belittle her accomplishments, lower her aspirations, learn to be a receptive listener in her relations with boys, but will be as true to her growing sense of self as her brother and male friends are. She will not marry before her adolescence and schooling are completed, but will be willing and able to view the college years as a "moratorium" from deeply intense cross-sex commitments, a period of life during which her identity can be "at large and open and various." Her intellectual aggressiveness as well as her brother's tender sentiments will be welcomed and accepted as *human* characteristics, without the self-questioning doubt of latent homosexuality that troubles many college-age men and women in our era when these qualities are sex-linked. She will not cling to her parents, nor they to her, but will establish an increasingly larger sphere of her own independent world in which she moves and works, loves and thinks, as a maturing young person. She will learn to take pleasure in her own body and a man's body and to view sex as a good and wonderful experience, but not as an exclusive basis for an ultimate commitment to another person, and not as a test of her competence as a female or her partner's competence as a male. Because she will have a many-faceted conception of her self and its worth, she will be free to merge and lose herself in the sex act with a lover or a husband.

Marriage for our hypothetical woman will not mark a withdrawal from the life and work pattern that she has established, just as there will be no sharp discontinuity between her early childhood and youthful adult years. Marriage will be an enlargement of her life experiences, the addition of a new dimension to an already established pattern, rather than an abrupt withdrawal to the home and a turning in upon the marital relationship. Marriage will be a "looking outward in the same direction" for both the woman and her husband. She will mary and bear children only if she deeply desires a mate and children, and will not be judged a failure as a person if she decides against either. She will have few children if she does have them, and will view her pregnancies, childbirth and early months of motherhood as one among many equally important highlights in her life, experienced intensely and with joy but not as the exclusive basis for a sense of self-fulfillment and purpose in life. With planning and foresight, her early years of child bearing and rearing can fit a long-range view of all sides of herself. If her children are not to suffer from "paternal deprivation," her husband will also anticipate that the assumption of parenthood will involve a weeding out of nonessential activities either in work, civic or social participation. Both the woman and the man will feel that unless a man can make room in his life for parenthood, he should not become a father. The woman will make sure, even if she remains at home during her child's infancy, that he has ample experience of being with and cared for by other adults be-

194

sides herself, so that her return to a full-time position in her field will not constitute a drastic change in the life of the child, but a gradual pattern of increasing supplementation by others of the mother. The children will have a less intense involvement with their mother, and she with them, and they will all be the better for it. When they are grown and establish adult lives of their own, our woman will face no retirement twenty years before her husband, for her own independent activities will continue and expand. She will be neither an embittered wife, an interfering mother-in-law nor an idle parasite, but together with her husband she will be able to live an independent, purposeful and satisfying third act in life.[6]

The third selection in this chapter was written by two English psychiatrists, R. D. Laing and Aaron Esterson. Laing and Esterson are concerned with the learning and production of insanity, particularly schizophrenia. The excerpt in this chapter comes from their book, *Sanity, Madness and the Family*, in which the authors describe and reproduce interviews with a number of families in which daughters have been diagnosed as schizophrenic. They show how the families helped produce and induce that aberration. Early socialization patterns of these families involved the denial of the experiences of the child, the confusion of double messages, the repression of their own or the child's sexuality, and the refusal to accept the child's quest for independence. The authors argue that schizophrenia is not a biological fact, but is induced through the socialization pattern of the family. As with all children, the schizophrenic woman's sense of self is produced by interaction. I did not find the Irwin family so bizarre that I could not identify with some aspects of its socialization process. Most of us have probably internalized some sense of the self that is similar to that of Mary Irwin.

This chapter does not speak directly to all issues concerning women. I do not feel that women can be treated as a homogeneous aggregate. Certainly the position of black women cannot be compared to that of white women. Nor can the issue of white women's liberation, with its focus on man as the oppressor, be equally relevant to black women. Although black women, like white women, are subjected to sexism and discrimination, they also are aligned with the struggle of the black male for liberation.

NOTES

1. Roger Brown, *Social Psychology* (New York: Free Press, 1965), pp. 194–95.

2. William James, *The Principles of Psychology Vol. I* (New York: Holt, Rinehart and Winston, 1890).

3. Charles Horton Cooley, *Human Nature and the Social Order* (New York: Schocken Books, 1964), pp. 183–87.

4. George Herbert Mead, *Mind, Self and Society* (Chicago: University of Chicago Press, 1934).

5. Mead, *Mind, Self, and Society*, pp. 140–41.

6. Alice Rossi, "Institutional Levers for Achieving Sex Equality," *Daedalus.*

Cultural Contradictions and Sex Roles

* * *

This article sets forth in detail the nature of certain incompatible sex roles imposed by our society upon the college woman. It is based on data collected in 1942 and 1943. Members of an undergraduate course on the family were asked for two successive years to submit auto-biographical documents focused on the topic; 73 were collected. In addition, 80 interviews, lasting about an hour each, were conducted with every member of a course in social psychology of the same institution—making a total of 153 documents ranging from a minimum of five to a maximum of thirty typewritten pages.

The generalization emerging from these documents is the existence of serious contradictions between two roles present in the social environment of the college woman. The goals set by each role are mutually exclusive, and the fundamental personality traits each evokes are at points diametrically opposed, so that what are assets for one become liabilities for the other, and the full realization of one role threatens defeat in the other.

One of these roles may be termed the "feminine" role. While there are a number of permissive variants of the feminine role for women of college age (the "good sport," the "glamour girl," the "young lady," the domestic "home girl," etc.), they have a common core of attributes defining the proper attitudes to men, family, work, love, etc., and a set of personality traits often described with reference to the male sex role as "not as dominant, or aggressive as men" or "more emotional, sympathetic."

The other and more recent role is, in a sense, no *sex* role at all, because it partly obliterates the differentiation in sex. It demands of the woman much the same virtues, patterns of behavior, and attitude that it does of the men of a corresponding age. We shall refer to this as the "modern" role.

Both roles are present in the social environment of these women throughout their lives, though, as the precise content of each sex role varies with age, so does the nature of their clashes change from one stage to another. In the period under discussion the conflict between the two roles apparently centers about academic work, social life, vocational plans, excellence in specific fields of endeavor, and a number of personality traits.

One manifestation of the problem is in the inconsistency of the goals set for the girl by her family.

Forty, or 26 percent, of the respondents expressed some griev-

Mirra Komarovsky, "Cultural Contradictions and Sex Roles," *American Journal of Sociology* 52 (November 1946): 184–89. Copyright © 1946 by the University of Chicago. Reprinted by permission of the author and the University of Chicago Press.

196 ance against their families for failure to confront them with clearcut and consistent goals. The majority, 74 per cent, denied having had such experiences. One student writes:

> How am I to pursue any course single-mindedly when some way along the line a person I respect is sure to say, "You are on the wrong track and are wasting your time." Uncle John telephones every Sunday morning. His first question is: "Did you go out last night?" He would think me a "grind" if I were to stay home Saturday night to finish a term paper. My father expects me to get an "A" in every subject and is dis-appointed by a "B." He says I have plenty of time for social life. Mother says, "That 'A' in Philosophy is very nice dear. But please don't become so deep that no man will be good enough for you." And, finally, Aunt Mary's line is careers for women. "Prepare yourself for some profession. This is the only way to insure yourself independence and an interesting life. You have plenty of time to marry."

A Senior writes:

> I get a letter from my mother at least three times a week. One week her letters will say, "Remember that this is your last year at college. Subordinate everything to your studies. You must have a good record to secure a job." The next week her letters are full of wedding news. This friend of mine got married; that one is engaged; my young cousin's wedding is only a week off. When, my mother wonders, will I make up my mind? Surely, I wouldn't want to be the only unmarried one in my group. It is high time, she feels, that I give some thought to it.

A student reminisces:

> All through high school my family urged me to work hard because they wished me to enter a first-rate college. At the same time they were always raving about a girl schoolmate who lived next door to us. How pretty and sweet she was, how popular, and what taste in clothes! Couldn't I also pay more attention to my appearance and to social life? They were overlooking the fact that this carefree friend of mine had little time left for school work and had failed several subjects. It seemed that my family had expected me to become Eve Curie and Hedy Lamar wrapped up in one.

Another comments:

> My mother thinks that it is very nice to be smart in college but only if it doesn't take too much effort. She always tells me not to be too intellectual on dates, to be clever in a light sort of way. My father, on the other hand, wants me to study law. He thinks that if I applied myself I could make an excellent lawyer and keeps telling me that I am better fitted for this profession than my brother.

Another writes:

> One of my two brothers writes: "Cover up that high forehead and act a little dumb once in a while"; while the other always urges upon me the importance of rigorous scholarship.

The students testified to a certain bewilderment and confusion caused by the failure on the part of the family to smooth the passage from one role to another, especially when the roles involved were con-tradictory. It seemed to some of them that they had awakened one morning to find their world upside down: what had hitherto evoked praise and rewards from relatives, now suddenly aroused censure. A **197** student recollects:

I could match my older brother in skating, sledding, riflery, ball, and many of the other games we played. He enjoyed teaching me and took great pride in my accomplishments. Then one day it all changed. He must have suddenly become conscious of the fact that girls ought to be feminine. I was walking with him, proud to be able to make long strides and keep up with his long-legged steps when he turned to me in annoyance, "Can't you walk like a lady?" I still remember feeling hurt and bewildered by his scorn, when I had been led to expect approval.

Once during her freshman year in college, after a delightful date, a student wrote her brother with great elation:

"What a wonderful evening at ———— fraternity house! You would be proud of me, Johnny! I won all ping-pong games but one!"
"For heavens sake," came the reply, "when will you grow up? Don't you know that a boy likes to think he is better than a girl? Give him a little competition, sure, but miss a few serves in the end. Should you join the Debate Club? By all means, but don't practice too much on the boys." Believe me I was stunned by this letter, but then I saw that he was right. To be a success in the dorms one must date, to date one must not win too many ping-pong games. At first I resented this bitterly. But now I am more or less used to it and live in hope of one day meeting a man who is my superior so that I may be my natural self.

It is the parents and not the older sibling who reversed their expectations in the following excerpt:

All through grammar school and high school my parents led me to feel that to do well in school was my chief responsibility. A good report card, an election to student office, these were the news Mother bragged about in telephone conversations with her friends. But recently they suddenly got worried about me: I don't pay enough attention to social life, a woman needs *some* education but not that much. They are disturbed by my determination to go to the School of Social Work. Why my ambitions should surprise them after they have exposed me for four years to some of the most inspired and stimulating social scientists in the country, I can't imagine. They have some mighty strong arguments on their side. What is the use, they say, of investing years in training for a profession, only to drop it in a few years? Chances of meeting men are slim in this profession. Besides, I may become so preoccupied with it as to sacrifice my social life. The next few years are, after all, the proper time to find a mate. But the urge to apply what I have learned, and the challenge of this profession is so strong that I shall go on despite the family opposition.

The final excerpt illustrates both the sudden transition of roles and the ambiguity of standards:

198

I major in English composition. This is not a completely "approved" field for girls so I usually just say "English." An English Literature major is quite liked and approved by boys. Somehow it is lumped with all the other arts and even has a little glamour. But a composition major is a girl to beware of because she supposedly will notice all your grammar mistakes, look at your letters too critically, and consider your ordinary speech and conversation as too crude.

I also work for a big metropolitan daily as a correspondent in the city room. I am well liked there and may possibly stay as a reporter after graduation in February. I have had several spreads (stories running to more than eight or ten inches of space), and this is considered pretty good for a college correspondent. Naturally, I was elated and pleased at such breaks, and as far as the city room is concerned I'm off to a very good start on a career that is hard for a man to achieve and even harder for a woman. General reporting is still a man's work in the opinion of most people. I have a lot of acclaim but also criticism, and I find it confusing and difficult to be praised for being clever and working hard and then, when my efforts promise to be successful, to be condemned and criticized for being unfeminine and ambitious.

Here are a few of these reactions:

My father: "I don't like this newspaper setup at all. The people you meet are making you less interested in marriage than ever. You're getting too educated and intellectual to be attractive to men."

My mother: "I don't like your attitude toward people. The paper is making you too analytical and calculating. Above all, you shouldn't sacrifice your education and career for marriage."

A lieutenant with two years of college: "It pleased me greatly to hear about your news assignment—good girl."

A Navy pilot with one year of college: "Undoubtedly, I'm old fashioned, but I could never expect to feel right about a girl giving up a very promising or interesting future to hang around waiting for me to finish college. Nevertheless, congratulations on your job on the paper. Where in the world do you get that wonderful energy? Anyway I know you were thrilled at getting it and feel very glad for you. I've an idea that it means the same to you as that letter saying 'report for active duty' meant to me."

A graduate metallurgist now a private in the Army: "It was good to hear that you got that break with the paper. I am sure that talent will prove itself and that you will go far. But not too far, as I don't think you should become a career woman. You'll get repressed and not be interested enough in having fun if you keep after that career."

A lieutenant with a year and a half of college: "All this career business is nonsense. A woman belongs in the home and absolutely no place else. My wife will have to stay home. That should keep her happy. Men are just superior in everything, and women have no right to expect to compete with them. They should do just what will keep their husbands happy."

A graduate engineer—my fiance: "Go right ahead and get as far as you can in your field. I am glad you are ambitious and clever, and I'm as anxious to see you happily successful as I am myself. It is a shame to let all those brains go to waste over just dusting and washing dishes. I think the usual home life and children are small sacrifices to make if a career will keep you happy. But I'd rather see you in radio because I am a bit wary of the effect upon our marriage of the way of life you will have around the newspaper."

Sixty-one, or 40 percent, of the students indicated that they have occasionally "played dumb" on dates, that is, concealed some academic honor, pretended ignorance of some subject, or allowed the man the last word in an intellectual discussion. Among these were women who "threw games" and in general played down certain skills in obedience to the unwritten law that men must possess these skills to a superior degree. At the same time, in other areas of life, social pressures were being exerted upon these women to "play to win," to compete to the utmost of their abilities for intellectual distinction and academic honors. One student writes:

I was glad to transfer to a women's college. The two years at the co-ed university produced a constant strain. I am a good student; my family expects me to get good marks. At the same time I am normal enough to want to be invited to the Saturday night dance. Well, everyone knew that on campus a reputation of a "brain" killed a girl socially. I was always fearful lest I say too much in class or answer a question which the boys I dated couldn't answer.

Here are some significant remarks made from the interviews:

When a girl asks me what marks I got last semester I answer, "Not so good—only one 'A'," When a boy asks the same question, I say very brightly with a note of surprise, "Imagine, I got an 'A!'"

I am engaged to a southern boy who doesn't think too much of the woman's intellect. In spite of myself, I play up to his theories because the less one knows and does, the more he does for you and thinks you "cute" into the bargain. . . . I allow him to explain things to me in great detail and to treat me as a child in financial matters.

One of the nicest techniques is to spell long words incorrectly once in a while. My boy-friend seems to get a great kick out of it and writes back, "Honey, you certainly don't know how to spell."

When my date said that he considers Ravel's *Bolero* the greatest piece of music ever written, I changed the subject because I knew I would talk down to him.

A boy advised me not to tell of my proficiency in math and not to talk of my plans to study medicine unless I knew my date well.

My fiance didn't go to college. I intend to finish college and work hard at it, but in talking to him I make college appear a kind of a game.

Once I went sailing with a man who so obviously enjoyed the role of a protector that I told him I didn't know how to sail. As it turned out he didn't either. We got into a tough spot, and I was torn between a desire to get hold of the boat and a fear to reveal that I had lied to him.

It embarrassed me that my "steady" in high school got worse marks than I. A boy should naturally do better in school. I would never tell him my marks and would often ask him to help me with my homework.

I am better in math than my fiance. But while I let him explain politics to me, we never talk about math even though, being a math major, I could tell him some interesting things.

Mother used to tell me to lay off the brains on dates because glasses make me look too intellectual anyhow.

I was once at a work camp. The girls did the same work as the boys.

200

If some girls worked better the boys resented it fiercely. The director told one capable girl to slow down to keep peace in the group.

How to do the job and remain popular was a tough task. If you worked your best, the boys resented the competition; if you acted feminine, they complained that you were clumsy.

On dates I always go through the "I-don't-care-anything-you-want-to-do" routine. It gets monotonous but boys fear girls who make decisions. They think such girls would make nagging wives.

I am a natural leader and, when in the company of girls, usually take the lead. That is why I am so active in college activities. But I know that men fear bossy women, and I always have to watch myself on dates not to assume the "executive" role. Once a boy walking to the theater with me took the wrong street. I knew a short cut but kept quiet.

I let my fiance make most of the decisions when we are out. It annoys me, but he prefers it.

I sometimes "play dumb" on dates, but it leaves a bad taste. The emontions are complicated. Part of me enjoys "putting something over" on the unsuspecting male. But this sense of superiority over him is mixed with feeling of guilt for my hypocrisy. Toward the "date" I feel some contempt because he is "taken in" by my technique, or if I like the boy, a kind of a maternal condescension. At times I resent him! Why isn't he my superior in all ways in which a man should excel so that I could be my natural self? What am I doing here with him, anyhow? Slumming?

And the funny part of it is that the man, I think, is not always so unsuspecting. He may sense the truth and become uneasy in the relation. "Where do I stand? Is she laughing up her sleeve or did she mean this praise? Was she really impressed with that little speech of mine or did she only pretend to know nothing about politics?" And once or twice I felt that the joke was on me: the boy saw through my wiles and felt contempt for me for stooping to such tricks.

Another aspect of the problem is the conflict between the psychogenetic personality of the girl and the cultural role foisted upon her by the milieu.[1] At times it is the girl with "masculine" interests and personality traits who chafes under the pressure to conform to the "feminine" pattern. At other times it is the family and the college who thrusts upon the reluctant girl the "modern" role.

While, historically, the "modern" role is the most recent one, ontogenetically it is the one emphasized earlier in the education. of the college girl, if these 153 documents are representative. Society confronts the girl with powerful challenges and strong pressure to excel in certain competitive lines of endeavor and to develop certain techniques of adaptations very similar to those expected of her brothers. But, then, quite suddenly as it appears to these girls, the very success in meeting these challenges begins to cause anxiety. It is precisely those most successful in the earlier role who are now penalized.

It is not only the passage from age to age but the moving to another region or type of campus which may create for the girl similar problems. The precise content of sex roles, or, to put it in another way, the degree of their differentiation, varies with regional class, nativity, and other subcultures.

NOTES

1. Margaret Mead, *Sex and Temperament in Three Primitive Societies* (New York: Morrow & Co., 1935).

MARGARET M. POLOMA AND T. NEAL GARLAND

The Married Professional Woman: A Study in the Tolerance of Domestication

The 1960s have produced reams of research documenting the discrimination against employed women in American society. Data from the U.S. Department of Labor provide the "hard facts" of salary differentials, unemployment figures, and the clustering of women workers in lower paying jobs. Perhaps the most sophisticated research on the topic, however, has been done on the professionally employed woman. Women academicians, using the tools of their trade, have demonstrated the inequities existing in their profession.[1] Through the research of Epstein (1968) in law and Kaplan (1970) in medicine, the lack of equality for women in these professions has been exposed. Newspaper accounts of "first women" to break the barriers of previously all-male professions have become frequent during the late 1960s and into the 1970s, thus illustrating well the vast number of occupations from which women have been excluded. The facts supposedly speak for themselves; women do not have employment rights equal to those of men. Depending on the stance of the accusor, the villain is either well-meaning (or not-so-well-meaning) males or the capitalistic economic system bent on exploitation.

The vast majority of the articles and books dealing with discrimination against women in our society, however, present an incomplete thesis. While sexism is the reported cause of the unequal treatment, this is only a partial explanation. It does not explain why women themselves are often reluctant to accept the research findings reported on discrimination and why many women themselves deny ever being victim to discriminatory practices—a phenomenon that we will treat during the course of this paper. We wish to argue that

Margaret M. Poloma and T. Neal Garland, "The Married Professional Woman: A Study in the Tolerance of Domestication," *Journal of Marriage and the Family* (August 1971). Reprinted by permission of the authors and *National Council on Family Relations*.

202

underlying the discriminatory evidence uncovered by researchers is an institution of our society that most are very reluctant to attack— the institution of our family system. It is the family that stands in the way of a woman's career advancement and is perhaps a major reason for employers discriminating against women.[2] The demands of home and family make it impossible for married women (and the majority of employed women, both professionals and nonprofessionals, are married) to compete with their male colleagues who are not burdened with the daily routine of homemaking. Moreover, as we shall attempt to document later, research evidence is strong that the young single girl, being constrained by a traditionally ideal image of sex roles, is fettered by the marital institution long before she says "I do."

The thesis that marriage provides a form of captivity for the woman, of course, is not new. Both Karl Marx and Frederick Engels denounced the evils of the traditional family, but both felt that the capitalistic system ironically would create the conditions for its deterioration through the employment of women outside the home. While presumably changes in the economic system have allowed women greater freedom in accord with Engels and Marx's prediction, the question of equality remains an open one. In spite of the many changes in the social system, marriage continues to be the thread tying the dove to capitivity—a thread, as we shall observe, that many women are reluctant to sever. As de Beauvoir (1952:452–53) has astutely noted:

Many young households give the impression of being on the basis of perfect equality. But as long as the man retains economic responsibility for the couple, this is only an illusion. It is he who decides where they will live, according to the demands of his work; she follows him from city to country or vice versa, to distant possessions, to foreign countries; their standard of living is set according to his income; the daily, weekly, annual rhythms are set by his occupation; associations and friendships most often depend upon his profession ... But the basic inequity still lies in the fact that the husband finds concrete self-realization in his work and action, whereas for the wife, as such, liberty has only a negative aspect. ...

Marriage for the modern married woman (and a young single woman's hopes, plans, and aspirations of achieving marital bliss) continues to make a career undesirable for vast numbers of American women. Poloma and Garland (1971) have demonstrated how the professionally employed women in their study, by and large, had "jobs" without having the demands and commitments of "careers." Powers, et al. (1969) study of women physicians reveals that married respondents worked fewer hours than their single sisters, and both groups of women practiced fewer hours than their male colleagues. While Simon (1967, 230–31) found that the women Ph.D. in their study were as productive as their male counterparts, nearly a quarter of their female respondents with children were employed only on a part-time basis and another 16 percent were not employed at all. Almost all those who worked part-time rather than full-time indicated that they preferred it this way because of family responsibilities. Only 6 percent of the unemployed women claimed they were unable to find positions. McFarlane's (1968), Tropman's (1968) and Lewin's (1962) studies all underscore the desire of married social workers for part-time jobs rather than full-time careers.

This same theme is evident in research done on career aspirations of high-school girls and college coeds. Almquist and Angrist's (1970; Angrist, 1970) recent research on young coeds indicates an inverse relationship between career plans and romantic attachments. Their longitudinal four-year study revealed that a girl who had strong career aspirations before meeting the man of her life was likely to show a waning interest in career possibilities after becoming pinned or engaged. Ademek (1970:98), in a review of similar literature on college coeds and career commitment, observes:

Women thus seem oriented to adapting to men rather than to themselves. They generally perceive men, moreover, as valuing women who conform to the traditional female role. Perhaps reacting to this perception, most college women appear to be basically marriage and family oriented and plan their college programs with this in mind. Even the "career oriented" tend to drift toward marriage interests as they near graduation, both at the high school and college level.

Yet in spite of the adverse effect marriage and prospects of marriage have on a woman's career, marriage is rarely seen as the villain barring the road to complete feminine equality. Contemporary writers who have been willing to point out this relationship appear to be few in number. O'Neill (1969) in his excellent treatment of the "rise and fall of feminism" attributes the first feminist movement's demise to the unwillingness or inability of feminist groups to see the need for drastic changes in the institution of marriage. Rather, the achievement of suffrage was viewed by many as an end goal. A noteworthy exception were the socialists, who being steeped in the writings of Marx and Engels, preached the need to alter the family system. But the socialists and other writers (such as Charlotte Perkins Gilman) who attacked hearth and home were seen as extreme radicals" and as harmful to the success of the movement. To some extent, we find history repeating itself today. A large segment of the new feminist movement appears to be moderate, with a "Betty Frieden" bent. These members protest the inequities of the system but are reluctant to point an accusing finger at the institution of marriage. At best they attempt patch-up work (e.g., calling for child-care centers), but are unwilling to demand the drastic changes in the family system that are essential for complete equality. Only the so-called radical feminists have been willing to indict our present man-woman relationships.[3] Under the rebel leader Ti-Grace Atkinson, one such group, The Feminists have seriously discussed the notion that "marriage is slavery." Atkinson's disciple, Shelia Cronan, in writing on marriage proclaimed:

Since marriage constitutes slavery for women, it is clear that the Women's Movement must concentrate on attacking this institution.

Freedom for women cannot be won without the abolition of marriage. Attack on such issues as employment discrimination is superfluous. . ."

Admittedly a vast majority of American women would not accept this strong admonition of our marital institution. Social scientists, however, should be willing to probe beneath the rhetoric of radical indictments of marriage in an attempt to better understand the relationship between marriage and a woman's equality in the occupational world. The handicap that marriage places on a woman's career must be viewed as part of the total perspective in studying and discussing women in American society.

FEMALE TOLERANCE OF DOMESTICATION

After hypothesizing that the traditional institution of marriage was an underlying basis for the fall of the feminist movement and that sexual equality in fact means "revolutionizing our domestic life," O'Neill (1969:358) cautiously adds, "Perhaps we do not want it, do not need it, and should not have it. Nonetheless, such a revolution is what equality presupposes." Evidence is strong that vast numbers of women in our society are not ready for such a revolution. What we are attempting to do in this article is to insure that the marital dimension becomes part of future writings on discrimination. Van den Berghe (1970:376) observed well (and courageously) when he stated

Women get screwed, but married women get doubly screwed, if you will pardon the *double entendre*. And, at the risk of exciting the ire of my female colleagues, I suggest that a good part of the trouble is that so many women like it, or at least play the game rather than buck the system. By that I mean that they let themselves become domesticated and follow their husband's movements. I am not defending the male academic establishing, but I am saying, that we academics cannot be blamed qua academics for the part of the sex differential which is due to what we may call female tolerance of domestication.

The implication of van den Berghe's "tolerance of domestication" goes far beyond the academic world. Empirically it can be demonstrated from data that we have secured in our study of the dual profession family. In a recent study of 53 couples in which the wife was a practicing physician, college professor, or attorney, we found little evidence that women desire full equality—if equality means performing on an equal footing with their husbands and holding a man's *responsibility* for achieving career success. Three findings that have bearing on van den Berghe's "tolerance of domestication" will be dealt with: (1) the lack of egalitarian family structures among the couples we studied; (2) the fact that most of our female respondents had jobs and not careers; and (3) attitudes of the female respondents on the issue of discrimination. The first two points have been dealt with elsewhere and will only be briefly reviewed here;[4] the third issue will be treated in greater detail.

The Myth of the Egalitarian Family

While the notion of the egalitarian family has been popularized through family text books, its actual existence remains to be proven (Safilios-Rothschild, 1969:3). Only one case of our 53 couples interviewed could be classified as a truly egalitarian family—a family form which we feel is essential to allow the married professional woman the opportunity for equal achievement and advancement. This case consisted of two professors who made a conscious effort to *share* (not merely *help*) in both traditionally male and female role tasks. Both considered it their *responsibility* to cook, clean, and care for the children. More important, both considered it their responsibility to provide for the family's economic needs; and under no circumstances, was the husband's career deemed more important than the wife's. In all other cases, the wife was *responsible* for the traditional feminine tasks (although usually the husband did "help" in varying degrees) while her husband was *responsible* for providing the family with status and income.[5] While the degree of responsibilities and helping varied greatly from the traditional (i.e., extremely sex-segregated in terms of familial responsibilities) to the neo-traditional categories (i.e., couples in which the husband and wife freely assisted each other with the other's traditionally sex-determined family obligations), the fact remains that only one couple could be classified as egalitarian. Our data yield no indication that either men or women desired to see an equal *sharing* of both masculine and feminine role tasks in the family. Wives (so long as their husbands were able to provide adequately) preferred not to *have to* work in the same ways as their husbands did, leaving the provider role and its corresponding rights and duties as his domain. In return, they accepted their prime responsibility in the area of homemaking and child care.

Career or Jobs?

While more and more American women are demonstrating that it is possible to combine *work* and marriage, there is no evidence that they are in a position to combine a *career* with marital obligations. Our data indicate that even among highly trained professional women, a "career" in the sense of being "personally salient," "having a developmental sequence," and having a "high degree of commitment" (Rapoport and Rapoport, 1969:3) may not be widespread among American married women. Most of the women in our sample (especially those with children) did not want "career" responsibilities. The priority of the wife and mother role over professional obligations was expressed over and over in differing ways by the majority of the respondents. A physician working in the academic world stated:

I have succeeded in doing what I want to do—in fact, having achieved academically an assistant professorship. I am rather sure that I do not want any more responsibility. When I was asked to be chairman of our department, I decided this was the kind of thing that would be very difficult for me to balance with my home and marriage responsibilities, so I turned it down.

206   The respondents were aware of the fact that marriage, and especially children, limited their professional involvement, but they appeared content with the situation the way it was. In exchange for the limitations placed on their career by home and family demands, these wives had financial security provided by their husbands as breadwinners, while the women themselves enjoyed the option of working or not working. One female physician expressed it in the following way:

> This is where I feel that the woman has the tremendous advantage.
> You can choose what you want to do; and if you don't like doing it,
> you can stop. You don't have a family to feed.

Some women in our sample did have careers in the fullest sense of the term, but they usually started out as simply working in a profession, often on a part-time basis, in the capacity of a volunteer, or from their homes. One very successful academician divided her work history into the "job" stage and the "career" stage, the latter coming to be when her children were launched and coinciding with the publication of a very successful book. A few respondents moved from a "career" to a "job" or the discontinuance of work completely depending on the stage and the corresponding demands of the family life cycle. For example, at least three respondents who were "career-oriented" at this stage of the family cycle will undoubtedly modify their professional involvement as the family increases in size.

PERCEPTION OF DISCRIMINATION

With mounting evidence that women as a group have not achieved a position comparable to men, we were surprised to find that the vast majority of our respondents did not feel that they personally had met with any discriminatory practices. Thirty-seven of the 53 women interviewed gave an unqualified "no" to inquiries as to whether they had met with problems in their professions—all of which could be sex-typed as male professions. Many of these women were willing to admit that discrimination may exist, but expressed their conviction that they had never felt inequity's sting. A young and successful attorney observed:

> I really haven't felt any discrimination. I know that some women have,
> but if you really narrow it down, they are the older women. They com-
> plain of discrimination. I am not saying that there isn't any, but I haven't
> felt it.

Another young resident pathologist admitted that some men are against women training for the medical practice; but again, she refused to see herself as an object of discrimination.

> There are a few men who feel that women shouldn't be in medical
> school because they are likely not to use their training, but I am not
> sure you can call this "discrimination"—this is just their feeling based
> on the facts they observe. But then you sometimes have the feeling
> that things are the other way around and that the instructors are easier
> on women than on men students.

Many of the women expressed the belief that only the "unfeminine" women in their professions (i.e., the one who swears, takes no interest in her appearance, is overly demanding) have problems of discrimination. A young physician observed:

207

I am sure the person makes the difference. You have various personalities among women physicians as you have in any situation. I guess I always preferred being treated like a woman first and a physician second. Maybe that has made all the difference.

While the vast majority of the women who expressed the belief that they personally had not experienced discrimination were willing to accept the position that some women have problems, a few refused to see discrimination in this light. Some expressed the belief that incompetence is discriminated against—not the competent woman. A nationally known academic woman stated emphatically:

I have very little patience with those who are constantly trying to document discrimination against women. In the professional world, I don't see it.

The most severe protests regarding discrimination seemed to come from academic women—especially over both the official and unofficial nepotism rules they have encountered. Of the 16 who complained of some form of discrimination, nine were in academia. One young academic woman observed:

I think that initially my salary had a very important skirt differential in it, but I think that has changed over time and is no longer the case. If a woman wants to make it in a field dominated by men, she has got to make it in her 20s or she will never be taken seriously.

Three of the five second-career women (i.e., women who earned their Ph.D.'s after their children were grown) in academia claimed to experience some form of discrimination in the form of salaries and promotions, lending some empirical support to this young academic's observation.

Yet it should be pointed out that nearly all of the respondents who complained of discrimination had made numerous sacrifices in behalf of their marriages at the expense of their careers. These included taking part-time positions at some stage of the work history, relinquishing fellowships and scholarships, turning down a chairmanship, or being unable to accept another tempting job offer in another location because of the husband's career. Yet, of those who did perceive discrimination, few were willing to blame the institution of marriage for the problems they faced in their professions. The young woman quoted above who had felt the "skirt differential" in her salary had left an Ivy League school to marry and had to finish her Ph.D. at a much less prestigious institution. A lawyer who indicated that her salary was not as good as her male colleagues presently puts in fewer hours and ceased work completely for over two years at one point of

208   the family life cycle. A new Ph.D. in history found it difficult to get a suitable position—but she did obtain a position (which is more than some of her male colleagues were able to achieve in the tight labor market) in spite of the fact that, due to her husband's work, she could not leave the area. We would suggest that these cases (and we could cite many others) are not so much due to discrimination on the part of the employment structure as it is due to the family structure.

The reluctance of women to admit being victim to discriminatory practices was also noted by Epstein (1968:167) in her study of women attorneys:

> We found that regardless of the reality of discrimination, two-thirds of the sample did *not* feel they had been discriminated against in job hunting; 67 percent said they had no difficulty in getting their first job and only one-quarter reported encountering difficulties in their first efforts to find jobs.

Why the incongruity between statistics on discrimination and a woman's perception of discrimination? Many might argue that a woman's consciousness has not been sufficiently raised—that discriminatory practices are numerous but that a woman is unwilling to see herself as a victim. Perhaps. More likely, however, a woman has been socialized to tolerate domestication and she realizes that this may cost something in terms of career success. Yet, our respondents perceived themselves as having the best of two worlds: both of the professional world and of domestic life. Statistics on discrimination are unable to present the women who accept low-paying jobs (such as in family planning clinics or in small private schools) precisely because they are in a position to accept only work which they enjoy. An academic woman provides a good example of this phenomenon—one that we encountered a number of times.

> I think there may be some financial discrimination against women, but I am not even sure that's a discrimination really. For example, I can work at a job that pays less because I really enjoy it, because I have a husband who can support the family. . . I have taken jobs when they interested me, which a person who had to support a family couldn't have taken because the pay was so low. But the low pay was there; it wasn't changed because I was a woman.

The statistics on discrimination do not discriminate situations such as these. In a way, it could be said that married women are in a position to be the last of the genteel professions[6]—and many of them are unwilling to sacrifice this freedom for the cardiac condition or ulcers that their husbands may be cultivating. They can accept a position because they find the work challenging, exciting, or philanthropic—without worry about pay.

Nor do the statistics on discrimination show the professor who declines a chairmanship because it interferes with her familial obligations, the professional who is employed (or was employed) on a part-time basis in order to accommodate her family, the physician who refuses the directorship of a clinic because the demands of her children are perceived to be too great, or the woman who interrupts her career for five, ten, or more years while her children are young. Yet these are the kinds of situations encountered in varying degrees during the career histories of almost all of our respondents. Could it be that some women are reluctant to complain of discrimination because they themselves realize their professional involvement is not directly analogous to their male colleagues'? It would appear that if anything were to "blame", it would be the familial institution in our present culture—and this is something that our respondents were unwilling to alter.

SUMMARY AND CONCLUSION

Much has been written exposing the discrimination which exists against women who are employed in high-status positions of the professional world. We have suggested that some (although certainly not all) of the problem stems from the structure and both the ideal and real demands made on a woman by our present family system. Women have beeen socialized "to tolerate domestication." The vast majority of the female respondents in our study of the dual-career family certainly bore out this contention. They, for the most part, expressed great satisfaction in being able to combine marriage and a career, with the family role as the salient one and the professional role as supportive in the hole hierarchy. To our surprise, this attitude was no different on the part of the women 25 to 30 years of age from those 50 and over.

Merton's (1949:122) "fallacy of group soliloquies" points out that there is a certain danger when liberals talk only with liberals. In a like vein, it is misleading when advocates of complete feminine emancipation talk only to each other; it easily results in a faulty line of attack. Women have been socialized to accept marriage and the family as a primary goal, and the professional women in our sample were no exception. While very few perceived any conflict between marriage and their professional activities, most explained it in terms of making professional demands and aspirations secondary to the needs of the family. Moreover, they expressed great satisfaction with the status quo as they experienced it.

Of course, sexism on the part of employers and fellow workers alike does exist, but it is only part of the problem. An even greater barrier in the road to complete femine equality exists in the ideology and structure of our family system—a fact which many women have been unwilling to face, or which they have faced, and decided in favor of the family.

NOTES

1. For a selected bibliography on the status of women in American higher education, *see* Harris (1970) "The Second Sex in Academe." Worthy of special note is Bernard (1964) *Academic Women*, Epstein (1970 *Woman's Place: Options and Limits on Professional Careers*, and Astin (1970) *The Woman Doctorate.*

2. Vast differences exist between the problems of professionally employed women who are able to derive both intrinsic and extrinsic rewards from their

positions and women employed in jobs of lesser status and rewards. Many writers have proven themselves oblivious to the nature of their employed working-class sisters' needs. Joan Jordon (1970), herself a working woman who was automated out of her job, has been one of the few writers who demonstrates a solid knowledge and understanding of the working-class employed woman's problems. The present paper makes no pretense of dealing with *all* working women. Its thesis was designed primarily with the high-status professionally employed woman in mind.

3. For a discussion of the various feminist organizations from The Pussycat League to W.I.T.C.H. and other radical groups, see Ellis (1970) *Revolt of the Second Sex.*

4. For a discussion of "Jobs or Careers?" see Poloma and Garland (1971a). The presentation on "The Myth of the Egalitarian Family" by the same authors (1971b) was also presented at the 65th Annual Meeting of the American Sociological Association, September 1, 1970,

5. The exceptions to this statement were the five cases which were classified as "matriarchal." In these couples, the wife's income was essential for the solidly middle-class standing, making it imperative for the wives to work. For the most part, these women resented the compulsion they felt in having to pursue a profession. They wished that either they could reduce their work to part-time positions or that they could cease working entirely.

6. In discussing our findings informally, Professor Warren Breed suggested the comparison of married women professionals with the gentility found in the professions in an earlier era. We felt this analogy was most intriguing and worthy of further study and consideration.

REFERENCES

Almquist, Elizabeth M. and Shirley S. Angrist. "Career Salience and Atypicality of Occupational Choice Among College Women." *The Journal of Marriage and the Family* 32 (May 1970) : 242–49.

Angrist, Shirley S. "Changes in Women's Work Aspirations During College (or Work Does Not Equal a Career)." Paper presented at the Ohio Valley Sociological Society Meeting, Akron, May 1970.

Adamek, Raymond J. "College Major, Work Commitment and Female Perceptions of Self, Ideal Woman, and Men's Ideal Woman." Social Forces 3 (Summer 1970) : 97–112.

Astin, Helen. *The Woman Doctorate.* Basic Books, 1970.

Bernard, Jessie. *Academic Women.* Pennsylvania State University, 1964.

Cronan, Shelia. "Marriage." *The Feminists.* 120 Liberty Street. New York, New York 10006.

Epstein, Cynthia Fuchs. The Case of the Woman Lawyer. Unpublished Ph.D. Dissertation. Columbia University, 1968.
Woman's Place: Options and Limits in Professional Careers. University of California Press, 1970.

Ellis, Julie. *Revolt of the Second Sex.* Lancer. New York, 1970.

Kaplan, Harold I. "Women Physicians: The More Effective Recruitment and Utilization of Their Talents and the Resistance to It—The Final Conclusions of a Seven-Year Study." *Woman Physician* 25 (September 1970).

Harris, Ann Sutherland. The Second Sex in Academe." *AAUP Bulletin* 56 (September 1970) : 283–95.

Jordan, Joan. "Comment: Working Women and the Equal Rights Amendment." *Trans*-action 8 (November/December 1970) : 16–22.

Lewin, Thomas F. "The Employment Experience of Married Women Social Caseworkers: A Study of One Hundred Graduates of the

New York School of Social Work, Columbia University." Unpublished doctoral dissertation. University of Chicago, 1965.

McFarlane, Patricia. "A Study of the Work Patterns of Selected Married Women Social Workers from thhe Columbia University School of Social Work." Unpublished master's thesis, University of Washington, 1968.

Merton, Robert K. "Discrimination and the American Creed." In *Discrimination and National Welfare*, R. M. MacIver, ed. New York (Harper) : 99–126.

O'Neill, William. *Everyone Was Brave: The Rise and Fall of Feminism.* Chicago: Quadrangle Books (1969).

Poloma, Margaret, and T. Neal Garland. "Job or Careers? The Case of the Professionally Employed Married Woman." In Andree' Michel, ed. special issue of the *International Journal of Comparative Sociology on Family Issues of Employed Women,* 1971.

"The Myth of the Egalitarian Family: Familial Roles and the Professionally Employed Wife." In Athena Theodore, *The Professional Woman* (Schenkman Publishing Co., 1971, forthcoming).

Powers, Lee; Rexford D. Parmelle; and Harry Wissenfelder. "Practice Patterns of Women and Men Physicians." *Journal of Medical Education* 44 (June 1970) : 481–85.

Rapoport, Rhona, and Robert Rapoport. "The Dual-Career Family: A Variant Pattern and Social Change." *Human Relations* 22 (February 1970) : 3–30.

Safilios-Rothschild, Constantina. "Marital Expectations and Marital Experience: Why Such a Discrepancy." Paper read at the ICOFA Meetings in Rennes, France, April 3–7, 1969.

Simon, Rita James; Shirley M. Clark; and Kathleen Galway. "The Woman Ph.D.: A Recent Profile." *Social Problems* 15 (1967) : 221–36.

Tropman, John E. "The Married Professional Social Worker." *Journal of Marriage and the Family* 30 (November 1968) : 661–65.

van den Berghe, Pierre L. "The Two Roles of Women." *American Sociologist* 5 (November 1970) : 375–76.

The Irwins

CLINICAL PERSPECTIVE

Mary is twenty. She is a plump, attractive girl, whose actions and words are slow and carefully chosen.

Her illness had followed the typical dementia praecox sequence. She had apparently been well until fifteen. Then she began to lose interest in her work at school and lost her position in class.

She had previously been happy and social. She became morose, and gave up her friends.

On leaving school, she could not decide what she wanted to do, but with prompting went into an office. She held the job for two years, then left because of lack of interest. Thereafter she did not want to do anything, but with prompting took another job. She was sacked after three months for incompetence. Over the next nine months she was sacked from two more jobs for the same reason. Shortly afterwards she was admitted to hospital for the first time.

About the time she left school she developed various 'habits', such as sniffing and coughing. She would sit or stand still for over an hour at a time. Later, in hospital, she would sniff, cough, or grimace, and sit or stand motionless unless prompted to move.

When seen by us she was being re-admitted for the third time, having spent twenty-two months of the previous twenty-four in two other mental hospitals.

During her stays in hospital, she had been in seclusion, had gained a reputation for smashing in states of catatonic excitement, hand been tranquillized by daily electro-shocks, and 'maintained' by electro-shocks and Stelazine.

Since her illness her parents found her to be unmanageable at home. Although they wanted her to get better, they felt unable to cope with her illness until she had made a "reasonable recovery."

The list of schizophrenic symptoms and signs included thought-blocking and over-inclusion, vagueness, speculative woolly thinking about the meaning of life, inability to face life's difficulties and aggressively to overcome them.

Emotional apathy and effective-cognitive incongruence were noted, and delusions of persecution, for example, that her mother was killing her mind, were also found.

Her emotional apathy was said suddenly to give way to accesses of senseless and uncontrolled excitement and violence.

Various stereotyped movements, grimacing, catatonic immo-

R. D. Laing and Aaron Esterson, "The Irwins," from *Sanity, Madness and the Family*. Reprinted by permission of the publisher Tavistock Publications Limited.

bility, negativsm, occasional mild flexibilitas cerea, automatic obedience, and so on, were also recorded.

Her family history was negative, and no relationship was felt
to exist between her various symptoms and her environment.

This case is particularly interesting in that the girl had been
investigated especially closely from a clinical psychiatric point of
view, because of a suspected encephalitic illness pre-dating the first
psychotic manifestations. These investigations were negative for organic findings.

Her parents' view of this girl as "ill" was essentially congruent
with the clinical psychiatric gestalt.

We shall here present a radically different gestalt, in which
the *attribution* of illness becomes socially intelligible. We shall see
how this attributed illness comes to be taken as a fact, and how she
is treated accordingly. Such is the spell cast by the make-believe of
everyone treating her as if she were ill, that one has constantly to
pinch oneself to remind oneself that there is no evidence to substantiate this assumption, except the actions of the others, who by acting
in terms of this assumption conjure up a feeling of conviction that the
experience and actions in question are the unintelligible outcome of
process, rather than the entirely intelligible expression of Mary's
praxis, in a social field where her position is untenable and where
her "moves" (her praxis) are explained on the presumption that they
are generated by a mysterious, indubitable, yet indefinable pathological process.

Once more, we have to show to what extent the experiences
and actions that are taken to be symptoms and signs of organic or
psychic pathological process are explicable as social praxis within the
context of the praxis-process of the social system of her family.

Here, as before, we are putting entirely in parenthesis the
validity of any attributions of illness.

We shall review the experiences and behavior of Mary, as
seen through the eyes of her mother, father, older sister, psychiatrists,
nurses, and ourselves; and, finally, as seen through the eyes of Mary
herself.

*   *   *

THE FAMILY SITUATION

According to her father, the trouble began when Mary was fifteen.
She had always been very meek and cooperative, but then she
started to question her parents and to show lack of respect for them.
She became defiant.

INTERVIEWER: What was the first thing you can remember her being
defiant over?

FATHER: Well one thing that sticks in my mind was—she was always
very well-behaved and suchlike you know, and she came home from
school this day—the children had to ask the teacher questions, and
she'd asked the teacher if he thought it was right that teachers

should be allowed to smack the children—something to that effect anyway it was—as her mate the day before had been smacked you know, at school. Well I was surprised at Mary's sticking up for that. You'd never have thought she would do anything like that before.

INTERVIEWER: Say such a thing?

FATHER: Yes.

INTERVIEWER: She told you this—that she'd said?

FATHER: Aye, she came home like and she told us. We never said anything at the time, but it just stuck in my mind at the time.

INTERVIEWER: You were quite surprised?

FATHER: I was. I was very surprised at it, because she was always so very meek and well-behaved. There's nothing wrong with that I suppose, but it was a bit impertinent to the teacher like.

This was the start. Then things went from "bad" to "worse." They thought she might just be obstinate and stubborn, but the 'real start of it' was when she left school.

INTERVIEWER: Well what was happening then?

FATHER: Well I think she used to pick her head first of all, and she was always told to stop picking her head—that was the first thing. And she would sit and waggle her foot, you know—these sort of things, and she seemed to sort of do everything to try and annoy you. That was the start of it.

INTERVIEWER: Like picking her head and waggling her foot?

FATHER: Yes. She was told to stop but she wouldn't do it—sniffing when you spoke to her (sniffs twice). That's another thing you see.

Her father, however, has not got as good a memory as his wife. We have to place her mother's view in the context of her picture of herself and Mary since Mary was born. She feels that she and Mary were an ideal couple.

INTERVIEWER: Now Mary, when she was a baby, can you tell me about her? I mean what sort of baby would she be?

MOTHER: Happy. Just the kind of baby everybody wants.

INTERVIEWER: What would that be?

MOTHER: She was happy. She was no trouble. She'd eat anything you gave her. You couldn't look at her without having a smile because she was such a bonny baby, golden curls, big blue eyes, fat chubby legs. She was clean. She was beautiful. She went to bed half-past six to seven up till she went to school—never any trouble. She played outside, had fun, climbed walls—um—got her bottom smacked occasionally—but she was an absolutely normal child.

And of herself as a mother she says:

"I was always told I was the most wonderful mother."

INTERVIEWER: Who would tell you this?

MOTHER: Just everybody I came into contact with. My husband's employer used to say, 'What a wonderful mother'. His wife said she'd never seen such beautiful children, they were so good and lovely.

They were really good without any smacking or shouting at them or anything. They were just happy.

Her mother currently addresses Mary, so it seems to us, as though she were about three years old, and it seems likely that she tended to treat her as a three-year-old both before and after she reached this age.

She says, for instance:

MOTHER: I used to think to myself, "How on *earth* will I ever get her trained." But when we got in our own house I put her to bed and I talked to her, I sat beside her and I just let her cry and at first she cried for nearly two hours.

INTERVIEWER: This was between six and ten? (p.m.)

MOTHER: Yes.

INTERVIEWER: She woke up about eight o'clock did she?

MOTHER: No she woke up about half-past six—she just went off to sleep and woke up.

INTERVIEWER: She'd be about a year at this time?

MOTHER: She would be getting on for a year.

INTERVIEWER: So you sat beside her.

MOTHER: Yes. I said, "Now be a good girl and go off to sleep," and she used to turn round to me and she'd say "Shut your eyes and go to sleep," and she'd cuddle down then, then she'd start again, crying. Well she said this *after* a while, when she started talking.

INTERVIEWER: I see. But you talked to her.

MOTHER: I'd talk to her firm and say, "It's bedtime and Angela's sleeping." And it gradually got less until after about three weeks of it she wasn't any more bother.

A further feature of Mrs. Irwin's attitude is that she treats Mary as a nurse might do. To her Mary is a little child who is ill, whom she has to see through a difficult, trying time, but it is her duty to do so.

Yet, according to her, Mary and she were alike in many ways —when Mary was well, that is to say.

MOTHER: We have the same sort of tastes, we like the same sort of colours and, um, well, until recently—And now Mary's tastes are different, she's gone for chunky jumpers and sloppy joes and I don't like those—but up to her being seventeenish, I could go and buy something for her or she could go and buy something for me and it would be just what we wanted, you know, exactly—that we'd both like the same thing.

All went satisfactorily until Mary became "ill." Then she started to "shut herself off from me," she became selfish, defiant, too full of herself, and cheeky.

MOTHER: Now I'm completely haywire with her, I don't know what she's doing or what she's thinking. I've *got* to think she's ill or I wouldn't put up with it.

This is by now a familiar story. What Mrs. Irwin finds particularly upsetting is the developing distance between herself and Mary. They used to be the same, and now they are different. It is this difference that, for her mother, seems to be the essence of the illness. Signs of disjunction are met with negations or attributions of badness (selfish, defiant, cheeky, stubborn, etc.) or madness.

But this is not all. Mrs. Irwin had a "dreadful old mother." Although she hated her, she was terrified of her, and had managed to leave home only after a great internal struggle, to get married, when she was twenty-two. Her mother had always made out that she was ill, to get things done for her. She was selfish. Her father was strict, and had funny ways—he would say one thing when he meant another, but if you knew how to take him, as she did, you could get along with him very well.

She is proud to feel that she models herself in relation to Mary on her father, now dead. As a friend told her, ". . . as long as you're there your father's still alive."

Although Mrs. Irwin feels she is her father in relation to Mary (who, then, is Mary?), she, unbeknown to herself, behaves toward Mary like her own mother, and appears to encourage Mary to see her as she had seen her mother, and to say and do to *her* what she (mother) had not said and done in relation to her own mother.

That is, Mrs. Irwin sees herself in relation to Mary as:

(i) a good mother—
"I was always told I was a wonderful mother," etc.
(ii) a bad mother—
"I feel it's me that's done something wrong."
and
(iii) her own father.

In addition, she is identified with Mary, and induces Mary to see her as "a terrible mother."

The following are two examples of the confusing ways in which Mrs. Irwin acts towards Mary.

Mrs. Irwin says, as we have seen, that she is her father all over again with Mary: "I'm aware of it with Mary, but not with anyone else."

Now her father had a great sense of humour. An example of *her* sense of humour is the way in which she used to make fun of Mary and her boy-friend. She used to joke that he sniffed a lot and blinked his eyes. "We had great fun with Mary and her boy-friends." As she saw it, Mary thought it was fun too, but Mary said the very opposite. She resented her mother's "fun" bitterly. This resentment was another sign of her illness that her mother hoped the hospital would help her to get over.

Another example given by Mrs. Irwin shows both her "humour"

and her way of "encouraging" Mary. When Mary left hospital the second time she took a job in an office, but gave it up after a few weeks. In hospital the third time, she was frightened to take another office job because after two years in hospital she had become too used to hospital ways, and had lost confidence in herself.

MOTHER: We came to see her on Sunday and she was worried stiff about going out to work on Monday—"I won't manage it, I know I can't do it. No, I won't do it right." I said, "No, that's right, you won't will you? You'll make a proper mess of it." And I was trying to joke it off this way.

INTERVIEWER: Oh I see, you were sort of saying that in a jocular manner?

MOTHER: Yes, but she worries about everything.

We shall return to the interaction between Mary and her mother after we have gathered more about Mary's experiences and actions from Mary herself.

Mary says that what she is trying to do is to *establish herself as a person*, especially towards her mother. She feels that her mother is killing her "personality" or her "mind." She resents her mother for this, but feels unable to get the better of her. She claims that her mother tells her to do one thing, and then asks her why she did not do the opposite. She feels that her mother muddled her about her boy-friend, and that her mother manoeuvred her into giving him up. She now feels that if she had known her own feelings at the time she would not have done so. Her mother is very kind, and has done a great deal for her, but she (mother) puts her under a debt of obligation for everything. She wants nothing more from her mother or from anyone like her, and is not asking for anything.

Her mother sees this as ingratitude and selfishness—another facet of her illness.

Mary says that her mother has always put thoughts into her head and had never let her have a "mind of her own." What she has been trying to do since she was sixteen is to keep her mother out. She feels that, although not entirely successful, up to a point she has held her own.

At school what she was really interested in was painting but "this wasn't education" to her parents. If she could get back to that she feels she might discover her own life again.

Her parents agree that Mary did well at music and painting at school. But they have an explanation for this.

MOTHER: I think she got away with a lot did Mary, because she had such winning ways. Everybody took to her, everybody made a fuss of her.

INTERVIEWER: How do you mean?

MOTHER: Well, where the sort of tests—I don't mean arithmetic and English and things that *couldn't* be marked any other way but one way—but say art, composition—she might get higher marks than a

218   less attractive child might get that was writing the same thing, because it was Mary.

INTERVIEWER: And did you think that at the time?

MOTHER: Yes.

INTERVIEWER: You thought that at the time?

MOTHER: Yes, yes.

INTERVIEWER: And your husband, did he think that at the time?—In other words, that she was being over-valued?

MOTHER: Yes, he did.

For Mary, her trouble with her mother had begun when she was eleven, after her mother had had an operation on her thyroid. According to Mary, her mother changed towards her after this operation. She picked on her and she went on and on at her. Instead of doing things, she just talked and talked. She could not stop her mother talking at her all the time, and her mother's talk began to get her muddled. She tried to stem her mother's flood of words by various stratagems. The following are some of them. We must remember that such obvious stratagems as *leaving* or telling her mother to *shut up* directly, were not feasible if our observations in the present are some index of the past.

1. She would go *rigid inside*

INTERVIEWER: Supposing you had an opinion, you see, and your mother puts forward the opposite opinion, and supposing—I mean it could happen that your mother's opinion could be right—supposing you saw that your mother was right—you could see that she really was right—what would you do? Would you agree with her or would you still maintain your opinion?

MARY: I'd be too busy fighting to see that she was right. Tell you what I do, I sort of go rigid so that nobody can get at me.

INTERVIEWER: The whole of your body?

MARY: Yes, so that she can't get at me, nobody can, so that nobody can alter my opinion.

INTERVIEWER: Could you show me how you do that?

MARY: No, I can't show you because it's something I do so—

INTERVIEWER: Do you sort of go like this, or what—or what do you do?

MARY: I just sort of go like that. It doesn't show because—

INTERVIEWER: You mean inside?

MARY: Yes.

INTERVIEWER: Oh I see, inside—you stiffen up inside?

MARY: That's right.

INTERVIEWER: And does your mother not notice that?

MARY: No, I can do that now because she doesn't know, but I can't keep it up.

2. She tried to *shut everyone out*

With her mother, and later with the nurses in hospital, she tried to be like them, but this was forbidden. So she shut everyone out.

MARY: I got to thinking—trying—being like the nurses, but I made everything too difficult, more difficult than it really was.

INTERVIEWER: In hospital?

MARY: Yes.

INTERVIEWER: In what way?

MARY: Well, I shut everything out then I had to get at it somehow again and I found there was a sort of bridge—I had to get out again.

3. When she was about fifteen she began to see her mother as "nasty." She felt also that her mother was putting her (mother's) thoughts into her mind, and not letting her think her own thoughts. However, she was frightened to see her mother in this light, and, confused and ashamed, would deliberately muddle herself up.

To herself, she was not herself if she thought what her mother wanted her to think, and, to her mother, she was mad or bad if she did not.

The following passage occurs after Mrs. Irwin has been saying she thinks something was wrong with Mary.

MARY: What do you think was wrong with me?

MOTHER: Well I think your nerves were in a state. I mean to say there might have been something bothering you that you couldn't tell me.

MARY: There wasn't.

MOTHER: Well you say there wasn't and that's it, but I'm only telling you what I thought then.

MARY: I've never—(pause)—Oh I see, yes. Well it was you that was bothering me.

MOTHER: (laughs)

MARY: And I didn't realize it.

MOTHER: You didn't realize it was me that was bothering you?

MARY: Yes.

MOTHER: Maybe, it could have been, but I think myself it was your job that was bothering you.

MARY: Yes of course—it wouldn't be you would it?

MOTHER: Now that is cheeky and not a thing I expect a mother to get. It's no way to speak to any mother, and you do cheek me nowadays.

4. Holding her breath, standing still, sniffing, and coughing were all means of countering what she felt as her mother's impingements.

MARY: I used to hold my breath because my mother used to go on so quick and (pause).

INTERVIEWER: Moving you mean?

MARY: Yes.

INTERVIEWER: You mean your mother was moving about the house quickly.

MARY: Yes and everything.

INTERVIEWER: And what did you do?

MARY: Sort of stand like that.

INTERVIEWER: Can you demonstrate to me—sitting in a chair?

MARY: Yes. I just sort of (shows what she did).

INTERVIEWER: With your elbows?

MARY: I'd wait till she stopped talking and then maybe I'd be able to think again. She seemed to stop me from thinking.

INTERVIEWER: What was your mother doing?

MARY: She'd just go on and on about her jobs that she's got to do. She talks about her jobs that she's got to do and talks and talks.

INTERVIEWER: How do you feel when she's doing that?

MARY: Well the jobs are nothing to do with me. She ought to get on with her jobs if she's got them to do shouldn't she?

INTERVIEWER: Sure, sure, but I mean, how do you feel inside yourself when she does that?

MARY: Oh, I don't know, she seems to stop me from thinking. I can't explain how I feel—sort of all upset, you know.

INTERVIEWER: And is it at this time you hold your breath?

MARY: Yes.

INTERVIEWER: Mmm.

MARY: Yes. To stop her from affecting me, you know. It seems to affect my head and everything you know.

Further evidence, showing that such so-called catatonic behaviour was praxis, is contained in two stories told by Mary's sister Angela and her mother respectively.

ANGELA: She had the habit of—um—going all stiff, and she wouldn't move, and she just would suddenly sit in the chair and she'd just go all stiff and rigid—you couldn't move her, you couldn't—you couldn't speak to her, get through to her at all.

INTERVIEWER: How long would she stay like that?

ANGELA: Oh she'd stay like that for half an hour or more. There was one particular time, I remember, she went through into the front room and stood with one hand on the setee and one hand on the chair, bent over like that, and she stayed there for—Oh I don't know, perhaps it was an hour. And she wouldn't move. And they had to get the doctor to her in the end because they thought perhaps there *was* something wrong (smiling). And meanwhile we were living in rooms in a big house, and the landlady came through into the front room, and when Mary saw her she stopped and you know, was quite natural. And as soon as the landlady went out and my father went into her again she started again (laughs).

INTERVIEWER: So that you feel this was something that Mary had control of?

ANGELA: Oh yes, yes. Oh it was definitely under her control. I'm *sure* of that.

Mother tells how Mary got "better" for her sister's wedding. **221**

MOTHER: Mary got better for the wedding and Mary was bridesmaid.

INTERVIEWER: She got *better* for the wedding?

MOTHER: Yes. Because it happened very suddenly. I went to see her on the Sunday, three weeks before the wedding and I said to her, "What about Angela's wedding, you always were going to be bridesmaid," I said. "Are you going to get better for the wedding?" —And this is how I tried to talk her out of that. "Oh go on!" she says. I said, "Well Mary, Angela's in a *difficult* position because," I said, "she'll need a bridesmaid," and I said, "Her friend is going to stand in for you if you're not able to be there," and I said, "If you are able Angela will have the two of you." So either that night or the next morning she took I don't know how many aspirin tablets, but I never knew of that for a long long time.

INTERVIEWER: Tried to kill herself?

MOTHER: Yes. And when she came to, she was as right as rain.

INTERVIEWER: How do you mean "she was as right as rain?"

MOTHER: Well she seemed to be perfectly normal to everybody.

So Mary was perfectly normal to everybody for the wedding, and then went back to hospital immediately.

Mary, however, recognizes some of the consequences of the perilous stratagems that she has used, since they are not always easy to give up at will, and secondary consequences may ensue which were not intended.

For instance, if you shut people off, and put things out of your mind, you may come to a stop, feel empty, and necessarily fearful of the inrush or implosion of reality in a persecuting form.

MARY: I'm scared I'm going to stop and then all that I've shoved back will come rushing forward and hit me and knock me over.

INTERVIEWER: How do mean stop?

MARY: Well—well—that I won't be able to—(pause).

INTERVIEWER: You mean you're afraid somehow you will stop living, or what?

MARY: That I won't be able to come to, or I do come to—Oh, I don't know, I just can't seem to think any more, if you know what I mean, and it's only because I—Oh, I don't know—(pause).

INTERVIEWER: Only because?

MARY: Well, I (pause)—put everything away from myself, I can't go on putting it away from me can I? It gets to the point when there is nothing more to put away I suppose, that is when I come to a stop.

INTERVIEWER: You mean putting away your problems and so on, or thinking about your problems, or what?

MARY: No, just people.

INTERVIEWER: Putting away getting on with people or what? Trying to shut people out of your life I suppose?

MARY: Yes.

INTERVIEWER: Mmm?

MARY: That's what I do—shut people out of my life and—(pause).

INTERVIEWER: Is that what you meant when you said putting things away?

MARY: I don't do it deliberately but em—Oh, I know what it is, what I mean is I stop putting good things away and then I meet bad things.

INTERVIEWER: You stop putting good things—

MARY: I get away from the—(pause). Oh I don't know, I have lost touch with reality, I seem to lose touch with reality. It's ridiculous (pause)—Is it right to think? You should think shouldn't you?

To come to a stop like this would be to die existentially if not biologically.

As has been partly shown so far, Mary was put in an untenable position, from which she could not make any of the more usual moves, for instance, leaving the field, controlling the others, identification, without the negative pay-off being too high. The only moves that it seemed feasible to make were of the order of coughing, sniffing, holding her breath, standing or staying still, going rigid inside, stopping her thoughts, shutting everyone out. But if she sees the whole world as her mother, she is liable to act towards everyone on the presupposition that everyone acts towards her in the same way as her mother.

In this way she was at a disadvantage. Transference is a normal phenomenon. When she went from home to hospital, she could hardly be expected to discriminate between the two social systems. Her home was only too similar to a mental hospital, since her mother had defined their relationship as a nurse-patient one from an early age.

As at home, she had to ask permission to go out, she was allowed no money of her own, she was told she was "ill," and she was expected to get well. But to be ill is to suffer from obstinacy, defiance, and ingratitude. It is to lack emotions or to have emotions of the wrong kind. She was in a ward of women, and when she got fond of a male patient she was told not to get emotionally involved, and so on.

Our observations in this case extend over a period in which Mary was beginning to achieve some measure of genuine autonomy and independence. At every point this was met by the counter-attribution from her parents that what *we* take to be independence is selfishness and conceit.

MARY: My mother said it was wrong when I came home the first time but I was very happy then. I was happier than I have been—I really felt on top of the world, sort of thing and em—I felt confident as well, and, em, she says that I was too full of myself.

MOTHER: You know that's not what I mean Mary. You came home and you jumped immediately into a job.

MARY: When I was coming home for weekends you said that I wasn't well and that I was selfish and too full of myself, and all the rest of it.

MOTHER: Well you were selfish then Mary. It was because you were ill.

MARY: Sick.

MOTHER: Well that's how it appeared to us that you were selfish.

MARY: How was I selfish?

MOTHER: Well I can't remember now, but I do know that—

MARY: No, you won't tell me now, so I don't know how—so if I get better again I won't know if I'm right or wrong or when I'm going to crack up again or what I'm going to do.

MOTHER: Now that's what I call selfishness, thrusting your opinion on me and not listening to mine.

MARY: Well you were thrusting your opinion on me and not listening to *mine*. You see it works both ways.

MOTHER: I know.

MARY: But I always have to take it when I'm home from you, because you're my mother. See—I can't be selfish—but if you're selfish that's not wrong. You're not ill because you're selfish, you're just my mother and it's right if you can do it.

MOTHER: I know what you mean.

INTERVIEWER: What was she actually doing when you thought she was either selfish or ill—what was she actually doing?

MOTHER: Well I can't remember.

INTERVIEWER: You can't remember?

MOTHER: But I mean I can remember saying she was selfish.

Investigation has failed to reveal in what way Mary is selfish, except that she no longer tells her mother everything, does not seek her advice or permission to do things, and so on.

It is hard for Mrs. Irwin not to see Mary as ill, for instance, when Mary tells her she feels in a rut at home, and would like to get away on her own.

MARY: I've told you it before haven't I?

MOTHER: Yes, you've told me it before, but it's *worse* now.

MARY: Well I wouldn't say it's worse.

MOTHER: Well it's stronger then.

MARY: I wouldn't say it's worse. I wouldn't count it as an illness that's got *worse* (pause). It's just something I *want*. If you want something it's not an *illness* that you want it. If you wanted to get married you wouldn't say you were ill would you?

MOTHER: No.

MARY: Well it's just like saying you want a career isn't it? You keep saying, 'Well wait till you find something that you really want.' I'll never find it will I? Folks say, "Well don't just sit and wait for something." You don't know what you're to go by.

MOTHER: I've said, "Have patience till you're *better*."

Again, Mary has been talking about being independent. This involves, she says, establishing herself as a person, finding out for

224   herself what she wants to do with her life. It might even involve leaving home.

MOTHER: Well I think Mary's idea of being independent—it doesn't mean being able to do what you want to do, it means being able to model a course for your life—finding ways and means of carrying it out. But to be independent doesn't mean you walk out of the door and don't tell anybody where you are going, and you're worried stiff about where she is—that's not independence to me.

MARY: I didn't walk out thinking I was going to be independent— for goodness' sake—

MOTHER: Oh I don't mean at the time you went away.

INTERVIEWER: But you wouldn't see that as inconsistent with being independent would you?

MOTHER: Well it may be independence of a kind but it's not the right kind of independence. She can be independent. She can make her arrangements and then say, "I'll go away a week on Monday" or whenever it was—"I've got a nice job so-and-so"—and let's know and go decently.

INTERVIEWER: But supposing she didn't say that sort of thing to you?

MOTHER: Well if she didn't want me to know she could say, "Well, look, Mummy, I'm going away, but I'd rather you didn't know or bother about where I'm going." I would say, "All right, then." That's still the right way isn't it?

MARY: But when do I go the wrong way then?

MOTHER: When you leave us wondering how you are getting on and what you are doing.

MARY: When did I do that?

MOTHER: You've never done it, it's the way that you're talking about doing things—about independence.

MARY: Oh heck—I'm nothing of the kind.

MOTHER: Well you say you want to stand on your own feet and establish yourself, don't you?

MARY: I don't know whether I want to do that now—(pause)—Why I was going to leave home was because I just didn't think I could get on with you.

MOTHER: Yes, well I've always advised you to go away from home haven't I? Even when we were at Exeter we advised you—go away. We tried to get you to join the Army and you wouldn't hear of it.

One has to remind oneself that Mrs. Irwin is talking about something that never happened. The most that happened was that on one occasion Mary walked out after a row without saying where she was going, and came back in a few hours. Her mother is impervious to the point that Mary repeatedly makes, that she does not want to be ordered to be autonomous.

Patterns of
Social Organization

PART **3**

The second section of this book focused on the ways in which socialization, via interaction, builds and supports broad cultural patterns in groups. The actual criteria and patterns of organized group life have been ignored so far. In this section I will develop criteria for establishing and evaluating social organization which can be applied to any group, large or small. Then I will describe the patterns of relationships which appear in social organizations.

The stable group properties that intervene between a population and its environment can be described in various ways. Some of these group properties are patterns of *loyalty*, *exchange*, and *imperative order*. Patterns of social organization can be mutually reinforcing, but I will consider them separately in the following chapters because each is important in its own right. Each pattern refers to a configuration of relationships and influence, a form of interaction which helps bind members to other members and to the group. The final chapter in this section is concerned with *normative order*, or the development of an organized way of life that includes all of these patterns.

Survival
SECURITY
Commitment
Control
Crisis
Phylogeny
RECAPITULATES
CONTINUITY
DOMINATION
JINGOISM
Stability
SOLIDARITY
Bolshevism
PROTECTION
SOCIALISM
Integration
Equilibrium
Commune
EFFECTIVENESS
Support
INVOLVEMENT
Longevity
Participation

Study Questions

1. Do you agree or disagree with Kanter's criterion of success of a social organization? What would be your criteria?
2. Think about the social organization that has been most meaningful in your life. Does it still exist? In what ways have the criteria of stability, effectiveness, and integration been met, or not met?
3. In the most successful organization that you know of, have there been instances of internal or external crisis? If so, how have they affected the organization?
4. When an organization fails, as in "Death by Dieselization" or the "Cincinnati Social Experiment," what happens to its members? Try to give examples from your own experience.
5. Was the demise of the "Cincinnati Experiment" due to its lack of organization or its success?

Definition and Criteria of Social Organization

7

By now, you may be feeling overwhelmed with concepts and terms. The initial definition of sociology—the study of human group life —may seem very broad and confusing, with the inclusion of such topics as culture, interaction, and socialization. Organized human group life seems to be everywhere. Perhaps this is an appropriate time to sharpen the definition of social organization.

GENERIC CONCEPT OF SOCIAL ORGANIZATION

Social organization can be fundamentally conceived as the phenomenon that mediates between a population and its environment. Imagine two deaf and blind persons who are attempting to move an 18-foot-long board. Because they are too far away from each other to communicate their desired direction at any moment of time, they may do more to hinder than to help one another. If they were not deaf and blind, they could follow each other's verbal and visual cues regarding when to lift, when to turn, and where to walk; they could interact with one another; they would be able to relate in concert to the environment and to the common task; they would have social organization. In this example, we have a population (two people) and an environment (space, a board, the ground, etc.). Social organization, if it existed in this situation, would permit the two people to complete their work. It would permit them to interlock roles in pursuit of a common goal.

PATTERNS OF SOCIAL ORGANIZATION

As we have seen in the example of two people coming together temporarily to complete a task, social organizations need not be formal. They can range over populations of every size from a group of two to a society. Social organization occurs wherever there is collective activity; wherever persons are relating to each other; wherever they are pursuing common tasks or competing tasks. It exists in all the patterns of mutual relationship and interaction which bind together a group, or an individual and a group, and which facilitate the pursuit of individual (element) or collective (part) goals.

Social organization can be clarified in terms of its relationship to our discussion of social morphology in chapter 3. Social organization refers to the activities of groups, while social morphology refers to the numbers and forms in a group. The morphology of a baseball team includes the number of players and a description of their spatial distribution. Through this perspective, however, we would not be able to explain the interrelationship of the positions on the team. Only by analyzing the social organization of the team would we be able to discover how the positions relate to one another, how players respond to each other, how players are prevented from bumping into fellow teammates, and how team spirit encourages hard playing.

CRITERIA FOR EVALUATING SOCIAL ORGANIZATIONS

What are some of the criteria we may use to evaluate organizations? What determines the durability and longevity of certain organized groups? It is important to consider these questions because social organizations have a life beyond those of the individuals involved. There are boundaries and criteria necessary for an organization's development, maintenance, growth, and survival. Unfortunately, we know little about the factors that contribute to the success or failure of social organizations. We have no systematic studies of their origins, growth, decline, and dissolution. I have, however, included in this chapter some examples of different organizational relations and outcomes.

Social units have certain prerequisites for their maintenance and continued survival. I have implied that there are several ways that organizations might relate to their environment or to each other. Social organizations may succeed or fail. They may conflict with each other, and one might eventually come to dominate the other. They may support and maintain other social units, in which case they are involved in interdependent relationships. Whether an organization will die, survive, be dominated, dependent, independent, or interdependent with another organization is problematic. The criteria of stability, effectiveness, and integration may help us to understand these alternative outcomes. These criteria may be used to evaluate any social organization or unit, from a family to a society.

Stability

Stability implies the presence of sufficient strength and flexibility to endure over time. It involves two distinct concepts: continuity and equilibrium. Continuity, one aspect of organizational survival, pertains to the longevity of the organization. The state of California, for example, has defined administrative roles that deal with expected population growth and its consequent problems. In this way, governmental administrators can plan new schools, roads, and parks. Thus, the maintenance of the organization is ensured by anticipating and

230   planning for future changes. Continuity, then, refers to the perpetuation of the organization on a routine basis. In addition, continuity has an *internal* and an *external* focus. Internal continuity is ensured, for example, by continued employee loyalty, and external continuity is ensured by continued applications for employment.

Equilibrium is the second aspect of stability. Most organizations go through times of periodic or random crisis. They also provide mechanisms which allow them to return to a state of balance. Lovers, for instance, may have a quarrel and leave each other for a time to allow one another to calm down. Many role occupants of an organization desire constant stability because of the complications of unsettling conditions. However, an occasional crisis may be used constructively by an ongoing, effective social unit as a means of increasing or mobilizing its capacities. In contrast, constant crisis not only weakens an organization but tends to disrupt that which may already be weak. Crisis can also be internal or external. For instance, crisis may arise concerning increased job resignations, or may involve external factors such as loss of a market or of a client. It is said that Dow Chemical Company stopped the manufacture of napalm because of the boycott of its products and a considerable number of threatened resignations.

Effectiveness

The ability of an organization to achieve collective goals as well as unit goals is a measure of its effectiveness. Collective goals refer to the goals of the organization as a whole; unit goals refer to goals of individuals or subgroups within the organization. For instance, one may ask about the effectiveness of our government's substantial involvement in foreign countries (a collective goal of defense) while waging a war on poverty (a unit goal for poor people). Effectiveness also has an internal and an external focus. Collective goals are external (Is the school system educating its children?), and unit goals are internal. (Are teachers happy with their salaries?)

A number of problems are connected with determining effectiveness. First of all, it is difficult to identify goals. Secondly, even when goals are identified, their meanings can be very complex. For instance, what does it mean to say that this nation seeks social justice or a more perfect union? The third complication is the problem of multiple goals. Many complex organizations have many goals, and not all of these are compatible. With increasingly complex organizations, the attainment and achievement of goals and the specific nature of the goals themselves become more difficult to ascertain.

Integration

High integration means that the parts of units are well-coordinated. Like stability, integration has two separate aspects: *coordination* and *cohesion*. Coordination in social organization involves the role occupants or actors as complementary or supplementary to each other. Cohesion refers to the capacity of an organization to maintain solidarity. A highly cohesive group is one in which the members are attached and attracted to the social unit or to other members of the unit. The more cohesive a group is, the more likely that it will be able to set behavioral standards for its members, and the more likely that deviant members' behavior will be modified to meet those standards. When an individual is genuinely attached to a group and is in close continuous contact with the group, his group-related views and behavior are extremely resistant to change. Thus, the group can exercise control over its members. The group influences the members, provides them with support, reinforcement, security, protection, and rationalizations, and can punish its deviants by ridicule, dislike, shame, threat, or expulsion. In an important pioneering study, Samuel Stouffer found that soldiers who were in cohesive groups felt more confident about carrying out the duties of a soldier, and were less likely to capitulate and surrender under stress.[1]

Groups can be coordinated and cohesive with one another as well as being internally coordinated and cohesive. Cohesiveness between groups, or the expression of solidarity between different collective units, are examples of the external aspects of cohesion.

The first selection in this chapter is an article by W. F. Cottrell written in 1951. Cottrell, in "Death by Dieselization," illustrates how an organization's effectiveness at one level may lead to its dissolution at another level. Cottrell describes how the town of Caliente was brought together and made into a cohesive unit. The study then describes the town's disorganization and ultimate demise because of an external factor—the advance of technology. This single article illustrates the problematic natures of *stability, effectiveness,* and *integration.*

The second selection deals mainly with the issue of stability. Rosabeth Kanter, a sociologist, is concerned with group properties and social organization. She asks: How does a group ensure that its organization will endure beyond the lives of its individual members? Kanter's sample consists of utopian communities, and she examines historical data concerning their growth, success, or failure. While Leavitt and Merei in their articles in chapter 2, focus on *how* members are related in a group, Kanter examines *why* members remain in a group and why groups survive over time. She locates the answer to that question within the structure of the group itself. She discovers that certain organizational mechanisms or strategies promote commitment and bind actors to the group and to each other. Thus, she broadens our understanding of group properties.

Kanter's article is a report of one of the few studies I know which compares successful and unsuccessful organizations in a systematic fashion. Her description and analysis help us to focus on the individual's involvement in and commitment to his organization— the commune in which he lives. She does not detail the nature of the transactions that a social organization has with other organizations, nor does she tell us why the unsuccessful communities failed; however, her work shows the positive correlation between personal commitment mechanisms and organizational survival, and this may provide clues about the reasons for failure of some social organizations.

Kanter's conceptual framework and methodology, while difficult to apprehend, have broad implications for the study of all types of groups. Since commitment is an issue for all organizations, whether banks or fraternities, families or gangs, her analysis permits the student to critically analyze his own social group. She offers the student an analysis that is relevant to the concerns of an increasing number of students. In some later works, she describes the function of present-day communes and makes some predictions concerning the probable success of different types of communes.[2]

Some students may challenge the criterion that Kanter uses to evaluate utopian communities. Longevity may or may not be an appropriate criterion for success. Longevity says little about the member's personal satisfaction, nor do we know whether these mechanisms have the potential for promoting commitment to organizations while still allowing for personal growth and freedom.

The demise of Caliente can be contrasted with the resurrection of a number of other towns that died. In *La Raza*, Stan Steiner writes about the vitality and reorganization that is required to establish viable social units. The villages, when run by outsiders such as officials of the Office of Economic Opportunity, fail to survive as units or to achieve their goals. They become viable when the inhabitants begin to build their own social organization. Steiner describes the nature of the efforts and struggles of the village people to construct their own way of life.

The final article in this chapter is written by a social worker and community organizer. In "The Cincinnati Social Unit Experiment" Anatole Shaffer describes an experiment in participatory democracy that occurred just prior to World War I. The article is of immediate concern to anyone interested in community action programs. The article is, however, more than a case study of an organization that succeeded and then failed. The "Cincinatti Block Plan" failure was not due to technology or a lack of organization as in the case of Caliente. Its failure was perhaps determined by its success. Professor Shaffer correctly points to the similarities of the attacks on the Cincinatti plan with the current attacks on community action efforts.

NOTES

1. Samuel Stouffer, et al, *The American Soldier: Combat and Aftermath Studies in Social Psychology in World War II* (Princeton, N.J.: Princeton Univeristy Press, 1949).

2. Rosabeth Kanter, "Communes," *Psychology Today* 4, no. 2 (July 1970): 53–57, 78.

W. F. COTTRELL   **233**

Death by Dieselization:
A Case Study in the Reaction to
Technological Change

In the following instance it is proposed that we examine a community confronted with radical change in its basic economic institution and to trace the effects of this change throughout the social structure. From these facts it may be possible in some degree to anticipate the resultant changing attitudes and values of the people in the community, particularly as they reveal whether or not there is a demand for modification of the social structure or a shift in function from one institution to another. Some of the implications of the facts discovered may be valuable in anticipating future social change.

The community chosen for examination has been disrupted by the dieselization of the railroads. Since the railroad is among the oldest of those industries organized around steam, and since therefore the social structure of railroad communities is a product of long-continued processes of adaptation to the technology of steam, the sharp contrast between the technological-requirements of the steam engine and those of the diesel should clearly reveal the changes in social structure required. Any one of a great many railroad towns might have been chosen for examination. However, many railroad towns are only partly dependent upon the railroad for their existence. In them many of the effects which take place are blurred and not easily distinguishable by the observer. Thus, the "normal" railroad town may not be the best place to see the consequences of dieselization. For this reason a one-industry town was chosen for examination.

In a sense it is an "ideal type" railroad town, and hence not complicated by other extraneous economic factors. It lies in the desert and is here given the name "Caliente" which is the Spanish adjective for "hot." Caliente was built in a break in an eighty-mile canyon traversing the desert. It's reason for existence was to service the steam locomotive. There are few resources in the area to support it on any other basis, and such as they are they would contribute more to the growth and maintenance of other little settlements in the vicinity than to that of Caliente. So long as the steam locomotive was in use, Caliente was a necessity. With the adoption of the diesel it became obsolescent.

This stark fact was not, however, part of the expectations of the residents of Caliente. Based upon the "certainty" of the railroad's

W. F. Cottrell, "Death by Dieselization: A Case Study in the Reaction to Technological Change," *American Sociological Review* 16 (June 1951) : 358–65. Reprinted by permission of the author and the American Sociological Association.

234   need for Caliente, men built their homes there, frequently of concrete and brick, at the cost, in many cases, of their life savings. The water system was laid in cast iron which will last for centuries. Business men erected substantial buildings which could be paid for only by profits gained through many years of business. Four churches evidence the faith of Caliente people in the future of their community. A twenty-seven bed hospital serves the town. Those who built it thought that their investment was as well warranted as the fact of birth, sickness, accident and death. They believed in education. Their school buildings represent the investment of savings guaranteed by bonds and future taxes. There is a combined park and play field which, together with a recently modernized theatre, has been serving recreational needs. All these physical structures are material evidence of the expectations, morally and leagally sanctioned and financially funded, of the people of Caliente. This is a normal and rational aspect of the culture of all "solid" and "sound" communities.

Similarly normal are the social organizations. These include Rotary, Chamber of Commerce, Masons, Odd Fellows, American Legion and the Veterans of Foreign Wars. There are the usual unions, churches, and myriad little clubs to which the women belong. In short, here is the average American community with normal social life, subscribing to normal American codes. Nothing its members had been taught would indicate that the whole pattern of this normal existence depended completely upon a few elements of technology which were themselves in flux. For them the continued use of the steam engine was as "natural" a phenomenon as any other element in their physical environment. Yet suddenly their life pattern was destroyed by the announcement that the railroad was moving its division point and with it destroying the economic basis of Caliente's existence.

Turning from this specific community for a moment, let us examine the technical changes which took place and the reasons for the change. Division points on a railroad are established by the frequency with which the rolling stock must be serviced and the operating crews changed. At the turn of the century when this particular road was built, the engines produced wet steam at low temperatures. The steel in the boilers was of comparatively low tensile strength and could not withstand the high temperatures and pressures required for the efficient use of coal and water. At intervals of roughly a hundred miles the engine had to be disconnected from the train for service. At these points the cars also were inspected and if they were found to be defective they were either removed from the train or repaired while it was standing and the new engine being coupled on. Thus the location of Caliente, as far as the railroad was concerned, was a function of boiler temperature and pressure and the resultant service requirements of the locomotive.

Following World War II, the high tensile steels developed to create superior artillery and armor were used for locomotives. As a consequence it was possible to utilize steam at higher temperatures and pressure. Speed, power, and efficiency were increased and the distance between service intervals was increased.

The "ideal distance" between freight divisions became approximately 150 to 200 miles whereas it had formerly been 100 to 150. Wherever possible, freight divisions were increased in length to that formerly used by passenger trains, and passenger divisions were lengthened from two old freight divisions to three. Thus towns located at 100 miles from a terminal became obsolescent, those at 200 became freight points only, and those at three hundred miles became passenger division points.

The increase in speed permitted the train crews to make the greater distance in the time previously required for the lesser trip, and roughly a third of the train and engine crews, car inspectors, boilermakers and machinists and other service men were dropped. The towns thus abandoned were crossed off the social record of the nation in the adjustment to these technological changes in the use of the steam locomotive. Caliente, located midway between terminals about six hundred miles apart, survived. In fact it gained, since the less frequent stops caused an increase in the service required of the maintenance crews at those points where it took place. However, the introduction of the change to diesel engines projected a very different future.

In its demands for service the diesel engine differs almost completely from a steam locomotive. It requires infrequent, highly skilled service, carried on within very close limits, in contrast to the frequent, crude adjustments required by the steam locomotive. Diesels operate at about 35 per cent efficiency, in contrast to the approximately 4 per cent efficiency of the steam locomotives in use after World War II in the United States. Hence diesels require much less frequent stops for fuel and water. These facts reduce their operating costs sufficiently to compensate for their much higher initial cost.

In spite of these reductions in operating costs the introduction of diesels ordinarily would have taken a good deal of time. The change-over would have been slowed by the high capital costs of retooling the locomotive works, the long period required to recapture the costs of existing steam locomotives, and the effective resistance of the workers. World War II altered each of these factors. The locomotive works were required to make the change in order to provide marine engines, and the cost of the change were assumed by the government. Steam engines were used up by the tremendous demand placed upon the railroads by war traffic. The costs were recaptured by shipping charges. Labor shortages were such that labor resistance was less formidable and much less acceptable to the public than it would have been in peace time. Hence the shift to diesels was greatly facilitated by the war. In consequence, every third and sometimes every second division point suddenly became technologically obsolescent.

Caliente, like all other towns in similar plight, is supposed to accept its fate in the name of "progress." The general public, as

236

shippers and consumers of shipped goods, reaps the harvest in better, faster service and eventually perhaps in lower charges. A few of the workers in Caliente will also share the gains, as they move to other division points, through higher wages. They will share in the higher pay, though whether this will be adequate to compensate for the costs of moving no one can say. Certain it is that their pay will not be adjusted to compensate for their specific losses. They will gain only as their seniority gives them the opportunity to work. These are those who gain. What are the losses, and who bears them?

The railroad company can figure its losses at Caliente fairly accurately. It owns 39 private dwellings, a modern clubhouse with 116 single rooms, and a twelve-room hotel with dining-room and lunch-counter facilities. These now become useless, as does much of the fixed physical equipment used for servicing trains. Some of the machinery can be used elsewhere. Some part of the roundhouse can be used to store unused locomotives and standby equipment. The rest will be torn down to save taxes. All of these costs can be entered as capital losses on the statement which the company draws up for its stockholders and for the government. Presumably they will be recovered by the use of the more efficient engines.

What are the losses that may not be entered on the company books? The total tax assessment in Caliente was $9,946.80 for the year 1948, of which $6,103.39 represented taxes assessed on the railroad. Thus the railroad valuation was about three-fifths that of the town. This does not take into account tax-free property belonging to the churches, the schools, the hospital, or the municipality itself which included all the public utilities. Some ideas of the losses sustained by the railroad in comparison with the losses of others can be surmised by reflecting on these figures for real estate alone. The story is an old one and often repeated in the economic history of America. It represents the "loss" side of a profit and loss system of adjusting to technological change. Perhaps for sociological purposes we need an answer to the question "just who pays?"

Probably the greatest losses are suffered by the older "non-operating" employees. Seniority among these men extends only within the local shop and craft. A man with twenty-five years' seniority at Caliente has no claim on the job of a similar craftsman at another point who has only twenty-five days' seniority. Moreover, some of the skills formerly valuable are no longer needed. The boilermaker, for example, knows that jobs for his kind are disappearing and he must enter the ranks of the unskilled. The protection and status offered by the union while he was employed have become meaningless now that he is no longer needed. The cost of this is high both in loss of income and in personal demoralization.

Operating employees also pay. Their seniority extends over a division, which in this case includes three division points. The older members can move from Caliente and claim another job at another point, but in many cases they move leaving a good portion of their life savings behind. The younger men must abandon their stake in railroad employment. The loss may mean a new apprenticeship in another occupation, at a time in life when apprenticeship wages are not adequate to meet the obligations of mature men with families. A steam engine hauled 2,000 tons up the hill out of Caliente with the aid of two helpers. The four-unit diesel in command of one crew handles a train of 5,000 tons alone. Thus, to handle the same amount of tonnage required only about a fourth the man-power it formerly took. Three out of four men must start out anew at something else.

The local merchants pay. The boarded windows, half-empty shelves, and abandoned store buildings bear mute evidence of these costs. The older merchants stay, and pay; the younger ones, and those with no stake in the community will move; but the value of their property will in both cases largely be gone.

The bondholders will pay. They can't foreclose on a dead town. If the town were wiped out altogether, that which would remain for salvage would be too little to satisfy their claims. Should the town continue there is little hope that taxes adequate to carry the overhead of bonds and day-to-day expenses could be secured by taxing the diminished number of property owners or employed persons.

The church will pay. The smaller congregations cannot support services as in the past. As the church men leave, the buildings will be abandoned.

Homeowners will pay. A hundred and thirty-five men owned homes in Caliente. They must accept the available means of support or rent to those who do. In either case the income available will be far less than that on which the houses were built. The least desirable homes will stand unoccupied, their value completely lost. The others must be revalued at a figure far below that at which they were formerly held.

In a word, those pay who are, by traditional American standards, *most moral*. Those who have raised children see friendships broken and neighborhoods disintegrated. The childless more freely shake the dust of Caliente from their feet. Those who built their personalities into the structure of the community watch their work destroyed. Those too wise or too selfish to have entangled themselves in community affairs suffer no such qualms. The chain store can pull down its sign, move its equipment and charge the costs off against more profitable and better located units, and against taxes. The local owner has no such alternatives. In short, "good citizens" who assumed family and community responsibility are the greatest losers. Nomads suffer least.

The people of Caliente are asked to accept as "normal" this strange inversion of their expectations. It is assumed that they will, without protest or change in sentiment, accept the dictum of the "law of supply and demand." Certainly they must comply in part with this dictum. While their behavior, in part reflects this compliance, there are also other changes perhaps equally important in their attitudes and values.

The first reaction took the form of an effort at community self-preservation. Caliente became visible to its inhabitants as a real entity,

238   as meaningful as the individual personalities which they had hitherto
been taught to see as atomistic or nomadic elements. Community survival was seen as prerequisite to many of the individual values that
had been given precedence in the past. The organized community
made a search for new industry, citing elements of community organization themselves as reasons why industry should move to Caliente. But
the conditions that led the railroad to abandon the point made the
place even less attractive to new industry than it had hitherto been.
Yet the effort to keep the community a going concern persisted.

There was also a change in sentiment. In the past the glib assertion that progress spelled sacrifice could be offered when some
distant group was a victim of technological change. There was no
such reaction when the event struck home. The change can probably
be as well revealed as in any other way by quoting from the Caliente
Herald:

... (over the) years ... (this) ... railroad and its affiliates ...
became to this writer his ideal of a railroad empire. The (company)
... appeared to take much more than the ordinary interest of big railroads
in the development of areas adjacent to its lines, all the while doing a
great deal for the communities large and small through which the
lines passed.

Those were the days creative of (its) enviable reputation as one of
the finest, most progressive—and most human—of American railroads,
enjoying the confidence and respect of employees, investors, and
communities alike!

One of the factors bringing about this confidence and respect was
the consideration shown communities which otherwise would have
suffered serious blows when division and other changes were effected.
A notable example was ... (a town) ... where the shock of division
change was made almost unnoticed by installation of a rolling stock
reclamation point, which gave (that town) an opportunity to hold its
community intact until tourist traffic and other industries could get
better established—with the result that ... (it) ... is now on a firm
foundation. And through this display of consideration for a community,
the railroad gained friends—not only among people of ... (that town)
... who were perhaps more vocal than others, but also among thousands
of others throughout the country on whom this action made an indelible
impression.

But things seem to have changed materially during the last few years,
the ... (company) ... seems to this writer to have gone all out for
glamor and the dollars which glamorous people have to spend, sadly
neglecting one of the principal factors which helped to make ...
(it) ... great: that fine consideration of communities and individuals,
as well as employees, who have been happy in cooperating steadfastly
with the railroad in times of stress as well as prosperity. The loyalty
of the people and communities seems to count for little with the ...
(company) ... of this day, though other "Big Business" corporations
do not hesitate to expend huge sums to encourage the loyalty of community and people which old friends of ... (the company) ... have
been happy to give voluntarily.

Ever since the ... railroad was constructed ... Caliente has been a key
town on the railroad. It is true, the town owed its inception to the rail-

road, but it has paid this back in becoming one of the most attractive communities on the system. With nice homes, streets and parks, good school . . . good city government . . . Caliente offers advantages that most big corporations would be gratified to have for their employees—a homey spot where they could live their lives of contentment, happiness and security.

Caliente's strategic location, midway of some of the toughest road on the entire system has been a lifesaver for the road several times when floods have wreaked havoc on the roadbed in the canyon above and below Caliente. This has been possible through storage in Caliente of large stocks of repair material and equipment—and not overlooking manpower—which has thus become available on short notice.

. . . But (the railroad) or at least one of its big officials appearing to be almost completely divorced from policies which made this railroad great, has ordered changes which are about as inconsiderate as anything of which "Big Business" has ever been accused! Employees who have given the best years of their lives to this railroad are cut off without anything to which they can turn, many of them with homes in which they have taken much pride; while others, similarly with nice homes, are told to move elsewhere and are given runs that only a few will be able to endure from a physical standpoint, according to common opinion.

Smart big corporations the country over encourage their employees to own their own homes—and loud are their boasts when the percentage of such employees is favorable! But in contrast, a high (company) official is reported to have said only recently that "a railroad man has no business owning a home!" Quite a departure from what has appeared to be (company) tradition.

It is difficult for the Herald to believe that this official however "big" he is, speaks for the . . . (company) . . . when he enunciates a policy that carried to the letter, would make tramps of (company) employees and their families!

No thinking person wants to stand in the way of progress, but true progress is not made when it is overshadowed by cold-blooded disregard for the loyalty of employees, their families, and the communities which have developed in the good American way through the decades of loyal service and good citizenship.

This editorial, written by a member of all the service clubs, approved by Caliente business men, and quoted with approbation by the most conservative members of the community, is significant of changing sentiment.

The people of Caliente continually profess their belief in "The American Way," but like the editor of the *Herald* they criticize decisions made solely in pursuit of profit, even though these decisions grow out of a clear-cut case of technological "progress." They feel that the company should have based its decision upon consideration for loyalty, citizenship, and community morale. They assume that the company should regard the seniority rights of workers as important considerations, and that it should consider significant the effect of permanent unemployment upon old and faithful employees. They look upon community integrity as an important community asset. Caught between the support of a "rational" system of "economic" forces and laws, and sentiments which they accept as significant

240   values, they seek a solution to their dilemma which will at once permit them to retain their expected rewards for continued adherence to past norms and to defend the social system which they have been taught to revere but which now offers them a stone instead of bread.

IMPLICATIONS

We have shown that those in Caliente whose behavior most nearly approached the ideal taught are hardest hit by change. On the other hand, those seemingly farthest removed in conduct from that ideal are either rewarded or pay less of the costs of change than do those who follow the ideal more closely. Absentee owners, completely anonymous, and consumers who are not expected to co-operate to make the gains possible are rewarded most highly, while the local people who must cooperate to raise productivity pay dearly for having contributed.

In a society run through sacred mysteries whose rationale it is not man's privilege to criticize, such incongruities may be explained away. Such a society may even provide some "explanation" which makes them seem rational. In a secular society, supposedly defended rationally upon scientific facts, in which the pragmatic test "Does it work?" is continually applied, such discrepancy between expectation and realization is difficult to reconcile.

Defense of our traditional system of assessing the costs of technological change is made on the theory that the costs of such change are more than offset by the benefits to "society as a whole." However, it is difficult to show the people of Caliente just why *they* should pay for advances made to benefit others whom they have never known and who, in their judgment, have done nothing to justify such rewards. Any action that will permit the people of Caliente to levy the costs of change upon those who will benefit from them will be morally justifiable to the people of Caliente. Appeals to the general welfare leave them cold and the compulsions of the price system are not felt to be self-justifying "natural laws" but are regarded as being the specific consequence of specific bookkeeping decisions as to what should be included in the costs of change. They seek to change these decisions through social action. They do not consider that the "American Way" consists primarily of acceptance of the market as the final arbiter of their destiny. Rather they conceive that the system as a whole exists to render "justice," and if the consequences of the price system are such as to produce what they consider to be "injustice" they proceed to use some other institution as a means to reverse or offset the effects of the price system. Like other groups faced with the same situation, those in Caliente seize upon the means available to them. The operating employees had in their unions a device to secure what they consider to be their rights. Union practices developed over the years make it possible for the organized workers to avoid some of the costs of change which they would otherwise have had to bear. Featherbed rules, make-work practices, restricted work weeks, train length legislation and other similar devices were designed to permit union members to continue work even when "efficiency" dictated that they be disemployed. Members of the "Big Four" in Caliente joined with their fellows in demanding not only the retention of previously existing rules, but the imposition of new ones such as that requiring the presence of a third man in the diesel cab. For other groups there was available only the appeal to the company that it establish some other facility in Caliente, or alternatively a demand that "government" do something. One such demand took the form of a request to the Interstate Commerce Commission that it require inspection of rolling stock at Caliente. This request was denied.

It rapidly became apparent to the people of Caliente that they could not gain their objectives by organized community action nor individual endeavor but there was hope that by adding their voices to those of others similarly injured there might be hope of solution. They began to look to the activities of the whole labor movement for succor. Union strategy which forced the transfer of control from the market to government mediation or to legislation and operation was widely approved on all sides. This was not confined to those only who were currently seeking rule changes but was equally approved by the great bulk of those in the community who had been hit by the change. Cries of public outrage at their demands for make-work rules were looked upon as coming from those at best ignorant, ill-informed or stupid, and at worst as being the hypocritical efforts of others to gain at the workers' expense. When the union threat of a national strike for rule changes was met by government seizure, Caliente workers like most of their compatriots across the country welcomed this shift in control, secure in their belief that if "justice" were done they could only be gainers by government intervention. These attitudes are not "class" phenomena purely nor are they merely occupational sentiments. They result from the fact that modern life, with the interdependence that it creates, particularly in one-industry communities, imposes penalties far beyond the membership of the groups presumably involved in industry. When make-work rules contributed to the livelihood of the community, the support of the churches, and the taxes which maintain the schools; when feather-bed practices determine the standard of living, the profits of the business man and the circulation of the press; when they contribute to the salary of the teacher and the preacher; they can no longer be treated as accidental, immoral, deviant or temporary. Rather they are elevated into the position of emergent morality and law. Such practices generate a morality which serves them just as the practices in turn nourish those who participate in and preserve them. They are as firmly a part of what one "has a right to expect" from industry as are parity payments to the farmer bonuses and pensions to the veterans, assistance to the aged, tariffs to the industrialist, or the sanctity of property to those who inherit. On the other hand, all these practices conceivably help create a structure that is particularly vulnerable to changes such as that described here.

Practices which force the company to spend in Caliente part of what has been saved through technological change, or failing that, to reward those who are forced to move by increased income for the same service, are not, by the people of Caliente, considered to be un-justifiable. Confronted by a choice between the old means and resultant "injustice" which their use entails, and the acceptance of new means which they believe will secure them the "justice" they hold to be their right, they are willing to abandon (in so far as this particular area is concerned) the liberal state and the omnicompetent market in favor of something that works to provide "justice."

The study of the politics of pressure groups will show how widely the reactions of Caliente people are paralleled by those of other groups. Amongst them it is in politics that the decisions as to who will pay and who will profit are made. Through organized political force railroaders maintain the continuance of rules which operate to their benefit rather than for "the public good" or "the general welfare." Their defense of these practices is found in the argument that only so can their rights be protected against the power of other groups who hope to gain at their expense by functioning through the corporation and the market.

We should expect that where there are other groups similarly affected by technological change, there will be similar efforts to change the operation of our institutions. The case cited is not unique. Not only is it duplicated in hundreds of railroad division points but also in other towns abandoned by management for similar reasons. Changes in the location of markets or in the method of calculating transportation costs, changes in technology making necessary the use of new materials, changes due to the exhaustion of old sources of materials, changes to avoid labor costs such as the shift of the textile industry from New England to the South, changes to expedite decentralization to avoid the consequence of bombing, or those of congested living, all give rise to the question, "Who benefits, and at whose expense?"

The accounting practices of the corporation permit the entry only of those costs which have become "legitimate" claims upon the company. But the tremendous risks borne by the workers and frequently all the members of the community in an era of technological change are real phenomena. Rapid shifts in technology which destroy the "legitimate" expectations derived from past experience force the recognition of new obligations. Such recognition may be made voluntarily as management forsees the necessity, or it may be thrust upon it by political or other action. Rigidity of property concepts, the legal structure controlling directors in what they may admit to be costs, and the stereotyped nature of the "economics" used by management make rapid change within the corporation itself difficult even in a "free democratic society." Hence while management is likely to be permitted or required to initiate technological change in the interest of profits, it may and probably will be barred from compensating for the social consequences certain to arise from those changes. Management thus shuts out the rising flood of demands in its cost-accounting only to have them reappear in its tax accounts, in legal regulations or in new insistent union demands. If economics fails to provide an answer to social demands then politics will be tried.

It is clear that while traditional morality provides a means of protecting some groups from the consequences of technological change, or some method of meliorating the effects of change upon them, other large segments of the population are left unprotected. It should be equally clear that rather than a quiet acquiescence in the finality and justice of such arrangements, there is an active effort to force new devices into being which will extend protection to those hitherto expected to bear the brunt of these costs. A good proportion of these inventions increasingly call for the intervention of the state. To call such arrangements immoral, unpatriotic, socialistic or to hurl other epithets at them is not to deal effectively with them. They are as "natural" as are the "normal" reactions for which we have "rational" explanations based upon some pre-scientific generalization about human nature such as "the law of supply and demand" or "the inevitability of progress." To be dealt with effectively they will have to be understood and treated as such.

ROSABETH MOSS KANTER

Commitment and Social Organization: A Study of Commitment Mechanisms in Utopian Communities

This paper defines commitment and proposes three types, continuance, cohesion, and control commitment, which bind personality systems to areas of social systems, linking cognitive, cathectic, and evaluative orientations to roles, relationships, and norms, respectively. Two processes underlie the development of each of the three types of commitment: sacrifice and investment support continuance; renunciation and communion support cohesion; and mortification and surrender support control. On the basis of these processes, a large number of commitment mechanisms, or commitment-producing organizational strategies, are set forth. Use of these strategies generally distinguishes successful (enduring) and unsuccessful (short-lived) nineteenth century American utopian communities.

Commitment is a consideration which arises at the intersection of organizational requisites and personal experience. On the one hand,

Rosabeth Moss Kanter, "Commitment and Social Organization: A Study of Commitment Mechanisms in Utopian Communities," *American Sociological Review* 33:4 (August 1968): 499–516. Reprinted by permission of the author and American Sociological Association.

244

social systems organize to meet systemic "needs"; and on the other hand, people orient themselves positively and negatively, emotionally and intellectually, to situations. Since social orders are supported by people, one problem of collectivities is to meet organizational requisites in such a way that participants at the same time become positively involved with the system—loyal, loving, dedicated, and obedient. This requires solutions to organizational or systemic problems that are simultaneously mechanisms for insuring commitment through their effects on individuals—their experience and orientations. Commitment, then, refers to the willingness of social actors to give their energy and loyalty to social systems, the attachment of personality systems to social relations which are seen as self-expressive. As such, the concept is of major theoretical importance, since it promises to join structural-functional considerations with phenomenology. At the same time, it has practical importance in a society in which many social problems are seen as stemming from lack of commitment. Yet, according to Becker (1960:32), "there has been little formal analysis of the concept of commitment and little attempt to inegrate it explicitly with current sociological theory." (And, I may add, little attempt to utilize it in organizational research, even though it is central to the understanding of both human motivation and system maintenance.) Such an integration and utilization is attempted here. By focusing on a kind of organization for which the securing of commitment is crucial to success, this paper will describe a number of structural arrangements and organizational strategies which promote and sustain commitment.

THEORETICAL CONSIDERATIONS

Commitment may be defined as the process through which individual interests become attached to the carrying out of socially organized patterns of behavior which are seen as fulfilling those interests, as expressing the nature and needs of the person. This definition bears some conceptual similarities to Parsons' notion of "institutionalization": "The integration of the expectations of actors in a relevant interactive system of roles with a shared normative pattern of values." (Parsons and Shils, 1962:20). What is added here, however, is a broader conception of commitment, in which actors become committed not only to norms but also to other aspects of a social system.

We may distinguish three major social system problems involving the commitment of actors: *social control, group cohesiveness*,[1] and *continuation* as an action system (retaining participants).[2] Continuance, cohesion, and control are three analytically distinct problems, with potentially independent solutions. An actor may be committed to continuing his membership but be continually deviant within the system, uncommitted to its control. For example, a rebellious teenager may reject his parents' control but be unwilling to withdraw from the family system. Furthermore, an actor may be very solidary with a group in a social system but be uncommitted to continued participation in the system, because of other circumstances. An office worker, for example, may take a better job even though her best friends work in her former office. The inmate of a prison may form close ties with fellow prisoners and even with guards, yet certainly wish to leave the system at the earliest opportunity. In specific social systems, one or another of these commitment problems may be of paramount importance; e.g., a business organization may concentrate on solving problems of continuance rather than cohesion. In other cases the three may be causally related; in fact, solutions to all three problems may be mutually reinforcing and multiply determined. But it is analytically possible to distinguish *continuance, cohesion,* and *control* as the social system axes of commitment.

What aspects of the personality system exhibit a good "fit" with or "support" these areas of a social system? On the basis of social action theory (Parsons and Shils, 1962:4–6), it is proposed that *cognitive, cathectic,* and *evaluative* orientations form the personality system axes of commitment, and that each of these personal orientations would seem to be able to support a particular social system area. Positive cognition can support continuance, positive cathexis can support group cohesion, and positive evaluation can support social control. It is proposed here that commitment of actors to participating in the system, remaining members, (*continuance commitment*) involves primarily their *cognitive* orientations. When profits and costs are considered, participants find that the cost of leaving the system would be greater than the cost of remaining: "profit" compels continued participation. (Considerations of cognitive consistency enter here.) Continuance commitment, in a more general sense, can be conceptualized as commitment to a social system role. Commitment of actors to group solidarity, to a set of social relationships, (*cohesion commitment*) involves primarily their forming positive *cathectic* orientations; affective ties bind members to the community, and gratifications stem from involvement with all the members of the group. Solidarity is high; "infighting" and jealousy low. A cohesive system can withstand threats to its existence; members "stick together." Commitment of actors to uphold norms and obey the authority of the group (*control commitment*) involves primarily their forming positive *evaluative* orientations. Demands made by the system are evaluated as right, as moral, as just, as expressing one's own values, so that obedience to these demands is a normative necessity, and sanctioning by the system is regarded as appropriate.[3] It is interesting to note that evaluative control commitment resembles in some respects the concept of a super-ego which binds the evaluative components of the personality system to the norms of a social system; the notion of super-ego, of course, formulated in much more intra-psychic terms than are used here.

The three kinds of commitment proposed here can be seen to cover the major aspects of the linking of the individual, as a personality system, to a social system,[4] and, as such, articulate with other formulations concerning a person's willingness to carry out socially organized lines of behavior. Cognitive-continuance commitment is commitment to social *roles,* or evaluation attached to the role; the role merely has a positive valence. This is on a similar level to what Kelman (1958) has termed "compliance," acting in terms of rewards and punishments, profits and costs. Cathectic-cohesion commitment is attachment to social *relationships*, which absorb the individuals' fund of affectivity, but again do not have internal moral imperatives attached to them. This resembles Kelman's "identification." Finally, evaluative-control commitment is commitment to *norms*, the values and inner convictions which morally obligate the individual. This resembles Kelman's third type, "internalization," in which the individual accepts influence which appears congruent with and even necessitated by his inner core of beliefs. The three kinds of commitment can also be seen to form a scale similar to that which may be proposed for the development of morality in children; the child first obeys social system demands because of rewards and punishments, then because of emotional attachment to others, and finally in terms of an internalized moral code.[5]

What the present formulation emphasizes that others do not, however, are the implications of the types of commitment not merely for the individual but for the social system. First, it is to different areas of the social system that the three personal orientations are attached, so that different consequences stem from different kinds of commitment. Groups in which members have formed cognitive-continuance commitments should manage to hold their members. Groups in which members have formed cathectic-cohesion commitments should be able to withstand threats to their existence, should have more "stick-together-ness." Groups in which members have formed evaluative-control commitments should have less deviance, challenge to authority, or ideological controversy—of course ignoring for the moment all the other diverse sources of influence on group life. Systems with all three kinds of commitment, with total commitment, should be more successful in their maintenance than those without.

At the same time, the reasons for gaining this commitment exist on the social system level—in the way the system is organized, in the implications of social arrangements for whether or not actors *do* tend to positively cognize, cathect, and evaluate the system. Since the social order is the *object* of commitment, differences in social organization should affect commitment. Thus, a criterion for the success of a social system in gaining commitment is whether or not it implements a program of social arrangements which tend to involve and bind participants' orientations. Such programs represent one kind of "social management of experience," a perspective taking into account both social-structural and phenomenological variables. When people are committed to social orders, structure and phenomenology are mutually reinforcing, and maintenance of the social system is intimately linked with maintenance of the self.

The proposition follows, then, that groups whose existence is dependent on the commitment of their participants should be more successfully maintained if they utilize social arrangements which promote commitment of all three types. Such commitment mechanisms can be proposed and their efficacy tested.

THE EMPIRICAL SETTING AND RESEARCH DESIGN

Utopian communities provide an interesting universe of organizations in which to study commitment mechanisms because in them certain problems are highlighted. Since they represent attempts to establish ideal social orders, but exist within a larger society, they, especially, must vie with the outside for members' loyalties. They must insure high member involvement despite external competition without sacrificing their distinctiveness or ideals. They must often *contravene* earlier socialization in securing obedience to new demands. They must calm internal dissension in order to present a united front to the world. The problem of securing total commitment, i.e., in all three organizational areas, is central.

In addition, historical material permits a direct comparison of communities of relatively long duration (which we may term "successful")[6] with those of relatively short duration (which we may term "unsuccessful") under a fairly similar set of external social conditions. (Thus we can, in a sense, hold external variables constant while we examine differences in internal organization.) About a hundred utopian communities were born and died in the nineteenth century America, most founded before 1850. Some of these lasted as long as 180 years (the Shaker Villages),[7] while others were in existence only six months (Yellow Springs, Ohio). The population of utopias chosen for examination, then, were those founded in the United States between the Revolutionary and the Civil Wars (roughly 1780 to 1860). This population, although experiencing similar external conditions, varied in type as well as in longevity. Some were more or less sectarian, some primarily secular; some were celibate, others favored free love. Some utopias derived from immigrant groups and spoke a foreign language. There was a Catholic community, Owenite communes, Fourierite phalanxes (phalansteries), and even one community derived from a literary utopia (Icaria, after Etienne Cabet's *Voyage en Icarie*). While many of the 19th century American utopian communities shared general values, they often implemented them in different ways. This variation in organizational characteristics, then, affords the opportunity for testing comparative hypotheses. Finally, these communities share an advantage of historical rather than contemporary research in that their ultimate historical fate is known: their entire life-span is accessible to the analyst.

A list of 91 utopian communities, representing a population of American utopias founded between 1780 and 1860, was generated from historical sources. A single instance of a community, a unit utopia, was defined using the following criterion: identity of organizational structure with some centralized control over successive or simultaneous locations. Thus, the Shakers, for example, are considered one case, even though they had at various times 22 villages in different locations. This list was divided into "successful" and "unsuccessful" cases and a sample of each drawn. Success was measured by length of time in existence: a system had to exist as a utopian community for at least 25 years in order to be considered successful (a sociological definition of a generation). A case was

248   considered a utopian community as long as all relevant relations among members were centrally controlled by a single organization. Thus, for example, Oneida was considered to be finished as a utopian community when it shifted to formal organization as an economic system and gave up jurisdiction over members' social and marital relations. Its duration as a utopian community was 33 years, even though as some kind of social system it has persisted 119 years. The utility of the 25-year criterion was tested on the whole population, and it was found that only one successful utopia lasted less than 33 years, and no unsuccessful case lasted more than 16 years. The population was found to include 11 successful utopias, 79 unsuccessful ones, and one case that proved to be unclassifiable (Icaria).

The sample consisted of 9 successful and 21 unsuccessful cases, communities for which there were available at least two independent sources of information.[8] Of the 11 successful cases in the population, two could not be included in the sample because of a scarcity of information on their social organization, although some data on one of them was collected; 9 successful cases therefore comprised the sample. (The sample of successful utopias thus nearly exhausts the population.) Twenty-one out of the 79 unsuccessful utopias were included, with another 9 cases on which some data had been collected thrown out for lack of information. Availability of data was not the only criterion used for selection of the 21 unsuccessful cases, however, for an attempt was made to make this sample relatively representative and independent. All major types and time periods are included in the sample, and most of those not studied were either similar in type and ideology to those examined or very small in size and short in duration. (The average life of the entire population of unsuccessful cases was less than two years.) Finally, within the sample of unsuccessful cases, those of relatively longer duration were over-represented. This was partly due to the availability of materials, for the longer a community's existence the greater the likelihood that it would attract the notice of history. However it was also deliberate, designed to increase the meaningfulness and validity of the comparison between successful and unsuccessful cases. Social organization does not usually arise suddenly and *in toto*; it often requires slow periods of getting organized. To include only 3 communities of less than two full years' duration and 14 of at least three full years tends to insure that the differences between successful and unsuccessful cases will not be wholly due to differences in their stage of organizational development but rather to differences in the kinds of organization they do establish.

Data were collected from sources representing four categories of informants: central members, such as leaders; peripheral members, such as deviants and apostates; visitors and first-hand observers; and historians. In addition, a number of documents, such as constitutions and financial records, were examined. Information from these sources pertaining to a large number of variables was recorded as though it represented responses to a flexible, open-ended interview schedule.

Data were then sorted into categories representing answers to questions suggested by theory and hypotheses about a large number of variables and their changes over time. To minimize bias the following precautions were taken: First, information on all critical variables was taken in as many instances as possible from at least two independent sources and from two informants who represented different perspectives, e.g., a member of the community and a nonmember visitor or historian. Secondly, once information had been categorized, internal checks were used to determine whether other related data tended to confirm or discredit that information. Independent judges who did not know the hypotheses of the study made these internal checks.

It was then necessary to devise a data reduction technique so that hypotheses could be tested quantitatively. Toward this end a data summary was constructed to generate a protocol for each community. This consisted of a series of questions dealing with practices, occurrences, rules and procedures in which the concepts and variables bearing on the hypotheses were operationally defined. The data summary permitted a transformation of the hypotheses into concrete and therefore measurable terms. This summary asked 260 questions about particular events and organizational strategies. The data summaries for all 31 utopian communities in the sample were completed by five independent judges who had some sociological training but did not know the hypotheses of the study. Inter-judge agreement was $r = +0.79$.[9] Essentially the procedure was analogous to having informants fill out questionnaires, but in this case the information was possessed by judges who had studied the information from many informants. The protocols for each community were then coded, converting the information in quantitative form.

For each kind of commitment defined earlier, cognitive-continuance, cathectic-cohesion, and evaluative-control, two processes were conceptualized—one a dissociative process, which would operate to free the personality system from other commitments, and one an associative process, operating to attach the personality to the current object of commitment. Commitment mechanisms were derived in terms of these processes and a series of hypotheses tested by comparing successful and unsuccessful utopias in their use of the mechanisms. The data were then analyzed, with certain underlying assumptions. Since for individual commitment processes there are a number of functional alternatives, it was considered inappropriate to compute tests of statistical significance on individual indicators. It was predicted only that a *class* of mechanisms must be utilized and that groups may use any combination of strategies from a pool of possibilities, so that the presence or absence of a *single* indicator was not considered definitive evidence. Furthermore, the mechanisms themselves are not analytically pure.[10] Accordingly the data on single measures were analyzed in the form of raw and percentaged frequencies. At the same time, however, the extent to which systems implement *programs* of commitment-producing arrangements can be tested. Thus, summary scores which compare the utilization of entire classes of mechanisms by successful and unsuccessful communities were derived, and tests of significance employed.

CONTINUANCE COMMITMENT MECHANISMS

Commitment to continued participation involves securing a person's positive *cognitive* orientations, inducing the individual to cognize participation in the organization as profitable when considered in terms of rewards and costs. Cognitive orientations are those which view objects and attach positive or negative valences to them, merely perceiving the properties of the objects; in a purely cognitive judgment there is no notion of emotional gratification (cathexis) or of morality (evaluation) attached to the object. For positive cognition to become attached to a social system, then, the system must be organized in such a way that it is viewed as rewarding. The individual who makes a cognitive-continuance commitment finds that what is profitable to him is bound up with his position in the organization, is contingent on his participating in the system—he commits himself to a role. For the actor there is a "profit" associated with continued participation and a "cost" associated with leaving. Thus sacrifice (negative) and investment (positive) are among the components of cognitive-continuance commitments. Sacrifice involves the giving up of something considered valuable or pleasurable in order to belong to the organization; this stresses the importance of role of member to the individual. Sacrifice means that membership becomes more costly and is therefore not lightly regarded or likely to be given up easily.[11] Investment is a process whereby the individual gains a stake in the organization, commits current and future profits to it so that he must continue to participate if he is going to realize them. Investment generally involves the tying of a person's present and potential resources to the organization, future gain to be received from present behavior. Organizational strategies which promote cognitive-continuance commitments work through sacrifice and investment, and the use of such mechanisms should distinguish between successful and unsuccessful utopian communities.

Sacrifice

The process of sacrifice asks members to give up something as a price of membership; once members agree to make the "sacrifice," their motivation to remain participants should increase. Membership should become more "sacred," more valuable and meaningful.[12] (The issue here is not how the organization induces the original concessions or manages to recruit people willing to make them; rather, it is proposed that those systems exacting sacrifices will survive longer because sacrifice is functional for their maintenance.) Sacrifice operates on the basis of a simple principle from cognitive consistency theories: the more it "costs" a person to do something, the more "valuable" he will have to consider it, in order to justify the psychic "expense" and remain internally consistent. Thus, it has been demonstrated in a laboratory setting that when people work for very small rewards they must justify their doing so on the basis of belief or commitment, and they come to believe strongly in what they are doing (Festinger and Carlsmith, 1959). To continue to do it would justify the sacrifice involved. In many religions, finally, sacrifice has been conceptualized as an act of consecration, bringing one closer to and more worthy of the deity. A vow of poverty, for example, may aid commitment. In the eyes of the group and in the mind of the individual, sacrifice for a cause indeed makes it sacred and inviolable. It is also a gesture of trust in the group, indicating the importance of membership. Sacrifice symbolizes to the group the lengths to which members are willing to go in order to belong—how positively cognized membership is.

Organizational arrangements involving abstinence and austerity support sacrifice. The following were considered indicators of a utopian community's use of sacrifice to secure cognitive-continuance commitment: abstention from any oral gratification (tobacco, alcohol, meat, etc.); abstention from personal adornment or indulgence (e.g., dancing, reading); celibacy, or sexual abstinence; and, as a measure of austerity, that the community had to build its own buildings, indicating primitive or rudimentary beginnings. Such sacrifices should aid commitment and hence success.

These arrangements were found more often in successful than in unsuccessful utopias, as shown in Table 1. In general, a larger proportion of successful than unsuccessful groups tended to use these strategies at some time in their history. On a more stringent summary measure of the sample's use of sacrifice mechanisms, sacrifice was also found to be related to success. An overall index was computed

Table 1. Frequency of Presence of Sacrifice Mechanisms

| | Communities employing mechanisms at any time in their history | | | |
| | Successful | | Unsuccessful | |
	n/N*	%	n/N*	%
Abstinence:				
Oral abstinence	7/9	78	11/20	55
Celibacy	8/9	89	2/21	9
Other abstinence	5/7	71	4/14	28
Austerity:				
Community built own buildings	9/9	100	18/21	83

*The symbol N represents the number of communites for which the presence or absence of the indicator was ascertainable; the "n" represents the number in which the indicator was present.

in which each community received a score based on the number of mechanisms used, in how strong a form, and whether they were present throughout the community's history or only for part of its history. In the use of sacrifice a total score of nine was possible, if a community had all the mechanisms in their more stringent forms throughout its history. Table 2 indicates that successful communities tended to score higher on this index than unsuccessful ones, with the difference significant at the 0.10 level.

Table 2.   Use of Sacrifice Mechanisms

Mean of successful cases	6.4	
(N = 9)		Standard deviation of difference 2.4
Mean of unsuccessful cases	3.2	
(N = 20)*		
t = 1.3 (d.f. = 27)	(p < .10)	(one-tailed test)

*One community was eliminated from the analysis because of missing data on 2 of the 4 indicators comprising this measure.

Investment

The process of investment provides the individual with a stake in the fate of the organization; he commits his "profit" to the organization, so that leaving it would be costly. Investment allows a person future gain from present involvement. It can be a simple economic process involving tangible resources or it can involve intangibles like time and energy. If an organization desires a set of committed members, it should require them to devote their time and energy to the system, to commit their present as well as potential profits, and to derive gain only from the system because of this commitment. Utopian communities thus should not have non-resident members, people who can share in organizational benefits without active participation; active involvement of time and energy should be a requirment in order to gain anything at all from belonging to the system.

Through investment individuals become integrated with the system, since their time and resources have become part of its economy. They have, in effect, purchased a share in the proceeds of the organization and now have a stake in its continued good operation. Often, in fact, organizations themselves can *give* members the basis for this kind of commitment, by providing them with a share in the benefits of success. In addition, when individuals invest their resources in one system rather than in other potential paths, they tie their rewards and the future usefulness of their resources, in effect, to the success of this system, burning other bridges, cutting themselves off from other ways to allocate resources. Here Becker's (1960) concept of commitment is relevant. Becker describes the unanticipated involvement of other sources of reward or other aspects of a person once a line of action is chosen. One's reputation, for example, or the utility of one's skills, become involved in any social pathway, making it difficult to disengage onself from the "career" and turn to others on the same terms as before the commitment. Becker is talking primarily of continuance—the conditions under which an individual will continue a line of action once undertaken; he attributes this to the making of "side bets," the unanticipated investment of other, often intangible, resources once a person is a member of a system. The "side bet" is that the line of action chosen will be satisfactory or rewarding. Thus investment aids commitment; for a person to realize his gains, to reap his rewards, he must continue to support the system.

Investment is made tangible by such requirements as financial donations by new members, assigning of recruits' property to the community, and giving over any money or property received while in the community. It can be further reinforced by emphasizing its irreversibility, that investment in utopia, committing oneself to it, is for all time. A variety of strategies can indicate irreversibility; no records kept of contributions of property or capital; or an official policy of no refunds to defectors for their original contributions or for their service to and labor in the community, along with a history of no refunds in actual practice. It is proposed that commitment should be stronger and utopias more successful if investment and its irreversibility are emphasized.

Table 3. Frequency of Presence of Investment Mechanisms

	Communities employing mechanisms at any time in their history			
	Successful		Unsuccessful	
	n/N*	%	n/n*	%
Physical participation				
Non-resident members prohibited	6/7	86	7/17	41
Financial investment				
Financial contribution for admission	4/9	44	9/20	45
Property signed over at admission	9/9	100	9/20	45
Sign over property received while member	4/7	57	6/14	43
Irreversibility of investment				
No records of contributions	4/8	50	4/14	28
Defectors not reimbursed for property—official policy	3/7	43	5/12	42
Defectors not reimbursed for property—in practice	2/6	33	0/6	0
Defectors not reimbursed for labor—official policy	6/7	86	7/13	54
Defectors not reimbursed for labor—in practice	6/7	86	3/9	33

*The symbol N represents the number of communities for which the presence or absence of the indicator was ascertainable; the "n" represents the number of communities in which the indicator was present.

Table 3 indicates that, in general this proposition is warranted: a higher proportion of successful than of unsuccessful groups tends to employ these investment strategies. On an overall index of the use of investment, using summary scores computed in a similar way to those for sacrifice, with a total possible score of 18, successful communities tended to score higher than unsuccessful ones, the difference being significant at the 0.15 level.

COHESION COMMITMENT MECHANISMS

Cohesion commitment involves the attaching of an individual's fund of effectivity and emotion to the group; emotional gratification stems from participation in and from identification with all the members of a close-knit group. Cathectic-cohesion commitment is commitment to a set of social relationships. The individual cathects each member of the group, and his loyalty and allegiance are thus to the group as a whole. Hence, if members form such attachments, the ties that bind the group should be strong enough to withstand threats to group existence, to maintain the brotherhood even in the face of adverse circumstance.

This kind of commitment requires, first, that members relinquish any attachments which might compete with their emotional involvement with the entire group. Second, it requires that members be brought into meaningful contact with a collective whole, that they experience the fact of one-ness with the group. Two general processes work toward these ends: renunciation (of other ties) and communion (with the group as a whole). The use of mechanisms supporting renunciation and communion should thus distinguish successful and unsuccessful utopian communities.

Renunciation

Renunciation involves the relinquishing of any relationships potentially disruptive to group cohesion, thereby heightening the relationship of individual to group. Seeking renunciation, an organization discourages relationships with certain categories of others, with conflicting collectivities, in order to provide maximum internal cohesiveness. Behavioral rules specify relationships members of the community may and may not have; no loyalties which might conflict with members' obligations to the group should be permitted. According to Bittner (1963), it is functional for radical groups in general to require that all traditional extra-group ties be suspended; Coser (1954, 1967) has made a similar point with respect to sex. Structural arrangements which insure that the individual give up relationships outside the group and with any number less than the total group concentrate not only his loyalties and allegiances but also his emotional attachments and gratifications within the social system. Thus, under such arrangements a great fund of affectivity and involvement should bind members, increasing their collective strength and ability to withstand threats to group existence. Mechanisms which promote renunciation of extra-group ties are thus functional for cathectic-cohesion commitment and hence for the success of a utopian community. Renunciation may center around relationships in three categories: with the outside world, in the dyad, and in the family.

Renunciation of the outside world can be promoted by the development of a set of insulating boundaries—rules and structural arrangements which minimize contact with the outside, place clear-cut barriers between members and the outside, and "reduce the influence of the outside when contact necessarily occurs." (Wilson, 1959:11). Insulation may take the form of geographical isolation, "the ecological segregation of group life," (Stinchcombe, 1965:186) as measured by the community's distance from neighbors and accessibility to transportation such as waterways and railroads. Stinchcombe's (1965) concept of "institutional completeness" is another arrangement involving insulation, as measured by a community's provision of medical services. A special term for the outside world, a negative attitude toward the outsider, the failure to read outside newspapers or to celebrate national patriotic holidays, a distinctive language, and distinctive styles of dress also promote insulation. Control of movements across community boundaries so that these do not threaten the group's insulation or permit attachments outside the group serves as a correlate of insulation. In communities with such control, ordinary members should leave the group infrequently, e.g., less than yearly, with control strategies such as confession required for those who leave and return, and rules should be provided restricting and controlling members interaction with visitors. In Oneida, for example, the problem of renouncing the outside was complicated by the large number of outsiders visiting the community; various practices were accordingly instituted to reinforce renunciation. Thus, after daily visitors left, those members most exposed to contact with them were required to submit to mutual criticism, so as to be "freed from contamination by worldly influences." (Estlake, 1900:11). Furthermore, the whole group joined together for a ritualistic scrubbing "bee," to "purify" the community.

Dyadic renunciation[13] can take the form of free love or celibacy, experientially opposite but functionally alternative organizational arrangements which forbid individualistic ties. With free love, each member is expected to have intimate relations with *all* others; celibacy permits *no* member to have relations with *any* other. In both cases, individual ties are structurally minimized and the ties of the actor to the total group are thereby emphasized. Successful groups should require either of these practices or, at the very least, encourage or prefer them and reward their adoption. Furthermore, they should regulate both practices so as to prevent dyadic attachments. Free love at Oneida, for example, was not really free; the group controlled both the quantity of sexual relations and who could have relations with whom. *Fidelity* was negatively sanctioned.

Renunciation of the family, finally, involves family ties both inside and outside of the community, competing loyalties which must be erased. A Shaker hymn (Andrews, 1962:20) portrays this renunciation:

> Of all the relations that ever I see
> My old fleshly kindred are furthest from me
> So bad and so ugly, so hateful they feel
> To see them and hate them increases my zeal
>> O how ugly they look!
>> How ugly they look!
>> How nasty they feel!

That the purpose of this requirement is to increase in-group cohesiveness is indicated elsewhere in the same hymn:

> My *gospel relations* are dearer to me
> Than all the flesh kindred that ever I see ...
>> O how pretty they look! ...

It is proposed, then, that successful communities should not permit families to share a dwelling unit and should separate children from parents.

In general, a larger proportion of successful than unsuccessful groups tended to make use of these renunciation strategies to promote cohesion commitment, as Table 4 indicates. On an overall index of the sample's use of renunciation, with a total score of 35 possible if all indicators were present in their more stringent forms, successful communities tended to score higher than unsuccessful ones, with the difference significant at the 0.10 level.

Communion

The process of communion may be defined as becoming part of a whole, the mingling of self with the group, and relinquishing separateness in order to identify with all the members of the collective whole. Communion generates what various writers have termed "we-feeling" or "we-sentiment." Blumer (1953:199), in fact, has defined the membership of a social-movement as a collectivity of individuals characterized by a "we-consciousness." Infield (1944:136–152) has included "we-sentiment" among "associative elements," i.e., integrating elements, in the Kibbutz. The function such communion processes serve for group cohesion is well stated by Turner and Killian (1957:442):

A social movement must weld [members]into a group with a strong in-group sense and enthusiasm for the "fellowship" or "comradeship" of the movement and give them determination to continue in the face of obstacles.

Accordingly, the emphasis in communion mechanisms is on group participation, with members as homogeneous, equal parts of a whole, rather than as differentiated individuals. The need for mem-

Table 4. Frequence: of Presence of Renunciation Mechanisms

| | Communities employing mechanisms at any time in their history | | | |
| | Successful | | Unsuccessful | |
	n/N*	%	n/N*	%
Insulation				
Ecological separation	9/9	100	21/21	100
Institutional completeness				
medical service provided)	7/7	100	10/18	55
Special term for outside	4/7	57	0/17	0
Outside conceptualized as evil, wicked	2/7	28	0/19	0
Uniform worn	8/9	89	5/17	30
Foreign language spoken	5/9	56	3/21	14
Slang, jargon, special terms used	2/9	22	2/19	11
Outside newspapers not read	3/6	50	1/16	6
American patriotic holidays not				
celebrated	3/4	75	4/6	67
Cross-boundary control				
Average member rarely left community	2/2	100	0/7	0
Rules for interaction with visitors	3/7	43	1/15	7
Dyadic renunciation				
Free love or celibacy	9/9	100	6/21	29
Controls on free love, celibacy, or				
sexual relations	7/9	73	1/21	5
Renunciation of family				
Parent-child separation	3/8	48	3/20	15
Families did not share dwelling unit	3/9	33	1/20	5

*The symbol N represents the number of communities for which the presence or absence of the indicator was ascertainable; the "n" represents the number in which the indicator was present.

bers' equality, fellowship, group consciousness, and group dependence may be supported by various kinds of structural arrangements. These arrangements include homogeneity of religious, class, and ethnic background, as well as prior acquaintance; communistic sharing, in which the individual relinquishes both control over his own goods and private symbols of identity, in favor of group control and owner-ship; communistic labor, which emphasizes joint effort, with all members performing all tasks for equal reward, including communal work efforts like "bees"; and regularized group contact, via communal dwellings and dining halls, limited opportunity for privacy, and frequent group meetings, which insure participation and involvement. Group ritual, which involves collective participation in ceremonies or recurring events of symbolic importance, also enhances communion. Ritual provides symbols under which "the group loyalty is commonly raised to the level of the universal and abiding." (Boisen, 1939; Blumer, 1953). Community songs and group singing may be used as measures of ritual, as well as celebration of special community occasions or important community dates. Finally, an experience of persecution welds the group together in the face of a common threat and "heightens the symbolic intensity of a group's values." (Turner and Killian, 1957:399). The persecution experience can serve as a kind of "social vaccination," in which the group's defenses are built and strengthened, and the group becomes immune to more extreme future attacks, whether in the form of natural disasters or out-group discrimination. Facing collective problems then, aids communion.[14]

The use of social arrangements involving communion distinguishes rather strongly between successful and unsuccessful utopias. When various forms of communion were further operationalized and their presence in the sample communities noted, it was found that in general a larger proportion of successful than unsuccessful groups had them at some time in their history, as Table 5 indicates. On an overall index of the sample's use of communion, with a total score of 51 possible if all indicators were present in their more stringent forms, successful communities tended to score higher than unsuccessful, with the difference significant at the 0.05 level.

CONTROL COMMITMENT MECHANISMS

Commitment to social control, or commitment to norms, involves securing a person's positive *evaluative* orientations, redefining his symbolic environment so that the system's demands are considered right in terms of his self-identity, and obedience to authority becomes a moral necessity. An individual whose personality system is attached to the norms of a social system should see himself as carrying out the dictates of a higher-order system, a system which orders and gives meaning to his life. This kind of commitment requires that the individual see himself as humble and hapless without the group, that he reformulate his identity in terms of meeting the ideal conditions set by the system. And, at the same time, he must experience the great power represented by the organization, so that he will attach the meaning of his life to the carrying out of the demands of this power. Thus, mortification (a negative process) and surrender (a positive process) are among the components of evaluative-control commitments. Mortification involves the submission of private states to social control, the exchanging of a private identity for one provided by the organization, one subject to its control. Surrender is a process whereby an individual attaches his decision-making prerogative, jurisdiction over even private domains, to a greater power. Organizational strategies which aid the processes of mortification and surrender promote evaluative-control commitment, and these strategies should distinguish successful and unsuccessful utopian communities.

Mortification

Mortification processes emphasize the individual's smallness before the greatness of the organization; they reduce his sense of autonomous identity, so that he can have no self-esteem unless he commits him-

Table 5.   Frequency of Presence of Communion Mechanisms

	Communities employing mechanisms at any time in their history			
	Successful		Unsuccessful	
	n/N*	%	n/N*	%
Homogeneity				
Common religious background	8/9	89	10/20	50
Similar economic, educational status	7/8	88	10/16	63
Common ethnic background	6/9	67	3/20	15
Prior acquaintance of members	8/8	100	17/20	85
Communistic sharing				
Property signed over at admission	9/9	100	9/20	45
Sign over property received while member	4/7	57	6/14	43
Community as whole owned land	8/9	89	16/21	76
Community as whole owned buildings	3/9	89	15/21	71
Community as whole owned furniture, tools, equipment	8/8	100	15/19	79
Community as whole owned clothing, personal effects	6/9	67	5/18	28
Legal title in name of community (not in name of individuals)	7/8	88	18/21	83
Communistic labor				
No compensation for labor	8/8	100	7/17	41
No charge for community services	7/7	100	9/19	47
No skills requirement for admission	7/8	88	13/17	77
Job rotation	3/6	50	8/18	44
Communal work efforts	7/7	100	7/14	50
Regularized group contact				
Communal dwellings	3/9	33	14/21	67
Communal dining halls	5/9	56	15/19	79
Little opportunity, place for privacy	2/9	22	2/16	13
More than 2/3 of typical member's day spent with other people	5/8	63	3/13	23
Regular group meetings	9/9	100	13/16	81
Group meetings held daily	5/9	56	1/16	6
Ritual				
Songs about community	5/8	63	2/14	14
Group singing	7/7	100	8/11	73
Special community occasions celebrated	5/6	83	5/10	50
Persecution experience				
Violence, economic discrimination suffered	5/8	63	10/20	50

*The symbol N represents the number of communities for which the presence or absence of the indicator was ascertainable; the "n" represents the number in which the indicator was present.

self to the norms of the group, evaluating its demands as just and morally necessary. These processes attempt to convince him that he is of little worth without the guidance and meaning provided by the organization, that he must instead open his self-concept to direction by the group. In order to be totally committed to the group, an individual may reserve no private areas of himself, no domains not subject to the group's awareness, at the very least, if not its jurisdiction. Mortification processes provide a new set of criteria for evaluating the self, and they transmit the message that the self is adequate, whole, and fulfilled only when it conforms to the model offered by the collectivity. In more or less extreme forms these kinds of processes have been noted in the military (Dornbusch, 1954; Vidich and Stein, 1960), in concentration camps (Abel, 1951; Cohen, 1954), in religious communities (Hulme, 1956; Stunkard, 1951), and in general in total institutions (Goffman, 1961), organizations which demand total involvement and submission to social control. One intended consequence of mortification processes in these settings is to strip away aspects of an individual's identity, make him dependent on authority for direction, and place him in a position of uncertainty with respect to appropriate behavior. Goffman (1961), in particular, describes in detail "mortification of the self," which operates by removing the individual's sense of self-determination, and making him acutely aware of the presence of others.

In less extreme and less coercive forms of mortification, religious groups often attempt to erase the "sin of pride," the sin of being too independent or self-sufficient, substituting instead a self which is subject to the influence of the collectivity. Hoffer (1963:66) calls this "the effacement of individual separateness." In noncoercive groups, such as sensitivity training groups, mortification can be a sign of trust in the group, a willingness to share weaknesses, failings, doubts, problems, and one's innermost secrets with others. At the same time, its use is also a sign that the group cares about the individual, about his thoughts and feelings, about the content of his inner world. It thus facilitates commitment of the evaluative-control type and generates loyalty, binding the evaluative components of the personality system to the norms of the social system, through the system's invasion of phenomenological privacy.

Many kinds of mortification strategy may be proposed. Confession, self-criticism, and mutual criticism all promote mortification; in these sessions the individual "bares his soul" to the social control of the group, which is present either actually or symbolically. The functions served by such events are attested to in a pamphlet published by Oneida, in which the experiences of members undergoing mutual criticism were recounted; in Bethel and Aurora, as another example, confession was deliberately and consciously used to ensure humility. (Bek, 1909:276). Confession and mutual criticism may be supported by some kind of surveillance of the behavior of members either by the members themselves or by leaders. Stratification can also promote mortification, if it takes a form such as "spiritual differentiation," which recognizes achievement in the spiritual or moral domain and rewards it. An absence of stratification based on skill, intelligence or expertise is also important, for mortification requires that only achievements relevant to group identification and humility be recognized. Spiritual differentiation is supported by certain kinds of socialization practice: instruction in esoteric community doctrines, revealing the recruit's ignorance; provision of rules or information which recruits must master; segregation of new members from old; and a formal probationary period.

Mortifying sanctions may also be employed, including public denouncement, removal of some privilege of membership, not allowing a deviant to participate in a valued community activity, and punishment within the group rather than expulsion. Finally, a variety of de-individuating mechanisms may be present, which anchor a person's identity in things which are collective or communal rather than individual, including a uniform style of dress, communal dwellings and dining halls, and little opportunity or place for privacy.

The use of some mortification processes was found in a higher proportion of successful than unsuccessful utopias, although other measures fail to distinguish between the two groups. Often there was a great deal of missing data; in the case of mortifying sanctions, in particular, there were few recorded instances of deviance in the data gathered; this made it impossible to determine the use of various kinds of sanctions. (See Table 6.) However, on an overall index of the sample's use of mortification, with a total score of 33 possible if all the indicators were present in their more stringent form, successful communities still tended to score higher than unsuccessful ones.

Surrender

Surrender involves the attaching of a person's decision-making prerogative to a greater power, total involvement with a larger system of authority which gives both meaning and direction to an individual's life. In surrender, personal identity is fused with the social entity, so that the carrying out of system demands becomes a moral necessity for the maintenance of the self. For surrender to occur, the individual must first experience great power and meaning residing in the organization. Weber has proposed that this experience is transmitted through the quality of charisma, a felt connection with some central and meaningful feature of existence, generally related to the presence of charismatic leaders. But for surrender to result in more or less permanent commitments, persisting over long periods of time and independent of the presence or existence of any one person, charisma diffused throughout the corporate group is required. I call charisma in this form "institutionalized awe," a characteristic of an on-going, formalized social system which imbues the system with power and meaning. Shils (1965:200) also reformulates the meaning of charisma in this way, as a possible property of a social system, its "awe-arousing centrality."

Table 6. Frequency of Presence of Mortification Mechanisms

| | Communities employing mechanisms at any time in their history | | | |
| | Successful | | Unsuccessful | |
	n/N*	%	n/N*	%
Confession and mutual criticism				
Regular confession	4/9	44	0/20	0
Confession upon joining	4/8	50	0/19	0
Mutual criticism, group confession	4/9	44	3/19	26
Mutual surveillance	2/7	29	0/17	0
Surveillance by leaders	3/7	43	1/17	6
Spiritual differentiation				
Members distinguished on moral, spiritual grounds	5/9	56	3/20	15
Formally structured deference to those of higher moral status	4/9	44	1/20	5
No skill, intelligence distinctions	9/9	100	15/17	88
Instruction in community doctrines	3/8	38	2/11	18
Learning of rules, dictates required	2/8	25	2/11	18
New members segregated from old	2/7	26	0/17	0
Formal probationary period with limited privileges for new members	5/8	63	8/15	53
Mortifying sanctions				
Public denouncement of deviants	6/9	67	3/16	19
Removal of a privilege of membership as sanction	2/8	25	2/16	12
Participation in a community function prohibited to deviant	3/8	38	2/15	14
Deviants more often punished within community than expelled from it	4/6	67	2/5	40
De-individuating mechanisms				
Uniform worn	8/9	89	5/17	30
Communal dwellings	3/9	33	14/21	67
Communal dining halls	5/9	56	15/19	79
Same meals eaten by all	3/7	43	4/10	40

*The symbol N represents the number of communities for which the presence or absence of the indicator was ascertainable; the "n" represents the number in which the indicator was present.

Institutionalized awe consists of ideological systems and structural arrangements which order and give meaning to the individual's life and attach this order and meaning to the social system. These not only satisfy the individual's "need for meaning," (Cantril, 1941: 141) but also provide a sense of rightness, certainty, and conviction (Hartmann, 1952:588) that promotes a moral-evaluative commitment and surrender to collective authority. Such arrangements should also elevate the group to the level of the sacred, setting it apart as something wonderful, remarkable, and awful, and, at the same time, indicate the system's mastery of or control over human existence. This can involve, for example, a pervasive philosophy on the one hand and minute regulation of behavior on the other. All of this enhances and makes tangible and meaningful surrender to the collective will.

Ideology can contribute to institutionalized awe in a variety of ways. Ideologies which include any of the following characteristics should be related to this property of a system: explanations of human nature, of the essential character of man; a comprehensive elaborate philosophical system; provision for the investing of power in persons with particular awe-inspiring qualities, e.g., wisdom, age, spiritualness, inspiration;[15] legitimation of demands made on members by reference to a higher order principle, e.g., justice, the will of nature, the will of God[16]; imputation of special or magical powers to members by virtue of their belonging; taking as evidence of good standing in the group the possession of magical or special powers; and linking the system to great figures of historical importance. If ideologies with these features are actually to serve surrender functions, they should be a potent part of the life of the organization, a factor both in decisions and in day-to-day operations.

Institutionalized awe may be structurally reinforced in several ways. One means is to increase the distance and mystery of the decision-making process for ordinary members, to enhance the sense of "tremendous mystery" surrounding the organization, so that obedience and moral conviction must be absolute. Distance and mystery may be promoted by several mechanisms; an authority hierarchy, insulated from members; physical separation of leaders from members; special leadership prerogatives (special privileges or immunities); and an irrational basis for decisions (inspiration, intuition, or magic as opposed to logic, scientific reasoning, pragmatism, or democratic consent). Insulation of an authority hierarchy may occur through choosing leaders not directly by democratic means but by other criteria, e.g., they founded the organization, were named by their predecessors, or groomed for leadership by them; and providing no impeachment or recall privileges over leaders.

In addition to institutionalized awe, surrender may also be promoted by programming (provision of a specific program of behavioral rules); by requiring ideological conversion for membership; and by the existence of tradition. The existence of programming is indicated by a more or less fixed daily routine, detailed specification of the daily routine, and personal conduct and deportment rules for members. All of these reinforce the role of the organization as an order-creating power which is responsible for and gives shape to every aspect of a member's life. Shaker programming, for example, extended even to such minor activities as dressing and getting out of bed. At the first "trump" (bell) everyone arose according to the following program:

Put your right foot out of bed first. Place your right knee where your foot first touched the floor in kneeling to pray. Do not speak, but if absolutely necessary whisper to the room leader. (Webber, 1959:67)

Reguiring ideological conversion, which can be measured in a variety of ways ensures that members share a faith that gives meaning and legitimacy to the organization. Tradition, finally, imbues group demands with what Weber called "the authority of the eternal yesterday." This can be utilized by a utopian community if it derives from a prior organization or organized group, and one of relatively long duration.

The use of these surrender mechanisms was generally found in a higher proportion of successful than unsuccessful utopias, as Table 7 indicates—even those organizational arrangements like a daily routine that would appear to be minimal requirements for organizational functioning. Finally, on an overall index of the sample's use of surrender, with a total score of 49 possible if all the indicators were present in their more stringent forms, successful communities tended to score higher than unsuccessful ones, with the difference significant at the 0.05 level.

CONCLUSION

This article has presented a discussion of commitment as a process binding actors into social systems. Commitment has been conceptualized as involving the areas of continuance, cohesion, and control, each being supported by a dissociative and an associative process, and operationalized in terms of specific mechanisms—organizational practices and arrangements—which distinguish successful from unsuccessful commitment-requiring organizations.

The results help explain why it is that members of some groups are highly committed while members of others are not; it locates this problem in the structure of the groups and in the phenomenological impact of their organizational arrangements. Systems which employ the kinds of mechanisms enumerated here, whether in the specific forms described or in others which serve the same functions, should find their participants dedicated, obedient, loyal, and involved. It is possible, furthermore, that alienation is related to arrangements in which the commitment processes proposed here are absent or negated.

The commitment-producing strategies discussed here are applicable to commitment on many levels and to many diverse kinds of system. The conceptual framework is potentially useful in analyzing any organization which seeks to establish strong ties with its members, maintain control over behavior, and, in general, integrate individuals into social systems. The mechanisms apply, for example, to small groups such as sensitivity-training groups, to resocialization institutions such as professional schools or brain-washing camps, to business organizations such as sales companies, to residential communities such as the urban negro ghetto, to political parties, and to nations. This paper is a further step toward the understanding of human loyalty and involvement in social groupings.

Table 7. Frequency or Presence of Surrender Mechanisms

	Communities employing mechanisms at any time in their history			
	Successful		Unsuccessful	
	n/N*	%	n/N*	%
Institutionalized awe (ideology)				
Ideology explained essential nature of man	9/9	100	16/19	84
Ideology a complete, elaborated philosophical system	8/9	89	15/20	75
Power to be invested in persons with special, magical characteristics	7/9	78	4/21	20
Demands legitmated by reference to a higher order principle	9/9	100	11/19	53
Special, magical powers imputed to members	8/9	89	3/20	15
Possession of special powers taken as evidence of good standing	6/8	75	2/19	10
Ideology related community to figures of historical importance	8/9	89	5/21	24
Ideology, values, the ultimate justification for decisions	6/7	86	7/17	41
Institutionalized awe (power and authority)				
Authority hierarchy	4/9	44	8/20	40
Top leaders founders or named or groomed by predecessors	9/9	100	10/20	50
No impeachment or recall privileges	7/8	88	7/12	58
Special leadership prerogatives	7/9	78	3/18	16
Special leadership immunities	5/8	63	3/18	16
Separate, special residence for leaders	6/8	75	1/15	7
Special forms of address for leaders	6/9	67	2/19	10
Irrational basis for decisions	4/7	57	3/20	15
Programming				
Fixed daily routine	6/6	100	8/15	54
Detailed specification of routine	4/6	67	2/15	13
Personal conduct rules (demeanor)	5/8	63	6/19	31
Ideological conversion				
Commitment to ideology required	5/9	56	4/21	19
Recruit expected to take vows	7/8	88	6/21	29
Procedure for choosing members	6/8	75	13/17	77
Prospective members often rejected	3/6	50	6/11	54
Tests of faith for community children to receive adjult membership status	7/9	78	5/21	24
Tradition				
Community derived from prior organization or organized group	7/9	78	13/21	62
Prior organization in existence at least 10 years before community began	5/9	56	1/21	5

*The symbol N represents the number of communities for which the presence or absence of the indicator was ascertainable; the "n" represents the number in which the indicator was present.

266 NOTES

1. In very complex systems it might seem likely that group cohesiveness would be limited to peer groups. However, if cohesiveness is defined not in terms of sociability and mutual attraction but rather in terms of the ability to withstand disruptive forces and threats from outside the group ("sticking together") it would apply to systems of any degree of complexity. This improved meaning of cohesiveness has been proposed by Gross and Martin (1952).

2. While *recruitment* of actors would seem at first glance to be as important for continuation of a system as *retention* of actors, recruitment and retention are two analytically distinct problems, solved by different kinds of organizational strategies. I would argue that recruitment does not particularly require commitment but may be accomplished in many other ways, with non-committed actors; e.g., birth, accident, and external organizational phenomena may serve to recruit uncommitted individuals. However, once a person has performed any single act within a system, the problem arises of committing him to further and future participation. Thus, the *commitment* necessary for continuation deals with retaining participants. Recruiting them is not a commitment problem (although, of course, the ways in which they are recruited have implications for commitment).

3. Social control is possible without control commitments by participants, of course, i.e., without their positive evaluative or normative orientations, but it should not be as efficient or effective.

4. There is one additional aspect of commitment, concerning cognitive orientations, which should be mentioned, although it is not central to the present analysis. Commitment can also link the personality system to the cultural system, creating a cognitive-cultural commitment, in which the individual comes to internalize group symbols and to see things as the group sees them. (This idea was suggested by Leon H. Mayhew.)

5. This becomes apparent when one attempts to integrate the many findings on moral development embodying diverse points of view. It is suggested, for example, by the juxtaposition of studies reviewed by Roger Brown (1960: 381–417).

6. "Success" as used here is measured solely by longevity, although it is of course recognized that there may be other criteria for successful maintenance. With respect to utopian communities, however, it is possible to make a case for the argument that one of their primary aims is the creation of an enduring social world.

7. In fact, the Shakers today have a very tenuous hold on life; the remnants of two Shaker villages still exist, but populated by a few old women.

8. The sample consisted of the following communities, listed in order of longevity: *Successful*: Shakers (180 years), Harmony (100), Amana (90), Zoar (81), Snowhill (70), St. Nazianz (42), Bethel and Aurora (36), Jerusalem (33), and Oneida (33); *Unsuccessful*: Hopedale (15), Modern Times (15), Bishop Hill (14), North American Phalanx (13), Communia (8), Oberlin (8), Brook Farm (6), Wisconsin Phalanx (6), Northampton (4), Utopia (4), Kendal (3), Nasboba (3), First Mormon United Order (3), Skaneateles (3), Iowa Pioneer Phalanx (2), Jasper (2), New Harmony (2), Preparation (2), Blue Spring (1), Fruitlands (8 months), and Yellow Springs (6 months).

9. For no community did the agreement fall below 0.71. The agreement scores ranged from 0.71 to 0.85.

10. This has several implications for the understanding of the indicators and the description of commitment mechanisms to follow. The indicators conceptualized here are, first of all, only particular concrete possibilities; groups may concretely implement the *general* kinds of processes that produce commitment in radically different ways. So in some sense the indicators used in this study are certainly not exhaustive; they are representatives of a larger population of commitment strategies serving the same functions. In addition, the concrete practices themselves often serve more than one function at the same time, over-

lapping my conceptual categories. For this reason I have tended to place them in categories according to my conception of their primary function.

11. Sacrifice is considered functional for *continuance;* it has, of course, different and possibly dysfunctional implications for recruitment. As mentioned in note 2, retention of members and recruitment of members may occur on very different grounds and for very different reasons.

12. This is similar to an idea formulated by Jerome P. Boime.

13. Slater (1963) states very well the problem of "dyadic withdrawal" for larger collectivities and points out the importance of giving up intimate dyadic ties for the welfare of collectivities.

14. The common threat or shared fate as a builder of cohesiveness is widely documented. See, for example, Simmel (1964); Coser (1964); Blumer (1953); Freud (1962:61. A field experiment by the Sherifs demonstrates the phenomenon rather dramatically. (See Sherif and Sherif, 1953).

15. Amana, for example, was officially called "The Society of True Inspiration." The particular quality that its ideology defined as necessary for authority in the group was "inspiration," or the ability to receive directly divine messages and guidance.

16. Shils (1965:207) has proposed that a charismatic social order must also seem to be connected with a transcendent moral order.

REFERENCES

Abel, Theodore M. "The Sociology of Concentration Camps." *Social Forces* 30 (December 1951) :150–55.

Andrews, Edward Deming. *The Gift to be Simple: Songs, Dances, and Rituals of the American Shakers.* New York: Dover, 1962.

Becker, Howard S. "Notes on the Concept of Commitment." *American Journal of Sociology* 66 (July 1960) : 32–40.

Bek, William G. "The Community at Bethal, Missouri, and Its Offspring at Aurora, Oregon." *German American Annals* n.s. 7 (September 1909) :257–76, 306–28.

Bittner, Egon. "Radicalism and the Organization of Radical Movements." *American Sociological Review* 28 (December 1960) : 928–40.

Blumer, Herbert. "Collective Behavior." In A. M. Lee, ed., Principles of Sociology, pp. 167–222. New York: Barnes and Noble, 1953.

Bolme, Jerome P. Personal Communication. 1967.

Boisen, Anton T. "Economic Distress and Religious Experience: A Study of the Holy Rollers." *Psychiatry* 2 (May 1939) : 185–94.

Brown, Roger. Social Psychology. New York: Free Press, 1965.

Cantril, Hadley. The Pyschology of Social Movements. New York: Wiley, 1941.

Cohen, Elle. Human Behavior in the Concentration Camp. London: Jonathan Cape, 1954.

Coser, Lewis A. "Sects and Sectarians." *Dissent* 1 (Autumn 1954) : 360–69.

———. The Function of Social Conflict. New York: Free Press, 1964.

———. "Greedy Organizations." *European Journal of Sociology* 8 (October 1967) : 196–215.

Dornbusch, Sanford. "The Military Academy as an Assimilating Institution." *Social Forces* 33 (May 1954) : 316–21.

Estlake, Allan. The Oneida Community. London: George Redway, 1900.

Festinger, Leon and Carlsmith, J. "Cognitive Consequences of Forced Compliance." *Journal of Abnormal and Social Psychology* 58 (March 1959) : 203–10.

268

Freud, Sigmund. Civilization and Its Discontents. Translated by James Strachey. New York: Norton, 1962.

Goffman, Erving. Asylums. Garden City, New York: Doubleday Anchor, 1961.

Gross, Neal and Martin, William E. "On Group Cohesiveness." *American Journal of Sociology* 57 (December 1952): 533–46.

Hartman, George W. "The Psychology of American Socialism." In Donald Drew Egbert and Stow Persona, eds., Socialism and American Life, pp. 557–97. Princeton: Princeton University Press, 1952.

Hoffer, Eric. The True Believer: Thoughts on the Nature of Mass Movements. New York: Time, Inc., 1962.

Hulme, Kathryn. The Nun's Story. Boston: Little, Brown, 1956.

Infield, Henrik F. Cooperative Living in Palestine. New York: The Dryden Press, 1944.

Kelman, Herbert C. "Compliance, Identification, and Internalization: Three Processes of Attitude Change." *Journal of Conflict Resolution* 2 (March 1958): 51–60.

Mayhew, Leon H. Personal Communication. 1967.

Parsons, Talcott, and Shils, Edward A., ed.s, Toward A General Theory of Action. New York: Harper & Row, 1962.

Sherif, Muanfer, and Sherif, Carolyn. Groups in Harmony and Tension. New York: Harper & Row, 1953.

Shils, Edward A. "Charisma, Order, and Status." *American Sociological Review* 30 (April 1965): 199–213.

Sinunel, Georg. Conflict. Translated by Kurt H. Wolff. New York: Free Press, 1964.

Slater, Philip E. "On Social Regression." *American Sociological Review* 28 (June 1963): 339–64.

Stinchcombe, Arthur. "Social Structure and Organization." In James G. March, ed., Handbook of Organizations, pp. 141–91. Chicago: Rand McNally, 1965.

Stunkard, A. "Some Interpersonal Aspects of an Oriental Religion." *Psychiatry* 14 (November 1951): 419–31.

Turner, Ralph H. and Killian, Lewis M. Collective Behavior. Englewood Cliffs, New Jersey: Prentice-Hall, 1957.

Vidich, Arthur J. and Stein, Maurice R. "The Dissolved Identity in Military Life." In Maurice R. Stein, et al., eds., Identity and Anxiety, pp. 493–505. Glencoe, Illinois: Free Press, 1960.

Webber, Everett. Escape to Utopia: The Communal Movement in America. New York: Hastings House, 1959.

Wilson, Bryan R. "An Analysis of Sect Development." *American Sociological Review* 24 (February 1959): 1–15.

The Cincinnati Social Unit Experiment: 1917-19

It is perhaps inevitable that each generation rediscovers a problem, or set of problems, the solution of which is deemed to be central to the process of man's growth and continued achievement. It is in this light that one can perhaps best view the periodic concern, at least for the past two centuries, with the development of patterns of participatory social and political organization. During the last century, the concern with participation has also served to sustain the development of an urban-industrial technocracy.

Just as problems are again identified, so too are solutions. The decade of the 1960s saw the concept of community action come to fruition as a matter of public social policy. On the basis of the experience of the Ford Foundation Grey Area Projects, community action was translated into a national program in the "war on poverty." Almost as quickly, community-action programs became mired in controversy as the unintended consequences of the "sentimental" phase, "maximum feasible participation," began to unfold, in particular with regard to the possible shift of locus in decision-making authority (20, 41).

For some, with the benefit of immediate hindsight, the outcome of community-action efforts was inevitable (24). They were described as politically naive, rooted in a fragile constituency, and contrary to the technological imperatives of society. This analysis is readily acceptable to many, given the apparent failure of community action to establish itself and have an identifiable impact on problems of poverty and alienation. In the tradition of the pragmatist, that which fails must be shed. The impending dismemberment of the Office of Economic Opportunity and community action will only bring to an official end that which has ceased to function and, in this line of reasoning, should therefore no longer survive. If one reads Moynihan correctly, this is not only right but good. It permits the development of the "technocrat supreme," who is freed of the unnecessary accountability to those who receive. Instead, the technocrat can turn his full attention to those who have power and whose hegemony over the public-industrial complex has survived unchanged since the early 1900s.

Yet, for those concerned with "participatory democracy," the failure of community action should be nothing other than the expected. As Rubin, Levitan, and Moynihan have demonstrated, the effort was never intended to result in a restructuring of the social order. At best, participation was to be an educative device by which the status quo would be maintained, perhaps with a slightly broadened con-

Anatole Shaffer, "The Cincinnati Social Unit Experiment: 1917-19," *Social Service Review* 45, no. 2 (June 1971), © 1971 by The University of Chicago. Reprinted by permission of The University of Chicago Press.

stituency. It may be too early to gather sufficient conclusive data to support such a view of the poverty program. Fortunately, we have an analogous situation, sufficiently removed in time to be analyzed dispassionately while we keep an eye on the immediate past. This paper reviews the development of the social unit plan during the early part of the century and describes the effort at demonstrating the feasibility of community action through the instrument of the Cincinnati Social Unit Organization.

THE SOCIAL UNIT PLAN

Originally drafted in 1914-15, the social unit plan, on which the Cincinnati Social Unit Organization was based, had its origins in the work of Mr. Wilbur C. Phillips with the New York Milk Fund. This position, as well as the joint experience of Phillips and his wife as co-executive staff to the Milwaukee Child Welfare Commission in 1912-13, provided the practical base for the development of the idea. These experiences, coupled with their activity in the Socialist party and their commitment to a "cooperative commonwealth," combined to generate the shape and detail of the social unit plan.

After graduation from Harvard, where he had prepared himself for a career in journalism, Mr. Phillips went to work for the New York Milk Fund to conduct a campaign of public education to advance the Fund's interest in pure milk. The Fund, a creation of the New York Association for Improving the Condition of the Poor, had assumed the responsibility for improving the milk supply available to children and dealing with the problems of infant sickness resulting from impurities in milk. In rather short order the Fund found itself embroiled in such controversies as pasteurization versus certification and breast feeding versus bottle feeding. To keep pace, Phillips found himself being drawn away from public information activity and into the development of an action program to achieve the Fund's goals.

In an effort to resolve the issues confronting the pure-milk advocates, Phillips established infant milk stations to provide "controlled" tests of the various questions involved in the dispute. The success of the stations convinced Phillips of the value of the "scientific method" as a means for selecting among contending alternatives. From this experience he also gained an appreciation for the potential of local neighborhood-based programs; the value of nursing service as an educational as well as a medical effort; and the capacity of poor, uneducated, immigrant women to learn and apply principles of sound child health and child-rearing practices through meaningful involvement with professional staff members (35:25–52).

By 1911 the work of the Milk Committee was complete. The milk-station experience had led to the establishment of a national commission on milk standards. A demonstration dairy had been developed, and new methods of milk-processing and distribution were being devised. Commercial dairies were beginning to adopt purification methods. Phillips, who saw the work of the committee settling into a routine. sought new challenges (35:52–56).

At this time he met and married Elsie LaGrange Cole, an active member of the Socialist party. At her urging he resigned from the Milk

Committee and traveled to Milwaukee, where the first Socialist municipal government had just been elected. He persuaded the new administration to establish a municipal child welfare commission to undertake new experimental programs to enhance child welfare and to extend some of the New York work. The new Socialist government, flushed with victory, accepted the idea, and the Phillipses were invited to become co-executives of the new commission (35:60–63).

Although short-lived, the Milwaukee experience proved to be the testing ground for more of the ideas that ultimately emerged as the social unit plan. Mr. and Mrs. Phillips first developed a child health center and a district medical-nursing committee. They developed a committee of neighborhood women to gather data and encourage their friends to use the health center. They became convinced that developing programs in a single district and then expanding district by district was the soundest approach to introducing new services. Finally, as they saw neighborhood residents identifying with the health center as a "part of their neighborhood," they became convinced that the notion of a "cooperative commonwealth" was indeed feasible (36:40–48).

The Milk Committee and the Milwaukee Commission provided the practical seedbed for framing the ideas that went into the social unit plan. The actual drafting of the plan, however, resulted from the loss of Socialist control over Milwaukee city government, the subsequent discharge of "the comrades" Phillips, and their enforced "semiretirement" in 1914, which provided them the opportunity for reflection and writing. This sudden reversal in Socialist party fortunes, and what they saw as the success of demogoguery in partisan politics, convinced Mr. and Mrs. Phillips that, for democracy to become a reality, government must be restructured along nonpartisan lines, with the block as the basic political unit.

Toward these ends they drafted the social unit plan with the goal of "making democracy genuine and efficient—providing a machinery through which the people can express their desires easily and continuously, and putting at the disposal of all of the people a consensus of expert skill." The plan would operate through democratic social units, on a neighborhood basis, focusing on block development, coordination of expert resources, and a community council (32). To initiate the program the Phillipses set about establishing the National Social Unit Organization to sponsor the plan.

THE NATIONAL SOCIAL UNIT ORGANIZATION

The NSUO consisted of a diverse and somewhat unusual group of people who had been brought together by the attractiveness of the social unit plan and by the Phillips's persistent efforts. After completing the draft of the social unit proposal in 1915, Mr. and Mrs. Phillips turned for support to their acquaintances active in philanthropic circles.

*   *   *

The excitement about the social unit idea and the sense of participating in an important experiement probably did much to bring together so broad and improbable a group. However, it seems equally reasonable that the very diversity of the group and the varied interests represented suggest some of the reasons that brought the NSUO into being at that time.

Certainly the Phillips's dream of a "cooperative common-wealth," a true democracy, was attractive in its own terms and was an ideal shared by many. The NSUO offered a plan of action by which the dream might be fulfilled. For those who joined the movement, the plan was especially important in that it denied the inevitability of class warfare and violent revolution, and it offered the possibility of a means by which the social disintegration wracking Europe might be avoided. Finally, in this vein, the social unit promised to recapture the "idyllic" village life of the past within the confines of the city and thereby to overcome the "unfortunate consequences" of urban life and industrial capitalism.

For Croly, Straight, Frankfurter, Pinchot, and others involved in the liberal intellectual circles of the day, the social unit offered the oportunity of demonstrating, in microcosm, the feasibility and potential of the ideology of "new nationalism." Here was an opportunity to show that the Jeffersonian ideal of local sovereignty and individual freedom could be effectively joined to the Hamiltonian notion of a strong and vital federal government (15). The NSUO, a strong and prestigious national body, would provide funds and assistance to the CSUO, a locally based, democratically organized, independent unit, for the solution of social problems.

The "social work/philanthropist" interest in coordinating social service in order to enhance efficiency and eliminate duplication would be accomplished by the social unit program. In addition, the growing interest in shifting philanthropic efforts from charity to self-help was the essence of the social unit orientation. In announcing the NSUO, Pinchot emphasized this concern. He commented:

> Money contributed for social welfare work is wasted through dupli-cation, and also when so many uninvited strangers break in upon the privacy of the families of the poor, it must seem to them to be both an intrusion and an affront to their self respect. . . . Most of us who contribute to philanthropic endeavor profess . . . to be interested not so much in doing things for people as in helping them do things themselves.
>
> The one is charity, the other is democracy. A system of social effort which aims merely at the dispensation of various . . . services to the poor and makes no attempt to aid them to organize to study their own needs and themselves become the power back of such a program as will meet these needs, is only scratching the surface [3:10].

Coupled with the interest in efficiency, coordination, and self-help was the growing support for "scientific inquiry." All problems were capable of solution if one applied the rational and unbiased skills of the pure, and somewhat idealized, scientist. Pinchot referred to the Cincinnati program as a "social laboratory" (3:10). NSUO publica-tions made constant reference to the program as an "experiment" and highlighted the plan for evaluating its results. If those results were positive, the plan called for extending social unit organization to other neighborhoods and cities (31). The plan extended from laboratory to application—the "complete scientific model."

Finally, the plan offered a means of heading off the dangers many believed confronted the nation or, at least, their own interests. The upheaval in Europe had produced uncertainty and political shifts. The number of strikes, like those that had rocked Lawrence and Paterson, was growing, as was the influence of "radicals." The war and competition from the "wobblies" had badly split the ranks of the Socialist party. For some socialists, personified perhaps by Spargo, Stelzle, and Mr. and Mrs. Phillips, the program offered hope for a "reasonable" political alternative to the challenge from the left—a challenge that was to grow with the advent of the Russian Revolution.

The reasons advanced by the NSUO to explain its choice of Cincinnati as the site for the experiment lend support to this analysis of the factors that produced the social unit plan. Cincinnati was favorably disposed to service efficiency and coordination, as testified to by (a) the existence of a Council of Social Agencies which "favored" the social unit idea and coordination of services; (b) a director of public welfare who offered his full cooperation; and (c) generally favorable public opinion toward the social unit plan and its goals, with particular support from the Chamber of Commerce, as well as the social agencies. The latter had committed themselves to abandon their own programs in the experimental district in favor of the social unit (8:121). The scientific interest was reflected in the demographic attractiveness of Cincinnati, which was located at the approximate center of the United States population, was considered a "typical" American city, and was compoesd of distinct districts which made experimentation in a single area feasible (8:117). As for the "cooperative commonwealth," Cincinnati was thought to be fertile ground because of the "cooperation" among business, professional, and labor interests; the public ownership of utilities, a municipal railroad, and rapid transit, the existence of a municipal university and a modern municipal hospital; and the city's new spirit of political reform, which had resulted in the deposing of "Boss" Cox after thirty years of rule (25:9). Finally, the political-science interest of the NSUO in demonstrating new ways of national-local cooperation was reflected in the selection of Cincinnati because there were available and committed local leaders who would make such cooperation possible. These leaders, active in pursuing the program for Cincinnati, had shown no fear or hesitancy about outside interference in local affairs. They committed themselves to financial support, if after three years of demonstration the program proved successful (22:8, 117).

When the Phillipses arrived in Cincinnati they felt fully prepared to launch their "adventure for democracy." They were representatives of a potent national organization which was soundly financed. The social unit plan had been competed for by sixteen cities, and the most supportive and compatible city had been selected. All that remained was to set the wheels in motion.

THE CINCINNATI SOCIAL UNIT ORGANIZATION

The Cincinnati Social Unit Organization was initiated on January 1, 1917. The first experimental application of the social unit idea was direct and simple in both form and structure. Consisting of a tripartite structure—a citizens' council, occupational council, and a general council—the plan was to operate in the Mohawk-Brighton district of Cincinnati with the general goal of "restoring the advantages of village life to city people" (29:2). The councils were to provide the channel through which social and political programs important in the neighborhood and geared to achieving democracy were to develop.

The Mohawk-Brighton district was divided into 31 blocks, each of which was organized into a block council with as close to 100 percent participation of the residents as possible. Everyone over the age of eighteen was entitled to participate in the affairs of the block council and to vote in the selection of a block worker from among their number. In turn, the block workers constituted the membership of the citizens' council, which had the responsibility of uncovering the needs of the total district and guaranteeing that plans and programs were developed to meet these needs (29:5, 10:2).

Although detailed development of specific service plans and programs was the responsibility of the occupational council, the general direction and content of the program emerged from the block councils acting through the citizens' council. Such direction and need identification was to be the result of formal block planning meetings and the general work of the block workers. Paid to work about eight hours per week, the block worker was responsible for collecting data, disseminating information in the district, developing resident participation, and "servicing the block" as a social worker and advocate in regard to securing social services (17:671–74).

Complementing the citizens' council was the occupational council. Persons belonging to a particular occupational group and working or living in the district were organized into occupational councils. Thus, doctors were to be organized into a doctor's council, social workers into a welfare council, workers and industrialists into an industrial council, and so on. Each of these groups in turn selected one of its number to represent it on the district occupational council. This overall council, with its constituent subgroups, provided technical advice and expert management skill for the development, specification, and implementation of the programs requested by the community (29:3–4).

The general council was the third component of the organization. Composed of the citizens' council and occupational council meeting together, this group was responsible for overall policy-making and budgeting for the district organizational and programmatic effort. The general council did not involve itself in the daily work of the program, which was to develop in the direct relations between the citizens' council and the various occupational groups (10:3).

The expected daily operation of the program was described by example as follows:

When the Citizens Council discovers a health need in the district, it will put the problem up to the doctor group. . . . [Then] the doctors will be responsible for the finding of a solution to the problem and for submitting the plan they devise to the Citizens Council. If the block workers in the Citizens Council find that there are many men out of work . . . the business and labor groups will be held responsible for

working out some plan to meet the problem. In this way, everyone in
the Social Unit District will . . . work for the whole community, at the
same time that he is working for himself [29:6].

In order to guarantee the daily operation of the program and to provide staff services, each council elected its own staff director. Mr. and
Mrs. Phillips were chosen executives by the general council, Mr. Courtenay Dinwiddie became the staff member of the occupational council,
and Miss Mary Hicks was elected executive of the citizens' council
(31).
    Participants believed that this structure, underscored by com-
mitment to the idea that need should be defined and met by those
affected operating through small geographic units, would inevitably
result in operationalizing democracy. Such a "participatory democracy" was clearly the ultimate goal of the program. Mr. Phillips stated
it thus:

> [The purpose is] to build democracy both genuine and efficient.
> . . . Genuine because it inheres in the life of the people; because they
> are truly self-governing, understanding their own needs, and analyzing
> their own difficulties; efficient, because it is developing leadership;
> because it is recognizing the skill at its command and mobilizing it for
> action [35:176–77].

    To achieve these ends, an initial and fairly specific service
through which the social unit could mobilize the district was needed.
The first such service was a child health center, which provided medical
care and preventive health services to babies. Selection of health service as the first effort reflected various interests. The large number of
children in the district and the lack of health services indicated the
need for such a center. Participants believed that the goal of organizing
block councils could be most easily reached by approaching adults who
would be interested in the health needs of their children and the services of the center. The center also reflected the interests of Dr. J. H.
Landis, city health officer and a major supporter of the social unit plan
(35:209–16), and the Anti-Tuberculosis League, which was concerned
with the unusually high tuberculosis rate in the city, particularly among
children (22:557). The Phillips's previous experience had convinced
them that health services, in addition to being needed, were a most
effective means of reaching families, organizing doctors, and dramatically demonstrating the plan. Finally, they reasoned that, if high participation in planning and service could be achieved in the development of democratic medical services, the CSUO could easily extend into
other service sectors.

CINCINNATI SOCIAL UNIT ORGANIZATION IN ACTION

Coincident with the organization of the health center, the doctors'
council, and the nurses' council, the block workers were employed, and
block organizing began. The early experiences of the center and the
work of the block workers stimulated the development of a social
worker council to plan programs to deal with the social needs discovered as a result of the medical program (12:506).

276   The health center was originally conceived as providing "well baby" services, but its scope was soon expanded to encompass the interest of the Anti-Tuberculosis League in case-finding and the interest of the Children's Bureau in providing medical examination and treatment for all preschool children during "Children's Year" (1918) and in providing public health education and medical services during the influenza epidemic. The "output" of the clinic was impressive, not only in relation to scope and case service, but in concept as well. The CSUO was acclaimed as having been able to develop the most advanced program of public health administration in the United States (46:5).

Specifically, the CSUO was praised for developing a unique system of gathering and maintaining up-to-date community statistics. The health center, with only four nurses, provided nursing care to one-half of the district population, gave complete medical examinations to 90 percent of the children under six years of age, provided nursing care to all the infants and preschool children found to be in poor health, achieved a fourfold increase in tuberculosis supervision and a fivefold increase in the care of sick children and adults, gave prenatal services to 45 percent of the expectant mothers, established the first special clinic for examination and treatment of persons convalescing from influenza, and provided information on symptoms and treatment of influenza within twenty-four hours of receiving such requests from public health officials (46:5).

About the less quantifiable aspects of the program, Dinwiddie commented:

The results of the unit plan, in the conduct of neighborhood services, indicate that it should have an important contribution to make to the handling of larger issues. But the exact part [the social unit] can play in dealing with other problems, those that are more technical and remote from the daily experience of the average citizen, is a matter for further experimentation [10:39].

Despite this somewhat qualified praise, he went on to say that the work and skills of the medical staff were greatly improved as a result of their close ties to the residents and that "the appreciation by the local physicians of their responsibilities and opportunities, as part of a neighborhood organization, developed in a way that was unique in any similar group of local practitioners" (10:48). He concluded:

The organization effected, and the work accomplished by the physician group . . . constituted the most significant development in group organization that grew out of this experiment . . . especially when it is considered that [physicians'] interests, as private practitioners with habits and traditions of exaggerated individualism, were apparently in direct conflict with their interests as members of a neighborhood organization campaigning for the prevention of disease [10:48].

Clearly, the experience of the health program was a major step toward accomplishing a public good—sound health—through the operationalizing of that strange idea of "genuine and efficient democracy." **277** But could the clinic experience be generalized? Was the success in fact indicative of the kind of response that would develop in other sectors of neighborhood life?

The short life of the program and the lack of opportunity to expand preclude the possibility of definitive answers. However, some initial expansion of the program was undertaken in the provision of social services, development of recreation, and some aspects of landlord-tenant relations. These efforts derived in large measure from the work of the block workers in case-finding, performance of friendly visitor functions, and the conduct of advocacy efforts in behalf of their neighbors. The degree of success of the work was commented on by E. T. Devine, who reported that the Associated Charities received more referrals from Mohawk-Brighton than from any other district, with greater follow-up by the local community than was normally found. Similarly, the Better Housing League reported greater cooperation in the district than elsewhere. The Schools Vocational Bureau credited the Citizens' Council with generating the influence necessary for creation of new services. The Ohio Humane Society relinquished its casework in the district to the block workers. The Domestic Relations Court praised the cooperation of the social unit (8:121). In summing up the nonmedical work of the CSUO Devine said: "I am of the opinion that definite, tangible and substantial results have been obtained. . . . [The CSUO] has added substantially to the physical and moral well-being of the residents . . . [and it has] prompted neighborliness and sociability not to be found elsewhere" (8:122).

In general, the contention that the CSUO made a significant contribution to the reorganization of community life along democratic lines is supported by the available literature. However, the success of the working relationships between the citizens' council and the occupational council, while not to be negated, must be tempered by an appreciation of the commitment and leadership of Mr. and Mrs. Phillips. In addition, one must recognize the potent effect of the national organization, the NSUO, which provided not only the philosophical and economic support to the experiment but significant political impact as well. Given such strength, why did the Cincinnati program disappear?

THE DEMISE OF THE SOCIAL UNIT PLAN

Most of the first year of CSUO was spent getting the program organized. Offices were established, preliminary organization was undertaken, and an elaborate process of selecting the experimental district was completed (12:498; 43). As a result, the health center did not open until December 1917 (12:499), and it was only the beginning of the second year that the block councils held elections of block workers.

The block workers who had been working during most of the first year had been selected by the Phillipses. The election signaled the transfer of this authority. The block workers were all reelected, and the voter turnout was a great encouragement to social unit leaders. With an average of 100 eligible voters per block, the number of votes cast ranged from a low of 22 in one block to a high of 143 in another. Voter turnout in the district as a whole averaged 71 percent, a figure far in excess of voter participation in local elections. In addition, the voting rate was correlated to the date of block organization, as those blocks organized earliest showed the greatest voter response (35:276–78).

The success of the program during the second year also encouraged social unit advocates. Its work was attracting national attention and support. In March 1919, the NSUO announced that Secretary of the Interior Franklin K. Lane had accepted the honorary national chairmanship of the movement. In accepting the office Lane said:

> The object of the movement is ... to organize communities so that every citizen can take part in the community programs and so that the people as a whole may be drawn in to close and continued relationship with the experts [18:6].

He continued:

> I believe the [NSUO] has great potentialities for bringing government close to the lives of the people; and for ensuring the cooperation of all classes in the most democratic way imaginable; for developing the community as a unit of the nation to provide its people with the municipal and civic life fulfilling their desires [18:6].

Lane also chose this occasion to announce that the NSUO was making plans to expand the experiment to other communities.

On the same day, Cincinnati's Mayor Galvin declared that he had discovered the social unit program to be "a dangerous type of socialism." He said: "I consider it a dangerous institution in our city and but one step away from Bolshevism. It aims at establishing a government within a government" (2:6).

To support his charges the mayor produced a letter from Dr. Landis to Mr. Phillips, in which the late health officer had expressed concern about the past Socialist party membership of the Phillipses and their continuing belief in the need to socialize the politico-economic system. The mayor neglected to point out that, despite these personal reservations, Dr. Landis expressed continuing support for the social unit. Instead, Galvin linked the Landis letter to his own discovery that the NSUO had secret and subversive intentions which were revealed in statements by Pinchot, Lane, and Phillips (35:299–300). These subversive goals were the establishment of a "cooperative commonwealth" and "a democracy both genuine and efficient."

In response to the mayor's attack, Dinwiddie, speaking for the NSUO, issued a statement that the social unit "is the most sane and constructive effort in community service now going on in America." He concluded by saying: "Just such constructive measures to achieve the highest ideals of our great Republic are the best answer to Bolshevism and class measures of all kind" (2:6). The exchange of charge and defense did not long occupy public attention. However, it became quickly apparent that the "broad local support" that had brought the program to Cincinnati was fast dwindling.

The Council of Social Agencies announced that it was withdrawing the minimal funds it had allocated to the social unit. It further threatened to cut off support to any agency that gave funds to the social unit. It then appointed a committee to investigate the charges, and, although the committee found no support for them, the Council stood fast by its decision to renege on its promise to provide financial support to the program (7:870). In his evaluation of the program, E. T. Devine indicated that the action of the Council of Social Agencies had been dictated by conservative political and financial interests, which had threatened to withdraw support from the annual fund campaign (8:119). ("Sentence first and trial after," said the Queen city.)

With firm belief in the democratic process, social unit leaders adopted various means of telling the story and attempting to reverse the sudden negative trend. A series of articles appeared in various journals. In one such article in the *Review*, Mrs. Tiffany argued that the accusation of "Bolshevism" and Sovietism" could be made against small town rural government or the Chamber of Commerce as easily as the CSUO. In regard to the social unit she said:

> The Social Unit philosophy is distinctly not Bolshevist. . . . The Social Unit has no *a priori* social, political or economic program. . . . [It] is based upon the conception that the collective intelligence of the whole community—not any one section or part—so organized that it can continuously express itself, is to be relied upon as against the will or intelligence of any individual, group, or class [49:12].

In addition to these efforts at rational discussion of the social unit idea, the NSUO sought and received editorial support from the press, most notably the *New Republic* (50) and the *New York Times* (34).

Somewhat naively, Phillips wrote an impassioned letter to Mayor Galvin attempting to describe the philosophical roots of the program and to show how social unit democracy was superior to party politics. In concluding the letter Phillips proposed that the mayor convene a public meeting, under his own chairmanship, to evaluate the unit. At the conclusion of the meeting those present, representing the full spectrum of Cincinnati life, would vote for or against the social unit, on the basis of the testimony they had heard. The social unit would accept the vote as binding.

The mayor ignored the letter (35:301–7). Undaunted, Phillips announced that the social unit would rely on the decision of the people. A plebiscite was organized by an independent citizens' committee in the Mohawk-Brighton district on April 10, 1919 (30:53). When the votes were tallied, 4,154 residents of an estimated seven thousand eligible voters had cast their ballots. Only 120 voted in opposition to the CSUO.

Despite the impressive show of support, the "committed and capable leadership" of Cincinnati had made a firm decision. By exercising its control over the Council of Social Agencies and the local political machinery and acting on the fears engendered by wartime jingoism, a mounting red scare, and postwar economic uncertainty,

280 community leaders had succeeded in ending the experiment for "genuine democracy," thereby making Cincinnati safe for themselves. The doors were closed on the CSUO. Although the NSUO attempted to mount a program elsewhere, it met with little success or interest. In March 1921 a brief notice on the financial page of the *New York Times* announced that the NSUO had been placed in receivership to satisfy outstanding debt (39). The social unit had completed the cycle.

DISCUSSION

Obviously, the effort to develop a broadened participatory base in social decision-making did not end with the demise of the NSUO. However, the social unit approach, tested and shown workable, disappeared, and the social work profession of the day, which had shown such great interest during the experiment, turned its community organizing interests away from such "hare-brained" schemes. With a wisdom unique to social work, it turned its attention to the solution of the "real" problem of the time—federated financing and community chest development.

In his evaluation of the CSUO, Devine, in what seemed a desperate effort to remind social workers of their roots, wrote:

> The Social Unit conception of democracy . . . goes deeper than particular political institutions or forms of government. It penetrates to the very heart of the social order and raises the challenge as to whether the people are or are not capable of deciding, with stimulated and socially controlled expert assistance, what their needs are and how they stall be met. This conception of democracy . . . may not be compatible with some aspects of party government or with some interpretation put upon existing constitutions. . . . There is no reason to think that [syndicalism, national guildism, or the soviet idea] or any of the features which have distinguished these three systems . . . are expected in connection with the Social Unit, except their democracy.
>
> It is in other words a political substitute for existing political government and for existing voluntary social agencies. . . . Thus the democracy which they are advocating and which they wish to extend is perhaps only another name for social progress. That its triumph however would make unnecessary most of our present political machinery . . . is hardly open to question [8:120].

Devine saw the controversy surrounding the social unit plan as clearly an issue between politicians and self-perpetuating boards of "altruists" against local democratic community organization. He concluded:

> The real question is whether [the critics] do not in fact object to the inherent tendencies of the Social Unit: to its democracy in the sense that it calls not ony for the consultation with the rank and file of small contributors, which is so rare to be almst nonexistent in social work, but also for consultation with beneficiaries, which is so rare as to be almost unheard of. . . .
>
> It is not surprising that a clear cut proposal to put into practice the democratic method may frighten into open opposition public officials who feel responsible for administering our existing institutions, busi-

nessmen who are concerned not only about prosperity but about profits, social agencies committed to present methods of finance and administration, and conservative citizens who are disturbed merely because new and strange methods are proposed, or perhaps for the better reason that they see the implications and do not like them [8:124–25].

Devine's clear challenge could not overcome the effect of the economic uncertainties of the ensuing decades or the mounting "red scare" and witch hunt of the early 1920s. The rush of social work to adopt the psychoanalytic model for treatment and the notion of federated financing as the "true path" to solving social problems could not be diverted. Instead, the Phillips's dream, Devine's challenge, and the search for a political-social-economic democracy rooted in participation of all the people were largely forgotten. When the issues resurfaced during the poverty war, particularly in regard to participation, it was necessary to build anew. Time had obliterated remembrances and the effects of such earlier beginnings as the social unit.

If one is allowed a biological analogy, the maxim that "ontogeny recapitulates phylogeny" seems appropriate. Although separated in time by fifty years, the parallels between the community-action experience and the social unit plan are startlingly apparent. The convergence of forces acting on the community-action program, while varying in form from those of the social unit, are amazingly similar. The growing challenge to the status quo came now from a militant civil-rights movement rather than a growing working-class consciousness. The emphasis on federal-local partnership generated renewed efforts at unifying the Hamiltonian and Jeffersonian perspectives. Social welfare interest returned to a search for new methods of effecting social change and shifting the focus from charity to self-help. The evils of urban life were rediscovered, and the search for recreating the lost, and perhaps romanticized, rural past was reawakened. Finally, for some, the dream of a "democracy, genuine and efficient," continued to stir.

Unfortunately, the parallels are not limited to motivation and goals alone. Present political attacks upon participatory efforts are at least as serious as those faced by the CSUO. Wartime jingosim, fear of riot and rebellion, and economic uncertainty bolster and support these attacks, which seem designed not so much to solve problems as to preserve the social-political status quo. If history does indeed repeat itself, then we may be entering another fifty-year period of forgetting and avoidance. If, on the other hand, history serves to teach, then perhaps the effort may be sustained and strengthened and a "democracy both genuine and efficient" can be realized.

REFERENCES

1. Black, Warwick. "Social Unit Ended in Cincinnati." *National Municipal Review* 10 (January 1921) : 72–73.
2. "Calls Unit Socialistic: Lane Experiment in Cincinnati near Socialism, Mayor Asserts." *New York Times*, 11 March 1919.
3. "Cincinnati's Social Welfare Scheme." *New York Times*, April 15, 1917, S. 8.

282

4. Community Chest of Cincinnati and Hamilton County. *The First Twenty Years, 1915–1935.* Cincinnati, 1935.
5. Council of Social Agencies (Cincinnati). *Special Committee Investigation of Charges against the Social Unit Organization: Report.* June 1919.
6. "Democracy on the Social Unit Pattern." *Survey* 39 (February 16, 1918) : 550–51.
7. Devine, Edward T. "Cincinnati Experiment." *Survey* 42 (September 20, 1919) : 869–70.
8. ———. "Social Unit in Cincinnati: An Experiment in Organization." *Survey* 43 (November 15, 1919) : 115–26.
9. ———. "Social Unit Plan in the Epidemic." *Survey* 41 (January 11, 1919) : 503–4.
10. Dinwiddie, Courtenay. *Community Responsibility: A Review of the Cincinnati Social Unit Experiment.* New York: New York School of Social Work, 1921.
11. ———. "Cooperation and Coordination in Public Health." In *Proceedings of the National Conference of Social Work, 1920.* New York: Columbia University Press, 1920.
12. ———. "Work Accomplished by the Cincinnati Social Unit." In *Proceedings of the National Conference of Social Work,* 1918. New York: Columbia University Press, 1918.
13. Duzanne, P. "County Neighborliness in City Blocks." *World Outlook* 5 (July 1919) : 12–13.
14. Eldridge, Seba. "Community Organization and Citizenship." *Social Forces* 7 (September 1928) : 132–40.
15. Forcey, Charles. *The Crossroads of Liberalism.* New York: Oxford University Press, 1961.
16. Hibble, Charles R., and Goodwin, Frank P. *The Citizen's Book.* Cincinnati: Stewart & Kidd Co., 1916.
17. Hicks, M. L., and Eastman, R. S. "Block Workers as Developed under the Social Unit Experiment in Cincinnati." *Survey* 44 (September 1, 1920) : 671–74.
18. "Lane to Serve as Social Unit Head." *New York Times,* March 11, 1919.
19. Leebron, H. "Democratic Community." *Survey* 44 (June 19, 1920) : 409–10.
20. Levitan, Sar A. "Planning the Anti-Poverty Strategy." *Poverty and Human Resources Abstracts* 2 (March-April 1967) : 5–16.
21. Lindeman, Eduard C. *The Community.* New York: Association Press, 1921.
22. Lowrie, S. G. "Social Unit: An Experiment in Politics." *National Municipal Review* 9 (September 1920) : 553–66.
23. "Mr. and Mrs. Wilbur C. Phillips' Big Idea." *Everybody's* 34 (June 1916) : 784–85.
24. Moynihan, Daniel P. *Maximum Feasible Misunderstanding.* New York: Free Press, 1969.
25. National Social Unit Organization. *Bulletin No. 1: History of the Unit Plan.* January 17, 1918.
26. ———. *Bulletin No. 2: Outline of the Unit Plan.* January 17, 1918.
27. ———. *Bulletin No. 2A: Statement on the Practical Experience on Which the Unit Plan Is Based.* March 18, 1918.
28. ———. *Bulletin No. 3: Creation and Purpose of the Cincinnati Social Unit Organization.* March 18, 1918.
29. ———. *Bulletin No. 4: Description of the Unit Plan Used in the Pre-*

liminary Organizing Work in the Mohawk-Brighton District. March **283**
18, 1918.

30. ———. *Bulletin No. 5: Beginning Work in the Social Unit.* August 1,
1918.
31. ———. *Bulletin No. 6: The Social Unit Experiment.* October 1, 1919.
32. ———. *Wanted: A Program for Community Organization.* October
1919.
33. Neely, R. T. "New Community Plan." *Ladies Home Journal* 35
(September 1918) : 20–21.
34. "New Yorkers to Have Social Units." *New York Times,* 30 June 1919.
35. Phillips, Wilbur C. *Adventuring for Democracy.* New York: Social
Unit Press, 1940.
36. ———. "Community Planning for Infant Welfare Work." In *Proceedings of the National Conference of Charities and Correction,
1912.*
37. ———. "Democracy and the Unit Plan." In *Proceedings of the National Conference of Social Work, 1919.* New York: Columbia
University Press, 1919.
38. ———. "Health and Commonwealth." In *Proceedings of the National
Conference of Social Work, 1917.* New York: Columbia University
Press, 1917.
39. "Receiver Asked for Social Unit." *New York Times,* 30 March 1921.
40. Reed, A. L. "The 'Social Unit' in Cincinnati." *American Review of Reviews* 59 (May 1919) : 523–24.
41. Rubin, Lillian M. "Maximum Feasible Participation." *Poverty and
Human Resources Abstracts* 2 (November-December 1967) : 5–18.
42. Shelby, G. M. "Extending Democracy: What the Cincinnati Social
Unit Has Accomplished." *Harper's,* April 1920, pp. 688–95.
43. "Social Unit District Chooses Itself." *Survey* 38 (July 21, 1917) :
355–56.
44. "Social Unit Plan." *Outlook,* July 23, 1919, pp. 460–62.
45. "Social Work by Blocks." *Literary Digest* 63 (December 6, 1919) :
34–35; 90–91.
46. Thompson, Dorothy. "A Community Experiment Which Has Succeeded." *New York Times Magazine,* 16 March 1919.
47. ———. "Social Unit Organization, Cincinnati, Ohio." *Social Service
Review* (Washington, D.C.) 8 (September 1918) : 12–13.
48. ———. "Unit Plan of Health Administration." *National Municipal
Review* 7 (November 1918) : 596–99.
49. Tiffany, K. L. "Social Unit at Cincinnati: Is It a Soviet?" *Review* 2
(January 3, 1920) : 11–12.
50. "Who Makes Bolshevism in Cincinnati?" *New Republic,* April 19,
1919, pp. 365–67.
51. Work Projects Administration Writers Program. *Cincinnati: A Guide
to the Queen City and Its Neighbors.* Cincinnati: Wiesen-Hart
Press, 1943.

284   STAN STEINER

The Death and Resurrection
of the Rural Village

One cold winter not too long ago a young reporter journeyed into the villages in the state of New Mexico. He saw death. The houses were boarded up, half of their people gone. "A man splits wood for his stove. And only a dog hears the noise of his ax," Peter Nabokov wrote in the Santa Fe *New Mexican.* "The villages are dying."

Years before the coming of mechanized farming the villages were "doomed." In the colonial Spanish era in the old Southwest it was evident that "beyond a mere livelihood incentive stopped, bowing to a stone wall of inevitability. And a dry rot set in," the Reverend Ross Calvin wrote twenty years ago in his *Sky Determines: An Interpretation of the Southwest.* His requiem was the usual one of the Anglo for those whom he had conquered: "A stronger race came and took away their inheritance."

And yet what else could one expect from the "illiterate, half savage proletariat," as the historical writer Harvey Fergusson has contemptuously described the Hispano villagers of the Southwest.

In the villages the earth too was dead. The earth was no longer sacred: it was fertilized by chemicals, not by the sun, plowed by machines, not by men, measured by market prices, not by its own beauty.

The strangers, many of them, were city men before they came into the wilderness. Who among them worships the gods of the earth? The Hispano villagers of New Mexico do. So do the Mexican farm workers of the Southwest, the descendants of Indian and Spanish farmers, who lived in communal villages, with a reverence for the earth. They sowed seeds to grow food, not to profit. They were outmoded, bypassed by progress.

"The destruction of the Spanish American village economy and social structure" is at hand, Dr. Clark Knowlton of the University of Texas informed a recent meeting of the Rural Sociological Society. His gloomy view, so common among the knowing, beholds the villages as "a largely distressed region marked by poverty, functional illiteracy, unemployment, high rates of welfare payments, poor educational features, emigration, apathy and ethnic bitterness." Elsewhere Dr. Knowlton has questioned the "continued existence" of the villages. "Problematical," he guesses.

It is true that emigration from the farms to the cities in the past twenty years has been greater than the flood of European immigrants into the ghettos during the peak years of the exodus—1896 to 1915. The refugees from the countryside numbered 17.5 million from 1940 to 1960. And still they come at the rate of almost one million a year. Mostly the young and restless, they fill the new ghettos with longing and discontent. Lopsided crowding has squeezed 70 percent of the people into 3 percent of the land. The trail of the refugees is everywhere the same as in the Southwest.

The folks down on the farms have decreased from 32 million in 1910 to 12.3 million in 1965. So, too, have the farms disappeared in those years, from 6,361,502 to about 3,000,000 today. Half of those remaining are barely subsistence farms, whose crops account for a mere 3 per cent of the agricultural market. Jobs in rural areas have evaporated. In the years before World War I one-third of the people labored on the land, but by the mid-1960's only 6 percent of the people had rural employment.

In a doomsday prophecy titled "The Decline and Fall of the Small Town," in the emporium of social scientism *Trans-action* (April, 1967), two moody sociologists, William Simon and John H. Gagnon, dissected the corpus delicti of three small towns in Southern Illinois —with little glee but no regrets. Simon and Gagnon, senior researchers at the Institute for Sexual Research at the University of Indiana —where they are specialists in the study of "adjustment of male homosexuals"—deviated from their normal scholarly pursuits to excoriate the ghosts of small-town life. They tried, but they failed.

Life in these small towns is "doomed," the sociologists decided. The "local amenities must deteriorate," the towns themselves "will become isolated and decayed," and soon only "the aged, the inept, the very young—and the local power elite" will be left on the dilapidated and dying Main Streets.

Not that the small towns cannot compete with the cities, but they won't, the sociologists wrote. "Redevelopment is not a promise but a threat to the ideologies of small town life."

Quiet and neighborly concerns, the belief in traditional ways, and "a strongly anti-urban system of values," such as a "rejection of purely mercenary values," convinced the sociologists that small towns were a drag on progress, an anachronism that had to succumb to history. "They must lose their best people," who presumably do not believe in these outmoded ideas, and those "who return will be failures," who are satisfied with "the second best in our competitive society."

The perverse and bygone literary farmer from Texas, Stanley Walker, extended this harsh view into the countryside. In his tirade of a few years ago, *The Myth of the Family Farm*, he wrote: "Far from being sturdy, valiant yeomen who should be preserved these people are for the most part born leeches. They hate their work. They make rural slums."

The requiem varies, yet it is everywhere the same. The ghost towns of the old mining camps in the Rockies, the abandoned farm towns on the Dakota plains, the deserted country crossroads in the

286   cotton delta, the decaying adobes of the Hispano villages—these are all ruins of a dying way of life. Our countryside has become a cemetery of beautiful memories. . . .

Alex Mercure, a quiet man not given to outbursts, is nonetheless angered by the prophecies of doom. He is the State Director of the Home Education Livelihood Program (HELP) of New Mexico, probably the most successful attempt at the revival of village economy and pride in the whole country.

"Villages are not dead," he says. "Some of the experts believe that rural life is no longer functional. That rural society has collapsed beyond any possibility of rebuilding. It is not so!

"What do the experts know of our village life?" Mecure scoffs. "Our villages have many human resources. People!" They know how to organize and run their own Cattle Growers Associations, and how to manage Water Users and Ditch Associations. They practice their own village democracy. They have religious strengths. They have the framework of strong families, though these have been weakened by the welfare system. They have their native skills—woodworking and weaving—that could be profitable for them. Most of all, says Mercure, "they know how to enjoy life."

"Communal life still exists in the villages," Mecure says. "It is not entirely the shadow that the experts see from the outside. It is a reality. And that communal life may be our greatest strength. These are the seeds of the revival of village life. Can these seeds be regenerated? I think so.

"Gandhi in India advocated a cottage industry. That may have been all right for India. But not here. What is cottage industry in an industrial country such as this but handicrafts and art crafts? That benefits just one man. And a Gifte Shoppe. It is archaic. It won't help a whole village. Look what the government's Indian Arts and Crafts program has done to stop poverty on the reservations. Not much.

"We need village industry," he says. "Small village industry that can revive the village. A village does not need a large plant, or huge investment. That would only destroy the village completely. No, we need native industry that would employ maybe ten, or twenty, people. Because ten jobs would feed one hundred people. That will mean more jobs in the grocery store, the post office, the gas station, the tavern. That's all a village needs to survive."

More than fifty village industries and cooperatives have been begun by the HELP project. Established in 1965 under the sponsorship of the New Mexico Council of Churches and the Roman Catholic Archdiocese of Santa Fe, and supported by Ford Foundation and OEO grants, HELP seeks to aid "the poorest of the poor" in the villages, who "never had a true sense of community." Its aims are straightforward and simple. The training of job skills "based on the skill needs of the community" is a prosaic enough beginning. So too is its second goal: the setting up of farming cooperatives to help stabilize "small family-sized farms." And finally, it hopes to help "small business enterprises to utilize existing handcraft skills."

"We are rebuilding the villages," Mercure says. "You know why we are succeeding where so many have failed? Because we practice old-fashioned democracy. I am very conservative about that."

"The most conservative program in existence today," Governor Cargo of New Mexico agrees. But the old ranchers, with hard-lined faces, are leery of HELP's program to encourage the self-reliance of the Hispano villagers. They cite an accusation of nefarious subversion, "The Communist Plot to Grab the Southwest," by Alan Strang, that appeared in *American Opinion*, a supposed John Birch publication, which implied that Mercure and the HELP program were part of a "plot" to "grab" the land of the Anglos.

"I thought the conservatives would support us," Mercure says, shaking his head with a bewildered smile. "All we are doing is encouraging individualism and free enterprise and old-fashioned initiative. Isn't that what everybody always says they want?

"Everybody is suspicious of our 'power.' What power? Look at our directors," he says. "On the Board of Trustees of HELP are six farm workers, five church lay leaders; in the villages, two ministers, one banker, one businessman, and a Catholic nun. What's suspicious about that?"

In the villages the self-help programs are run by the villagers themselves. One village has a woodworkers' cooperative where they make chairs for kindergartens; another makes wooden crates. There are farm-machinery cooperatives and apple-marketing cooperatives and vegetable farmers' cooperatives. There are health clinics that the villagers build and run. In one village famous for its weaving, until recently a dying art, the craftsmen are encouraged to establish a weavers' cooperative. The villagers decide on their needs and develop solutions that the farmers and artisans wish.

"Too many decisions are forced (on the poor) and consequently are resented rather than responsibly met," Mecure says. His philosophy is simple to help the villages decide what to do, with capital loans and technical aid. Eight of these villages have set up credit unions run by and for the poor farmers and farm workers.

"If you want to help people let them tell you what they need," Mercure says. "Let them decide. Never impose your needs on them. You are only fooling yourself that you are helping them. You aren't fooling them.

"All this middle-class nonsense of trying to teach people to be middle class on $1,500 a year. What good does it do?" The urban programs thought up in government offices by middle-class planners just confuse the villagers, he says. "Rural people don't need them. Learning to push an elevator button! Now what good does that do a farmer?" Even though these programs may be offered with the best of intentions he feels they stifle the initiative of the rural poor.

" 'We want to do something *for* you,' they say. They can't do anything *for* us. They don't understand that," Mercure says.

In the beginning of the War on Poverty he thought these government programs might offer new hope. He fears that hope has been betrayed, as do many others. "We thought that they would be of some

288

service to the people," says Fecundo Valdez, who too has worked on OEO projects. "But as it turned out, on many occasions they have been a deterrent. In a way the War on Poverty has speeded up the actual displacement of people in the rural areas."

The frustrations of villagers brought about by governmental promises and congressional withdrawals has been picaresquely portrayed by Lauro Garcia, a young village leader in the farm workers' community of Guadalupe, Arizona:

"It's like having a beautiful woman. She excites you. She entices you. You are ready. Then she closes her legs. And you get nothing. Just frustrated. You feel humiliated. You feel like killing her. That's the way you get frustrated by the promise of these government programs. Because they don't deliver what they promise. And you are left holding the bag.

"We have a saying for that in Spanish," says Garcia, "but it's not polite."

The Lord giveth and the Lord taketh attitude of the agencies dealing with the Hispano villages is not the creation of the OEO. It is the traditional way of the government. "Our people do not trust the government. *Gobierno!* That's almost a curse word," says Fecundo Valdez; the *patron* and the peon have too often been preserved in the attitudes, procedures, and institutions of the government.

Much of the rural Southwest, and most of New Mexico, is treated like a colony by the rest of the country, Mercure says. "We export our raw materials and we import the finished products. Isn't that the way it is in the colonial country?" he asks bitterly. "Like poor colonials we are kept in a state of dependency and indebtedness. And condescension is the political expression of this.

"I told this to the executive Committee of the New Mexico Legislature," Mercure says. "I told them, Do you know that of all the hides of all the cattle in this state not one hide is tanned in this state? Do you know that all the hay and straw that is grown for brooms, that the villages could make into brooms if they had small industry, that all this hay and straw is sent out of the state? Do you know that we import 70 per cent of the food we eat in this state, though this is an agricultural state?

"We *are* a colonial country. That's why we are poor. And we will have to change that ourselves."

The villages are not dying, says Fecundo Valdez: the villages are being methodically and deliberately killed by the urbanization policy of the government. "It's a sociological murder!" he says.

"No effort is really made to increase the land base of these people. Their lands are taken from them. Why? Because all government programs are geared to complete urbanization," Valdez charges. "Not just by centralization of bureaucracy, but of rural life. Services are further and further removed from the villages. The villages are depleted. If the schools are consolidated, for example, that means the people in the rural areas have to move nearer the schools. Why? Because there are no roads, good roads, in many of these villages. The government builds superhighways that bypass the villages entirely and kill the small businesses. But they are reluctant to build country roads. Yes, we have more of these micro-urban cities. And the extended villages are killed.

"Bureaucratic bumbling? Yes, but it is also a conscious effort to displace the people from rural areas," he says.

In an article written for *Fortune* magazine, "The Southern Roots of Urban Crisis" (August, 1968), Roger Beardwood searchingly explores "the malaise of the rural South." He finds it no economic accident. "Since World War II, U.S. agricultural policy has encouraged the sweeping mechanization of farming in the South," Beardwood writes. "The resulting migrations are inexorable results of polices and programs devised by the agricultural committees of Congress in which white Southerners have long had a dominant voice. Encouraged and financially aided by the Department of Agriculture, southern farmers are using modern technology that constantly raises the productivity of both labor and land. But abundance produces surpluses. To reduce them, the department pays farmers not to cultivate some of their land. On the land they do cultivate, white southern farmers need less labor each year. On the land they take out of production, they need almost none."

For the large farmers and urban consumers these "policies have been beneficial," Beardwood writes. But what of the rural poor?

"So far, the government and business have focused their problem-solving powers on urban problems, and blinkered themselves to rural ones," Beardwood concludes. "But every additional migrant is another burden to the cities, and the urban crisis will not be cured, or even arrested, until the South becomes more attractive to its black population than the urban North. The slums are in part a result of the malaise of the rural and smalltown South; the violence in northern streets is a product of frustrations born in the southern fields."

It is merely necessary to substitute brown for black, and the Southwest for the South, to depict the migrations and the miseries of the Chicanos in the barrios of Los Angeles, Phoenix, or El Paso.

The vanishing farms have been helped into oblivion by the Census Bureau. In the mid-1950s the statisticians eliminated hundreds of thousands of farms, and thus Department of Agriculture services to them, by moving a decimal point. Farms of less than ten acres were declared not to be farms any more, and were not counted. Tens of thousands of the Hispano farmers in New Mexico, and throughout the Southwestern *colonias,* with their garden plots and small pastures, were thereby rendered nonexistent.

Alex Mercure is neither infuriated nor dismayed by the plight of these villagers. "The villagers are stubborn people," he says. "So am I." He was born into this troubled world. "I come from a rural village," he says. Lumberton, the mountain community where his family lives, is in the midst of the old Spanish land-grant country. The Jicarilla Apache Reservation is nearby. "I grew up with Apache boys," he says. The strength of these Apaches is in his patience.

When he became a schoolteacher he stayed near his village, teaching in Chama, a lumber town in the mountains. Even when he went to the university to study business administration and economics he kept close to the way of the villagers. "I was even a local bartender," he says.

"Now I can go into any village and the people will say, 'You come from Lumberton. You are one of us.' A man has to begin with himself. He has to know himself. He has to know where he comes from and know who he is."

Mercure lives in the suburbs of North Albuquerque now, in the farthest-out community he could find without leaving the city. "I got as near to the farms as I could." Along the wall of his driveway he grows rows of corn, and by the patio behind his suburban home there are patches of strawberries. On the wire fence that separates his lawn from the irrigation ditch, he has planted grapevines.

The village has not left him, though he has left the village. His philosophy is still that of a villager: Like an old man the earth may grow tired. Unlike an old man the earth cannot die. In the spring every seed is an act of resurrection. Men may erode, cut up, fence in, sell, and disfigure the earth. But the earth will outlive them. This is his belief.

"Our allegiance is to the land. The villager couldn't care less about politics in the United States, or even Mexico. He cares about his land. Sometimes people will ask me why the villager doesn't move. There is nothing in the village, they say. There are no jobs. That may be so. But it is our homeland. It is the land we were born on, and where we have lived for hundreds of years."

He tells the story of a man from the village of Portales. The man was asked if he would like to relocate to Albuquerque, where there were jobs, since there were no jobs in Portales. His way would be paid. The man said, "I have been to Albuquerque." He thought about it a while longer, then he added, "I would rather *live* in Portales than *work* in Albuquerque."

The man from Portales is not alone. A national opinion poll has shown that the majority of people who work in the cities would prefer to live in the country—if there was work. Urban living was the preference of a small minority. Irving Kristol, citing this poll in a critique of urban "myths," feels that it indicates that rural life is not merely an idyllic memory; it is a living reality in the minds of most city dwellers. The "myths" of urban utopias are tenuous, Kristol writes in the *New York Times*; for the better the job the urbanite has, the farther away from the city he tends to live.

The exodus to the cities has been slowing down in the last few years, Mercure believes. In the most recent statistics of the Census Bureau this estimate is affirmed; the "urban boom" has begun to level off, the *New York Times* reports, and fewer rural immigrants are on the roads. At the height of the trek to the cities, in the 1960's, more than 30 percent of the people still lived in the rural areas. That population is "becoming more stable," Mercure says, "and the people are not moving from the villages as *eagerly* as they once did. They are returning to their villages more often. I think more would return if we had village industries. Jobs!

"Life in the villages may be a resource for the entire country," Mecure says. "Cybernetics and the computer revolution may soon mean that most workers won't have anything to do. Then we will be in a real crisis. We may be in it already. We, in the villages, may then have to teach the country how to live in leisure.

"Riots in the cities may be a symptom of this age of cybernetics. The ghetto people who have 'nothing' to do, who have no jobs, are taught to feel ashamed and useless, to feel guilty. So they try to assert their manhood, to do something, anything. They riot. It's this neurotic idea city people have that 'doing nothing' is somehow a crime.

"In the villages we know how to 'do nothing.' To live at a leisurely pace. To enjoy life. No one has to teach the villager how to live in the age of cybernetics. He is ready, willing, and able. He is not neurotic about 'doing nothing.' That's one of the strengths of the village, and one of the reasons the village has endured. So, if the villages disappear our nation may lose its most precious resource—the solution to its urban problems.

"The villages had better be rebuilt," Mercure says, with matter-of-fact severity. "Where else can urban man go to find peace of mind?"

Fecundo Valdez has an equally disregarded rural view of urban crisis: "The root of the riots, ghetto poverty, and crime is the decline of rural life. And that's something all these Presidential Commissions on urban problems just ignore. Unless something is done at the roots it's just going to get worse and worse. I thing it's high time that a serious attempt is made to halt the growth, break up and decentralize our industrial cities.

"If we wish to save our cities, we will have to save the villages," Valdez says. "But who will do that?"

In the village of Penasco, high in the Sangre de Cristo Mountains, wedged in between the 13,102-foot peak of Truchas Mountain and the 11,947-foot Cerro Vista, the farmers no longer bemoan the "doom" of their village. They are too busy sowing seeds.

The farmers of Penasco have formed a Vegetable Cooperative. In the past these farmers were too poor to buy tractors, and their plots of land were too small to be profitably farmed in an era of supermarket farming. Every year the families left the village to seek work in the cities. Now they farm cooperatively to compete with the factory farms and save their village.

"We don't say, Wipe out the fences. Instead we say, Let's join hands, cooperate, and work together to make it feasible to farm the area. Instead of buying forty tractors, we'll buy four, and all forty farmers can use them," says Alex Mercure, who helped organize the Penasco Vegetable Cooperative, with the aid of HELP. He foresees a time when the poor farmers' farms, whose meager harvests bring $25 to $50 an acre, will increase their harvests to $250 to $1,000 an acre. "These farmers could earn $4,500 a year."

Across the high mountains, in the village of Tierra Amarilla, where the men of Tijerina had come with their rifles two summers before, the farmers are building their own agricultural cooperative. They have laid down their rifles and have taken up their plows.

In the spring of 1969 there were several meetings in the mountain village. The winds of March had not blown away the snow and frost when the farmers began to gather to talk once more of Zapata's dreamed-of *"La tierra le pertence al hombre que trabaja, con sus propias manos"*—"The land belongs to those who work it, with their own hands." Couldn't they reclaim their land?

Some of the farmers were skeptical. How could they, who had nothing, finance a cooperative? A few thought the cooperative would fail. "It is a mistake to give our sweat to a dream that will evaporate," one man said.

They had no money. A farmer offered his tractor. One villager donated his *molino* (a grinding mill for flour and cornmeal). Still another gave "a squealing pig." Acre by acre the farmers of Tierra Amarilla gathered their land together, until they had offered two hundred "well-rested" acres to begin their cooperative with.

If they cooperated, one village could help another, said young Pedro Archuleta, a leader of the Comancheros del Norte. Velarde, a nearby village, had lost all its fruit the year before. The apples, pears, and peaches had "dried up" on the trees, because the market prices were so low the farmers let the fruit rot. "We could trade beans, potatoes, and pumpkins for the fruit of the Velarde people," Archuleta explained, if the villages would cooperate. "That way, we could have both vegetables and fruits."

In the villages of Coyote and Las Vegas, and the cities of Espanola and Albuquerque, the women put up "donation boxes" to gather food for the cooperative farmers. Every week they collected canned goods and dried meat so that the workers in the fields would have something to eat during the long summer, before the harvest was gathered.

"Our ancestors could make it pretty well; then we can now," declared a village woman, Senora Juan Martinez.

A woman in the village of San Cristobal, the dark and intense Enriqueta Longeaux de Vasquez, who is a voice of the cooperative movement, wrote in *El Grito del Norte* ("The Cry of the North"): "Land is a beautiful part of man's relationship to nature. I see land as something that belongs to everyone. Land is like air and life. It is part of each and every one of us."

"The gringo doesn't understand the way we feel about the land," the villagers' newspaper editorialized. "He uses the land to make money from. The land for us is not to make money. Nor is the water or the trees. *'Elos son de Dios'* These are of God! He gave them to us to feed our families with, and not to make a lot of money.

"Our people in Tierra Amarilla are going to revive the old traditions of working together to feed our people, because this is the revolution, also," wrote *El Grito del Norte*. "What good is it to fight for the land when our children grow up without food? Without a culture? Our children belong to the tomorrow when our revolution will bear fruit."

And so the farmers voted to set up their "COOPERATIVA AGRICOLA DEL PUEBLO TIERRA AMARILLA." They issued a proclamation: "We are going to work together this summer to grow such crops as beans, potatoes, wheat to grind for flour, onions, garlic, and squash: just to name a few vegetables. We are going to work together so our children will not go hungry next winter. Our people are hungry and have to practically beg for food from the government. We beg the same government which took our land, or supported those who took it. We don't want to beg any more. We want to grow the food we need, so we don't have to go on welfare, or to the store which robs us in credit charges. We will store the food we grow and next winter give it to those of our people who helped grow it and to those who are hungry."

As the summer approached the call went out to the mountain villages: "The Tierra Amarilla Co-op needs volunteers. Come work with your brothers and sisters. Work! So that people may eat. Work! For unity and power. Work! To be independent of the bloodsuckers."

In *El Grito del Norte* the beautiful Enriqueta Longeaux de Vasquez wrote: "Let's go back to being more self-sufficient. Why do we have to support Mr. Safeway, whoever or wherever he may be? Let's work the land. Then the land will come back to the people and it will belong to those who plant the seeds, water the fields and gather the crops."

The defiant slogan of the farmers, in honor of the hero of the Cuban revolution, had been rewritten. Once it had read: "Che Is Alive and Hiding in Tierra Amarilla." Now it had been changed to:

CHE IS ALIVE

AND FARMING

IN TIERRA AMARILLA!

Identity
UNITY
Strain
PRODUCTIVITY
Initiation
SANCTION
Loyalty
CEREMONY
Hostility
Leadership
FRIENDSHIP
Attraction
HARMONY
Goal
CONFLICT
Cohesion
SECRECY

Study Questions

1. What multiple loyalties do you have? Have you had to re-solve competing loyalties? How?
2. What is the basis of attraction in your classroom? What is the basis for cohesion?
3. Could Lysistrata be an effective leader in American society?
4. Does secrecy operate in any of your membership groups? Does it help to ensure loyalties?
5. How do you account for the similarities or differences in the way deviants have been handled in the various groups to which you belong?

Patterns of Loyalty

8 Loyalty is the outgrowth of the distinctive types of attraction and cohesion that coexist in all social organizations. I shall discuss each of these variables individually.

ATTRACTION

The bases for attraction to a group may vary greatly. Attraction depends upon the goals, size, position, or status of the group in the community or upon those personal needs of the members which can be satisfied and mediated by the group. The source of attraction may be the group itself. In this situation, individuals are interested in the members of the group or in the activities of the group. George Homans, a social psychologist, has related attraction and interaction in the following way: "If the frequency of interaction between two or more persons increases, the degree of their liking for one another will increase and vice versa."[1]

Groups may also be attractive because they provide a means for achieving something desirable in the environment. Arnold Rose found that workers became union members because membership meant higher wages and job security.[2] The attractiveness of the union was its capacity to achieve goals outside of activities of the group itself. Students who join fraternities or sororities, in which the major benefit of membership is the prestige that is obtained in the community, are attracted for reasons similar to those of union members.

Sometimes the basis for attraction is not at all obvious. In a laboratory study, two social psychologists, Elliot Aronson and Judson Mills, varied the severity of initiation into a group in order to determine the attractiveness of the group to its new members. In this experiment the subjects, all women, were told that they were going to participate in a discussion on the psychology of sex. In order to do this they were required to read embarrassing sexual material aloud. The control group was given unembarrassing material or was not given anything to read. All the participants were accepted as members and attended a dull, banal group discussion. Those who had read the highly embarrassing material perceived the discussion group as more attractive than those who had read unembarrassing content or nothing. Aronson and Mills explained the results in terms of the severity of the initiation rites.[3]

COHESION

Cohesion is the pattern of relations that helps keep members in a group after they have been attracted to it. Cohesion depends upon the meaningfulness of the group's activities to its members and upon the coordination of members' efforts. Highly cohesive groups exhibit different behavior than those that are less cohesive. They can make greater demands on their members and can level stronger sanctions against deviants.

In one laboratory experiment on the consequences of cohesion, two social psychologists, Albert Pepitone and George Reichling, created laboratory groups which differed in the amount of cohesiveness. First, subjects were randomly assigned to one of the two groups. The creation of different degrees of cohesiveness was accomplished by telling subjects either that they were well matched and were going to like each other or that they were ill suited and were not expected to get along very well together. The groups were left alone and told that a discussion leader would arrive. A person then entered the room and proceeded to make insulting and disparaging remarks to the groups. After leaving, the person (an instructor unknown to the subjects) went behind his one-way mirror and observed that the highly cohesive group freely engaged in hostile remarks against him, while those in the group with low cohesiveness sat quietly or spoke about issues that were irrelevant to their embarrassing experience.[4]

Cohesive social organizations are those whose members work together to achieve group goals and take responsibility for group tasks. Such organizations defend their membership from criticism or attack.

Cohesive groups do more than simply teach their members about loyalty and obligations. They celebrate these bonds. Through ceremony and ritual, group members express the loyalties they feel toward their group and their participation in social life. The social bonds of attraction, cohesion, and obligation are affirmed and reaffirmed as members achieve certain important positions within the group. Even when members leave a group to participate in another social unit, the first group may honor their performances and accomplishments.

PRIMARY GROUPS

When the group is small and is itself the object of attraction, it is a potential primary group. Primary groups are those in which there are close face-to-face relationships. The individual participates and belongs as a total person rather than one role or another. The concept of the primary group was developed by Charles Horton Cooley, whose theory of early socialization was discussed in chapter 6. Cooley used "primary groups" to cover neighborhood and family groups, and related the concept to the development of self-consciousness and character.[5] In the primary group, members are made aware of the fundamental values of the society, and internalize these values through interaction. The primary group is not limited to families and neighborhood groups; groups with primary relations exist in all areas of human behavior. No matter how large, impersonal, or bureaucratic an organization may appear to be, analysis usually reveals the existence of networks of small, informal, face-to-face relations which can operate to support or undermine the larger unit. Because of their cohesion, primary groups exert great influence upon their members. Their goals often run counter to those of the larger social organization, and strong group loyalties occur within them.

PROBLEMS OF MULTIPLE MEMBERSHIP

Few groups satisfy all of their members' desires and needs. Therefore, people may seek membership in additional groups, thus creating competing or multiple loyalties. Often, these competing loyalties cause strain within an organization or between organizations. Some of the mechanisms which are employed to alleviate these strains are contracts, initiations, and departure ceremonies. Social arrangements can be developed which recognize and legitimize multiple memberships in groups. The first meeting of the year for students returning to school can be both a celebration of the participation in the new group and the recognition of other valid group memberships.

Occasionally group demands are so great that membership requires total commitment, to the exclusion of participation in other social units. Revolutionary groups, for example, because of the nature of their activities, often require denunciation of other ties.

CONFLICT

At first glance, conflict and cohesion seem to be opposite concepts, but they need not be inconsistent with each other. In fact, conflict within or between groups may lead to greater cohesion. After the Watts riot in Los Angeles in 1965, loyalty and cohesion seemed to increase among black residents of southwest Los Angeles. Everett K. Wilson says that "intra-group harmony is related to inter-group antipathy."[6] (This idea pertains to a theory of Jewish identity which states that when the Jewish people are no longer the target of prejudice and discrimination, they will not feel the need to be Jews.) Not only cohesion, but also self-identity, may arise out of group conflict.

Two experiments help illustrate the phenomena of cohesion and conflict. In the first, Robert Black and Jane Mouton arranged people into problem-solving groups that met for about six to eight hours at a time. The groups developed a great deal of solidarity; the members had a sense of accomplishment and unity because they had worked on, and solved, certain problems as a group. In the second experiment, Blake and Mouton asked each group to elect a representative to defend the group's position in a debate with other group leaders. They found that the representatives were so motivated to win that, when the debate came to a vote, each representative was defiantly loyal to his or her own group. Out of 62 representatives, only 2 voted against their own group's position.[7] [Sometimes loyalties may be so binding that they preclude objective decision making, rational action or evaluation. In this situation members may blindly adhere to traditions or feelings regardless of the situation. The phrase "My country, right or wrong," has a touch of this ethnocentric quality.]

One way to circumvent the problem of group loyalty that takes on ethnocentric qualities is to develop superordinate goals. Muzafer Sherif, in his study called "Experiments in Group Conflict," developed in-group cohesion and out-group hostility between two childrens' camp groups. The groups played against each other and competition developed between them. Sherif then arranged for both groups of children to appear at the same place for ice cream, but one group was allowed to arrive first and devour it all. After the incident, the groups began to steal from and cheat each other when they played together. A great deal of antagonism grew up between them. After a period of escalated hostilities, Sherif was able to establish cooperation between the groups through the development of unifying goals.[8]

The first excerpt in this chapter is over 2,000 years old and was written by the Greek dramatist Aristophanes. In the play *Lysistrata*, Aristophanes deals with the themes of war and sexual love. He lived during the war that Athens had been waging for 21 years against Sparta—another war that was going to make the world safe for democracy. He wrote four plays attacking the war and was accused of being a traitor and defeatist. Some citizens sought to have him exiled and his last play is an indictment of the demagogues, scoundrels, and profiteers who equate loyalty at any cost with patriotism. In this play, Aristophanes speaks against war through the voice of Lysistrata, who asks all women to participate in a severe initiation rite. Their sacrifice and Lysistrata's leadership bind them to each other and contribute to an effective social organization. The play illustrates the transformation of an aggregation into a cohesive social unit. An aggregation is a social organization that is relatively spontaneous in origin and of temporary duration. The fears and concerns of the women in the play who take the pledge bring us back to Komarovsky and Rossi.

The second selection deals with the consequences of multiple-role membership and competing loyalties. Lewis Killian, a sociologist, examines what happens to individuals who come face-to-face with disaster and must make choices between family and community, work and home, property and person. Killian is able to show the various ways that people resolve these dilemmas. There are situations when individuals have exclusive loyalties. Revolutionary groups, for example exert tremendous demand upon their members. The loyalties of members in turn makes for an effective group. During the French-Algerian War, the colonial powers were determined to break the resistance of the Algerians, and to do this they had to undermine their loyalties. A police officer describes the interrogation methods used:

Sometimes we almost wanted to tell them that if they had a bit of consideration for us they'd speak out without forcing us to spend hours tearing information out of them word by word. But you might as well talk to the wall. To all the questions we asked they'd only say "I don't know." Even when we asked them what their name was. If we asked them where they lived, they'd say "I don't know." So of course, we have to go through with it. But they scream too much. At the beginning that made me laugh. But afterward I was a bit shaken. Nowadays as soon as I hear someone shouting I can tell you exactly at what stage of the questioning we've got to. The chap who's had two blows of the fist and a belt of the baton behind his ear has a certain way of speaking, of shouting, and of saying he's innocent. After he's been left two hours strung up by his wrists he has another kind of voice. After the bath, still another. And so on.[9]

The third article, by sociologist William Westley, describes the way loyalty functions to ensure secrecy in a police unit. In "Secrecy and the Police," Westley analyzes the functions of secrecy and its importance in police work. He shows that, while loyalty may contribute to short-run efficiency, it can cause the erosion of community support.

NOTES

1. George Homans, *The Human Group* (New York: Harcourt Brace Jovanovich, 1950), p. 112.

2. Arnold Rose, *Union Solidarity* (Minneapolis: Univ. of Minn. Press, 1952).

3. Elliot Aronson and Judson Mills, "The Effect of Severity of Initiations or Liking for a Group Initiation," *Journal of Abnormal and Social Psychology* 59 (1959): 171–81.

4. Albert Pepitone and George Reichling, "Group Cohesiveness and The Expression of Hostility," *Human Relations* 8 (1955): 327–37.

5. Charles H. Cooley, *Social Organization* (New York: Schocken Books, 1909, 1962).

6. Everett K. Wilson, *Sociology; Rules, Roles and Relationships* (Homewood, Illinois: Dorsey Press, 1966), p. 468.

7. Robert Blake and Jane Mouton, "Loyalty of Representatives to In-Group Positions During Inter-Group Competitions," *Sociometry* 24 (1961): 177–94.

8. Muzafer Sherif, "Experiments in Group Conflict," *Scientific American*, November 1956, pp. 54–58.

9. Frantz Fanon, *The Wretched of The Earth* (New York: Grove Press, 1968), p. 265.

ARISTOPHANES   **301**

Lysistrata

ACT 1

Daybreak on the sloping hill which rises from the lower to the upper
city of Athens. 411 B.C., that is, in the twenty-first year of the war between Athens and Sparta. At the top of the hill, the facade of a temple.
Lysistrata is discovered, ill at ease, in the cold dawn, impatient and
angry. From the foot of the slope rises the sound of women's voices;
and the chorus of old women come up the hill.

LEADER OLD WOMEN CHORUS: Hard is the path of man's life. He
stumbles and falls. In the days of his childhood his mother upholds him.
His feet are uncertain. He runs to his mother and cries—then he laughs.
At the end of his life his knees grow weary. He stumbles again. He
cries, but no laughter follows his tears. Old age is a sorrow.

OLD WOMEN CHORUS: Old age is a sorrow: Old age is a sickness
for which there's no comfort, no cure or physician.

LEADER OLD WOMEN CHORUS: This is the common lot of man.
But for women a worse fate comes with the years. Their beauty departs
and their strength is no more. The children they bear forsake and
desert them. The men they have served forget and deny them.

OLD WOMEN CHORUS: Thin arms, grey hair, breasts shrunken,
alone.

LEADER OLD WOMEN CHORUS: What should a woman expect at
the end of her days? So long as peace reigns she may hope for contentment, a small bowl of gruel, a quiet bed.

OLD WOMEN CHORUS: All these are denied us.

LEADER OLD WOMEN CHORUS: Our grandchildren march off to
fight with the Spartans. Our sons go about to fit out the ships, to treat
with allies for more arms and provisions. The farms are unworked,
weeds grow in the gardens, the vine and the figtree wither and perish.

OLD WOMEN CHORUS: Aye, like the figtree we wither and perish.

LEADER OLD WOMEN CHORUS: Yet one thing we have which the
gods still allow us. One thing we take down to the brink of the grave.
The days of our lives when we lived rich and happy, our men by our
sides, our children around us—we can still remember.

OLD WOMEN CHORUS: We still can remember. A plague and a
torment, the days of our youth, when we look back upon them.

LEADER OLD WOMEN CHORUS: Not torment to us who have nothing to hope for. The gift of Pandora is not in our power. We have no
more hope. We can live in despair. O, Pallas Athena! We who have
lived have nothing to ask you, but there are the others. Such women
as we were twenty years gone, young women whose blood still runs hot
through their bodies, zestful to live with their appetites keen. Sad is

Aristophanes, *Lysistrata*, trans. Gilbert Seldes (New York: The Heritage
Press, 1962), pp. 24–55. Reprinted by permission of the Estate of Gilbert Seldes.

302

their lot who live now in Athens, loveless, despairing, with no men to serve.

OLD WOMEN CHORUS: Hard is the fate of a woman who's dying, but harder still for a woman whose life is as yet unfulfilled.

LEADER OLD WOMEN CHORUS: Lysistrata! *(The old women proceed out of sight up the hill, leaving a few of their number behind)*

OLD WOMEN CHORUS: Lysistrata! We have done it!

LYSISTRATA: Praise to the Goddess who stands guard on the Temple.

LEADER OLD WOMEN CHORUS: Is that all we've to do?

LYSISTRATA: All for you. But the others—*They* have not come. Not one of them!

LEADER OLD WOMEN CHORUS: *We* are here, Lysistrata.

LYSISTRATA: Yes, you! *Old* women. Widows of the first year of this twenty-year-old war. You, with your sons and grandsons standing watch on the battlefield or lying dead along the picket-lines. You, who can barely lift the water-jug. . . . You are here! But where are the *young* women?

SECOND OLD WOMAN: Young women are where young ones always are—where you would be if your husband were at home.

THIRD OLD WOMAN: Or if you had someone to take his place while he is away. . . .

LEADER OLD WOMEN CHORUS: Can we take the place of the young women, Lysistrata?

LYSISTRATA: No, what you were called to do, you have begun well. The rest you cannot do. You are too old.

THIRD OLD WOMAN: Old age makes women willing.

LEADER OLD WOMEN CHORUS: Shall we go home then?

LYSISTRATA: I beg you, finish your work in the citadel. You have been faithful. You have obeyed me. Blindly, not knowing what my purpose was, you served me.

LEADER OLD WOMEN CHORUS: You said it was for Athens, for our children and our grandchildren. What joy is left to women old as we are except to serve their city and their children?

LYSISTRATA: The younger women have a city too. Their children lie in mortal danger still. Their farms are still untended and their crops, choked by rank weeds, rot in the fruitless fields. I sent a messenger to everyone, saying for Athens' sake, for your husband's sake, for the great common happiness of all, meet me this morning. And they have not come!

LEADER OLD WOMEN CHORUS: Look, Lysistrata. At least one young woman is coming.

SECOND OLD WOMAN: Kalonika, I think. *(The remaining old women proceed up the hill as Kalonika, a young woman, enters sleepily)*

KALONIKA: Oh, Lysistrata.

LYSISTRATA: You've come, Kalonika.

KALONIKA: But of course I've come, my dear. You look so gloomy. *(She moves toward Lysistrata with an endearing gesture, but Lysistrata throws her off)* You're really angry, Lysistrata. What has happened? It doesn't make you look pretty to scowl like that and draw **303** your lovely eyebrows down.

LYSISTRATA: Look pretty! Oh, Kalonika, my heart is broken. I'm ashamed of our sex. Men have always said that we are untrustworthy and sly and trivial—

KALONIKA: Just between ourselves, don't you think that they're right?

LYSISTRATA: They're too kind. What would the men say if they knew that today the women of Athens were called on a matter of vital importance—secret and urgent and permitting no delay—and, instead of coming, lay sleeping in their beds.

KALONIKA: Oh, I assure you, my dear, they will come. But give them time. You know it isn't easy for a woman to slip out of her bed. She tries to go and her husband sleepily puts his arm about her and draws her back. Or perhaps, just as she leaves, her baby begins to bawl and she has to put him to sleep again. Or perhaps wash its face, or give it breakfast.

LYSISTRATA: Important things. Desperately important to wash the baby's face or lie down again beside her lover. I tell you, Kalonika, what we have to do outranks these things a thousand times.

KALONIKA: Still, I don't see why all of us are summoned to this place at such an hour. The things we women do best, we do alone. Unless—oh, Lysistrata, are you preparing for the feast of Adonis? Has some new wine come in from Samos for our revels? I thought that might be it.

LYSISTRATA: It's not a feast I called you for. I have a project— something big.

KALONIKA: If I had only known, I would have been here earlier.

LYSISTRATA: For weeks I've not slept, thinking what to do about it, how to handle it, turning it this way and that way to see what I could do.

KALONIKA: Who can it be gives you such delightfully sleepless nights, my dear?

LYSISTRATA: You know what I am talking about. If it were what you mean, you'd all be here, no doubt. Kalonika, I tell you if Greece is to be saved, it is the *women* who must do it.

KALONIKA (*Not impressed*): The women? Why, then, Greece will be a long time being saved.

LYSISTRATA: It will be saved by us—or be forever ruined.

KALONIKA: But, Lysistrata, even so, what makes you think that women can do what our great statesmen have failed to do? They always *try* for peace.

LYSISTRATA (*Sardonically*): They *say* they try.

KALONIKA: They are men with great minds. They think of everything.

LYSISTRATA: They make us believe they do.

KALONIKA: And when their great peace conferences fail, they can go to war. But we, Lysistrata, we know nothing about great affairs. We sit there, waiting for the men to come to tell us what they have done, dressed in transparent gowns of yellow silk, flowing about so that we can hardly walk, with flowers in our hair and embroidered slippers.

LYSISTRATA: You have just recited the catalogue of our most powerful weapons.

KALONIKA: Weapons?

LYSISTRATA (*As she speaks, Kalonika touches her own clothes as if not quite understanding the argument, but merely verifying the fact that these things exist*): The filmy yellow tunic. Yes. The intoxicating perfume and your dainty slippers. Yes. Your lotions and your rouge and your provocative flowing robe.

KALONIKA: What about them?

LYSISTRATA: These are the weapons by which every woman can make the men of Greece lay down their arms.

KALONIKA: If that were true, I'd get myself a dress so thin I'd be embarrassed even before my husband.

LYSISTRATA: I ask you now, if we have such power, should we not use it?

KALONIKA: We should, indeed. Why, Lysistrata, you've hit upon a really grand idea. Each one of us will buy new clothes and jewels and lovely perfumes and seduce our husbands—and the war will end. Why, who'd have thought it?

LYSISTRATA: There's more than that to do, but, to commence with—that is enough. I tell you, Kalonika, we can do it—just as I say— and ought not every honest Grecian woman come to help us? (*A group of young women, including Myrrhina, approaches*)

YOUNG WOMEN CHORUS: My beauty sleep's gone. Ye gods! How I hated to get up in the dark, in the cold before daybreak. And what's it all for? Lysistrata said come, and, like fools, we obey her.

LEADER YOUNG WOMEN CHORUS: Now what's all this bother? I don't want to worry. My husband is coming. He won't want to hear that long before dawn I was tramping the hillsides. He'll never believe it wasn't a lover.

KALONIKA: Oh. look, Lysistrata, someone is coming now— down there, way down the hill.

YOUNG WOMEN CHORUS: He'll never believe that it wasn't a lover. Why should he, indeed? But it wasn't a lover.

LEADER YOUNG WOMEN CHORUS: Lysistrata's all right, but she's full of ideas. She's always discussing the war and its problems.

MYRRHINA: Oh, Lysistrata, Lysistrata! Oh, Lysistrata, don't tell me we're late. I came just as fast as I could. I really did. You aren't angry?

LYSISTRATA: I really don't think much of you, Myrrhina. You knew it was desperately important that you all get here before dawn. You couldn't have hurried very much.

MYRRHINA: Well, I couldn't find my girdle—it was pitch dark when I had to get up to get here at all. But if you're in such a hurry, tell us what's the matter. We're here *now*.

LYSISTRATA: Not until you have all arrived. We've waited so

long, we might as well wait longer till the women come from Thebes **305**
and the Spartan women—

KALONIKA: The Spartan women coming? Why, Lysistrata, this
is treachery. They're our enemies.

MYRRHINA: We want no Spartan women here in Athens. Why,
I've heard that they're worse than the men, those *demon* Spartans.

LYSISTRATA: They've come to help us put an end to war.

KALONIKA: Well, I don't care. My husband's at the front and
I don't think a faithful wife ought ever to have social relations with
the enemy.

MYRRHINA: Just the same I don't approve of this.

KALONIKA: Well, I won't speak to them, that's one thing certain.

MYRRHINA: I think you're right and, Lysistrata, if you say
anything against our city—well—just be careful. Some of us are loyal.

LYSISTRATA: Yes—you're loyal—but to what, my sister? You're
loyal to the war that bleeds us white, that ruins Attica and ruins
Greece, that maims our husbands and destroys our city. Do you doubt
I'm loyal, Myrrhina, loyal to peace and to the good of Athens, to the
great glory of our city and to the joy and happiness of men?

KALONIKA: Here come the Spartans, now.

MYRRHINA: Look, there's Lampito. *(Lampito, a powerfully
built Spartan woman, followed by several others, comes in)*

LYSISTRATA: Good morning, Lampito darling. It was splendid
of you to come all the way from Sparta. You must be tired. And how
magnificent you look!

LAMPITO: Let's drop the compliments, *dear* Lysistrata. We
came away from Sparta with your pledge that what you had to say
was for our good. We know that things in Athens, here, are different.
You women aren't so keen about this war.

MYRRHINA: You lie, you *wicked* woman.

LAMPITO: We have our ways of finding out about you. My
husband told me when he last was home that all the Athenian soldiers
are so thin, there's hardly place to run a spearhead in.

KALONIKA: Oh, you've heard that? Well, that's a pretty story,
when all the Spartan commissary does is send out rotten turnips and
fresh water. Your men are bloated and you women, you're keen to have
your men keep up the war—and yet, two weeks ago, we heard three
thousand men came running home to Sparta from the front.

LAMPITO: That's just the sort of thing you would hear, you
Athenians. You've never yet learned how to tell the truth. And what
now? You, Lysistrata, you invited us, not these cheap chatterboxes.
What do you want? I warn you, we're in no mood to help you Athenians in this war.

LYSISTRATA: Lampito, I have summoned you not to bring aid
to Athens, though we need it.

MYRRHINA: No! No! We need no help.

LYSISTRATA: Quiet, Myrrhina. Yes, Lampito—Athens needs
help but just as Sparta needs it and Thebes and Corinth. This is no

306 trick, but by the gods I swear it, we meet here only for our mutual good.

LAMPITO: That's fair enough. And, after all, today begins the truce between our armies. If *they* lay down their arms and rest a fortnight, we can afford to lay aside our anger.

FIRST SPARTAN WOMAN: The truce, Lampito, that's the worst of it. Today our men are coming home to Sparta and they'll not find us there. And we'll not find them—

MYRRHINA: That's right and I ought to be gone too. A lot of little things I left undone. Kinesias likes to see the house all tidy when he comes home.

LYSISTRATA: Take my word for it there will be no loss. I'm glad we meet here now as friends, Lampito. It's years since last I saw you, but the passing years are generous to you. Look, girls, isn't she strong? *(Lampito puts up both arms in the gesture of a "strong-man")*

KALONIKA: Why, I bet she could strangle an ox.

MYRRHINA: *(Timidly):* Oh, I wish I were as strong as that.

LAMPITO: You city women! We're *all* strong. Look at her.

KALONIKA: Oh, what do you eat?

FIRST SPARTAN WOMAN: Everything. We get our strength from exercise and dancing. Have you tried the new kick-step? Try this one, Lysistrata. *(She does the kick-step. Myrrhina awkwardly imitates her)*

LYSISTRATA: And who are these, Lampito? Where are they from?

LAMPITO: They joined us down the road. She's another great lady from Thebes.

LYSISTRATA: Your journey down from Thebes doesn't seem to have tired you. You're as fresh as a garden.

KALONIKA *(Aside to Myrrhina):* A vegetable garden, maybe.

LYSISTRATA: And who are these?

LAMPITO: These came from Corinth—virtuous women. *(The Corinthian women beam)*

LYSISTRATA: If they are from Corinth then they must be virtuous.

KALONIKA: As virtue goes in Corinth.

LYSISTRATA: Then all of Greece is here. Be welcome, friends.

LAMPITO: Now, Lysistrata, tell us what you want.

LYSISTRATA: It's not an easy thing to tell. We must do something we have never done before, my friends. Something no woman, since the beginning of time, has dreamed of doing.

MYRRHINA, KALONIKA, LAMPITO, FIRST, SECOND CORINTHIAN WOMEN *(Together):* Not even dreamed of doing, Lysistrata? Why, it must be unheard of. Is it something the gods forbid? I can do anything that you can think of. What can women do that's so unheard of? And what haven't women heard of that we can do?

LYSISTRATA: Question no more. Your thoughts are all misleading. But listen to me. *(She moves so that she begins to dominate the group)* Are you not sad and sorry that the fathers of your children are at the front—far away from you, in danger, without twenty-four hours' leave once in six months? Has any one of you seen her husband in the last half year?

YOUNG WOMEN CHORUS: The gods help us! Bring them safely back to us.

KALONIKA: It's just six months since he went back to Thrace.

MYRRHINA: It's seven since my husband went to Pilos.

LAMPITO: And mine—why, if he ever does get leave, what good's it to me?

LYSISTRATA: And what lovers have you? Not the strong vigorous men because they are all away—only the bent, the old or sick. Now tell me, if I bring your husbands back and end the war, will you be with me?

MYRRHINA: But how can you bring our husbands back to us?

FIRST CORINTHIAN WOMAN: Will you seduce the whole Athenian army and have time left for the Corinthian men?

LAMPITO: You take a great deal on yourself to think that you alone can do so much.

LYSISTRATA: Tell me this—if I show you the way to end the war and bring our men back safely—if today, after this truce, they'll never march again, will you be with me?

MYRRHINA: Of course we'll be with you. *If* you can bring them back. I would pawn the dress off my back—*if*——

KALONIKA *(Spitefully)*: If you could spend the money on good wine.

MYRRHINA *(Contemptuously)*: And you, Kalonika?

KALONIKA: Why, if we could have peace, I'd split myself in two and be gutted like a fish.

LAMPITO: I'd scramble to the top of the highest hill in Sparta.

MYRRHINA: Now tell us, Lysistrata.

LYSISTRATA: My sisters, to compel our men to sign a pact of peace, we must make war.

FIRST THEBAN WOMAN: Me?

MYRRHINA, KALONIKA, LAMPITO, FIRST, SECOND CORINTHIAN WOMEN, ARMENIAN WOMAN *(Together)*: What? We make war? With shield and spear? You'll be general, I suppose. A war with whom? A woman's war!

LAMPITO: Put me in the cavalry. I have a good seat—on a horse.

LYSISTRATA: Yes, war! But not as men make war. Yet—be prepared for a great sacrifice.

MYRRHINA: We have to die?

KALONIKA: My sight is bad. You really must excuse me.

MYRRHINA: And oh, my poor sore feet—the arches are broken.

LAMPITO: I'm undersize for service, Lysistrata.

LYSISTRATA: Oh, have no fears. It's not your lives you must give up. You must give up——

YOUNG WOMEN CHORUS: What?

KALONIKA: Whatever it is, so long as it's not my life, I'll give it up although I die in the attempt.

LYSISTRATA: You'll not die—you'll only promise never to lie——

308   *(She speaks impressively. The women cry out incredulously and laugh)*

KALONIKA: Never to lie?

FIRST CORINTHIAN WOMAN: Never to lie?

YOUNG WOMEN CHORUS: Never to lie!

LYSISTRATA: With any man, until the war is ended.

MYRRHINA: Is that your big idea?

KALONIKA: You call that a stiff job? Why, you've gone crazy.

LAMPITO: Have you brought us all the way from Sparta for a silly joke?

FIRST CORINTHIAN WOMAN: If we don't lie with our men, who will, I want to know?

YOUNG WOMEN CHORUS: Never to lie——

LYSISTRATA *(The passion in her tones shocks them out of their levity):* Never to lie with any man again. Never to admit one to your bed. Never to know delight or give delight to man until the war is over. Never to let a soldier home on leave, starved for your soft white arms and the great embrace of love, have joy of you. But hold yourself aloof—refuse, deny what they and you yourselves desire——Abstain from love! *(The women turn from her despairingly)* Why, now you turn away! Where are you going? Back to your beds to wait your men's return, eager to welcome them and let them go again to starve and kill and be killed too? Why, now you see that something's to be done, you bite your lips. You really look quite pale. And you're crying. Why, what have I said? These six months you have lived without your men. Another month——

MYRRHINA: These six months he's been gone. At noon today, or earlier, he will be back on leave. I was waiting for him. The bedspread I have woven while he was away is spread. For two weeks I have thought only of him. *(Hysterically)* I will not do it! Let the war go on.

LYSISTRATA *(Turning from her with contempt, she addresses Kalonika):* And *you*, my fish—ready to be split and gutted.

KALONIKA: Well, take a knife then, slash me head to foot, broil me alive—I'll do that! But not this, Lysistrata—not give up the sweetest joy of life.

LYSISTRATA: And you?

LAMPITO: Never on earth! Make peace at *that* price now that Sparta's winning! *(Lysistrata stands silent with a look of pity and contempt on her face as the women grow more and more bitter and finally begin to tear at each other)*

FIRST ATHENIAN WOMAN: Oh—so Sparta's winning?

LAMPITO: The Spartans always win.

FIRST THEBAN WOMAN: Who supplies the men? The Theban phalanx crashes through the line.

FIRST CORINTHIAN WOMAN: Yes, they crash through when the line is held by children. You're fine allies, you Thebans, in a battle.

KALONIKA: The lot of you—great heroes every one, but when the Persians came, who won the war?

FIRST THEBAN WOMAN: The Athenians won the war. The

Athenians won the war. Oh, yes, they won the war—with *Theban* soldiers.

LAMPITO: Who held the pass when the first Persian horde swept down at Thermopylae? The Athenians? No! Leonidas and three hundred Spartans. Whenever Greece was saved, the Spartans saved her.

KALONIKA: Perhaps the Spartans won at Marathon?

FIRST CORINTHIAN WOMAN: And just because the Athenians had some ships you think you own all of Greece, and Corinth is only a province. Why, this is all a plot to make us lay down our arms—and Athens triumphs.

LAMPITO: You're right, Corinthian! Those Athenians are wily. They're orators. We must be careful. Lysistrata, you think that you can fool us—country cousins, just stupid women without the advantages of your Athenian education. Well, cats don't argue with philosophers, but cats can smell a rat as well as you can. Back I go to Sparta and report this noble plot.

MYRRHINA *(She flies at Lampito and the other women begin fighting)*: Who needs a plot to beat the Spartan dogs?

FIRST CORINTHIAN WOMAN: Why, every friend of Athens has deserted because we all know the Athenian pledges are written in water. You, good Thebans, you've had your fill of these sweet promises.

LAMPITO: Your men put you up to this. I know it.

SECOND CORINTHIAN WOMAN: A plot, a plot.

FIRST SPARTAN WOMAN: A foul conspiracy.

MYRRHINA: You Spartan liars.

LAMPITO: A typical Athenian trick.

FIRST THEBAN WOMAN: It's a plot.

KALONIKA: It's not a plot, you stupid Spartan wench.

MYRRHINA: Stop trampling on me, you mare.

LAMPITO: Get out of my way, you toad.

KALONIKA: I'll save you, Myrrhina. *(She gets Myrrhina out of Lampito's hold and turns furiously to Lysistrata)* Now, Lysistrata, now you see what comes of asking enemies to come to Athens. Let's drive——

LYSISTRATA *(Magnificently)*: May all the gods save Greece! Or rather, great Zeus, send down your thunderbolts! Annihilate this wanton race. Destroy them all before they ruin Greece. Look at yourselves—come here to save our country, and everyone is fighting with the others.

FIRST CORINTHIAN WOMAN: The Athenians started it. They always do.

LYSISTRATA *(Quelling the resumption of the riot)*: For once then, let the Athenians end the war, with Corinth at her side and Thebes and Sparta. Oh, women of Greece, stand together! We can forget our ancient wrongs, the lies they teach the children to make them hate their brothers. Stand by me.

LAMPITO: And if I do, will these others drop the quarrel?

FIRST THEBAN WOMAN: I'm all for peace. I always am.

MYRRHINA: And you?

FIRST CORINTHIAN WOMAN: I only said——

KALONIKA: Don't start again. We all know what you said. You vote for peace? Now, Lysistrata. See, we're all agreed. I've brought them round.

LAMPITO: We're all agreed but we were all agreed when we first came. Yes, I'm for peace, my dear Athenian friend, but why must I lie alone in bed?

KALONIKA: And if we do, the gods forbid—will that bring peace?

LYSISTRATA: Oh, can't you see it? When our men come home, ravening for us like wolves for prey, what do we do? First we sit indoors and never run to meet them in the portico. They see the bright expectant flush upon our cheeks—the rouge pot serves for that—and when they come in, flinging their shield and spear upon the floor, we rise and our transparent gowns cling to our bodies. We lie down on the accustomed couch and when we put out our arms, they go mad and fall upon us——

YOUNG WOMEN CHORUS *(With excitement)*: And then——

LYSISTRATA *(Deliberately)*: Why then, we turn away and say, "You must be tired", and put them off and talk about—the cobbler down the street and say, "How nice to see you back", "I've really missed you", or "Did you have a good trip?" or "What charming weather". And then they *will* go mad—and if you tell them: "Never until the war is over"—they'll make peace.

LAMPITO: You're right. King Menelaus threw away his sword to rest his head on Helen's dazzling breast.

KALONIKA: Oh, Helen—yes. Not all of us are Helens. Suppose our husbands go to someone else?

FIRST CORINTHIAN WOMAN: The way they always do, the gods be praised.

KALONIKA: Suppose my husband drags me by the hair into our bedroom?

LYSISTRATA: Hold on to the door posts.

MYRRHINA: But if he beats me?

LYSISTRATA: Beat him back.

FIRST CORINTHIAN WOMAN: But if they fly into a rage and rape us? You know, men are sometimes stubborn.

LYSISTRATA: Much good it does them. If you're beaten down, yield to their wishes, but be surly. But why should I tell you? Since when do Grecian women need to be instructed to make their men impassioned? All you have to learn is to deny them—and yourselves. For there is no joy a man can have if woman doesn't share it.

MYRRHINA: Well, Lysistrata, some women may do this and only infuriate their men, but——

SECOND CORINTHIAN WOMAN: You have to learn the art from other women.

LAMPITO: I think it can be done. By Hercules, we'll do it.

LYSISTRATA: Lampito, you're a woman in ten thousand. I knew

that I could count on you at least. Now, by the sweet-tongued god that gives you persuasion, convince these women that they must do like-wise.

LAMPITO: Suppose we knock them down, good Lysistrata? That's one way we'll be sure that they'll obey us.

KALONIKA: Now don't get rough, Lampito. Of course, we'll do it—at least we'll try—I mean if Lysistrata wants us to—but I can't see my husband roaring back from war to find me—unaccommodating.

MYRRHINA: Kinesias will go mad. He'll kill me, Lysistrata. And then I'll cry. And when I cry, Kinesias gets so tender, I can't resist him.

LAMPITO: Myrrhina, this is no time for little women. We women must be big.

KALONIKA: We'll not grow big from sleeping without men.

MYRRHINA: Well, I won't do it. There! I've said it now. I think the whole thing's just silly. Besides, I want Kinesias. He's my husband.

FIRST CORINTHIAN WOMAN: Myrrhina's right. I won't give up my—husband.

KALONIKA: She means her lover.

LYSISTRATA: Husband or lover—you'll do as I say. Lampito—you'll help me. By the gods, can't you see? It's the one thing to do—the one way to save Greece. Lampito——

LAMPITO: I'll help you. I'll stand guard if you ask me.

LYSISTRATA: Stand guard and keep these little fools locked up here.

LAMPITO: I will.

KALONIKA: You promise, Lysistrata, that it's only a few days we must hold off. It's not forever, Lysistrata, is it?

LYSISTRATA: A day. Two days. Three, at the utmost. Can't you understand that all this time the men back from the armies, in far worse case than you, will languish burning for you; and if you stay away just these first days when they are back from the front, our work is over.

YOUNG ATHENIAN WOMEN: *Three* days is a long time.

KALONIKA: Well, I'll try.

MYRRHINA: Just *one* night, Lysistrata. I can't promise much more than that. But at least the first night after Kinesias comes back I'll lock the door on him.

KALONIKA: All right—I promise, too.

LYSISTRATA: So be it then. So much is gained. Come, like the men we'll swear a fearful oath.

LAMPITO: You say the words and we'll repeat them after.

LYSISTRATA: That's splendid. Here, you, bring the sacred en-trails for the oath.

KALONIKA: Suppose we sacrifice a bull?

MYRRHINA: I don't think bulls would be appropriate.

LYSISTRATA: And even if they were we have no bulls.

KALONIKA: Well, in that case, maybe not. Suppose we get a skin of wine.

MYRRHINA: Thasian wine! I love the taste of it.

FIRST CORINTHIAN AND SECOND ATHENIAN WOMAN: Thasian wine!

LYSISTRATA: Go fetch a skin of wine.

MYRRHINA *(Darting after the departing women and whispering loudly):* Thasian wine!

KALONIKA: And we will swear—that we will never dilute it with a drop of water.

LAMPITO: Now that—there's a thing to swear to, I agree.

LEADER OLD WOMEN CHORUS *(From off-stage):* Oh ho—Lysistrata!

LAMPITO: Who's that?

LYSISTRATA: The old women have taken the Acropolis.

LEADER OLD WOMEN CHORUS *(Appearing):* We've got it, Lysistrata. Here—catch.

FIRST THEBAN WOMAN: What's this?

LEADER OLD WOMEN CHORUS: The key to the treasure house.

LYSISTRATA: Now you may be sure that Athens will not man another ship or send another soldier to the front against our will. And you, dear friends, whose work is done so well, leave a small guard up there and join us here to take the oath in which all Greece is pledged.

LEADER OLD WOMEN CHORUS: How do you take the oath?

MYRRHINA: In Thasian wine.

KALONIKA: Oh, dear, when I drink wine I get—excited.

FIRST CORINTHIAN WOMAN: Oh, so do I. It makes my husband sleepy but—there's someone else I know who lets me drink cup for cup with him.

LAMPITO: Well, there's a cup that you and someone else would be a long time drinking. *(The bowl is brought in and a wine-skin, the women clustering around it as Lysistrata pronounces the invocation)*

LYSISTRATA: Let each one touch this noble sacrifice. Almighty goddess of the subtle tongue, mistress of argument, who gives victory in persuasion; Goddess of Love, whom we this once forswear; and thou, great bowl of flowing wine, comrade of every joy and happiness, receive this sacrifice and be propitious to us women. *(She strikes a knife into the wine-skin and the wine flows into the bowl)*

KALONIKA: Ah, the beautiful red blood—look at it spurting.

LAMPITO: It makes me thirsty just to look at it.

FIRST CORINTHIAN WOMAN: And what a fine bouquet! This must be vintage.

LYSISTRATA: Now I'll swear first and drink.

YOUNG WOMEN CHORUS: No! No! No! All together! Let's draw lots! An equal share for all.

LYSISTRATA: Well, just as you like. Let's all put hands together round the rim. I'll say the oath and one of you repeat it for all the rest. Myrrhina!

MYRRHINA: Why me? I'll take the oath—I promise—but I couldn't say it.

LAMPITO: Come, now!

LYSISTRATA: Now, every word I say, you say it after. From this day forth until peace is declared——

MYRRHINA *(Tearfully)*: From this day forth until peace is declared——

YOUNG WOMEN CHORUS: From this day forth until peace is declared——

LYSISTRATA: Although my heart aches for my husband's love——

MYRRHINA: Although my heart aches for my husband's love——

YOUNG WOMEN CHORUS: Although my heart aches for my husband's love——

LYSISTRATA: Or any lover comes, afire with passion——

MYRRHINA: Or any lover comes, afire with passion——*(Her responses become more and more tremulous and the other women murmur their responses hastily)*

YOUNG WOMEN CHORUS: Or any lover comes, afire with passion——

LYSISTRATA: I never will take man into my bed.

MYRRHINA: I never will——*(She breaks into hysterical weeping)* I can't—I can't! I will not take the oath.

LAMPITO: You must, you little fool.

MYRRHINA: Let someone else repeat: I'll just hold hands.

LYSISTRATA: Kalonika, then, say after me: I never will take man into my bed.

KALONIKA *(She speaks firmly and clearly but gradually her responses also grow weak)*: I never will take man into my bed.

YOUNG WOMEN CHORUS: I never will take man into my bed.

LYSISTRATA: But I will live at home austere and chaste——

KALONIKA: But I will live at home austere and chaste——*(Her voice breaks a little on the word "chaste")*

YOUNG WOMEN CHORUS: But I will live at home austere and chaste——

LYSISTRATA: Dressed in a saffron robe and amorus——

KALONIKA: Dressed in a saffron robe and amorous——

YOUNG WOMEN CHORUS: Dressed in a saffron robe and amorous——

LYSISTRATA: So that my husband or my lover faints to hold me——

KALONIKA: So that my husband or——*(Hysterically)* Oh, Polydorus, Polydorus—I can't—I can't.

LYSISTRATA *(Mercilessly)*: Faints to hold me——

LAMPITO *(Firmly)*: Faints to hold me——

YOUNG WOMEN CHORUS: Faints to hold me.

LYSISTRATA: And never shall he have his way with me——

LAMPITO: And never shall he have his way with me——

YOUNG WOMEN CHORUS: And never shall he have his way with me——

LYSISTRATA: Of my free will——

LAMPITO: Of my free will——

314

YOUNG WOMEN CHORUS: Of my free will——*(A Corinthian woman sobs as she murmurs the words; a Theban woman mutters and shakes her head)*

LYSISTRATA: And if he overcomes me by sheer force——

LAMPITO: And if he overcomes me by sheer force——

YOUNG WOMEN CHORUS: And if he overcomes me by sheer force——

LYSISTRATA: I'll lie as cold as ice and not respond——

LAMPITO: I'll lie as cold as ice and not respond——

YOUNG WOMEN CHORUS: I'll lie as cold as ice and not respond.

LYSISTRATA: I will not give him joy in any way.

KALONIKA AND LAMPITO: I will not give him joy in any way.

YOUNG WOMEN CHORUS: I will not give him joy in any way.

LYSISTRATA: Or crouch like a lion on a hunting knife.

MYRRHINA, KALONIKA AND LAMPITO: Or crouch like a lion on a hunting knife.

YOUNG WOMEN CHORUS: Or crouch like a lion on a hunting knife.

LYSISTRATA: And if I keep my oath, let my blood be red as wine.

MYRRHINA, KALONIKA, LAMPITO AND YOUNG WOMEN CHORUS: And if I keep my oath, let my blood be red as wine.

LYSISTRATA: But if I break it—let it turn to water.

MYRRHINA, KALONIKA, LAMPITO AND YOUNG WOMEN CHORUS: But if I break it, let it turn to water.

LYSISTRATA: You've taken the oath. Now pledge it in the wine. *(The tension is relieved and the women grow gay with the wine. The slow muffled tramping of feet is heard off-stage)*

KALONIKA: Let's drink the rest to show we are all friends. Take care not to drink too much. You know some women aren't responsible. And for the first time in my life, I'll drink with the women of Corinth. *(One of the Theban women stands immovable by the bowl and drinks with a slow and steady motion)*

FIRST CORINTHIAN WOMAN: Oh, I'm afraid if I get tipsy now——

KALONIKA: Oh, come along. There are several things I'd like you to tell me. You know you Corinthians have such a reputation. I've often wondered what your special charm was.

SECOND CORINTHIAN WOMAN: Oh, she would hardly know. But let me tell you. I have a reputation now in Corinth—if you could only ask some of my friends.

KALONIKA: I wish I could.

LAMPITO *(Embracing Myrrhina)*: Why, now you're feeling better, aren't you, darling?

MYRRHINA: I am better but I wish you were Kinesias.

LAMPITO: Still thinking of your husband! You'll forget him.

FIRST CORINTHIAN WOMAN *(Murmuring)*: If he were only here——

LYSISTRATA: And now, Lampito, all our work is to be done

and you must start. Fly back to Sparta. Organize things there, and when you've done your work, come back to us.

LAMPITO (*Slightly tipsy*): I'll do it, Lyshishtrata.

KALONIKA (*She looks down the hill and speaks very seriously*): Oh, look who's coming there. All is lost! The flower of our army returns to capture us.

LYSISTRATA: Fly, Lampito! All of you quick—take the back way over the hill——

LEADER YOUNG WOMEN CHORUS: What splendid men! Their shields shine in the sun.

MYRRHINA: What brawny arms! What legs—what glorious men!

KALONIKA: See how they march—so perfectly in step. Look, Myrrhina, a battering ram.

MYRRHINA: We must retreat.

LYSISTRATA: I knew there was a truce, but they've come too early. Why, these tireless soldiers must have marched for twenty hours and still so vigorous and still so handsome and so powerful. Hail, saviors of Athens! (*Lysistrata's tone becomes sarcastic just as the dilapidated chorus of old men comes in sight, out of step, ragged, scrawny and altogether comic*)

OLD WOMEN CHORUS: Hail, saviors of Athens! (*A great shout of laughter from all the women as they scutter up the hill and out of sight. The chorus of old men now occupies the foreground of the entire stage. They carry fagots and fire-pan and the front ones have a huge log on their shoulders. The leader of the old men is an ill-tempered fellow who speaks as if he were addressing a magnificent army*)

LEADER OLD MEN CHORUS: In step there! Close ranks! (*The old men stagger forward clumsily*) Quick march, now! Forward!

SECOND OLD MAN: Let's fall out, Drakes—for just a minute.

LEADER OLD MEN CHORUS: Silence in the ranks!

SECOND OLD MAN: Oh, we know you're a hero, but don't rub it in.

TENTH OLD MAN: My shoulder is rubbed enough by this great log.

THIRD OLD MAN: My knees won't stand this. I say, Drakes, go easy.

LEADER OLD MEN CHORUS: Come—quick, march! Time flies. (*They sit*) Strip tunics! Fall in! Mark time! Left, left, left. (*They rise again, and proceed up the hill*) Forward!

One more dash and we are there. Then we storm the fortress. You attend to the others, and I will go in and with my own hands I'll draw out Lysistrata.

NINTH OLD MAN: Yes, drag out Lysistrata.

FOURTH OLD MAN: Tie her ankles and hands.

SECOND OLD MAN: We know that at Marathon you were a good soldier, but we were there too, and well we remember the terms of command and how to obey them; but, by all the gods, in those days we were younger.

THIRD OLD MAN: And in those days, Strymodorus, we fought with the spear and the javelin—against whom? The Persian barbarian. Now *that* I call warfare. That's fighting. A man likes a battle like that. But now we are sent by the rulers of Athens to fight with these women. What sort of battle can you fight with women?

LEADER OLD MEN CHORUS: You wait here a moment, and I will go up and demand their surrender and if they refuse—press close on beside me. Let the women see that the old men of Athens are ready to punish their insolent actions.

LEADER OLD MEN CHORUS *(Approaching the temple):* By order of the Council of Seven and the Senate of Athens, I command you to open! *(There is no answer)* By order of the Council of Seven and the Senate of Athens, I command you women to open your gates! *(The women become visible before the temple)* Well, here's a pretty sight. A swarm of women—a regular army of them posted along the walls.

SECOND OLD MAN: Just tell them to come down. Let's have no nonsense.

LEADER YOUNG WOMEN CHORUS *(Looking down on them. All the women throughout this scene have the higher level of the hill):* Just tell them to come up. Let's have no nonsense. Why, you impotent old lechers!

LEADER OLD MEN CHORUS: Attention! To your posts, my brave veterans! You—forward!

LEADER YOUNG WOMEN CHORUS: Why, what can this be? Who are all these graybeards?—these spindle-shanked men who tremble as they walk?—and what have they here—what is that strange looking thing they carry?

LEADER OLD MEN CHORUS: As I said before, in the name of the Council of Seven and——

LEADER YOUNG WOMEN CHORUS: There is someone below there who thinks he is important. A slave, I suspect. Ho, slavie, who sent you?

THIRD OLD MAN: Well, Drakes, what are we waiting for? Let's smash the gate down.

LEADER OLD MEN CHORUS: In the name of the Council of Seven and the Senate——

LEADER OLD WOMEN CHORUS: Has the Council of Seven sent you here to set fire to the temple of Pallas? Go away, you old fool.

LEADER OLD MEN CHORUS: Will you let us pass?

LEADER OLD WOMEN CHORUS: Yes—that way.

LEADER OLD MEN CHORUS: Come, veterans, on with your torches.

LYSISTRATA *(Appearing above the old women):* Now, Pallas Athena, the women of Athens appeal to you to save and protect them. See these vicious old men all wrinkled and puffing, bring up fire and flame to destroy your great temple. Suffer them not to commit desecration and join with Poseidon, the God of the Waters, to give us full strength and full jars to beat off these men.

TENTH OLD MAN: Jars? Jars?

LEADER OLD MEN CHORUS: Jars, what can they do with jars?

OLD MEN CHORUS: Let's trample them down.

OLD WOMEN CHORUS: Yaaaaaaah, you living dead men, walking corpses. Come near us and we'll gut you tooth and nail.

THIRD OLD MAN: Now you see the wisdom of the poets. Doesn't Euripides say that in every species of man or beast, the female is more deadly than the male? *(The old men surround the leader of the old women)*

LEADER OLD WOMEN CHORUS: Let go of me, you doddering old fool! Kalyke, help me!

AN OLD WOMAN: Let go of that young lady.

LEADER OLD WOMEN CHORUS: Help! Help! *(She breaks away and rejoins the others. The old men move forward with their fire and fagots)*

LEADER OLD MEN CHORUS: Come, heroes, storm this breastwork.

THIRD OLD MAN: What are you doing up there, you harlots?

LEADER YOUNG WOMEN CHORUS: We intend to soften your ardor just a bit.

OLD MEN CHORUS: What? Put out our fire?

LEADER OLD WOMEN CHORUS: A little bath would make you better company.

OLD MEN CHORUS: A bath?

SECOND OLD MAN: And are you addressing me, you slut?

THIRD OLD WOMAN: The bridegroom always bathes before the wedding.

OLD MEN CHORUS: The insolence of women—vile wenches.

SEVENTH OLD WOMAN: I'm a free woman.

SECOND OLD MAN: All too free.

LEADER OLD MEN CHORUS: Now, to your posts. Every man his duty. Philurgus, you're at Number One Post. You, Strymodorus——

SECOND OLD MAN: I take the left flank.

LEADER OLD MEN CHORUS: And all the rest—stand ready when I count three.

LEADER OLD WOMEN CHORUS: Are you all ready? Here. Now, Kalyke, remember, don't get excited. Take your time, we'll wait for them.

LEADER OLD MEN CHORUS: Fire carriers—light up! Now ready! Close ranks! Now forward! One—two—three—in we go! *(As the fire starts, the old women drench all the men with water from their pots)*

LEADER OLD MEN CHORUS: Oh, Zeus, I'm drenched!

ELEVENTH OLD MAN: I'm scalded!

NINTH OLD MAN: I'm burned!

THIRD OLD MAN: The water is hot!

TWELFTH OLD MAN: It's cold!

EIGHTH OLD MAN: It's wet!

SIXTH OLD MAN: Oh, God, where has our fire gone?

OLD MEN CHORUS: Enough, enough, enough——

SECOND OLD WOMAN: What? Must you go so soon? Come back, dear friends, and get a second welcome.

LEADER OLD MEN CHORUS: Oh, Zeus, I'm wet!

THIRD OLD MAN: My limbs are shaking.

318

NINTH OLD MAN: I'll catch cold.

OLD MEN CHORUS: Enough, enough——

SECOND OLD MAN: On, Drakes, I told you——

OLD MEN CHORUS: I told you so! I told you so!

OLD WOMEN CHORUS: Alas, look at the heroes!

LEADER OLD WOMEN CHORUS: The war is over and we are unwounded and now our hearts break when we think of those proud, handsome men, how they are maimed and disfigured. Surely this is a battle that Athens will always remember. Even when Marathon is forgotten, old men will tell their children how they ran to the defense of the Acropolis and the children will ask, "What happened then, Daddy?" and the old men will say they broke down the gate and——

OLD WOMEN CHORUS: Out came the women of Athens.

LEADER OLD WOMEN CHORUS: And the children will say, "But where is the scar from your wound, my brave daddy?" And the old men will say——

OLD WOMEN CHORUS: We were wet.

LEADER OLD MEN CHORUS: Once more to the gate! We still have our vigor.

LEADER OLD WOMEN CHORUS: Yes—form for the attack again. We've plenty of ammunition left. *(The women withdraw)*

LEWIS M. KILLIAN

The Significance of Multiple-Group Membership in Disaster

Although the importance of multiple-group membership as one of the salient features of modern social life is widely recognized by sociologists and psychologists, the task of exploring its many implications has only just been begun. Cooley, a pioneer in the study of the importance of group membership for the individual, recognized the existence of multiple-group memberships, describing the individual in modern society as a point through which numerous arcs, representing different group memberships, pass.[1] Before him, William James declared that a man has "as many social selves . . . as there are distinct groups of persons about whose opinion he cares."[2]

In recent years other students have begun a more systematic

Lewis M. Killian, "The Significance of Multiple-Group Membership in Disaster," *American Journal of Sociology* 57:4 (January 1952): 309–14. Copyright © 1952 by the University of Chicago. Reprinted by permission of the author and the University of Chicago Press.

exploration of the implications of identification with several different groups for the individual and for the society of which he is a part. The creation of psychological problems for the individual and the development of new strata in the social structure as the result of some types of multiple-group membership are discussed in the work of Robert E. Park,[3] Everett Stonequist,[4] and E. C. Hughes.[5] Hughes has demonstrated that possession of contradictory roles in different groups may create "dilemmas and contradictions of status" for the individual.

Muzafer Sherif, in his elaboration of the concepts of "membership group" and "reference group," has furnished valuable conceptual tools for the analysis of multiple-group identifications and conflicting group loyalties.[6] He suggests, furthermore, that identification with numerous different reference groups and the lack of a unitary ego are the keys to the understanding of inconsistencies in certain types of behavior, such as intergroup relations.[7]

In the study of the reactions of people in four Southwestern communities to physical disasters—explosions and tornadoes—made by the University of Oklahoma Research Institute, it was found that conflicting group loyalties and contradictory roles resulting from multiple-group membership were significant factors affecting individual behavior in critical situations. The dilemmas created by the disasters also brought to light latent contradictions in roles not ordinarily regarded as conflicting.

In spite of the fact that multiple-group memberships do create dilemmas and inconsistencies, the majority of people in modern urban society manage to function efficiently as members of many groups, often being only vaguely aware of contradictions in their various roles. Sherif points out that the individual is often not aware of the derivation of the "cross-pressures" which cause inconsistent behavior.[8] Newcomb declares that many role prescriptions are "relatively nonconflicting" and says:

> Most of us, most of the time, manage to take quite different roles, as prescribed by the same or by different groups, without undue conflict. . . . Indeed, it is rather remarkable how many different roles most of us manage to take with a minimum of conflict.[9]

He points out that many roles are "nonoverlapping." A man may play the role of a businessman, acting in terms of the work situation, during most of the day. For a few hours in the evening he may play the role of "the family man," leaving his work at the office. In a small community he may, on certain occasions, act as a functionary of the town government, as a volunteer fireman, or as a town councilman. Simultaneously, he has other group memberships which call for certain behavior—in a social class group, in a racial group, in the community of which he is a citizen, and in "society-at-large."[10]

When catastrophe strikes a community, many individuals find that the latent conflict between ordinarily nonconflicting group loyalties suddenly becomes apparent and that they are faced with the dilemma of making an immediate choice between various roles. In his classic study of the Halifax disaster, S. H. Prince noted this conflict when he wrote:

> But the earliest leadership that could be called social, arising from the public itself, was that on the part of those who had no family ties, much of the earliest work being done by visitors in the city. The others as a rule ran first to their homes to discover if their own families were in danger.[11]

People who had been present in the explosion port of Texas City and in three Oklahoma tornado towns during disasters were asked, among other questions, "What was the first thing you thought of after the disaster struck?" and "What was the first thing you did?" Their answers revealed not only the conflict between loyalties to the family and to the community, described by Prince, but also dilemmas arising from conflicting roles derived from membership in other groups. The individuals concerned were not always conscious of the dilemmas or of the existence of "cross-pressures," but even in such cases the choice of roles which the person made was significant in affecting the total pattern of group reaction to the disaster. In some cases subjects indicated that they recognized *after* the emergency that their reaction had been of critical social importance. On the basis of the experiences of people involved in these four community disasters it is possible to suggest the types of groups between which dilemmas of loyalty may arise in modern communities. Tentative generalization as to how these dilemmas will be resolved and as to their significance for *group* reactions to disaster may also be formulated.

The choice required of the greatest number of individuals was the one between the family and other groups, principally the employment group or the community. Especially in Texas City, many men were at work away from their families when disaster struck and presented a threat to both "the plant" and "the home." In all the communities there were individuals, such as policemen, firemen, and public utilities workers, whose loved ones were threatened by the same disaster that demanded their services as "trouble-shooters." Even persons who had no such definite roles to play in time of catastrophe were confronted with the alternatives of seeing after only their own primary groups or of assisting in the rescue and relief of any of the large number of injured persons, regardless of identity. Indeed, only the unattached person in the community was likely to be free of such a conflict.

How these conflicts between loyalty to the family group and loyalty to other membership groups, including the community and "society-at-large," were resolved was of great significance for the reorganization of communities for rescue, relief, and prevention of further disaster. In Texas City, at the time of the first ship explosion, many men were working in oil refineries, where failure to remain on the job until units were shut down could result in additional fires and explosions. In all the communities studied, failure of community functionaries, such as firemen and policemen, to perform the duties appropriate to their positions could result in the absence of expected and badly needed leadership in a disorganized group. This, in turn, could cause costly delay in the reorganization of the community for emergency rescue, traffic control, and fire-fighting activity. Preoccupation of large numbers of able survivors with their own small primary groups could result in the atomization of the community into small, unco-ordinated groups, again delaying reorganization into a relatively well-integrated, unified, large group. As Prince indicated in his statement, quoted above, this would increase the dependence of the community on outside sources of leadership.

The great majority of persons interviewed who were involved in such dilemmas resolved them in favor of loyalty to the family or, in some cases, to friendship groups. Much of the initial confusion, disorder, and seemingly complete disorganization reported in the disaster communities was the result of the rush of individuals to find and rejoin their families. Yet in none of the four communities studied did the disastrous consequences contemplated above seem to have materialized. In the first place, there were important exceptions to the tendency to react first in terms of the family. Most of the refinery workers in Texas City did stay on the job until their units were safely shut down, as they had been trained to do. The significance of conflicting group loyalties in a disaster situation is underlined, however, by the importance of the actions taken by a few exceptional individuals in each town who were not confronted with such conflicts. In Texas City the chief of police remained at his post from the moment of the first explosion until seventy-two hours later, never returning to his home during the entire period of playing a vital part in the reorganization of the community. He ascribed his ability to give undivided attention to his official duties to the fact that he knew that his family was safely out of town, visiting relatives, at the time of the explosion. One member of the volunteer fire department of a tornado town told of the thin margin by which his community escaped a disastrous fire following the "twister":

I was at my home, right on the edge of where the storm passed, when it hit. Neither me nor my wife was hurt. The first thing I though of was fire. I knew there'd be some, so I went to the fire station right away. On the way I could see that there was a fire right in the middle of the wreckage —a butane tank had caught fire. I got out of the truck, drove over there, and fought the fire by myself until the army got there to help me.

All the rest of the firemen had relatives that were hurt, and they stayed with them. Naturally they looked after them. If it hadn't been that my wife was all right, this town probably would have burned up. It's hard to say, but I kind of believe I would have been looking after my family, too.

Devotion to the family as the primary object of loyalty did not always redound to the detriment of aid to other groups, however. Many people who served as rescue workers, assisting injured people whom they did not even know, were drawn to the areas of heavy casualties because of concern for members of their own families whom they believed to be there. Apparently they found their identification with society-at-large, and the emphasis of American culture upon the importance of human life, too great to permit them to pass an injured stranger without assisting him. Hence, many stayed to assist in the common community task of rescuing the injured; in both Texas City and in the tornado towns. In one of the latter a man sensed the approach of the tornado only minutes before it struck. In spite of great personal danger he rushed through the storm to a theater where his children were attending a movie. There he prevented the frightened audience from pouring forth into the storm by holding the doors closed. Later he was acclaimed as a hero whose quick action had saved the lives of many of his fellow-citizens. He himself denied that he had any thought of taking the great risk that he took for the sake of the anonymous audience itself; he was thinking only of his own children.

A second, but less common, type of conflict was found in the case of people who were confronted with the alternatives of playing the "heroic" role of rescue worker and of carrying out what were essentially "occupational roles." In terms of group loyalty, they were impelled, on the one hand, to act as sympathetic, loyal members of society-at-large and to give personal aid to injured human beings. On the other hand, they were called to do their duty as it was indicated by their membership in certain occupational groups.

One such person was a minister in Texas City, who, upon hearing the explosion, started for the docks with the intention of helping in the rescue work. On the way he became conscious of the choice of roles which confronted him. He said:

After I heard the first explosion my first impulse was to go down to the docks and try to help there. But on the way down I saw two or three folks I knew who had husbands down there. I saw then that my job was with the families—not doing rescue work. I had a job that I was peculiarly suited for, prepared for, and I felt that I should do that.

More important for the reorganization of a tornado-stricken town was the choice made by a state patrolman between his role as a police officer and his role as friend and neighbor to the people of the community in which he was stationed. His story was:

As I drove around town after the tornado had passed I realized that the best thing I could do was to try to make contact with the outside and get help from there. I started out to drive to the next town and try to call from there. As I drove out of town people I knew well would call me by name and ask me to help them find their relatives. Driving by and not stopping to help those people who were looking to me as a friend was one of the hardest things I ever had to do.

As a result of this difficult decision, this man became the key figure in the development of organized rescue work, after he recruited and organized a large force of rescue workers in a near-by community.

A similar dilemma faced many public utilities workers who were forced to disregard the plight of the injured if they were to perform **323** their task of restoring normal community services. Unlike the minister and the patrolman, these workers reported no awareness of a conflict of roles, regarding it as a matter of course that they concentrated on their often quite dangerous jobs. Some indicated that preoccupation with the job was so intense that they were scarcely aware of what went on around them. Yet the instances of devotion to prosaic duty cited above were exceptional. Many policemen, firemen, and other functionaries acted heroically but quite outside the framework and discipline of their organizations.

For people whose usual occupational roles bore little or no relationship to the needs created by a disaster, identification with the community as a whole and disregard of their occupational roles came still more easily. Many merchants and clerks rushed from their stores to aid in rescue work, leaving both goods and cash on the counters. The postmaster in one tornado town left the post office completely unguarded, even though the windows were shattered and mail was strewn about the floor. This was, it is true, an extreme case of abandonment of the occupational role.

A third type of conflict of loyalties was that between the loyalty of employees to "the company" as an organization and to fellow-employees as friends and human beings. It might seem that the choice, essentially one between life and property, should have been an easy one; but the fact that different choices were made by men with different degrees of identification with other workers reveals that a basic conflict was present. In Texas City many plant officials were also residents of the community and friends of the workers. After the explosions, in which several top executives were killed, some men found themselves suddenly "promoted" to the position of being in charge of their company's damaged property. At the same time men with whom they had worked daily for several years were injured or missing. The most common, almost universal, reaction was to think of the men first and of the plant later. One plant official, active in rescue work in spite of a broken arm and numerous lacerations, described his reaction to the sudden, dramatic conflict between loyalty to the company and loyalty to the workers as follows:

Property! Nobody gave a damn for property! All that was important was life. I've often wondered just how it would be to walk off and let a plant burn up. That was the way it was. We didn't even consider fighting the fire.

In sharp contrast to this reaction, however, was that of a man in charge of a neighboring plant. While he was in Texas City at the time of the first blast, he had never lived in the community and scarcely knew his workers. He described his first reaction in the following words:

I got in my car and drove over to another refinery to find out what had happened. The assistant superintendent told me that their top men had been killed and asked me what I thought he should do. I told him, "You should take charge of the company's property. That's what the president of your company would tell you if he were here. You look after the property. I'm going over to Galveston to call our president, and I'll call yours at the same time."

While this reaction was exceptional, it is significant as suggesting an alternate way of resolving the conflict between loyalty to "the company" and "the men."

Finally, some individuals suddenly discovered, in the face of disaster, that there was a conflict between loyalty to the community and loyalty to certain extra-community groups. At the time of two of the disasters telephone workers in the Southwest were on strike. In both communities the striking workers were allowed to return to duty by union leaders but were ordered to walk out again a few days later. In both cases the union officials considered the emergency to be over sooner than did the townspeople of the stricken communities. In one town the workers obeyed the union's orders only to find themselves subjected to harsh criticism by their fellow-townsmen. In the other community the workers resigned from the union rather than forsake their loyalty to their other membership group. It was almost a year before union officials were able to reorganize the local in this town, and some workers never rejoined.

As was pointed out earlier, the individual may, under normal circumstances, carry out roles appropriate to membership in several groups without having to make a choice between basically conflicting group loyalties. He may even do so without seriously impairing his performance of any of his roles. The worker may wish that he could spend more time at home with his family but resigns himself to the fact that he cannot if he is to keep the job he wants. On his way to work he may pass the scene of a fire and be vaguely conscious that, as a citizen, he is indirectly responsible for the protection of life and property; but he assumes that the limit of his direct responsibility for action extends only to notifying the fire department, if it is not already there. The employer may, within certain limits, think of the workers as persons and friends and still not be disloyal to the company's interests. In the crisis induced by disaster, however, these individuals may find that it is impossible to serve two masters, to act in two roles. An immediate choice is demanded, but it may be difficult because the demands of the competing groups may appear equally urgent. The nature of the choice made by the individual, particularly if one of his roles is associated with a key position in the community, may have important consequences for the reorganization of the community. Large-scale reorganization, co-ordination, and direction of efforts is necessary to speedy rescue work and the restoration of normalcy. Activities carried on in terms of the demands of many diverse, competing groups act as an impediment to this reorganization.

Further research is needed to make possible the prediction of the choices that will be made by individuals in these conflicts. The frequency with which individuals thought and acted first in terms of family and close friends suggests that loyalty to primary groups stands first in the hierarchy of group loyalties, as might be expected. On the other hand, important exceptions in which persons played relatively impersonal roles as leaders or working with materiel, rather than people, indicate that some factors, such as training or feelings of responsibility, may predispose the individual to adhere to secondary-group demands even in a disaster. Knowledge of what these factors are and how they may be induced would contribute to greater understanding of group reactions to disorganization and of methods of facilitating group reorganization.

NOTES

1. Charles H. Cooley, *Human Nature and the Social Order* (New York: Charles Scribner's Sons, 1902), p. 114.

2. William James, *Principles of Psychology* (New York: Henry Holland & Co., 1890), I, 294.

3. "Human Migration and the Marginal Man," *American Journal of Sociology* 33 (1928): 881-93.

4. *The Marginal Man* (New York: Charles Scribner's Sons, 1937).

5. Dilemmas and Contradictions of Status," *American Journal of Sociology* 50 (1945): 353–59.

6. *An Outline of Social Psychology* (New York: Harper & Bros., 1948), pp. 122–25.

7. "The Problems of Inconsistency in Intergroup Relations," *Journal of Social Issues* 5 (1949): 32–37.

8. Ibid., p. 37.

9. Theodore Newcomb, *Social Psychology* (New York: Dryden Press, 1950), p. 449.

10. Ibid., p. 544.

11. *Catastrophe and Social Change* ("Columbia University Studies in History, Economics, and Public Law," vol. 94 (New York: Columbia University Press, 1921), p. 61.

326   WILLIAM A. WESTLEY

Secrecy and the Police

The stool pigeon, the squealer, the one who tells, is anathema to any social group. The label symbolizes the sanction against breaking secrecy which is found in many groups, ranging from the school class, through the production line, to the criminal gang. Secrecy maintains group identity, and supports solidarity since it gives something in common to those who belong and differentiates those who do not. A breech of secrecy is thus a threat to the group.

Secrecy would seem to be a phenomenon which is generic to social groups and therefore of special concern to the sociologist. Yet, except for occasional theoretical references[1] there is little research or writing which indicates its genesis, incidence, or function in modern society.

This paper concerns secrecy among the police. It reports part of a larger study of a municipal police department in a midwestern industrial city.[2] The report is based upon close observation of all phases of police work over a period of two years which included intensive interviews with approximately fifty percent of the men in the department and a large number of case histories.

This study of one police force has shown that the maintenance of secrecy is a fundamental rule. The generic characteristics of this rule were suggested by August Vollmer twenty-five years ago. "Eradication of disgruntled agitators, incompetent policemen, police crooks and grafters takes much time since it is next to impossible to induce police officers to inform on each other. *It is an unwritten law in police departments that police officers must never testify against their brother officers.*"[3]

THE STRENGTH OF SECRECY

In the course of the above study a special effort was made to confirm the existence of this norm and to determine its relative value and areas of applicability. Two questions were devised, any answer to which would reveal the policeman's orientation to secrecy.

The questions were as follows:

1. You and your partner pick up a drunk who is breaking up a bar. While you are patting him down you discover that he has five hundred dollars on him. You take him back to the station in a car and your partner sits in the back with him to keep him quiet. When you check him in with the turnkey the money is gone. You realize that your partner has clipped him. What would you do?

William A. Westley, "Secrecy and the Police," *Social Forces* 34:3 (March 1956): 254–57. Reprinted by permission of the University of North Carolina Press.

When they had replied the following question was asked:

2. The drunk finds his money gone and prefers charges against you. In court your partner testifies that the drunk had no money on him when you discovered him. There are no other witnesses. How would you testify?

Table 1.   Number and Percent of Policemen Willing to
Report Other Policemen for Stealing

Response	Frequency	Percentage
Total	15	100
Yes	4	27
No	11	73

Table 2.   Number and Percent of Policemen Willing to
Testify Against Other Policemen

Response	Frequency	Percentage
Total	13*	100
Yes	3	23
No	10	77

*Two men refused to answer this question.

These questions put the men in a dilemma because a refusal to answer *looked* incriminating, to refuse to report the partner and/or to testify against him *was* incriminating, and to agree to report or testify against the partner meant breaking secrecy.

The question was presented to 15 men in a series, and then dropped because of large-scale cancellations of interviews. Therefore the sample is very small, but not necessarily biased. Tables 1 and 2, above, present the results. Only one man stated that he would both report and testify against his partner. He was a rookie.

The results show that 73 percent of the men would not report their partners, and that 77 percent would PERJURE themselves rather than testify against their partners. While the limited size of the sample does not permit statistical generalization to the remainder of the force, other information strongly suggests that these results are representative.

To understand the full significance of these findings the reader must take into consideration the following facts: (a) the support and enforcement of the law are the basic legal functions of the police, and they are fully conscious of this fact; (b) policemen themselves maintain that biased testimony only leads to trouble in the long run; and (c) the detection of perjury would result in the suspension of the man from the force, the loss of his pension time, make him liable to imprisonment, and probably ruin his career. If so, why do these

328 men feel that they would prefer to break the law, to perjure themselves, rather than break secrecy; *and* why did they tell this to an outside observer? To answer this question it is necessary to refer to the sanctions supporting secrecy, the functions of secrecy, and the manner in which new men are indoctrinated into the rule of secrecy.

SANCTIONS SUPPORTING SECRECY

The men who were questioned were asked to explain their answers. Their replies delineate the sanctions supporting secrecy. This is illustrated by the following excerpts:

> It would give you the name of a stool pigeon ... and once you get that name you are an outcast from the police force. Nobody wants to say anything to you. Nobody talks to you. Nobody wants to be around you and you never get to know what's going on in the department.
> If I did say that I saw the money, he would get the sack and, although everybody would think I was right, they would always remember that I had been down on my buddy. But, I would not say anything. I would always remember, though, that he had rolled the drunk, and one of my rules is that if we make a dollar, we split fifty-fifty.
> If I turned the man in everybody would be out to get me. They wouldn't talk to me. They would go out of their way to get me in trouble.
> The other men would treat me with contempt. They would regard me as an unsafe officer.

The successful policeman needs the full support of his partners in order to act in tricky situations (many of which require illegal or semi-legal decisions), and in dangerous situations which every policeman meets from time to time. He needs access to the police grapevine because some of the most important orders are never put on paper, and he must be immediately familiar with day to day shifts in political orientation or the mood of the chief, if he is to keep in good standing. The person who breaks secrecy loses the confidence of his colleagues and in serious cases may be deprived of their support. He is always cut off from the grapevine. This represents an intolerable situation. Therefore, it is the most powerful sanction the police can devise.

THE FUNCTIONS OF SECRECY

The functions of secrecy among the police are closely related to the manner in which the policeman is defined in the American community. Frequently, the people in the community has a low regard for the police and consider them corrupt, brutal, and incompetent.[4] Policemen are sensitive to this definition and in turn tend to regard the public as an enemy. To this extent the police, who are supposedly the pillars of the official morality, are in fact a conflict group. The manifest functions of secrecy are related to these conditions. Secrecy stands as a shield against the attacks of the outside world; against bad newspaper publicity which would lower the reputation of the police; against public criticism from which the police feel that they suffer too much; against the criminal who is eager to know the moves of the police; against the law which the police all too frequently abrogate. The activities of the police usually involve them in the illegal use of violence,[5] and often involve them in politics and corruption. They are constantly subject to investigations. Therefore they need secrecy.

Among the latent functions of the secrecy code one of the most important seems to be that it makes the individual policeman identify with other policemen, and distinguish himself from non-policemen. Thus, it functions as a social bond among the police, by giving them something in common (if only a sense of mutual incrimination). However, while secrecy fosters the sense of mutual identification, it does not produce a sense of trust. In fact, it seems clear that an unanticipated consequence of the emphasis on secrecy is that the police become intensely suspicious of each other. Thus, they are constantly testing each other to find out if the other is a stool pigeon. This is delineated in the following statement:

It's a good idea to keep your mouth shut about what happens in the department. Not long ago I had a man test me out. When we were in a restaurant he told me a really terrific story about an incident in which a number of policemen were involved. Boy, it was really something. I could hardly wait to run over to tell my partner about it. But then I got to thinking and I decided to keep my mouth shut and later it turned out that he had told me the story just to see whether or not it came back to him.

Each man is careful to talk only about impersonal things and to stay out of dangerous areas of discussion, of which the most important are the affairs of other men in the department. Naturally, this varies with the garrulousness of the particular individual, but in general, policemen are closemouthed and tend to be suspicious of each other. Thus, another policeman stated:

It's more or less a rule that if you have any beefs, you keep them in your family. Don't start talking to people outside. If you are in the department for a while you eventually develop a survival of the fittest attitude. Everybody builds a barrier around himself . . . around his personal affairs. When you work with guys and they get to nosing around, they generally get to know too much about your personal life.

INDOCTRINATION IN THE NEED FOR SECRECY

The chief threat to the code of secrecy is the initiate, for he is yet largely a member of the outer world, with no emotional involvement with the group. Therefore, in the beginning care must be taken that he is not given premature access to secrets, and full acceptance occurs only when he is told the secrets. Among the police, the "rookie" is carefully observed and assessed, at the same time that he is constantly told about the need for secrecy. In fact, there is no area of police work where the code of secrecy is made more evident.

Fifty percent of the rookies (men in training) were asked what the experienced men had told them. *All* reported that *every* experienced man with whom they had been in contact had empha-

330

sized the need for secrecy with statements like: "Keep your mouth shut—never squeal on a fellow officer." They had this dinned into their ears by man after man, as they went the rounds of training, and the admonition was related to every conceivable kind of situation. They were all told to beware of stool pigeons who were regularly characterized in disparaging terms. This is what finally drove the lesson home. The rookies became aware of stool pigeons and learned to fear them. They became suspicious. The following statements by two rookies are illustrative:

> There are some guys you can't trust. They are just looking out for themselves. The men won't tell you who they are. I don't want to work with a man who won't back you up.
> There was one guy who did tell the names of some of these stoolies. I tried to find out, you know, because I don't like the idea of trial and error method, in a thing like that. But, when the guy gave me the names, I figured the reason he gave me the names is because he isn't much liked in the department and so was probably one of the stoolies himself. Most of the police won't tell you who the guys are. I think they don't want to because they are afraid you will reveal the source.

The experienced men, in turn, evaluated the rookies chiefly in terms of their discretion. Forty experienced officers (representing approximately 35 percent of the patrolmen) were asked what they considered to be the most desirable characteristic in a rookie. Forty-seven percent said that "he should keep his mouth shut" and another thirteen percent said that "he shouldn't be a stool pigeon."

Thus, the role was so important that it was made explicit to every new man by every experienced man; and the ability to keep secrets was considered essential to acceptance and a successful career.

CONCLUSION

It appears, then, that today in a midwestern city secrecy within the police group is an unwritten law, that Vollmer's statement of a generation ago might be expected to fit most city police departments today. The data suggest that the norm of secrecy emerges from common occupational needs, is collectively supported, and is considered of such importance that policemen will break the law to support it.

NOTES

1. The most prominent is that of Georg Simmel. See: *The Writing of Georg Simmel*, trans. by Kurt Wolff (Glencoe, Ill.: Free Press, 1950), pp. 317–79.

2. William A. Westley. The Police: A Sociological Study of Law, Custom and Morality, unpublished Ph.D dissertation, Department of Sociology, University of Chicago, 1951.

3. U. S. National Committee on Law Observance and Enforcement, *Report on the Police* (Washington: Government Printing Office, 1960), p. 48, the italics are mine.

4. Westley, op. cit., pp. 99–107.

5. See William A. Westley, "Violence and the Police," *American Journal of Sociology* 59 (July 1953): 34–41.

Stability

REWARD

DRAWBACK

SPECIALIZATION

Credit

Dehumanization

Interdependence

Cost

Benefit

RESPONSIBILITY

Humanism

Study Questions

1. Cite some examples in your life of patterns of exchange. Are they at work in your personal relationships? In organizations to which you belong? How?
2. Both Olsen and Friedman acknowledge the division of labor in intellectual life, but each sees the consequences of this functional differentiation very differently. With whom do you agree, and why? If you agree with neither, discuss your personal views of this phenomenon.
3. Is the division of labor in your classroom linked to the sex of the members?
4. What is mechanical and organic solidarity? Is it present in the groups to which you belong? Describe the basis for the two forms of solidarity.

Patterns of Exchange

9 The second pattern of social organization described in this section is the pattern of social exchange, the pattern of mutual influence in which individuals or collectivities evaluate the costs and rewards of social interaction. Patterns of loyalty are also rewarding, or can be so. How then is exchange differentiated from loyalty as a pattern of social organization? While actors may be bound by loyalty, the pattern of social exchange helps to produce greater or lesser amounts of loyalty. Moreover, loyalty itself may be conceptualized in terms of the costs and rewards involved, or may function as an independent variable to bring about changes in the quantity and quality of exchange. For example, increased affection for and loyalty to a friend or one's country may encourage greater sacrifice of time, energy, or even life. Loyalty can be looked at through an exchange perspective in terms of the costs and profits to the actor or collectivity.

In an exchange pattern, after weighing potential benefits and drawbacks, individuals act or behave in ways that are rewarding to them. Interaction is often sustained by the equilibrium of costs and rewards, and may well cease if the costs are too great or the rewards not meaningful enough. From the asymmetrical contingencies of employee-employer relations to the mutual contingencies of close friendships, patterns of exchange help shape and guide human relationships. Exchange involves the notion that people have a balance sheet with which to assess the credits and debits of their affairs. It is said to be a pervasive phenomenon of collective life.

Exchange involves a basic fact of human social intercourse: others have what we want and need. Since each of us is an "other" to someone else, patterns of exchange are inevitable in relating to one another. From the interpersonal perspective, Swanson noted the dangers involved when counting is introduced in loving relationships. From the social organization perspective, exchange is significant as the process by which organizations and actors acquire goods and services, and the process by which actors are bound to one another and to the overall goals of the organization. The flow of goods and services, of ideas and sentiments, between social units and actors is the process of exchange.

INTERDEPENDENCE

Exchange, both within and between social organizations, is based on interdependence. When you think of all the items that you have used in the last 24 hours that you yourself did not produce, you can begin to understand the extent of interdependence in modern life. It is an omnipresent fact in a complex society. The quotation from Linton about the "100 percent American" in chapter 4 gives us an appreciation of the amount and pervasiveness of exchange of ideas, technology, and philosophy that has occurred throughout history.

FUNCTIONAL DIFFERENTIATION

Another fundamental fact about social exchange and human groupings, in addition to the notion of interdependence, is the concept of division of labor, or "functional differentiation." Division of labor is a fundamental structural characteristic of all social organizations and as a group property is linked with exchange. It refers to the process by which people in groups adopt different roles and positions. A study by R. F. Bales demonstrates that in small discussion groups which start off as completely undifferentiated units, individuals tend to develop certain roles over time. Bales found that in groups which had a problem to solve through discussion, roles of leadership emerged that were recognized by the participants of the group.[1]

Even in relatively undifferentiated societies, such as folk societies, functional differentiation occurs on the basis of sex, age, and natural ability. Men with specific skills—those who can run faster or those who possess greater or lesser strength—play particular roles in the hunt. Differentiations based on sex and age are important in all societies, from the most simple to the most complex. In order for a group or society to attain functional differentiation of any scope, however, the society must develop a technology that will support specialists—those who do not take an active part in the ongoing technology. In order to have a full-time "specialist" in religion, a hunting or food-gathering society must have resources and technology to provide the specialist with at least his minimal needs. This implies that there must be an economic system that produces a certain amount of surplus goods. Technology can create the surplus goods that allow for the support of political, social, cultural, and religious specialists who are not directly related to the productive economic system.

FUNCTIONAL INTEGRATION

The concept of division of labor also implies a certain degree of complementarity of roles, or "functional integration." As roles come to be differentiated from one another, role inhabitants become specialized in their activities. The interdependence which is created by this specialization necessitates the formation of exchange relationships. Patterns of exchange, which occur among individuals or units as a

336 result of the loss of self-sufficiency, create complementary relationships in which each individual or group survives or is enhanced by its dealings with others. When specialized and interdependent elements or parts are unified in a mutually beneficial way, functional integration has occurred.

SPECIALIZATION AND ALIENATION

To say that groups and group members exchange goods and services and sentiments means that all groups depend upon both likeness and difference. Emile Durkheim used this theme in a book entitled *The Division of Labor in Society*.[2] Durkheim pointed out that social cohesion in primitive societies rests upon the fact that members of the society hold common values. Group unity, Durkheim said, is built upon similarity and likeness, or "mechanical solidarity." In a changing industrial order, where society is increasingly complex, Durkheim observed the breakdown of social cohesion which rests on similarity. Division of labor in this situation seems to create specialists with differing interests and views, a condition that contributes to the disintegration of society.

We have seen that functional differentiation occurs in all societies. But modern technology makes the division of labor contingent on acquired skills rather than ascribed characteristics. In this situation, a large number of specialists contribute to the great variety of available goods and services.

To summarize, social exchange is a pattern of social organization in which goods and services are being exchanged with consideration of the costs and benefits to the social actors. The fact that many people continue in costly social relationships is explained either by the concept of loyalty or by the phenomenon of control and power (chapter 10). The importance of exchange is that it can link diverse and different peoples into socially organized units facilitated by division of labor. In the small groups of Bales, we discovered that group members who have little in common with each other become linked to one or another while facing a task that is accomplished through differentiation. In large modern societies, men are linked by an elaborate division of labor.

While differentiation and exchange resulting from the division of labor increase the integration of the social unit through interdependence, specialization also means that people interact less as total beings and more as role players. Durkheim argued that the newly emerging industrial society would be functionally integrated. The new division of labor and specialization was going to be the basis for a new form of solidarity. He called this form "organic solidarity." Marx, on the other hand, focused on the divisive aspects of the newly emerging industrial order. These phenomena of specialization and alienation, of integration and divisiveness, as operative in the exchange pattern, are explored in two of the readings in this chapter. The first article, by Marvin E. Olsen, discusses the nature of personal autonomy and the possibilities for its existence. Many of the concepts that I have used in this chapter are developed in Olsen's description of the ways in which modern society provides opportunities for autonomy and responsibility. Olsen indicates that functional specialization, the diversification of groups, and the routinization of work are valuable in facilitating the growth of knowledge and stability and in enhancing freedom of choice. The pattern of exchange in social organization operates, according to Olsen, in such a way that stability, routinization, and specialization are exchanged for enhanced personal vocational choice, diversified group interest, and personal autonomy.

This position is in direct contrast to that of Samuel Friedman, who examines our educational institutions. Friedman argues that students have come to question the exchange value of their education. He describes the alienative nature of educational training, the deleterious effects of increasing specialization in education, and the loss of autonomy and freedom. Friedman says, in essence, that the rewards or exchange values of money, security and status are no longer satisfying enough to maintain the loyalties of students and future professionals.

The third selection in this chapter, by sociologist Erving Goffmann, focuses upon the personal, face to face encounter, rather than the societal aspects of exchange. In "On Face Work," Goffman analyzes the ways in which a social actor attempts to define and present him or herself. Goffmann's meticulous descriptions and analysis of the ritualistic elements involved in the creation and maintenance of a particular type of face and his concern with the ways in which actors seek to "make" help remind us of the omnipresence of exchange in daily life. Goffman also brings us back to the issue of human nature, discussed in chapter 4. He argues that people possess human nature, in relation to the moral codes that are established by the social organization. The question of the variability of human nature has its limits in the types of interaction each collectively encourages.

NOTES

1. R. F. Bales, *Interaction Process Analysis: A Method for the Study of Small Groups* (Cambridge, Mass., Addison-Wesley, 1950).

2. Emile Durkheim, *The Division of Labor in Society*, trans. George Simpson (New York: Free Press of Glencoe, 1947).

338 MARVIN E. OLSEN

The Mature Society: Personal Autonomy and Social Responsibility

The quest for personal autonomy within a framework of social responsibility is not unique to our era. In fact, it is as old as mankind itself, and might well be termed the "basic human dilemma."

On the one hand, the individual human being is always dependent on other people, and hence by his very nature is committed to a social life with his fellow men. The utter helplessness of the newborn infant is only the most obvious form of human dependency; throughout our lives we continually rely on others for the satisfaction of countless physical, mental, emotional, and social needs. All the knowledge we possess, as well as our total personality structure, must be learned from other people. Hell is not physical torture, Sartre suggests in his play *No Exit*, but simply aloneness. Recent psychological studies of the destructive psychological effects of extreme social isolation fully support his basic contention. Finally, no human society of any kind could exist without the constant interaction and cooperation of large numbers of individuals.

On the other hand, however, human existence is a continual effort to increase independence of thought and action. Not only in childhood, but throughout his entire life, the individual is growing and developing—always reaching for the goal of greater personal autonomy. Life is a never-ending process of "becoming," to use Gordon Allport's[1] term. On a much broader scale, the entire sweep of human history, from "cave man" to "space man," may be seen as man's struggle to free himself from the bonds of his natural environment and his own ignorance.

The main point I wish to make in this essay is that conditions of autonomy and responsibility do not confront mankind with a dilemma to be resolved through compromise, as is commonly assumed. On the contrary, we should speak of them as a paradox. *Personal autonomy and social responsibility can be mutually reinforcing*, so that an increase in one condition may also produce an increase in the other. The rest of this paper will attempt to explain and illustrate this seemingly self-contradictory proposition by drawing on several contemporary theories and descriptions of social organization.

What is meant by "social organization"? In bare outline, the idea is as follows: Man is a social creature, he cannot exist alone. In order to satisfy their countless needs—ranging from food and sex to emotional security and intellectual stimulation—individuals are forced

Marvin E. Olsen, "The Mature Society: Personal Autonomy and Social Responsibility," *Michigan Quarterly Review* 3 (July 1964): 148–59. Reprinted by permission of the publisher.

to relate their actions to each other. They form social groups in order to join efforts toward securing common goals. Many such cooperative ventures prove fruitless, and are sooner or later abandoned. Some groups do succeed in achieving some of their goals, though, and hence prove satisfying to their members. In order to maintain and perpetuate these collective efforts, the members organize their relationships into certain patterned forms. (This process is often unintended and unplanned, but it can also be purposefully directed.) Furthermore, group members, through symbolic communication, come to identify themselves with the other members and with the organized social relationships which comprise the group. When this happens, individuals are willing to take action to defend the organization from both internal or external disruptions.

These social structures—or organized patterns of social relationships—are "real" in that they have observable effects on their members. If social relationships are to be organized and perpetuated, the actions of the individual members must be controlled so as to make social interaction stable and predictable. Rules of behavior, or social norms, are therefore created by the group and applied to all members. If one wishes to remain a member of the group, he must act in accordance with these group norms. To enforce social norms, two basic types of social controls are established: External controls consist of social sanctions, or rewards and punishment, which are applied by agents of the group to deviant members. Much more efficient is internal social control, in which members are taught (often in early childhood) to value the group norms and to want to abide by them without external sanctions. When norms are internalized in this manner, the social organization not only increases its influence over its members, but it also gains greater cohesion and stablilty.

Thus far we have been describing social organization as it occurs in relatively small, informal groups. As the population of a group and its accumulated body of knowledge (or culture) increases in size, the social structure of the group almost invariably becomes more complex. Individual members begin to specialize in particular types of activities, and to assume formally designated social roles. (Some role playing occurs in all groups, especially along age and sex lines, but in more complex organizations the number of specialized roles increases rapidly.) Numerous role expectations in turn impose an even greater number of social demands on the group members. Furthermore, increasing division of labor necessitates a more formally organized social structure. If multitudes of specialized activities are to be coordinated and integrated so as to achieve over-all group goals, individuals must be assigned to specified positions in the social structure, and some form of centralized controlling body, or government, must be established. This requires an even greater elaboration of social duties and obligations, with a corresponding spiralling of social responsibilities on group members.

In capsule form, this picture of social organization indicates that organized and controlled group activities are absolutely necessary for the satisfaction of human needs. If groups are to achieve their goals

340 and satisfy their members, these members must take upon themselves many kinds of social responsibilities, including adherence to social norms, performance of role expectations, and assumption of functional obligations. Responsibility is inherent to social life!

A fundamental generalization about contemporary societies on which virtually all social scientists agree is that social organization is constantly becoming more and more complex. The combined pressures of increasing populations and rapidly growing bodies of technical and scientific knowledge are inevitably leading to greater specialization of functions and elaboration of structures. This trend is most evident in Western societies today, but its seeds can be seen sprouting throughout the world.

*   *   *

The central importance of this dominant trend for our consideration of autonomy and responsibility is quite plain: Social responsibility is inherent in all aspects of social life, but as social organization becomes increasingly complex and bureaucratic, the demands made on individuals by their social environment mount astronomically. Things we take for granted, such as our responsibility to be at work at 8 A.M. and to remain there until 5 P.M., are anathemas to members of simpler peasant societies when they are recruited into a factory for the first time.

What does this seemingly irreversible trend toward large, complex, bureaucratic organization in all spheres of social life mean for the individual member of such a society? More pointedly, what is the future of personal autonomy in "Organizational Society"? The answers given to this question by most contemporary social theorists share one common feature—gloomy pessimism. They see the individual slowly and reluctantly, but nevertheless inevitably, surrendering larger and larger portions of his personal freedom to a monolithic society. The individual eventually becomes nothing but a numbered cog in a vast, impersonal, mechanical organization, and has no choice but to conform to what others (either superiors or peers, or both) demand of him. The result of mass conformity, say these critics, is "dehumanization" of the individual—mankind exists, but man does not. Not only is choice among available actions lost, but also the awareness of the possibility of choice. The individual is left without an identity of his own.

Within this community of despair two fairly distinct schools of thought can be identified:

1.) The older and more traditional picture of the loss of individual freedom to organized society is quite straightforward. Any time an individual joins a group he relinquishes part of his personal freedom to the group, and allows it to control some of his actions. It follows, then, that the larger and more complex the scale of social organization, the more social responsibilities an individual will acquire, and the less autonomy he will retain. The end result of this process is a world in which each person's actions are largely predetermined, and individuals are conditioned to cheerfully carry out whatever tasks are assigned to them. As a corollary to this position, many social philosophers—ranging from Plato to Ortega y Gasset[2]—have stressed the importance of exempting a small elite group from the demands made on the other members of the society. The function of this elite group is to guide and direct the rest of the population, and hence keep the social system functioning smoothly and make human civilization possible. More recently, however, other observers have pointed out that an isolated elite is not necessary to keep a society functioning. Once a full-scale bureaucratic structure is established, they say, it continues to virtually "run itself," regardless of what individuals wish or do. This is the process which Whyte[3] is describing when he warns of the pervasiveness of "the organization."

Regardless of whether one adopts the "elitist" or the "bureaucratic" side of this picture, the result is the same for the vast majority of the population. Mankind is forced to conform to some type of superior authority. The name most commonly given to this type of society, in which the people are virtual slaves to a central controlling authority, be it an elite group or an impersonal bureaucracy or some combination of the two, is *totalitarian society*. The dominant feature of a fully developed totalitarian society is that the governing body exercises absolute and unrestricted control over almost all aspects of human life. To skeptics who scoff at the possibility of ever maintaining complete control over all human actions, these prophets of doom merely point to the remarkable "success" of Nazism and Communism despite their crude techniques. It could very well happen here, they add.

2.) In recent years, a second conception of "Organizational Society" has been developed by a number of social and political theorists. As in the first case, they also see loss of individualism and surrender to conformity as the result of the growth of complex social organization. The crucial difference, however, lies in the direction of this conformity and the nature of the standards to which one conforms. Instead of obeying orders from above, people slavishly seek to abide by the demands of their peers. The result is a *mass society* of socially isolated or "atomized" individuals. The only guides for behavior are the expectations of an amorphous "they," as perpetuated by mass culture. Control by the masses can be even more destructive of individual autonomy than is control by a centralized authority, these commentators suggest, since the person does not even know who is dominating him. David Riesman's[4] sketch of the "other-directed" individual is the prototype of this "mass man," while C. Wright Mills'[5] description of the "personality market" among white collar workers gives an idea of the effects of mass society on the individual.

* * *

Although these theories of totalitarian and mass societies differ in many details, there is no reason why they should be incompatible. In fact, to the extent that they are combined, as in the writings of Erich Fromm,[6] their effects on the individual are mutually reinforcing.

Certainly there would be very little room for personal autonomy in a society totally dominated by a powerful elite group working through a centralized bureaucratic structure which allowed no effective or meaningful participation by the masses of the people, but kept them satiated with the mental pabulum of mass culture.

Thus far we have struck a uniformly pessimistic note concerning the possibilities for individual autonomy in both present and future societies. We have purposefully given considerable attention to these theories of despair because they dominate so much thinking in contemporary social science. Furthermore, there is certainly no denying the possibility that one or both of these predictions could easily come true, however reprehensible the results might be. But is there no way out of this seemingly unavoidable trend toward increasing limitations on individual freedom? Must social responsibility inevitably wipe out personal autonomy?

This is a question of vital concern to many intellectuals in America. They are aware of the possibilities of our becoming either a totalitarian or a mass society, and they are urgently searching for a means of stemming the tide before it is too late. Most of these "solutions of desperation" can be grouped into two broad categories, which Winston White[7] has labeled the "moralistic" and the "reform" approaches.

Moralists tend to hold the individual responsible for any conditions of mass servitude or conformity that may occur. Loss of personal autonomy, they say, is caused by the weakening of basic individualistic values. This situation is often attributed to a preoccupation with science and technology, so that concern for instrumental means undermines commitments to more enduring humanistic values. These writers do not deny the existence or power of complex social organizations, but they hold that it is the individual's responsibility to recognize this power and to "assert himself against it."[8] To be capable of such resistance, they suggest, the individual must be transformed into a new kind of person. Thus Riesman[9] holds out the possibility of combining "inner-directed" and "other-directed" character types into what he terms "autonomous man." This kind of individual possesses a self-awareness that enables him to carry out those social responsibilities which are functionally necessary, while at the same time remaining free to choose when and how to conform to society and when to assert his unique identity. Quite similar is Fromm's[10] "spontaneously creative" individual who is capable of transforming necessary instrumental actions into creative and meaningful activities which in themselves have value for the person. Needless to say, these ideas appear to offer the perfect solution to our problem—until one asks how they can be achieved in practice. The moralists offer us an ultimate goal, but not a specific plan of action.

Reformers, on the other hand, place the blame for loss of autonomy on the structure of society, not on the individual. If basic individualistic values have been weakened, they say, it is because unsatisfactory social conditions are inhibiting personal growth and development. The individual is essentially a product of his social environment, so that his values will reflect whatever social forces play upon him. The solution to the problem of over-conformity offered by the reformers therefore involves social change. What is needed is a vast, interlocking network of "mediating groups" to fill the structural gap between the individual's personal world of primary relationships and the realm of complex bureaucracies and total societies. These "intermediate groups" are large enough and powerful enough to give the individual member a sense of control over his social destiny and of meaning to his life. At the same time, they are small enough to allow him to retain his unique identity. The prototype of such a mediating group is the special-interest, voluntary association—ranging in size and function from stamp collectors' clubs to labor unions. It is of crucial importance, however, that there be a great many such groups in a society, and that they have overlapping memberships. In this way they can act as checks and balances on each other's power, so that no one group comes to dominate completely the lives of its members, while at the same time they mutually reinforce each other's activities. This idea of the role of intermediate groups in preserving personal autonomy has a long history in social theory, extending from de Tocqueville[11] to Emile Durkheim[12] to William Kornhauser.[13] The reformers without doubt give us a definite plan of action, but their suggestions lack the contribution offered by the moralists—a long-range goal.

It is my contention that although both the moralists and the reformers offer many valuable ideas which should not be ignored, both schools of thought are nevertheless committing a grave oversight. As mentioned previously, most of these writers are looking for "solutions" to the "problem" of loss of autonomy. That is, they have accepted the thesis that increasing social organization inevitably produces greater social control over individuals, and hence reduces personal freedom. This process is seen as a non-problematic phenomenon which perhaps may be limited and re-directed, but which cannot be reversed. This is not to say that increasing social organization could not result in either a totalitarian or a mass society; both forms of complete social conformity are distinct possibilities, given the present drift of world affairs. But we must not overlook a third type of society which could also result from the basic trend toward greater complexity of social organization. Unlike the first two models, it magnifies personal autonomy as well as social responsibility. It, too, is only a possibility for the future—and perhaps not a very likely possibility—but it should not be dismissed on these grounds. I shall call this third model a *mature society*,[14] although social maturity is implied only in relation to the present, and not in any absolute sense. Furthermore, as a conceptual model, or "pure type," it does not represent any real society, although it can serve as an ideal by which actual societies may be evaluated.

To describe this concept of the mature society, we must squarely face the seemingly paradoxical question of how individual feerdom can be expanded in a world of increasing social responsibilities. First of all, we must guard against making two common logical errors. One of these is "zero-sum" thinking, to borrow a term from game theory.

This approach assumes that there is a fixed quantity of choices available in a situation, so that a gain on one side must result in a loss on the other. While many games, both parlor and serious, do operate on this principle, there is no basis for assuming that it must also apply to the functioning of all social life. Increased social demands may, but do not necessarily, result in decreased personal freedom. In fact, there is no logical reason why both conditions could not increase simultaneously.

The second logical error to be avoided can be called the fallacy of "uncritical induction." Even though a particular relationship between two variables does exist in several specific instances, this is no basis for automatically assuming that it is a general rule applicable to all situations. There may be many other cases which flatly contradict the generalization. Thus, even if the growing complexity of social organization does impose greater social responsibility on individuals in some areas of life, this is no reason for assuming that personal autonomy in a general sense is being surrendered. We may be gaining much more than we are losing.

The next step after noting these two logical pitfalls is to examine the concept of autonomy in greater detail. The dictionary synonyms of "independent" and "self-governing" are inadequate when the term is applied to the totality of human life. Taken too literally, such definitions could lead one to the conclusion that an amoeba is the most autonomous form of animal life, since its actions are minimally dependent on other animals. The concept of human freedom has a long history of intellectual debate and development, which can briefly be summarized in the form of five conditions which must be met before personal autonomy is possible. (1) As emphasized by German philosophers beginning with the Reformation, the individual must be aware of, and committed to, some transcendent values and principles with which he can judge passing historical events. Only in this manner can man escape the fate of all other creatures of being entirely bound to their immediate existence. (2) Thinkers of the Enlightenment added to this idea the necessity of possessing adequate rational and scientific knowledge to enable the individual to express his ideas in action, and thus bring the world more in line with his ideals. (3) Liberal political theorists, of whom Locke is the best example, have argued that the individual must also be freed from constraining external restraints on his activities, so that it is realistically possible for him to take action to reach his goals. (4) More recent philosophers, beginning with Hegel and Marx, have pointed out that action by the individual can only be successful to the extent that his social world is ordered or organized in such a way that instrumental activities will result in desired ends. (5) Finally, contemporary psychologists from Freud to Fromm have added the observation that the individual will still be incapable of acting in an autonomous manner unless he has achieved sufficient personality development to be able to take on the burdens of independent action without relying on dominating external support. Taken together these ideas suggest that the autonomous individual must have meaningful values and goals, adequate practical knowledge, freedom of action, an ordered social environment, and a high level of personal integration. All these conditions, I suggest, are not only fully possible in a world of complex social organization, but actually require a very elaborate degree of societal development for their fullest expression.

How can a mature society provide these prerequisites for autonomy? A discussion of four major characteristics of mature societies will provide an answer to this question. The first of these characteristics is elaborate functional specialization, or division of labor, which we have already seen as an inevitable factor in the growth of complex and social organization. Individuals will be required to play a wide range of quite diversified social roles. Without doubt this will increase a person's burden of social responsibilities, since he must become familiar with many different role expectations. But as Durkheim[15] and Talcott Parsons[16] have pointed out, it also results in greater opportunities for individual freedom of action. Most role definitions do not minutely prescribe required behavior, but rather provide only broad outlines of obligations and privileges for the individual. Within these guidelines there is normally extensive room for personal modifications and variations. And as the number of roles in a social system increases, the rigidity of the role definitions normally declines. Therefore, if the person is limited to playing a few traditional roles, such as in most primitive societies, it is very difficult for him to escape the "cake of custom" which controls so much of his life. With a high degree of division of labor, on the other hand, the individual gains greater flexibility to select the particular roles which he wants to occupy and to play them as he desires. He is released from many of the bonds of ascribed social characteristics such as age, sex, race, and family, and can pursue social positions which are based on individual achievement. Of course, the person may choose to bind himself to customs and traditions—for example to "carry on the business just as Dad would have wanted"—but at least the possibility of choice of action does exist. This opportunity for the individual to select and play social roles which are compatible with his particular temperament, personality, interests, and talents, is absolutely necessary if he is to achieve autonomy of action.

Second, a trend toward more complex social organization can also produce increased structural differentiation, or diversification of groups and social institutions. Because social roles involve reciprocal behavior, they must always be interrelated within social structures. And the more specialized the roles, the more diversified are the structures which they comprise. In most simple societies one type of group —usually the extended family—performs all of the major social functions, including economic, political, religious, educational, welfare, socialization, affectual, and defense activities. This arrangement works fairly well in a society of 200 people, but with 200 million people it would prove disastrous for personal freedom. The family in such a society would become such a dominant social institution that it would control the entire lives of its members. The modern example of attempted structural unity is the totalitarian society, in which all social

346   functions are controlled by the central government. By contrast, in a structurally differentiated society there is a proliferation of limited, but relatively independent, social groups. In this type of social structure, each person has greater opportunities to participate effectively in groups oriented toward his particular values and goals. At the same time, no one group is strong enough to gain complete domination over all his activities.

*   *   *

A third major characteristic of a mature society is routinization of normal functioning. Any social system must somehow deal with a number of basic problems, or functional imperatives, if it is to survive for long. These include acquiring and training new members, procuring resources and transforming and distributing them to meet the needs of the members, maintaining order so that social interaction can take place with a minimum of disruption, proctecting the system against threatening forces, preserving its knowledge and values, and directing and coordinating its overall functioning. In groups that are relatively new, inexperienced, or simply organized, many of these requirements are often handled on an *ad hoc* basis. Unfortunately, many of these "spur of the moment" solutions are inefficient or completely ineffective. Moreover, the members are forced to spend a great deal of their time, efforts, and resources dealing with these basic problems, so that the life of the group frequently centers around the struggle for group survival. A more adequate way of satisfying these functional imperatives is obviously to establish organized, stable social structures which are specifically designed to handle such requirements. Each specialized subsystem can anticipate, plan for, and more effectively solve its particular problems. Thus a complex society with well developed social institutions is much more stable and durable than a simple folk society which lacks this degree of social organization.

*   *   *

In more general terms, we are saying that with the growth of complex social organization, problems that previously had to be solved at each occurrence and at great expense to the individual can now be handled relatively automatically through established, routinized procedures. Social life thus becomes more predictable and rewarding. Personal choice is restricted in some areas, but the total autonomy of the individual is greatly enhanced. He is freed from many of the mundane burdens of staying alive, and is given the time and resources to devote himself to more personal endeavors. Complex social organization, and its consequent routinization of some areas of life, actually increases the total number of possible activities and choices within the system. Consequently, the number of choices gained by the individual through this process can be much greater than the number relinquished to the social order. Once again, though, this outcome is never inevitable. For instance, a rigid stratification system which assigned a large portion of the population to menial servitude for the benefit of a small elite would certainly deprive many people of any meaningful autonomy.[17]

The final characteristic of our model of a mature society—encouragement of creativity—is a direct result of functional routinization. Complex social organization gives the individual many opportunities for non-sustenance activities, but what will he do with this free time? Conceivably, he could choose to spend it all amusing himself, or in a drunken stupor. The quality of the choices made by the individual —whether or not they add to the development of both his personality and the society—is largely shaped by his social and cultural environment. If his society does not give him the opportunity, motivation, and education necessary to make wise decisions and seek valuable goals, his personal freedom will be hollow and meaningless. In Fromm's[18] terms, the individual must have "freedom to" participate in creative activities as well as "freedom from" external restraints. The results of turning people loose from prescribed social relationships without also providing them with the skills necessary to use their freedom include such phenomena as feelings of apathy and alienation, perpetual attempts to escape via the mass media, support for strong authoritarian social movements, socially deviant behavior, mental illness, and even suicide. To say that society must shape these more personal activities of the individual does not imply that once again personal autonomy is lost; the ultimate choice of creative activities must remain with the individual. But if his freedom of decision is to have any real meaning, appropriate social conditions must exist to guide him in worthwhile directions.

A mature society can encourage individual creativity by providing these social conditions that make possible and probable the upgrading of human activity to higher levels of achievement. It is a curious fact of human existence that our collective problems are never eliminated. As a society develops various social institutions to "solve," or routinize, old problems, these social arrangements themselves raise many new questions of a higher order for the society to face. Modern society may have solved the problem of maintaining sustenance, but a primitive group would never face the issues of technological unemployment. Utopia, it appears, is never attained by arresting the process of social evolution at any given stage. Life is a continual series of challenges; as we meet and conquer one hurdle, we are inextricably led down the path toward other more demanding challenges which call forth in us even higher levels of performance.

* * *

On the other hand, the members of a society might at any time choose to endure rather than attempt to solve present problems, and hence effectively halt the process of social development. Social, cultural, and personality growth will occur only if individuals continually face toward the future rather than the past, and are always willing to confront increasingly demanding challenges. To encourage such attitudes, the society must possess a body of transcendent and en-

348

during values which will serve as goals and guides in all social activities. At this point, then, we must include the suggestions of the "moralists" in our model of a mature society. As with the reformers, we are using these ideas not as "solutions of desperation," but rather as essential elements of the total picture of a mature society. The main emphasis of the moralists, it will be remembered, is on the necessity for strengthening basic values within the individual, so as to better equip him to meet the demands of a complex society. They are insisting that we not lose sight of the elementary truth that the ultimate worth of any society, no matter how mature it may be, lies in its contribution to human betterment. At the same time, a society is only as strong as the social relationships among the individuals who comprise it, and these in turn depend ultimately on the values which shape and guide human action. If socially mature values—such as the importance and dignity of the individual, the right of freedom of thought and action, and the necessity of always considering the consequences of our behavior for other people—are not institutionalized in the functioning of a society and internalized within most of its members, that society may well become nothing but an elaborate prison which confines and destroys its inmates.

As a means of integrating our thoughts up to this point, let us review the five criteria for personal freedom discussed earlier, to see if our model of a mature society has fulfilled all of them. These five requirements were meaningful values and goals, adequate functional knowledge, freedom of action, and ordered social environment, and a high level of personal integration. The first characteristic of a mature society—elaborate division of labor—facilitates the growth of knowledge in all fields of endeavor by freeing individuals from ascribed positions and customs and allowing them to specialize in those roles to which they are best suited and in which they can make the greatest contribution to society. The second characteristic—increased structural differentiation—ensures freedom of individual action by distributing social influence and power among a variety of relatively independent groups which hold each other in check while at the same time giving expression to all shades of opinion and interest. The third characteristic—functional routinization—provides an ordered and stable social environment by establishing definite procedures for dealing with the everyday problems of individual and societal maintenance, so that these factors do not dominate people's lives. The final characteristic of a mature society—encouragement of creativity—makes possible the upgrading of human activity and the development of higher levels of personality integration by providing opportunities and stimulation for the growth of human creativity, which in turn also preserves and strengthens basic values and goals of personal autonomy. It is for these reasons, then, that I propose the concept of the mature society as a model of a social system which integrates personal freedom and autonomy with complex social organization and responsibility, so that each supports and reinforces the other. The individual's potential for personal autonomy is a direct consequence of his interdependence with others in society. Our basic paradox of autonomy *and* responsibility is thus resolved.

As a concluding note, we should stress again a point which has been mentioned repeatedly throughout our discussion of the mature society. The trend toward increasingly complex social organization which we are witnessing today can lead toward several different types of future societies. Unfortunately, the two types which are the least desirable from the point of view of individual freedom—totalitarian and mass societies—are perhaps the easiest paths to follow, since blind inertia alone will provide much pressure in both of these directions. On the other hand, the model of a mature society presented in this essay offers probably the most difficult goal of all for societal development. There is nothing inherent in complex social organization which insures inevitable evolution toward more mature forms of social life. In fact, there are so many hazards and pitfalls along this path that we should ask if it is even possible for any society to approach the goal of social maturity, however relative that goal may be. My answer to this question is that relative social maturity is indeed possible, though never inevitable, if certain pre-conditions are continually met.

First, the society must develop techniques for controlling and directing social change. Any society with a high degree of social organization is bound to experience many structural and functional strains; the extreme complexity of the system virtually prohibits perfect harmony among all its parts, and there will be unlimited opportunities for real conditions to depart radically from ideal conceptions. The result of these strains will be continuous and extensive social change within the society. Although this change does produce many problems for the system, it is not undesirable in itself, since only in this manner can the society keep moving along the never-ending path toward greater social maturity. However, sheer exhaustion from dealing with perpetual strains and changes can also cause a social system to disintegrate. If a society is to successfully overcome the challenges and problems which are inevitable in human social life, it must develop some skill in handling social change, so that progress can be achieved with a minimum amount of disruption to the system.

Second, the society and its individual members must always be guided in their actions by fundamental humanistic values. We must never lose sight of the fact that in all social life the individual person is an end in himself, and not merely a means to some other goal. Not only are these basic values an essential element of the mature society, as we saw previously, but they also play a crucial role in leading us toward that goal. The path toward increasing social maturity is easily lost; a depression or would-be demigod can often lead a society astray, as seen in Germany in the 1930s. This path can be successfully followed only if these humanistic values continually light the way and guide our struggles. These values cannot be hollow slogans and rituals, but must be built into the structure and functioning of all social institutions, and deeply internalized by most individuals.

The third pre-condition for the attainment of a mature society

350 is deceptively simple—a great deal of purposeful and dedicated human effort. Certainly no degree of social maturity throughout a whole society can be attained in even a few years. We must be content to do the best we can today, and then look to succeeding generations for the fruition of our efforts. To give in to frustration, bitterness, and despair at the slowness of the process is only to admit defeat. The struggle can be eased somewhat, though, if we can learn to avoid blind, impetuous actions. To the extent that we rationally direct our social activities through objective analysis and purposeful planning, they are much more likely to achieve permanent and meaningful results. In short, the mature society will never just occur, but we can create it if we are willing to put forth the necessary effort.

The ultimate question is this: Will mankind come to understand the paradox of its own existence—that humanity fulfills its destiny only to the extent that both personal autonomy and social responsibility are maximized—before it is too late for us to choose our own path to the future?

NOTES

1. Gordon Allport, *Becoming* (New Haven: Yale University Press, 1955).

2. Jose Ortega y Gasset, *The Revolt of the Masses*, anonymous translation (New York: Mentor Books, 1950).

3. William H. Whyte, *The Organization Man* (Garden City: Doubleday and Co., 1956).

4. David Riesman with Reuel Denney and Nathan Glazer, *The Lonely Crowd* (New Haven: Yale University Press, 1950).

5. C. Wright Mills *White Collar* (New York: Oxford University Press, 1951).

6. Erich Fromm, *Escape from Freedom* (New York: Rolt, Rinehart and Winston, 1941).

7. Winston White, *Beyond Conformity* (Glencoe: Free Press, 1961).

8. Whyte, op. cit., p. 14.

9. Riesman, op. cit.

10. Fromm, op. cit.

11. Tocqueville, op. cit.

12. Emile Durkheim, *The Division of Labor in Society*, trans. George Simpson (Glencoe: Free Press, 1949).

13. Kornhauser, op. cit.

14. This term is mine, but I am indebted to Winston White, op. cit., and Talcott Parsons for several of the ideas presented in the following discussion. See Parsons and White, "The Link between Character and Society," in *Culture and Social Character*, edited by Seymour M. Lipset and Leo Lowenthal (Glencoe: Free Press, 1961), pp. 89–135.

15. Durkheim, op. cit.

16. Parsons and White, op. cit.

17. From this observation it could be argued that a mature society also requires relative homogeneity of social status, with a minimum of social distance between the lowest and the highest status levels. Furthermore, there should be no sharp boundaries between any two status levels, so that social mobility can easily occur. Such a condition of relative status equality and open mobility is being approached in the U. S. today.

18. Fromm, op. cit.

SAMUEL R. FRIEDMAN **351**

The American Student Movement: Causes and Implications

The American student movement of the 1960s and 1970s is a topic of much discussion in the mass media and social sciences. Analysts have looked at the personal characteristics of students who take part,[1] the changes in colleges that have caused the movement,[2] the concept of the "generation gap,"[3] and the various issues raised and struggled over by the student movement.[4] By focusing on these parts of the picture, analysts often lose sight of its broad framework. Thus, in all the thousands of pages written on this subject, very few have dealt with the question, "What has changed in the structure of society that has led to the formation of a mass student movement?" This paper attempts to answer this question, and in doing so, finds that the student movement is a direct product of modern capitalism (and perhaps of other industrialized class societies such as that of the USSR) and that the conditions that cause it lead the movement to challenge the basic structure of this society.

The most obvious fact about students' relationship to society is that they are being trained to fill various roles after graduation, and that most students are being prepared for jobs as "intellectual laborers." The average student is in training for a job as a teacher, a lawyer, a nurse, a social worker, an engineer, a technician, or another paid position in which part of the job requires the use of knowledge (or social graces) learned in school, instead of being in school to prepare for a life in top management, as a self-employed businessman, or as a housewife who never is employed. One should thus look at changes in the nature of work as an intellectual laborer as a possible source of student unrest.

Two commonplace findings of social science shed further light on this. First, since the economic and political need for coordination and innovation has been growing larger as American society becomes more complex and technological, the role of intellectual labor in the society has been expanding. As a consequence, so has the enrollment in colleges and universities. Thus, the number of professional and technical workers in the United States increased from 3.9 million in 1940 to 10.3 million in 1968 (an increase from 7.5 percent of total employment to 13.6 percent) and the number of all white collar workers from 16 million to 35.6 million (an increase from 31.1 percent of total employment to 46.8 percent).[5] Second, the nature of an intellectual laborer's work has been changing rapidly. It is increasingly conducted by groups rather than by individuals, and under bureaucratic planning

This article was written especially for this book.

rather than at the intellectual laborer's discretion. The intellectual laborer is then faced with a situation in which his or her work is less and less a product of individual initiative and creativity, and more and more a set of tasks defined by others in pursuit of others' goals.

A closer look at the change in the nature of intellectual labor indicates an increase in alienation in the Marxist sense. Intellectual laborers decreasingly control the nature of their work, the uses to which it is put, and the scheduling and conditions under which it is performed. Furthermore, their labor and the products thereof are increasingly valued in commodity terms, with prices set for buying and selling by impersonal market mechanisms rather than in more individualized ways. The market criteria of value often force the intellectual laborer to emphasize quantity over quality. These criteria tend to transform intellectual work from artisanry, whose products involve creativity and care, to mass production, in which production is on an assembly-line or batch basis. As intellectual labor becomes a large–scale operation that requires heavy capital investment (in computers, classrooms, laboratories, and other necessary items), the intellectual laborer is personally unable to own the facilities or equipment needed for his or her work, and is forced to work at alienated labor in which work is a commodity in all the above ways.

The plight of the college professor may help to illustrate the concepts of intellectual labor and alienation. Since research is the chief basis of evaluation, and since the various disciplines have become mass nationwide markets in which it is impossible for one's work to become known except through the journals in the field, one's market value (and hence job security, salary, and promotion) is based on the number of articles published in the "leading" journals. A need to produce such articles is thus created, with several consequences:

1. Research becomes less and less a matter of individual creativity and one's own desire to produce, and more and more a matter of adding to one's commodity value by getting something published.
2. The professor is induced to do research in those areas in which granting agencies are willing to provide funding. This is in part a consequence of the fact that research is becoming a rationalized and expensive part of the productive and governmental processes of society.
3. The professor finds it prudent to do research in areas in which the leading journals are interested, using methods of research of which they approve. This means that the nature of a professor's research work is to some extent taken out of his or her hands and put into those of the journals.
4. Since quantity is increasingly important, research becomes less a matter of thinking things through and more a matter of "getting the article out."

Elements of alienation of labor are also increasing on the teaching side of professordom. The expansion of class size forces professors toward assembly-line lecturing and grading, in which personal contact with students is minimized and "the lecture" becomes a product to be passed on to listening students. Control over conditions and scheduling of work is placed in administrative hands. Semesters are changed to quarters and then to trimesters, and professors' objections are ignored.

With the decline of the "free intelligentsia" as a source of alternative employment (which is based on the economic limits of the market for academic or semi-academic articles) the professor is forced into alienated labor. Available employment which uses his or her special skills outside the college or university is generally limited to research firms or government agencies which use similar criteria of evaluation and offer similar working conditions (except there are no students).

Thus, we see that under the pressures to mass-produce intellectual laborers and to turn out research for the rest of the economy, professors themselves are becoming part of the alienated labor force. The professor and his or her work are commodities, and control over the conditions, scheduling, goals, uses, and form of this labor is in the hands of market forces or distant bureaucracies.

The work of an electronics engineer is another example of alienated labor. To an increasing extent, electronics engineers are employed in large corporations involved in military (or other) research, development, or production. Their tasks are set, within narrow limits, by their supervisors. Each project requires a great deal of coordination of manpower, and this means that the engineer must complete each job on schedule or the timetable for the project will be disrupted. Furthermore, the product of this work must fit preconceived assumptions on which other tasks were assigned.

Electronics engineers generally do not control the uses of their research. There are instances—such as the Manhattan Project during World War II—in which engineers are not even told what the project is all about until it is over. Furthermore, given the budget priorities of the 1960s at least, many of them are unable to find employment on the kinds of projects which would be meaningful to them. Thus, in one case I know of a man who had to work in defense electronics even though he could contribute a lot in medical electronics. The electronics engineer, with little control over his work situation, is forced to relate to work more as a chore to be done than as personal fulfillment. His or her labor is a commodity sold to the employer rather than an element of creative power and initiative.

A great many students in the 1960s became aware of the change in the nature of intellectual labor. Increasingly, they turned away from the business world as a source of employment and towards social service careers such as teaching, social welfare, and the Peace Corps. They hoped this work would be less alienating; but since the alienation of intellectual labor included even these jobs, they became more bitter and dissatisfied. As the student movement developed, it discovered that social service institutions as well as businesses are involved in racism, male supremacy, imperialism, and militarism. Students reject employer goals and the means of achieving them, and sense the futility of their own desires and efforts to exercise control over their own work.

Thus, the student comes to see no place for himself (or herself) in the society. This leads, on the one hand, to dropping out (whether as the Beats of the 1950s or psychedelics of the 1960s) and, on the other, attempting to set up new and meaningful life styles. For those who do not drop out, or who do so but remain close to a campus, it may produce a willingness to take part in activist movements. On many campuses action has been directed at policies which are most alien to student goals (as they have developed politically—examples are war research and whites-only admissions) and which symbolize students' lack of control over their own lives both as students and afterwards. In addition, many of America's traditional sanctions against radical political behavior have lost their impact, since the fear of being expelled from school or of being blacklisted from employment is greatly minimized for a person who sees very little value in the employment for which school is training her (or him).

Students have begun to perceive the way in which changes in the nature of intellectual labor will affect their own lives, and they are less willing to put up with unpleasant conditions or arbitrary authority while in school to secure such work. Yet the very fact that intellectual labor has become a major sector of the economy (and of government) means that the conditions students face in school have become more unpleasant. Increased enrollment in colleges and universities results in large, impersonal classes, in mass grading techniques, and in student ghettoization. Attempts to be creative run afoul of the impersonal drive to process batches of students as quickly as possible. As a result of increasing demands on their time which stem both from the larger number of students and from the research–oriented side of their jobs, faculty and administrators have become more arbitrary in their behavior. Thus, the alienated nature of professors' work increases the burdens on students, too. Following Moore's analysis of the conditions under which peasant movements break out, we can view this as an increase in exploitation (since greater sacrifices at school are being rewarded with less return in the form of creative work than was previously the case) that results in students being more willing to take action to change the society.[6]

These changes in college life have an important *subjective* impact on students. The grading system and the impersonal nature of education carry a message about the nature of intellectual jobs. It is clear to students that grades are the mechanism by which they are given their commodity value for these job markets; and it is clear that they are being trained for routinized and bureaucratized labor on relatively narrow projects. The mechanisms necessitated by the change to an economy in which intellectual labor is used on a mass scale serve to alienate students from their studies and to inform them of the fate awaiting them after graduation.

To summarize the argument as it stands so far, these changes in the nature of intellectual labor create the preconditions for student political action. There remain four questions to be answered: How and why have the preconditions been followed by an actual movement? How does this analysis tie in with the international existence of student movements? How well does this analysis fit the findings of other researchers? What are the implications of this analysis for the student movement?

The fact that a category of people are subject to forces that incline them to social activism does not have to mean that they become active. The continued existence of oppression without large-scale opposition in many areas throughout the world attests to this, as does the relative quiescence of American students throughout the 1950s, even in the face of these changes in the nature of intellectual labor (which were partially described by Mills in 1951).[7] The activation of the student movement in America is not the inevitable result of changes in the nature of intellectual labor; a number of *political* factors also had a necessary part to play. Very briefly, the apathy of the 1950s was replaced by the activism of the 1960s because of several interrelated phenomena:

1. The rapid growth of the market for intellectual labor as a result of the post-Sputnik attempt to expand America's technological resources (and as a social-welfare response to the civil rights and related movements) intensified the alienation of intellectual labor in the society as a whole.
2. The decline of extreme anti-Communism made political action more possible. It is worth noting that the first campuses to become active were those in which political restrictions were lowest.
3. A leadership base developed out of civil rights activism and the early peace movement. Much of the ideology of the student movement in its first years came from these sources.
4. The Vietnam War and the continued Black Liberation struggle intensified and speeded up the development of the student movement, and greatly influenced its direction, but were probably not essential for its continued existence. Similarly, the elitist beliefs about themselves which students hold increased the poignancy and anger of the movement as students discovered they were valued as future labor power rather than as whole human beings, but this was probably not necessary for the movement to continue either.

The student movement is international in many ways. There are student movements in France, Britain, India, Mexico, Japan, South Africa, and other countries.

The thesis of this paper is that student movements will be likely to develop where intellectual labor is becoming alienated labor. Analy-

356 ses of the movements in France and Britain indicate that this may well be the case in those countries, though no work bearing directly on this point has come to my attention.[8] It is probable that similar patterns hold true in other heavily industrialized countries, such as Japan and West Germany, since many of the changes in their economies are very similar to those in the United States economy. As to student movements in countries such as Mexico and India, they may well have causes different from those we have just considered. College graduates go on to occupy relatively elite administrative positions in these countries, rather than to become part of a massive force of intellectual laborers, except in those countries where many of them remain unemployed or under-employed for much of their lives. In Mexico students increasingly are graduating into jobs that are heavily bureaucratized; indeed, this is one of the themes of their student activists. There is no reason to believe, then, that student activism in such a context is the product of the same causes as in advanced capitalist societies, even though bonds of comradeship and emulation of each other's actions may well occur among activists from different countries.

Richard Flacks summarizes a number of studies that indicate that the parents of activists tend to be intellectual laborers and not businessmen, blue-collar workers, or other white–collar workers; that activists as well as a large number of apolitical students have great difficulty in deciding on a career or vocation because they find the available choices unsatisfactory*; and that revulsion with these available adult roles and careers *predates* movement involvement for many students.[9] These findings support the contention that changes in the nature of intellectual labor underlie the student revolt. The finding that activists tend disporportionately to be intellectual laborers' children can be explained as follows. It is to be expected that the intellectual laborers of the previous generation, who had children in the period before the proletarianization of intellectual labor was well established, had values appropriate to such labor. Thus, they passed on to their children values and expectations such as those Flacks describes: intellectualism, the desire to be socially useful and creative, independence, and autonomy.[10] These children then found that their values, which were fairly well suited to the intellectual labor of their parents' generation, did not correspond to the career opportunities of the America in which they live. That they and their friends became activists earlier and in greater proportion than others in their age group is thus not surprising.

What lies ahead for the American student movement? It is certain that the movement will be with us for many years, although there may be periods of quiescence interspersed with periods of activism. As long as intellectual labor is alienated labor, the basis for a

---

*Flacks explains this in terms of incompatibility between students' ideals and the political and social functions of these jobs. I do not disagree with him on this, but point to the nature of the work involved in intellectual labor as both prior to and more basic than this moral incompatibility.

mass student movement will continue to exist, and the dynamics of American capitalism will probably continue to intensify and extend this alienation for many years to come. It seems unlikely that intellectual laborers will be any more able to protect themselves against the rationalizing, bureaucratizing, and alienating tendencies of modern capitalism, with its market forces and political power, than were manual laborers before them. A segment of the student movement is already attempting to bring about an alliance of all workers in the society, whether blue or white collar, male or female, black or white. It can be predicted that this attempt will be expanded as lesser social forces are found inadequate to solve the problems faced by intellectual laborers.

NOTES

1. Richard Flacks, "The Liberated Generation: An Exploration of the Roots of Student Protest," *Journal of Social Issues* 23 (July 1967) : 52–75. Kenneth Kenniston, *Young Radicals* (New York: Harcourt, Brace Jovanovich, 1968). David L. Westby, and Richard G. Braungart, "Class and Politics in the Family Backgrounds of Student Political Activists," *American Sociological Review* 31 (October 1966) : 690–92.

2. Jerome H. Skolnick, *The Politics of Protest* (New York: Ballatine Books, 1969), pp. 111–20.

3. Michael Brown, *The Politics and the Anti-Politics of the Young* (Beverly Hills, Calif.; Glencoe Press, 1969). See particularly Brown's Introduction. Theodore Roszak, "Youth and the Great Refusal," reprinted in Brown, *Politics and Anti-Politics*, pp. 3–21, from *Nation* (1968).

4. Skolnick, *Politics of Protest*, pp. 79–124. James O'Brien, "A History of the New Left, 1960–1968" (Boston: New England Free Press, 1969).

5. Compiled from: *Historical Statistics of the United States, Colonial Times to 1957* (U.S. Bureau of the Census, 1960), p. 74; and *Monthly Labor Review* April 1969 (U. S. Department of Labor, Bureau of Labor Statistics), p. 98.

6. Barrington Moore, Jr., *Social Origins of Dictatorship and Democracy: Lord and Peasant in the Making of the Modern World* (Boston: Beacon Press, 1966), pp. 469–74.

7. C. Wright Mills, *White Collar: The American Middle Classes* (New York: Oxford University Press, 1951).

8. Gareth Stedman Jones, "*The Meaning of the Student Revolt,*" in *Student Power: Problems, Diagnosis, Action*, edited by Alexander Cockburn and Robin Blackburn (Baltimore: Penguin Books, 1969), pp. 25–56. Patrick Seale, and Maureen McConville, *Red Flag/Black Flag: French Revolution 1968* (New York: Ballantine Books, 1968), pp. 27–31.

9. Richard Flacks, "Social and Cultural Meanings of Student Revolt: Some Informal Comparative Observations," *Social Problems* 17 (Winter 1970) : 340–57.

10. Flacks, "Social and Cultural Meanings of Student Revolt," pp. 346–48.

On Face Work: An Analysis of Ritual Elements in Social Interaction

Every person lives in a world of social encounters, involving him either in face-to-face or mediated contact with other participants. In each of these contacts, he tends to act out what is sometimes called a *line*—that is, a pattern of verbal and nonverbal acts by which he expresses his view of the situation and through this his evaluation of the participants, especially himself. Regardless of whether a person intends to take a line, he will find that he has done so in effect. The other participants will assume that he has more or less willfully taken a stand, so that if he is to deal with their response to him he must take into consideration the impression they have possibly formed of him.

The term *face* may be defined as the positive social value a person effectively claims for himself by the line others assume he has taken during a particular contact.[1] Face is an image of self delineated in terms of approved social attributes—albeit an image that others may share, as when a person makes a good showing for his profession or religion by making a good showing for himself.

A person tends to experience an immediate emotional response to the face which a contact with others allows him; he cathects his face; his 'feelings' become attached to it. If the encounter sustains an image of him that he has long taken for granted, he probably will have few feelings about the matter. If events establish a face for him that is better than he might have expected, he is likely to "feel good"; if his ordinary expectations are not fulfilled, one expects that he will "feel bad" or "feel hurt." In general, a person's attachment to a particular face, coupled with the ease with which disconfirming information can be conveyed by himself and others, provides one reason why he finds that participation in any contact with others is a commitment. A person will also have feelings about the face sustained for the other participants, and while these feelings may differ in quantity and direction from those he has for his own face, they constitute an involvement in the face of others that is as immediate and spontaneous as the involvement he has in his own face. One's own face and the face of others are constructs of the same order; it is the rules of the group and the definition of the situation which determine how much feeling one is to have for face and how this feeling is to be distributed among the faces involved.

A person may be said to *have*, or *be in*, or *maintain* face when the line he effectively takes presents an image of him that is internally

From Erving Goffman, "On Face-Work: An Analysis of Ritual Elements in Social Interaction." Reprinted by special permission of The William Alanson White Psychiatric Foundation, Inc. *Psychiatry* 18, no. 3 (August 1955): 213–31. Copyright © 1955 by The William Alanson White Psychiatric Foundation.

consistent, that is supported by judgments and evidence conveyed by other participants, and that is confirmed by evidence conveyed through impersonal agencies in the situation. At such times the person's face clearly is something that is not lodged in or on his body, but rather something that is diffusely located in the flow of events in the encounter and becomes manifest only when these events are read and interpreted for the appraisals expressd in them.

The line maintained by and for a person during contact with others tends to be of a legitimate institutionalized kind. During a contact of a particular type, an interactant of known or visible attributes can expect to be sustained in a particular face and can feel that it is morally proper that this should be so. Given his attributes and the conventionalized nature of the encounter, he will find a small choice of lines will be open to him and a small choice of faces will be waiting for him. Further, on the basis of a few known attributes, he is given the responsibility of possessing a vast number of others. His coparticipants are not likely to be conscious of the character of many of these attributes until he acts perceptibly in such a way as to discredit his possession of them; then everyone becomes conscious of these attributes and assumes that he willfully gave a false impression of possessing them.

Thus while concern for face focuses the attention of the person on the current activity, he must, to maintain face in this activity, take into consideration his place in the social world beyond it. A person who can maintain face in the current situation is someone who abstained from certain actions in the past that would have been difficult to face up to later. In addition, he fears loss of face now partly because the others may take this as a sign that consideration for his feelings need not be shown in the future. There is nevertheless a limitation to this interdependence between the current situation and the wider social world: an encounter with people whom he will not have dealings with again leaves him free to take a high line that the future will discredit, or free to suffer humiliations that would make future dealings with them an embarrassing thing to have to face.

A person may be said to be *in wrong face* when information is brought forth in some way about his social worth which cannot be integrated, even with effort, into the line that is being sustained for him. A person may be said to *be out of face* when he participates in a contact with others without having ready a line of the kind participants in such situations are expected to take. The intent of many pranks is to lead a person into showing a wrong face or no face, but there will also be serious occasions, of course, when he will find himself expressively out of touch with the situation.

When a person senses that he is in face, he typically responds with feelings of confidence and assurance. Firm in the line he is taking, he feels that he can hold his head up and openly present himself to others. He feels some security and some relief—as he also can when the others feel he is in wrong face but successfully hide these feelings from him.

When a person is in wrong face or out of face, expressive

events are being contributed to the encounter which cannot be readily woven into the expressive fabric of the occasion. Should he sense that he is in wrong face or out of face, he is likely to feel ashamed and inferior because of what has happened to the activity on his account and because of what may happen to his reputation as a participant. Further, he may feel bad because he had relied upon the encounter to support an image of self to which he has become emotionally attached and which he now finds threatened. Felt lack of judgmental support from the encounter may take him aback, confuse him, and momentarily incapacitate him as an interactant. His manner and bearing may falter, collapse, and crumble. He may become embarrassed and chagrined; he may become shamefaced. The feeling, whether warranted or not, that he is perceived in a flustered state by others, and that he is presenting no usable line, may add further injuries to his feelings, just as his change from being in wrong face or out of face to being shamefaced can add further disorder to the expressive organization of the situation. Following common usage, I shall employ the term *poise* to refer to the capacity to suppress and conceal any tendency to become shamefaced during encounters with others.

In our Anglo-American society, as in some others, the phrase "to lose face" seems to mean to be in wrong face, to be out of face, or to be shamefaced. The phrase "to save one's face" appears to refer to the process by which the person sustains an impression for others that he has not lost face. Following Chinese usage, one can say that "to give face" is to arrange for another to take a better line than he might otherwise have been able to take,[2] the other thereby gets face given him, this being one way in which he can gain face.

As an aspect of the social code of any social circle, one may expect to find an understanding as to how far a person should go to save his face. Once he takes on a self-image expressed through face he will be expected to live up to it. In different ways in different societies he will be required to show self-respect, abjuring certain actions because they are above or beneath him, while forcing himself to perform others even though they cost him dearly. By entering a situation in which he is given a face to maintain, a person takes on the responsibility of standing guard over the flow of events as they pass before him. He must ensure that a particular *expressive order* is sustained—an order which regulates the flow of events, large or small, so that anything that appears to be expressed by them will be consistent with his face. When a person manifests these compunctions primarily from duty to himself, one speaks in our society of pride; when he does so because of duty to wider social units, and receives support from these units in doing so, one speaks of honor. When these compunctions have to do with postural things, with expressive events derived from the way in which the person handles his body, his emotions, and the things with which he has physical contact, one speaks of dignity, this being an aspect of expressive control that is always praised and never studied. In any case, while his social face can be his most personal possession and the center of his security and pleasure, it is only on loan to him from society; it will be withdrawn unless he conducts himself in a way that is worthy of it. Approved attributes and their relation to face make of every man his own jailer; this is a fundamental social constraint even though each man may like his cell.

Just as the member of any group is expected to have self-respect, so also he is expected to sustain a standard of considerateness; he is expected to go to certain lengths to save the feelings and the face of others present, and he is expected to do this willingly and spontaneously because of emotional identification with the others and with their feelings.[3] In consequence, he is disinclined to witness the defacement of others.[4] The person who can witness another's humiliation and unfeelingly retain a cool countenance himself is said in our society to be "heartless," just as he who can unfeelingly participate in his own defacement is thought to be "shameless."

The combined effect of the rule of self-respect and the rule of considerateness is that the person tends to conduct himself during an encounter so as to maintain both his own face and the face of the other participants. This means that the line taken by each participant is usually allowed to prevail, and each participant is allowed to carry off the role he appears to have chosen for himself. A state where everyone temporarily accepts everyone else's line is established.[6] This kind of mutual acceptance seems to be a basic structural feature of interaction, especially the interaction of face-to-face talk. It is typically a 'working' acceptance, not a 'real' one, since it tends to be based not on agreement of candidly expressed heartfelt evaluations, but upon a willingness to give temporary lip service to judgments with which the participants do not really agree.

The mutual acceptance of lines has an important conservative effect upon encounters. Once the person initially presents a line, he and the others tend to build their later responses upon it, and in a sense become stuck with it. Should the person radically alter his line, or should it become discredited, then confusion results, for the participants will have prepared and committed themselves for actions that are now unsuitable.

Ordinarily, maintenance of face is a condition of interaction, not its objective. Usual objectives, such as gaining face for oneself, giving free expression to one's true beliefs, introducing depreciating information about the others, or solving problems and performing tasks, are typically pursued in such a way as to be consistent with the maintenance of face. To study face-saving is to study the traffic rules of social interaction; one learns about the code the person adheres to in his movement across the paths and designs of others, but not where he is going, or why he wants to get there. One does not even learn why he is ready to follow the code, for a large number of different motives can equally lead him to do so. He may want to save his own face because of his emotional attachment to the image of self which it expresses, because of his pride or honor, because of the power his presumed status allows him to exert over the other participants, and so on. He may want to save the others' face because of his emotional attachment to an image of them, or because he feels that his coparticipants have a moral right to this protection, or because he wants to avoid the hostility that may be directed toward him if they lose their face. He may feel that an assumption has been made that he is the

362   sort of person who shows compassion and sympathy toward others, so that to retain his own face, he may feel obliged to be considerate of the line taken by the other participants.

By *face-work* I mean to designate the actions taken by a person to make whatever he is doing consistent with face. Face-work serves to counteract 'incidents'—that is, events whose effective symbolic implications threaten face. Thus poise is one important type of face-work, for through poise the person controls his embarrassment and hence the embarrassment that he and others might have over his embarrassment. Whether or not the full consequences of face-saving actions are known to the person who employs them, they often become habitual and standardized practices; they are like traditional plays in a game or traditional steps in a dance. Each person, subculture, and society seems to have its own characteristic repertoire of face-saving practices. It is to this repertoire that people partly refer when they ask what a person or culture is "really" like. And yet the particular set of practices stressed by particular persons or groups seems to be drawn from a single logically coherent framework of possible practices. It is as if face, by its very nature, can be saved only in a certain number of ways, and as if each social grouping must make its selections from this single matrix of possibilities.

The members of every social circle may be expected to have some experience in its use. In our society, this kind of capacity is sometimes called tact, *savoir-faire*, diplomacy, or social skill. Variation in social skill pertains more to the efficacy of face-work than to the frequency of its application, for almost all acts involving others are modified, prescriptively or proscriptively, by considerations of face.

If a person is to employ his repertoire of face-saving practices, obviously he must first become aware of the interpretations that others may have placed upon his acts and the interpretations that he ought perhaps to place upon theirs. In other words, he must exercise perceptiveness.[6] But even if he is properly alive to symbolically conveyed judgments and is socially skilled, he must yet be willing to exercise his perceptiveness and his skill; he must, in short, be prideful and considerate. Admittedly, of course, the possession of perceptiveness and social skill so often leads to their application that in our society terms such as politeness or tact fail to distinguish between the inclination to exercise such capacities and the capacities themselves.

I have already said that the person will have two points of view—a defensive orientation toward saving his own face and a protective orientation toward saving the others' face. Some practices will be primarily defensive and others primarily protective, although in general one may expect these two perspectives to be taken at the same time. In trying to save the face of others, the person must choose a tack that will not lead to loss of his own; in trying to save his own face, he must consider the loss of face that his action may entail for others.

In many societies there is a tendency to distinguish three levels of responsibility which a person may have for a threat to face that his actions have created. First, he may appear to have acted innocently; his offense seems to be unintended and unwitting, and those who perceive his act can feel that he would have attempted to avoid it had he foreseen its offensive consequences. In our society one calls such threats to face *faux pas, gaffes*, boners, or bricks. Secondly, the offending person may appear to have acted maliciously and spitefully, with the intention of causing open insult. Thirdly, there are incidental offenses; these arise as an unplanned but sometimes anticipated by-product of action—action which the offender performs in spite of its offensive consequences, although not out of spite. From the point of view of a particular participant, these three types of threat can be introduced by the participant himself against his own face, by himself against the face of the others, by the others against their own face, or by the others against himself. Thus the person may find himself in many different relations to a threat to face. If he is to handle himself and others well in all contingencies, he will have to have a repertoire of face-saving practices for each of these possible relations to threat.

THE BASIC KINDS OF FACE-WORK

The Avoidance Process

The surest way for a person to prevent threats to his face is to avoid contacts in which these threats are likely to occur. In all societies one can observe this in the avoidance relationship[7] and in the tendency for certain delicate transactions to be conducted by go-betweens.[8] Similarly, in many societies, members know the value of voluntarily making a gracious withdrawal before an anticipated threat to face has had a chance to occur.[9]

Once the person does chance an encounter, other kinds of avoidance practices come into play. As defensive measures, he keeps off topics and away from activities which would lead to the expression of information that is inconsistent with the line he is maintaining. At opportune moments he will change the topic of conversation or the direction of activity. He will often present initially a front of diffidence and composure, suppressing any show of feeling until he has found out what kind of line the others will be ready to support for him. Any claims regarding self may be made with belittling modesty, with strong qualifications, or with a note of unseriousness; by hedging in these ways he will have prepared a self for himself that will not be discredited by exposure, personal failure, or the unanticipated acts of others. And if he does not hedge his claims about self, he will at least attempt to be realistic about them, knowing that otherwise events may discredit him and make him lose face.

Certain protective maneuvers are as common as these defensive ones. The person shows respect and politeness, making sure to extend to others any ceremonial treatment which might be their due. He employs discretion; he leaves unstated facts which might implicitly or explicitly contradict and embarrass the positive claims made by others.[10] He employs circumlocutions and deceptions, phrasing his replies with careful ambiguity so that the others' face is preserved even if their welfare is not.[11] He employs courtesies, making slight modifications of his demands on or appraisals of the others so that they will be able to define the situation as one in which their self-respect is not threatened. In making a belittling demand upon the others, or in imputing uncomplimentary attributes to them, he may employ a joking manner, allowing them to take the line that they are good sports, able to relax from their ordinary standards of pride and honor. And before engaging in a potentially offensive act, he may provide explanations as to why the others ought not to be affronted by it. For eample, if he knows that it will be necessary to withdraw from the encounter before it has terminated, he may tell the others in advance that it is necessary for him to leave, so that they will have faces that are prepared for it. But neutralizing the potentially offensive act need not be done verbally; he may wait for a propitious moment or natural break—for example, in conversation, a momentary lull when no one speaker can be affronted—and then leave, in this way using the context instead of his words as a guarantee of inoffensiveness.

When a person fails to prevent an incident, he can still attempt to maintain the fiction that no threat to face has occurred. The most blatant example of this is found where the person acts as if an event which contains a threatening expression has not occurred at all. He may apply this studied nonobservance to his own acts—as when he does not by any outward sign admit that his stomach is rumbling—or to the acts of others, as when he does not 'see' that another has stumbled.[12] Social life in mental hospitals owes much to this process; patients employ it in regard to their own peculiarities, and visitors employ it, often with tenuous desperation, in regard to patients. In general, tactful blindness of this kind is applied only to events which, if perceived at all, could be perceived and interpreted only as threats to face.

A more important, less spectacular kind of tactful overlooking is practiced when a person openly acknowledges an incident as an event that has occurred, but not as an event that contains a threatening expression. If he is not the one who is responsible for the incident, then his blindness will have to be supported by his forbearance; if he is the doer of the threatening deed, then his blindness will have to be supported by his willingness to seek a way of dealing with the matter which leaves him dangerously dependent upon the cooperative forbearance of the others.

Another kind of avoidance occurs when a person loses control of his expressions during an encounter. At such times he may try not so much to overlook the incident as to hide or conceal his activity in some way, thus making it possible for the others to avoid some of the difficulties created by a participant who has not maintained face. Correspondlingly, when a person is caught out of face because he had not expected to be thrust into interaction, or because strong feelings have disrupted his expressive mask, the others may protectively turn away from him or his activity for a moment, to give him time to assemble himself.

The Corrective Process

When the participants in an undertaking or encounter fail to prevent the occurance of an event that is expressively incompatible with the judgments of social worth that are being maintained, and when the event is of the kind that is difficult to overlook, then the participants are likely to give it accredited status as an incident—to ratify it as a threat that deserves direct official attention—and to proceed to try to correct for its effects. At this point one or more participants find themselves in an established state of ritual disequilibrium or disgrace, and an attempt must be made to re-establish a satisfactory ritual state for them. I use the term *ritual* because I am dealing with acts through whose symbolic component the actor shows how worthy he is of respect or how worthy he feels others are of it. The imagery of equilibrium is apt here because the length and intensity of the corrective effort is nicely adapted to the persistence and intensity of the threat.[13] One's face, then, is a sacred thing, and the expressive order required to sustain it is therefore a ritual one.

The sequence of acts set in motion by an acknowledged threat to face, and terminating in the re-establishment of ritual equilibrium, I shall call an *interchange*.[14] Defining a message or move as everything conveyed by an actor during a turn at taking action, one can say that an interchange will involve two or more moves and two or more participants. Obvious examples in our society may be found in the sequence of "Excuse me" and "Certainly," and in the exchange of presents or visits. The interchange seems to be a basic concrete unit of social activity and provides one natural empirical way to study interaction of all kinds. Face-saving practices can be usefully classified according to their position in the natural sequence of moves which comprise this unit. Aside from the event which introduces the need for a corrective interchange, four classic moves seem to be involved.

There is, first, the challenge, by which participants take on the responsibility of calling attention to the misconduct; by implication they suggest that the threatened claims are to stand firm and that the threatening event itself will have to be brought back into line.

The second move consists of the offering, whereby a participant, typically the offender, is given a chance to correct for the offense and re-establish the expressive order. Some classic ways of making this move are available. On the one hand, an attempt can be made to show that what admittedly appeared to be a threatening expression is really a meaningless event, or an unintentional act, or a joke not meant to be taken seriously, or an unavoidable, 'understandable' product of extenuating circumstances. On the other hand, the meaning of the event may be granted and effort concentrated on the creator of it. Information may be provided to show that the creator was under the influence of something and not himself, or that he was under the command of somebody else and not acting for himself. When a person claims that an act was meant in jest, he may go on and claim that the self that seemed to lie behind the act was also projected as a joke. When a person suddenly finds that he has demonstrably failed in capacities that the others assumed him to have and to claim for himself—such as the capacity to spell, to perform minor tasks, to talk without malapropisms, and so on—he may quickly add, in a serious or unserious way, that he claims these incapacities as part of his self. The meaning of the threatening incident thus stands, but it can now be incorporated smoothly into the flow of expressive events.

As a supplement to or substitute for strategy of redefining the offensive act or himself, the offender can follow two other procedures: he can provide compensations to the injured—when it is not his own face that he has threatened; or he can provide punishment, penance, and expiation for himself. These are important moves or phases in the ritual interchange. Even though the offender may fail to prove his innocence, he can suggest through these means that he is now a re-newed person, a person who has paid for his sin against the expressive order and is once more to be trusted in the judgmental scene. Further, he can show that he does not treat the feelings of the others lightly, and that if their feelings have been injured by him, however inno-cently, he is prepared to pay a price for his action. Thus he assures the others that they can accept his explanations without this acceptance constituting a sign of weakness and a lack of pride on their part. Also, by his treatment of himself, by his self-castigation, he shows that he is clearly aware of the kind of crime he would have committed had the incident been what it first appeared to be, and that he knows the kind of punishment that ought to be accorded to one who would commit such a crime. The suspected person thus shows that he is thoroughly capable of taking the role of the others toward his own activity, that he can still be used as a responsible participant in the ritual process, and that the rules of conduct which he appears to have broken are still sacred, real, and unweakened. An offensive act may arouse anxiety about the ritual code; the offender allays this anxiety by showing that both the code and he as an upholder of it are still in working order.

After the challenge and the offering have been made, the third move can occur: the persons to whom the offering is made can accept it as a satisfactory means of re-establishing the expressive order and the faces supported by this order. Only then can the offender cease the major part of his ritual offering.

In the terminal move of the interchange, the forgiven person conveys a sign of gratitude to those who have given him the indul-gence of forgiveness.

The phases of the corrective process—challenge, offering, ac-ceptance, and thanks—provide a model for interpersonal ritual be-havior, but a model that may be departed from in significant ways. For example, the offended parties may give the offender a chance to initiate the offering on his own before a challenge is made and before they ratify the offense as an incident. This is a common courtesy, ex-tended on the assumption that the recipient will introduce a self-challenge. Further, when the offended persons accept the corrective offering, the offender may suspect that this has been grudgingly done from tact, and so he may volunteer additional corrective offerings, not allowing the matter to rest until he has received a second or third ac-

ceptance of his repeated apology. Or the offended persons may tactfully take over the role of the offender and volunteer excuses for him
that will, perforce, be acceptable to the offended persons.

An important departure from the standard corrective cycle
occurs when a challenged offender patently refuses to heed the warning and continues with his offending behavior, instead of setting the
activity to rights. This move shifts the play back to the challengers. If
they countenance the refusal to meet their demands, then it will be
plain that their challenge was a bluff and that the bluff has been called.
This is an untenable position; a face for themselves cannot be derived
from it, and they are left to bluster. To avoid this fate, some classic
moves are open to them. For instance, they can resort to tactless, violent retaliation, destroying either themselves or the person who had
refused to heed their warning. Or they can withdraw from the undertaking in a visible huff—righteously indignant, outraged, but confident
of ultimate vindication. Both tacks provide a way of denying the offender his status as an interactant, and hence denying the reality of
the offensive judgment he has made. Both strategies are ways of sal-
vaging face, but for all concerned the costs are usually high. It is partly to forestall such scenes that an offender is usually quick to offer
apologies; he does not want the affronted persons to trap themselves
into the obligation to resort to desperate measures.

It is plain that emotions play a part in these cycles of response, as when anguish is expressed because of what one has done to
another's face, or anger because of what has been done to one's own.
I want to stress that these emotions function as moves, and fit so precisely into the logic of the ritual game that it would seem difficult to
understand them without it.[15] In fact, spontaneously expressed feelings
are likely to fit into the formal pattern of the ritual interchange more
elegantly than consciously designed ones.

MAKING POINTS—THE AGGRESSIVE USE OF FACE-WORK

Every face-saving practice which is allowed to neutralize a particular threat opens up the possibility that the threat will be willfully introduced for what can be safely gained by it. If a person knows
that his modesty will be answered by others' praise of him, he can
fish for compliments. If his own appraisal of self will be checked
against incidental events, then he can arrange for favorable incidental
events to appear. If others are prepared to overlook an affront to them
and act forbearantly, or to accept apologies, then he can rely on this
as a basis for safely offending them. He can attempt by sudden withdrawal to force the others into a ritually unsatisfactory state, leaving
them to flounder in an interchange that cannot readily be completed.
Finally, at some expense to himself, he can arrange for the others
to hurt his feelings, thus forcing them to feel guilt, remorse, and sustained ritual disequilibrium.[16]

When a person treats face-work not as something he need be
prepared to perform, but rather as something that others can be
counted on to perform or to accept, then an encounter or an undertaking becomes less a scene of mutual considerateness than an arena

in which a contest or match is held. The purpose of the game is to preserve everyone's line from an inexcusable contradiction, while scoring as many points as possible against one's adversaries and making as many gains as possible for oneself. An audience to the struggle is almost a necessity. The general method is for the person to introduce favorable facts about himself and unfavorable facts about the others in such a way that the only reply the others will be able to think up will be one that terminates the interchange in a grumble, a meager excuse, a face-saving I-can-take-a-joke laugh, or an empty stereotyped comeback of the "Oh yeah?" or "That's what you think" variety. The losers in such cases will have to cut their losses, tacitly grant the loss of a point, and attempt to do better in the next interchange. Points made by allusion to social class status are sometimes called snubs; those made by allusions to moral respectability are sometimes called digs; in either case one deals with a capacity at what is sometimes called "bitchiness."

In aggressive interchanges the winner not only succeeds in introducing information favorable to himself and unfavorable to the others, but also demonstrates that as interactant he can handle himself better than his adversaries. Evidence of this capacity is often more important than all the other information the person conveys in the interchange, so that the introduction of a 'crack' in verbal interaction tends to imply that the initiator is better at footwork than those who must suffer his remarks. However, if they succeed in making a successful parry of the thrust and then a successful riposte, the instigator of the play must not only face the disparagement with which the others have answered him but also accept the fact that his assumption of superiority in footwork has proven false. He is made to look foolish; he loses face. Hence it is always a gamble to 'make a remark.' The tables can be turned and the aggressor can lose more than he could have gained had his move won the point. Successful ripostes or comebacks in our society are sometimes called squelches or toppers; theoretically it would be possible for a squelch to be squelched, a topper to be topped, and a riposte to be parried with a counterriposte, but except in staged interchanges this third level of successful action seems rare.[17]

THE CHOICE OF APPROPRIATE FACE-WORK

When an incident occurs, the person whose face is threatened may attempt to reinstate the ritual order by means of one kind of strategy, while the other participants may desire or expect a practice of a different type to be employed. When, for example, a minor mishap occurs, momentarily revealing a person in wrong face or out of face, the others are often more willing and able to act blind to the discrepancy than is the threatened person himself. Often they would prefer him to exercise poise,[18] while he feels that he cannot afford to overlook what has happened to his face and so becomes apologetic and shamefaced, if he is the creator of the incident, or destructively assertive, if the others are responsible for it.[19] Yet on the other hand, a person may manifest poise when the others feel that he ought to have broken down into embarrassed apology—that he is taking undue advantage of their helpfulness by his attempts to brazen it out. Sometimes a person may himself be undecided as to which practice to employ, leaving the others in the embarrassing position of not knowing which tack they are going to have to follow. Thus when a person makes a slight *gaffe*, he and the others may become embarrassed not because of inability to handle such difficulties, but because for a moment no one knows whether the offender is going to act blind to the incident, or give it joking recognition, or employ some other face-saving practice.

COOPERATION IN FACE-WORK

When a face has been threatened, face-work must be done, but whether this is initiated and primarily carried through by the person whose face is threatened, or by the offender, or by a mere witness,[20] is often of secondary importance. Lack of effort on the part of one person induces compensatory effort from others; a contribution by one person relieves the others of the task. In fact, there are many minor incidents in which the offender and the offended simultaneously attempt to initiate an apology.[21] Resolution of the situation to everyone's apparent satisfaction is the first requirement; correct apportionment of blame is typically a secondary consideration. Hence terms such as tact and *savoir-faire* fail to disinguish whether it is the person's own face that his diplomacy saves or the face of the others. Similarly terms such as *gaffe* and *faux pas* fail to specify whether it is the actor's own face he has threatened or the face of other participants. And it is understandable that if one person finds he is powerless to save his own face, the others seem especially bound to protect him. For example, in polite society, a handshake that perhaps should not have been extended becomes one that cannot be declined. Thus one accounts for the *no-blesse oblige* through which those of high status are expected to curb their power of embarrassing their lessers,[22] as well as the fact that the handicapped often accept courtesies that they can manage better without.

Since each participant in an undertaking is concerned, albeit for differing reasons, with saving his own face and the face of others, then tacit cooperation will naturally arise so that the participants together can attain their shared but differently motivated objectives.

One common type of tacit cooperation in face-saving is the face exerted in regard to face-work itself. The person not only defends his own face and protects the face of the others, but also acts so as to make it possible and even easy for the others to employ face-work for themselves and him. He helps them to help themselves and him. Social etiquette, for example warns men against asking for New Year's Eve dates too early in the season, lest the girl find it difficult to provide a gentle excuse for refusing. This second order tact can be further illustrated by the widespread practice of negative-attribute etiquette. The person who has an unapparent negatively valued attribute often finds it expedient to begin an encounter with an unobtrusive admission of his failing, especially with persons who are uninformed about him. The others are thus warned in advance against making disparaging remarks about his kind of person and are saved from the contradiction of acting in a friendly fashion to a person toward whom they are unwittingly being hostile. This strategy also prevents the others from automatically making assumptions about him which place him in a false position and saves him from painful forbearance or embarrassing remonstrances.

Tact in regard to face-work often relies for its operation on a tacit agreement to do business through the language of hint—the language of innuendo, ambiguities, well-placed pauses, carefully worded jokes, and so on.[23] The rule regarding this unofficial kind of communication is that the sender ought not to act as if he had officially conveyed the message he has hinted at, while the recipients have the right and the obligation to act as if they have not officially received the message contained in the hint. Hinted communication, then, is deniable communication; it need not be faced up to. It provides a means by which the person can be warned that his current line or the current situation is leading to loss of face, without this warning itself becoming an incident.

Another form of tacit cooperation, and one that seems to be much used in many societies, is reciprocal self-denial. Often the person does not have a clear idea of what would be a just or acceptable apportionment of judgments during the occasion, and so he voluntarily deprives or depreciates himself while indulging and complimenting the others, in both cases carrying the judgments safely past what is likely to be just. The favorable judgments about himself he allows to come from the others; the unfavorable judgments of himself are his own contributions. This 'after you, Alphonse' technique works, of course, because in depriving himself he can reliably anticipate that the others will compliment or indulge him. Whatever allocation of favors is eventually established, all participants are first given a chance to show that they are not bound or constrained by their own desires and expectations, that they have a properly modest view of themselves, and that they can be counted upon to support the ritual code. Negative bargaining, through which each participant tries to make the terms of trade more favorable to the other side, is another instance; as a form of exchange perhaps it is more widespread than the economist's kind.

A person's performance of face-work, extended by his tacit agreement to help others perform theirs, represents his willingness to abide by the ground rules of social interaction. Here is the hallmark of his socialization as an interactant. If he and the others were not socialized in this way, interaction in most societies and most situations would be a much more hazardous thing for feelings and faces. The person would find it impractical to be oriented to symbolically conveyed appraisals of social worth, or to be possessed of feelings—that is, it would be impractical for him to be a ritually delicate object. And as I shall suggest, if the person were not a ritually delicate object, occasions of talk could not be organized in the way they usually are. It is no wonder that trouble is caused by a person who cannot be relied upon to play the face-saving game.

THE RITUAL ROLES OF THE SELF

So far I have implicitly been using a double definition of self: the self as an image pieced together from the expressive implications of the full flow of events in an undertaking; and the self as a kind of player in a ritual game who copes honorably or dishonorably, diplomatically or undiplomatically, with the judgmental contingencies of the situation. A double mandate is involved. As sacred objects, men are subject to slights and profanation; hence as players of the ritual game they have had to lead themselves into duels, and wait for a round of shots to go wide off the mark before embracing their opponents. Here is an echo of the distinction between the value of a hand drawn at cards and the capacity of the person who plays it. This distinction must be kept in mind, even though it appears that once a person has gotten a reputation for good or bad play this reputation may become part of the face he must later play at maintaining.

Once the two roles of the self have been separated, one can look to the ritual code implicit in face-work to learn how the two roles are related. When a person is responsible for introducing a threat to another's face, he apparently has a right, within limits, to wriggle out of the difficulty by means of self-abasement. When performed voluntarily these indignities do not seem to profane his own image. It is as if he had the right of insulation and could castigate himself qua actor without injuring himself qua object of ultimate worth. By token of the same insulation he can belittle himself and modestly underplay his positive qualities, with the understanding that no one will take his statements as a fair representation of his sacred self. On the other hand, if he is forced against his will to treat himself in these ways, his face, his pride, and his honor will be seriously threatened. Thus, in terms of the ritual code, the person seems to have a special license to accept mistreatment at his own hands that he does not have the right to accept from others. Perhaps this is a safe arrangement because he is not likely to carry this license too far, whereas the others, were they given this privilege, might be more likely to abuse it.

Further, within limits the person has a right to forgive other participants for affronts to his sacred image. He can forbearantly overlook minor slurs upon his face, and in regard to somewhat greater injuries he is the one person who is in a position to accept apologies on behalf of his sacred self. This is a relatively safe prerogative for the person to have in regard to himself, for it is one that is exercised in the interests of the others or of the undertaking. Interestingly enough, when the person commits a *gaffe* against himself, it is not he who has the license to forgive the event; only the others have that prerogative, and it is a safe prerogative for them to have because they can exercise it only in his interests or in the interests of the undertaking. One finds, then, a system of checks and balances by which each participant tends to be given the right to handle only those matters which he will have little motivation for mishandling. In short, the rights and obligations of an interactant are designed to prevent him from abusing his role as an object of sacred value.

372   SPOKEN INTERACTION

Most of what has been said so far applies to encounters of both an immediate and mediated kind, although in the latter the interaction is likely to be more attenuated, with each participant's line being gleaned from such things as written statements and work records. During direct personal contacts, however, unique informational conditions prevail and the significance of face becomes especially clear. The human tendency to use signs and symbols means that evidence of social worth and mutual evaluations will be conveyed by very minor things, and these things will be witnessed, as will the fact that they have been witnessed. An unguarded glance, a momentary change in tone of voice, an ecological position taken or not taken, can drench a talk with judgmental significance. Therefore, just as there is no occasion to talk in which improper impressions could not intentionally or unintentionally arise, so there is no occasion of talk so trivial as not to require each participant to show serious concern with the way in which he handles himself and others present. Ritual factors which are present in mediated contacts are here present in an extreme form.

In any society, whenever the physical possibility of spoken interaction arises, it seems that a system of practices, conventions, and procedural rules comes into play which functions as a means of guiding and organizing the flow of messages. An understanding will prevail as to when and where it will be permissible to initiate talk, among whom, and by means of what topics of conversation. A set of significant gestures is employed to initiate a spate of communication and as a means for the persons concerned to accredit each other as legitimate participants.[24] When this process of reciprocal ratification occurs, the persons so ratified are in what might be called a *state of talk*—that is, they have declared themselves officially open to one another for purposes of spoken communication and guarantee together to maintain a flow of words. A set of significant gestures is also employed by which one or more new participants can officially join the talk, by which one or more accredited participants can officially withdraw, and by which the state of talk can be terminated.

A single focus of thought and visual attention, and a single flow of talk, tends to be maintained and to be legitimated as officially representative of the encounter. The concerted and official visual attention of the participants tends to be transferred smoothly by means of formal or informal clearance cues, by which the current speaker signals that he is about to relinquish the floor and the prospective speaker signals a desire to be given the floor. An understanding will prevail as to how long and how frequently each participant is to hold the floor. The recipients convey to the speaker, by appropriate gestures, that they are according him their attention. Participants restrict their involvement in matters external to the encounter and observe a limit to involvement in any one message of the encounter, in this way ensuring that they will be able to follow along whatever direction the topic of conversation takes them. Interruptions and lulls are regulated so as not to disrupt the flow of messages. Messages that are not part of the **373** officially accredited flow are modulated so as not to interfere seriously with the accredited messages. Nearby persons who are not participants visibly desist in some way from exploiting their communication position and also modify their own communication, if any, so as not to provide difficult interference. A particular ethos or emotional atmosphere is allowed to prevail. A polite accord is typically maintained, and participants who may be in real disagreement with one another give temporary lip service to views that bring them into agreement on matters of fact and principle. Rules are followed for smoothing out the transition, if any, from one topic of conversation to another.[25]

These rules of talk pertain not to spoken interaction considered as an on-going process, but to *an* occasion of talk or episode of interaction as a naturally bounded unit. This unit consists of the total activity that occurs during the time that a given set of participants have accredited one another for talk and maintain a single moving focus of attention.[26]

The conventions regarding the structure of occasions of talk represent an effective solution to the problem of organizing a flow of spoken messages. In attempting to discover how it is that these conventions are maintained in force as guides to action, one finds evidence to suggest a functional relationship between the structure of the self and the structure of spoken interaction.

The socialized interactant comes to handle spoken interaction as he would any other kind, as something that must be pursued with ritual care. By automatically appealing to face, he knows how to conduct himself in regard to talk. By repeatedly and automatically asking himself the question, "If I do or do not act in this way, will I or others lose face?" he decides at each moment, consciously or unconsciously, how to behave. For example, entrance into an occasion of spoken interaction may be taken as a symbol of intimacy or legitimate purpose, and so the person must, to save his face desist from entering into talk with a given set of others unless his circumstances justify what is expressed about him by his entrance. Once approached for talk, he must accede to the others in order to save their face. Once engaged in conversation, he must demand only the amount of attention that is an appropriate expression of his relative social worth. Undue lulls come to be potential signs of having nothing in common, or being insufficiently self-possessed to create something to say, and hence must be avoided. Similarly, interruptions and inattentiveness may convey disrespect, and must be avoided unless the implied disrespect is an accepted part of the relationship. A surface of agreement must be maintained by means of discretion and white lies, so that the assumption of mutual approval will not be discredited. Withdrawal must be handled so that it will not convey an improper evaluation.[27] The person must restrain his emotional involvement so as not to present an image of someone with no self-control or dignity who does not rise above his feelings.

The relation between the self and spoken interaction is further displayed when one examines the ritual interchange. In a conversational encounter, interaction tends to proceed in spurts, an interchange at a time, and the flow of information and business is parcelled out into these relatively closed ritual units.[28] The lull between interchanges tends to be greater than the lull between turns as talking in an interchange, and there tends to be a less meaningful relationship between two sequential interchanges than between two sequential speeches in an interchange.

This structural aspect of talk arises from the fact that when a person volunteers a statement or message, however trivial or commonplace, he commits himself and those he addresses, and in a sense places everyone present in jeopardy. By saying something, the speaker opens himself up to the possibility that the intended recipients will affront him by not listening or will think him forward, foolish, or offensive in what he has said. And should he meet with such a reception, he will find himself committed to the necessity of taking face-saving action against them. Furthermore, by saying something the speaker opens his intended recipients up to the possibility that the message will be self-approving, presumptuous, demanding, insulting, and generally an affront to them or to their conception of him, so that they will find themselves obliged to take action against him in defense of the ritual code. And should the speaker praise the recipients, they will be obliged to make suitable denials, showing that they do not hold too favorable an opinion of themselves and are not so eager to secure indulgences as to endanger their reliability and flexibility as interactants.

Thus when one person volunteers a message, thereby contributing what might easily be a threat to the ritual equilibrium, someone else present is obliged to show that the message has been received and that its content is acceptable to all concerned or can be acceptably countered. This acknowledging reply, of course, may contain a tactful rejection of the original communication, along with a request for modification. In such cases, several exchanges of messages may be required before the interchange is terminated on the basis of modified lines. The interchange comes to a close when it is possible to allow it to do so—that is, when everyone present has signified that he has been ritually appeased to a degree satisfactory to him.[29] A momentary lull between interchanges is possible, for it comes at a time when it will not be taken as a sign of something untoward.

In general, then, a person determines how he ought to conduct himself during an occasion of talk by testing the potentially symbolic meaning of his acts against the self-images that are being sustained. In doing this, however, he incidentally subjects his behavior to the expressive order that prevails and contributes to the orderly flow of messages. His aim is to save face; his effect is to save the situation. From the point of view of saving face, then, it is a good thing that spoken interaction has the conventional organization given it; from the point of view of sustaining an orderly flow of spoken messages, it is a good thing that the self has the ritual structure given it.

I do not mean, however, to claim that another kind of person related to another kind of message organization would not do as well.

More important, I do not claim that the present system is without weaknesses or drawbacks; these must be expected for everywhere in social life a mechanism or functional relation which solves one set of problems necessarily creates a set of potential difficulties and abuses all its own. For example, a characteristic problem in the ritual organization of personal contacts is that while a person can save his face by quarreling or by indignantly withdrawing from the encounter, he does this at the cost of the interaction. Furthermore, the person's attachment to face gives others something to aim at; they can not only make an effort to wound him unofficially, but may even make an official attempt utterly to destroy his face. Also, fear over possible loss of his face often prevents the person from initiating contacts in which important information can be transmitted and important relationships re-established; he may be led to seek the safety of solitude rather than the danger of social encounters. He may do this even though others feel that he is motivated by 'false pride'—a pride which suggests that the ritual code is getting the better of those whose conduct is regulated by it. Further, the 'after you, Alphonse' complex can make the termination of an interchange difficult. So, too, where each participant feels that he must sacrifice a little more than has been sacrificed for him, a kind of vicious indulgence cycle may occur—much like the hostility cycle that can lead to open quarrels—with each person receiving things he does not want and giving in return things he would rather keep. Again, when people are on formal terms, much energy may be spent in ensuring that events do not occur which might effectively carry an improper expression. And on the other hand, when a set of persons are on familiar terms and feel that they need not stand on ceremony with one another, then inattentiveness and interruptions are likely to become rife, and talk may degenerate into a happy babble of disorganized sound.

The ritual code itself requires a delicate balance, and can be easily upset by anyone who upholds it too eagerly or not eagerly enough, in terms of the standards and expectations of his group. Too little perceptiveness, too little *savoir-faire*, too little pride and considerateness, and the person ceases to be someone who can be trusted to take a hint about himself or give a hint that will save others embarrassment. Such a person comes to be a real threat to society; there is nothing much that can be done with him, and often he gets his way. Too much perceptiveness or too much pride, and the person becomes someone who is thin-skinned, who must be treated with kid gloves, requiring more care on the part of others than he may be worth to them. Too much *savoir-faire* or too much considerateness, and he becomes someone who is too socialized, who leaves the others with the feeling that they do not know how they really stand with him, nor what they should do to make an effective long-term adjustment to him.

In spite of these inherent 'pathologies' in the organization of talk, the functional fitness between the socialized person and spoken interaction is a viable and practical one. The person's orientation to

376   face, especially his own, is the point of leverage that the ritual order has in regard to him; yet a promise to take ritual care of his face is built into the very structure of talk.

FACE AND SOCIAL RELATIONSHIPS

When a person begins a mediated or immediate encounter, he already stands in some kind of social relationship to the others concerned, and expects to stand in a given relationship to them after the particular encounter ends. This, of course, is one of the ways in which social contacts are geared into the wider society. Much of the activity occurring during an encounter can be understood as an effort on everyone's part to get through the occasion and all the unanticipated and unintentional events that can cast participants in an undesirable light, without disrupting the relationships of the participants. And if relationships are in the process of change, the object will be to bring the encounter to a satisfactory close without altering the expected course of development. This perspective nicely accounts, for example, for the little ceremonies of greeting and farewell which occur when people begin a conversational encounter or depart from one. Greetings provide a way of showing that a relationship is still what it was at the termination of the previous coparticipation, and, typically, that this relationship involves sufficient suppression of hostility for the participants temporarily to drop their guards and talk. Farewells sum up the effect of the encounter upon the relationship and show what the participants may expect of one another when they next meet. The enthusiasm of greetings compensates for the weakening of the relationship caused by the absence just terminated, while the enthusiasm of farewells compensates the relationship for the harm that is about to be done to it by separation.[30]

It seems to be a characteristic obligation of many social relationships that each of the members guarantees to support a given face for the other members in given situations. To prevent disruption of these relationships, it is therefore necessary for each member to avoid destroying the others' face. At the same time, it is often the person's social relationship with others that leads him to participate in certain encounters with them, where incidentally he will be dependent upon them for supporting his face. Furthermore, in many relationships, the members come to share a face, so that in the presence of third parties an improper act on the part of one member becomes a source of acute embarrassment to the other members. A social relationship, then, can be seen as a way in which the person is more than ordinarily forced to trust his self-image and face to the fact and good conduct of others.

THE NATURE OF THE RITUAL ORDER

The ritual order seems to be organized basically on accommodative lines, so that the imagery used in thinking about other types of social order is not quite suitable for it. For the other types of social order a kind of schoolboy model seems to be employed: if a person wishes to sustain a particular image of himself and trust his feeling to it, he must work hard for the credits that will buy this self-enhancement for him;

should he try to obtain ends by improper means by cheating or theft, he will be punished, disqualified from the race, or at least made to start all over again from the beginning. This is the imagery of a hard, dull game. In fact, society and the individual join in one that is easier on both of them, yet one that has dangers of its own.

Whatever his position in society, the person insulates himself by blindnesses, half-truths, illusions, and rationalizations. He makes an 'adjustment' by convincing himself, with the tactful support of his intimate circle, that he is what he wants to be and that he would not do to gain his ends what the others have done to gain theirs. And as for society, if the person is willing to be subject to informal social control —if he is willing to find out from hints and glances and tactful cues what his place is, and keep it—then there will be no objection to his furnishing this place at his own discretion, with all the comfort, elegance, and nobility that his wit can muster for him. To protect this shelter he does not have to work hard, or join a group, or compete with anybody; he need only be careful about the expressed judgments he places himself in a position to witness. Some situations and acts and persons will have to be avoided; others, less threatening, must not be pressed too far. Social life is an uncluttered, orderly thing because the person voluntarily stays away from the places and topics and times where he is not wanted and where he might be disparaged for going. He cooperates to save his face, finding that there is much to be gained from venturing nothing.

Facts are of the schoolboy's world—they can be altered by diligent effort but they cannot be avoided. But what the person protects and defends and invests his feelings in is an idea about himself, and ideas are vulnerable not to facts and things but to communications. Communications belong to a less punitive scheme than do facts, for communications can be by-passed, withdrawn from, disbelieved, conveniently misunderstood, and tactfully conveyed. And even should the person misbehave and break the truce he has made with society, punishment need not be the consequence. If the offense is one that the offended persons can let go by without losing too much face, then they are likely to act forbearantly, telling themselves that they will get even with the offender in another way at another time, even though such an occasion may never arise and might not be exploited if it did. If the offense is great, the offended persons may withdraw from the encounter, or from future similar ones, allowing their withdrawal to be reinforced by the awe they may feel toward someone who breaks the ritual code. Or they may have the offender withdrawn, so that no further communication can occur. But since the offender can salvage a good deal of face from such operations, withdrawal is often not so much an informal punishment for an offense as it is merely a means of terminating it. Perhaps the main principle of the ritual order is not justice but face, and what any offender receives is not what he deserves but what will sustain for the moment the line to which he has committed himself, and through this the line to which he has committed the interaction.

Throughout this paper it has been implied that underneath

their differences in culture, people everywhere are the same. If persons have a universal human nature, they themselves are not to be looked to for an explanation of it. One must look rather to the fact that societies everywhere, if they are to be societies, must mobilize their members as self-regulating participants in social encounters. One way of mobilizing the individual for this purpose is through ritual; he is taught to be perceptive, to have feelings attached to self and a self expressed through face, to have pride, honor, and dignity, to have considerateness, to have tact and a certain amount of poise. These are some of the elements of behavior which must be built into the person if practical use is to be made of him as an interactant, and it is these elements that are referred to in part when one speaks of universal human nature.

Universal human nature is not a very human thing. By acquiring it, the person becomes a kind of construct, built up not from inner psychic propensities but from moral rules that are impressed upon him from without. These rules, when followed, determine the evaluation he will make of himself and of his fellow-participants in the encounter, the distribution of his feeling, and the kinds of practices he will employ to maintain a specified and obligatory kind of ritual equilibrium. The general capacity to be bound by moral rules may well belong to the individual, but the particular set of rules which transforms him into a human being derives from requirements established in the ritual organization of social encounters. And if a particular person or group or society seems to have a unique character all its own, it is because its standard set of human-nature elements is pitched and combined in a particular way. Instead of much pride, there may be little. Instead of abiding by the rules, there may be much effort to break them safely. But if an encounter or undertaking is to be sustained as a viable system of interaction organized on ritual principles, then these variations must be held within certain bounds and nicely counterbalanced by corresponding modifications in some of the other rules and understandings. Similarly, the human nature of a particular set of persons may be specially designed for the special kind of undertakings in which they participate, but still each of these persons must have within him something of the balance of characteristics required of a usable participant in any ritually organized system of social activity.

NOTES

1. For discussions of the Chinese conception of face, *see* the following: Hsien Chin Hu, "The Chinese Concept of 'Face,'" *Amer. Anthropologist* (1944) n.s. 46:45–64. Martin C. Yang, *A Chinese Village*; New York, Columbia Univ. Press, 1945; pp. 167–72. J. Macgowan, *Men and Manners of Modern China*; London, Unwin. 1912; pp. 301–12. Arthur H. Smith, *Chinese Characteristics*; New York, Fleming H. Revell Co., 1894; pp. 16–18. For a comment on the American Indian conception of face, *see* Marcel Mauss, *The Gift* (Ian Cunnison, tr.) ; London, Cohen & West, 1954; p. 38.

2. *See*, for example, Smith, reference footnote 1; p. 17.

3. Of course, the more power and prestige the others have, the more a person is likely to show consideration for their feelings, as H. E. Dale suggests in *The*

Higher Civil Service of Great Britain (Oxford, Oxford Univ. Press, 1941), p. 126*n*. "The doctrine of 'feelings' was expounded to me many years ago by a very eminent civil servant with a pretty taste in cynicism. He explained that the importance of feelings varies in close correspondence with the importance of the person who feels. If the public interest requires that a junior clerk should be removed from his post, no regard need be paid to his feelings; if it is a case of an Assistant Secretary, they must be carefully considered, within reason; if it is a Permanent Secretary, his feelings are a principal element in the situation, and only imperative public interest can override their requirements."

4. Salesmen, especially street 'stemmers,' know that if they take a line that will be discredited unless the reluctant customer buys, the customer may be trapped by considerateness and buy in order to save the face of the salesman and prevent what would ordinarily result in a scene.

5. Surface agreement in the assessment of social worth does not, of course, imply equality; the evaluation consensually sustained of one participant may be quite different from the one consensually sustained of another. Such agreement is also compatible with expression of differences of opinion between two participants, provided each of the disputants shows 'respect' for the other, guiding the expression of disagreement so that it will convey an evaluation of the other that the other will be willing to convey about himself. Extreme cases are provided by wars, duels, and barroom fights, when these are of a gentlemanly kind, for they can be conducted under consensual auspices, with each protagonist guiding his action according to the rules of the game, thereby making it possible for his action to be interpreted as an expression of a fair player openly in combat with a fair opponent. In fact, the rules and etiquette of any game can be analyzed as a means by which the image of a fair player can be expressed, just as the image of a fair player can be analyzed as a means by which the rules and etiquette of a game are sustained.

6. Presumably social skill and perceptiveness will be high in groups whose members frequently act as representatives of wider social units such as lineages or nations, for the player here is gambling with a face to which the feelings of many persons are attached. Similarly, one might expect social skill to be well developed among those of high station and those with whom they have dealings, for the more face an interactant has, the greater the number of events that may be inconsistent with it, and hence the greater the need for social skill to forestall or counteract these inconsistencies.

7. In our own society an illustration of avoidance is found in the middle- and upper-class Negro who avoids certain face-to-face contacts with whites in order to protect the self-evaluation projected by his clothes and manner. See, for example, Charles Johnson, *Patterns of Negro Segregation;* New York, Harper, 1943; ch. 13. The function of avoidance in maintaining the kinship system in small preliterate societies might be taken as a particular illustration of the same general theme.

8. An illustration is given by K. S. Latourette, *The Chinese: Their History and Culture* [New York, Macmillan, 1942]: "A neighbor or a group of neighbors may tender their good offices in adjusting a quarrel in which each antagonist would be sacrificing his face by taking the first step in approaching the other. The wise intermediary can effect the reconciliation while preserving the dignity of both" (vol. 2: p. 211).

9. In an unpublished paper Harold Garfinkel has suggested that when the person finds that he has lost face in a conversational encounter, he may feel a desire to disappear or "drop through the floor," and that this may involve a wish not only to conceal loss of face but also to return magically to a point in time when it would have been possible to save face by avoiding the encounter.

10. When the person knows the others well, he will know what issues ought not to be raised and what situations the others ought not to be placed in, and he will be free to introduce matters at will in all other areas. When the others are strangers to him, he will often reverse the formula, restricting himself to specific areas he knows are safe. On these occasions, as Simmel suggests, ". . . discretion

consists by no means only in the respect for the secret of the other, for his specific will to conceal this or that from us, but in staying away from the knowledge of all that the other does not expressly reveal to us." See *The Sociology of George Simmel* (Kurt H. Wolff, tr. and ed.); Glencoe, Ill., Free Press, 1950; pp. 320–21.

11. The Western traveler used to complain that the Chinese could never be trusted to say what they meant but always said what they felt their Western listener wanted to hear. The Chinese used to complain that the Westerner was brusque, boorish, and unmannered. In terms of Chinese standards, presumably, the conduct of a Westerner is so gauche that he creates an emergency, forcing the Asian to forgo any kind of direct reply in order to rush in with a remark that might rescue the Westerner from the compromising position in which he had placed himself. (See Smith, reference footnote 1; ch. 8, "The Talent for Indirection.") This is an instance of the important group of misunderstandings which arise during interaction between persons who come from groups with different ritual standards.

12. A pretty example of this is found in paradeground etiquette which may oblige those in a parade to treat anyone who faints as if he were not present at all.

13. This kind of imagery is one that social anthropologists seem to find naturally fitting. Note, for example, the implications of the following statement by Margaret Mead in her "Kinship in the Admiralty Islands" [*Anthropological Papers of the American Museum of Natural History*, 34:183–358]: "If a husband beats his wife, custom demands that she leave him and go to her brother, real or officiating, and remain a length of time commensurate with the degree of her offended dignity" (p. 274).

14. The notion of interchange is drawn in part from Eliot D. Chapple, "Measuring Human Relations," *Genetic Psychol. Monographs* (1940) 22:3–147, especiall pp.26–30, and from A. B. Horsfall and C. A. Arensberg, Teamwork and Productivity in a Shoe Factory," *Human Organization* (1949) 8:13–25, especially p. 19. For further material on the interchange as a unit see E. Goffman, "Communication Conduct in an Island Community," unpublished Ph.D. dissertation, Department of Sociology, University of Chicago, 1953, especially chs. 12 and 13, pp. 165–95.

15. Even when a child demands something and is refused, he is likely to cry and sulk not as an irrational expression of frustration but as a ritual move, conveying that he already has a face to lose and that its loss is not to be permitted lightly. Sympathetic parents may even allow for such display, seeing in these crude strategies the beginnings of a social self.

16. The strategy of maneuvering another into a position where he cannot right the harm he has done is very commonly employed but nowhere with such devotion to the ritual model of conduct as in revengeful suicide. See, for example, M. D. W. Jeffreys, "Samsonic Suicide, or Suicide of Revenge Among Africans," *African Studies* (1952) 11:118–22.

17. In board and card games the player regularly takes into consideration the possible responses of his adversaries to a play that he is about to make, and even considers the possibility that his adversaries will know that he is taking such precautions. Conversational play is by comparison surprisingly impulsive, people regularly make remarks about others present without carefully designing their remarks to prevent a successful comeback. Similarly, while feinting and sandbagging are theoretical possibilities during talk, they seem to be little exploited.

18. Folklore imputes a great deal of poise to the upper classes. If there is truth in this belief it may lie in the fact that the upper-class person tends to find himself in encounters in which he outranks the other participants in ways additional to class. The ranking participant is often somewhat independent of the good opinion of the others and finds it practical to be arrogant, sticking to a face regardless of whether the encounter supports it. On the other hand, those who are in the power of a fellow-participant tend to be very much concerned with the valuation he makes of them or witnesses being made of them, and so find it difficult to maintain a slightly wrong face without becoming embarrassed and

apologetic. It may be added that people who lack awareness of the symbolism in minor events may keep cool in difficult situations, showing poise that they do not really possess.

19. Thus, in our society, when a person feels that others expect him to measure up to approved standards of cleanliness, tidiness, fairness, hospitality, generosity, affluence, and so on, or when he sees himself as someone who ought to maintain such standards, he may burden an encounter with extended apologies for his failings, while all along the other participants do not care about the standard, or do not believe the person is really lacking in it, or are convinced that he is lacking in it and see the apology itself as a vain effort at self-elevation.

20. Thus one function of seconds in actual duels, as well as the figurative ones, is to provide an excuse for not fighting that both contestants can afford to accept.

21. *See* for instance Jackson Toby, "Some Variables in Role Conflict Analysis" [*Social Forces* (1952) 30:323–37]: "With adults there is less likelihood for essentially trivial issues to produce conflict. The automatic apology of two strangers who accidentally collide on a busy street illustrates the integrative function of etiquette. In effect, each of the parties to the collision says, 'I don't know whether I am responsible for this situation, but *if* I am, you have a right to be angry with me, a right that I pray you will not exercise.' By defining the situation as one in which both parties must abase themselves, society enables each to keep his self-respect. Each may feel in his heart of hearts, 'Why can't that stupid ass watch where he's going?' But overtly *each plays the role of the guilty party* whether he feels he has been miscast or not" (p. 325).

22. Regardless of the person's relative social position, in one sense he has power over the other participants and they must rely upon his considerateness. When the others act toward him in some way, they presume upon a social relationship to him, since one of the things expressed by interaction is the relationship of the interactants. Thus they compromise themselves, for they place him in a position to discredit the claims they express as to his attitude toward them. Hence in response to claimed social relationships every person of high estate or low, will be expected to exercise *noblesse oblige* and refrain from exploiting the compromised position of the others.

Since social relationships are defined partly in terms of voluntary mutual aid, refusal of a request for assistance becomes a delicate matter, potentially destructive of the asker's face. Chester Holcombe, *The Real Chinaman* [New York, Dodd, Mead, 1895] provides a Chinese instance: "Much of the falsehood to which the Chinese as a nation are said to be addicted is a result of the demands of etiquette. A plain, frank 'no' is the height of discourtesy. Refusal or denial of any sort must be softened and toned down into an expression of regretted inability. Unwillingness to grant a favor is never shown. In place of it there is seen a chastened feeling of sorrow that unavoidable but quite imaginary circumstances render it wholly impossible. Centuries of practice in this form of evasion have made the Chinese matchlessly fertile in the invention and development of excuses. It is rare, indeed, that one is caught at a loss for a bit of artfully embroidered fiction with which to hide an unwelcome truth" (pp.274–75).

23. Useful comments on some of the structural roles played by unofficial communication can be found in a discussion of irony and banter in Tom Burns, "Friends, Enemies, and the Polite Fiction," *Amer. Sociol. Rev.* 18 (1943) : 654–62.

24. The meaning of this status can be appreciated by looking at the kinds of unlegitimated or unratified participation that can occur in spoken interaction. A person may overhear others unbeknownst to them; he can overhear them when they know this to be the case and when they choose either to act as if he were not overhearing them or to signal to him informally that they know he is overhearing them, in all of these cases, the outsider is officially held at bay as someone who is not formally participating in the occasion. Ritual codes, of course, require a ratified participant to be treated quite differently from an unratified one. Thus, for example, only a certain amount of insult from a ratified participant can be ignored without this avoidance practice causing loss of face to the insulted

persons; after a point they must challenge the offender and demand redress. However, in many societies apparently, many kinds of verbal abuse from unratified participants can be ignored, without this failure to challenge constituting a loss of face.

25. For a further treatment of the structure of spoken interaction *see* Goffman, reference footnote 14; part 4.

26. I mean to include formal talks where rules of procedure are explicitly prescribed and officially enforced, and where only certain categories of participants may be allowed to hold the floor—as well as chats and sociable talks where rules are not explicit and the role of speaker passes back and forth among the participants.

27. Among people who have had some experience in interacting with one another, conversational encounters are often terminated in such a way as to give the appearance that all participants have indpendently hit upon the same moment to withdraw. The disbandment is general, and no one may be conscious of the exchange of cues that has been required to make such a happy simultaneity of action possible. Each participant is thus saved from the compromising position of showing readiness to spend further time with someone who is not as ready to spend time with him.

28. The empirical discreteness of the interchange unit is sometimes obscured when the same person who provides the terminating turn at talking in one interchange initiates the first turn at talking in the next. However, the analytical utility of the interchange as a unit remains.

29. The occurrence of the interchange unit is an empirical fact. In addition to the ritual explanation for it, others may be suggested. For example, when the person makes a statement and receives a reply at once, this provides him with a way of learning that his statement has been received and correctly received. Such 'metacommunication' would be necessary on functional grounds even were it unnecessary on ritual ones.

30. Greetings, of course, serve to clarify and fix the roles that the participants will take during the occasion of talk and to commit participants to these roles, while farewells provide a way of unambiguously terminating the encounter. Greetings and farewells may also be used to state, and apologize for, extenuating circumstances—in the case of greetings for circumstances that have kept the participants from interacting until now, and in the case of farewells for circumstances that prevent the participants from continuing their display of solidarity. These apologies allow the impression to be maintained that the participants are now more warmly related socially than may be the case. This positive stress, in turn, assures that they will act more ready to enter into contacts than they perhaps really feel inclined to do, thus guaranteeing that diffuse channels for potential communication will be kept open in the society.

Influence

SANCTION

LABELING

FREEDOM

ORDER

Obedience

Punishment

Control

RESISTANCE

Legitimacy

Coercion

Threat

RESOURCES

NORMS

Power

Compromise

Deviance

INVASION

Legitimate

Authority

FORCE

Compliance

Study Questions

1. When have you been the recipient of social control imposed by others? How did you act and react? How do you feel about control which is external? Is control in a society achieved more through internalization or through external force or pressure?
2. Describe a situation, formal or informal, where you have exercised control. Was it effective? Why or why not?
3. What kind of social organization produces the patterned interactions witnessed in Milgram's study? Do you feel that at least some obedience to authority is necessary for an organization's survival? Explain.
4. Distinguish between influence and authority and give some examples of how each of these is operative in a social organization.
5. Do you agree with Kitano's conclusion that evacuation and internment are no longer possible in our country?
6. If you were a guard at the New Jersey State Prison, would your control of prisoners' behavior be much different than that depicted in Sykes' article? In what ways?

Patterns of Control

Imagine a very busy intersection at rush hour with no provisions for facilitating the flow of traffic. In a very short time, cars would be backed up and traffic blocked. There would be a great deal of mutual interference without the establishment of some kind of order. Putting up signal lights at the intersection would be one way to remedy this disorganized situation. People would recognize the red and green lights and would respond accordingly. They would adjust their actions on the basis of shared meanings. We can thus create organization by means of substantive norms, which tell men *what* they should do, and procedural norms, which tell men *how* they should proceed. Social order can be established when men are ready and willing to respond to rules.

IMPERATIVE ORDER AND SOCIAL CONTROL

Loyalty, exchange, and impersonal norms, working independently or together, are ways of creating and maintaining social order. Another way of influencing behavior is the establishment of imperative order. An example of imperative order is the presence of a policeman directing traffic at the busy intersection at rush hour. Imperative order, in which men direct other men, is part of a broader concept known as social control.

It may seem to you that traffic became organized by means of an exchange pattern rather than by control. The cost of a traffic ticket or arrest is greater than the cost of conformity. The driver exchanges his conforming behavior for a reward: another day without a ticket. Exchange is one way to conceptualize the occurrences at the traffic corner, but the situation can be perceived more appropriately as an example of the pattern of social organization known as social control. And the effectiveness of the control is dependent upon the amount of power held by the controller.

DEFINITION OF POWER

Power is an aspect or variable of all organized social roles and social units. It is another way of viewing the patterns of mutual influence. Any pattern of social organization in which influence is achieved by the use of power is an example of social control. Power may affect the loyalties of individuals. The amount or type of exchange may be the basis for differentiated power relations. In any case, each of the patterns—loyalty, exchange, and social control—can be said to reinforce the others. It should be noted however, that the fundamental influence of power rests not upon loyalties or exchange, but on the capacity to impose sanctions.

The concept of power has been referred to or defined in a number of ways by different sociologists. Among these definitions are:

1. Power is the ability to impose one's will.
2. Power is the ability to impose one's will by imposing sanctions.
3. Power is the ability to make binding decisions for a group.
4. Power is the ability to effect or prevent decisions.

A general definition of power would include the capacity to affect others' behavior through the imposition of sanctions. Power is built into all social relationships, and sanctions are present in all social roles. The very concept of position or role implies the existence of more or less power which goes with the position. Power operates in many areas, in many ways. Congress passes or fails to pass laws that affect us; parents' discipline and set limits for their children; teachers assign homework; TV networks delete our favorite programs; sit-ins, strikes, and boycotts occur. All of these affect our daily lives and our long-range plans.

SOURCES OF POWER

Power generally rests on the control of valued resources and the dependencies which result from this control. It flows from basic interdependencies of social actors for goods and services, ideas and sentiments. Since most individuals are not totally self-sufficient, patterns of exchange of resources emerge within social organizations. Different types of power depend on the kinds of resources exchanged.

The large variety of available resources implies multiple sources of power. When different groups have different sources of power, they may be in competition with each other, or they may neutralize each other's attempts at domination.

The most obvious type of resource is economic: the control of goods, money, and jobs makes it possible for people to influence others. Another kind of resource is the possession of wanted skills and knowledge. Control over the means of violence is yet another kind of resource. In modern society the state has the ultimate source of power insofar as the militia and guard or military force are concerned. An-

388   other resource for power is legislative power or the various legal aspects of power which reside in many legally constituted bodies, such as our legislatures and courts.

These are finite power resources, which are depleted as they are used. Another type of resource is not finite and has great importance in social life. This type of resource is multiplied rather than depleted with use. Knowledge is such a resource. When you share knowledge, you do not lose it. Indeed, the fact that others now share your knowledge may mean that they can add to yours in a reciprocal, multiplicative process. Love is another resource similar to knowledge. Loving and educating can add to and enhance the resources of an organization. When this occurs, power is shared and it grows.

RESISTANCE TO POWER

The notions of power, social control, and imperative order can also be considered in terms of the kinds of goods and services the controlled can withhold from the controller, as a way of resisting power. If you have something that the powerful wants, you can exchange that "something" for a decision from the power authority to refrain from imposing his will. You can, for example, withhold your vote or your buying power. You can also obtain goods and services elsewhere in order to free yourself of dependency on a powerful person. For instance, a student who flunks out of a school but still wants to obtain his degree may go to another school. Another form of resistance to power occurs when force is used. A demand or request from a person with power may be dealt with by a show or threat of force. President Kennedy, in his handling of the Cuban missile crisis, used this type of strategy in resisting power. Indifference to the rewards of the powerful is another way of dealing with power. Many young people today refuse some of the conventional material rewards that result from educational or occupational achievement and seek fulfillment elsewhere.

To summarize, power is control over means and outcomes, or the ability to bring about a condition that is desired. Of course, one may have power without using it. Many of us have power to do countless things that we do not choose to do. One major consequence of the process of loving, described by Swanson in chapter 5, is for the loved one to develop new skills and competencies which are reservoirs of power. Education, in a general and positive sense, may be seen as a way of making people more powerful when it helps knowledge, or new ways of gaining knowledge to grow. Through this book, I hope to contribute to your knowledge—to your potential—to clarify power, and the relationship between power and freedom. A person must have a certain amount of freedom before he can have power, but a free person is not necessarily powerful. The possession of power is contingent upon the use of certain means upon the ability to exercise control. If a person has no control and therefore is powerless, can he still be free? The answer to that question is a qualified yes. Men can choose among goals and can form plans independent of their ability to carry out the plans or to move towards desired outcomes. This conception of

389

freedom without power is difficult to apprehend for it is not commonly used. You have the freedom to decide that a textbook is bad, but you may not have the power to stop your instructor from using it in his classes. The power to escape from a concentration camp during World War II was practically unattainable, but the freedom to nurture desires and plans for escape was limitless. Only when people are deprived of the will to resist as well as the possibility are they deprived of freedom as well as power.

LEGITIMACY, DEVIANCE, AND THE LABELLING THEORY

So far, I have talked mainly of the coercive aspects of power and resistance to power. However, power may also be accepted willingly. It may be seen as legitimate or right; as correct or moral. Jean Jacques Rousseau, in *The Social Contract*, said, "The strongest is never strong enough to be always the master, unless he transforms strength into right and obedience into duty. When power is legitimate, we accede to the demands of others.[1] The fact that power is inherent in a system means that decisions about who should be obedient and what is appropriate behavior may be in the hands of those who are agents of social control. In modern society, we have teachers, policemen, and probation officers who play such roles. In holding a legitimate position, the agent may decide who is deviant or insane, who is immoral or delinquent. You have been exposed to this idea in some of the previous readings. In the article by Scheff on "negotiating reality" (chapter 5) the power of the psychiatrist is evident. Studies show that decisions about insanity are less a matter of objective fact than of social judgement. The view that deviance is dependent upon the reaction of sanctioned officials is known as "labelling theory." The crux of this theory is that the essential feature of a deviant act is external to the act. What matters is the reaction and not the act itself. Kai Erikson describes this approach:

> [T]ransactions taking place between deviant persons on the one side and agencies on the other are boundary-maintaining mechanisms. They mark the outside limits of the area in which the norm has jurisdiction, and in this way assert how much diversity and variability can be contained within the system before it begins to lose its distinct structure, its unique shape.[2]

But deviance is more than the reaction of others. Deviance can be organized around patterned evasion, as in groups which adhere to deviant value systems or subcultures. Thus, while knowledge of the labelling theory serves in helping to understand rates of deviance or reactions to deviance, it is not a sufficient explanation of the variations among a population or of certain organized patterns of deviance. In the discussion of labelling theory, it is essential to note that social control can facilitate deviance as well as order.

The existence of agents for social control means that power has in some measure been legitimized by social groups. The idea of legitimate power may be considered in two ways. The powerful may

390

have the right to demand and command. There may be norms that give him these rights. He may be unintelligent or have any number of other limitations but he is powerful by virtue of laws, rules, or norms. A second way that power may be legitimized is through the personal qualities of the powerful. A person may be powerful only because he is bright, articulate, or persuasive. His leadership develops as a role because of personal qualities rather than because of an established, legitimate position. This suggests the following important distinction between influence and authority: a person has authority when he can make a binding decision for a group, and a person has influence when he can affect a person in authority.

The four selections included in this chapter illustrate some of the concepts of social control and power. The first, by Stanley Milgram, is a study of the degree to which individuals will acquiesce to authority. Milgram is concerned with the conditions under which feelings of obedience supercede a sense of accountability toward another human being. After reading this experiment, you may want to consider the real or imagined sources of power Milgram's subjects attributed to him. You may also want to reflect, as Milgram did, on the pervasiveness of this pattern thruout our society. The brief follow up article by Milgram investigates the conditions under which men remain firm and resolute in their beliefs and disengage themselves from the commands of an authority when the appropriateness of these commands is in doubts.

The third selection in this chapter on control is perhaps as removed from real life as the laboratory groups of Milgram or the prison of Gresham Sykes in the last article. "The Wartime Evacuation" was written by a colleague of mine, Harry H. L. Kitano, who teaches in the School of Social Welfare at UCLA. The exerpt describes the American government's treatment of Japanese Americans during World War II. I grew up in the eastern part of the United States and as a child and teenager knew nothing of the internment of the Japanese. In my third year of college, in a Constitutional Law course, I discovered what happened to the Issei and Nisei. I was shocked and dismayed by the potential destructiveness of the abuse of power and its counterpart—accession to power and control without resistance. At the conclusion of his article, Kitano makes a prediction that relocation camps will never again be used in this country. There are many who make a very different prediction about the readiness of camps for occupancy. Milgram and Kitano in their writings help pinpoint the factors which contribute to obedience and control and lend substance to the arguments of those who feel that camp containment is a very real possibility.

The last selection, "The Defects of Total Power," was written by a sociologist, Gresham Sykes, who describes the interaction between guards and inmates in a maximum security prison in Trenton, New Jersey. Sykes studied the prison in order to analyze the dynamics of power. In the prison, the staff had a monopoly on the legitimate sources of coercion—the control of rewards and privileges and the right to punish. Sykes was able to show how this power could be undermined and compromised by the prisoners.

NOTES

1. Jean Jacques Rousseau, *The Social Contract* (Chicago: H. Regnery, 1954).

2. Kai T. Erikson, "Notes on the Sociology of Deviance." *Social Problems* 9 (Spring 1962) : 310.

3. Allan R. Bosworth, *America's Concentration Camps* (New York: W. W. Norton & Co.).

STANLEY MILGRAM

Some Conditions of Obedience and Disobedience to Authority

The issue under examination in this article is the extent to which an individual (the subject) will obey the commands of a legitimate authority (the experimenter) to inflict painful punishment on another individual. The experimental situation created by Milgram placed the subject (surprisingly enough) in a highly conflictful situation—to be a "good" subject and fulfill the requirements of the experiment meant harming another person.

This research is extremely important because it calls into question many assumptions that Americans—who profess democratic, humanitarian values—have about themselves. It demonstrates that even citizens of a democracy will abdicate personal responsibility for their actions under the commands of an authority figure. Perhaps more of us are potential Eichmanns that we ever imagined.

The situation in which one agent commands another to hurt a third turns up time and again as a significant theme in human relations. It is powerfully expressed in the story of Abraham, who is commanded by God to kill his son. It is no accident that Kierkegaard (1843), seeking to orient his thought to the central themes of human experience, chose Abraham's conflict as the springboard to his philosophy.

War too moves forward on the triad of an authority which commands a person to destroy the enemy, and perhaps all organized hostility may be viewed as a theme and variation on the three elements of authority, executant, and victim. We describe an experimental program, recently concluded at Yale University, in which a particular expression of this conflict is studied by experimental means. . . .

One aim of the research was to study behavior in a strong situ-

From Stanley Milgram, "Some Conditions of Obedience and Disobedience to Authority," *Human Relations* 18 (1965) : 57–75. Reprinted by permission of Plenum Publishing Company.

ation of deep consequence to the participants, for the psychological forces operative in powerful and lifelike forms of the conflict may not be brought into play under diluted conditions.

This approach meant, first, that we had a special obligation to protect the welfare and dignity of the persons who took part in the study; subjects were, of necessity, placed in a difficult predicament, and steps had to be taken to ensure their wellbeing before they were discharged from the laboratory. Toward this end, a careful post-experimental treatment was devised and has been carried through for subjects in all conditions.[1]

TERMINOLOGY

If Y follows the command of X we shall say that he has obeyed X; if he fails to carry out the command of X, we shall say that he has disobeyed X. The terms *to obey* and *to disobey*, as used here, refer to the subject's overt action only, and carry no implication for the motive or experimental states accompanying the action. . . .

A subject who complies with the entire series of experimental commands will be termed an *obedient* subject; one who at any point in the command serries defies the experimenter will be called a *disobedient* or *defiant* subject. As used in this report, the terms refer only to the subject's performance in the experiment, and do not necessarily imply a general personality disposition to submit to or reject authority.

SUBJECT POPULATION

The subjects used in all experimental conditions were male adults, residing in the greater New Haven and Bridgeport areas, aged 20 to 50 years, and engaged in a wide variety of occupations. Each experimental condition described in this report employed 40 fresh subjects and was carefully balanced for age and occupational types. The occupational composition for each experiment was: workers, skilled and unskilled: 40 per cent; white collar, sales, business: 40 per cent; professionals: 20 per cent. The occupations were intersected with three age categories (subjects in 20s, 30s, and 40s, assigned to each condition in the proportions of 20, 40, and 40 percent respectively).

THE GENERAL LABORATORY PROCEDURE

The focus of the study concerns the amount of electric shock a subject is willing to administer to another person when ordered by an experimenter to give the 'victim' increasingly more severe punishment. The act of administering shock is set in the context of a learning experiment, ostensibly designed to study the effect of punishment on memory. Aside from the experimenter, one naive subject and one accomplice perform in each session. On arrival each subject is paid $4.50. After a general talk by the experimenter, telling how little scientists know about the effect of punishment on memory, subjects are informed that one member of the pair will serve as teacher and one as learner. A rigged drawing is held so that the naive subject is always the teacher, and the accomplice becomes the learner. The learner is taken to an adjacent room and strapped into an "electric chair."

The naive subject is told that it is his task to teach the learner a list of paired associates, to test him on the list, and to administer punishment whenever the learner errs in the test. Punishment takes the form of electric shock, delivered to the learner by means of a shock generator controlled by the naive subject. The teacher is instructed to increase the intensity of electric shock one step on the generator on each error. The learner, according to plan, provides many wrong answers, so that before long the naive subject must give him the strongest shock on the generator. Increases in shock level are met by increasingly insistent demands from the learner that the experiment be stopped because of the growing discomfort to him. However, in clear terms the experimenter orders the teacher to continue with the procedure in disregard of the learner's protests. *Thus, the naive subject must resolve a conflict between two mutually incompatible demands from the social field. He may continue to follow the orders of the experimenter and shock the learner with increasing severity, or he may refuse to follow the orders of the experimenter and heed the learner's pleas. The experimenter's authority operates not in a free field, but against ever-mounting countervailing pressures from the person being punished.*

A few technical points need to be considered before the findings of the study are described. For the purpose of delivering shock, a simulated shock generator is used, with 30 clearly marked voltage levels that range from 15 to 450 volts (and each activated by one of 30 individual lever switches set in a horizontal line). The naive subject is given a sample shock of 45 volts to convince him of the authenticity of the instrument. The generator bears verbal designations that range from "Slight Shock" to "Danger: Severe Shock."

The responses of the victim are standardized on tape, and each protest is coordinated to a particular voltage level on the shock generator. Starting with 75 volts the learner begins to grunt and moan. At 150 volts he demands to be let out of the experiment. At 180 volts he cries out that he can no longer stand the pain. At 300 volts he refuses to provide any more answers to the memory test, insisting that he is no longer a participant in the experiment and must be freed. In response to this last tactic, the experimenter instructs the naive subject to treat the absence of an answer as equivalent to a wrong answer, and to follow the usual shock procedure. The experimenter reinforces his demand with the statement: "You have no other choice, you must go on!" (This imperative is used whenever the naive subject tries to break off the experiment.) If the subject refuses to give the next higher level of shock, the experiment is considered at an end. A quantitative value is assigned to the subject's performance based on the maximum intensity shock he administered before breaking off. Thus any subject's score may range from zero (for a subject unwilling to administer the first shock level) to 30 (for a subject who proceeds to the highest voltage level on the board). For any particular subject and for

394

any particular experimental condition the degree to which participants have followed the experimenter's orders may be specified with a numerical value, corresponding to the metric on the shock generator. . . .

PILOT STUDIES

Pilot studies for the present research were completed in the winter of 1960; they differed from the regular experiments in a few details; for one, the victim was placed behind a silvered glass, with the light balance on the glass such that the victim could be dimly perceived by the subject (Milgram, 1961).

Though essentially qualitative in treatment, these studies pointed to several significant features of the experimental situation. At first no vocal feedback was used from the victim. It was thought that the verbal and voltage designations on the control panel would create sufficient pressure to curtail the subject's obedience. However, this was not the case. In the absence of protests from the learner, virtually all subjects, once commanded, went blithely to the end of the board, seemingly indifferent to the verbal designations ("Extreme Shock" and "Danger: Severe Shock"). This deprived us of an adequate basis for scaling obedient tendencies. A force had to be introduced that would strengthen the subject's resistance to the experimenter's commands, and reveal individual differences in terms of a distribution of breakoff points.

This force took the form of protests from the victim. Initially, mild protests were used, but proved inadequate. Subsequently, more vehement protests were inserted into the experimental procedure. To our consternation, even the strongest protests from the victim did not prevent all subjects from administering the harshest punishment ordered by the experimenter; but the protests did lower the mean maximum shock somewhat and created some spread in the subject's performance; therefore, the victim's cries were standardized on tape and incorporated into the regular experimental procedure.

The situation did more than highlight the technical difficulties of finding a workable experimental procedure: it indicated that subjects would obey authority to a greater extent than we had supposed. It also pointed to the importance of feedback from the victim in controlling the subject's behavior.

One further aspect of the pilot study was that subjects frequently averted their eyes from the person they were shocking, often turning their heads in an awkward and conspicuous manner. One subject explained: "I didn't want to see the consequences of what I had done."

This suggested that the salience of the victim may have, in some degree, regulated the subject's performance. If, in obeying the experimenter, the subject found it necessary to avoid scrutiny of the victim, would the converse be true? If the victim were rendered increasingly more salient to the subject, would obedience diminish? The first set of regular experiments was designed to answer this question.

IMMEDIACY OF THE VICTIM   **395**

This series consisted of four experimental conditions. In each condition the victim was brought "psychologically" closer to the subject giving him shocks.

In the first condition (Remote Feedback) the victim was placed in another room and could not be heard or seen by the subject, except that, at 300 volts, he pounded on the wall in protest. After 315 volts he no longer answered or was heard from.

The second condition (Voice Feedback) was identical to the first except that voice protests were introduced. As in the first condition the victim was placed in an adjacent room, but his complaints could be heard clearly through a door left slightly ajar, and through the walls of the laboratory.[2]

The third experimental condition (Proximity) was similar to the second, except that the victim was now placed in the same room as the subject, and $1\frac{1}{2}$ feet from him. Thus he was visible as well as audible, and voice cues were provided.

The fourth, and final, condition of the series (Touch-Proximity) was identical to the third, with this exception: the victim received a shock only when his hand rested on a shockplate. At the 150-volt level the victim again demanded to be let free and, in this condition, refused to place his hand on the shockplate. The experimenter ordered the naïve subject to force the victim's hand onto the plate. Thus obedience in this condition required that the subject have physical contact with the victim in order to give him punishment beyond the 150-volt level.

Forty adult subjects were studied in each condition. The data revealed that obedience was significantly reduced as the victim was rendered more immediate to the subject. . . .

Expressed in terms of the proportion of obedient to defiant subjects, the findings are that 34 per cent of the subjects defied the experimenter in the Remote condition, 37.5 percent in Voice Feedback, 60 per cent in Proximity, and 70 percent in Touch-Proximity.

How are we to account for this effect? A first conjecture might be that as the victim was brought closer the subject became more aware of the intensity of his suffering and regulated his behavior accordingly. This makes sense, but our evidence does not support the interpretation. There are no consistent differences in the attributed level of pain across the four conditions (i.e. the amount of pain experienced by the victim as estimated by the subject and expressed on a 14-point scale). But it is easy to speculate about alternative mechanisms.

Empathic Cues

In the Remote and to a lesser extent the Voice Feedback condition, the victim's suffering possesses an abstract, remote quality for the subject. He is aware, but only in a conceptual sense, that his actions cause pain to another person; the fact is apprehended, but not felt. . . . It is

396

possible that the visual cues associated with the victim's suffering trigger empathic responses in the subject and provide him with a more complete grasp of the victim's experience. Or it is possible that the empathic responses are themselves unpleasant, possessing drive properties which cause the subject to terminate the arousal situation. Diminishing obedience, then, would be explained by the enrichment of empathic cues in the successive experimental conditions.

Denial and Narrowing of the Cognitive Field

The Remote condition allows a narrowing of the cognitive field so that the victim is put out of mind. The subject no longer considers the act of depressing a lever relevant to moral judgement, for it is no longer associated with the victim's suffering. When the victim is close it is more difficult to exclude him phenomenologically. He necessarily intrudes on the subject's awareness since he is continuously visible. In the Remote conditions, his existence and reactions are made known only after the shock has been administered. The auditory feedback is sporadic and discontinuous. In the Proximity conditions his inclusion in the immediate visual field renders him a continuously salient element for the subject. The mechanism of denial can no longer be brought into play. One subject in the Remote condition said: "It's funny how you really begin to forget that there's a guy out there, even though you can hear him. For a long time I just concentrated on pressing the switches and reading the words."

Reciprocal Fields

If in the Proximity condition the subject is in an improved position to observe the victim, the reverse is also true. The actions of the subject now come under proximal scrutiny by the victim. Possibly, it is easier to harm a person when he is unable to observe our actions than when he can see what we are doing. His surveillance of the action directed against him may give rise to shame, or guilt, which may then serve to curtail the action. Many expressions of language refer to the discomfort or inhibitions that arise in face-to-face confrontation. It is often said that it is easier to criticize a man "behind his back" than to "attack him to his face". . . . In short, in the Proximity condition, the subject may sense that he has become more salient in the victim's field of awareness. Possibly he becomes more self-conscious, embarrassed, and inhibited in his punishment of the victim.

Phenomenal Unity of Act

In the Remote condition it is more difficult for the subject to gain a sense of *relatedness* between his own actions and the consequences of these actions for the victim. There is a physical and spatial separation of the act and its consequences. The subject depresses a lever in one room, and protests and cries are heard from another. The two events are in correlation, yet they lack a compelling phenomenological unity. The structure of a meaningful act—*I am hurting a man*—breaks down because of the spatial arrangements, in a manner somewhat analogous to the disappearance of phi phenomena when the blinking lights are spaced too far apart. The unity is more fully achieved in the Proximity condition as the victim is brought closer to the action that causes him pain. It is rendered complete in Touch–Proximity.

Incipient Group Formation

Placing the victim in another room not only takes him further from the subject, but the subject and the experimenter are drawn relatively closer. There is incipient group formation between the experimenter and the subject, from which the victim is excluded. The wall between the victim and the others deprives him of an intimacy which the experimenter and subject feel. In the Remote condition, the victim is truly an outsider, who stands alone, physically and psychologically.

When the victim is placed close to the subject, it becomes easier to form an alliance with him against the experimenter. Subjects no longer have to face the experimenter alone. They have an ally who is close at hand and eager to collaborate in a revolt against the experimenter. Thus the changing set of spatial relations leads to a potentially shifting set of alliances over the several experimental conditions.

Acquired Behavior Dispositions

It is commonly observed that laboratory mice will rarely fight with the litter mates. Scott (1958) explains this in terms of passive inhibition. He writes: "By doing nothing under . . . circumstances [the animal] learns to do nothing, and this may be spoken of as passive inhibition . . . this principle has great importance in teaching an individual to be peaceful, for it means that he can learn not to fight simply by not fighting." Similarly, we may learn not to harm others simply by not harming them in everyday life. Yet this learning occurs in a context of proximal relations with others, and may not be generalized to that situation in which the person is physically removed from us. Or possibly, in the past, aggressive actions against others who were physically close resulted in retaliatory punishment which extinguished the original form of response. In contrast, aggression against others at a distance may have only sporadically led to retaliation. Thus the organism learns that it is safer to be aggressive toward others at a distance, and precarious to be so when the parties are within arm's reach. Through a pattern of rewards and punishments, he acquires a disposition to avoid aggression at close quarters, a disposition which does not extend to harming others at a distance. And this may account for experimental findings in the remote and proximal experiments. . . .

CLOSENESS OF AUTHORITY

If the spatial relationship of the subject and victim is relevant to the degree of obedience, would not the relationship of subject to experimenter also play a part?

There are reasons to feel that, on arrival, the subject is oriented primarily to the experimenter rather than to the victim. He has come to the laboratory to fit into the structure that the experimenter—not the

398   victim—would provide. He has come less to understand his behavior than to *reveal* that behavior to a competent scientist, and he is willing to display himself as the scientist's purposes require. Most subjects seem quite concerned about the appearance they are making before the experimenter, and one could argue that this preoccupation in a relatively new and strange setting makes the subject somewhat insensitive to the triadic nature of the social situation. In other words, the subject is so concerned about the show he is putting on for the experimenter that influences from other parts of the social field do not receive as much weight as they ordinarily would. This overdetermined orientation to the experimenter would account for the relative insensitivity of the subject to the victim, and would also lead us to believe that alterations in the relationship between subject and experimenter would have important consequences for obedience.

In a series of experiments we varied the physical closeness and degree of surveillance of the experimenter. In one condition the experimenter sat just a few feet away from the subject. In a second condition, after giving initial instructions, the experimenter left the laboratory and gave his orders by telephone; in still a third condition the experimenter was never seen, providing instructions by means of a tape recording activated when the subjects entered the laboratory.

Obedience dropped sharply as the experimenter was physically removed from the laboratory. The number of obedient subjects in the first condition (Experimenter Present) was almost three times as great as in the second, where the experimenter gave his orders by telephone. Twenty-six subjects were fully obedient in the first condition, and only 9 in the second (Chi square obedient *vs* defiant in the two conditions, 1 $df=14.7$; $p<.001$). Subjects seemed able to take a far stronger stand against the experimenter when they did not have to encounter him face to face, and the experimenter's power over the subject was severely curtailed.

Moreover, when the experimenter was absent, subjects displayed an interesting form of behavior that had not occurred under his surveillance. Though continuing with the experiment, several subjects administered lower shocks than were required and never informed the experimenter of their deviation from the correct procedure. (Unknown to the subjects, shock levels were automatically recorded by an Esterline-Angus event recorder wired directly into the shock generator; the instrument provided us with an objective record of the subject's performance.) Indeed, in telephone conversations some subjects specifically assured the experimenter that they were raising the shock level according to instruction, whereas in fact they were repeatedly using the lowest shock on the board. This form of behavior is particularly interesting; although these subjects acted in a way that clearly undermined the avowed purposes of the experiment, they found it easier to handle the conflict in this manner than to precipitate an open break with authority.

Other conditions were completed in which the experimenter was absent during the first segment of the experiment, but reappeared at the point that the subject definitely refused to give higher shocks when commanded by telephone. Although he had exhausted his power via telephone, the experimenter could frequently force further obedience when he reappeared in the laboratory.

Experiments in this series show that the physical *presence* of an authority is an important force contributing to the subject's obedience or defiance. Taken together with the first experimental series on the proximity of the victim, it would appear that something akin to fields of force, diminishing in effectiveness with increasing psychological distance from their source, have a controlling effect on the subject's performance. As the victim is brought closer, the subject finds it harder to administer shocks to him. When the victim's position is held constant relative to the subject, and the authority is made more remote, the subject finds it easier to break off the experiment. This effect is substantial in both cases, but manipulation of the experimenter's position yielded the more powerful results. . . .

TENSIONS

The description of final scores does not fully convey the character of the subjects' performance, and it would be useful to interrupt our reporting of quantitative relationships to remark on the subjects' general reaction to the situation.

One might suppose that a subject would simply break off or continue as his conscience and temperament dictated. Yet this is very far from what happened. There were powerful reactions of tension and emotional strain in a substantial proportion of the participants. Persons were observed to sweat, tremble, stutter, bite their lips, and groan as they found themselves increasingly implicated in the experimental conflict. Some sense of the subjects' mood can be gotten from a transcript of their remarks at breakoff point. Here are the remarks of two defiant subjects:

Is he banging? . . . Is he hurt out there? Well, I don't want to be responsible for anything that happens to him. No I can't go on with it. I don't know whether he's all right or not. I mean he may have a heart condition or something; I wouldn't feel right doing it. He's banging for help. He's evidently in trouble or he wouldn't bang . . . I don't see any sense to this —to knocking him out or something. I just can't see it.

(Subject refuses to administer shocks) (Subject 0108)

The man is banging. He wants to get out . . . I'm sorry. If the man wants to get out I'd just as soon stop . . . I don't want to administer any more [extremely excited] . . . I will gladly refund the check, but I will not harm this man . . . I'm sorry, I will not give him any more if he obviously wants to get out. There is no money in the world that will make me hurt another individual. *(Subject 010X)*.

And here is a transcript from an obedient subject. He began the experiment calmly, but became increasingly tense as the experi-

400 ment proceeded. After administering the 150-volt shock, he began
to address the experimenter in agitated tones:

150 volts delivered. You want me to keep going?
165 volts delivered. That guy is hollering in there. There's a lot of them
here. He's liable to have heart condition. You want me to go on?
180 volts delivered. He can't stand it! I'm not going to kill that man in
there! You hear him hollering? He's hollering. He can't stand it. What
if something happens to him? . . . I'm not going to get that man sick
in there. He's hollering in there. You know what I mean? I mean I refuse
to take responsibility. He's getting hurt in there. He's in there hollering.
Too many left here. Geez, if he gets them wrong. There's too many of
them left. I mean who is going to take responsibility if anything happens to that gentleman?
(The experimenter accepts responsibility.) All right.
195 volts delivered. You see he's hollering. Hear that. Gee. I don't know.
(The experimenter says: "The experiment requires that you go on.")
—I know it does, sir, but I mean—hugh—he don't know what he's in for.
He's up to 195 volts.
210 volts delivered
225 volts delivered
240 volts delivered. Aw, no. You mean I've got to keep going up with
the scale? No sir. I'm not going to kill that man! I'm not going to give
him 450 volts! *(The experimenter says: "The experiment requires that
you go on.")*—I know it does, but that man is hollering in there, sir . . .

Despite his numerous, agitated objections, which were constant ac-
companiments to his actions, the subject unfailingly obeyed the experimenter, proceeding to the highest shock level on the generator. He
displayed a curious dissociation between word and action. Although
at the verbal level he had resolved not to go on, his actions were fully
in accord with the experimenter's commands. This subject did not
want to shock the victim, and he found it an extremely disagreeable
task, but he was unable to invent a response that would free him from
the experimenter's authority. Many subjects cannot find the specific
verbal formula that would enable them to reject the role assigned to
them by the experimenter. Perhaps our culture does not provide adequate models for disobedience.

One puzzling sign of tension was the regular occurrence of
nervous laughing fits. In the first four conditions 71 of the 160 subjects showed definite signs of nervous laughter and smiling. The
laugher seemed entirely out of place, even bizarre. Full-blown, uncontrollable seizures were observed for 15 of these subjects. On one occasion we observed a seizure so violently convulsive that it was necessary to call a halt to the experiment. In the post-experimental interviews subjects took pains to point out that they were not sadistic types
and that the laughter did not mean they enjoyed shocking the victim.

In the interview following the experiment subjects were asked
to indicate on a 14-point scale just how nervous or tense they felt at the
point of maximum tension. . . . [O]bedient subjects reported themselves as having been slightly more tense and nervous than the defiant
subjects at the point of maximum tension. . . .

BACKGROUND AUTHORITY

In psychophysics, animal learning, and other branches of psychology, the fact that measures are obtained at one institution rather than another is irrelevant to the interpretation of the findings, so long as the technical facilities for measurement are adequate and the operations are carried out with competence.

But it cannot be assumed that this holds true for the present study. The effectiveness of the experimenter's commands may depend in an important way on the larger institutional context in which they are issued. The experiments described thus far were conducted at Yale University, an organization which most subjects regarded with respect and sometimes awe. In post-experimental interviews several participants remarked that the locale and sponsorship of the study gave them confidence in the integrity, competence, and benign purposes of the personnel; many indicated that they would not have shocked the learner if the experiments had been done elswhere.

This issue of background authority seemed to us important for an interpretation of the results that had been obtained thus far; moreover it is highly relevant to any comprehensive theory of human obedience. Consider, for example, how closely our compliance with the imperatives of others is tied to particular institutions and locales in our day-to-day activities. On request, we expose our throats to a man with a razor blade in the barber shop, but would not do so in a shoe store; in the latter setting we willingly follow the clerk's request to stand in our stockinged feet, but resist the command in a bank. . . . *One must always question the relationship of obedience to a person's sense of the context in which he is operating.*

To explore the problem we moved our apparatus to an office building in industrial Bridgeport and replicated experimental conditions, without any visible tie to the university. . . . The experiments were conducted in a three-room office suite in a somewhat run-down commercial building located in the downtown shopping area. The laboratory was sparsely furnished, though clean, and marginally respectable in appearance. When subjects inquired about professional affiliations, they were informed only that we were a private firm conducting research for industry. . . .

As it turned out, the level of obedience in Bridgeport, although somewhat reduced, was not significantly lower than that obtained at Yale. A large proportion of the Bridgeport subjects were fully obedient to the experimenter's commands (48 percent of the Bridgeport subjects delivered the maximum shock *vs.* 65 percent in the corresponding condition at Yale). . . .

LEVELS OF OBEDIENCE AND DEFIANCE

. . . The proportion of obedient subjects greatly exceeded the expectations of the experimenter and his colleagues. At the outset, we had conjectured that subjects would not, in general, go above the level of "Strong Shock." In practice, many subjects were willing to administer the most extreme shocks available when commanded by the ex-

402 perimenter. For some subjects the experiment provides an occasion for aggressive release. And for others it demonstrates the extent to which obedient dispositions are deeply ingrained, and are engaged irrespective of their consequences for others. Yet this is not the whole story. Somehow, the subject becomes implicated in a situation from which he cannot disengage himself. . . .

In Figure 1, we compare the predictions of forty psychiatrists at a leading medical school with the actual performance of subjects in the experiment. The psychiatrists predicted that most subjects would not go beyond the tenth shock level (150 volts; at this point the victim makes his first explicit demand to be freed). They further predicted that by the twentieth shock level (300 volts; the victim refuses to answer) 3.73 percent of the subjects would still be obedient; and that only a little over one-tenth of one percent of the subjects would administer the highest shock on the board. But, as the graph indicates, the obtained behavior was very different. Sixty-two percent of the subjects obeyed the experimenter's commands fully. Between expectation and occurrence there is a whopping discrepancy.

Why did the psychiatrists underestimate the level of obedience? Possibly, because their predictions were based on an inadequate conception of the determinants of human action, a conception that focuses on motives *in vacuo*. This orientation may be entirely adequate for the repair of bruised impulses as revealed on the psychiatrist's couch, but as soon as our interest turns to action in larger settings, attention must be paid to the situations in which motives are expressed. A situation exerts an important press on the individual. It exercises constraints and may provide push. In certain circumstances it is not so much the kind of person a man is, as the kind of situation in which he is placed, that determines his actions.

Figure 1. Predicted and Obtained Behavior in Voice Feedback

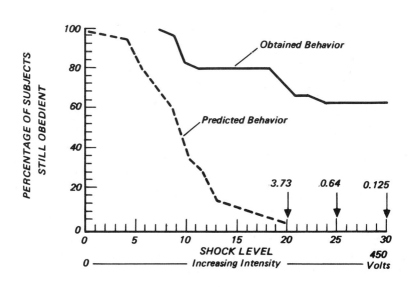

Many people, not knowing much about the experiment, claim that subjects who go to the end of the board are sadistic. Nothing could be more foolish as an overall characterization of these persons. It is like saying that a person thrown into a swift-flowing stream is necessarily a fast swimmer, or that he has great stamina because he moves so rapidly relative to the bank. The context of action must always be considered. The individual, upon entering the laboratory, becomes integrated into a situation that carries its own momentum. The subject's problem then is how to become disengaged from a situation which is moving in an altogether ugly direction.

The fact that disengagement is so difficult testifies to the potency of the forces that keep the subject at the control board. Are these forces to be conceptualized as individual motives and expressed in the language of personality dynamics, or are they to be seen as the effects of social structure and pressures arising from the situational field?

A full understanding of the subject's action will, I feel, require that both perspectives be adopted. The person brings to the laboratory enduring dipositions toward authority and aggression, and at the same time he becomes enmeshed in a social structure that is no less an objective fact of the case. . . .

But whatever the motives involved—and it is far from certain that they can ever be known—action may be studied as a direct function of the situation in which it occurs. This has been the approach of the present study, where we sought to plot behavioral regularities against manipulated properties of the social field. Ultimately, social psychology would like to have a compelling *theory of situations* which will, first, present a language in terms of which situations can be defined; proceed to a typology of situations; and then point to the manner in which definable properties of situations are transformed into psychological forces in the individual.

POSTSCRIPT

. . . With numbing regularity good people were seen to knuckle under the demands of authority and perform actions that were callous and severe. Men who are in everyday life responsible and decent were seduced by the trappings of authority, by the control of their perceptions, and by the uncritical acceptance of the experimenter's definition of the situation, into performing harsh acts. . . .

The results, as seen and felt in the laboratory, are to this author disturbing. They raise the possibility that human nature, or—more specifically—the kind of character produced in American democratic society, cannot be counted on to insulate its citizens from brutality and inhumane treatment at the direction of malevolent authority . . .

In an article titled "The Dangers of Obedience," Harold J. Laski (1929) wrote:

. . . civilization means, above all, an unwillingness to inflict unnecessary pain. Within the ambit of that definition, those of us who heedlessly accept the commands of authority cannot yet claim to be civilized men.

. . . Our business, if we desire to live a life not utterly devoid of mean-

404

ing and significance, is to accept nothing which contradicts our basic experience merely because it comes to us from tradition or convention or authority. It may well be that we shall be wrong; but our self-expression is thwarted at the root unless the certainties we are asked to accept coincide with the certainties we experience. That is why the condition of freedom in any state is always a widespread and consistent skepticism of the canons upon which power insists.

NOTES

1. It consisted of an extended discussion with the experimenter and, of equal importance, a friendly reconciliation with the victim. It is made clear that the victim did not receive painful electric shocks. After the completion of the experimental series, subjects were sent a detailed report of the results and full purposes of the experimental program. A formal assessment of this procedure points to its overall effectiveness. Of the subjects, 83.7 percent indicated that they were glad to have taken part in the study; 15.1 percent reported neutral feelings; and 1.3 percent stated that they were sorry to have participated. A large number of subjects spontaneously requested that they be used in further experimentation. Four fifths of the subjects felt that more experiments of this sort should be carried out, and 74 percent indicated that they had learned something of personal importance as a result of being in the study. Furthermore, a university psychiatrist, experienced in outpatient treatment, interviewed a sample of experimental subjects with the aim of uncovering possible injurious effects resulting from participation. No such effects were in evidence. Indeed, subjects typically felt that their participation was instructive and enriching.

2. It is difficult to convey on the printed page the full tenor of the victim's responses, for we have no adequate notation for vocal intensity, timing, and general qualities of delivery. Yet these features are crucial to producing the effect of an increasingly severe reaction to mounting voltage levels. (They can be communicated fully only by sending interested parties the recorded tapes.) In general terms, however, the victim indicates no discomfort until the 75-volt shock is administerd, at which time time there is a light grunt in response to the punishment. Similar reactions follow the 90- and 105-volt shocks, and at 120 volts the victim shouts to the experimenter that the shocks are becoming painful. Painful groans are heard on administration of the 135-volt shock, and at 150 volts the victim cries out, "Experimenter, get me out of here! I won't be in the experiment any more! I refuse to go on!" Cries of this type continue with generally rising intensity, so that at 180 volts the victim cries out, "I can't stand the pain," and by 270 volts his response to the shock is definitely an agonized scream. Throughout, he insists that he be let out of the experiment. At 300 volts the victim shouts in desperation that he will no longer provide answers to the memory test; and at 315 volts, after a violent scream, he reaffirms with vehemence that he is no longer a participant. From this point on, he provides no answers, but shrieks in agony whenever a shock is administered; this continues through 450 volts. Of course, many subjects will have broken off before this point.

Liberating Effects of Group Pressure

*As Hollander and Willis (1967) point out, the overwhelming
preoccupation of social psychologists has been to study the
negative effects of group pressure—i.e., conformity—where the
individual changes his opinion so that it is more in line with
that of the group. In this experiment, Milgram utilizes essentially the same situation as in his obedience study except
that this time he introduces experimental stooges who
at pre-arranged times refuse to continue participating in
the experiment. In this way, Milgram pits the influence
of a disobedient peer group against the power of the legitimate authority (the experimenter) to find out once again how
obedient individual subjects will be. The section closes
with this study because it points us in a direction sorely
neglected by students of social influence—namely the identification of conditions under which subjects will not conform
but will disobey.*

In laboratory research, the effect of group pressure has most often
been studied in its negative aspect; the conspiratorial group is shown
to limit, constrain, and distort the individual's responses (Asch, 1951;
Blake & Brehm, 1954; Milgram, 1964). Edifying effects of the group,
although acknowledged, have rarely been demonstrated with the clarity and force of its destructive potential. Particularly in those areas
in which a morally relevant choice is at issue, experimentalists typically
examine pressures that diminish the scope of individual action. They
have neglected effects that enhance the individual's sense of worth,
enlarge the possibilities for action, and help the subject resolve conflicting feelings in a direction congruent with his ideals and values.
Although in everyday life occasions arise when conformity to group
pressures is constructive, in the laboratory "thinking and investigation
have concentrated almost obsessively on conformity in its most sterile
forms [Asch, 1959].[1]

There are technical difficulties to demonstrating the value enhancing potential of group pressure. They concern the nature of the
base line from which the group effect is to be measured. The problem
is that the experimental subject ordinarily acts in a manner that is socially appropriate. If he has come to the laboratory to participate in
a study on the perception of lines, he will generally report what he
sees in an honest manner. If one wishes to show the effects of group
influence by producing a change in his performance, the only direction open to change is that of creating some deficiency in his performance, which can then be attributed to group influences.... The
experimental problem for any study of *constructive* conformity is to
create a situation in which undesirable behavior occurs with regular-

From Stanley Milgram, "Liberating Effects of Group Pressure," *Journal of
Personality and Social Psychology* 1 (1965): 127–34. Reprinted by permission
of the author and the American Psychological Association.

406   ity and then to see whether group pressure can be applied effectively in the direction of a valued behavior outcome.

EXPERIMENT 1: BASE-LINE CONDITION

A technique for the study of destructive obedience (Milgram, 1963, 1965) generates the required base line. In this situation a subject is ordered to give increasingly more severe punishment to a person. Despite the apparent discomfort, cries, and vehement protests of the victim, the experimenter instructs the subject to continue stepping up the shock level.

Results and Discussion

In this situation a subject is instructed to perform acts that are in some sense incompatible with his normal standards of behavior. In the face of the vehement protests of an innocent individual, many subjects refuse to carry out the experimenter's orders to continue with the shock procedure. They reject the role assignment of *experimental subject*, assert themselves as persons, and are unwilling to perform actions that violate personal standards of conduct. . . . Fourteen of the 40 subjects withdraw from the experiment at some point before the completion of the command series.

The majority of subjects, however, comply fully with the experimenter's commands, despite the acute discomfort they often experience in connection with shocking the victim. Typically these obedient subjects report that they do not wish to hurt the victim, but they feel obligated to follow the orders of the experimenter. On questioning they often state that it would have been "better" not to have shocked the victim at the highest voltage levels. . . .

There is additional evidence that, in shocking the victim to the end of the command series, subjects are engaging in behavior which they disvalue and see as antithetical to personal and social ideals:

Spontaneous shock levels

In an experimental control reported elsewhere (Milgram, 1964), subjects administer any voltage level they wish in the absence of group or authoritarian pressure. Under this condition the mean maximum shock for 40 subjects is 82.5 volts (level=5.50); in contrast, under command of the experimenter (in the base-line condition described above) the mean maximum shock is 368.25 volts (level= 24.55). When left on their own, subjects administer far lower shock levels than when under command.

Self image

When persons who have not performed in the experiment are provided with a description of the experimental situation, and are asked to predict their own performance, almost all subjects see themselves as defying the experimenter at some point in the command series. Moreover, they justify their hypothetical behavior in terms of positive qualities of character, employing such statements as "I'm not the kind of person who is willing to hurt others even for the cause of science.". . .

Moral judgment

Twenty undergraduates were asked to render a moral judgment on the issue of obeying or disobeying the experimenter. . . .

There is a clear consensus that the only behavior consistent with social values and individual conscience is to defy the experimenter at some point before the completion of the command series. Yet there is a marked discrepancy between this value judgment and the actual performance of subjects in the laboratory. Despite their protests and obvious conflict in shocking the victim, a substantial number of subjects are unable to defy the experimenter's authority, and proceed to administer the highest shock levels commanded by him.

EXPERIMENT II: GROUPS FOR DISOBEDIENCE

We may now examine in what degree group influence can release the subject from authoritarian control, and allow him to act in a direction congruent with his values and personal standards.

The strategy is to replicate Experiment I, but with this difference: the subject is placed in the midst of two peers who defy the experimenter and refuse to punish the victim against his will. In what degree will the pressure created by their action affect the naive subject's behavior?

Technique

Forty fresh subjects were studied in this condition. The procedure is identical to Experiment I with these exceptions: Four persons appear at the laboratory to take part in an experiment on "the effects of collective teaching and punishment on memory and learning." Three subjects are confederates of the experimenter and one is a naive subject. The experimenter explains that three teachers and one learner are to be used in the study, and by means of a rigged drawing, the naive subject is assigned the position of Teacher 3. The roles of Teacher 1, Teacher 2, and learner are filled by the confederates. The learner is strapped into the electric chair and the three teachers are seated before the shock generator. Teacher 1 is told to read the list of word pairs, Teacher 2 informs the subject if he is correct or incorrect in his answers, and Teacher 3 (the naive subject) administers punishment. As in Experiment I, the subjects are instructed to raise the shock level one step each time the learner makes an error. (More detailed descriptions of the group technique can be found in Milgram, 1964.)

Behavior of Confederates

The confederates comply with the experimenter through the 150-volt shock. After the 150-volt level is administered Teacher 1 informs the experimenter that he does not wish to participate further, because of the learner's complaints. (It is at the 150-volt shock level that the learner makes his first vehement protest.) The experimenter insists that the subject continue. However, Teacher 1 is not swayed by the experimenter's commands, gets up from his chair in front of the shock generator, and takes a seat in another part of the room. Since the experimenter's efforts to get the subject to return to the generator are futile, the experimenter instructs the remaining two subjects to continue with the experiment. Teacher 3 (the naive subject) is to handle the reading of word pairs, in addition to his regular job of administering electric shock to the learner.

After Shock Level 14 (210 volts) is administered, Teacher 2, expressing concern for the learner, refuses to participate further. The experimenter makes strong efforts to have him continue, but he too leaves his chair in front of the generator and seats himself at an opposite corner of the room saying "I'm willing to answer any of your questions, but I'm not willing to shock that man against his will; I'll have no part of it.

At this point the naive subject is seated alone in front of the shock generator. He has witnessed the defiant actions of two peers. The experimenter orders the naive subject to continue with the experimental procedure by himself, indicating that it is essential that the experiment be completed.

Results and Discussion

... Comparing the proportion of obedient to defiant subjects in Experiments I and II, we see that the effect of the confederates' pressure was substantial. In Experiment I, 26 subjects proceeded to the end of the command series; less than one-sixth of this number obeyed fully in the group setting (obedient versus defiant subjects $\chi^2=25.81$, $df=1$, $p<.001$). These results are presented graphically in Figure 1. The mean maximum shock in Experiment II (16.45) was also significantly lower than in Experiment I (24.55, $p<.001$).[2]

After Shock Level 14 the second confederate defies the experimenter. Before Level 15 is administered, 25 naive subjects have followed the defiant group, while at the corresponding point in Experiment I only 8 subjects have refused to follow the experimenter's orders. The confederates appear to exert some influence however, even on those

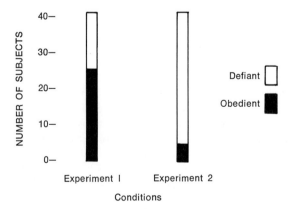

Figure 1. Proportion of Obedient and Defiant Subjects in Experiments I and II

subjects who do not follow them immediately. Between Voltage Levels 17 and 29, 11 subjects in Experiment II break off, while only 6 subjects do so in Experiment I.

In sum, in the group setting 36 of the 40 subjects defy the experimenter while the corresponding number in the absence of group pressure is 14. The effects of peer rebellion are most impressive in undercutting the experimenter's authority. Indeed, of the score of experimental variations completed in the Yale study on obedience none was so effective in undermining the experimenter's authority as the manipulation reported here.

How should we account for the powerful effect of the experimental manipulation? It is probable that in Experiment I many subjects come near to performing the defiant action but cannot quite bring themselves to the point of disobedience. The additional pressure of the group members leads to an increment in the forces oriented toward defiance; the increment is of sufficient strength so that, in combination with pressures for defiance already present, many subjects are carried over the threshold of disobedience. . . .

Reactions to the confederates

The reactions of naive subjects to the defiant confederates varied considerably and were in part dependent on the exact point where the subject defied the experimenter. A subject who quit simultaneously with the first confederate stated, "Well, I was already thinking about quitting when the guy broke off." Most defiant subjects praised the confederates with such statements as "I thought they were men of good character, yes I do. When the victim said 'Stop,' they stopped (Shock Level 11)."[3] "I think they were very sympathetic people . . . and they were totally unaware of what was in store for them (Shock Level 14)."

A subject who defied the experimenter at Level 21 qualified his approval: "Well I think they should continue a little further, but I don't blame them for backing out when they did."

A few subjects acknowledged the importance of the confederates in leading to their own defiance: "The thought of stopping didn't enter my mind until it was put there by the other two (Shock Level 14)." "The reason I quit was that I did not wish to seem callous and cruel in the eyes of the other two men who had already refused to go on with the experiment (Shock Level 14). The majority of subjects, however, denied that the confederates' action was the critical factor in their own defiance.[4]

The fact that obedient subjects failed to follow the defiant group should not suggest that they did not feel the pressure of the confederates' action. One obedient subject stated:

I felt that I would just look like a real Simon Legree to these guys if I just went on coolly and just kept administering lashes. I thought they reacted normally, and the first thing that came to my mind was to react as they did. But I didn't, because if they reacted normally, and stopped the experiment, and I did the same, I don't know how many months and days you'd have to continue before you got done.

410   Thus this subject felt the burden of the group judgment, but sensed
that in the light of two defections he had a special obligation to help
the experimenter complete his work. Another obedient subject, when
asked about the nervousness he displayed in the experiment, replied:

> I think it was primarily because of their actions. Momentarily I was
> ready to go along with them. Then suddenly I felt that they were just
> being ridiculous. What was I doing following the crowd? ... They
> certainly had a right to stop, but I felt they lost all control of themselves.

And a third obedient subject criticized the confederates more directly,
stating:

> I don't think they should have quit. They came here for an experiment,
> and I think they should have stuck with it.

A closer analysis of the experimental situation points to a number of specific factors that may contribute to the group's effectiveness:

1. The peers instill in the subject the *idea* of defying the experimenter. It may not have occurred to some subjects as
   a response possibility.
2. The lone subject has no way of knowing whether, in defying the experimenter, he is performing in a bizarre manner or whether this action is a common occurrence in the
   laboratory. The two examples of disobedience he sees suggest that defiance is a natural reaction to the situation.
3. The reactions of the defiant confederates define the act of
   shocking the victim as improper. They provide social confirmation to the naïve subject's suspicion that it is wrong
   to punish a man against his will, even in the context of a
   psychological experiment.
4. The defiant confederates remain in the laboratory even
   after withdrawing from the experiment (they have agreed
   to answer post-experimental questions). Each additional
   shock administered by the naïve subject now carries with
   it a measure of social disapproval from the two confederates.
5. As long as the two confederates participate in the experimental procedure there is a dispersion of responsibility
   among the group members for shocking the vicitim. As the
   confederates withdraw, responsibility becomes focused onto
   the naïve subject.[5]
6. The naïve subject is a witness to two instances of disobedience and observes the *consequences* of defying the experimenter to be minimal.
7. There is identification with the disobedient confederates
   and the possibility of falling back on them for social support when defying the experimenter.
8. Additionally, the experimenter's power may be diminished
   by the very fact of failing to keep the two confederates
   in line, following the general rule that every failure of
   authority to exact compliance to its command weakens the
   perceived power of the authority (Homans, 1961).

Hypothesis of Arbitrary Direction of Group Effects **411**

The results examined thus far show that group influence serves to liberate individuals effectively from submission to destructive commands. There are some who will take this to mean that the direction of group influence is arbitrary, that it can be oriented toward destructive or constructive ends with equal impact, and that group pressure need merely be inserted into a social situation on one side of a standard or the other in order to induce movement in the desired direction. . . .

A competing view would be that the direction of possible influence of a group is not arbitrary, but is highly dependent on the general structure of the situation in which influence is attempted.

To examine this issue we need to undertake a further experimental variation, one in which the group forces are thrown on the side of the experimenter, rather than directed against him. The idea is simply to have the members of the group reinforce the experimenter's commands by following them unfailingly, thus adding peer pressures to those originating in the experimenter's commands.

EXPERIMENT III: OBEDIENT GROUPS

Forty fresh subjects, matched to the subjects in Experiments I and II for sex, age, and occupational status, were employed in this condition. The procedure was identical to that followed in Experiment II with this exception: at all times the two confederates followed the commands of the experimenter; at no point did they object to carrying out the experimental instructions. Nor did they show sympathy for or comment on the discomfort of the victim. If a subject attempted to break off they allowed the experimenter primary responsibility for keeping him in line, but contributed background support for the experimenter; they indicated their disapproval of the naïve subject's attempts to leave the experiment with such remarks as: "You can't quit *now*; this experiment has got to get done." As in Experiment II the naïve subject was seated between the two confederates, and in his role of Teacher 3, administered the shocks to the victim.

Results and Discussion

The results show that the obedient group had very little effect on the overall performance of subjects. In Experiment I, 26 of the 40 subjects complied fully with the experimenter's commands; in the present condition this figure is increased but 3, yielding a total of 29 obedient subjects. This increase falls far short of statistical significance ($\chi^2=.52$, $df=1$, $p>.50$). Nor is the difference in mean maximum shocks statistically reliable. The failure of the manipulation to produce a significant change cannot be attributed to a ceiling artifact since an obedient shift of even 8 of the 14 defiant subjects would yield the .05 significance level by chi square.

Why the lack of change when we know that group pressure often exerts powerful effects? One interpretation is that the authoritarian pressure already present in Experiment I has preempted subjects who would have submitted to group pressures. Conceivably, the subjects who are fully obedient in Experiment I are precisely those who would

412

be susceptible to group forces, while those who resisted authoritarian pressure were also immune to the pressure of the obedient confederates. The pressures applied in Experiment III do not show an effect because they overlap with other pressures having the same direction and present in Experiment I; all persons responsive to the initial pressure have already been moved to the obedient criterion in Experiment I. This possibility seems obvious enough in the present study. Yet every other situation in which group pressure is exerted also possesses a field structure (a particular arrangement of stimulus, motive, and social factors) that limits and controls potential influence within that field.[6] Some structures allow group influence to be exerted in one direction but not another. Seen in this light, the hypothesis of the arbitrary direction of group effects is inadequate.

In the present study Experiment I defines the initial field: the insertion of group pressure in a direction opposite to that of the experimenter's commands (Experiment II) produces a powerful shift toward the group. Changing the direction of each group movement (Experiment III) does not yield a comparable shift in the subject's performance. The group success in one case and failure in another can be traced directly to the configuration of motive and social forces operative in the starting situation (Experiment I).

Given any social situation, the strength and direction of potential group influence is predetermined by existing conditions. We need to examine the variety of field structures that typify social situations and the manner in which each controls the pattern of potential influence.

NOTES

1. Exceptions become more numerous in moving from the experimental domain to the practice of group therapy and training groups. And surely the *philosophy* of group dynamics stresses the productive possibilities inherent in groups (Cartwright & Zander, 1960).

2. Of course the mean maximum shock in the experimental condition is tied to the precise point in the voltage series where the confederates' break-off is staged. In this experiment it is not until Level 14 that both confederates have defied the experimenter.

3. Numerals in parentheses indicate the break-off point of the subject quoted.

4. Twenty-seven of the defiant subjects stated that they would have broken off without the benefit of the confederates' example: four subjects definitely acknowledged the confederates' rebellion as the critical factor in their own defiance. The remaining defiant subjects were undecided on this issue. In general, then, subjects underestimate the degree to which their defiant actions are dependent on group support.

5. See Wallach, Kogan & Bem (1962) for treatment of this concept dealing with risk taking.

6. See, for example, the study of Jones, Wells, & Torrey (1958). Starting with the Asch situation they show that through feedback, the experimenter can foster greater independence in the subject, but not significantly greater yielding to the erring majority. Here, too, an initial field structure limits the direction of influence attempts.

HARRY H. L. KITANO   **413**

The Wartime Evacuation

Many of the adverse conditions of Japanese immigration, however, appear no different from those facing other immigrant groups. In common with the others, most Japanese came to the United States during the great industrial and agricultural expansion that took place between the end of the Civil War and the beginning of World War I. Most were poor and had little capital to set up their own enterprises. Most were minimally educated, so that entrance into professions and fields of skilled labor was denied them. The majority could not communicate in English. Further, most Japanese had unrealistic ideas about America; many expected to make their fortunes and return to the old country in a short period of time. They were often attacked by nativist and racist groups and were forced to settle in the slums. Inevitably they started at the bottom of the occupational ladder, and felt too socially inferior to seek much intercourse with the majority group. But as Daniels indicates, these were the conditions facing most newcomers to America.[1] A comparison of such scars is a standoff.

There are, however, several factors that make an "ideal" immigrant—ideal in that he epitomizes the expectations of influential segments of the core culture. In most cases, he should be white, Anglo-Saxon, Protestant, and come from a nation that has been friendly to the United States. It is presumed that such an immigrant adjusts, adapts, acculturates, and merges into the "melting pot" with a minimum of difficulty. From this perspective, the Japanese immigrant represented the opposite in every respect. He was nonwhite, Oriental, non-Christian, and was from a nation that would eventually be engaged in a full-scale war against the United States. It was no wonder that life in the United States was one of continuous hardship and discrimination. It can truly be said that he came to the wrong country and the wrong state (California) at the wrong time (immediately after the Chinese "problem"), with the wrong race and skin color, with the wrong religion, and from the wrong country.

MOUNTING ANTAGONISM

The Japanese attack on Pearl Harbor on December 7, 1941, provided impetus for the "final victory" for forces opposing the Japanese-American group. Nevertheless, plans for a final solution were never that clear. Instead, the months after the Japanese attack and the ensuing declaration of war were troubled and confusing ones. The question of what was to be done with the Japanese in the United States can probably be best understood in the context of this confusion, since even today it is difficult to ascertain accurately the roles of various in-

Harry H. L. Kitano, *Japanese Americans: The Evolution of a Subculture*, © 1969. Reprinted by permission of Prentice-Hall, Inc., Englewood Cliffs, New Jersey.

414   dividuals, officials, and institutions in relation to the decision to evacuate the Japanese from the West Coast.

Immediately after Pearl Harbor, selected enemy aliens, including 2,192 Japanese, were arrested by the FBI. Curfew regulations and
other precautions were also instituted. These steps might have been
sufficient for protective purposes, except in light of the continued
battle between Californians and the Japanese. The Hearst papers presented the issue vigorously; for example, the *Los Angeles Examiner*
on December 16, 1941, led off with the headline, "Fifth Column Treachery Told," using a quotation from Secretary of the Navy Knox, but
omitting the fact that Knox was discussing only rumors against the
Japanese. The *San Francisco Examiner* picked up the cry, then the
American Legion, then the Chambers of Commerce, then the farm
groups, and finally the politicians—"all Japanese are traitors."

Evidence to the contrary was ignored. Bill Henry, conservative
columnist for the *Los Angeles Times*, wrote on December 26, 1942:

The FBI chief says the yarns about the dead Jap flyers with McKinley
High School [Honolulu] rings on their fingers, the stories of the arrows
in the cane fields pointing towards Pearl Harbor, and the yarns about Jap
vegetable trucks blocking the roadway to Pearl Harbor that day are all
unadulterated bunk.

But the rumors continued to fly and were picked up on a national level. On January 29, 1942, Henry McLemore, a syndicated
Hearst columnist wrote:

I am for the immediate removal of every Japanese on the West Coast
to a point deep in the interior . . . let 'em be pinched, hurt, hungry.
Personally, I hate Japanese. And that goes for all of them.

Austin Anson of the Grower-Shippers Association in Salinas,
writing in the *Saturday Evening Post* of May 9, 1942, said:

If all the Japs were removed tomorrow, we'd never miss them . . . because the white farmer can take over and produce everything the Jap
grows, and we don't want them back when the war ends either.

The Japanese handicaps of race and nationality, compounded
by social and legal discrimination, isolated ghetto lives, and the out-
break of war, were even too much for the spirit of American democracy and fair play. Very few Caucasians really knew the Japanese
Americans; their general ignorance about this group helped to foster
and maintain negative stereotypes. The range of those attacking the
Japanese was truly remarkable—the American Legion, the State Federation of Labor, the Native Sons of the Golden West, the California
State Grange, the leftist parties, and individuals such as then California Attorney General Earl Warren and "liberal" columnist Walter
Lippmann, as well as the usual racists. The major newspapers in California kept up a constant attack and were joined by local and national
magazines. Also as damaging to the future of the Japanese was the
silence of the standard liberal organizations. Only some Quaker groups

and the American Civil Liberties Union (ACLU) provided visible **415**
support.

A SMOOTH EVACUATION

On January 29, 1942, the first of a series of orders by U.S. Attorney
General Francis Biddle established security areas along the Pacific
Coast that required the removal of all enemy aliens from these areas.
On February 13, a West Coast Congressional delegation wrote to President
Roosevelt urging immediate evacuation of all Japanese, whether
citizens or aliens, from California, Oregon, and Washington, and on
February 19, 1942, President Roosevelt signed Executive Order 9066,
which (1) designated military areas where military commanders
could exclude persons, and (2) authorized the building of "relocation"
camps to house those people excluded. This set the stage for the evacuation
of more than 100,000 Japanese, both citizens and aliens, from
the West Coast.

On March 2, 1942, General John De Witt, then Commander
in charge of the Western Defense Area, issued an order to evacuate
all persons of Japanese ancestry (defined as children with as little as
$1/8$ Japanese blood), from the Western half of the three Pacific Coast
States and the southern third of Arizona. More than 110,000 of the
126,000 Japanese in the United States were affected by the order. Of
this group, two-thirds were United States citizens.

On March 22, the first large contingent of Japanese, both aliens
and citizens were moved from Los Angeles to the Manzanar Assembly
Center in California. Prior to this, there was initial governmental encouragement
of voluntary movement away from the designated strategic
areas, followed by an order on March 27 to halt voluntary emigration.

From then on, all evacuation procedures were controlled by
the Army, and by August 7, 1942, the more than 110,000 West Coast
Japanese had been removed from their homes. The evacuation proceeded
in two stages—first into temporary Assembly Centers at such
places as the Tanforan and Santa Anita racetracks in California (under
control of the Army and the Wartime Civilian Control Agency), and
then to more permanent camps under the jurisdiction of the War
Relocation Authority (WRA). The permanent camps and their listed
capacities were:

California:	Manzanar (10,000)
	Tule Lake (16,000)
Arizona:	Poston (20,000)
	Gila River (15,000)
Idaho:	Minidoka (10,000)
Wyoming:	Heart Mountain (10,000)
Colorado:	Granada (8,000)
Utah:	Topaz (10,000)
Arkansas:	Rohwer (10,000)
	Jerome (10,000)

By November 3, 1942, the transfer from Army to WRA jurisdiction and from the temporary assembly centers to the permanent camps was complete.

The evacuation was rapid, smooth, and efficient, primarily because of the cooperativeness of the Japanese population, who responded to the posted notices to register, to assemble voluntarily on time at designated points, and to follow all orders. The manner in which the Japanese obediently marched to the trains and busses hauling them to camp presaged a conflict-free camp life.

The Santa Anita Riot

But there was some conflict. The writer, then an evacuated high school student, remembers one such incident. At the Santa Anita Assembly Center, a riot began in response to rumors that a group of evacuee policemen was illegally confiscating electrical appliances and other material for personal use. During this direct confrontation between those interned and those representing the United States Government, there were cries of *"Ko-ro-se"* ("Kill them!") and *"Inu!"* ("Dog"). A crowd of around 2,000 Japanese, including large numbers of teenagers, ran aimlessly and wildly about, rumors flew, property was destroyed, and finally an accused policeman was set upon during a routine inspection and badly beaten. The incident was controlled through the intervention of 200 Army MPs, installation of martial law, and stricter security. It was significant that the policeman was non-Caucasian (part Korean), since in most instances of conflict throughout the evacuation period Japanese turned on other Japanese (e.g., generation against generation, or pro-American against anti-American Japanese) rather than the Caucasian administrators.

A letter written by one of the evacuees dated August 9, 1942, illustrates the significance of this riot to one observer:

> Although the censored version of the "rioting" in the newspapers gives a black eye to Center residents by not explaining the extenuating circumstances under which the uprising arose, it seems to have raised their spirits in anticipation of brighter prospects to come. The residents now feel that they shouldn't allow themselves to be imposed upon too much, that occasionally they should assert their rights and not to lie supinely on their backs when injustice is being done.[2]

CONCENTRATION CAMPS AND THEIR EFFECTS

It is often asked if the war relocation camps were concentration camps. In most senses they were. The writer remembers when, on his second day in Topaz, he walked past the barbed-wire boundaries with a group of his high school friends, in a typically adolescent attempt to test established limits—despite the fact that the camp was located in the middle of a desert and there was virtually no place to go. After walking about fifty yards past a break in the wired fence, we were surrounded by military policemen with drawn guns, interrogated, our names recorded, warned, loaded on jeeps, and returned to camp. It was a frightening and sobering experience.

In other cases, Military Police actually shot evacuees who went beyond the fences, and the barbed wire and guard towers characteristic of concentration camps were always present.[3]

But there were important differences. One of the most important differences between the centers and concentration camps lay in the process of checking, clearing, and then releasing Japanese to areas of the United States away from the Western Defense Area. Some were students going to college, others were in search of employment. By the end of 1943, an estimated 35,000 evacuees, primarily Nisei, were attempting to establish themselves in the Midwest and East. It was the second voluntary emigration for the Japanese—in some ways resembling the first migration of the Issei from Japan. The immigrants, too, were a young, highly motivated group and were drawn primarily from those who could not stand the confines of barracks life. They characteristically held high expectations for upward mobility, either through further education or employment. Most of them presented a positive picture to those Americans who had never been in contact with the group before and they carried on the pattern of selective migration that their Issei fathers had laid down a generation before.[4]

The benefits worked both ways. Most of the group had an opportunity to see themselves as Japanese in new situations; being a Japanese in Chicago was often different from being a Japanese in California, and the experience greatly broadened the horizons of a large group of Nisei.

Conversely, Americans from other parts of the country, coming into contact for the first time with Japanese Americans, generally found themselves impressed with and well disposed toward this intelligent, ambitious, and highly motivated group.

For those forced to remain in the camps, life was not so promising. Daily existence was desultory, monotonous, and self-defeating. Dillon Meyer, Director of the camps wrote:

[Being] cut off from the main currents of American life does things to people. It saps the initiative, weakens the instincts of human dignity and freedom, creates doubts, misgivings and tensions. Even more important, the mere act of putting people in camps and keeping them there establishes precedents which are not healthy or hopeful for a democratic nation. Over the past three years, we have watched some of these formerly enterprising energetic people become steadily obsessed with feelings of hopelessness, personal insecurity and inertia.[5]

Obviously both positive and negative features of the evacuation must be evaluated. But the most relevant point for our purpose is that the wartime evacuation aided the acculturation of the Japanese, especially the Nisei. New exposure, new opportunities, the dissolution of old institutions and structures, and life away from the ghetto hastened change.

Some effects were felt immediately. The ghettos and "Jap Towns" in coastal cities were broken up, replaced by tar-paper barracks and community mess halls in the interiors of California, Arizona, Utah, Wyoming, Idaho, Colorado, and Arkansas. The invisible walls erected by housing discrimination had now become highly visible barbed-wire fences and guard towers.

Many Japanese families were ruined economically. Their property had been lost, stolen, sold, or confiscated. Camp jobs paid only 16 to 19 dollars a month, so there was no hope of savings or financial recovery at this time. Such a bleak outlook in turn caused unmeasurable damage to the self-respect of a proud independent group of people.

Financial ruin, together with the camp policies of using American citizens (Nisei) in positions of camp responsibility, worked to shift power and influence away from the Issei and onto the shoulders of the Nisei. This exerted a definite influence on the structure of the Japanese family, and operated to free the Nisei from Issei influence.

The family structure was reordered, too, by the physical conditions of camp life. Community mess halls and other facilities required certain basic changes in roles and expectations. A young father complained:

The worst part of it is not being able to bring up the baby right. He's just 18 months. . . . Naturally he cries some. If you were living alone in your own home, you could let him cry when he did it and not spoil him. But here you've got to pay attention to it. You don't feel like letting him bother the people on the other side of the partition. They can hear everything that goes on. We've got to shut him up some way. So you have to fuss around with his crying and pay attention to him. That's not good for the baby.

And in the mess halls, parental problems often became acute. One mother said:

My small daughter and I used to eat at a table where two little boys ate with their mothers. They had become so uncontrollable that the mothers had given up, and let them eat as they pleased. They behaved so badly that I stopped eating there . . . but my daughter was fascinated. They would come running into the mess hall and the first thing both of them did was to take off their shoes and stockings and jump up and down on the seat. Then they would start yelling for their food. . . . Now these little boys had older brothers and sisters, and if they had eaten at one table with both parents, things like that couldn't have happened, for the other children would have protested out of pride, and the father probably would have forbidden it.[7]

In general, under the influence of mess hall conditions, eating ceased to be a family affair. Mothers and small children usually ate together, but the father often ate at separate tables with other men, and older children joined peers of their own age. Thus family control and the basic discipline of comportment while eating changed character rapidly, and different family standards became merged into a sort of common mess-hall behavior. Family groups ceased to encourage the enforcement of customary family rituals associated with the mealtime gathering of the group. The social control exerted by the family under more normal circumstances seemed to be loosening.

The changes also affected the roles of husband and wife. All husbands were no longer in the position of serving as the major bread-winner; in some families the wife and the children were drawing the same wage as the husband. There was an accompanying loss of prestige on the part of the husband and a gain in independence on the part of the wife and, in some cases, the children.

Immediate economic needs were not pressing; the provision of food, shelter, and minimum clothing was removed from the area of family responsibility and taken over entirely by the government. For some evacuees with higher economic aspirations, a way was open through departure from camp with government security clearance.[8] In general, the evacuation tended toward the destruction of established family patterns of behavior.

Other behavioral patterns were also changed. Riots, assaults, and other forms of violence "not typically Japanese" were now encountered for the first time in the Japanese-American group. The effects of the special situation can clearly be seen in the fact that such behavior ceased as soon as the camps were closed. For the first time, large numbers of older Japanese became recipients of formal social welfare services. Dependence on the government, a concept heretofore rare among the Japanese, assumed a major role in camp life.

On the more positive side, Japanese Americans were exposed here for the first time to an American model of a small community. Block votes, community services, community decisions, and the like, provided a taste of "ideal" American community democracy, the likes of which few Americans have actually ever seen.

The camp schools were uneven in quality. For example, the writer's high school in Topaz, Utah, was oriented toward state standards of education, but some courses were taught by local evacuees who were not yet college graduates, and others were taught by Caucasian Ph.D.'s (among them conscientious objectors). All typical high school activities—a yearbook, football and basketball teams, cheerleaders, student body organization, scholarship society—were available, and, for the first time, young Nisei were able to feel themselves in the majority, and to run things. They became student body leaders, athletic, political, and social heroes—roles usually reserved for Caucasians in the everyday world.

Similarly, other community positions became available for the first time to adult Japanese. They became block leaders, firemen, policemen, foremen, supervisors, timekeepers, and almost every other type of non-administrative job was available to them. The variable of ethnicity was held constant so that competition rested primarily upon qualifications and achievement.

The evacuation forced Japanese Americans to consider carefully their nationality and their ethnic identity. They now had choices to make, choices that previously had been delayed or repressed. Were they Japanese or Americans? The decision was difficult for many Issei and Kibei, and perhaps an easier choice for Nisei, who, as a group, remained completely loyal to the United States.

The question of national identity was more easily resolved than the very personal question of ethnic identity. Fisher writes that only 2,300 of the 110,000 evacuees asked to be sent back to Japan.[9] This

420

was a surprisingly low figure from a group that might conceivably have seen little future for it in the United States.

Ethnic identity had to be faced squarely for the first time by many of the group. Prior to the evacuation, one could dream of being an "American," perhaps at the 100 per cent level, or deny that one was a hyphenated citizen. Now that they were behind barbed wire for simply having a common ancestry, many Japanese had to reevaluate their identity. The phrases, "I'm a 'bootchie' " and "I'm a Buddha-head" became popular in camp and were used to refer to being Japanese. One could be a smart Buddhahead or a dumb one, or a good-looking one or an ugly one—all the definitions referred to a common element, the ethnic identity. Fortunately, the elements of the identity were not all negative so that a reevaluation of their ancestry contained many healthy perceptions.

NOT ALL ACQUIESCED

The handful of Japanese who resisted the wartime evacuation by taking their cases to the courts eventually brought an end to the camps. In their quiet way, each of these Nisei were heroes—they faced the court decision almost alone, since many of the evacuated Japanese either did not know of their efforts or deplored the possible negative effects upon the rest of the Japanese population.

Gordon Hirabayashi, a senior-student at the University of Washington, and Minoru Yasui, a young attorney in Portland, Oregon, both challenged the evacuation orders. Hirabayashi wrote:

The violation of human personality is the violation of the most sacred thing which man owns. This order for the mass evacuation of all persons of Japanese descent denies them the right to live. It forces thousands of energetic, law-abiding individuals to exist in miserable psychological conditions and a horrible physical atmosphere. This order limits to almost full extent the creative expressions of those subjected. It kills the desire for a higher life. Hope for the future is exterminated. Human personalities are poisoned. . . . If I were to register and cooperate under these circumstances, I would be giving helpless consent to the denial of practically all of the things which give me incentive to live. I must maintain my Christian principles. I consider it my duty to maintain the democratic standards for which this nation lives. Therefore, I must refuse this order of exacution.[10]

Hirabayashi was arrested, convicted, and jailed for violating the evacuation orders. Yasui was also found guilty, fined $5,000, and sentenced to one year in jail. Subsequent appeals led to a unanimous U.S. Supreme Court ruling of June 21, 1943 which said:

We cannot close our eyes to the fact, demonstrated by experience, that in time of war, residents having ethnic affiliations with an invading enemy may be a greater source of danger than those of a different ancestry.[11]

These were words from the Supreme Court of the United States, and not from nativist or racist groups in California.

Fred Korematsu attempted a different tactic to avoid evacuation. He hoped to change his name and to alter his features.[12] But the FBI caught up with him; he was found guilty of violating the exclusion order and was given a suspended sentence and probationary status. His was a potentially difficult case—his probation meant he was under court rather than Army authority, and therefore at large. But the Army immediately threw him into an assembly center and his case was finally heard by the Supreme Court, which ruled that Korematsu was excluded not because of hostility to him or to his race but because of the war with the Japanese Empire and the military urgency of the situation. This decision was not unanimous: Justices Black, Rutledge, Reed, Douglas, Frankfurter, and Chief Justice Stone delivered the majority opinion, but Justices Murphy, Jackson, and Roberts dissented.

The most influential case in the cause of regaining Japanese-American liberty was that of Miss Mitsuye Endo of Sacramento, California. In July, 1942, she petitioned for a writ of habeas corpus, contending that her detention in camp was unlawful. She represented a test case for James Purcell, a young attorney who questioned that the War Relocation Authority had a right to detain a loyal American citizen for any of the various reasons used by the Army to justify the evacuation. Purcell carried the case to the Supreme Court, and finally, on December 18, 1944, the court ruled that Miss Endo should be given her liberty. All nine of the justices agreed that the WRA had no right to detain loyal American citizens in camps. It was no accident that, after this ruling, the commander of the Western Defense Area announced that the West Coast mass exclusion orders would be revoked, effective January 2, 1945.[13]

The Endo case and the continued success of the Pacific war meant the close of the evacuation camps before the end of 1945, and the termination of the entire program by the middle of June, 1946. Ironically, it turned out to be difficult to move some of the Japanese out of the camps. They had almost completely adapted to the closed environment. Perhaps, along with the reservation Indian, the reservation Japanese might have come into existence as one result of the Second World War.

RETURN TO THE COAST

Part of the reluctance of many evacuees to leave the camps derived from their fear of returning to their former homes and hostile neighbors. Secretary of the Interior Ickes reported that by May 14, 1945, there had been 24 incidents of terrorism and violence—15 shooting attacks, 1 attempted dynamiting, 2 arson cases, and 5 threatening visits.[14]

An especially notorious event occurred in Hood River, Oregon, about this time. The local American Legion attempted to exclude all Nisei soldiers' names from the "honor roll." They removed 16 Japanese names—of these, 14 had served overseas, two had been killed in action against the Nazis, ten had been awarded the Purple Heart, one was to die in Leyte, and another was the regimental interpreter in the Pacific, who volunteered for a dangerous mission and was killed in action. Yet, a headline advertisement in the *Hood River Sun* (February 2, 1945) read, "So sorry please, Japs are not wanted in Hood River."[15]

In such ways, toward the close of World War II, the outlook for West Coast Japanese was gloomy. Although some were returning to their homes in California, most were afraid, and others had simply resettled in other parts of the country. A final attempt was made in California, through a number of escheat cases, to seize property owned by the Nisei under clouded titles. (It should be recalled that since the Issei were ineligible to purchase land, many had put their property under the names of their American-born children.)

The two most critical events occurred in 1946. One was the Oyama case, which involved Kajiro Oyama, an alien "ineligible to citizenship" because of his race, who bought a tract of land for his citizen son, Fred. The California Supreme Court unanimously upheld the right of the State to escheat the Oyama property.

It looked as though the final solution to the "Japanese problem" was at hand. The state could claim much of their land, even that in the hands of the Nisei, and the losses the group had suffered during the evacuation would almost ensure a permanent inferior status. But the constitutionality of the California Alien Land Law was placed under scrutiny and, although the Oyama case did not involve a direct ruling on this issue, the U.S. Supreme Court reversed the decision of the California Supreme Court on Oyama's citizenship rights. The tide appeared to be turning.

The second and possibly most influential event was the California vote on Proposition 15 in 1946. Proposition 15 was in effect an attempt to amend the State Constitution in order to incorporate the entire Alien Land Law of 1920 and to strengthen racist attacks upon Nisei property. The voters of California overwhelmingly defeated the proposition.

The Tide Turns

The sharp defeat of Proposition 15 marked the first retreat of the high tide of discrimination and the beginning of a series of acts designed to heal some of the scars of the last several decades. Politicians, instead of crying for more blood, now began to issue statesmanlike pronouncements about democracy, equality, and justice for all. It is difficult to pinpoint the elements that turned the tide. One was undoubtedly the record of Japanese-American soldiers, especially in the campaigns in Italy and France. The 442nd and the 100th battalions, composed of Japanese Americans from the mainland and Hawaii, suffered more than 9,000 casualties, had more than 600 killed in action, and became known as the most decorated unit in American military history. There was also a significant contribution by Nisei in the Pacific against Japanese of their own ancestry. Returning servicemen often told and retold the exploits of the Japanese Americans and were quick to rise to their defense. Part of the change may have been reaction-formation, and may have come in part through a feeling of guilt. It is possible, too, that the evacuation and many other anti-Japanese acts were foisted upon an apathetic majority by a small but active minority. And, perhaps unfortunately, part of the diminishing hostility against the Japanese may also be explained by the increased concern over the activities and problems presented by other ethnic and minority groups.

MOTIVATING FACTORS IN THE EVACUATION

Two questions are involved in any explanation of the wartime evacuation. First, why did the American government intern the Japanese in violation of fundamental traditions? Second, why did the Japanese cooperate so willingly with the authorities during their evacuation and internment?

Plausible answers to the first question were covered earlier—racism, pressure from individuals and groups, the background of anti-Oriental prejudice, wartime conditions, the neutrality of many liberal organizations, and the general lack of knowledge about the Japanese held by most Americans.

White Racism

It is difficult to avoid the conclusion that the primary cause of the wartime evacuation was West Coast racism. Hawaii, the scene of the initial attack, was theoretically more vulnerable to a Japanese invasion and had a Japanese population of 150,000. Among them were 40,000 aliens, unable to read or write English, but there was no mass evacuation in Hawaii.

There were important differences between Hawaiian and mainland Japanese. The Japanese in Hawaii were a more integral part of the economy, while, on the West Coast, Japanese had only a peripheral role or were viewed as an economic threat by some groups. Hawaii was more liberal toward nonwhites, and Hawaiian military leaders had an enlightened view of potential dangers from the Japanese population. Finally, it would have been difficult and expensive to move Hawaii's large Japanese population to mainland camps.

Canada also treated its Japanese shamefully. Mass evacuations, incarceration, and the denial of constitutional privileges were their fate as well.[16] Japanese in Latin America were generally ignored, except in Peru and Mexico. Meanwhile, individuals of German and Italian extraction were generally left alone in the United States.

But on the U.S. mainland, anti-Japanese prejudice was not confined to the West Coast. Bloom and Riemer, comparing attitudes of Pacific Coast and Midwestern college samples, find general agreement concerning the wartime evacuation.[17] Of 2,647 students of 17 colleges and universities tested in 1943, 63 percent on the West Coast and 73 percent in the Midwest felt that the handling of the Japanese was correct. Conversely, only 6 percent of the Pacific Coast sample and 19 percent of the Midwesterners felt that American-born Japanese (Nisei) should be allowed complete freedom as in peacetime. Attitudes toward the Issei noncitizens were even more severe.

The authors also cite a National Opinion Research Center article reported in *Opinion News* on January 23, 1945, which classified responses to the following question: "After the war, do you think that Japanese living in the United States should have as good a chance as white people to get any kind of job?" Sixty-one percent of the respondents answered "No," that the whites should have the first chance!

It is hard to single out a villain to take the blame for the evacuation. General John De Witt deserves his share of the opprobrium for his role as West Coast Theater Commander. He issued the evacuation orders and summed up his feelings at the time with the remark, "Once a Jap, always a Jap." However, Bosworth reports that the general regretted his actions before he died and felt that he had been the victim of bad advice.[18] Earl Warren, then California attorney general, played a role in the evacuation and may also have been the "victim" of poor advice. In any case, it does little good to point accusingly. Silence, denials, or the usual rejoinders about "doing one's duty" obscure the truth still, and perhaps it is not really important to affix guilt.

The shock of the wartime evacuation is that for the first time in its history the United States used the concept of collective guilt and initiated group incarceration, even though there was no evidence of prior wrongdoing. The important lesson of the evacuation was that it could and did happen in the United States, and to American citizens.

Japanese Nonresistance

Answers to the second question—why the Japanese did not resist—provide illuminating insights into norms of Japanese behavior. The explanations are both political and psychological.

Prewar Japanese on the U.S. mainland were politically powerless—the Issei were denied citizenship rights, and the Nisei were just reaching voting age. Further, there were no prominent Japanese public figures on the political front or on any other. Therefore, the American public was often only intellectually aware of the evacuation and felt rather detached from the process. It is not facetious to suggest that the Italians could never have been handled in the same manner because of baseball hero Joe DiMaggio. One can well imagine the publicity, the hue and cry for political scalps and investigations if first and second generation Italians, including the famous baseball player, had been sent away.

Economic considerations also help to explain the behavior of the Japanese. There was a short period prior to the evacuation when the Japanese could have migrated to the Midwest and the far East but few did. Most were poor so that the financial risk of moving to other parts of the country was too overwhelming. Further, the economic structure of the Japanese community—low pay, small business, and high interdependence within the system meant that very few Japanese could move out, or into non-Japanese systems easily. The overall economic picture of the nation, too, was against any easy mobility.

Although there is an interdependence among all of the reasons the social-psychological explanations of Japanese behavior appear to be the most relevant. Future chapters will describe the Japanese-American "culture"—its community and family structures, its norms, values, and personality, and Japanese behavior. Japanese reactions to the wartime evacuation provide an example of the working of the system.

For example, the community structure with its many small

interdependent groups, the critical role of the Issei in terms of leadership, of understanding the system, of wielding power, and of providing for the social control and cohesion of the community, meant that when many Issei leaders were rounded up and incarcerated by the FBI, the system began to fall apart. Many Japanese families were affected by the incarceration, too, so that a group whose primary strength lay in the community and family structure found itself under extremely vulnerable conditions.

The emphasis on norms—the "how to behave in situations" direction of the Japanese culture also contributed to their docility. Norms and values emphasizing conformity and obedience meant that those in power (e.g., the U.S. Army) were able to use this position to gain the cooperation of the evacuated population.

There were also some primary psychological reasons for Japanese behavior. Many Japanese held low expectations for any sort of "break" in America so that a wartime evacuation was viewed as a validation of this point of view (e.g., "What else can a poor Japanese expect in America?"); others used the explanation of shi-ka-ta-ga-nai ("it can't be helped") so that the fate of an individual was tied to forces beyond one's control. Other Japanese used a relatively common Japanese point of view—"I'll become an even better American—I'll cooperate more than 100 percent to prove it." The high need for love and acceptance among many Japanese often leads them to pattern their behavior according to their perception of the expectations of those in authority.

There is also a personality characteristic that is probably not peculiar to the ethnic group but is often found among individuals facing extreme stress. It is the denial of reality—the attitude that says, "It can't happen to me." It is a phenomenon that can be found among soldiers on the battle line and was observed among the Jews at Buchenwald and was present with the Japanese at the time of the evacuation. It was a naive belief that nothing was really going to happen—that the notices to evacuate really meant something else; that the buses and trains were really not taking them anywhere; that the barbed wire fences and guard towers were really not for them, and finally, when in camp, that the situation was not real.

There were no models of resistance or of rebellion—some turned to Caucasian friends, who invariably counseled cooperation. Therefore, with no one to turn to, with their structures and institutions dismantled, with little political or economic power, with cultural norms and values emphasizing conformity and nonconflictual behavior, with a lack of feasible alternatives and facing the awesome might and power of the United States government, the Japanese marched into camp. Could they really have done otherwise?

Can It Happen Again?

Melancholy traces of the evacuation remain today. Rumors that the evacuation camp at Tule Lake was ready for "enemies" were afloat during the McCarthy period and occasionally are heard today. Peterson mentions that Chinese citizens wonder if the same thing can happen to them if hostilities develop between China and the United States.[19] The Japanese evacuation set a precedent whereby a wartime emergency can justify the nullification of other constitutional guarantees. Justice Jackson, in his minority dissent on the Korematsu case, warned against the principle of sanctioning racial discrimination in criminal procedure.

The principle then lies about like a loaded weapon ready for the hand of any authority that can bring forward a plausible claim for an urgent need.... I should hold that a civil court cannot be made to enforce an order which violates constitutional limitations even if it is a reasonable exercise of military authority. The courts can exercise only the judicial power, can only apply law, and must abide by the Constitution, or they cease to be civil courts and become instruments of military policy.[20]

Some of the external conditions leading to the evacuation appear to be ever present. There are pressure groups; there are targets; there is hate, discrimination, prejudice, and irrationality and there is the noncommitted, fence-sitting majority. And periods in our history record what has happened to individuals and groups—the hanging of witches, the treatment of the Indian, and the guilt by association era during the 1950s. But never was there such a mass evacuation of American citizens.

However, when the question of another possible evacuation is raised, we believe that the prospects will be low, especially since an evacuation needs a docile, cooperative population. It is this very docility that made the evacuation possible—no massive resistance, no confrontation, no huge fuss, no dramatic, all-out court battles, no counter-mobilization, no sophisticated use of power and counterstrategies. In our opinion, never will any American group submit to such treatment without fighting back—if only because of the lesson learned from the wartime evacuation of the Japanese.

NOTES

1. Roger Daniels, *The Politics of Prejudice* (Berkeley: University of California Press, 1962).

2. Harry H. L. Kitano, private interviews with members of the Japanese community, 1964.

3. Allan R. Bosworth, *America's Concentration Camps* (New York: W. W. Norton & Co., 1967).

4. Robert O'Brien, "Selective Dispersion as a Factor in the Solution of the Nisei Problem," *Social Forces* (December 1944), pp. 140–47. O'Brien makes the point that these Nisei college students made "ideal ambassadors" since they entered into the American scene in the noncompetitive (in the economic sense) student role as contrasted to other immigrants who were economic competitors.

5. Dillon S. Meyer, "The WRA Says 'Thirty,'" *New Republic*, June 1945.

6. U.S. Department of the Interior War Relocation Authority, *Impounded People* (Washington, D.C.: U.S. Government Printing Office, n.d.), p. 68.

7. Ibid.

8. A resettlement program to non-Pacific Coast areas was in effect from the early days of the evacuation. Wives of servicemen were usually the first to leave, followed by students, then by those seeking employment. Major cities for emigration included Chicago, Minneapolis, Cleveland, and New York.

9. Anne R. Fisher, *Exile of a Race* (Seattle, Wash.: F. & T. Publishers, 1965), p. 103.

10. Ibid.

11. Ibid., p. 114.

12. It should be noted that, as a group, very few Japanese have lost their identity through deliberate name changes or face alterations. The only group to use name changes with some frequency is in the entertainment industry, where such changes are common.

13. Jacobus ten Broek, Edward Barnhart, and Floyd Matson, *Prejudice, War and the Constitution* (Berkeley, California: University of California Press, 1954). See especially pp. 211–223, which cover the episodes in court, including the Hirabayashi, Endo, and Korematsu cases.

14. Bosworth, op. cit. The exclusion order was lifted in December, 1944. These incidents were noted along the Pacific Coast, primarily in California.

15. Fisher, op. cit., p. 199.

16. Forest E. LaViolette, "Canada and its Japanese," in E. Thompson and E. C. Hughes (eds), *Race* (Glencoe, Illinois: The Free Press, 1958), pp. 149–55.

17. Leonard Bloom and Ruth Riemer, "Attitudes of College Students Toward Japanese Americans" *Sociometry* 8, no. 2 (May 1945) ; 166.

18. Bosworth, op. cit.

19. William Peterson, article, *The New York Times Magazine*, 9 January 1966.

20. Fisher, op. cit., p. 181.

GRESHAM M. SYKES

The Defects of Total Power

"For the needs of mass administration today," said Max Weber, "bureaucratic administration is completely indispensable. The choice is between bureaucracy and dilettantism in the field of administration."[1] To the officials of the New Jersey State Prison the choice is clear, as it is clear to the custodians of all maximum security prisons in the United States today. They are organized into a bureaucratic administrative staff—characterized by limited and specific rules, well-defined areas of competence and responsibility, impersonal standards of performance and promotion, and so on—which is similar in many respects to that of any modern, large-scale enterprise; and it is this staff which must see to the effective execution of the prison's routine procedures.

* * *

The most striking fact about this bureaucracy of custodians is

Selections from Gresham M. Sykes, *The Society of Captives: A Study of a Maximum Security Prison* (copyright © 1958 by Princeton University Press; Princeton Paperback, 1971), pp. 40–61. Omission of footnotes. Reprinted by permission of Princeton University Press.

428   its unparalleled position of power—in formal terms, at least—vis-a-vis
the body of men which it rules and from which it is supposed to extract
compliance. The officials, after all, possess a monopoly on the legitimate means of coercion (or, as one prisoner has phrased it succinctly,
"They have the guns and we don't") ; and the officials can call on
the armed might of the police and the National Guard in case of an
overwhelming emergency. The 24-hour surveillance of the custodians
represents the ultimate watchfulness and, presumably, noncompliance on the part of the inmates need not go long unchecked. The rulers
of this society of captives norminally hold in their hands the sole right
of granting rewards and inflicting punishments and it would seem
that no prisoner could afford to ignore their demands for conformity. Centers of opposition in the inmate population—in the form of
men recognized as leaders by fellow prisoners—can be neutralized
through the use of solitary confinement or exile to other State institutions.

*   *   *

It is true, of course, that the power position of the custodial
bureaucracy is not truly infinite. The objectives which the officials pursue are not completely of their own choosing and the means which
they can use to achieve their objectives are far from limitless. The
custodians are not total despots, able to exercise power at whim, and
thus they lack the essential mark of infinite power, the unchallenged
right of being capricious in their rule. It is this last which distinguishes
terror from government, infinite power from almost infinite power,
and the distinction is an important one. Neither by right nor by intention are the officials of the New Jersey State Prison free from a
system of norms and laws which curb their actions. But within these
limitations the bureaucracy of the prison is organized around a grant
of power which is without an equal in American society; and if the
rulers of any social system could secure compliance with their rules
and regulations—however sullen or unwilling—it might be expected that
the officials of the maximum security prison would be able to do so.

When we examine the New Jersey State Prison, however, we
find that this expectation is not borne out in actuality. Indeed, the
glaring conclusion is that despite the guns and the surveillance, the
searches and the precautions of the custodians the actual behavior of
the inmate population differs markedly from that which is called for
by official commands and decrees. Violence, fraud, theft, aberrant
sexual behavior—all are common-place occurrences in the daily round
of institutional existence in spite of the fact that the maximum security prison is conceived by society as the ultimate weapon for the
control of the criminal and his deviant actions.

*   *   *

In our examination of the forces which undermine the power
position of the New Jersey State Prison's custodial bureaucracy, the
most important fact is, perhaps, that the power of the custodians is
not based on authority.

Now power based on authority is actually a complex social relationship in which an individual or a group of individuals is recognized as possessing a right to issue commands or regulations and those
who receive these commands or regulations feel compelled to obey
by a sense of duty. In its pure form, then, or as an ideal type, power
based on authority has two essential elements: a rightful or legitimate
effort to exercise control on the one hand and an inner, moral compulsion to obey, by those who are to be controlled, on the other. In
reality, of course, the recognition of the legitimacy of efforts to exercise control may be qualified or partial and the sense of duty, as a
motive for compliance, may be mixed with motives of fear or self-
interest. But it is possible for theoretical purposes to think of power
based on authority in its pure form and to use this as a baseline in
describing the empirical case.

It is the second element of authority—the sense of duty as a
motive for compliance—which supplies the secret strength of most
social organizations. Orders and rules can be issued with the expectation that they will be obeyed without the necessity of demonstrating
in each case that compliance will advance the subordinate's interests.
Obedience or conformity springs from an internalized morality which
transcends the personal feelings of the individual; the fact that an
order or a rule is an order or a rule becomes the basis for modifying
one's behavior, rather than a rational calculation of the advantages
which might be gained.

In the prison, however, it is precisely this sense of duty which
is lacking in the general inmate population. The regime of the custodians is expressed as a mass of commands and regulations passing
down a hierarchy of power. In general, these efforts at control are
regarded as legitimate by individuals in the hierarchy, and individuals
tend to respond because they feel they "should," down to the level of
the guard in the cellblock, the industrial shop, or the recreation yard.

* * *

Since the Officials of prison possess a monopoly on the means
of coercion, as we have pointed out earlier, it might be thought that
the inmate population could simply be forced into conformity and
that the lack of an inner moral compulsion to obey on the part of the
inmates could be ignored. Yet the combination of a bureaucratic staff
—that most modern rational form of mobilizing effort to exercise control—and the use of physical violence—that most ancient device to
channel man's conduct—must strike us as an anomaly and with good
reason. The use of force is actually grossly inefficient as a means for
securing obedience, particularly when those who are to be controlled
are called on to perform a task of any complexity. A blow with a club
may check an immediate revolt, it is true, but it cannot assure effective performance on a punch-press. A "come-along," a straitjacket or
a pair of handcuffs may serve to curb one rebellious prisoner in a
crisis, but they will be of little aid in moving more than 1200 inmates through the messhall in a routine and orderly fashion. Furthermore, the custodians are well aware that violence once unleashed is

430

not easily brought to heel and it is this awareness that lies behind the standing order that no guard should ever strike an inmate with his hand—he should always use a night stick. This rule is not an open invitation to brutality but an attempt to set a high threshold on the use of force in order to eliminate the casual cuffing which might explode into extensive and violent retaliation. Similarly, guards are under orders to throw their nightsticks over the wall if they are on duty in the recreation yard when a riot develops. A guard without weapons, it is argued, is safer than a guard who tries to hold on to his symbol of office, for a mass of rebellious inmates may find a single night stick a goad rather than a restraint and the guard may find himself beaten to death with his own means of compelling order.

In short, the ability of the officials to physically coerce their captives into the paths of compliance is something of an illusion as far as the day-to-day activities of the prison are concerned and may be of doubtful value in moments of crisis. Intrinsically inefficient as a method of making men carry out a complex task, diminished ineffectiveness by the realities of the guard-inmate ratio, and always accompanied by the danger of touching off further violence, the use of physical force by the custodians has many limitations as a basis on which to found the routine operation of the prison. Coercive tactics may have some utility in checking blatant disobedience—if only a few men disobey. But if the great mass of criminals in prison are to be brought into the habit of conformity, it must be on other grounds. Unable to count on a sense of duty to motivate their captives to obey and unable to depend on the direct and immediate use of violence to insure a step-by-step submission to the rules, the custodians must fall back on a system of rewards and punishments.

Now if men are to be controlled by the use of rewards and punishments—by promises and threats—at least one point is patent: The rewards and punishments dangled in front of the individual must indeed be rewards and punishments from the point of view of the individual who is to be controlled. It is precisely on this point, however, that the custodians' system of rewards and punishments founders. In our discussion of the problems encountered in securing conscientious performance at work, we suggested that both the penalties and the incentives available to the officials were inadequate. This is also largely true, at a more general level, with regard to rewards and punishments for securing compliance with the wishes of the custodians in all areas of prison life.

In the first place, the punishments which the officials can inflict—for theft, assaults, escape attempt, gambling, insolence, homosexuality, and all the other deviations from the pattern of behavior called for by the regime of the custodians—do not represent a profound difference from the prisoner's usual status. It may be that when men are chronically deprived of liberty, material goods and services, recreational opportunities and so on, the few pleasures that are granted take on a new importance and the threat of their withdrawal is a more powerful motive for comformity than those of us in the free community can realize. To be locked up in the solitary confinement wing, that prison within a prison; to move from the monotonous, often badly prepared meals in the mess-hall to a diet of bread and water; to be dropped from a dull, unsatisfying job and forced to remain in idleness —all, perhaps, may mean the difference between an existence which can be borne, painful though it may be, and one which cannot.

* * *

In the second place, the system of rewards and punishments in the prison is defective because the reward side of the picture has been largely stripped away. Mail and visiting privileges, recreational privileges, the supply of personal possessions—all are given to the inmate at the time of his arrival in one fixed sum. Even the so-called Good Time—the portion of the prisoner's sentence deducted for good behavior—is automatically subtracted from the prisoner's sentence when he begins his period of imprisonment.

* * *

In short, the New Jersey State Prison makes an initial grant of all its rewards and then threatens to withdraw them if the prisoner does not conform. It does not start the prisoner from scratch and promise to grant its available rewards one by one as the prisoner proves himself through continued submission to the institutional regulations. As a result a subtle alchemy is set in motion whereby the inmates cease to see the rewards of the system as rewards, that is, as benefits contingent upon performance; instead, rewards are apt to be defined as obligations. Whatever justification might be offered for such a policy, it would appear to have a number of drawbacks as a method of motivating prisoners to fall into the posture of obedience. In effect, rewards and punishments of the officials have been collapsed into one and the prisoner moves in a world where there is no hope of progress but only the possibility of further punishments. Since the prisoner is already suffering from most of the punishments permitted by society, the threat of imposing those few remaining is all too likely to be a gesture of futility.

Unable to depend on that inner moral compulsion or sense of duty which eases the problem of control in most social organizations, acutely aware that brute force is inadequate, and lacking an effective system of legitimate rewards and punishments which might induce prisoners to conform to institutional regulations on the grounds of self interest, the custodians of the New Jersey State Prison are considerably weakened in their attempts to impose their regime on their captive population. The result, in fact, is, as we have already indicated, a good deal of deviant behavior or noncompliance in a social system where the rulers at first glance seem to possess almost infinite power.

Yet systems of power may be defective for reasons other than the fact that those who are ruled do not feel the need to obey the orders and regulations descending on them from above. Systems of power may also fail because those who are supposed to rule are unwilling to do so. The unissued order, the deliberately ignored disobedience, the duty left unperformed—these are cracks in the mono-lith just as surely as are acts of defiance in the subject population. The "corruption" of the rulers may be far less dramatic than the in-surrection of the ruled, for power unexercised is seldom visible as power which is challenged, but the system of power still falters.

Now the official in the lowest ranks of the custodial bureaucracy —the guard in the cellblock, the industrial shop, or the recreation yard —is the pivotal figure on which the custodial bureaucracy turns. It is he who must supervise and control the inmate population in concrete and detailed terms. It is he who must see to the translation of the custodial regime from blueprint to reality and engage in the specific battles for conformity. Counting prisoners, periodically reporting to the center of communications, signing passes, checking groups of in-mates as they come and go, searching for contraband or signs of at-tempts to escape—these make up the minutiae of his eight-hour shift. In addition, he is supposed to be alert for violations of the prison rules which fall outside his routine sphere of surveillance. Not only must he detect and report deviant behavior after it occurs; he must curb deviant behavior before it arises as well as when he is called on to prevent a minor quarrel among prisoners from flaring into a more dangerous situation. And he must make sure that the inmates in his charge perform their assigned tasks with a reasonable degree of efficiency.

The expected role of the guard, then, is a complicated com-pound of policeman and foreman, of cadi, counsellor, and boss all rolled into one. But as the guard goes about his duties, piling one day on top of another (and the guard too, in a certain sense, is serving time in confinement), we find that the system of power in the prison is defective not only because the means of motivating the inmates to con-form are largely lacking but also because the guard is frequently re-luctant to enforce the full range of the institution's regulations. The guard frequently fails to report infractions of the rules which have occurred before his eyes. The guard often transmits forbidden infor-mation to inmates, such as plans for searching particular cells in a surprise raid for contraband. The guard often neglects elementary se-curity requirements and on numerous occasions he will be found join-ing his prisoners in outspoken criticisms of the Warden and his as-sistants. In short, the guard frequently shows evidence of having been "corrupted" by the captive criminals over whom he stands in theoreti-cal dominance. This failure within the ranks of the rulers is seldom to be attributed to outright bribery—bribery indeed, is usually un-necessary, for far more effective influences are at work to bridge the gap supposedly separating captors and captives.

In the first place, the guard is in close and intimate association with his prisoners throughout the course of the working day. He can remain aloof only with great difficulty, for he possesses few of those devices which normally serve to maintain social distance between the rulers and the ruled. He cannot withdraw physically in symbolic af-firmation of his superior position; he has no intermediaries to bear the brunt of resentment springing from orders which are disliked; and he cannot fall back on a dignity adhering to his office—he is a *hack* or a *screw* in the eyes of those he controls and an unwelcome display of officiousness evokes that great destroyer of unquestioned power, the ribald humor of the dispossessed.

There are many pressures in American culture to "be nice," to be a "good Joe," and the guard in the maximum security prison is not immune. The guard is constantly exposed to a sort of moral blackmail in which the first signs of condemnation, estrangement, or rigid aherence to the rules is countered by the inmates with the threat of ridicule or hostility. And in this complex interplay, the guard does not always start from a position of determined opposition to "being friendly." He holds an intermediate post in a bureaucratic structure between top prison officials—his captains, lieutenants, and sergeants—and the prisoners in his charge. Like many such figures, the guard is caught in a conflict of loyalties. He often has reason to resent the actions of his superior officers—the reprimands, the lack of ready appreciation, the incomprehensible order—and in the inmates he finds willing sympathizers: They too claim to suffer from the unreasonable irritants of power. Furthermore, the guard in many cases is marked by a basic ambivalence toward the criminals under his supervision and control. It is true that the inmates of the prison have been condemned by society through the agency of the courts, but some of these prisoners must be viewed as a success in terms of a worldly system of the values which accords high prestige to wealth and influence even though they may have been won by devious means; and the poorly paid guard may be gratified to associate with a famous racketeer. Moreover, this ambivalence in the guard's attitudes toward the criminals nominally under his thumb may be based on something more than a *sub rosa* respect for the notorious. . . . In the eyes of the custodian, the inmate tends to become a man in prison rather than a criminal in prison and the relationship between captor and captive is subtly transformed in the process.

In the second place, the guard's position as a strict enforcer of the rules is undermined by the fact that he finds it almost impossible to avoid the claims of reciprocity. To a large extent the guard is dependent on inmates for the satisfactory performance of his duties; and like many individuals in positions of power, the guard is evaluated in terms of the conduct of the men he controls. A troublesome, noisy, dirty cellblock reflects on the guard's ability to "handle" prisoners and this ability forms an important component of the merit rating which is used as the basis for pay raises and promotions. As we have pointed out above, a guard cannot rely on the direct application of force to achieve compliance nor can he easily depend on threats of punishment. And if the guard does insist on constantly using the last few negative sanctions available to the institution—if the guard turns in Charge Slip after Charge Slip for every violation of the rules which he encounters—he becomes burdensome to the top officials of the prison bureaucratic staff who realize only too well that their apparent dominance rests on some degree of co-operation. . . .

The guard, then, is under pressure to achieve a smoothly run-

434   ning tour of duty not with the stick but with the carrot, but here again his legitimate stock is limited. Facing demands from above that he achieve compliance and stalemated from below, he finds that one of the most meaningful rewards he can offer is to ignore certain offenses or make sure that he never places himself in a position where he will discover them. Thus the guard—backed by all the power of the State, close to armed men who will run to his aid, and aware that any prisoner who disobeys him can be punished if he presses charges against him —often discovers that his best path of action is to make "deals" or "trades" with the captives in his power. In effect, the guard buys compliance or obedience in certain areas at the cost of tolerating disobedience elsewhere.

* * *

In the third place, the theoretical dominance of the guard is undermined in actuality by the innocuous encroachment of the prisoner on the guard's duties. Making out reports, checking cells at the periodic count, locking and unlocking doors—in short, all the minor chores which the guard is called on to perform—may gradually be transferred into the hands of inmates whom the guard has come to trust. The cellblock runner, formally assigned the tasks of delivering mail, housekeeping duties, and so on, is of particular importance in this respect. Inmates in this position function in a manner analogous to that of the company clerk in the Armed Forces and like such figures they may wield power and influence far beyond the nominal definition of their role. For reasons of indifference, laziness or naïvete, the guard may find that much of the power which he is supposed to exercise has slipped from his grasp.

* * *

It is apparent, then, that the power of the custodians is defective, not simply in the sense that the ruled are rebellious, but also in the sense that the rulers are reluctant. We must attach a new meaning to Lord Acton's aphorism that power tends to corrupt and absolute power corrupts absolutely. The custodians of the New Jersey State Prison, far from being converted into brutal tyrants, are under strong pressure to compromise with their captives, for it is a paradox that they can insure their dominance only by allowing it to be corrupted. Only by tolerating violations of "minor" rules and regulations can the guard secure compliance in the "major" areas of the custodial regime. Ill-equipped to maintain the social distance which in theory separates the world of the officials and the world of the inmates, their suspicions eroded by long familiarity, the custodians are led into a modus vivendi with their captives which bears little resemblance to the stereotypical picture of guards and their prisoners.

The fact that the officials of the prison experience serious difficulties in imposing their regime on the society of prisoners is sometimes attributed to inadequacies of the custodial staff's personnel. These inadequacies, it is claimed, are in turn due to the fact that more than

50 percent of the guards are temporary employees who have not passed a Civil Service examination.

* * *

Now the guard at the New Jersey State Prison receives a salary of $3,240 per year when he is hired and he can reach a maximum of $3,840 per year; and there is little doubt that the low salary scale accounts for much of the prison's high turnover rate. The fact that the job of the guard is often depressing, dangerous, and possesses relatively low prestige adds further difficulties. There is also little doubt that the high turnover rate carries numerous evils in its train, as the comments of the Deputy Commissioner have indicated. Yet even if higher salaries could counterbalance the many dissatisfying features of the guard's job—to a point where the custodial force consisted of men with long service rather than a group of transients—there remains a question of whether or not the problems of administration in the New Jersey State Prison would be eased to a significant extent.

* * *

We are not arguing, of course, that the quality of the personnel in the prison is irrelevant to the successful performance of the bureaucracy's tasks nor are we arguing that it would be impossible to improve the quality of the personnel by increasing salaries. We are arguing, however, that the problems of the custodians far transcend the size of the guard's pay check or the length of his employment and that better personnel is at best a palliative rather than a final cure. It is true, of course, that it is difficult to unravel the characteristics of a social organization from the characteristics of the individuals who are its members; but there seems to be little reason to believe that a different crop of guards in the New Jersey State Prison would exhibit an outstanding increase in efficiency in trying to impose the regime of the custodians on the population of prisoners. *The lack of a sense of duty among those who are held captive, the obvious fallacies of coercion, the pathetic collection of rewards and punishments to induce compliance, the strong pressures toward the corruption of the guard in the form of friendship, reciprocity, and the transfer of duties into the hands of trusted inmates—all are structural defects in the prison's system of power rather than individual inadequacies.*

NOTES

1. Max Weber, *The Theory of Social and Economic Organization,* edited by Talcott Parsons, New York: Oxford University Press, 1947, p. 337.

VALUES

NORMS

Deviant

Peace

Standards

Indoctrination

GANG

SANCTIONS

CHANGE Symbolism

IMPLEMENTATIONS

Study Questions

1. Are the four processes in the development of normative order operative in your sociology class? Do you consider the class a social organization? Or an example of normative order?
2. Is there any indoctrination in your class? How do you decide what is indoctrination?
3. Did the Provo boys have more or less freedom than you?
4. What changes might occur in your education if America was a nation devoted to peace?
5. Did the Provo experiment depend on exchange and loyalty as well as control?

The Establishment of
a Normative Order

11 Perhaps this is an appropriate place to review and integrate some of the major concepts we have explored so far. I have defined social organization in terms of patterns of mutual influence: loyalty, exchange, and imperative order. I have noted that these patterns are not necessarily mutually exclusive; in fact, they often reinforce each other. Each of them may exist singly or together, within any social unit, although certain patterns seem to predominate in particular social units. Within the family, loyalty and exchange are usually more salient than power, but in most families the notions of power and imperative order also are implicit as certain roles come to interact with each other. Police units and communities are organized around the concept of social control, but patterns of loyalty and exchange are operative within them also. As we shall see in the next section on the background of contemporary society, folk and feudal societies can be characterized by differences in *emphasis* in their patterns of social organization as well as by differences in the patterns themselves.

THE IMPORTANCE OF NORMATIVE ORDER

Comprehension of the differences in the patterns and in their emphasis is not sufficient, however, for an understanding of the establishment of normative order in a social organization. Normative order is essentially equivalent to social organization, but I am using normative order as a new concept for two reasons. First, norms may vary in their degree of acceptance. Roughly speaking, when norms are both widely accepted in a group and deeply inculcated in the personalities of its members, we have a normative order. Sociologists say that a norm which is inculcated and accepted is institutionalized. Second, the concept of normative order is the dependent variable, or that which is to be explained. Accordingly, it helps us focus on the processes of establishing the social unit on a firm basis. Normative order, then, involves norms, rules, or standards, and the patterns of exchange, loyalty, and power. In a normative order, institutionalized rules, or norms, guide the behavior of individuals in their various positions, roles, and transactions.

There is a distinction between norms and values which bears repetition so that the concept of normative order can be clearly understood. Values can be defined as general principles for deciding upon desired ends. They exist at the cultural level. They are held by individuals, are conceptions of the desirable, and never imply sanctions. Norms, by definition, are group properties. They exist at the social level, are rules for behavior, and do imply sanctions. Norms are based upon shared values.

TYPES OF NORMS

Chapter 10 discusses two kinds of norms—procedural and substantive. Substantive norms regulate the content of behavior. They repress certain actions by imposing restraints. Procedural norms, on the other hand, do not prescribe what to do but how to do it, if behavior is to be considered valid or legitimate. Both kinds of norms facilitate the creation of order. Procedural and substantive norms, and the values on which they are based, are reflected in the establishment and development of an organized social unit.

Processes in the Development of a Normative Order

Let us imagine an interaction involving a number of pre-delinquent boys. I could be talking about medical school students, or members of a revolutionary organization instead, for the concept to be examined is the evolution of the normative order of a group, which is universal. In the ongoing or developing delinquent gang, or in any social unit, there are four identifiable processes that occur in the establishment of a normative order. The first process is called *indoctrination*. The delinquent boy does what he *has* to do. In order to be accepted as a member of a "steady" gang, he has to steal. Indoctrination can promote his willingness to submit to this pattern of expected behavior. Indoctrination can be reinforced by loyalty, by exchange of goods or services, or by control.

The levelling of *sanctions* is the second process that occurs in the development of a normative order. Sanctions consist of the rewards and punishments that members of a group receive as a result of their actions. In a delinquent gang, the boy who does not steal can be verbally abused, threatened, or actually beaten. In larger organizations, a special role or a sub-group is set up to handle deviants. The truant officer is an example of a specialized role, created to deal with infractions of rules. Special classrooms in the educational system exemplify a sub-group mechanism for handling deviants. Sanctions can be imposed in any of the three patterns of loyalty, exchange, or control.

A third process, *symbolization*, expresses the relationship of the act to the values of the group. Thus, ceremonies after a gang war celebrate the bravery of particular gang members. Symbolization seems to involve the patterns of loyalty and exchange more than the pattern of imperative order or control.

440

Finally, the gang or social organization must be concerned with *implementation*. The group must develop mechanisms to ensure conformity. Social arrangements need to be developed so that members' actions may be consistent with group expectations. If we want drivers to be able to drive safely, we need to be able to evaluate and license them. If we want gang members to steal, we have to provide places and tools. The implementation of activities allows the group to achieve its goals.

The first selection in this chapter is a description and analysis of how a new organization comes to be. The organizational goal in this case is the "rehabilitation of recidivistic delinquent boys." The description of the way Provo Boys are presented with certain choices may seem a bit severe. These choices, however, are similar to the choices of many new members or recruits in other organizations. The fact that the Provo Boys are not volunteers should not confuse the issue. Voluntarism in social life is a relative phenomenon. As you read about the Provo Experiment, try to select the passages that refer to the indoctrination phase, or orientation period, in which peer groups were involved in initiating others. The sanctions of the peer group were particularly vital aspects of the Provo program. The peer group had the power to reward a boy with release from the program. The concept of symbolization was only indirectly relevant to the program. In group discussions, the boys could symbolize the success of Provo by referring to graduates of the program who had prior reputations in the community as "hoods" or thieves. "If Provo could help——, then why can't it help you?" Implementation of the program, aside from the method of selecting the boys and some aspects of the group treatment, is not discussed. The selection of the boys and their relationships with the school, courts, community, and police are not detailed. You should discuss and try to analyze the pattern of exchange, the shifting loyalties, and the changing patterns of control in the Provo Experiment.

The establishment of a normative order involves more than small social units like delinquent gangs or treatment centers. Often an entire way of life or an entire nation or society may be involved. The second article in this chapter is a speculative piece about the transformation of American society, written by Kenneth Boulding, an economist. Boulding discusses the war-like organization and value orientation that Americans have had. He notes that peace has never been a major value for American society. He suggests a strategy for the peace movement that is consistent with his analysis of developing a value of pacifism within the normative order.

441

The Provo Experiment in
Delinquency Rehabilitation

Despite the importance of sociological contributions to the understanding of delinquent behavior, relatively few of these contributions have been systematically utilized for purposes of rehabilitation.[1] The reason is at least partially inherent in the sociological tradition which views sociology primarily as a research discipline. As a consequence, the rehabilitation of delinquents has been left, by default, to people who have been relatively unaware of sociological theory and its implications for treatment.

This situation has produced or perpetuated problems along two dimensions. On one dimension are the problems engendered in reformatories where authorities find themselves bound, not only by the norms of their own official system, but by the inmate system as well. They are unable to work out an effective program: (1) because the goals of the two systems are incompatible; and (2) because no one knows much about the structure and function of the inmate system and how it might be dealt with for purposes of rehabilitation.[2] Furthermore, the crux of any treatment program has ultimately to do with the decision-making process utilized by delinquents in the community, *not* in the reformatory. Yet, the decisions which lead to success in "doing time" in the reformatory are not of the same type needed for successful community adjustment. Existing conditions may actually be more effective in cementing ties to the delinquent system than in destroying them.[3]

The second dimension of the problem has to do with the traditional emphasis upon "individualized treatment."[4] This emphasis stems from two sources: (1) a humanistic concern for the importance of human dignity and the need for sympathetic understanding;[5] and (2) a widespread belief that delinquency is a psychological disease and the offender a *"sick"* person.[6] If, however, sociologists are even partially correct regarding the causes for delinquency, these two points of view overlook the possibility that most persistent delinquents do have the support of a meaningful reference group and are not, therefore, without the emotional support and normative orientation which such a group can provide. In fact, a complete dedication to an individualistic approach poses an impasse: How can an individual who acquired delinquency from a group with which he identifies strongly be treated individually without regard to the persons or norms of the system from whom he acquired it?[7]

A successful treatment program for such a person would require

La Mar T. Empey and Jerome Rabow, "The Provo Experiment in Delinquency Rehabilitation," *American Sociological Review* 26:5 (October 1961). Reprinted by permission of the authors and the American Sociological Association.

techniques not normally included in the individualized approach. It should no more be expected that dedicated delinquents can be converted to conventionality by such means than that devout Pentecostals can be converted to Catholicism by the same means. Instead, different techniques are required for dealing with the normative orientation of the delinquent's system, replacing it with new values, beliefs, and rationalizations and developing means by which he can realize conventional satisfactions, especially with respect to successful employment.

This does not suggest, of course, that such traditional means as probation for dealing with the first offender or psychotherapy for dealing with the disturbed offender can be discarded. But it does suggest the need for experimental programs more consistent with sociological theory, and more consistent with the sociological premise that most *persistent* and *habitual* offenders are active members of a delinquent social system.[8]

This paper presents the outlines of a program—the Provo Experiment in Delinquency Rehabilitation—which is derived from sociological principles to rehabilitation. Because of its theoretical ties, the concern of the Experiment is as much with a systematic evaluation and reformulation of treatment consistent with findings as with the administration of treatment itself. For that reason, research and evaluation are an integral part of the program. Its theoretical orientation, major assumptions, treatment system, and research design are outlined below.

THEORETICAL ORIENTATION

With regards to causation, the Provo Experiment turned to a growing body of evidence which suggests two important conclusions: (1) that the greater part of delinquent behavior is not that of individuals engaging in highly secretive deviations, but is a group phenomenon—a shared deviation which is the product of differential group experience in a particular subculture,[9] and (2) that because most delinquents tend to be concentrated in slums or to be the children of lower class parents, their lives are characterized by learning situations which limit their access to success goals.[10]

Attention to these two conclusions does not mean that emotional problems,[11] or "bad" homes,[12] can be ignored. But only occasionally do these variables lead by themselves to delinquency. In most cases where older delinquents are involved other intervening variables must operate, the most important of which is the presence of a delinquent system—one which supplies status and recognition not normally obtainable elsewhere. Whether they are members of a tight knit gang or of the amorphous structure of the "parent" delinquent subculture,[13] habitual delinquents tend to look affectively both to their peers and to the norms of their system for meaning and orientation. Thus, although a "bad" home may have been instrumental at some early phase in the genesis of a boy's delinquency, it must be recognized that it is now other delinquent boys, not his parents, who are current sources of support and identification. Any attempts to change him, therefore, would have to view him as more than an unstable isolate without a meaningful reference group. And, instead of concentrating on changing his parental relationships, they would have to recognize the intrinsic nature of his membership in the delinquent system and direct treatment to him as a part of that system.

There is another theoretical problem. An emphasis on the importance of the delinquent system raises some question regarding the extent to which delinquents are without any positive feeling for conventional standards. Vold says that one approach to explaining delinquency "... operates from the basic, implicit assumption that in a delinquency area, delinquency is the normal response of the normal individual—that the non-delinquent is really the 'problem case,' the nonconformist whose behavior needs to be accounted for."[14] This is a deterministic point of view suggesting the possibility the delinquents view conventional people as "foreigners" and conventional norms and beliefs as anathema. It implies that delinquents have been socialized entirely in a criminal system and have never internalized or encountered the blandishments of conventional society.[15]

Actually, sociological literature suggests otherwise. It emphasizes, in general, that the sub-parts of complex society are intimately tied up with the whole,[16] and, specifically, that delinquents are very much aware of conventional standards; that they have been socialized in an environment dominated by middle-class morality;[17] that they have internalized the American success ideal to such a degree that they turn to illegitimate means in an effort to be successful[18] (or, failing in that, engage in malicious, or retreatist activities) ;[19] that they are profoundly ambivalent about their delinquent behavior;[20] and that in order to cope with the claims of respectable norms upon them, they maintain a whole series of intricate rationalizations by which to "neutralize" their delinquent behavior.[21]

This suggests that delinquents are aware of conventional structure and its expectations. In many conventional settings they can, and usually do, behave conventionally. But it also suggests that, like other people, they are motivated by the normative expectations of their own subsystem. Consequently, when in the company of other delinquent boys, they may not only feel that they have to live up to minimal delinquent expectations but to appear more delinquent than they actually are, just as people in church often feel that they have to appear more holy than they actually are.

If this is the case, the problem of rehabilitation is probably not akin to converting delinquents to ways of behavior and points of view about which they are unaware and which they have never seriously considered as realistic alternatives. Instead, the feeling of ambivalence on their parts might be an element which could be used in rehabilitation.

An important sociological hypothesis based on this assumption would be that the ambivalence of most habitual delinquents is not primarily the result of personality conflicts developed in such social *microcosms* as the family but is inherent in the structure of the societal *macrocosm*. A delinquent sub-system simply represents an alternative means for acquiring, or attempting to acquire, social and economic goals idealized by the societal system which are acquired by other people through conventional means.

If this hypothesis is accurate, delinquent ambivalence might actually be used in effecting change. A rehabilitation program might seek: (1) to make conventional and delinquent alternatives clear; (2) to lead delinquents to question the ultimate utility of delinquent alternatives; and (3) to help conventional alternatives assume some positive valence for them. It might then reduce the affective identification which they feel for the delinquent subsystem and tip the scales in the opposite direction.

MAJOR ASSUMPTIONS FOR TREATMENT

In order to relate such theoretical premises to the specific needs of treatment, the Provo Experiment adopted a series of major assumptions. They are as follows:

1. Delinquent behavior is primarily a group product and demands an approach to treatment far different from that which sees it as characteristic of a "sick," or "well-meaning" but "misguided," person.

2. An effective program must recognize the intrinsic nature of a delinquent's membership in a delinquent system and, therefore, must direct treatment to him as a part of that system.

3. Most habitual delinquents are affectively and ideologically dedicated to the delinquent system. Before they can be made amenable to change, they must be made anxious about the ultimate utility of that system for them.

4. Delinquents must be forced to deal with the conflicts which the demands of conventional and delinquent systems place upon them. The resolution of such conflicts, either for or against further law violations, must ultimately involve a community decision. For that reason, a treatment program, in order to force realistic decision-making, can be most effective if it permits continued participation in the community as well as in the treatment process.

5. Delinquent ambivalence for purposes of rehabilitation can only be utilized in a setting conducive to the free expression of feelings— both delinquent and conventional. This means that the protection and rewards provided by the treatment system for *candor* must exceed those provided either by delinquents for adherence to delinquent roles or by officials for adherence to custodial demands for "good behavior." Only in this way can delinquent individuals become aware of the extent to which other delinquents share conventional as well as delinquent aspirations and, only in this way, can they be encouraged to examine the ultimate utility of each.

6. An effective program must develop a unified and cohesive social system in which delinquents and authorities alike are devoted to one task—overcoming lawbreaking. In order to accomplish this the program must avoid two pitfalls: (a) it must avoid establishing authorities as "rejectors" and making inevitable the creation of two social systems within the program; and (b) it must avoid the institutionaliza-

tion of means by which skilled offenders can evade norms and escape sanctions.[22] The occasional imposition of negative sanctions is as necessary in this system as in any other system.

7. A treatment system will be most effective if the delinquent peer group is used as the means of perpetuating the norms and imposing the sanctions of the system. The peer group should be seen by delinquents as the primary source of help and support. The traditional psychotherapeutic emphasis upon transference relationships is not viewed as the most vital factor in effecting change.

8. A program based on sociological theory may tend to exclude lectures, sermons, films, individual counseling, analytic psychotherapy, organized athletics, academic education, and vocational training as primary treatment techniques. It will have to concentrate, instead, on matters of another variety: changing reference group and normative orientations, utilizing ambivalent feelings resulting from the conflict of conventional and delinquent standards, and providing opportunities for recognition and achievement in conventional pursuits.

9. An effective treatment system must include rewards which are realistically meaningful to delinquents. They would include such things as peer acceptance for law-abiding behavior or the opportunity for gainful employment rather than badges, movies or furlough privileges which are designed primarily to facilitate institutional control. Rewards, therefore, must only be given for realistic and lasting changes, not for conformance to norms which concentrate upon effective custody as an end in itself.

10. Finally, in summary, a successful program must be viewed by delinquents as possessing four important characteristics: (a) a social climate in which delinquents are given the opportunity to examine and experience alternatives related to a realistic choice between delinquent or non-delinquent behavior; (b) the opportunity to declare publicly to peers and authorities a belief or disbelief that they can benefit from a change in values; (c) a type of social structure which will permit them to examine the role and legitimacy (for their purposes) of authorities in the treatment system; and (d) a type of treatment interaction which, because it places major responsibilities upon peer-group decision-making, grants status and recognition to individuals, not only for their own successful participation in the treatment interaction, but for their willingness to involve others.

THE TREATMENT SYSTEM[23]

The Provo Program, consistent with these basic assumptions, resides in the community and does not involve permanent incarceration. Boys live at home and spend only a part of each day at Pinehills (the program center). Otherwise they are free in the community.[24]

History and Locale

The Provo Program was begun in 1956 as an "in-between" program designed specifically to help those habitual delinquents whose persistence made them candidates, in most cases for a reformatory. It was instigated by a volunteer group of professional and lay people known as the *Citizens' Advisory Council to the Juvenile Court.* It has never had formal ties to government except through the Juvenile Court. This lack of ties has permitted considerable experimentation. Techniques have been modified to such a degree that the present program bears little resemblance to the original one. Legally, program officials are deputy probation officers appointed by the Juvenile Judge.

The cost of treatment is financed by county funds budgeted through the Juvenile Courts. So near as we can estimate the cost per boy is approximately one-tenth of what it would cost if he were incarcerated in a reformatory. Research operations are financed by the Ford Foundation. Concentrated evaluation of the program is now in its second year of a six year operation. Because both the theoretical orientation and treatment techniques of the program were in developmental process until its outlines were given final form for research purposes, it is difficult to make an objective evaluation of the over-all program based on recidivism rates for previous years, especially in the absence of adequate control groups. Such an evaluation, however, is an integral part of the present research and is described below.

Relations with welfare agencies and the community, *per se,* are informal but extremely co-operative. This is due to three things: the extreme good will and guiding influence of the Juvenile Court Judge, Monroe J. Paxman, [25] the unceasing efforts of the Citizens' Advisory Council to involve the entire county as a community, and the willingness of city and county officials, not only to overcome traditional fears regarding habitual offenders in the community, but to lend strong support to an experimental program of this type.

Community co-operation is probably enhanced by strong Mormon traditions. However, Utah County is in a period of rapid transition which began in the early days of World War II with the introduction of a large steel plant, allied industries, and an influx of non-Mormons. This trend, both in industry and population, has continued to the present time. The treatment program is located in the city of Provo but draws boys from all major communities in the county—from a string of small cities, many of which border on each other, ranging in size from four to forty thousand. The total population from which it draws its assignees is about 110,000.

Despite the fact that Utah County is not a highly urbanized area, when compared to large metropolitan centers, the concept of a "parent" delinquent subculture has real meaning for it. While there are no clear-cut gangs, *per se,* it is surprising to observe the extent to which delinquent boys from the entire county, who have never met, know each other by reputation, go with the same girls, use the same language, or can seek each other out when they change high schools. About half of them are permanently out of school, do not participate in any regular institutional activities, and are reliant almost entirely upon the delinquent system for social acceptance and participation.

Assignees

Only habitual offenders, 15–17 years, are assigned to the program. In the absence of public facilities, they are transported to and from home each day in automobiles driven by university students. Their offenses run the usual gamut: vandalism, trouble in school, shoplifting, car theft, burglary, forgery, and so forth. Highly disturbed and psychotic boys are not assigned. The pre-sentence investigation is used to exclude these people. They constitute an extremely small minority.

Number in Attendance

No more than twenty boys are assigned to the program at any one time. A large number would make difficult any attempts to establish and maintain a unified, cohesive system. This group of twenty is broken into two smaller groups, each of which operates as a separate discussion unit. When an older boy is released from one of these units, a new boy is added. This is an important feature because it serves as the means by which the culture of the system is perpetuated.

Length of Attendance

No length of stay is specified. It is intimately tied to the group and its processes because a boy's release depends not only upon his own behavior, but upon the maturation processes through which his group goes. Release usually comes somewhere between four and seven months.

Nature of Program

The program does not utilize any testing, gathering of case histories, or clinical diagnosis. One of its key tools, peer group interaction, is believed to provide a considerably richer source of information about boys and delinquency than do clinical methods.

The program, *per se*, is divided into two phases. Phase I is an intensive group program, utilizing work and the delinquent peer group as the principal instruments for change. During the winter, boys attend this phase three hours a day, five days a week, and all day on Saturdays. Activities include daily group discussions, hard work, and some unstructured activities in which boys are left entirely on their own. During the summer they attend an all-day program which involves work and group discussions. However, there are no practices without exceptions. For example, if a boy has a full-time job, he may be allowed to continue the job in lieu of working in the program. Other innovations occur repeatedly.

Phase II is designed to aid a boy after release from intensive treatment in Phase I. It involves two things: (1) an attempt to maintain some reference group support for a boy; and (2) community action to help him find employment. Both phases are described below.

PHASE I: INTENSIVE TREATMENT

Every attempt is made in Phase I to create a social system in which social structure, peer members, and authorities are oriented to the one task of instituting change. The more relevant to this task the system is, the greater will be its influence.

448   Social Structure

There is little formal structure in the Provo Program. Patterns are abhorred which might make boys think that their release depends upon *refraining* from swearing, engaging in open quarrels or doing such *"positive"* things as saying "yes sir," or "no sir." Such criteria as these play into their hands. They learn to manipulate them in developing techniques for beating a system. Consequently, other than requiring boys to appear each day, and working hard on the job, there are no formal demands. The only other daily activities are the group discussions at which attendance is optional.

The absence of formal structure helps to do more than avoid artificial criteria for release. It has the positive effect of making boys more amenable to treatment. In the absence of formal structure they are uneasy and they are not quite sure of themselves. Thus, the lack of clear-cut definitions for behavior helps to accomplish three important things: (1) It produces anxiety and turns boys towards the group as a method of resolving their anxiety; (2) It leaves boys free to define situations for themselves: leaders begin to lead, followers begin to follow, and manipulators begin to manipulate. It is these types of behavior which must be seen and analyzed if change is to take place; (3) It binds neither authorities nor the peer group to prescribed courses of action. Each is free to do whatever is needed to suit the needs of particular boys, groups, or situations.

On the other hand, the absence of formal structure obviously does not mean that there is no structure. But, that which does exist is informal and emphasizes ways of thinking and behaving which are not traditional. Perhaps the greatest difference lies in the fact that a considerable amount of power is vested in the delinquent peer group. It is the instrument by which norms are perpetuated and through which many important decisions are made. It is the primary source of pressure for change.

The Peer Group

Attempts to involve a boy with the peer group begin the moment he arrives. Instead of meeting with and receiving an orientation lecture from authorities, he receives no formal instructions. He is always full of such questions as, "What do I have to do to get out of this place?" or "How long do I have to stay?", but such questions as these are never answered. They are turned aside with, "I don't know," or "Why don't you find out?" Adults will not orient him in the ways that he has grown to expect, nor will they answer any of his questions. He is forced to turn to his peers. Usually, he knows someone in the program, either personally or by reputation. As he begins to associate with other boys he discovers that important informal norms do exist, the most important of which makes *inconsistency* rather than *consistency* the rule. That which is approprite for one situation, boy, or group may not be appropriate for another. Each merits a decision as it arises.

Other norms center most heavily about the daily group discussion sessions. These sessions are patterned after the technique of

"Guided Group Interaction" which was developed at Fort Knox during World War II and at Highfields.[26] Guided Group Interaction emphasizes the idea that only through a group and its processes can a boy work out his problems. From a peer point of view it has three main goals: (1) to question the utility of a life devoted to delinquency; (2) to suggest alternative ways for behavior; and (3) to provide recognition for a boy's personal reformation and his willingness to reform others.[27]

Guided Group Interaction grants to the peer group a great deal of power, including that of helping to decide when each boy is ready to be released. This involves "retroflexive reformation."[28] If a delinquent is serious in his attempts to reform others he must automatically accept the common purpose of the reformation process, identify himself closely with others engaged in it, and grant prestige to those who succeed in it. In so doing, he becomes a genuine member of the reformation group and in the process may be alienated from his previous pro-delinquent groups.[29] Such is an ideal and long term goal. Before it can be realized for any individual he must become heavily involved with the treatment system. Such involvement does not come easy and the system must include techniques which will impel him to involvement. Efforts to avoid the development of formal structure have already been described as one technique. Group processes constitute a second technique.

Before a group will help a boy "solve his problems" it demands that he review his total delinquent history. This produces anxiety because, while he is still relatively free, it is almost inevitable that he has much more to reveal than is already known by the police or the court. In an effort to avoid such involvement he may try subterfuge. But any reluctance on his part to be honest will not be taken lightly. Norms dictate that no one in the group can be released until everyone is honest and until every boy helps to solve problems. A refusal to come clean shows a lack of trust in the group and slows down the problem-solving process. Therefore, any recalcitrant boy is faced with a real dilemma. He can either choose involvement or relentless attack by his peers. Once a boy does involve himself, however, he learns that some of his fears were unwarranted. What goes on in the group meeting is sacred and is not revealed elsewhere.

A second process for involvement lies in the use of the peer group to perpetuate the norms of the treatment system. One of the most important norms suggests that most boys in the program are candidates for a reformatory. This is shocking because even habitual delinquents do not ordinarily see themselves as serious offenders.[30] Yet, the tradition is clear; most failures at Pinehills are sent to the Utah State Industrial School. Therefore, each boy has a major decision to make: either he makes serious attempts to change or he gets sent away.

The third process of involvement could only occur in a community program. Each boy has the tremendous problem of choosing between the demands of his delinquent peers outside the program and the demands of those within it. The usual reaction is to test the situa-

450

tion by continuing to identify with the former. Efforts to do this, however, and to keep out of serious trouble are usually unsuccessful. The group is a collective board on delinquency; it usually includes a member who knows the individual personally or by reputation; and it can rely on the meeting to discover many things. Thus, the group is able to use actual behavior in the community to judge the extent to which a boy is involved with the program and to judge his readiness for release. The crucial criterion for any treatment program is not what an individual does while in it, but what he does while he is *not* in it.

The fourth process involves a number of important sanctions which the group can impose if a boy refuses to become involved. It can employ familiar techniques such as ostracism or derision or it can deny him the status and recognition which come with change. Furthermore, it can use sanctions arising out of the treatment system. For example, while authorities may impose restrictions on boys in the form of extra work or incarceration in jail, the group is often permitted, and encouraged, to explore reasons for the action and to help decide what future actions should be taken. For example, a boy may be placed in jail over the week-end and told that he will be returned there each week-end thereafter until his group decides to release him. It is not uncommon for the group, after thorough discussion, to return him one or more weekends despite his protestations. Such an occurrence would be less likely in an ordinary reformatory because of the need for inmates to maintain solidarity against the official system. However, in this setting it is possible because boys are granted the power to make important decisions affecting their entire lives. Rather than having other people do things to them, they are doing things to themselves.

The ultimate sanction possessed by the group is refusal to release a boy from the program. Such a sanction has great power because it is normative to expect that no individual will be tolerated in the program indefinitely. Pinehills is not a place where boys "do time."

Authorities

The third source of pressure towards change rests in the hands of authorities. The role of an authority in a treatment system of this type is a difficult one. On one hand, he cannot be seen as a person whom skillful delinquents or groups can manipulate. But, on the other hand, he cannot be perceived permanently as a "rejector." Everything possible, therefore, must be done by him to create an adult image which is new and different.

Initially, authorities are probably seen as "rejectors." It will be recalled that they do not go out of their way to engage in regular social amenities, to put boys at ease, or to establish one-to-one relationships with boys. Adult behavior of this type is consistent with the treatment philosophy. It attempts to have boys focus upon the peer group, not adults, as the vehicle by which questions and problems are resolved.

Second, boys learn that authorities will strongly uphold the norm which says that Pinehills is not a place for boys to "do time." If, therefore, a boy does not become involved and the group is unwilling or unable to take action, authorities will. Such action varies. It might involve requiring him to work all day without pay, placing him in jail, or putting him in a situation in which he has no role whatsoever. In the latter case he is free to wander around the Center all day but he is neither allowed to work nor given the satisfaction of answers to his questions regarding his future status.

Boys are seldom told why they are in trouble or, if they are told, solutions are not suggested. To do so would be to provide them structure by which to rationalize their behavior, hide other things they have been doing, and escape the need to change. Consequently, they are left on their own to figure out why authorities are doing what they are doing and what they must do to get out of trouble.

Situations of this type precipitate crises. Sometimes boys run away. But, whatever happens, the boy's status remains amorphous until he can come up with a solution to his dilemma. This dilemma, however, is not easily resolved.

There is no individual counseling since this would reflect heavily upon the integrity of the peer group. Consequently, he cannot resolve his problems by counseling with or pleasing adults. His only recourse is to the group. But since the group waits for him to bring up his troubles, he must involve himself with it or he cannot resolve them. Once he does, he must reveal why he is in trouble, what he has been doing to get into trouble or how he has been abusing the program. If he refuses to become involved he may be returned to court by authorities. This latter alternative occurs rarely, since adults have more time than boys. While they can afford to wait, boys find it very difficult to "sweat out" a situation. They feel the need to resolve it.

As a result of such experiences, boys are often confused and hostile. But where such feelings might be cause for alarm elsewhere, they are welcomed at Pinehills. They are taken as a sign that a boy is not in command of the situation and is therefore amenable to change. Nevertheless, the treatment system does not leave him without an outlet for his feelings. The meeting is a place where his anger and hostility can be vented—not only against the program but against the adults who run it. But, in venting his confusion and hostility, it becomes possible for the group to analyze not only his own behavior, but that of adults, and to determine to what end the behavior of all is leading. Initial perceptions of adults which were confusing and provoking can now be seen in a new way. The treatment system places responsibility upon a boy and his peers for changing delinquent behavior, not upon adults. Thus, adult behavior which was initially seen as rejecting can now be seen as consistent with this expectation. Boys have to look to their own resources for solutions of problems. In this way they are denied social-psychological support for "rejecting the rejectors," or for rejecting decisions demanded by the group. Furthermore, as a result of the new adult image which is pressed upon

452 them, boys are led to examine their perceptions regarding other authorities with whom they had difficulties previously in a new, nonsterotyped fashion.

WORK AND OTHER ACTIVITIES

Any use of athletics, handicrafts, or remedial schooling involves a definition of rehabilitation goals. Are these activities actually important in changing delinquents? In the Provo Experiment they are not viewed as having an inherent value in developing non-delinquent behavior. In fact, they are viewed as detrimental because participation in them often becomes criteria for release. On the other hand, work habits are viewed as vitally important. Previous research suggests that employment is one of the most important means of changing reference from delinquent to law-abiding groups.[31] But, such findings simply pose the important question: How can boys be best prepared to find and hold employment?

Sociologists have noted the lack of opportunity structure for delinquents, but attention to a modification of the structure (assuming that it can be modified) as the sole approach to rehabilitation overlooks the need to prepare delinquents to utilize employment possibilities. One alternative for doing this is an education program with all its complications. The other is an immediate attack on delinquent values and work habits. The Provo Experiment chose the latter alternative. It hypothesized that an immediate attack on delinquent values, previous careers, and nocturnal habits would be more effective than an educational program. Sophisticated delinquents, who are otherwise very skillful in convincing peers and authorities of their good intentions, are often unable to work consistently. They have too long believed that only suckers work. Thus concentration is upon work habits. Boys are employed by the city and county in parks, streets, and recreation areas. Their work habits are one focus of group discussion and an important criterion for change. After release, they are encouraged to attend academic and vocational schools should they desire.

THE STARTER MECHANISM:
PUTTING THE SYSTEM IN MOTION

There are both theoretical and practical considerations relative to the purposeful creation of the social structure at Pinehills and the process by which it was developed. The foregoing discussion described some of the structural elements involved and, by inference, suggested the means by which they were introduced. However, the following is presented as a means of further clarification.

The first consideration involved the necessity of establishing structure which could pose realistically and clearly the alternatives open to habitually delinquent boys. What are these alternatives? Since in most cases delinquents are lower-class individuals who not only lack many of the social skills but who have been school failures as well, the alternatives are not great. Some may become professional criminals but this is a small minority. Therefore, most of them have two principal choices: (1) they can continue to be delinquent and expect, in most cases, to end up in prison; or (2) they can learn to live a rather marginal life in which they will be able to operate sufficiently within the law to avoid being locked up. Acceptance of the second alternative by delinquents would not mean that they would have to change their entire style of living, but it does mean that most would have to find employment and be willing to disregard delinquent behavior in favor of the drudgery of everyday living.

Until these alternatives are posed for them, and posed in a meaningful way, delinquents will not be able to make the necessary decisions regarding them. The need, therefore, was for the type of structure at Pinehills which could pose these alternatives initially without equivocation and thus force boys to consider involvement in the rehabilitative process as a realistic alternative for them.

By the time delinquents reach Pinehills they have been cajoled, threatened, lectured, and exhorted—all by a variety of people in a variety of settings: by parents, teachers, police, religious leaders, and court officials. As a consequence, most have developed a set of manipulative techniques which enable them to "neutralize" verbal admonitions by appearing to comply with them, yet refraining all the while from any real adherence. For that reason, it was concluded that *deeds*, not *words*, would be required as the chief means of posing clearly the structural alternatives open to them.

Upon arrival the first delinquents assigned to Pinehills had every reason to believe that this was another community agency for which they possessed the necessary "techniques of neutralization." It was housed in an ordinary two-story home, and authorities spent little time giving instructions or posing threats. It must have seemed, therefore, that Pinehills would not constitute a serious obstacle for which they could not find some means to avoid involvement.

The following are examples of happenings which helped to establish norms contrary to this view. After attending only one day, a rather sophisticated boy was not at home to be picked up for his second day. Instead, he left a note on his front door saying he was at the hospital visiting a sick sister. Official reaction was immediate and almost entirely opposite to what he expected. No one made any efforts to contact him. Instead, a detention order was issued by the court to the police who arrested the boy later that evening and placed him in jail. He was left there for several days without the benefit of visits from anyone and then returned to Pinehills. Even then, no one said anything to him about his absence. No one had to; he did not miss again. Furthermore, he had been instrumental in initiating the norm which says that the principal alternative to Pinehills is incarceration.

A second occurrence established this norm even more clearly. After having been at Pinehills for two months and refusing to yield to the pressures of his group, a boy asked for a rehearing in court, apparently feeling that he could manipulate the judge more successfully than he could the people at Pinehills. His request was acted upon immediately. He was taken to jail that afternoon and a hearing arranged for the following morning. The judge committed him to the State Reformatory.[32] Since that time there has never been another request for a rehearing. In a similar way, especially during the first year, boys who continued to get in serious trouble while at Pinehills were re-called by the court for another hearing and assigned to the reforma-tory. These cases became legendary examples to later boys. How-ever, adults have never had to call attention to them; they are passed on in the peer socialization process.

Once such traditions were established, they could yet be used in another way. They became devices by which to produce the type of uncertainty characteristic of social settings in which negative sanc-tions should be forthcoming but do not appear. The individual is left wondering why. For example, not all boys who miss a day or two at Pinehills now are sent to jail. In some cases, nothing is said to the individual in question. He is left, instead, to wonder when, and if, he will be sent. Likewise, other boys who have been in serious trouble in the community are not always sent to the State Reformatory but may be subjected to the same kind of waiting and uncertainty. Efforts are made, however, to make it impossible for boys to predict in ad-vance what will happen in any particular case. Even adults cannot predict this, relying on the circumstances inherent in each case. Thus, both rigidity and inconsistency are present in the system at the same time.

The same sort of structural alternatives were posed regarding work. Boys who did not work consistently on their city jobs, where they were being paid, were returned to Pinehills to work for nothing. At Pinehills, they were usually alone and had to perform such oner-ous tasks as scrubbing the floor, washing windows, mowing the lawn or cutting weeds. They might be left on this job for hours or weeks. The problem of being returned to work with the other boys for pay was left to them for their own resolution, usually in the group. So long as they said nothing, nothing was said to them except to assign them more work.

This type of structure posed stark but, in our opinion, realistic alternatives. It was stark and realistic because boys were still living in the community, but for the first time could sense the omnipresence of permanent incarceration. However, another type of structure less stringent was needed by which boys could realistically resolve prob-lems and make choices. Since, as has been mentioned, peer-group de-cision-making was chosen as the means for problem-resolution, at-tention was focussed upon the daily group meetings as the primary source of information. It became the focal point of the whole treatment system.

The first group, not having any standards to guide it (except those which suggested resistance to official pressures), spent great por-tions of entire meetings without speaking. However, consistent with the idea that deeds, not words, count, and that a group has to resolve its own problems, the group leader refused to break the silence except at the very end of each meeting. At that time he began standardizing one common meeting practice: he summarized what had been accom-plished. Of silent meetings he simply said that nothing had been accomplished. He did point out, however, that he would be back the next day—that, in fact, he would be there a year from that day. Where would they be, still there? The problem was theirs.

When some boys could stand the silence no longer, they asked the group leader what they might talk about. Rather than making it easy for them he suggested something that could only involve them further: he suggested that someone might recite all the things he had done to get in trouble. Not completely without resources, however, boys responded by citing only those things they had been caught for. In his summary, the leader noted this fact and suggested that whoever spoke the next time might desire to be more honest by telling all. Boys were reluctant to do this but, partly because it was an opportunity to enhance reputations and partly because they did not know what else to do, some gave honest recitations. When no official action was taken against them, two new and important norms were introduced: (1) the idea that what is said in the meeting is sacred to the meeting; and (2) that boys can afford to be candid—that, in fact, candor pays.

The subsequent recitals of delinquent activities ultimately led to a growing awareness of the ambivalence which many delinquents feel regarding their activities. In the social climate provided by the meeting some boys began to express feelings and receive support for behavior which the delinquent system with its emphasis on ideal-typical role behavior could not permit.

Eventually, the meeting reached a stage where it began to discuss the plethora of happenings which occurred daily, both at Pinehills and elsewhere in the community. These happenings, rather than impersonal, easily speculated-about material, were urged as the most productive subject matter. For example, many boys had reached the stage of trying devious rather than direct methods of missing sessions at Pinehills. They came with requests to be excused for normally laudatory activities: school functions, family outings, and even religious services. But, again adults refused to take the traditional course of assuming responsibility and making decisions for boys. Boys were directed to the meeting instead. This not only shifted the responsibility to them, but provided the opportunity to develop five important norms: (1) those having to do with absences; (2) the idea that the place for problem-solving is in the meeting; (3) that everyone, not just adults, should be involved in the process; (4) that if a boy wants the meeting to talk about his problems, he has to justify them as being more important than someone else's; and (5) that any request or point of view has to be substantiated both by evidence and some relevance to the solution of delinquent problems.

It became obvious that even simple requests could be complicated. Boys found themselves using their own rationalizations on each other, often providing both humorous and eye-opening experiences. The climate became increasingly resistant to superficial requests and more conducive to the examination of pressing problems. Boys who chose to fight the system found themselves fighting peers. A stubborn boy could be a thorn in the side of the whole group.

The daily meeting summaries took on increased importance

456

as the leader helped the group: (1) to examine what had happened each day; (2) to examine to what ends various efforts were leading—that is, to examine what various boys were doing, or not doing, and what relevance this had for themselves and the group; (3) to suggest areas of discussion which had been neglected, ignored, or purposely hidden by group members; and (4) to describe the goals of the treatment system in such a way that boys could come to recognize the meaning of group discussions as a realistic source of problem-resolution.

The structural lines associated with the meeting eventually began to define not only the type of subject matter most relevant to change, but the general means for dealing with this subject matter. However, such structure was extremely flexible, permitting a wide latitude of behavior. Great care was taken to avoid the institutionalization of clear-cut steps by which boys could escape Pinehills. Problem solving was, and still is, viewed as a process—a process not easily understood in advance, but something which develops uniquely for each new boy and each new group.

Finally, in summary, the Pinehills system, like many social systems, has some rigid prerequisites for continued membership. The broad structural outlines carefully define the limits beyond which members should not go. However, unlike most extreme authoritarian systems, there is an inner structure, associated with the meeting, which does not demand rigid conformity and which instead permits those deviations which are an honest expression of feelings.

The admission of deviations within the structural confines of the meeting helps to lower the barriers which prevent a realistic examination of their implications for the broader authoritarian structure, either at Pinehills or in society at large. Boys are able to make more realistic decisions as to which roles, conventional or delinquent, would seem to have the most utility for them.

This brief attempt to describe a complex system may have been misleading. The complexities involved are multivariate and profound. However, one important aspect of the experiment has to do with the theoretical development of, and research on, the nature of the treatment system. Each discussion session is recorded and efforts are made to determine means by which treatment techniques might be improved, and ways in which group processes can be articulated. All would be very useful in testing theory which suggests that experience in a cohesive group is an important variable in directing or changing behavior.

PHASE II: COMMUNITY ADJUSTMENT

Phase II involves an effort to maintain reference group support and employment for a boy after intensive treatment in Phase I. After his release from Phase I he continues to meet periodically for discussions with his old group. The goal is to utilize this group in accomplishing three things: (1) acting as a check on a boy's current behavior; (2) serving as a law-abiding reference group; and (3) aiding in the solution of new problems. It seeks to continue treatment in a different and perhaps more intensive way than such traditional practices as probation or parole.

Efforts to find employment for boys are made by the Citizens' Advisory Council. If employment is found, a boy is simply informed that an employer needs someone. No efforts are taken by some well-meaning but pretentious adult to manipulate the boy's life.

These steps, along with the idea that delinquents should be permitted to make important decisions during the rehabilitative process, are consistent with structural-functional analysis which suggests that in order to eliminate existing structure, or identification with it, one must provide the necessary functional alternatives.[33]

APPROPRIATENESS OF TECHNIQUES

Many persons express disfavor with what they consider a harsh and punitive system at Pinehills. If, however, alternatives are not great for habitual delinquents, a program which suggests otherwise is not being honest with them. Delinquents are aware that society seldom provides honors for *not* being delinquent; that, in fact, conventional alternatives for them have not always promised significantly more than delinquent alternatives.[34] Therefore, expectations associated with the adaption of conventional alternatives should not be unrealistic.

On the other hand it should be remembered that, in terms familiar to delinquents, every effort is made at Pinehills to include as many positive experiences as possible. The following are some which seem to function:

1. Peers examine problems which are common to all.

2. There is a recurring opportunity for each individual to be the focal point of attention among peers in which his behavior and problems become the most important concern of the moment.

3. Delinquent peers articulate in front of conventional adults without constraint with regard to topic, language, or feeling.

4. Delinquents have the opportunity, for the first time in an institutional setting, to make crucial decisions about their own lives. This in itself is a change in the opportunity structure and is a means of obligating them to the treatment system. In a reformatory a boy cannot help but see the official system as doing things to him in which he has no say: locking him up, testing him, feeding him, making his decisions. Why should he feel obligated? But when some important decision-making is turned over to him, he no longer has so many grounds for rejecting the system. Rejection in a reformatory might be functional in relating him to his peers, but in this system it is not so functional.

5. Delinquents participate in a treatment system that grants status in three ways: (a) for age and experience in the treatment process—old boys have the responsibility of teaching new boys the norms of the system—; (b) for the exhibition of law-abiding behavior, not only in a minimal sense, but for actual qualitative changes in specific role behavior at Pinehills, home or with friends; and (c) for the willingness to confront other boys, in a group setting, with their delinquent behavior. (In a reformatory where he has to contend with

the inmate system a boy can gain little and lose much for his willingness to be candid in front of adults about peers, but at Pinehills it is a primary source of prestige). The ability to confront others often reflects more about the *confronter* than it does about the *confronted*. It is an indication of the extent to which he has accepted the reformation process and identified himself with it.[35]

6. Boys can find encouragement in a program which poses the possibility of relatively short restriction and the avoidance of incarceration.

7. The peer group is a potential source of reference group support for law-abiding behavior. Boys commonly refer to the fact that their group knows more about them than any other person: parents of friends.

RESEARCH DESIGN

An integral part of the Provo Experiment is an evaluation of treatment extending over a five year period. It includes means by which offenders who receive treatment are compared to two control groups: (1) a similar group of offenders who at time of sentence are placed on probation and left in the community; and (2) a similar group who at time of sentence are incarcerated in the Utah State Industrial School. Since it is virtually impossible to match all three groups, random selection is used to minimize the effect of sample bias. All three groups are drawn from a population of habitual delinquents who reside in Utah County, Utah, and who come before the Juvenile Court. Actual selection is as follows:

The Judge of the Court has in his possession two series of numbered envelopes—one series for selecting individuals to be placed in the *probation* treatment and control groups and one series for selecting the *reformatory* treatment and control groups. These series of envelopes are supplied by the research team and contain randomly selected slips of paper on which are written either *Control Group* or *Treatment Group.*

In making an assignment to one of these groups the Judge takes the following steps: (1) After hearing a case he decides whether he would ordinarily place the offender on probation or in the reformatory. He makes this decision as though Pinehills did not exist. Then, (2) he brings the practice of random placement into play. He does so by opening an envelope from one of the two series supplied him (See Table 1). For example, if he decides initially that he would ordinarily send the boy to the reformatory, he would select an envelope from the *reformatory* series and depend upon the designation therein as to whether the boy would actually go to the reformatory, and become a member of the *control* group, or be sent to Pinehills as a member of the *treatment* group.

This technique does not interfere with the judicial decision regarding the alternatives previously available to the Judge, but it does intercede, after the decision, by posing another alternative. The Judge is willing to permit the use of this alternative on the premise that, in the long run, his contributions to research will enable judicial

Table 1. Section of Treatment and Control Groups **459**

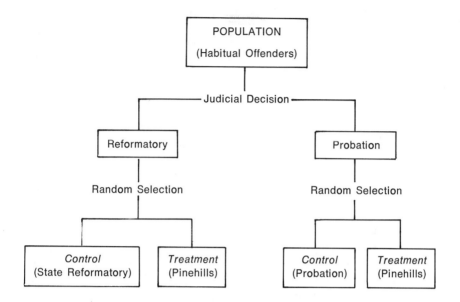

decisions to be based ultimately on a more realistic evaluation of treatment programs available.

In order to make the comparison of treatment and control groups more meaningful, additional research is being conducted on the treatment process. Efforts are made to examine the problems involved in relating causation theory to intervention strategy, the role of the therapist in Guided Group Interaction, and the types of group interaction that seem most beneficial. Finally, a detailed examination is being made of the ways in which boys handle "critical incidents"[36] after release from treatment as compared to the way they handled them prior to treatment.

SUMMARY AND IMPLICATIONS

This paper describes an attempt to apply sociological theory to the treatment of delinquents. It concentrates not only upon treatment techniques, *per se*, but the type of social system in which these techniques must operate. The over-all treatment system it describes is like all other social systems in the sense that it specifies generalized requirements for continued membership in the system. At the same time, however, it also legitimizes the existence of a sub-system within it— the meeting—which permits the discussion and evaluation of happenings and feelings which *may* or *may not* support the over-all normative structure of the larger system.

The purposeful creation of this subsystem simply recognized what seemed to be two obvious facts: (1) that the existence of contrary normative expectations among delinquent and official members of the over-all system would ultimately result in the creation of such a subsystem anyway; and (2) that such a system, not officially recognized, would pose a greater threat, and would inhibit to a greater degree, the realization of the over-all rehabilitative goals of the major system than would its use as a rehabilitative tool.

This subsystem receives not only official sanction but grants considerable power and freedom to delinquent members. By permitting open expressions of anger, frustration, and opposition, it removes social-psychological support for complete resistance to a realistic examination of the ultimate utility of delinquent versus conventional norms. At the same time, however, the freedom it grants is relative. So long as opposition to the demands of the larger system is contained in the meeting subsystem, such opposition is respected. But continued deviancy outside the meeting cannot be tolerated indefinitely. It must be seen as dysfunctional because the requirements of the over-all treatment system are identified with those of the total society and these requirements will ultimately predominate.

At the same time, the over-all treatment system includes elements designed to encourage and support the adoption of conventional roles. The roles it encourages and the rewards it grants, however, are peer-group oriented and concentrate mainly upon the normative expectations of the social strata from which most delinquents come: working- rather than middle-class strata. This is done on the premise that a rehabilitation program is more realistic if it attempts to change normative orientations towards lawbreaking rather than attempting (or hoping) to change an individual's entire way of life. It suggests, for example, that a change in attitudes and values toward work *per se* is more important than attempting to create an interest in the educational, occupational, and recreational goals of the middle-class.

The differences posed by this treatment system, as contrasted to many existing approaches to rehabilitation, are great. Means should be sought, therefore, in addition to this project by which its techniques and orientation can be treated as hypotheses and verified, modified, or rejected.

NOTES

1. Donald R. Cressy, "Changing Criminals: The Application of the Theory of Differential Association," *American Journal of Sociology* 61 (July 1955) : 116.

2. Daniel Glaser maintains that the prison social system has not received the study it merits. Most writing about prisons, he says, is "impressionistic," "moralistic," "superficial," and "biased," rather than "systematic" and "objective." "The Sociological Approach to Crime and Correction," *Law and Contemporary Problems* 23 (Autumn 1958) : 697; *see also* Gresham M. Sykes and Sheldon Messinger, "The Inmate Social System," in *Theoretical Studies in Social Organization of the Prison*, Social Science Research Council, March 1960, pp. 5–19; and Lloyd W. McCorkle and Richard Korn, "Resocialization Within Walls," *The Annals of The American Avademy of Political and Social Science*, 293 (May 1954) : 88–98.

3. Sykes and Messinger, op. cit., pp. 12–13; Richard McCleery, "Policy Change in Prison Management," *Michigan State University Political Research Studies*, No. 5, 1957; Richard A. Cloward, "Social Control in the Prison," in *Theoretical Studies in Social Organization of the Prison*, op. cit., pp. 20–48; and Stanton Wheeler, "Socialization in Correctional Communities," in this issue of the *Review*.

4. Cressey, op. cit., p. 116.

5. For example, see John C. Milner, "Report on an Evaluated Study of the Citizenship Training Program, Island of Hawaii," Los Angeles: University of Southern California School of Social Work, 1959, p. IV. Irving E. Cohen implies that anything which interferes with the establishment of "confidence, sympathy and understanding" between adult and offender interferes with the effectiveness of the individualizd approach. See "Twilight Zones in Probation," *Journal of Criminal Law and Criminology* 37, no. 4, p. 291.

6. Michael Hakeem, "A Critique of the Psychiatric Approach to Juvenile Delinquency," in *Juvenile Delinquency*, edited by Joseph S. Roucek, New York: Philosophical Library, 1958. Hakeem provides a large bibliography to which attention can be directed if further information is desired. See also Daniel Glaser, "Criminality Theories and Behavioral Images," *American Journal of Sociology*, 61 (1956) : 435.

7. Cressey, op. cit., p. 117. LaMay Adamson and H. Warren Dunham even imply that the clinical approach cannot work successfully with habitual offenders. *See* "Clinical Treatment of Male Delinquents: A Case Study in Effort and Result," *American Sociological Review* 21 (June 1956) : 320.

8. One program consistent with this premise is the Highfields Residential Group Center in New Jersey. Modern penology is indebted to it for the development of many unique and important aspects. *See* Lloyd W. McCorkle, Albert Elias, and F. Lovell Bixby, *The Highfields Story: A Unique Experiment in the Treatment of Juvenile Delinquency*, New York: Henry Holt & Co., 1958; H. Ashley Weeks, *Youthful Offenders at Highfields*, Ann Arbor: University of Michigan Press, 1958; and Albert Elias and Jerome Rabow, Post-Release Adjustment of Highfields Boys, 1955–57, *Welfare Reporter*, January 1960, pp. 7–11.

9. Richard A. Cloward and Lloyd E. Ohlin, *Delinquency and Opportunity: A Theory of Delinquent Gangs*, Glencoe, Ill.: The Free Press, 1960; Albert K. Cohen, *Delinquent Boys—The Culture of the Gang*, Glencoe: The Free Press, 1955; Albert K. Cohen and James F. Short, Jr., "Research in Delinquent Subcultures," *The Journal of Social Issues* 14 (1958) : 20–37; Solomon Kobrin, "The Conflict of Values in Delinquency Areas," *American Sociological Review*, 16 (October 1951) : 653–61; Robert K. Merton, *Social Theory and Social Structure*, Glencoe: The Free Press, 1957, Chapters IV–V; Walter B. Miller, "Lower Class Culture as a Generating Milieu of Gang Delinquency," *The Journal of Social Issues* 14 (1958) : 5–19; Clifford R. Shaw, *Delinquency Areas*, Chicago: University of Chicago Press, 1929; Clifford R. Shaw, Henry D. McKay, et al., *Juvenile Delinquency and Urban Areas*, Chicago: University of Chicago Press, 1931; Edwin H. Sutherland, *Principles of Criminology*, 4th ed., Philadelphia: Lippincott, 1947; Frank Tannenbaum, *Crime and the Community*, Boston: Ginn and Co., 1938; F. M. Thrasher, *The Gang*, Chicago: University of Chicago Press, 1936; William F. White, *Street Corner Society*, Chicago: University of Chicago Press, 1943.

10. Richard A. Cloward, "Illegitimate Means, Anomie, and Deviant Behavior," *American Sociological Review* 24 (April 1959) : 164–76; Cloward and Ohlin, op. cit.; Robert K. Merton, "Social Conformity, Deviation, and Opportunity-Structures; A Comment on the Contributions of Dublin and Cloward," *American Sociological Review* 24 (April 1959) : 177–89; Robert K. Merton, "The Social-Cultural Environment and Anomie," *New Perspectives for Research on Juvenile Delinquency*, edited by Helen Kotinsky, U.S. Department of Helath, Education, and Welfare, 1955, pp. 24–50; Merton, *Social Theory and Social Structure*, op. cit.

11. Erik H. Erikson, "Ego Identity and the Psycho-Social Moratorium," *New Perspectives for Research on Juvenile Delinquency*, op. cit. pp. 1–23.

12. Jackson Toby, "The Differential Impact of Family Disorganization," *American Sociological Review* 22 (October 1957) : 505–11; and F. Ivan Nye, *Family Relationships and Delinquent Behavior*, New York: John Wiley & Sons, 1958.

13. Cohen and Short, Jr., op. cit., p. 24.

14. George B. Vold, "Discussion of Guided Group Interaction and Correctional

462 Work," by F. Lovell Bixby and Lloyd W. McCorkle, *American Sociological Review* 16 (August 1951) : 460.

15. As Glaser points out, sociologists have tended to be deterministic and to ally themselves with psychiatrists in the struggle against classical legalists and religious leaders over the free will versus determinism issue. He labels this struggle as a "phony war," involving polemics more than reality. However, he says the war is losing its intensity because of a declining interest in metaphysical issues and a recognition of the importance of voluntaristic rather than reflexive conceptions of human behavior. Contrary to their protestations, the determinists, for example, recognize that humans are aware of alternative possible courses of behavior and make deliberate choices between them. *See* "The Sociological Approach to Crime and Correction," op. cit., pp. 686–87.

16. Sutherland, it will be recalled, maintained that "While criminal behavior is an expression of general needs and values, it is not explained by those general needs and values since non-criminal behavior is an expression of the *same needs and values.*" Op. cit., pp. 6–7, italics ours. The accuracy of the statement would hinge on the definition of "needs" and "values." *See also* David J. Bordua, *Sociological Theories and Their Implications for Juvenile Delinquency*, U.S. Department of Health, Education, and Welfare, 1960, p. 8, and Robin M. Williams, Jr., *American Society*, New York: Alfred A. Knopf, 1955, Chapter 11.

17. Cohen, op. cit., p. 133.

18. Merton, *Social Theory and Social Structure, op. cit.*

19. Cloward, op. cit., and Cloward and Ohlin, op. cit. *See also* Robert Dubin, "Deviant Behavior and Social Structure: Continuities in Social Theory," *American Sociological Review* 24 (April 1959) : 147–64.

20. Cohen, *Delinquent Boys*, op. cit., p. 133; Cohen and Short, op. cit., p. 21. *See also* John I. Kitsuse and David C. Dietrick, "Delinquent Boys: A Critique," *American Sociological Review* 24 (April 1959) : 211.

21. Gresham M. Sykes and David Matza, "Techniques of Neutralization: A Theory of Delinquency," *American Sociological Review* 22 (December 1957) : 664–70.

22. McCorkle and Korn, op. cit., pp. 88–91.

23. Except for the community aspects, the above assumptions and the treatment system are similar to those pioneered at Highfields. *See* McCorkle, Elias, and Bixby, op. cit. The Provo Program is especially indebted to Albert Elias, the present director of Highfields, not only for his knowledge about treatment techniques, but for his criticisms of the Provo Experiment.

24. The idea of a community program is not new. The Boston Citizenship Training Group, Inc., a non-residential program, was begun in 1934–36. However, it is for younger boys and utilizes a different approach. A similar program, initiated by Professor Ray R. Canning, in Provo, was a forerunner to this experiment. See "A New Treatment Program for Juvenile Delinquents," *Journal of Criminal Law and Criminology* 31 (March-April 1941) : 712–19.

25. Judge Paxman is a member of the Advisory Council of Judges to the National Council On Crime and Delinquency and is a member of the symposium preparing a work entitled, *Justice For the Child*, University of Chicago (forthcoming).

26. *See* F. Lovell Bixby and Lloyd W. McCorkle, "Guided Group Interaction and Correctional Work," *American Sociological Review* 16 (August 1951) : 455–59; McCorkle, Elias, and Bixby, *The Highfields Story*, op. cit.; and Joseph Abrahams and Lloyd W. McCorkle, "Group Psychotherapy on Military Offenders," *American Journal of Sociology* 51 (March 1946) : 455–64. These sources present a very limited account of techniques employed. An intimate knowledge would require attendance at group sessions.

27. Other goals relating to the emphasis upon group development, the role of the group therapist, and the nature of the therapeutic situations have been described briefly elsewhere. *See The Highfields Story*, op. cit., pp. 72–80.

28. Cressey, op. cit., p. 119.

29. Vold maintains that guided group interaction assumes that there is something wrong inside the individual and attempts to correct that. He is right in the sense that it emphasizes that an individual must accept responsibility for his own delinquencies and that no one can keep him out of prison unless he himself is ready to stay out. Vold, in our opinion, is incorrect if his remarks are taken to mean that the group does not discuss groups and group processes, what peers mean to a boy or how the orientations of delinquent groups differ from that of conventional society. Op. cit., p. 360.

30. Delinquents are like other people: The worst can never happen to them. *See also* Mark R. Moran, "Inmate Concept of Self in a Reformatory Society," unpublished Ph.D. Dissertation, Ohio State University, 1953.

31. Glaser, "A Sociological Approach to Crime and Corrections," op. cit., pp. 690–91.

32. Co-operation of this type between the Juvenile Courts and rehabilitative agencies is not always forthcoming. Yet, it also reflects two things: (1) the fact that Judge Paxman sentences only those boys to Pinehills who are habitual offenders; and (2) the fact that it is his conviction that rehabilitation must inevitably involve the Court's participation, both in posing alternatives for boys and in determining the effectiveness of various approaches.

33. Edwin M. Schur. "Sociological Analysis in Confidence Swindling," *Journal of Criminal Law, Criminology and Police Science* 48 (September-October 1957) : 304.

34. Gwynn Nettler has raised a question as to who perceives reality most accurately, deviants or "good" people. See "Good Men, Bad Men and the Perception of Reality." Paper delivered at the meetings of the American Sociological Association, Chicago: September 1959.

35. Support for this idea can be found in a recently developed matrix designed to measure the impact of group interaction. See William and Ida Hill, *Interaction Matrix for Group Psychotherapy*, mimeographed manuscript, Utah State Mental Hospital, Provo, Utah, 1960. This matrix has been many years in development.

36. John C. Flanagan, "The Critical Incident Technique," *Psychological Bulletin* 51 (July 1954) : 327–58.

KENNETH E. BOULDING

What the First "Teach-In" Taught Us

I participated in what may well turn out to have been an historic occasion, the first "teach-in" at the University of Michigan. This originated as a protest movement against the escalation of the war in Vietnam, by a group of Michigan faculty, mostly younger men. It developed from a simple protest into what turned out to be a unique educational experience, in which between two and three thousand students literally sat down and talked and argued all night. The movement spread rapidly to other campuses and organized a national teach-in which was held in Washington in May. It now begins to look like almost a national mobilization of university teachers and

Kenneth E. Boulding, "What the First 'Teach-In' Taught Us," *Dissent* (January-February 1966) : 10–15. Reprinted by permission of the author and the publisher.

464   students. In a way, the forerunner of this movement was the remarkable mobilization of faculty members on university campuses against
Goldwater, which represented political arousement on a scale which
has rarely, if ever, been seen before in these supposedly cloistered circles. The teach-in movement is clearly a response to Johnson's behaving like Goldwater, so in a way is part of this same arousal.

Nobody, unfortunately, is much concerned to study the effects
of all this, some of which may be quite different from what the people who are aroused by the arousal intend. I am constantly impressed
by the ironies of social systems, where action often produces quite the
reverse of the consequences which are intended. On the other hand,
presumably, the better our knowledge of social systems, the more likely
are we to avoid any unintentional consequences. It is important, therefore, for protesters to have some theory of protest, and to be sensitive
to those circumstances in which protest is effective in achieving its intended consequences, and those circumstances in which it is not.

Let me venture, then, on a few tentative suggestions for a possible theory of protest, in the form of some tentative propositions.

1. Protest arises when there is strongly felt dissatisfaction with
existing programs and policies of government or other organizations,
on the part of those who feel themselves affected by these policies but
who are unable to express their discontent through regular and legitimate channels, and who feel unable to exercise the weight to which
they think they are entitled in the decisionmaking process. When nobody is listening to us and we feel we have something to say, then
comes the urge to shout. The protester is the man in the advertisement
who does not read the *Philadelphia Bulletin*, but who has something
very important to say that clearly isn't in it. Furthermore, as he apparently has no access to the *Bulletin*, all he can do is to stand in the
middle of its complacent readers and scream. In the present case, the
State Department White Paper on Vietnam is clearly the *Philadelphia
Bulletin*; the protesters are those who see something quite obvious
that isn't in it.

2. Protest is most likely to be successful where it represents a
view which is in fact widespread in the society, but which has somehow not been called to people's attention. The protest of the man who
does not read the *Philadelphia Bulletin* is likely to be highly successful, as he is usually trying to call attention to events which obviously
ought to be in the *Bulletin*, being intrinsically newsworthy. Societies,
like solutions, get supersaturated or supercooled; that is, they reach
a situation in which their present state is intrinsically unstable but it
does not change because of the absence of some kind of nucleus around
which change can grow. Under these circumstances, protest is like the
seed crystal or the silver iodide in the cloud. It precipitates the whole
system toward a position which it really ought to be in anyway. We
see this exemplified in the relative success of the protest movements in
civil rights. Here we have a situation, as Myrdal saw very clearly in
The American Dilemma, in which certain fundamental images of
the American society were inconsistent with its practices, and where,
therefore, the protesters could appeal to an ideal which was very widely

held. Wherever there is hypocrisy, there is strong hope of change, for the hypocrite is terribly vulnerable to protest. On the other hand, in the absence of protest, the supersaturated society may go on for a long time without change, simply because of what physicists call the nucleation problem.

Where the society is not supersaturated, a protest movement has a much rougher time. It then has to move the society toward the new position, from which change can then crystallize out, and this is a much more difficult task than crystallizing change in a society that is ready for it. Furthermore, protest as a social form, which may be very effective and indeed necessary in crystallizing a supersaturated society, may be quite ineffective in moving a society which is not saturated for change toward a point where it is saturated. That is, the techniques for creating the preconditions of change, may be very different from the techniques required for crystallizing it. Where a society is divided and ambivalent, a protest movement designed to push it in one direction may easily arouse movements of counterprotest designed to resist the movement or to push it in the other direction. This is something to which protesters rarely give sufficient attention. Because they are themselves emotionally aroused, they tend to think that almost everybody must be in a similar frame of mind, which may not be true at all. It is quite possible, for instance, for protest movements to arouse counterprotests much larger than the original protests, and hence the net result of the protest is to move the system away from the direction in which the protesters want it to move. The Goldwater campaign was a good example of this. Goldwater was nominated as a Republican candidate as a result of a protest movement among discontented conservatives. The result, however, was the arousal of a much larger movement of counter-protest among those who were frightened and dismayed by Goldwater, which resulted in a quite unprecedented defeat.

4. The dynamic processes of social systems are not entirely random, and this means that any particular social system is more likely to go in some directions than it is in others. Obviously, a protest movement which is trying to push the social system in a direction in which it has a high probability of going anyway is more likely to be successful than one that is trying to push the social system in a direction that has a low probability. Unfortunately, it is by no means easy to assess the various probabilities of change; nevertheless, we can surely know something about it. At least we can be pretty sure, for instance, that movements toward absolute hereditary monarchies today have a pretty slim chance of success. We can identify certain cumulative processes in the history of social systems, such as the growth of knowledge, the widening of integrative systems, and so on, which have a certain long-run irreversibility about them, even if they may have short-run setbacks. Systems move, however painfully, towards payoffs. As we learn to understand the payoffs, we can identify those protest movements which have the best chance of success. On the other hand, it is not the "real" payoffs which determine human behavior, but the imagined ones, and there can often be a strong diver-

gence between the two, at least in the short run, and this short run can be painfully long.

5. We might perhaps distinguish between protest movements and educational movements, the one designed to crystallize a change for which a society is ready, the other to push the society toward a change for which it is not yet ready. The techniques of these two movements may be very different. A protest movement needs to be shrill, obstreperous, undignified, and careless of the pattern of existing legitimacy which it is seeking to destroy, in the interest of a new pattern which is waiting to emerge. Educational movements have to be low-keyed, respectful of existing legitimacies and tying into them wherever possible, and chary of arousing counterprotest. A good example of this in race relations is the work of the NAACP, which unquestionably laid the educational groundwork for the recent protest movement in civil rights. When the movement for protest arrives, however, the educational institution is often pushed aside, and perhaps properly so, as inappropriate in the circumstances. On the other hand, protest movements for which society has not been prepared by education, or which are seeking for improbable change, are virtually doomed to failure, like the IWW. The movement for social security in this country is an interesting example of one in which the educational process dominates it almost completely, and where the role of protest is almost negligible.

6. Even when a situation is ripe for a protest movement, it can go astray and be ineffective if it takes an inappropriate form. The form of a protest should be closely related to the object of protest. This is why, for instance, on the whole, the sit-ins have been very successful, whereas marches and parades are usually less so. It can be particularly disastrous to the protest movement if the protest takes a form which arouses a counterprotest over the form itself, and not over the object of protest. Any object of protest can easily be lost in argument and counterargument over the question as to whether the form of the protest is legitimate or appropriate.

7. Protest movements are also likely to be weakened if the object of protest is not clear, or if there are many different objects, some of them incompatible, combined in the same protest. Thus the strike in industrial conflict is usually a rather effective form of protest, particularly when it is directed toward a change that would have come anyway, because it is appropriate to the objective, and the objective itself is usually very clear. Political protest, by contrast, is apt to be diffuse; its objectives are unclear and often inconsistent. Political protest movements almost always run into the problem of strange bedfellows, and the less clear the objectives of protest, the less likely is anybody to fulfill them.

With these propsitions in mind, let us now take a look at the peace movement and the current movement of protest against the war in Vietnam. Unlike the civil rights movement, which had fulfilled almost all the conditions for successful protest, the peace movement only fulfills some of them. The condition which it fulfills is that related to the long-run payoff. There is no doubt that the payoffs of a stable peace are enormous. The $120 billion a year that the world spends on the war industry is an appalling waste which may well set back the achievement of world development by even hundreds of years, and might even prevent it altogether. The probability of long-run change toward a system of stable peace is therefore high, and the peace movement fulfills this one essential requirement for the success of a movement for social change. On the other hand, it fulfills practically none of the other conditions. Its objectives in terms of specific institutional and behavorial change are not clear. We still do not really know how to get stable peace, and what particular forms of behavior lead us toward rather than away from this goal. There is, furthermore, a great diversity of view as to immediate objectives within the peace movement.

It is clear also that American society at least is not supersaturated in regard to social change toward stable peace. In a sense, the task of the peace movement is fundamentally educational, rather than protest. Most of the communications which are received by Americans, whether in the formal educational system or in the informal contacts of face to face conversation, tend to create an image of the world in which war is a recurrent necessity, and in which, furthermore, for the United States, war has paid off pretty well. We tend to associate war with easy victories, like the war against Mexico or Spain, or with periods of economic prosperity and recovery from depression, as in the Second World War. We are not and never have been a peace-loving nation; we are not only ruthless and bloody but we feel no shame about it. There is nothing in our Constitution; in our national heroes, many of whom are generals; in our national origin, which came out of a war; in our greatest single national experience, which was the Civil War; or in anything which contributes to our national image which makes war illegitimate in the way racial discrimination is felt to be illegitimate and inconsistent with our national ideals. In the case of war we have very little hypocrisy, and change is very difficult. The peace movement is not simply trying to mobilize an already existing mass feeling or sentiment; it is trying to create a radical change in the national image, against which all the forces of ordinary legitimacy seem to be arrayed. In the case of the peace movement, therefore, protest arouses counterprotest with great ease. The hawks in our society far outnumber the doves, and those who flutter the dovecotes stand in danger of arousing clouds of hawks from their innumerable nests. It will take an extensive process of education and perhaps even the grim teacher of national disaster before we learn that the prevailing national image is incompatible with our well-being or even with our survival, and we have yet to learn that we are only one people among many, that we are not the rulers of the world, that power cannot be exercised without legitimacy, and that the costs of stable peace, significant and important as they are, are far less than the benefits.

The teach-in movement represents perhaps a partly subconscious recognition of the validity of some of the above principles. It began as a movement of pure protest and outrage. The motivations which inspired it were no doubt various. They included a genuine fear of escalation into nuclear warfare; they included also a sense of moral outrage at the use of such things as napalm and the "lazy dog," and the appalling sufferings which we are imposing on the Vietnamese in the supposed name of freedom and democracy. Coupled with this, unquestionably, were some people on the left who were politically sympathetic with the objectives of the Vietcong, though in the original movement there were few if any of these. I am inclined to think that the largest motivating factor was a sense of simple human sympathy with the sufferings of the Vietnamese, and a sense of outrage at the utterly inhuman weapons of the American air force, and a sense of outrage also that we were using Vietnamese as the guinea pigs in weapon experimentation. The method of protest first suggested by the original group at University of Michigan was a work moratorium and a one-day suspension of classes. This violated a good many of the above principles. It is a form of protest which is not related to the object of protest; it immediately aroused a large counterprotest over the means, as well as over the object of protest, and it was very strongly on the protest side of the spectrum and away from education. The teach-in, which was adopted as a substitute, was much more successful. It at least edged toward the education end of the spectrum, even though it still retained a good many of the qualities of protest, and it was appropriate to the situation. The teach-in movement, furthermore, seems to be developing more and more in the direction of dialogue rather than pure protest, and this itself reflects the fact that there is an educational task ahead rather than a task of pure protest. The basic problem here is change in the national image itself, and this is something which protest is singularly unable to do, for protest has to take the image for granted and call attention to certain inconsistencies and incompatibilities. It assumes a given national image and says, in effect, to the policymaker, "be consistent with it."

Under these circumstances, what is likely to be the best strategy for those of us who are interested in producing social change toward stable peace? The answer seems fairly clear. It should be a strategy of limited protest and extensive education. We should not, I think, abandon protest altogether, for there are many points even now at which, for instance, the conduct of the war in Vietnam violates a widespread national image of the United States as a reasonably decent and compassionate country. Protest, I suspect, should be directed mainly at the air force; it should be directed at the use of specific weapons and certainly fall under the heading of "cruel and unusual punishments," the moral feeling against which is securely enshrined in our Constitution and history. We have paid enough lip service to the United Nations also, to render protests on this score viable. The contrast between the shred of legitimacy which the United Nations gave us in Korea and the total absence of legitimacy in Vietnam is very striking, and protest could well be concentrated on this. We also have in our national image a high value on negotiation and willingness to negotiate, and our present interpretation of negotiation as the abject surrender of the other side can be protested fiercely and effectively. Beyond this, I suspect, protest will be ineffective, with one possible exception. Our deepest trouble in Vietnam arises out of the total failure of our China policy, and at this point it may well be that the country is ripe for change, and that, to continue this particular metaphor, protest will shake the tree. There is real danger lest in our obsession with Vietnam we forget the larger issue and we forget that the solution to Vietnam lies in our relationship with Peking.

Beyond this, social change toward stable peace can only come through education and research. The educational task is to convince people that stable peace is possible. Here we need to point to the many examples in which it has already been achieved. In the educational process, unlike in the process of protest, we want to tie in as far as possible with existing legitimacy, existing images, and familiar history. We need to play up how we got a security community with the British and the Canadians. We need to play up historical examples of peaceful coexistence, such as was achieved between Protestants and Catholics in the Treaty of Wesphalia in 1648. We need to emphasize the continuing dynamic that goes on in socialist countries as well as in our own, and to emphasize the learning process and our role as a teacher. We need to emphasize also the possible role of the United States not as a great power or as a world dominator, but as a leader in a world movement for stable peace. All these things can easily be fitted into existing images and existing legitimacies. Then at some point, a protest movement may be necessary to crystallize the image as a peace leader. This may be some time off, but we should be ready for it when it comes.

Background of Contemporary Society

PART **4**

The first three sections of this text have been devoted to some of the basic concepts used by sociologists to analyze organized social life, and to the description and analysis of some of the processes, patterns, and mechanisms that occur in collective units. I have emphasized a general approach to man and his patterns of social organizations rather than concentrated on specific historical periods. Kanter's article on Utopian communities, Boulding's on the "teach-in," and Friedman's on the American student movement touch upon time in their analyses and explanations of social phenomena. However, none of these articles make an attempt to deal with sequences of actual events. Rather, they describe and attempt to document some of the factors or variables which they believe are causally linked to the phenomena they discuss.

This section, *The Background of Contemporary Society*, attempts to furnish the student with some broad-ranging descriptions of the historical background of modern society. Knowledge of earlier societies and the sequence of major changes within them is essential for thorough understanding of modern life and modern man. The following chapter describes and analyzes the main patterns of social organization of the past, and the ways in which they have changed.

Affection

FACTORIES

FEUDALISM

Homogeneity

Transformation

Evolution

Guilds

Trade

MERCHANTS

KINSHIP

Industrialization

PRICE

HISTORY

MACHINE

FIEF

SOLIDARITY

MARKET

SELF-INTEREST

Craftsmen

ELITE

Artisans

CRITICISM

MYTHS

Tradition

WORKERS

URBANIZATION

Stories

VILLAGE

MORALE

Study Questions

1. What are the major differences and similarities between folk and feudal societies?
2. What is Sjoberg's major thesis?
3. How are societies changed, according to Marx and Engels?
4. What is a market situation?
5. What are the major consequences of industrialization?

Folk, Feudal, Preindustrial, and Urban-Agrarian Societies

12

Social scientists and philosophers have been very interested in the quality of life in different societies. Many have looked at life in small, undifferentiated societies and have tried to explain contemporary society as the result of an evolutionary sequence.

In this chapter I shall briefly mention some schemes used to analyze changes in societies, and then describe the social organization of folk, feudal, preindustrial, and urban-agrarian societies.

SOME VIEWS OF THE SHIFT

One of the first theories of major societal change was Sir Henry Maine's proposition that there was an evolutionary development from societies based on status to societies based on contract. He developed this idea through an analysis of legal thought in the Roman Empire. In his book, *Ancient Law*, written in 1854, Maine said that primitive societies are those in which individuals are born with certain rights, duties, and powers. Status is an ascribed rather than an achieved condition. These primitive societies tend to develop into societies where positions are based on performance rather than on personal attributes.[1]

A second scheme, developed by Ferdinand Toennies in 1887, employed the terms *Gemeinschaft* and *Gesellschaft* to describe two differing types of societies. In the former, there existed a community whose members were linked by close emotional ties of kinship and affection. As these patterns of social relations were broken, society moved toward new patterns of organization. In *Gesellschaft* society people are tied, not by common values and similar interests, but by complex networks of market relations which develop from self-interest.[2]

A third scheme, mentioned in chapter 4, is Durkheim's conception of mechanical and organic solidarity. Mechanical solidarity is based upon a common or collective consciousness, in which people coalesce around similar values and standards. The study of law and its changing form and emphasis convinced Durkheim that a new kind

474

of social cohesiveness was evolving. This type of solidarity, in which **475** social ties and relationships result from interdependent roles or roles which complement each other.[3]

Charles Horton Cooley, mentioned in chapter 4, was also interested in the changing form of society. He felt that the close emotional ties of primary groups were critical for individual socialization. He was very much concerned about the erosion of these relationships in modern society, and he speculated on ways in which these close emotional ties, necessary to make men human, might be maintained in an increasingly complex society. Although other views of societal change could be discussed here, they would only serve to add weight to the major point: societies have evolved, and this evolution has been of great concern to many social scientists. To describe the dimensions of shifts, it is necessary to examine preindustrial society in greater detail.

THE SOCIAL ORGANIZATION OF FOLK SOCIETY

In folk society, there is a high degree of solidarity and loyalty because there is great homogeneity. Common traditions and strong kinship ties contribute to an effective form of social control.

Certain patterns or forms of social organization characterize the folk society. First, there is neither imperative order nor formal government in the social unit. Instead, a primitive form of democracy and leadership exists. The division of labor, which may be relatively complex, does not contribute to the development of value differences because it has many ritualistic aspects. Thus, before or after a hunt or before members go out to sea, the society as a whole may celebrate or pray. These rites tend to unite members through an emphasis on their common values and interests. There are several important differences in the social organization and values of folk and modern societies.

Folk society is organized around kinship ties. This means that social relationships have a wide scope and carry diffuse obligations, rights, and privileges. In contrast to folk society our family obligations in modern societies are rather narrow and many family functions are more symbolic than real. In the modern family, the exchange of goods and resources is minimal. If a child wants to borrow money from his parents after he is 21 years old, the parents may lend it to him if they can, but they don't feel obligated to go out and find the money for him, no does the child feel that his parents must fulfill their obligations to him by obtaining outside funds for the loan.

The value system of a folk society is different from that of modern society in that there is greater agreement on values in folk society.

The values of folk society also stress tradition and spontaneity. The organization of folk society around kinship lines operationalizes these values. Values and beliefs in folk society are very directly connected to the way of life of the people. Emphasis upon tradition and strong kinship organization tends to discourage any challenge of societal values. The challenging of the value scheme comes about with the transformation of folk society.

476 FOLK URBAN CONTINUUM

An ideal picture of folk society is presented in the selection written by anthropologist Robert Redfield. "The Folk Society" is based upon Redfield's nine years of work in the Yucatan Peninsula from 1927 to 1936. This article describes ten variables that Redfield and his co-workers found useful in comparing and contrasting societies. Redfield's work is a useful benchmark for describing other social units, although there has been a fair amount of criticism directed toward his typology.

One of the main sources of this criticism is the work done by Oscar Lewis, who visited Tepoztlan on the Yucatan Peninsula in 1943. Lewis found that Tepoztlan was not as homogeneous, isolated, smoothly functioning, and well integrated as Redfield had pictured it. Lewis witnessed violence, disruption, cruelty, disease, suffering, and maladjustment, none of which had been described in the earlier study. According to Lewis, Redfield failed to note poverty, tensions between villages, lack of cooperation, schisms within the village, and the pervading qualities of fear, envy, and distrust in interpersonal relationships that existed.

Despite the cogent criticisms of Redfield's continuum, his study points out certain important characteristics of primitive societies and sheds some light on our effort to understand more complex society.

PREINDUSTRIAL CITY

The major implication of Redfield's position is that urbanization was the impetus for transformation in folk society. The second selection included in this chapter argues against the position taken by Redfield. In "The Preindustrial City," sociologist Gideon Sjoberg notes that early urban life had many traditional characteristics and that industrialization rather than urbanization was the major source of change.

In the preindustrial city, extensive trade brought about widened contacts with other cultures. New ideas were carried into the city and were modified and altered by their merging with already established ideas, values, and beliefs. Up until this point, scholars and philosophers were concerned with justifying the ways of God to man. Now myths and stories and recorded history were introduced, and were made available for analysis, discussion, and debate. These older stories, once they were recorded, functioned as ideals against which social reality could be weighed. A new process—social criticism—then arose out of conflicts among the ideologies of various social groups.

In the preindustrial city, structural conflict that was part of the fabric of the social organization arose for the first time. In the folk society there was conflict over property, resources, adultery, family relationships, or kin insults, but the conflict was always between similar units over specific objects or resources. In the preindustrial city, however, there was conflict between different units over different resources. The city created dissimilar interests and outlooks and a variety of sources of power. New groups and new alliances grew up which challenged the traditional forms of power as well as the traditional values.

477

URBAN-AGRARIAN SOCIETY

Surrounding the preindustrial city were peasant villages, and, although they approximated the folk society described by Redfield, they differed from it in important respects. These villages were linked to the preindustrial city through a market relationship. This relationship served as an impetus to change, for there began a slow process that may be described as the *rationalization of work*. Up until this point in time, agriculture and handicrafts served the needs of the village. The qualitative measure of work and the craftsman's creative "self" were necessities of existence. As urban-agrarian society evolved, work came to be measured in more quantitative or rational ways. How much was a crop worth? What percentage of the cultivated land belonged to the church or to the lord? What agricultural materials or tools were most productive?

At the same time, the exchange relationship between the city and the surrounding peasant villages and the resulting surplus of resources gave rise to a series of social roles that connected the city and the villages. Tax collectors, land renters, and outside tradesmen who practiced sharp trading practices appeared. The villages were no longer turned inward and self-contained, but became linked with the preindustrial city. The feudal order which emerged could be described as a network consisting of preindustrial cities and their surrounding peasant villages.

The social organization of the village was characterized by high solidarity among the peasants. The normative order was traditional or sacred. With the growth of the city, patterns of imperative order emerged and individuals began to deal with strangers regarding manufactured goods, agricultural products, taxes and other economic concerns. Within the peasant village, patterns of economic exchange enforced social solidarity, but as they developed between the village and the preindustrial city these patterns became detached from considerations of solidarity. The village society was characterized by elites that had vested economic interests and by a traditionally oriented mass of peasants. This society, which was strongly resistant to change, was radically transformed by industrialization.

Sjoberg's major point of disagreement with Redfield encompasses the issues of urbanization and industrialization. Redfield feels that urbanization itself is a major cause in the transformation of society. Sjoberg, on the other hand, argues that the preindustrial city differs sharply from the industrial city. The preindustrial city depends on animal or human sources of power, while the industrial city develops inanimate sources of power. There is little fragmentation of work in the preindustrial city, for work is organized around guilds. Most important, the economic system of the preindustrial city is nonrational, for there is no standardization of weights or measures, and fixed prices are rare. The imperative order in the preindustrial city consists of a literate elite that functions with an uneducated mass.

478 There is no mass communication system. The lack of social mobility enforces loyalty. The emphasis on kinship influences occupational recruitment as well as marriage. Religion infuses all aspects of life.

Sjoberg's central hypothesis is that industrialization accounts for many of the differences in social organization between the preindustrial city and the industrial city. It is impossible for a form of production based on inanimate sources of power to develop in the preindustrial city. This sort of production requires a rationalized and centralized economic organization, in which recruitment is based on universalistic rather than particularistic principles and on a value system in which status is acquired by achievement rather than by ascription.* Industrialization, Sjoberg says, not only provides a necessary kind of social structure but also provides the means for its establishment.

TRANSFORMATION OF THE FEUDAL ORDER

There are important differences between the feudal order and modern industrial society. Within industrial society there is extensive exchange and division of labor. People and communities form networks of economic interrelations. Exchange creates secularized communities in which large groups of people are brought together. It is said that trade was the significant factor in bringing about new forms of solidarity and exchange, but barter in itself does not imply a market. A true market is brought about by the development of a price mechanism. Price is impersonal. It reflects economic facts rather than traditional norms, values, or beliefs. As you have already read in the article by Cottrell in chapter 7, there is nothing sacred or traditional about the steam locomotive. The diesel engine was introduced because its use permitted the railroad to carefully estimate profits, expenses, and losses. The price mechanism allows for impersonal decisions. This is a market situation. In feudal society, trade was organized around imperative order and traditional norms, rather than by the impersonal relations of money markets. Royal patents not only authorized trade but set the amounts and prices of the goods to be traded. The terms of trade were the outcome of diplomatic agreements, and could not change with flucuating economic conditions as they would in a true market. The true market is the product of industrialized society. It was not trade that transformed the feudal order, because trade under feudalism was conducted by tradition rather than by impersonal market mechanisms. Industrialization and the money market it developed were responsible for the transformation to a different kind of social order.

With the evolution of a truly industrial economy, two important developments occurred: the handicraft industries were destroyed

---

*Universalistic principles of classification refer to some general or objective frame of reference. Particularistic criteria are standards which are applied when the person himself is involved. The criteria are basically cognitive (universalism) and cathectic (particularism), in the example above, one hires employees on the basis of tests and interviews (universalism) and not on the basis of kinship (particularism).

by the development of inanimate sources of power; and the traditional **479** controls of the market were torn away. In industrialized societies, impersonal forces shape the market. These forces are responsible for the development of functionally specific relationships, contractual and temporary relations. The most important change arising from the development of industrial order is the domination of the economy by machines and factories.

The feudal economy was based on the control of land. A small elite class owned the land, and the peasant mass cultivated it. Merchants and artisans composed only a small fraction of a population. With increasing trade and commerce, however, more goods were desired. As the demands for goods grew, there developed a class of free laborers and craftsmen who could satisfy them. These workers left the fief or estate of the noble and went to the cities or the newly developing towns. Groups of independent artisans organized and set up guilds. Specific crafts monopolies developed. The guilds formulated restrictions on membership, training requirements, and standards for their products. Under the feudal order production became guild-organized. But with the further increase in the demand for goods, guilds began eperiencing difficulties in controlling their products. Merchants who traveled and traded were close to market conditions and demands and began to dictate standards to the guildmasters and master craftsmen. They purchased raw materials and supplied them to the guilds, and the cost of this material was deducted from the cost of the finished product. The artisans and craftsmen found themselves at the mercy of the market and the merchants, who directed production. Guilds lost control of the market and merchants became increasingly important. Increasing rationalization of production was in the direct interest of the merchants, and through their travels and trade they acquired simple machines for new methods of production. But machine production itself did not suffice to change the old order. Maximum efficiency required the supervision of workers and the separation of work and home life. The providers of machines began to control the people who were producing; home industries were destroyed by the development of inanimate power. The development of a factory system was concomitant with the development of a labor market, where workers could offer their time and effort for wages.

Thus, industrialization had two important consequences for modern society: first, large groups of people were placed under a new form of discipline—the regulation of their time and skill by factory production; second, control over the entire trade apparatus of society passed into the hands of the owners of factories and the bourgeosie.

Included in this chapter's readings, in addition to the selections by Redfield and Sjoberg, is an exerpt from *The Communist Manifesto*, by Karl Marx and Friedrich Engels. It is a classic piece of revolutionary writing, and speaks to the issues of evolution and transformation from less to more complex social order. Marx and Engels decry the conditions created by industrialization and describe their vision of the way the industrial order will be changed.

480 NOTES

1. Sir Henry Maine, Sumner *Ancient Law* (London: Oxford University Press, The World's Classics. 1931).

2. Toennies *Gemeinschaft und Gessellschaft* (1st Ed., 1887), trans. and ed. C. P. Loomis in *Fundamental Concepts in Sociology* (New York: American Book Co., 1940).

3. Emile Durkheim, *The Division of Labor in Society*, trans. George Simpson (New York: The Free Press of Glencoe, Inc., 1947).

4. Charles Horton Cooley, *Social Organization* (New York: Schocken Books, 1962).

5. Oscar Lewis, *Tepoztlan: Village in Mexico* (New York: Holt, Rinehart and Winston, 1960).

ROBERT REDFIELD

The Folk Society

Understanding of society in general and of our own modern urbanized society in particular can be gained through consideration of the societies least like our own: the primitive, or folk, societies.[1] All societies are alike in some respects, and each differs from others in other respects; the further assumption made here is that folk societies have certain features in common which enable us to think of them as a type—a type which contrasts with the society of the modern city.[2]

This type is ideal, a mental construction. No known society precisely corresponds with it, but the societies which have been the chief interest of the anthropologist most closely approximate it. The construction of the type depends, indeed, upon special knowledge of tribal and peasant groups. The ideal folk society could be defined through assembling, in the imagination, the characters which are logically opposite those which are to be found in the modern city, only if we had first some knowledge of nonurban peoples to permit us to determine what, indeed, are the characteristic features of modern city living. The complete procedure requires us to gain acquaintance with many folk societies in many parts of the world and to set down in words general enough to describe most of them those characteristics which they have in common with each other and which the modern city does not have.

In short, we move from folk society to folk society, asking ourselves what it is about them that makes them like each other and

Robert Redfield, "The Folk Society," *American Journal of Sociology* 60 (January 1947): 293–308. Copyright © 1947 by the University of Chicago. Reprinted by permission of the author and the University of Chicago Press.

different from the modern city. So we assemble the elements of the **481** ideal type. The more elements we add, the less will any one real society correspond to it. As the type is constructed, real societies may be arranged in an order of degree of resemblance to it. The conception develops that any one real society is more or less "folk." But the more elements we add, the less possible it becomes to arrange real societies in a single order of degree of resemblance to the type, because one of two societies will be found to resemble the ideal type strongly in one character and weakly in another, while in the next society strong resemblance will lie in the latter character and not in the former. This situation, however, is an advantage, for it enables us to ask and perhaps answer questions, first, as to whether certain characters tend to be found together in most societies, and then, if certain of them do, why.

Anyone attempting to describe the ideal folk society must take account of and in large degree include certain characterizations which have been made of many students, each of whom has been attentive to some but not to all aspects of the contrast between folk and modern urban society. Certain students have derived the characterization from examination of a number of folk societies and have generalized upon them in the light of contrast provided by modern urban society; the procedure defined above and followed by the writer. This is illustrated by Goldenweiser's characterization of five primitive societies. He says that they are small, isolated, nonliterate; that they exhibit local cultures; that they are relatively homogeneous with regard to the distribution of knowledge, attitudes, and functions among the population; that the individual does not figure as a conspicuous unit; and that knowledge is not explicitly systematized.[3]

In other cases the students have compared the state of certain societies at an early time with the same, or historical descendant of the same, society at a later time. In this way Maine arrived at his influential contrasts between society based on kinship and society based on territory, and between a society of status and one of contract.[4] In the case of this procedure, as in the case of the next, broad and illuminating conceptions are offered us to apply to folk societies as we contrast them with modern urban society. We are to find out if one of the contrasting terms is properly applicable to folk society and the other term to modern urban society.

In the work of still other students there is apparent no detailed comparison of folk with urbanized societies or of early society with later; rather, by inspection of our own society or of society in general, contrasting aspects of all society are recognized and named. This procedure is perhaps never followed in the unqualified manner just described, for in the instances about to be mentioned there is evidence that folk or ancient society has been compared with modern urbanized society. Nevertheless, the emphasis placed by men of this group is upon characteristics which, contrasting logically, in real fact coexist in every society and help to make it up. Here belongs Tonnies' contrast between *Gemeinschaft* and *Gesellschaft*, or that aspect of society which appears in the relations that develop without the deliberate intention of anyone out of the mere fact that men live to-

482

gether, as contrasted with that aspect of society which appears in the relations entered into deliberately by independent individuals through agreement to achieve certain recognized ends.[5] Comparable is Durkheim's distinction between that social solidarity which results from the sharing of common attitudes and sentiments and that which results from the complementary functional usefulnesses of the members of the group. In the "social segment"—the form of society existing in terms of "mechanical solidarity"—the law is "repressive"; in the "social organ"—the form of society existing in terms of "organic solidarity"—the law is "restitutive."[6]

It may be asked how closely the constructed type arrived at by any one investigator who follows the procedure sketched above will resemble that reached by another doing the same. It may be supposed that to the extent to which the real societies examined by the one investigator constitute a sample of the range and variety of societies similar to the sample constituted by the societies examined by the other, and to the extent that the general conceptions tentatively held by the one are similar to those held by the other, the results will be (except as modified for other factors) the same. For the purposes of understanding which are served by the method of the constructed type, however, it is not necessary to consider the question. The type is an imagined entity, created only because through it we may hope to understand reality. Its function is to suggest aspects of real societies which deserve study, and especially to suggest hypotheses as to what, under certain defined conditions, may be generally true about society. Any ideal type will do, although it is safe to assert that that ideal construction has most heuristic value which depends on close and considered knowledge of real folk societies and which is guided by an effective scientific imagination—whatever that may be.

"The conception of a 'primitive society' which we ought to form," wrote Sumner, "is that of small groups scattered over a territory."[7] The folk society is a small society. There are no more people in it than can come to know each other well, and they remain in long association with each other. Among the Western Shoshone the individual parental family was the group which went about, apart from other families, collecting food; a group of families would assemble and so remain for a few weeks, from time to time, to hunt together; during the winter months such a group of families would form a single camp.[8] Such a temporary village included perhaps a hundred people. The hunting or food-collecting bands considered by Steward, representing many parts of the world, contained, in most cases, only a few score people.[9] A Southwestern Pueblo contained no more than a few thousand persons.

The folk society is an isolated society. Probably there is no real society whose members are in complete ignorance of the existence of people other than themselves; the Andamanese, although their islands were avoided by navigators for centuries, knew of outsiders and occasionally came in contact with Malay or Chinese visitors.[10] Nevertheless, the folk societies we know are made up of people who have little communication with outsiders, and we may conceive of the ideal folk society as composed of persons having communication with no outsider.

This isolation is one half of a whole of which the other half is intimate communication among the members of the society. A group of recent castaways is a small and isolated society, but it is not a folk society; and if the castaways have come from different ships and different societies, there will have been no previous intimate communication among them, and the society will not be composed of people who are much alike.

May the isolation of the folk society be identified with the physical immobility of its members? In building this ideal type, we may conceive of the members of the society as remaining always within the small territory they occupy. There are some primitive peoples who have dwelt from time immemorial in the same small valley, and who rarely leave it.[11] Certain of the pueblos of the American Southwest have been occupied by the same people or their descendants for many generations. On the other hand, some of the food-collecting peoples, such as the Shoshone Indians and certain aborigines of Australia, move about within a territory of very considerable extent; and there are Asiatic folk groups that make regular seasonal migrations hundreds of miles in extent.

It is possible to conceive of the members of such a society as moving about physically without communicating with members of other groups than their own. Each of the Indian villages of the midwest highlands of Guatemala is a folk society distinguishable by its customs and even by the physical type of its members from neighboring villages, yet the people are great travelers and in the case of one of the most distinct communities, Chichicastenango, most of the men travel far and spend much of their time away from home.[12] This does not result, however, in much intimate communication between those traveling villagers and other peoples. The gipsies have moved about among the various peoples of the earth for generations, and yet they retain many of the characteristics of a folk society.

Through books the civilized people communicate with the minds of other people and other times, and an aspect of the isolation of the folk society is the absence of books. The folk communicate only by word of mouth; therefore the communication upon which understanding is built is only that which takes place among neighbors, within the little society itself. The folk has no access to the thought and experience of the past, whether of peoples or of their own ancestors, such as books provide. Therefore, oral tradition has no check or competitor. Knowledge of what has gone before reaches no further back than memory and speech between old and young can make it go; behind "the time of our grandfathers" all is legendary and vague. With no form of belief established by written record, there can be no historical sense, such as civilized people have, no theology, and no basis for science in recorded experiment. The only form of accumulation of experience, except the tools and other enduring articles of manufacture, is the increase of wisdom which comes as the individual

484   lives longer; therefore the old, knowing more than the young can know until they too have lived that long, have prestige and authority.

The people who make up a folk society are much alike. Having lived in long intimacy with one another, and with no others, they have come to form a single biological type. This somatic homogeneity of local, inbred populations has been noted and studied. Since the people communicate with one another and with no others, one man's learned ways of doing and thinking are the same as another's. Another way of putting this is to say that in the ideal folk society, what one man knows and believes is the same as what all men know and believe. Habits are the same as customs. In real fact, of course, the differences among individuals in a primitive group and the different chances of experience prevent this ideal state of things from coming about. Nevertheless, it is near enough to the truth for the student of a real folk society to report it fairly well by learning what goes on in the minds of a few of its members, and a primitive group has been presented, although sketchily, as learned about from a single member. The similarity among the members is found also as one generation is compared with its successor. Old people find young people doing, as they grow up, what the old people did at the same age, and what they have come to think right and proper. This is another way of saying that in such a society there is little change.

The members of the folk society have a strong sense of belonging together. The group which an outsider might recognize as composed of similar persons different from members of other groups is also the group of people who see their own resemblances and feel correspondingly united. Communicating intimately with each other, each has a strong claim on the sympathies of the others. Moreover, against such knowledge as they have of societies other than their own, they emphasize their own mutual likeness and value themselves as compared with others. They say of themselves "we" as against all others, who are "they."[13]

Thus we may characterize the folk society as small, isolated, nonliterate, and homogeneous, with a strong sense of group solidarity. Are we not soon to acknowledge the simplicity of the technology of the ideal folk society? Something should certainly be said about the tools and tool-making of this generalized primitive group, but it is not easy to assign a meaning to "simple," in connection with technology which will do justice to the facts as known from the real folk societies. The preciseness with which each tool, in a large number of such tools, meets its needs in the case of the Eskimo, for example, makes one hesitate to use the word "simple." Some negative statements appear to be safe: secondary and tertiary tools—tools to make tools—are relatively few as compared with primary tools; there is no making of artifacts by multiple, rapid, machine manufacture; there is little or no use of natural power.

There is not much division of labor in the folk society: what one person does is what another does. In the ideal folk society all the tools and ways of production are shared by everybody. The "everybody" must mean "every adult man" or "every adult woman," for the obvious exception to the homogeneity of the folk society lies in the differences between what men do and know and what women do and know. These differences are clear and unexceptional (as compared with our modern urban society where they are less so). "Within the local group there is no such thing as a division of labor save as between the sexes," writes Radcliffe-Brown about the Andaman Islanders. ". . . Every man is expected to be able to hunt pig, to harpoon turtle and to catch fish, and also to cut a canoe, to make bows and arrows and all the other objects that are made by men."[14] So all men share the same interests and have, in general, the same experience of life.

We may conceive, also, of the ideal folk society as a group economically independent of all others: the people produce what they consume and consume what they produce. Few, if any, real societies are completely in this situation; some Eskimo groups perhaps most closely approach it. Although each little Andamanese band could get along without getting anything from any other, exchange of goods occurred between bands by a sort of periodic gift-giving.

The foregoing characterizations amount, roughly, to saying that the folk society is a little world off by itself, a world in which the recurrent problems of life are met by all its members in much the same way. This statement, while correct enough, fails to emphasize an important, perhaps the important, aspect of the folk society. The ways in which the members of the society meet the recurrent problems of life are conventionalized ways; they are the results of long intercommunication within the group in the face of these problems; and these conventionalized ways have become interrelated within one another so that they constitute a coherent and self-consistent system. Such a system is what we mean in saying that the folk society is characterized by "a culture." A culture is an organization or integration of conventional understandings. It is, as well, the acts and the objects, in so far as they represent the type characteristic of that society, which express and maintain these understandings. In the folk society this integrated whole, this system, provides for all the recurrent needs of the individual from birth to death and of the society through the seasons and the years. The society is to be described, and distinguished from others, largely by presenting this system.

This is not the same as saying, as was said early in this paper, that in the folk society what one man does is the same as what another man does. What one man does in a mob is the same as what another man does, but a mob is not a folk society. It is, so far as culture is concerned, its very antithesis.[15] The members of a mob (which is a kind of "mass") each do the same thing, it is true, but it is a very immediate and particular thing, and it is done without much reference to tradition. It does not depend upon and express a great many conventional understandings related to one another. A mob has no culture. The folk society exhibits culture to the greatest conceivable degree. A mob is an aggregation of people doing the same simple thing simultaneously. A folk society is an organization of people doing many different things successively as well as simultaneously. The

486

members of a mob act with reference to the same object of attention. The members of a folk society are guided in acting by previously established comprehensive and interdependent conventional understandings; at any one time they do many different things, which are complexly related to one another to express collective sentiments and conceptions. When the turn comes for the boy to do what a man does, he does what a man does; thus, though in the end the experiences of all individuals of the same sex are alike, the activities of the society, seen at a moment of time, are diverse, while interdependent and consistent.

The Papago Indians, a few hundred of them, constituted a folk society in southern Arizona. Among these Indians a war party was not so simple a thing as a number of men going out together to kill the enemy. It was a complex activity involving everybody in the society both before, during, and after the expedition and dramatizing the religious and moral ideas fundamental to Papago life.[16] Preparation for the expedition involved many practical or ritual acts on the part of the immediate participants, their wives and children, previously successful warriors, and many others. While the party was away, the various relatives of the wariors had many things to do or not to do—prayer, fasting, preparation of ritual paraphernalia, etc. These were specialized activities, each appropriate to just that kind of relative or other category of person. So the war was waged by everybody. These activities, different and special as they were, interlocked, so to speak, with each other to make a large whole, the society-during-a-war-expedition. And all these specialized activities obeyed fundamental principles, understood by all and expressed and reaffirmed in the very forms of the acts—the gestures of the rituals, the words of songs, the implied or expressed explanations and admonitions of the elders to the younger people. All understood that the end in view was the acquisition by the group of the supernatural power of the slain enemy. This power, potentially of great positive value, was dangerous, and the practices and rituals had as their purposes first the success of the war party and then the draining-off of the supernatural power acquired by the slaying into a safe and "usable" form.

We may say, then, that in the folk society conventional behavior is strongly patterned; it tends to conform to a type or a norm. These patterns are interrelated in thought and in action with one another, so that one tends to evoke others and to be consistent with the others. Every customary act among the Papago when the successful warriors return is consistent with and is a special form of the general conceptions held as to supernatural power. We may still further say that the patterns of what people think should be done are closely consistent with what they believe is done, and that there is one way, or a very few conventional ways, in which everybody has some understanding and some share, of meeting each need that arises.[17] The culture of a folk society is, therefore, one of those wholes which is greater than its parts. Gaining a livelihood takes support from religion, and the relations of men to men are justified in the conceptions held of the supernatural world or in some other aspect of the culture. Life, for the member of the folk society, is not one activity and then another and different one; it is one large activity out of which one part may not be separated without affecting the rest.

A related characteristic of the folk society was implied when it was declared that the specialized activities incident to the Papago war party obeyed fundamental principles understood by all. These "principles" had to do with the ends of living, as conceived by the Papago. A near-ultimate good for the Papago was the acquisition of supernatural power. This end was not questioned; it was a sort of axiom in terms of which many lesser activities were understood. This suggests that we may say of the folk society that its ends are taken as given. The activities incident to the war party may be regarded as merely complementarily useful acts, aspects of the division of labor. They may also, and more significantly, be seen as expressions of un-questioned common ends. The folk society exists not so much in the exchange of useful functions as in common understandings as to the ends given. The ends are not stated as matters of doctrine, but are im-plied by the many acts which make up the living that goes on in the society. Therefore, the morale of a folk society—its power to act con-sistently over periods of time and to meet crises effectively is not de-pendent upon discipline exerted by force or upon devotion to some single principle of action but to the concurrence and consistency of many or all of the actions and conceptions which make up the whole round of life. In the trite phrase, the folk society is a "design for living."

What is done in the ideal folk society is done not because somebody or some people decided, at once, that it should be done, but because it seems "necessarily" to flow from the very nature of things. There is, moreover, no disposition to reflect upon traditional acts and consider them objectively and critically. In short, behavior in the folk society is traditional, spontaneous, and uncritical. In any real folk society, of course, many things are done as a result of decision as to that particular action, but as to that class of actions tradition is the sufficient authority. The Indians decide now to go on a hunt; but it is not a matter of debate whether or not one should, from time to time, hunt.

The folkways are the ways that grow up out of long and inti-mate association of men with each other; in the society of our con-ception all the ways are folkways. Men act with reference to each other by understandings which are tacit and traditional. There are no formal contacts or other agreements. The rights and obligations of the in-dividual come about not by special arrangement; they are, chiefly, aspects of the position of the individual as a person of one sex or the other, one age-group or another, one occupational group or another, and as one occupying just that position in a system of relationships which are traditional in the society. The individual's status is thus in large part fixed at birth; it changes as he lives, but it changes in ways which were "foreordained" by the nature of his particular society. The institutions of the folk society are of the sort which has been called "crescive"; they are not of the sort that is created deliberately for special purposes, as was the juvenile court. So, too, law is made up of the traditional conceptions of rights and obligations and the custom-ary procedures whereby these rights and obligations are assured; legis-lation has no part in it.

If legislation has no part in the law of the ideal folk society, neither has codification, still less jurisprudence. Radin has collected material suggesting the limited extent to which real primitive people do question custom and do systematize their knowledge.[18] In known folk societies they do these things only to a limited extent. In the ideal folk society there is no objectivity and no systematization of knowl-edge as guided by what seems to be its "internal" order. The member of this mentally constructed society does not stand off from his cus-tomary conduct and subject it to scrutiny apart from its meaning for him as that meaning is defined in culture. Nor is there any habitual exercise of classification, experiment, and abstraction for its own sake, least of all for the sake of intellectual ends. There is common practical knowledge, but there is no science.

Behavior in the folk society is highly conventional, custom fixes the rights and duties of individuals, and knowledge is not criti-cally examined or objectively and systematically formulated; but it must not be supposed that primitive man is a sort of automaton in which custom is the mainspring. It would be as mistaken to think of primitive man as strongly aware that he is constrained by custom. Within the limits set by custom there is invitation to excel in perform-ance. There is lively competition, a sense of opportunity, and a feeling that what the culture moves one to do is well worth doing. "There is no drabness in such a life. It has about it all the allurements of per-sonal experience, very much one's own, of competitive skill, of things well done."[19] The interrelations and high degree of consistency among the elements of custom which are presented to the individual declare to him the importance of making his endeavors in the directions indi-cated by tradition. The culture sets goals which stimulate action by giving great meaning to it.[20]

It has been said that the folk society is small and that its mem-bers have lived in long and intimate association with one another. It has also been said that in such societies there is little critical or ab-stract thinking. These characteristics are related to yet another charac-teristic of the folk society: behavior is personal, not impersonal. A "person" may be defined as that social object which I feel to respond to situations as I do, with all the sentiments and interests which I feel to be my own; a person is myself in another form, his qualities and values are inherent within him, and his significance for me is not merely one of utility. A "thing," on the other hand, is a social object which has no claim upon my sympathies, which responds to me, as I conceive it, mechanically; its value for me exists in so far is it serves my end. In the folk society all human beings admitted to the society are treated as persons; one does not deal impersonally ("thing-fashion") with any other participant in the little world of that society. Moreover, in the folk society much besides human beings is treated personally. The pattern of behavior which is first suggested by the inner experience of the individual—his wishes, fears, sensitivenesses, and interests of all sorts—is projected into all objects with which he comes into contact. Thus nature, too, is treated personally; the elements, the features of the landscape, the animals, and especially anything in the environment which by its appearance or behavior suggests that it has the attributes of mankind—to all these are attributed qualities of the human person.[21]

In short, the personal and intimate life of the child in the family is extended, in the folk society, into the social world of the adult and even into inanimate objects. It is not merely that relations in such a society are personal; it is also that they are familial. The first contacts made as the infant becomes a person are with other persons; moreover, each of these first persons, he comes to learn, has a particular kind of relation to him which is associated with that one's genealogical position. The individual finds himself fixed within a constellation of familial relationships. The kinship connections provide a pattern in terms of which, in the ideal folk society, all personal relations are conventionalized and categorized. All relations are personal. But relations are not, in content of specific behavior, the same for everyone. As a mother is different from a father, and a grandson from a nephew, so are these classes of personal relationship, originating in genealogical connection, extended outward into all relationships whatever. In this sense, the folk society is a familial society. Lowie[22] has demonstrated the qualification that is to be introduced into the statement of Maine[23] that the primitive society is organized in terms of kinship rather than territory. It is true that the fact that men are neighbors contributes to their sense of belonging together. But the point to be emphasized in understanding the folk society is that whether mere contiguity or relationship as brother or as son is the circumstance uniting men into the society, the result is a group of people among whom prevail the personal and categorized relationships that characterize families as we know them, and in which the patterns of kinship tend to be extended outward from the group of genealogically connected individuals into the whole society. The kin are the type persons for all experience.

This general conception may be resolved into component or related conceptions. In the folk society family relationships are clearly distinguished from one another. Very special sorts of behavior may be expected by a mother's brother of his sister's son, and this behavior will be different from that expected by a father's brother of his brother's son. Among certain Australian tribes animals killed by a hunter must be divided so that nine or ten certain parts must be given to nine or ten corresponding relatives of the successful hunter—the right ribs to the father's brother, a piece of the flank to the mother's brother, and so on.[24] The tendency to extend kinship outward takes many special forms. In many primitive societies kinship terms and kinship behavior (in reduced degree) are extended to persons not known to be genealogically related at all, but who are nevertheless regarded as kin. Among the central Australians, terms of relationship are extended "so as to embrace all persons who come into social contact with one another. . . . In this way the whole society forms a body of relatives."[25] In

490   the folk society groupings which do not arise out of genealogical connection are few, and those that do exist tend to take on the attributes
of kinship. Ritual kinship is common in primitive and peasant societies in the forms of blood brotherhood, godparental relationships, and
other ceremonial sponsorships.[26] These multiply kinship connections;
in these cases the particular individuals to be united depend upon
choice. Furthermore, there is frequently a recognizedly fictitious or
metaphorical use of kinship terms to designate more casual relationships, as between host and guest or between worshipper and deity.[27]

The real primitive and peasant societies differ very greatly as
to the forms assumed by kinship. Nevertheless, it is possible to recognize two main types. In one of these the connection between husband
and wife is emphasized, while neither one of the lineages, matrilineal
or patrilineal, is singled out as contrasted with the other. In such a folk
society the individual parental family is the social unit, and connections with relatives outside this family are of secondary importance.
Such family organization is common where the population is small,
the means of livelihood are by precarious collection of wild food, and
larger units cannot permanently remain together because the natural
resources will not allow it. But where a somewhat larger population remains together, either in a village or in a migratory band, there often,
although by no means always, is found an emphasis upon one line of
consaguine connection rather than the other with subordination of the
conjugal connection.[28] There results a segmentation of the society into
equivalent kinship units. These may take the form of extended domestic groups or joint families (as in China) or may include many
households of persons related in part through recognized genealogical
connection and in part through the sharing of the same name or other
symbolic designation, in the latter case we speak of the groups as clans.
Even in societies where the individual parental family is an independent economic unit, as in the case of the eastern Eskimo, husband and
wife never become a new social and economic unit with the completeness that is characteristic of our own society. When a marriage in
primitive society comes to an end, the kinsmen of the dead spouse
assert upon his property a claim they have never given up.[29] On the
whole, we may think of the family among folk peoples as made up
of persons consanguinely connected. Marriage is, in comparison with
what we in our society directly experience, an incident in the life of
the individual who is born, brought up, and dies with his blood kinsmen. In such a society romantic love can hardly be elevated to a
major principle.

In so far as the consanguine lines are well defined (and in
some cases both lines may be of importance to the individual)[30] the
folk society may be thought of as composed of families rather than of
individuals. It is the familial groups that act and are acted upon. There
is strong solidarity within the kinship group, and the individual is
responsible to all his kin as they are responsible to him. "The clan is
a natural mutual aid society.... A member belongs to the clan, he
is not his own; if he is wrong, they will right him; if he does wrong,
the responsibility is shared by them.[31] Thus, in folk societies wherein

the tendency to maintain consanguine connection has resulted in joint families or clans, it is usual to find that injuries done by an individual are regarded as injuries against his kinship group, and the group takes the steps to right the wrong. The step may be revenge regulated by custom or a property settlement. A considerable part of primitive law exists in the regulation of claims by one body of kin against another. The fact that the folk society is an organization of families rather than an aggregation of individuals is further expressed in many of those forms of marriage in which a certain kind of relative is the approved spouse. The customs by which in many primitive societies a man is expected to marry his deceased brother's widow or a woman to marry her deceased sister's husband express the view of marriage as an undertaking between kinship groups. One of the spouses having failed by death, the undertaking is to be carried on by some other representative of the family group. Indeed, in the arrangements for marriage—the selection of spouses by their relatives, in brideprice, dowry, and in many forms of familial negotiations leading to a marriage—the nature of marriage as a connubial form of social relations between kindreds finds expression.

It has been said in foregoing paragraphs that behavior in the folk society is traditional, spontaneous, and uncritical, that what one man does is much the same as what another man does, and that the patterns of conduct are clear and remain constant throughout the generations. It has also been suggested that the congruence of all parts of conventional behavior and social institutions with each other contributes to the sense of rightness which the member of the folk society feels to inhere in his traditional ways of action. In the well-known language of Sumner, the ways of life are folkways; furthermore, the folkways tend to be also mores—ways of doing or thinking to which attach notions of moral worth. The value of every traditional act or object or institution is, thus, something which the members of the society are not disposed to call into question; and should the value be called into question, the doing so is resented. This characteristic of the folk society may be briefly referred to by saying that it is a sacred society. In the folk society one may not, without calling into effect negative social sanctions, challenge as valueless what has come to be traditional in that society.

Presumably, the sacredness of social objects has its source, in part, at least, in the mere fact of habituation; probably the individual organism becomes early adjusted to certain habits, motor and mental, and to certain associations between one activity and another or between certain sense experiences and certain activities, and it is almost physically uncomfortable to change or even to entertain the idea of change. There arises "a feeling of impropriety of certain forms, of a particular social or religious value, or a superstitious fear of change."[32] Probably the sacredness of social objects in the folk society is related also to the fact that in such well-organized cultures acts and objects suggest the traditions, beliefs, and conceptions which all share. There is reason to suppose that when what is traditionally done becomes less meaningful because people no longer know what the acts stand for, life becomes

492   more secular.[33] In the repetitious character of conventional action (aside from technical action) we have ritual; in its expressive character we have ceremony; in the folk society ritual tends also to be ceremonious, and ritual-ceremony tends to be sacred, not secular.

The sacredness of social objects is apparent in the ways in which, in the folk society, such an object is hedged around with restraints and protections that keep it away from the commonplace and the matter-of-fact.[34] In the sacred there is alternatively, or in combination, holiness and dangerousness. When the Papago Indians returned from a successful war expedition, bringing the scalp of a slain Apache, the head-hairs of the enemy were treated as loaded with a tremendous "charge" of supernatural power; only old men already successful warriors and purified through religious ritual, could touch the object and make it safe for incorporation into the home of the slayer. Made into the doll-like form of an Apache Indian, it was, at last, after much ceremonial preparation, held for an instant by the members of the slayer's family, addressed in respect and awe by kinship terms, and placed in the house, there to give off protective power.[35] The Indians of San Pedro de la Laguna, Guatemala, recognize an officer, serving for life, whose function it is to keep custody of ten or a dozen Latin breviaries printed in the eighteenth century and to read prayers from one or another of these books on certain occasions. No one but this custodian may handle the books, save his assistants on ceremonial occasions, with his permission. Should anyons else touch a book he would go mad or be stricken with blindness. Incense and candles are burnt before the chest containing the books, yet the books are not gods—they are objects of sacredness.[36]

In the folk society this disposition to regard objects as sacred extends, characteristically, even into the subsistence activities and into the foodstuffs of the people. Often the foodstuffs are personified as well as sacred. " 'My granduncle used to say to me,' explained a Navajo Indian, ' "if you are walking along a trail and see a kernel of corn, pick it up. It is like a child lost and starving." According to the legends corn is just the same as a human being, only it is holier. . . . . When a man goes into a cornfield he feels that he is in a holy place, that he is walking among Holy People. . . . . Agriculture is a holy occupation. Even before you plant you sing songs. You continue this during the whole time your crops are growing. You canot help but feel that you are in a holy place when you go through your fields and they are doing well.' "[37] In the folk society, ideally conceived, nothing is solely a means to an immediate practical end. All activities, even the means of production, are ends in themselves, activities expressive of the ultimate values of the society.

This characterization of the ideal folk society could be greatly extended. Various of the elements that make up the conception could be differently combined with one another, and this point or that could be developed or further emphasized and its relations shown to other aspects of the conception. For example, it might be pointed out that where there is little or no systematic and reflective thinking the customary solutions to problems of practical action only imperfectly take the form of really effective and understood control of the means appropriate to accomplish the desired end, and that, instead, they tend to express the states of mind of the individuals who want the end brought about and fear that it may not be. We say this briefly in declaring that the folk society is characterized by much magic, for we may understand "magic" to refer to action with regard to an end—to instrumental action—but only to such instrumental action as does not effectively bring about that end, or is not really understood in so far as it does, and which is expressive of the way the doer thinks and feels rather than adapted to accomplishing the end. "Magic is based on specific experience of emotional states . . . . in which the truth is revealed not by reason but by the play of emotions upon the human organism . . . . magic is founded on the belief that hope cannot fail nor desire deceive."[38] In the folk society effective technical action is much mixed with magical activity. What is done tends to take the form of a little drama; it is a picture of what is desired.

The nature of the folk society could, indeed, be restated in the form of a description of the folk mind. This description would be largely a repetition of what has been written in foregoing pages, except that now the emphasis would be upon the characteristic mental activity of members of the folk society, rather than upon customs and institutions. The man of the folk society tends to make mental associations which are personal and emotional, rather than abstractly categoric or defined in terms of cause and effect. ". . . . Primitive man views every action not only as adapted to its main object, every thought related to its main end, as we should perceive them, but . . . . he associates them with other ideas, often of a religious or at least a symbolic nature. Thus he gives to them a higher significance than they seem to us to deserve."[39] A very similar statement of this kind of thinking has been expressed in connection with the thinking of medieval man; the description would apply as well to man in the folk society:

From the causal point of view, symbolism appears as a sort of short-cut of thought. Instead of looking for the relation between two things by following the hidden detours of their causal connections, thought makes a leap and discovers their relation, not in a connection of cause or effects, but in a connection of signification or finality. Such a connection will at once appear convincing, provided only that the two things have an essential quality in common which can be referred to a general value. . . . Symbolic assimilation founded on common properties presupposes the idea that these properties are essential to things. The vision of white and red roses blooming among thorns at once calls up a symbolic association in the medieval mind: for example, that of virgins and martyrs, shining with glory, in the midst of their persecutors. The assimilation is produced because the attributes are the same: the beauty, the tenderness, the purity, the colours of the roses are also those of the virgins, their red color that of the blood of the martyrs. But this similarity will only have a mystic meaning if the middle-term connecting the two terms of the symbolic concept expresses an essentiality common to both; in other words, if redness and whiteness are something more than names for physical differences based on quantity, if they are conceived of as essences, as realities. The mind of the savage, of the child, and of the poet never sees them otherwise.[40]

The tendency to treat nature personally has recognition in the literature as the "animistic" or "anthropomorphic" quality of primitive thinking, and the contrast between the means-end pattern of thought more characteristic of modern urban man and the personal thought of primitive man has been specially investigated.[41]

In the foregoing account no mention has been made of the absence of economic behavior characteristic of the market in the folk society. Within the ideal folk society members are bound by religious and kinship ties, and there is no place for the motive of commercial gain. There is no money and nothing is measured by any such common denominator of value. The distribution of goods and services tends to be an aspect of the conventional and personal relationships of status which make up the structure of the society: goods are exchanged as expressions of good will and, in large part, as incidents of ceremonial and ritual activities. "On the whole, then, the compulsion to work, to save, and to expend is given not so much by a rational appreciation of the [material] benefits to be received as by the desire for social recognition, through such behavior."[42]

The conception sketched here takes on meaning if the folk society is seen in contrast to the modern city. The vast, complicated, and rapidly changing world in which the urbanite and even the urbanized country-dweller live today is enormously different from the small, inward-facing folk society, with its well-integrated and little-changing moral and religious conceptions. At one time all men lived in these little folk societies. For many thousands of years men must have lived so; urbanized life began only very recently, as the long history of man on earth is considered, and the extreme development of a secularized and swift-changing world society is only a few generations old.

The tribal groups that still remain around the edges of expanding civilization are the small remainders of this primary state of living. Considering them one by one, and in comparison with the literate or semi-literate societies, the industrialized and the semi-industrialized societies, we may discover how each has developed forms of social life in accordance with its own special circumstances. Among the polar Eskimos, where each small family had to shift for itself in the rigors of the arctic environment, although the ties of kinship were of great importance, no clans or other large unilateral kinship groups came into existence. The sedentary Haida of the Queen Charlotte Islands were divided into two oxogamous kinship groups, each composed of clans, with intense pride of decent and healthy rivalry between them. Among the warring and nomadic Comanche initiative and resourcefulness of the individual were looked on more favorably than among the sedentary and closely interdependent Zuni. In West Africa great native states arose, with chiefs and courts and markets, yet the kinship organization remained strong; and in China we have an example of slow growth of a great society, with a literate elite, inclosing within it a multitude of village communities of the folk type. Where cities have arisen, the country people dependent on those cities have developed economic and political relationships, as well as relationships of status, with the city people, and so have become that special kind of rural folk we call peasantry.[43] And even in the newer parts of the world, as in the United States, many a village or small town has, perhaps, as many points of resemblance with the folk society as with urban life.

Thus the societies of the world do not range themselves in the same order with regard to the degree to which they realize all of the characteristics of the ideal folk society. On the other hand, there is so marked a tendency for some of these characteristics to occur together with others that the interrelations among them must be in no small part that of interdependent variables. Indeed, some of the interrelations are so obvious that we feel no sense of problem. The smallness of the folk society and the long association together of the same individuals certainly is related to the prevailingly personal character of relationships. The fewness of secondary and tertiary tools and the absence of machine manufacture are circumstances obviously unfavorable to a very complex division of labor. Many problems present themselves, however, as to the conditions in which certain of these characteristics do not occur in association, and as to the circumstance under which certain of them may be expected to change in the direction of their opposites, with or without influencing others to change also.

A study of the local differences in the festival of the patron village saint in certain communities of Yucatan indicates that some interrelationship exists in that case.[44] In all four communities, differing as to their degrees of isolation from urban centers of modifying influence, the festival expresses a relationship between the village and its patron saint (or cross) which is annually renewed. In it a ritual and worship are combined with a considerable amount of play. The chief activities of the festival are a novena, a folk dance, and a rustic bullfight. In all four communities there is an organization of men and women who for that year undertake the leadership of the festival, handing over the responsibility to a corresponding group of successors at its culmination. So far the institution is the same in all the communities studied. The differences appear when the details of the ritual and play and of the festal organization are compared, and when the essential meanings of these acts and organizations are inquired into. Then it appears that from being an intensely sacred act, made by the village as a collectivity composed of familially defined component groups, with close relationship to the system of religious and moral understandings of the people, the festival becomes, in the more urbanized communities, chiefly an opportunity for recreation for some and of financial profit for others, with little reference to moral and religious conceptions.

In the most isolated and otherwise most folklike of the communities studied the organization of the festival is closely integrated with the whole social structure of the community. The hierarchy of leaders of the community, whose duties are both civil and religious, carry on the festival: It is the chiefs, the men who decide disputes and lead in warfare, who also take principal places in the religious proces-

496 sions and in the conduct of the ceremonies. The community, including several neighboring settlements, is divided into five groups, membership in which descends in the male line. The responsibility for leading the prayers and preparing the festal foods rests in turn on four groups. The festival is held at the head village, at the shrine house and cross patron of the entire community. The festival consists chiefly of solemnly religious acts: masses, rosaries, procession of images, kneeling of worshipers. The ritual offerings are presented by a special officer, in all solemnity, to the patron cross; certain symbols of divinity are brought from the temple and exposed to the kneeling people as the offerings are made. The transfer of the responsibility to lead the festival is attended by ceremony in an atmosphere of sanctity: certain ritual paraphernalia are first placed on the altar and then, after recitation of prayers and performance of a religious dance, are handed over, in view of all, from the custodians of the sacred charge for that year to their successors.

In the villages that are less isolated the festival is similar in form, but it is less well integrated with the social organization of the community, is less sacred, and allows for more individual enterprise and responsibility. These changes continue in the other communities studied, as one gets nearer to the city of Merida. In certain seacoast villages the festival of the patron saint is a money-getting enterprise of a few secular-minded townspeople. The novena is in the hands of a few women who receive no help from the municipal authorities; the bullfight is a commercial entertainment, professional bullfighters being hired for the occasion and admission charged; the folk dance is little attended. The festival is enjoyed by young people who come to dance modern dances and to witness the bullfight, and it is an opportunity to the merchants to make a profit. What was an institution of folk culture has become a business enterprise in which individuals, as such, take part for secular ends.

The principal conclusion is that the less isolated and more heterogeneous communities of the peninsula of Yucatan are the more secular and individualistic and the more characterized by disorganization of culture. It further appeared probable that there was, in the changes taking place in Yucatan, a relation of interdependence among these changing characteristics, especially between the disorganization of culture and secularization. "People cease to believe because they cease to understand, and they cease to understand because they cease to do the things that express the understandings."[45] New jobs and other changes in the division of labor bring it about that people cannot participate in the old rituals; and, ceasing to participate, they cease to share the values for which the rituals stood. This is, admittedly, however, only a part of the explanation.

The conception of the folk society has stimulated one small group of field workers to consider the interdependence or independence of these characteristics of society. In Yucatan isolation, homogeneity, a personal and "symbolic" view of nature, importance of familial relationships, a high degree of organization of culture, and sacredness of sanctions and institutions were all found in regular association with each other. It was then reported that in certain Indian communities on or near Lake Atitlan in Guatemala this association of characteristics is not repeated.[46] As it appeared that these Guatemalan communities were not in rapid change, but were persisting in their essential nature, the conclusion was reached that "a stable society can be small, unsophisticated, homogeneous in beliefs and practices," have a local, well-organized culture, and still be one "with relationships impersonal, with formal institutions dictating the acts of individuals, and with family organization weak, with life secularized, and with individuals acting more from economic or other personal advantage than from any deep conviction or thought of the social good." It was further pointed out that in these Guatemalan societies a "primitive world view," that is, a disposition to treat nature personally, to regard attributes as entities, and to make "symbolic" rather than causal connections, coexists with a tendency for relations between man and man to be impersonal, commercial, and secular, as they tend to be in the urban society.[47]

These observations lead, in turn, to reconsideration of the circumstances tending to bring about one kind of society or one aspect of society rather than another. The breakdown of familial institutions in recent times in Western society is often ascribed to the development of the city and of modern industry. If, as has been reported, familial institutions are also weak in these Guatemalan villages, there must be alternative causes for the breakdown of the family to the rise of industry and the growth of the city, for these Guatemalan Indians live on or near their farms, practice a domestic handicraft manufacture, and have little or nothing to do with cities. It has been suggested that in the case of the Guatemalan societies the development, partly before the Conquest and partly afterward, of a pecuniary economy with a peddler's commerce, based on great regional division of labor, together with a system of regulations imposed by an elite with the use of force, may be the circumstances that have brought about reduction in the importance of familial institutions and individual independence, especially in matters of livlihood.[48]

The secular character of life in these highland villages of the Lake Atitlan region is not so well established as in the individuated character of life, but if life is indeed secular there, it is a secularity that has developed without the influence of high personal mobility, of the machine, and of science. In a well-known essay Max Weber showed how capitalistic commercialism could and did get along with piety in the case of the Puritans.[49] So it may appear that under certain conditions a literate and, indeed, at least partly urbanized society may be both highly commercial and sacred—as witness, also, the Jews—while under certain other conditions an otherwise folklike people may become individualistic, commercial, and perhaps secular. It is, of course, the determination of the limiting conditions that is important.

NOTES

1. Neither the term "primitive" nor any other is denotative, and none has sufficient generally accepted precise meaning to allow us to know in just what characters of a society to discover the degree to which it is or is not "primitive,"

498

"simple," or whatever. The words "nonliterate" or preliterate" do call attention to a particular character, literacy, but understanding is still required as to when a society is "literate" and as what form or degree of literacy has significance. There are head-hunting tribes, in other respects as primitive as were the Pawnee Indians in the seventeenth century, that have knowledge of writing. In certain Mexican villages most children and many adults have formal knowledge of the arts of reading and writing, but in most other respects these village societies are much more like tribal societies than they are like our western cities.

The word "folk," which will be used in this paper, is no more precise than any other. It is used here because, better than others, it suggests the inclusion in our comparisons of peasant and rustic people who are not wholly independent of cities and because in its compounds, "folklore" and "folk song," it points, in a rough way, to the presence of folklore and folk songs, as recognized by the collector of such materials, as a sign of a society to be examined in making up the characterization of the ideal type with which we are here concerned. But the question of the word to be used is of small importance.

2. The reader may compare the conception developed in this paper with the ideal "sacred society" characterized by Howard Becker in "Ionia and Athens" (Ph.D. dissertation, University of Chicago, 1930), pp. 1–16; with similar conceptions developed in chapter i of *Social Thought from Lore to Science* by Harry Elmer Barnes and Howard Becker (Boston, New York: D. C. Heath & Co., 1938); and with the application of the conception in *The Sociology of the Renaissance* by Alfred von Martin (London: Kegan Paul, Trench, Truburn & Co., 1945).

3. A. A. Goldenweiser, *Early Civilization* (New York: Alfred A. Knopf, 1922), pp. 117–18.

4. Henry Maine, *Ancient Law* (London: J. Murray, 1861).

5. Ferdinand Tonnies, *Gemeinschaft und Gesellschaft* (1st ed., 1887), trans. and ed. Charles P. Loomis as *Fundamental Concepts of Sociology* (New York, Cincinnati, etc.: American Book Co., 1940).

6. *Emile Durkheim on the Division of Labor in Society*, a translation by George Simpson of *De la division du travail social* (New York: Macmillan Co., 1933); Howard Becker, "Constructive Typology in the Social Sciences," *American Sociological Review* 5, no. 1 (February 1940), 40–55; reprinted in Harry Elmer Barnes, Howard Becker, and Frances Bennett Becker (eds.), *Contemporary Social Theory* (New York: D. Appleton—Century Co., 1940), Part I.

7. W. G. Sumner, *Folkways* (Boston: Ginn & Co., 1907), p. 12.

8. Julian Steward, *Basin-Plateau Aboriginal Sociopolitical Groups* (Smithsonian Institution, Bureau of American Ethnology, Bull. 120 [Washington: Government Printing Office, 1938]), pp. 230–34.

9. Julian Steward, "Economic and Social Basis of Primitive Bands," *Essays in Anthropology Presented to A. L. Kroeber* (Berkeley: University of California Press, 1936), pp. 341–42.

10. A. R. Radcliffe-Brown. *The Andaman Islanders* (Cambridge: At the University Press, 1933), pp. 6–9.

11. A. L. Kroeber, *Handbook of Indians of California* (Smithsonian Institution, Bureau of American Ethnology, Bull. 78 [Washington: Government Printing Office, 1925]), p. 13.

12. Robert Redfield, "Primitive Merchants of Guatemala," *Quarterly Journal of Inter-American Relations*, I, no. 4, 42–56.

13. Sumner, op. cit., pp. 13–15.

14. Radcliffe-Brown, op. cit., p. 43.

15. Herbert Blumer, "Mass Behavior and the Motion Picture," *Publications of the American Sociological Society* 29, no. 3 (August 1935): 115–27.

16. Ruth Underhill, *The Autobiography of a Papago Woman* ("American Anthropological Association, Memoirs," no 46 [1936]).

17. Ralph Linton, *The Study of Man* (New York: D. Appleton—Century Co., 1936), chap. xvi, esp. p. 283.

18. Paul Radin, *Primitive Man as Philosopher* (New York: D. Appleton–Century Co., 1927).

19. A. A. Goldenweiser, "Individual Pattern and Involution," *Essays in Honor of A. L. Kroeber* (Berkeley: University of California Press, 1936), p. 102.

20. Ruth Benedict, *Patterns of Culture* (Boston and New York: Houghton Mifflin Co., 1934).

21. Ruth Benedict, "Animism," *Encyclopaedia of the Social Sciences.*

22. Robert H. Lowie, *The Origin of the State* (New York: Harcourt Brace Jovanovich, 1927), pp. 51–73.

23. Maine, op. cit.

24. A. W. Howitt, *The Native Tribes of Southeastern Australia* (New York: Macmillan Co., 1904), p. 759.

25. A. R. Radcliffe-Brown, "Three Tribes of Western Australia," *Journal of the Royal Anthropological Institute*, 48, 150–51.

26. Benjamin Paul, "Ritual Kinship: With Special Reference to Godparenthood in Middle America" (Ph.D. thesis, University of Chicago, 1942).

27. E. C. Parsons, *Notes on Zuni*, Part II ("American Anthropological Association Memoirs" 4, no. 4 [1917]).

28. Ralph Linton, *The Study of Society* (New York: Century Co.), p. 159.

29. Ruth Benedict, "Marital Property Rights in Bilateral Societies," *American Anthropologist* 38, no 3 (July-September 1936) : 368–73.

30. Peter Murdock, "Double Descent," *American Anthropologist* 42 (new ser.), no. 4, Part I (October-December 1940) : 555–61.

31. Edwin W. Smith and Andrew Murray Dale, *The Ila-Speaking Peoples of Northern Rhodesia* (London: Macmillan & Co., 1920), I, 296.

32. Franz Boas, *Primitive Art* (Oslo, 1927), p. 150.

33. Robert Redfield, *The Folk Culture of Yucatan* (Chicago: University of Chicago Press, 1941), p. 364.

34. Emile Durkheim, *The Elementary Forms of the Religious Life* (London: Allen & Unwin, 1926).

35. Underhill, op. cit., p. 18.

36. Benjamin Paul, unpublished MS.

37. W. W. Hill, *The Agricultural and Hunting Methods of the Navaho Indians* ("Yale University Publications in Anthropology," no 18 [New Haven: Yale University Press, 1938]), p. 53.

38. Bronislaw Malinowski, "Magic, Science and Religion," in *Science, Religion and Reality*, ed. Joseph Needham (New York: Macmillan Co., 1925), p. 80.

39. Franz Boas, *The Mind of Primitive Man* (New York: Macmillan Co., 1938), p. 226.

40. J. Huizinga, *The Waning of the Middle Ages* (London: Arnold & Co., 1924), pp. 184–85. This "symbolic"kind of thinking is related to what Levy-Bruhl called "participation" (see L. Levy-Bruhl, *How Natives Think* [New York: Alfred A. Knopf, 1925], esp. chap. ii.

41. Hans Kelsen, "Causality and Retribution," *Philosophy of Science* 8, no 4 (October 1941) : 533–56; and Kelsen, *Society and Nature* (Chicago: University of Chicago Press, 1944).

42. Raymond Firth, *Primitive Economics of the New Zealand Maori* (New York: E. P. Dutton & Co., 1929), p. 484. See also, Firth, *Primitive Polynesian Economy* (London: George Routledge & Sons, 1939), esp. chap. x, "Characteristics of a Primitive Economy."

43. Robert Redfield, "Introduction," in Horace Miner, *St. Denis: A French-Canadian Parish* (Chicago: University of Chicago Press, 1940).

44. Redfield, *The Folk Culture of Yucatan.*

45. Ibid., p. 364.

46. Sol Tax, "Culture and Civilization in Guatemalan Societies," *Scientific Monthly* , May 1939, p. 467.

47. Sol Tax, "World View and Social Relations in Guatemala," *American Anthropologist* 43 no. 1 (new ser.). (January–March 1941) : 27–42.

48. Redfield, *The Folk Culture of Yucatan*, pp. 365–67.

49. Max Weber, "Protestant Ethics and the Spirit of Capitalism," cited in Kemper Fullerton, "Calvinism and Capitalism," *Harvard Theological Review* 21: 163–95.

GIDEON SJOBERG

The Preindustrial City

In the past few decades social scientists have been conducting field studies in a number of relatively non-Western cities. Their recently acquired knowledge of North Africa and various parts of Asia, combined with what was already learned, clearly indicates that these cities are not like typical cities of the United States and other highly industrialized areas but are much more like those of medieval Europe. Such communities are termed herein "preindustrial," for they have arisen without stimulus from that form of production which we associate with the European industrial revolution.

Recently Foster, in a most informative article, took cognizance of the preindustrial city.[1] His primary emphasis was upon the peasantry (which he calls "folk") ; but he recognized this to be part of a broader social structure which includes the preindustrial city. He noted certain similarities between the peasantry and the city's lower class. Likewise the present author sought to analyze the total society of which the peasantry and the preindustrial city are integral parts.[2] For want of a better term this was called "feudal." Like Redfield's folk (or "primitive") society, the feudal order is highly stable and sacred; in contrast, however, it has a complex social organization. It is characterized by highly developed state and educational and/or religious institutions and by a rigid class structure.

Thus far no one has analyzed the preindustrial city per se, especially as it differs from the industrial-urban community, although Weber, Tonnies, and a few others perceived differences between the two. Yet such a survey is needed for the understanding of urban development in so-called underdeveloped countries and, for that matter, in parts of Europe. Such is the goal of this paper. The typological analysis should also serve as a guide to future research.

Gideon Sjoberg , "The Preindustrial City," *American Journal of Sociology* 60 (March 1955) : 438–45. Copyright © 1955 by the University of Chicago. Reprinted by permission of the author and the University of Chicago Press.

ECOLOGICAL ORGANIZATION   **501**

Preindustrial cities depend for their existence upon food and raw
materials obtained from without; for this reason they are marketing
centers. And they serve as centers for handicraft manufacturing. In addition, they fulfill important political, religious, and educational functions. Some cities have become specialized; for example, Benares in
India and Karbala in Iraq are best known as religious communities,
and Peiping in China as a locus for political and educational activities.

The proportion of urbanites relative to the peasant population
is small, in some societies about 10 percent, even though a few preindustrial cities have attained populations of 100,000 or more. Growth
has been by slow accretion. These characteristics are due to the nonin-
dustrial nature of the total social order. The amount of surplus food
available to support an urban population has been limited by the
unmechanized agriculture, transportation facilities utilizing primarily
human or animal power, and inefficient methods of food preservation
and storage.

The internal arrangement of the preindustrial city, in the
nature of the case, is closely related to the city's economic and social
structure.[3] Most streets are mere passageways for people and for animals used in transport. Buildings are low and crowded together. The
congested conditions, combined with limited scientific knowledge, have
fostered serious sanitation problems.

More significant is the rigid social segregation which typically
has led to the formation of "quarters" or "wards." In some cities (e.g.,
Fez, Morocco, and Aleppo, Syria) these were sealed off from each
other by walls, whose gates were locked at night. The quarters reflect
the sharp local social divisions. Thus ethnic groups live in special
sections. And the occupational groupings, some being at the same time
ethnic in character, typically reside apart from one another. Often a
special street or sector of the city is occupied almost exclusively by
members of a particular trade; cities in such divergent cultures as
medieval Europe and modern Afghanistan contain streets with names
like "street of the goldsmiths." Lower-class and especially "outcaste"
groups live on the city's periphery, at a distance from the primary
centers of activity. Social segregation, the limited transportation facilities, the modicum of residential mobility, and the cramped living
quarters have encouraged the development of well-defined neighborhoods which are almost primary groups.

Despite rigid segregation the evidence suggests no real specialization of land use such as is functionally necessary in industrial-urban
communities. In medieval Europe and in other areas city dwellings
often serve as workshops, and religious structures are used as schools
or marketing centers.[4]

Finally, the "business district" does not hold the position of
dominance that it enjoys in the industrial-urban community. Thus, in
the Middle East, the principal mosque, or in medieval Europe, the
cathedral, is usually the focal point of community life. The center of
Peiping is the Forbidden City.

502 ECONOMIC ORGANIZATION

The economy of the preindustrial city diverges sharply from that of the modern industrial center. The prime difference is the absence in the former of industrialism which may be defined as that system of production in which *inanimate* sources of power are used to multiply human effort. Preindustrial cities depend for the production of goods and services upon *animate* (human or animal) sources of energy— applied either directly or indirectly through such mechanical devices as hammers, pulleys, and wheels. The industrial-urban community, on the other hand, employs inanimate generators of power such as electricity and steam which greatly enhance the productive capacity of urbanites. This basically new form of energy production, one which requires for its development and survival a special kind of industrial complex, effects striking changes in the ecological, economic, and social organization of cities in which it has become dominant.

Other facets of the economy of the preindustrial city are associated with its particular system of production. There is little fragmentation or specialization of work. The handicraftsman participates in nearly every phase of the manufacture of an article, often carrying out the work in his own home or in a small shop near by and, within the limits of certain guild and community regulations, maintaining direct control over conditions of work and methods of production.

In industrial cities, on the other hand, the complex division of labor requires a specialized managerial group, often extra-community in character, whose primary function is to direct and control others. And for the supervision and co-ordination of the activities of workers, a "factory system" has been developed, something typically lacking in preindustrial cities. (Occasionally centralized production is found in preindustrial cities—e.g., where the state organized slaves for large-scale construction projects.) Mose commercial activities, also, are conducted in preindustrial cities by individuals without a highly formalized organization; for example, the craftsman has frequently been responsible for the marketing of his own products. With a few exceptions, the preindustrial community cannot support a large group of middlemen.

The various occupations are organized into what have been termed "guilds."[5] These strive to encompass all, except the elite, who are gainfully employed in some economic activity. Guilds have existed for merchants and handicraft workers (e.g., goldsmiths and weavers) as well as for servants, entertainers, and even beggars and thieves. Typically the guilds operate only within the local community, and there are no large-scale economic organizations such as those in industrial cities which link their members to their fellows in other communities.

Guild membership and apprenticeship are prerequisites to the practice of almost any occupation, a circumstance obviously leading to monopolization. To a degree these organizations regulate the work of their members and the price of their products and services. And the guilds recruit workers into specific occupations, typically selecting them according to such particularistic criteria as kinship rather than universalistic standards.

The guilds are integrated with still other elements of the city's social structure. They perform certain religious functions; for example, in medieval European, Chinese, and Middle Eastern cities each guild had its "patron saint" and held periodic festivals in his honor. And, by assisting members in time of trouble, the guilds serve as social security agencies.

The economic structure of the preindustrial city functions with little rationality, judged by industrial-urban standards. This is shown in the general nonstandardization of manufacturing methods as well as in the products and is even more evident in marketing. In preindustrial cities throughout the world a fixed price is rare; buyer and seller settle their bargain by haggling. (Of course, there are limits above which customers will not buy and below which merchants will not sell.) Often business is conducted in a leisurely manner, money not being the only desired end.

Furthermore, the sorting of goods according to size, weight, and quality is not common. Typical is the adulteration and spoilage of produce. And weights and measures are not standardized: variations exist not only between one city and the next but also within communities, for often different guilds employ their own systems. Within a single city there may be different kinds of currency, which, with the poorly developed accounting and credit systems, signalize a modicum of rationality in the whole of economic action in preindustrial cities.[6]

SOCIAL ORGANIZATION

The economic system of the preindustrial city, based as it has been upon animate sources of power, articulates with a characteristic class structure and family, religious, educational, and governmental systems.

Of the class structure, the most striking component is a literate elite controlling and depending for its existence upon the mass of the populace, even in the traditional cities of India with their caste system. The elite is composed of individuals holding positions in the government, religious, and/or educational institutions of the larger society, although at times groups such as large absentee landlords have belonged to it. At the opposite pole are the masses, comprising such groups as handicraft workers whose goods and services are produced primarily for the elite's benefit.[7] Between the elite and the lower class is a rather sharp schism, but in both groups there are gradations in rank. The members of the elite belong to the "correct" families and enjoy power, property, and certain highly valued personal attributes. Their position, moreover is legitimized by sacred writings.

Social mobility in this city is minimal; the only real threat to the elite comes from the outside—not from the city's lower classes. And a middle class—so typical of industrial-urban communities, where it can be considered the "dominant" class—is not known in the preindustrial city. The system of production in the larger society provides goods, including food, and services in sufficient amounts to support only a small group of leisured individuals; under these conditions an

504   urban middle class, a semileisured group, cannot rise. Nor are a middle class and extensive social mobility essential to the maintenance of the economic system.

Significant is the role of the marginal or "outcaste" groups (e.g., the Eta of Japan), which are not an integral part of the dominant social system. Typically they rank lower than the urban lower class, performing tasks considered especially degrading, such as burying the dead. Slaves, beggars, and the like are outcastes in most preindustrial cities. Even such groups as professional entertainers and itinerant merchants are often viewed as outcastes, for their rovings expose them to "foreign" ideas from which the dominant social group seeks to isolate itself. Actually many outcaste groups, including some of those mentioned above, are ethnic groups, a fact which further intensifies their isolation. (A few, like the Jews in the predominantly Muslim cities of North Africa, have their own small literate religious elite which, however, enjoys no significant political power in the city as a whole.)

An assumption of many urban sociologists is that a small, unstable kinship group, notably the conjugal unit, is a necessary correlate of city life. But this premise does not hold for preindustrial cities.[8] At times sociologists and anthropologists, when generalizing about various traditional societies, have imputed to peasants typically urban kinship patterns. Actually, in these societies the ideal forms of kinship and family life are most closely approximated by members of the urban literate elite, who are best able to fulfil the exacting requirements of the sacred writings. Kinship and the ability to perpetuate one's lineage are accorded marked prestige in preindustrial cities. Children, especially sons, are highly valued, and polygamy or concubinage or adoption help to assure the attainment of large families. The pre-eminence of kinship is apparent even in those preindustrial cities where divorce is permitted. Thus, among the urban Muslims or urban Chinese divorce is not an index of disorganization; here, conjugal ties are loose and distinctly subordinate to the bonds of kinship, and each member of a dissolved conjugal unit typically is absorbed by his kin group. Marriage, a prerequisite to adult status in the preindustrial city, is entered upon at an early age and is arranged between families rather than romantically, by individuals.

The kinship and familial organization displays some rigid patterns of sex and age differentiation whose universality in preindustrial cities has generally been overlooked. A woman, especially of the upper class, ideally performs few significant functions outside the home. She is clearly subordinate to males, especially her father or husband. Recent evidence indicates that this is true even for such a city as Lhasa, Tibet, where women supposedly have had high status.[9] The isolation of women from public life has in some cases been extreme. In nineteenth-century Seoul, Korea, "respectable" women appeared on the streets only during certain hours of the night when men were supposed to stay at home.[10] Those women in preindustrial cities who evade some of the stricter requirements are members of certain marginal groups (e.g., entertainers) or of the lower class. The role of the urban lower-class woman typically resembles that of the peasant rather than the urban upper-class woman. Industrialization, by creating demands and opportunities for their employment outside the home, is causing significant changes in the status of women as well as in the whole of the kinship system in urban areas.

A formalized system of age grading is an effective mechanism of social control in preindustrial cities. Among siblings the eldest son is privileged. And children and youth are subordinate to parents and other adults. This, combined with early marriage, inhibits the development of a "youth culture." On the other hand, older persons hold considerable power and prestige, a fact contributing to the slow pace of change.

As noted above, kinship is functionally integrated with social class. It also reinforces and is reinforced by the economic organization: the occupations, through the guilds, select their members primarily on the basis of kinship, and much of the work is carried on in the home or immediate vicinity. Such conditions are not functional to the requirements of a highly industrialized society.

The kinship system in the preindustrial city also articulates with a special kind of religious system, whose formal organization reaches fullest development among members of the literate elite.[11] The city is the seat of the key religious functionaries whose actions set standards for the rest of society. The urban lower class, like the peasantry, does not possess the education or the means to maintain all the exacting norms prescribed by the sacred writings. Yet the religious system influences the city's entire social structure. (Typically, within the preindustrial city one religion is dominant; however, certain minority groups adhere to their own beliefs.) Unlike the situation in industrial cities, religious activity is not separate from other social action but permeates family, economic, governmental, and other activities. Daily life is pervaded with religious significance. Especially important are periodic public festivals and ceremonies like Ramadan in Muslim cities. Even distinctly ethnic outcaste groups can through their own religious festivals maintain solidarity.

Magic, too, is interwoven with economic, familial, and other social activities. Divination is commonly employed for determining the "correct" action on critical occasions; for example, in traditional Japanese and Chinese cities, the selection of marriage partners. And nonscientific procedures are widely employed to treat illness among all elements of the population of the preindustrial city.

Formal education typically is restricted to the male elite, its purpose being to train individuals for positions in the governmental, educational, or religious hierarchies. The economy of preindustrial cities does not require mass literacy, nor, in fact, does the system of production provide the leisure so necessary for the acquisition of formal education. Considerable time is needed merely to learn the written language, which often is quite different from that spoken. The teacher occupies a position of honor, primarily because of the prestige of all learning and especially of knowledge of the sacred literature, and learning is traditional and characteristically based upon sacred writings.[12] Students are expected to memorize rather than evaluate and initiate, even in institutions of higher learning.

Since preindustrial cities have no agencies of mass communication, they are relatively isolated from one another. Moreover, the masses within a city are isolated from the elite. The former must rely upon verbal communication, which is formalized in special groups such as story tellers or their counterparts. Through verse and song these transmit upper-class tradition to nonliterate individuals.

The formal government of the preindustrial city is the province of the elite and is closely integrated with the educational and religious systems. It performs two principal functions: exacting tribute from the city's masses to support the activities of the elite and maintaining law and order through a "police force" (at times a branch of the army) and a court system. The police force exists primarily for the control of "outsiders," and the courts support custom and the rule of the sacred literature, a code of enacted legislation typically being absent.

In actual practice little reliance is placed upon formal machinery for regulating social life.[13] Much more significant are the informal controls exerted by the kinship, guild, and religious systems, and here, of course, personal standing is decisive. Status distinctions are visibly correlated with personal attributes, chiefly speech, dress, and personal mannerisms which proclaim ethnic group occupation, age, sex, and social class. In nineteenth-century Seoul, not only did the upper-class mode of dress differ considerably from that of the masses, but speech varied according to social class, the verb forms and pronouns depending upon whether the speaker ranked higher or lower or was the equal of the person being addressed.[14] Obviously, then, escape from one's role is difficult, even in the street crowds. The individual is ever conscious of his specific rights and duties. All these things conserve the social order in the preindustrial city despite its heterogeneity.

CONCLUSIONS

Throughout this paper there is the assumption that certain structural elements are universal for all urban centers. This study's hypothesis is that their form in the preindustrial city is fundamentally distinct from that in the industrial-urban community. A considerable body of data not only from medieval Europe, which is somewhat atypical,[15] but from a variety of cultures supports this point of view. Emphasis has been upon the static features of preindustrial city life. But even those preindustrial cities which have undergone considerable change approach the ideal type. For one thing, social change is of such a nature that it is not usually perceived by the general populace.

Most cities of the preindustrial type have been located in Europe or Asia. Even though Athens and Rome and the large commercial centers of Europe prior to the industrial revolution displayed certain unique features, they fit the preindustrial type quite well.[16] And many traditional Latin-American cities are quite like it, although

deviations exist, for, excluding pre-Columbian cities, these were affected to some degree by the industrial revolution soon after their
establishment.

It is postulated that industrialization is a key variable accounting for the distinctions between preindustrial and industrial cities.
The type of social structure required to develop and maintain a form
of production utilizing inanimate sources of power is quite unlike that
in the preindustrial city.[17] At the very least, extensive industrialization
requires a rational, centralized, extra-community economic organization in which recruitment is based more upon universalism than on
particularism, a class system which stresses achievement rather than
ascription, a small and flexible kinship system, a system of mass education which emphasizes universalistic rather than particularistic criteria, and mass communication. Modification in any one of these
elements affects the others and induces changes in other systems such
as those of religion and social control as well. Industrialization, moreover, not only requires a special kind of social structure within the
urban community but provides the means necessary for its establishment.

Anthropologists and sociologists will in the future devote increased attention to the study of cities throughout the world. They
must therefore recognize that the particular kind of social structure
found in cities in the United States is not typical of all societies. Miner's
recent study of Timbuctoo,[18] which contains much excellent data,
points to the need for recognition of the preindustrial city. His emphasis upon the folk-urban continuum diverted him from an equally
significant problem: How does Timbuctoo differ from modern industrial cities in its ecological, economic, and social structure? Society
there seems even more sacred and organized than Miner admits.[19]
For example, he used divorce as an index of disorganization, but in
Muslim society divorce within certain rules is justified by the sacred
scripture. The studies of Hsu and Fried would have considerably more
significance had the authors perceived the generality of their findings.
And, once the general structure of the preindustrial city is understood, the specific cultural deviations become more meaningful.

Beals notes the importance of the city as a center of acculturation.[20] But an understanding of this process is impossible without
some knowledge of the preindustrial city's social structure. Although
industrialization is clearly advancing throughout most of the world, the
social structure of preindustrial civilizations is conservative, often resisting the introduction of numerous industrial forms. Certainly many
cities of Europe (e.g., in France or Spain) are not so fully industrialized as some presume; a number of preindustrial patterns remain. The
persistence of preindustrial elements is also evident in cities of North
Africa and many parts of Asia; for example, in India and Japan,[21]
even though great social change is currently taking place. And the
Latin-American city of Merida, which Redfield studied, had many
preindustrial traits.[22] A conscious awareness of the ecological, economic, and social structure of the preindustrial city should do much
to further the development of comparative urban community studies.

508   NOTES

1. George M. Foster, "What Is Folk Culture?" *American Anthropologist* 55 (1953) : 159–73.

2. Gideon Sjoberg, "Folk and 'Feudal' Societies," *American Journal of Sociology* 58 (1952) : 231–39.

3. Sociologists have devoted almost no attention to the ecology of preindustrial centers. However, works of other social scientists do provide some valuable preliminary data. *See,* e.g., Marcel Clerget, *Le Caire: Etude de geographie urbaine et d'histoire economique* (2 vols.; Cairo: E. & R. Schindler, 1934) ; Robert E. Dickinson, *The West European City* (London: Routledge & Kegan Paul, 1951) ; Roger Le Tourneau, *Fes: Avant le protectorat* (Casablanca: Societe Marocaine de Librairie et d'Edition, 1949) ; Edward W. Lane, *Cairo Fifty Years Ago* (London: John Murray, 1896) ; J. Sauvaget, *Alep* (Paris: Librairie Orientaliste Paul Geuthner, 1941) ; J. Weulersse, "Antioche: Essai de geographic urbaine," *Bulletin d'etudes orientales,* IV (1934), 27–79; Jean Kennedy, *Here Is India* (New York: Charles Scribner's Sons, 1945) : and relevant articles in American geographical journals.

4. Dickinson, op. cit., p. 27; O. H. K. Spate, *India and Pakistan* (London: Methuen & Co., 1954), p. 183.

5. For a discussion of guilds and other facets of the preindustrial city's economy see, e.g., J. S. Burgess, *The Guilds of Peking* (New York: Columbia University Press, 1928) ; Edward T. Williams, *China, Yesterday and Today* (5th ed.; New York: Thomas Y. Crowell Co., 1932) ; T'ai-ch'u Liao, "The Apprentices in Chengtu during and after the War," *Yenching Journal of Social Studies* 4 (1948) : 90–106; H. A. R. Gibb and Harold Bowen, *Islamic Society and the West* (London: Oxford University Press, 1950), vol I, part I, chap. vi; Le Tourneau, op. cit.; Clerget, op cit.; James W. Thompson and Edgar N. Johnson, *An Introduction to Medieval Europe* (New York: W. W. Norton Co., 1937), chap. xx; Sylvia L. Thrupp, "Medieval Gilds Reconsidered," *Journal of Economic History* 2 (1942) : 164–73.

6. For an extreme example of unstandardized currency cf. Robert Coltman, Jr., *The Chinese* (Philadelphia: F. A. Davis, 1891), p. 52. In some traditional societies (e.g., China) the state has sought to standardize economic action in the city by setting up standard systems of currency and/or weights and measures; these efforts, however, generally proved ineffective. Inconsistent policies in taxation, too, hinder the development of a "rational" economy.

7. The status of the true merchant in the preindustrial city, ideally, has been low; in medieval Europe and China many merchants were considered "outcasts." However, in some preindustrial cities a few wealthy merchants have acquired considerable power even though their role has not been highly valued. Even then most of their prestige has come through participation in religious, governmental, or educational activities, which have been highly valued (see, e.g., Ping-ti Ho, "The Salt Merchants of Yang-Chou: A Study of Commercial Capitalism in Eighteenth-Century China," *Harvard Journal of Asiatic Studies* 17 (1954) : 130–68).

8. For materials on the kinship system and age and sex differasientiation *see,* e.g., Le Tourneau, op. cit.; Edward W. Lane, *The Manners and Customs of the Modern Egyptians* (3rd ed.; New York: E. P. Dutton Co., 1923) ; C. Snouck Hurgronje, *Mekka in the Latter Part of the Nineteenth Century,* trans. J. H. Monahan (London: Luzac, 1931) ; Horace Miner, *The Primitive City of Timbuctoo* (Princeton: Princeton University Press, 1953) ; Alice M. Bacon, *Japanese Girls and Women* (rev. ed.; Boston: Houghton Mifflin Co., 1902) ; J. S. Burgess, "Community Organization in China," *Far Eastern Survey* 14 (1945) : 371–73; Morton H. Fried, *Fabric of Chinese Society* (New York: Frederick A. Praeger, 1953) ; Francis L. K. Hsu, *Under the Ancestors' Shadow* (New York: Columbia University Press, 1948) ; Cornelius Osgood, *The Koreans and Their Culture* (New York: Ronald Press, 1951), chap. viii; Jukichi Inouye, *Home Life in Tokyo* (2d ed.; Tokyo: Tokyo Printing Co., 1911).

9. Tsung-Lien Shen and Shen-Chi Liu, *Tibet and the Tibetans* (Stanford: Stanford University Press, 1953), pp. 143–44.

10. Osgood, op. cit., p. 146.

11. For information on various aspects of religious behavior see, e.g., Le Tourneau, op. cit.; Miner, op. cit.; Lane, *Manners and Customs;* Hurgronje, op. cit.; Andre Chouraqui, *Les Juifs d'Afrique du Nord* (Paris: Presses Universitaires de France, 1952); Justus Doolittle, *Social Life of the Chinese* (London: Sampson Low, 1868); John K. Shryock, *The Temples of Anking and Their Cults* (Paris: Privately printed, 1931); Derk Bodde (ed.), *Annual Customs and Festivals in Peking* (Peiping: Henri Vetch, 1936); Edwin Benson, *Life in a Medieval City* (New York: Macmillan Co., 1920); Hsu, op. cit.

12. Le Tourneau, op. cit., Part VI; Lane, *Manners and Customs*, chap ii; Charles Bell, *The People of Tibet* (Oxford: Clarendon Press, 1928), chap. xix; O. Olufsen, *The Emir of Bokhara and His Country* (London: William Heinemann, 1911), chap. ix; Doolittle, op. cit.

13. Carleton Coon, *Caravan: The Story of the Middle East* (New York: Henry Holt & Co., 1951), p. 259; George W. Gilmore, *Korea from Its Capital* (Philadelphia: Presbyterian Board of Publication, 1892), pp. 51–52.

14. Osgood, op. cit., chap. viii; Gilmore, op. cit., chap iv.

15. Henri Pirenne, in *Medieval Cities* (Princeton: Princeton University Press, 1925), and others have noted that European cities grew up in opposition to and were separate from the greater society. But this thesis has been overstated for medieval Europe. Most preindustrial cities are integral parts of broader social structures.

16. Some of these cities made extensive use of water power, which possibly fostered deviations from the type.

17. For a discussion of the institutional prerequisites of industrialization *see*, e.g., Bert F. Hoselitz, "Social Structure and Economic Growth," *Economia internazionale* 6 (1953): 52–57, and Marion J. Levy, "Some Sources of the Vulnerability of the Structures of Relatively Non-industrialized Societies to Those of Highly Industrialized Societies," in Bert F. Hoselitz ed., *The Progress of Underdeveloped Areas* (Chicago: University of Chicago Press, 1952), pp. 114 ff.

18. Op. cit.

19. This point seems to have been perceived also by Asael T. Hansen in his review of Horace Miner's *The Primitive City of Timbuctoo, American Journal of Sociology* 59 (1954): 501–2.

20. Ralph L. Beals, "Urbanism, Urbanization and Acculturation," *American Anthropologist*, LIII (1951), 1–10.

21. *See*, e.g., D. R. Gadgil, *Poona: A Socio-economic Survey* (Poona: Gokhale Institute of Politics and Economics, 1952), Part II; N. V. Sovani, *Social Survey of Kolhapur City* (Poona: Gokhale Institute of Politics and Economics, 1951), vol. II; Noel P. Gist, "Caste Differentials in South India," *American Sociological Review* 19 (1954): 126–37; John Campbell Pelzel, "Social Stratification in Japanese Urban Economic Life" (unpublished Ph.D. dissertation, Harvard University, Department of Social Relations, 1950).

22. Robert Redfield, *The Folk Culture of Yucatan* (Chicago: University of Chicago Press, 1941).

KARL MARX AND FRIEDRICH ENGELS

Manifesto of the Communist Party

A spectre is haunting Europe—the spectre of Communism. All the powers of old Europe have entered into a holy alliance to exorcise this spectre: Pope and Czar, Metternich and Guizot, French Radicals and German police-spies.

Where is the party in opposition that has not been decried as communistic by its opponents in power? Where the Opposition that has not hurled back the branding reproach of Communism, against the more advanced opposition parties, as well as against its reactionary adversaries?

Two things result from this fact:

I. Communism is already acknowledged by all European powers to be itself a power.

II. It is high time that Communists should openly, in the face of the whole world, publish their views, their aims, their tendencies, and meet this nursery tale of the spectre of Communism with a manifesto of the party itself.

To this end, Communists of various nationalities have assembled in London, and sketched the following manifesto, to be published in the English, French, German, Italian, Flemish and Danish languages.

*   *   *

BOURGEOIS AND PROLETARIANS

The history of all hitherto existing society is the history of class struggles.

Freeman and slave, patrician and plebeian, lord and serf, guild-master and journeyman, in a word, oppressor and oppressed, stood in constant opposition to one another, carried on an uninterrupted, now hidden, now open fight, a fight that each time ended, either in a revolutionary reconstitution of society at large, or in the common ruin of the contending classes.

In the earlier epochs of history, we find almost everywhere a complicated arrangement of society into various orders, a manifold gradation of social rank. In ancient Rome we have patricians, knights, plebeians, slaves; in the Middle Ages, feudal lords, vassals, guild-masters, journeymen, apprentices, serfs; in almost all of these classes, again, subordinate gradations.

The modern bourgeois society that has sprouted from the ruins of feudal society, has not done away with class antagonisms. It has

Karl Marx and Friedrich Engels, "Manifesto of the Communist Party." This article is S-445 in The Bobbs-Merril Reprint Series.

but established new classes, new conditions of oppression, new forms of struggle in place of the old ones.

Our epoch, the epoch of the bourgeoisie, possesses, however, this distinctive feature: It has simplified the class antagonisms. Society as a whole is more and more splitting up into two great hostile camps, into two great classes directly facing each other—bourgeoisie and proletariat.

From the serfs of the Middle Ages sprang the chartered burghers of the earliest towns. From these burgesses the first elements of the bourgeoisie were developed.

The discovery of America, the rounding of the Cape, opened up fresh ground for the rising bourgeoisie. The East-Indian and Chinese markets, the colonisation of America, trade with the colonies, the increase in the means of exchange and in commodities generally, gave to commerce, to navigation, to industry, an impulse never before known, and thereby, to the revolutionary element in the tottering feudal society, a rapid development.

The feudal system of industry, in which industrial production was monopolised by closed guilds, now no longer sufficed for the growing wants of the new markets. The manufacturing system took its place. The guild-masters were pushed aside by the manufacturing middle class; division of labour between the different corporate guilds vanished in the face of division of labour in each single workshop.

Meantime the markets kept ever growing, the demand ever rising. Even manufacture no longer sufficed. Thereupon, steam and machinery revolutionised industrial production. The place of manufacture was taken by the giant, modern industry, the place of the industrial middle class, by industrial millionaires—the leaders of whole industrial armies, the modern bourgeois.

Modern industry has established the world market, for which the discovery of America paved the way. This market has given an immense development to commerce, to navigation, to communication by land. This development has, in its turn, reacted on the extension of industry; and in proportion as industry, commerce, navigation, railways extended, in the same proportion the bourgeoisie developed, increased its capital, and pushed into the background every class handed down from the Middle Ages.

We see, therefore, how the modern bourgeoisie is itself the product of a long course of development, of a series of revolutions in the modes of production and exchange.

Each step in the development of the bourgeoisie was accompanied by a corresponding political advance of that class. An oppressed class under the sway of the feudal nobility, it became an armed and self-governing association in the mediaeval commune; here independent urban republic (as in Italy and Germany), there taxable "third estate" of the monarchy (as in France); afterwards, in the period of manufacture proper, serving either the semi-feudal or the absolute monarchy as a counterpoise against the nobility, and, in fact, corner-stone of the great monarchies in general—the bourgeoisie has at last, since the establishment of modern industry and of the world market, conquered for itself, in the modern representative state, exclusive political sway. The executive of the modern state is but a committee for managing the common affairs of the whole bourgeoisie.

The bourgeoisie has played a most revolutionary role in history.

The bourgeoisie, wherever it has got the upper hand, has put an end to all feudal, patriarchal, idyllic relations. It has pitilessly torn asunder the motley feudal ties that bound man to his "natural superiors," and has left no other bond between man and man than naked self-interest, than callous "cash-payment." It has drowned the most heavenly ecstasies of religious fervour, of chivalrous enthusiasm, of philistine sentimentalism, in the icy water of egotistical calculation. It has resolved personal worth into exchange value, and in place of the numberless indefeasible chartered freedoms, has set up that single, unconscionable freedom—Free Trade. In one word, for exploitation, veiled by religious and political illusions, it has substituted naked, shameless, direct, brutal exploitation.

The bourgeoisie has stripped of its halo every occupation hitherto honoured and looked up to with reverent awe. It has converted the physician, the lawyer, the priest, the poet, the man of science, into its paid wage-labourers.

The bourgeoisie has torn away from the family its sentimental veil, and has reduced the family relation to a mere money relation.

The bourgeoisie has disclosed how it came to pass that the brutal display of vigour in the Middle Ages, which reactionaries so much admire, found its fitting complement in the most slothful indolence. It has been the first to show what man's activity can bring about. It has accomplished wonders far surpassing Egyptian pyramids, Roman aqueducts, and Gothic cathedrals; it has conducted expeditions that put in the shade all former migrations of nations and crusades.

The bourgoisie cannot exist without constantly revolutionising the instruments of production, and thereby the relations of production, and with them the whole relations of society. Conservation of the old modes of production in unaltered form, was, on the contrary, the first condition of existence for all earlier industrial classes. Constant revolutionising of production, uninterrupted disturbance of all social conditions, everlasting uncertainty and agitation distinguish the bourgeois epoch from all earlier ones. All fixed, fast-frozen relations, with their train of ancient and venerable prejudices and opinions, are swept away, all new-formed ones become antiquated before they can ossify. All that is solid melts into air, all that is holy is profaned, and man is at last compelled to face with sober senses his real conditions of life and his relations with his kind.

The need of a constantly expanding market for its products chases the bourgeoisie over the whole surface of the globe. It must nestle everywhere, settle everywhere, establish connections everywhere.

The bourgeoisie has through its exploitation of the world market given a cosmopolitan character to production and consumption in every country. To the great chagrin of reactionaries, it has drawn from under the feet of industry the national ground on which it stood. All old-established national industries have been destroyed or are daily being destroyed. They are dislodged by new industries, whose introduction becomes a life and death question for all civilised nations, by industries that no longer work up indigenous raw material, but raw material drawn from the remotest zones; industries whose products are consumed, not only at home, but in every quarter of the globe. In place of the old wants, satisfied by the production of the country, we find new wants, requiring for their satisfaction the products of distant lands and climes. In place of the old local and national seclusion and self-sufficiency, we have intercourse in every direction, universal inter-dependence of nations. And as in material, so also in intellectual production. The intellectual creations of individual nations become common property. National one-sidedness and narrow-mindedness become more and more impossible, and from the numerous national and local literatures there arises a world literature.

The bourgeoisie, by the rapid improvement of all instruments of production, by the immensely facilitated means of communication, draws all nations, even the most barbarian, into civilisation. The cheap prices of its commodities are the heavy artillery with which it batters down all Chinese walls, with which it forces the barbarians' intensely obstinate hatred of foreigners to capitulate. It compels all nations, on pain of extinction, to adopt the bourgeois mode of production; it compels them to introduce what it calls civilisation into their midst, i.e., to become bourgeois themselves. In a word, it creates a world after its own image.

The bourgeoisie has subjected the country to the rule of the towns. It has created enormous cities, has greatly increased the urban population as compared with the rural, and has thus rescued a considerable part of the population from the idiocy of rural life. Just as it has made the country dependent on the towns, so it has made barbarian and semi-barbarian countries dependent on the civilised ones, nations of peasants on nations of bourgeois, the East on the West.

More and more the bourgeoisie keeps doing away with the scattered state of the population, of the means of production, and of property. It has agglomerated population, centralised means of production, and has concentrated property in a few hands. The necessary consequence of this was political centralisation. Independent, or but loosely connected provinces, with separate interests, laws, governments and systems of taxation, became lumped together into one nation, with one government, one code of laws, one national class interest, one frontier and one customs tariff.

The bourgeoisie, during its rule of scarce one hundred years, has created more massive and more colossal productive forces than have all preceding generations together. Subjection of nature's forces to man, machinery, application of chemistry to industry and agriculture, steam-navigation, railways, electric telegraphs, clearing of whole continents for cultivation, canalisation of rivers, whole populations conjured out of the ground—what earlier century had even a presentiment that such productive forces slumbered in the lap of social labour?

We see then that the means of production and of exchange, which served as the foundation for the growth of the bourgeoisie, were generated in feudal society. At a certain stage in the development of these means of production and of exchange, the conditions under which feudal society produced and exchanged, the feudal organisation of agriculture and manufacturing industry, in a word, the feudal relations of property became no longer compatible with the already developed productive forces; they became so many fetters. They had to be burst asunder; they were burst asunder.

Into their place stepped free competition, accompanied by a social and political constitution adapted to it, and by the economic and political sway of the bourgeois class.

A similar movement is going on before our own eyes. Modern bourgeois society with its relations of production of exchange and of property, a society that has conjured up such gigantic means of production and of exchange, is like the sorcerer who is no longer able to control the powers of the nether world whom he has called up by his spells. For many a decade past the history of industry and commerce is but the history of the revolt of modern productive forces against modern conditions of production, against the property relations that are the conditions for the existence of the bourgeoisie and its rule. It is enough to mention the commercial crisis that by their periodical return put the existence of the entire bourgeois society on trial, each time more threateningly. In these crises a great part not only of the existing products, but also of the previously created productive forces, are periodically destroyed. In these crises there breaks out an epidemic that, in all earlier epochs, would have seemed an absurdity—the epidemic of over-production. Society suddenly finds itself put back into a state of momentary barbarism; it appears as if a famine, a universal war of devastation had cut off the supply of every means of subsistence; industry and commerce seem to be destroyed. And why? Because there is too much civilisation, too much means of subsistence, too much industry, too much commerce. The productive forces at the disposal of society no longer tend to further the development of the conditions of bourgeois property; on the contrary, they have become too powerful for these conditions, by which they are fettered, and no sooner do they overcome these fetters than they bring disorder into the whole of bourgeois society, endanger the existence of bourgeois property. The conditions of bourgeois society are too narrow to comprise the wealth created by them. And how does the bourgeoisie get over these crises? On the one hand by enforced destruction of a mass of productive forces; on the other, by the conquest of new markets, and by the more thorough exploitation of the old ones. That is to say, by paving the way for more extensive and more destructive crises, and by diminishing the means whereby crises are prevented.

The weapons with which the bourgeoisie felled feudalism to the ground are now turned against the bourgeoisie itself.

But not only has the bourgeoisie forged the weapons that bring death to itself; it has called into existence the men who are to wield those weapons—the modern working class—the proletarians.

In proportion as the bourgeoisie, i.e., capital, is developed, in the same proportion is the proletariat, the modern working class, developed—a class of labourers, who live only so long as they find work, and who find work only so long as their labour increases capital. These labourers, who must sell themselves piecemeal, are a commodity, like every other article of commerce, and are consequently exposed to all the vicissitudes of competition, to all the fluctations of the market.

Owing to the extensive use of machinery and to division of labour, the work of the proletarians has lost all individual character, and, consequently, all charm for the workman. He becomes an appendage of the machine, and it is only the most simple, most monotonous, and most easily acquired knack, that is required of him. Hence, the cost of production of a workman is restricted, almost entirely, to the means of subsistence that he requires for his maintenance, and for the propagation of his race. But the price of a commodity, and therefore also of labour, is equal to its cost of production. In proportion, therefore, as the repulsiveness of the work increases, the wage decreases. Nay more, in proportion as the use of machinery and division of labour increases, in the same proportion the burden of toil also increases, whether by prolongation of the working hours, by increase of the work exacted in a given time, or by increased speed of the machinery, etc.

Modern industry has converted the little workshop of the patriarchal master into the great factory of the industrial capitalist. Masses of labourers, crowded into the factory, are organised like soldiers. As privates of the industrial army they are placed under the command of a perfect hierarchy of officers and sergeants. Not only are they slaves of the bourgeois class, and of the bourgeois state; they are daily and hourly enslaved by the machine, by the over-looker, and above all, by the individual bourgeois manufacturer himself. The more openly this despotism proclaims gain to be its end and aim, the more petty, the more hateful and the more embittering it is.

The less the skill and exertion of strength implied in manual labour, in other words, the more modern industry develops, the more is the labour of men superseded by that of women. Differences of age and sex have no longer any distinctive social validity for the working class. All are instruments of labour, more or less expensive to use, according to their age and sex.

No sooner has the labourer received his wages in cash, for the moment escaping exploitation by the manufacturer, than he is set upon by the other portions of the bourgeoisie, the landlord, the shopkeeper, the pawnbroker, etc.

The lower strata of the middle class—the small tradespeople, shopkeepers, and retired tradesmen generally, the handicraftsmen and peasants—all these sink gradually into the proletariat, partly because their diminutive capital does not suffice for the scale on which modern industry is carried on, and is swamped in the competition with the large capitalists, partly because their specialised skill is rendered worthless by new methods of production. Thus the proletariat is recruited from all classes of the population.

The proletariat goes through various stages of development. With its birth begins its struggle with the bourgeoisie. At first the con-

516   test is carried on by individual labourers, then by the work people of a factory, then by the operatives of one trade, in one locality, against the individual bourgeois who directly exploits them. They direct their attacks not against the bourgeois conditions of production, but against the instruments of production themselves; they destroy imported wares that compete with their labour, they smash machinery to pieces, they set factories ablaze, they seek to restore by force the vanished status of the workman of the Middle Ages.

At this stage the labourers still form an incoherent mass scattered over the whole country, and broken up by their mutual competition. If anywhere they unite to form more compact bodies, this is not yet the consequence of their own active union, but of the union of the bourgeoisie, which class, in order to attain its own political ends, is compelled to set the whole proletariat in motion, and is moreover still able to do so for a time. At this stage, therefore, the proletarians do not fight their enemies, but the enemies of their enemies, the remnants of absolute monarchy, the landowners, the non-industrial bourgeois, the petty bourgeoisie. Thus the whole historical movement is concentrated in the hands of the bourgeoisie; every victory so obtained is a victory for the bourgeoisie.

But with the development of industry the proletariat not only increases in number; it becomes concentrated in greater masses, its strength grows, and it feels that strength more. The various interests and conditions of life within the ranks of the proletariat are more and more equalised, in proportion as machinery obliterates all distinctions of labour and nearly everywhere reduces wages to the same low level. The growing competition among the bourgeois, and the resulting commercial crises, make the wages of the worker ever more fluctuating. The unceasing improvement of machinery, ever more rapidly developing, makes their livlihood more and more precarious; the collisions between individual workmen and individual bourgeois take more and more the character of collisions between two classes. Thereupon the workers begin to form combinations (trade unions) against the bourgeoisie; they club together in order to keep up the rate of wages; they found permanent associations in order to make provision beforehand for these occasional revolts. Here and there the contest breaks out into riots.

Now and then the workers are victorious, but only for a time. The real fruit of their battles lies, not in the immediate result, but in the ever expanding union of the workers. This union is furthered by the improved means of communication which are created by modern industry, and which place the workers of different localities in contact with one another. It was just this contact that was needed to centralise the numerous local struggles, all of the same character, into one national struggle between classes. But every class struggle is a political struggle. And that union, to attain which the burghers of the Middle Ages, with their miserable highways, required centuries, the modern proletarians, thanks to railways, achieve in a few years.

This organisation of the proletarians into a class, and consequently into a political party, is continually being upset again by the competition between the workers themselves. But it ever rises up again, stronger, firmer, mightier. It compels legislative recognition of particular interests of the workers, by taking advantage of the divisions among the bourgeoisie itself. Thus the ten-hour bill in England was carried.

Altogether, collisions between the classes of the old society further the course of development of the proletariat in many ways. The bourgeoisie finds itself involved in a constant battle. At first with the aristocracy; later on, with those portions of the bourgeoisie itself whose interests have become antagonistic to the progress of industry at all times with the bourgeoisie of foreign countries. In all these battles it sees itself compelled to appeal to the proletariat, to ask for its help, and thus, to drag it into the political arena. The bourgoisie itself, therefore, supplies the proletariat with its own elements of political and general education, in other words, it furnishes the proletariat with weapons for fighting the bourgeoisie.

Further, as we have already seen, entire sections of the ruling classes are, by the advance of industry, precipitated into the proletariat, or are at least threatened in their conditions of existence. These also supply the proletariat with fresh elements of enlightenment and progress.

Finally, in times when the class struggle nears the decisive hour, the process of dissolution going on within the ruling class, in fact within the whole range of old society, assumes such a violent, glaring character, that a small section of the ruling class cuts itself adrift, and joins the revolutionary class, the class that holds the future in its hands. Just as, therefore, at an earlier period, a section of the nobility went over to the bourgeoisie, so now a portion of the bourgeoisie goes over to the proletariat, and in particular, a portion of the bourgeois ideologists, who have raised themselves to the level of comprehending theoretically the historical movement as a whole.

Of all the classes that stand face to face with the bourgeoisie today, the proletariat alone is a really revolutionary class. The other classes decay and finally disappear in the face of modern industry; the proletariat is its special and essential product.

The lower middle class, the small manufacturer, the shopkeeper, the artisan, the peasant, all these fight against the bourgeoisie, to save from extinction their existence as fractions of the middle class. They are therefore not revolutionary, but conservative. Nay more, they are reactionary, for they try to roll back the wheel of history. If by chance they are revolutionary, they are so only in view of their impending transfer into the proletariat; they thus defend not their present, but their future interests; they desert their own standpoint to adopt that of the proletariat.

The "dangerous class," the social scum *(Lumpenproletariat)*, that passively rotting mass thrown off by the lowest layers of old society, may, here and there, be swept into the movement by a proletarian revolution; its conditions of life, however, prepare it far more for the part of a bribed tool of reactionary intrigue.

The social conditions of the old society no longer exist for the

518 proletariat. The proletarian is without property; his relation to his wife and children has no longer anything in common with bourgeois family relations; modern industrial labour, modern subjection to capital, the same in England as in France, in America as in Germany, has stripped him of every trace of national character. Law, morality, religion, are to him so many bourgeois prejudices, behind which lurk in ambush just as many bourgeois interests.

All the preceding classes that got the upper hand, sought to fortify their already acquired status by subjecting society at large to their conditions of appropriation. The proletarians cannot become masters of the productive forces of society, except by abolishing their own previous mode of appropriation, and thereby also every other previous mode of appropriation. They have nothing of their own to secure and to fortify; their mission is to destroy all previous securities for, and insurances of, individual property.

All previous historical movements were movements of minorities, or in the interest of minorities. The proletarian movement is the self-conscious, independent movement of the immense majority, in the interest of the immense majority. The proletariat, the lowest stratum of our present society, cannot stir, cannot raise itself up without the whole superincumbent strata of official society being sprung into the air.

Though not in substance, yet in form, the struggle of the proletariat with the bourgeoisie is at first a national struggle. The proletariat of each country must, of course, first of all settle matters with its own bourgeoisie.

In depicting the most general phases of the development of the proletariat, we traced the more or less veiled civil war, raging within existing society, up to the point where that war breaks out into open revolution, and where the violent overthrow of the bourgeoisie lays the foundation for the sway of the proletariat.

Hitherto, every form of society has been based, as we have already seen, on the antagonism of oppressing and oppressed classes. But in order to oppress a class, certain conditions must be assured to it under which it can at least, continue its slavish existence. The serf, in the period of serfdom, raised himself to membership in the commune, just as the petty bourgeois, under the yoke of feudal absolutism, managed to develop into a bourgeois. The modern labourer, on the contrary, instead of rising with the progress of industry, sinks deeper and deeper below the conditions of existence of his own class. He becomes a pauper, and pauperism develops more rapidly than population and wealth. And here it becomes evident, that the bourgeoisie is unfit any longer to be the ruling class in society, and to impose its conditions of existence upon society as over-riding law. It is unfit to rule because it is incompetent to assure an existence to its slave within his slavery, because it cannot help letting him sink into such a state, that it has to feed him, instead of being fed by him. Society can no longer live under this bourgeoisie, in other words, its existence is no longer compatible with society.

The essential condition for the existence and sway of the bourgeois class, is the formation and augmentation of capital; the condition for capital is wage-labour. Wage-labour rests exclusively on competition between labourers. The advance of industry, whose involuntary promoter is the bourgeoisie, replaces the isolation of the labourers, due to competition, by their revolutionary combination, due to association. The development of modern industry, therefore, cuts from under its feet the very foundation on which the bourgeoisie produces and appropriates products. What the bourgeoisie therefore produces, above all, are its own grave-diggers. Its fall and the victory of the proletariat are equally inevitable.

Modern Society

PART **5**

The last section of this book examines man in modern society. Each of its three chapters appears as an entity, but in reality it is difficult to separate them. Bureaucracy, as a major fact of modern social life, cannot be studied without considering stratification and mass society also. Thus, the three chapters, while distinct from one another, describe and analyze modern life in a unified way. I will try to identify the major forces of modern society and describe them in terms of social organizational patterns.

INVERSE **DIRECT**
RATEBUSTER

Power

OSTRACIZED

RITUALISM

SABOTAGE

SANCTIONS

Structure

CHARISMA

Cooperation

METAPHYSICAL

NORMS

Demise

Authority

PRODUCTIVITY

Informal **Competition**

BUREAUCRATIC

RATIONALE

Study Questions

1. What is a rational power structure? Do you agree with the Weberian definition of a rational power structure?
2. Is charismatic leadership more attractive to you than traditional leadership? Why or why not?
3. How did the leadership differ in the various communes that Prof. Kanter described earlier in chapter 8?
4. Are there occasions when one type of leadership is more valuable than another type? What are these circumstances?
5. Why are competition and productivity inversely related for groups but directly related to individuals in competitive groups?
6. Do Professor Blau's findings confirm your own experiences? How would you go about deciding whether your classroom is run along competitive or cooperative lines?
7. Do you feel that the new mayor of Gary made any errors in the governing of the city? Why or Why not? What might you have done differently?

Bureaucracy

13

In the article on Caliente in chapter 7, the coming of the diesel engine forecast the fate of a small social unit. Caliente's demise was not extraordinary. As the scale of modern society increases—as businesses, schools, hospitals and the military establishment become larger—more and more small social units and individuals are absorbed into large organizations. Even though large-scale organizations need not be bureaucratic, they tend to develop bureaucratic patterns in their social organization.

Bureaucracy, as Max Weber, the renowned classical theorist of bureaucracy, first described and analyzed it, is the most efficient form of organization, although the term refers not to a particular social organization but to a type or form of social organization that certain social units develop.[1] In bureaucratically organized social units, actors enter into social relationships for specific goals. In exchange for services, the bureaucratic official receives certain benefits and rewards. Weber was interested in bureaucracy because it allowed him to pose a number of key questions. He asked:

1. What is the relationship between the power to control and the ability to justify that control?
2. What characterizes a rational power structure?
3. To what degree must authority be persuasive?

Most modern studies on bureaucracy use these questions as a basis for their research. More simply put, the problem is: How can men control other men so as to maximize effectiveness and minimize unhappiness? "Unhappiness" can be seen as that variable which unifies the many studies on productivity, absenteeism, and worker satisfaction. In order to grapple with these questions, we must clarify a number of terms and issues.

LEGITIMATION AND AUTHORITY

All organizations develop norms and need to enforce them, because they are necessary for organizational functioning even though members may not agree with them. If members do not comply with organizational norms, sanctions may be leveled against them. The exercise of power, however, has certain drawbacks; when people conform because of the threat of sanctions or the use of power, they are not likely to share information or show initiative. Nor will people cooperate unless cooperation is demanded by those in power. At times of organizational stress or strain, members are likely to substitute their personal values or the values of other groups for those of their organization if the values are not carefully observed.

525

In contrast to this, power may be seen as legitimate. When rules, orders, and norms conform to the values of members, they are legitimized, and members are more committed to the organization. This means that members are more concerned with the goals of the organization, they are more productive, and there is less waste. The elements and parts of an organization are fused. The use of power and the threat of sanctions are unnecessary.

The meaning and relationships of power, legitimacy, and authority are interwoven. Power, it will be recalled, was defined as the capacity to affect the behavior of others through the imposition of sanctions. Legitimacy refers to the acceptance of the exercise of power, and authority refers to power that is viewed as legitimate.

WEBER'S TYPOLOGY OF AUTHORITY

Weber was able to distinguish three types of authority: traditional, charismatic, and rational-legal or bureaucratic. Traditional authority rests upon the sanctity of custom, such as personal loyalty to a chief or leader whose authority is bounded by the limitations of the society's traditions. It occurs in the feudal order, where rules and traditions are sanctified, but it also occurs in the modern family. An example of the invocation of traditional authority is the response, "because your father says so," as a justification for rules. Wherever orders are justified on the grounds that this is the way it is or this is the way things are always done, traditional authority is present.

Charismatic authority rests upon devotion to a special person or heroic figure. Typical of charismatic authority is the justification of rules on the grounds of personality. If a certain person makes a rule, it is followed by group members without resistance. Contemporary figures such as Fidel Castro, John F. Kennedy, and Malcolm X are powerful by virtue of their personal magnetism.

Authority is often exerted and enforced by law, where law is a system of abstract rules. When group members agree to consider these abstract rules as legitimate, rational legal bureaucratic authority is in force. Weber felt that bureaucratic authority was the purest kind of legal authority. The identifying characteristics of legal authority are obedience to other persons in one's capacity as a member of an organization, definition of the legitimate means of compulsion, and delineation of each official's specific field or sphere of competence.

WEBER'S CRITERIA FOR BUREAUCRACY

Bureaucracy, then, is the exercise of legal authority through an administrative staff of officials. Weber listed ten criteria for bureaucracy:

1. Officials are personally free and subject to authority only with respect to impersonal and official obligations.
2. The administrative staff is organized into offices arranged hierarchically.
3. The office holder has a clearly defined sphere of competence.
4. The office is filled on the basis of contract.
5. Members are chosen by competence or according to performance.
6. There is a fixed salary, and supplementary renumeration is forbidden.
7. The office is the member's sole or prime occupation.
8. The office provides the member with a career, i.e., with a series of steps to progressive advancement.
9. Members are subject to strict discipline and control.
10. Members of the administrative staff are separated from the ownership of the means of production.[2]

Although these criteria overlap, Weber argued that only when they are all satisfied simultaneously is there a truly bureaucratic organization. In a bureaucracy, according to Weber, power does not depend on persons but is part of the organization of the system. Bureaucracy is efficient because it emancipates power from those who would quarrel for its possession.

CRITIQUE OF WEBER'S VIEWS

Weber exaggerated selected aspects of bureaucracy and ignored others. We know enough about social organizations by now to understand that no organization can function merely by written rules. Organizations must be flexible; individual authority must be delegated; there must be some decentralization of power. Weber also underestimated the role of informal communication. In bureaucracies, as in other social units, important information is transmitted by informal networks. Students do not learn how to function effectively in a large university by merely reading the official catalogue. Talking with other students who have gone through the process before them is usually more valuable. Finally, Weber did not see that there could be conflict between controllers and specialists. Technical workers may make decisions independent of the normal pyramid of command; they are often insulated from the hierarchy of power.

The most important criticism of Weber's work is that he failed to appreciate the significance of informal organization as potentially subversive or supportive of the formal organization's goals. Hiring practices and promotions often are supported by informal networks of friends, relatives, or fraternity members whose information brings qualified persons to the notice of the formal organization. Organizations cannot function efficiently if they merely fulfill the criteria of bureaucracy that Weber outlined.

One study on informal relations stands out as a classic. It was done during the years 1927 through 1932 by F. J. Roethlisberger and William J. Dickson at the Western Electric Works in Chicago.[3] One of the major aims of the research was to inform the management about the functioning of work groups. Accordingly, there was one intensive study of fourteen men who assembled switches. This work required some individual and group cooperation. The researcher found that there were uniformities in group behavior that were contrary to the formal organizational blueprint. These were the informal rules established by the work group. The norms set by the work group guided the amount of work and the treatment of ratebusters. Ratebusters who worked harder than the work group said they were supposed to were ostracized or punched in the arm.

Informal organizations form the networks of social relations that arise in a formal organization but which are not defined or prescribed by it and may help or hinder the formal organization's goal attainment.

BUREAUCRATIC PATHOLOGIES

There is another kind of problem that went unnoticed by Weber. He failed to take into account what I call "bureaucratic pathologies." There is a real potential for totalitarian control in bureaucratic organizations, because they do not allow for independent solidarity groupings. A member may have a friend or two, but there are no ongoing organizations that can intervene between members and the organization. "Death by Dieselization" is, again, a good example of this problem, for there was no mediating group between the workers and the railroad. The bureaucratic goal of efficiency may thus override other, individual goals, and the bureaucracy becomes a potential means of totalitarian domination.

Another *pathology* is that of *sabotage*. Bureaucracies can survive revolutions and can, therefore, undermine any changes which the government may wish to effect. For example, on a small scale, the secretary in a university department can have tremendous power, not because she is a secretary but because she makes important decisions and can schedule inconvenient appointments or prevent an applicant from seeing the chairman of the department.

Ritualism, another pathology, occurs when members of an organization begin to emphasize rules rather than goals. Bureaucracy is designed to attain precision, reliability, and efficiency, but where rules become too important, the organization is unable to handle special cases or individual differences. Closely allied to ritualism is ethical dilution. Here the organization, once committed to certain ends, becomes bogged down in routine. The maintenance of the organization, the tasks, and salaries, become more important than the realization of organization goals. In correction work, for example, social workers may continue to treat delinquents according to old routines without any longer being concerned with the efficacy of the treatment.

BUREAUCRACY AND METAPHYSICAL PATHOS

As organizations come to terms with the necessary conditions of survival, they must compromise. Universities struggling with funding problems do a certain amount of work for the Department of Defense;

parents who want their children to learn to act on principle also do not want them to rot in prisons. Bureaucracies are particularly subject to compromises of survival because their ruling oligarchies are comprised of careerists who interact segmentally; they remain in their positions through any upheaval. Philip Selznick, in his book *TVA and the Grass Roots*, analyzes the way in which an organization that is guided by democratic ideals is compromised. His hypothesis is that all organizations are concerned with survival and maintenance. Selznick despairs over the realities of organization life where bureaucratic patterns are operative.[4]

This despair is the subject of a response by Alvin Gouldner, "Metaphysical Pathos and the Theory of Bureaucracy." Gouldner takes issue with the stance of many social scientists, who see bureaucracy as the destroyer of ideals, especially the ideals of democracy. Instead, Gouldner develops his Iron Law of Democracy.[5] Gouldner notes that organizations are indeed concerned with maintenance and survival but at the same time they are oriented towards problems of change and growth. Gouldner argues that survival in Selznick's terms means the demise of the organization. For an organization to survive and come to terms with the environment, it must be flexible and ready for change. Thus security is balance of changes and maintenance is balance of growth. The potential for democracy exists even in a bureaucratic organization.

The first article in this chapter is Peter Blau's well-known study of cooperation and competition in an employment agency. Blau demonstrates how the informal organization, the cohesiveness of the group, and the value orientation of two groups in an employment agency produce different rates of productivity. He is able to explain how competition and productivity are inversely related for groups but directly related for individuals in the competition group.

The second article is by Edward Greer, a political scientist. "The 'Liberation' of Gary, Indiana" is a description of the way in which a new black mayor comes to grips with the environment. It is a documentation of the staying power of bureaucrats.

NOTES

1. H. H. Gertz, and C. Wright Mills, *From Max Weber: Essays in Sociology*, New York: Oxford University Press. *See especially* chapters 8 and 9.

2. Max Weber, *The Theory of Social and Economic Organization*, trans. A. M. Henderson and Talcott Parsons, ed. Talcott Parsons, p. 335.

3. F. J. Roethlisberger and William J. Dickson, *Management and the Worker* (Cambridge: Harvard University Press, 1939).

4. Philip Selznick, *TVA and The Grass Roots* (Berkeley and Los Angeles: University of California Press, 1949).

5. Alvin Gouldner, "Metaphysical Pathos and The Theory of Bureaucracy," *American Political Science Review* 49 (1955): 496–507.

PETER M. BLAU   **529**

Co-operation and Competition in a Bureaucracy

This paper discusses performance and variations in competitiveness among twelve interviewers in two small sections of a public employment agency.[1] The duties of the interviewers in both sections were essentially alike. They received requests for workers over the phone. The order forms on which job openings were described were filed in a common pool in each section. Most of the official's time was spent interviewing applicants for jobs. After ascertaining the client's qualifications, the interviewer searched the sectional files for suitable vacancies. If an acceptable job was found, he referred the client to it and later phoned the employer to determine whether the client had been hired.

"The statistics which show how many interviews and how many placements each person in the section did are passed around to all interviewers. Of course, you look at them and see how you compare with others. This creates a competitive spirit," said one of the interviewers, voicing the sentiments of most of his fellows. In a period of job shortages, competition took the form of trying to utilize job openings before anybody else did. Interviewers were so anxious to make placements that they even resorted to illicit methods. Said one:

When you take an order, instead of putting it in the box, you leave it on your desk. There was so much hiding of orders under the blotter that we used to ask, "Do you have anything under your rug?" when we looked for an order. You might leave an order you took on the desk, or you might leave it on the desk after you made no referral. . . . Or, you might take an order only partially; you write the firm's name, and a few things; the others you remember. And you leave it on the pad [of order blanks]. You keep on doing this, and all these orders are not in the box.

You can do some wrong filling out. For instance, for a rather low-salary job, you fill out "experience required." Nobody can make a placement on that except you, because you, alone, know that experience isn't required. Or, if there are several openings [on one order], you put the order into "referrals" [file category for *filled* job openings] after you make one placement. You're supposed to put it into "referrals" but stand it up, so that the others can see it. If you don't, you have a better chance of making the next placement than somebody else. And time and again you see four, five openings on one order filled by the same person. [In one case on file eight out of nine openings on one order had been filled by the same interviewer.]

Peter M. Blau, "Cooperation and Competition in a Bureaucracy," *American Journal of Sociology* 59 (May 1954): 530–35. Copyright © 1954 by the University of Chicago. Reprinted by permission of the author and the University of Chicago Press.

530

The major opportunity for competitive monopolization of job openings occurred when they were received from employers. Since illicit practices were concealed from the observer, the extent of competition could not be determined through questioning or direct observation[2] but was betrayed by the record of official transactions. The extent to which an interviewer filled the vacancies he had received over the phone with his own clients in excess of chance expectations furnishes an index of competitiveness. (Col. 4 in Table 1 shows this index; cols. 1–3 present the data on which it is based.)

STRUCTURAL CONDITIONS AND COMPETITIVENESS

The members of Section A were more competitive than those of Section B. The last two columns in Table 1 also show that the interviewer's competitiveness was related to his productivity in Section A (Pearsonian $\tau = +.92$), but this was not the case in Section B ($\tau = -.20$). In other words, hoarding of jobs was an effective way to improve an interviewer's placement record only in one of these two groups.

The members of Section B were more cooperative: they discouraged competitive practices by making them ineffective. When

Table 1. Competiveness and Productivity in
Section A and in Section B

	Openings Received* (1)	Referrals Made by Recipient (2)	Ratio of Referrals to Openings (3)	Competitiveness† (4)	Productivity‡ (5)	Number of Placements (6)
Section A:						
Adams	34	19	0.56	3.9	0.70	100
Ahman	62	27	.44	3.1	.49	70
Ajax	40	28	.70	4.9	.97	139
Akers	71	32	.45	3.2	.71	101
Ambros	69	18	.26	1.8	.45	65
Atzenberg	106	43	.41	2.9	.61	87
Auble	10	3	.30	2.1	.39	56§
Section B:						
Babcock	16	7	.44	2.2	.53	46
Beers	58	19	.33	1.6	.71	62
Bing	51	15	.29	1.5	.75	65
Borden	17	7	.41	2.1	.55	48§
Bush	43	19	0.42	2.1	0.97	84
Section A	392	170	0.43	3.0	0.59	590
Section B	185	67	0.36	1.8	0.67	289

*The great differences between interviewers in this column show that some were much more successful than others in inducing employers, or telephone operators, to channel requests for workers to them personally. This form of rivalry does not involve competitive interaction.

†Competitiveness index (col. 4): The proportion of job openings received to which the recipient made a referral (col. 3) times the number of members of the section. (This represents the observed divided by the expected frequency of referrals made by the recipient of a job opening.) Base period: First half of April 1949.

‡Productivity index (col. 5): The number of placements made (col. 6) divided by the number of job openings available, that is, the number of openings in the section per interviewer. Base period: April, 1949.

§The number of placements was adjusted for the two interviewers absent for more than five days during April. Since the sectional numbers of placements were not revised, the values in col. 6 add up to more than the two totals shown.

they learned about interesting vacancies, they often told one another, but an interviewer who manifested competitive tendencies was excluded from the network of reciprocal information and lost the respect of his co-workers. Any advantage of hoarding jobs was, at least, neutralized by such lack of cooperation, as is indicated by the absence of a relation between competitiveness and productivity in this group. Since competitive practices made an interviewer unpopular and failed to raise his productivity, they were infrequent.

These officials themselves attributed the greater competitiveness in Section A to the ambitiousness of several members: "There is usually one individual who starts it, who becomes a pace-setter. Once it has started, it is too late." The others, so interviewers claimed, have to follow suit. However, the most competitive member of Section A in recounting her reactions when production records were first introduced made it clear that this explanation of competition on the basis of personality characteristics is inadequate:

When they introduced statistics, I realized how fast I worked. I even wanted to drop lower. I didn't mind working fast as long as it didn't show, but when it showed up like that on the record, I wanted to work less. But you know what happened? Some of the others started to compete with each other and produced more than I did. Then I thought to myself, "Since I can do it, it's silly to let them get ahead of me." I'm only human. So I worked as fast as before.

When statistical records made the superior performance of this interviewer public knowledge, she decided to work less, possibly in response to pressures the others had brought to bear upon her. While complaining about her unfair standards, however, the other members of the section also improved their own performance. Consequently, this interviewer, just like the others, felt constrained by colleagues to compete for an outstanding record. One or two members of Section B, on the other hand, were also accused of competitive tendencies, but their colleagues successfully discouraged their expression in monopolistic practices. It is in this sense that the competitive practices of one group and the co-operative practices of the other were social factors, calling for explanation in sociological rather than psychological terms, as Durkheim has long since emphasized.[3]

Differential conditions affected the development of these two groups. First, the supervisor in Section A relied heavily on performance records in evaluating interviewers: "And here, in the production figures, is the answer to the question: How good are you? Here you see exactly how good the work you did was." Interviewers often mentioned the pressure thus exerted: "[Especially] around rating time, you get this competition. You don't care whether the best person gets the job, but you try to make the placement yourself." In contrast, the new supervisor in Section B surprised his subordinates by rating them more leniently than they had expected, and not primarily on the basis of production records. Consequently, as one interviewer reported, "we became less anxious about statistics; another experience like that, and we might forget all about placement credit."

532

Second, a common professional orientation existed only in Section B. While the members of Section A had been assigned, and had received their training, at different times, the majority of those in Section B received their training together after World War II, at a time when intensive counseling had been stressed, since many returning veterans needed occupational advice. One official said of this period:

When I first came here, in May, 1946, we had a very nice bunch. It was like an all-day consultation; we discussed placements with each other all day long. At that time, the veterans came back, and there was a lot of emphasis on counseling. Nobody asked you how many placements you made, then. The emphasis was on quality, and we consulted with each other all day.

In this situation, the group developed a common professional code, which discouraged speedy placement as constituting defective employment service. In effect, this orientation transformed competitive practices from illegitimate means for desirable ends into illegitimate means for worthless ends. If such practices did occur, they were vigorously opposed on moral grounds as violating the interest of clients. Nevertheless, as will be shown presently, competition could not have been effectively curbed if the supervisor's evaluation practice had engendered acute anxiety over productivity. However, the existence of this code would have made it difficult for the supervisor to judge performance mainly by productivity, since doing so would have stamped him as ignorant of the essentials of good employment service.

No opportunity for the development of a *common* professional code had existed in Section A. Since competitiveness prevailed in this group, the individual whose personal professional standards made him reluctant to compete either became the deviant whose productivity suffered or modified his standards and entered the race with the others.

Third, most members of Section A had been appointed to temporary civil service positions during World War II. They were on probation pending permanent appointments when production records were originally introduced and even afterward remained subject to layoffs due to reductions in staff. Their insecurity led them to strive to impress superiors with outstanding performance. In contrast, all but one of the members of Section B were veterans, whose employment could not be terminated except for cause. As one envious colleague put it, "They felt that nothing could happen to them, because they were veterans, and had super-seniority."

Differences in these three conditions—security of employment, opportunity for the development of a common professional orientation, and the evaluation practice of the supervisor—gave rise to two dissimilar social structures. Productivity was highly valued in Section A and became associated with the individual's standing in the group, while striving for sheer productivity was disparaged in Section B. Thus, whereas the most productive and most competitive member of Section A was considered the best interviewer by her co-workers and was most popular with them,[4] the most productive member of Section B was least respected and least popular. As a result of these structural differences, co-operative norms prevailed only in Section B.

The interviewers in *both* sections disliked working in a competitive atmosphere. A member of Section A said: "If I see that an interviewer keeps orders on her desk, I take them and put them in the box. . . . Of course, you don't make friends that way." Since the majority in this section, including its most popular members, were highly competitive, to antagonize them was to threaten one's own standing in the group. This deterred interviewers from discouraging competitive practices. Antagonizing a deviant, however, does not endanger one's status. Consequently, since a striver was unpopular in Section B, its members could use sanctions freely to combat competitive practices and enforce co-operative norms.

SOCIAL COHESION AND PRODUCTIVITY

Table 1 shows that the group most concerned with productivity was less productive than the other group. Fifty-nine percent of the job openings received in Section A were filled, in contrast to 67 percent in Section B. (The 8 percent difference is significant on the .01 level.) Another implicit paradox is that competitiveness and productivity were directly related for individuals in Section A but inversely related for the two groups.[5]

Anxious concern with productivity induced interviewers in Section A to concentrate blindly upon it at the expense of other considerations. In their eagerness to make many placements they often ignored their relationships with others as well as official rules. Competitiveness in this group weakened social cohesion, while co-operativeness in Section B strengthened it. This difference is further shown by the fact that usually none of the members of Section A spent their rest periods together, whereas all but one of those of Section B, a newcomer when this study was being made, did. Social cohesion enhanced operating efficiency by facilitating co-operation and by reducing status anxiety.

Although the members of both groups had occasion to assist one another, greater effort was required to elicit such co-operation in Section A. The social interaction that occurred in the office during the twenty-four busiest hours of one week was recorded and classified as official and private contacts, that is, those directly concerned with a specific job or client, and all others. The frequency of an interviewer's official contacts with colleagues was related to his productivity in Section A (rank correlation $= +.98$) but not in Section B (rank correlation $= +.08$). This suggests that only interviewers who kept, as one put it, "hopping around all the time" to retrieve job orders that others kept on their desks were able to make many placements in the competitive section. In the cohesive group, on the other hand, the co-operation needed for making placement occurred as a matter of course, and not only in response to special requests. This effort was not required for high productivity.

To maximize his placements, the interviewer in Section A

hoarded jobs and simultaneously tried to prevent others from doing so, thereby antagonizing his co-workers, whose co-operation he needed if he was to do well. The members of this section therefore attempted to conciliate colleagues whom their competitive practices had alienated. Often, shortly after having interfered with her operations, an interviewer paid another a compliment about her work or her apparel. The most competitive interviewer was in the habit of taking time out to joke with her co-workers and was proud of making more placements than anybody else, "nevertheless." Actually, this compensating friendliness, which made her popular despite her competitiveness, helped her to be productive.

In Section A, interviewers had to make special efforts at conciliation in order to make placements, but this was not necessary in Section B. At least, this impression is corroborated by the finding that frequency of private contacts with others was also related to productivity in Section A (rank correlation $= +.84$) but not in Section B (rank correlation $= +.13$). The members of the cohesive group, whose operating practices did not put colleagues at a disadvantage, did not have to devote time and energy to solicit and encourage co-operation, since it was not extended reluctantly. Their spontaneous co-operation improved operating efficiency.

Social cohesion also lessened the status anxiety generated by the evaluation system. Such anxiety is most acute in the individual who does not feel integrated in his work group and therefore seeks to derive social recognition from excelling at his task and from approval of superiors. Friendly relations with co-workers made the standing of the individual in the cohesive group independent of his productivity, particularly since fast work was disparaged as a sign of superficial service. The consequent reduction of anxiety in the antiproductivity-oriented group actually raised its productivity.

Fluctuations in productivity illustrate the dysfunction of status anxiety. Section B had not always operated more efficiently than Section A. Its productivity had been lower during the two months preceding the last rating but had abruptly increased then, while that of Section A had declined, as Table 2 shows.

Table 2. Productivity Before and After Rating

	Section A	Section B
December, 1948	0.64　(619)*	0.56 (317)
January, 1949	.70　(941)	.56 (472)
February, 1949 (rating)	.56 (1,342)	.60 (477)
March, 1949	.59 (1,335)	.71 (448)
April, 1949	0.59 (1,001)	0.67 (433)

*Numbers in parentheses are the numbers of job openings available on which the productivity index — the proportion of these openings that were filled — is based.

The two groups found themselves in different situations before and after they were rated. The members of Section A were familiar with the rating standards of their supervisor, for she had rated them in previous years. Their anxiety led them to work especially hard immediately before the annual rating. The members of Section B, on the other hand, had never before been rated by their new supervisor. They were also concerned about their record but could not calm their anxiety by concentrating upon certain tasks, because they did not know what the supervisor would stress; the explanation he gave to his subordinates was too vague and adhered too strictly to official procedures to help them to foresee his actual practices. This unfocused anxiety was particularly detrimental to efficient performance. Later, when the interviewers found out that they were not rated primarily on the basis of statistical records, their anxiety largely subsided and their productivity increased. In contrast, the experience of the members of Section A, whose rating was strongly influenced by their production records, intensified their status anxiety, but, when the rating was over, anxiety was no longer channeled into exceptionally hard work, with the result that their productivity declined below that of Section B.

Social cohesion is no guaranty against anxiety in a bureaucracy. Civil service status is too important to officials for them to remain immune to the threat of losing it. But when no such threat is felt, social cohesion reduces anxiety by divesting productivity of its significance as a symbol of status in the work group. Diminished anxiety as well as smoother co-operation then enable those in the cohesive group to perform their tasks more efficiently than the others.

In the absence of social cohesion, competitive striving for an outstanding performance record became a substitute means for relieving status anxiety in Section A. This psychological function of competition is illustrated by the following incident: The interviewers in this section became very irritable, and one of them even became physically ill, when a temporary supervisor, who tried to prevent competitive practices, interfered with their method of allaying anxiety. Status anxiety reduced operating efficiency. Even in the cohesive group, productivity was low when the unknown rating standards of a new supervisor produced acute and diffuse anxiety. Otherwise, however, the cohesive group was more productive, because social cohesion relieved status anxiety by making the individual's standing in the group independent of his productivity. The very competitive striving that undermined the group's cohesiveness also served to lessen the individual's status anxiety in a noncohesive situation. The hypothesis that the cohesiveness of the group and the competitiveness of the individual in the less cohesive group both reduce status anxiety explains the paradox that the *less competitive group* as well as the *more competitive individual* in the competitive group each was particularly productive.

NOTES

1. These data are part of a study on interpersonal relations in two government agencies conducted under a fellowship of the Social Science Research Council,

which is hereby gratefully acknowledged. The entire study is soon to be published under the title "The Dynamics of Bureaucracy."

There were seven interviewers in Section A and five in Section B. Seven of the twelve were women.

2. This is clearly indicated by the comment of one of a group of special interviewers, who were expected to use the job openings of the regular interviewers but usually had great difficulty in doing so: "Oh, they hide everything from us. We got more orders when you [the observer] sat in the middle of that section than ever before. We laughed about it. Interviewers would hand us orders asking whether we could use them—when you were looking. That had never happened before."

3. Emile Durkheim, *The Rules of Sociological Method* (Chicago: University of Chicago Press, 1938), pp. 110 and *passim*.

4. She was most often mentioned by members of her own section in answer to the questions, respectively, "Who are the best interviewers?" and "Who are your friends in the office?"

5. For another example of such disparity between individual and corresponding group data see the discussion of promotion opportunities and attitudes toward promotion in Samuel A. Stouffer et al., *The American Soldier* (Princeton: Princeton University Press, 1949), I, 250–54. Kendall and Lazarsfeld discuss the methodological significance of such findings in Robert K. Merton and Paul F. Lazarsfeld, eds., *Continuities in Social Research* (Glencoe, Ill.: Free Press, 1950), pp. 193–95.

EDWARD GREER

The "Liberation" of Gary, Indiana

In silhouette, the skyline of Gary, Indiana, could serve as the perfect emblem of America's industrial might—or its industrial pollution. In the half-century since they were built, the great mills of the United States Steel Corporation—once the largest steel complex on earth—have produced more than a quarter-trillion tons of steel. They have also produced one of the highest air pollution rates on earth. Day and night the tall stacks belch out a ruddy smoke that newcomers to the city find almost intolerable.

Apart from its appalling physical presence, the most striking thing about Gary is the very narrow compass in which the people of the city lead their lives. Three-quarters of the total work force is directly employed by the United States Steel Corporation. About 75 percent of all male employment is in durable goods manufacture and in the wholesale-retail trades, and a majority of this labor force is blue-collar. This means that the cultural tone of the city is solidly working-class.

From Edward Greer, "The 'Liberation' of Gary, Indiana," *Trans-action* 8, no. 3 (January 1971): 30–39, 63. Copyright © January 1971 by *Transaction*, Inc., New Brunswick, New Jersey.

But not poor. Most Gary workers own their own homes, and **537** the city's median income is 10 percent above the national average. The lives of these people, however, are parochial, circumscribed, on a tight focus. With the exception of the ethnic clubs, the union and the Catholic church, the outstanding social edifices in Gary are its bars, gambling joints and whorehouses.

COMPANY TOWN

The city of Gary was the largest of all company towns in America. The United States Steel Corporation began construction in 1905, after assembling the necessary parcel of land on the Lake Michigan shore front. Within two years, over $40 million had been invested in the project; by now the figure must be well into the billions.

Gary was built practically from scratch. Swamps had to be dredged and dunes leveled; a belt-line railroad to Chicago had to be constructed, as well as a port for ore ships and of course a vast complex of manufacturing facilities including coke ovens, blast furnaces and an independent electrical power plant. The city was laid out by corporation architects and engineers and largely developed by the corporation-owned Gary Land Company, which did not sell off most of its holdings until the thirties. Even though the original city plan included locations for a variety of civic, cultural and commercial uses (though woefully little for park land), an eminent critic, John W. Reps, points out that it "failed sadly in its attempt to produce a community pattern noticeably different or better than elsewhere."

The corporation planned more than the physical nature of the city. It also had agents advertise in Europe and the South to bring in workers from as many different backgrounds as possible to build the mills and work in them. Today over 50 ethnic groups are represented in the population.

This imported labor was cheap, and it was hoped that cultural differences and language barriers would curtail the growth of a socialist labor movement. The tough, pioneer character of the city and the fact that many of the immigrant workers' families had not yet joined them in this country combined to create a lawless and vice-ridden atmosphere which the corporation did little to curtail. In much more than its genesis and name, then, Gary is indelibly stamped in the mold of its corporate creators.

LABOR AND THE LEFT

During the course of the First World War, government and vigilante repression broke the back of the Socialist party in small-town America, though it was not very strong to begin with. Simultaneously, however, the Left grew rapidly as a political force among the foreign-born in large urban centers. As the war continued, labor peace was kept by a combination of prosperity (full employment and overtime), pressures for production in the "national interest," and Wilsonian and corporate promises of an extension of democracy in the workplace after the war was over. The promises of a change in priorities proved empty, and in 1919 the long-suppressed grievances of the steelworkers broke forth. Especially among the unskilled immigrant workers, demands for an industrial union, a reduction of the workday from 12 to eight hours and better pay and working conditions sparked a spontaneous movement for an industry-wide strike.

For a time it appeared that the workers would win the Great Steel Strike of 1919, but despite the capable leadership of William Z. Foster the strike was broken. The native white skilled labor aristocracy refused to support it, and the corporation imported blacks from the South to scab in the mills. This defeat helped set back the prospect of militant industrial trade unionism for almost a generation. And meanwhile, racism, a consumer-oriented culture (especially the automobile and relaxed sexual mores) and reforms from above (by the mid-twenties the eight-hour day had been voluntarily granted in the mills) combined to prevent the Left from recovering as a significant social force.

It was in this period between World War I and the depression that a substantial black population came to Gary. Before the war only a handful of black families lived there, and few of them worked in the mills. During World War I, when immigration from abroad was choked off, blacks were encouraged to move to Gary to make up for the labor shortage caused by expanding production. After the war this policy was continued, most spectacularly during the strike, but rather consistently throughout the twenties. In 1920 blacks made up 9.6 percent of the population; in 1930 they were 17.8 percent—and they were proportionately represented in the steel industry work force.

When the CIO was organized during the depression, an interracial alliance was absolutely essential to the task. In Gary a disproportionate number of the union organizers were black; the Communist party's slogan of "black and white unite and fight" proved useful as an organizing tactic. Nevertheless, it was only during World War II (and not as the result of the radicals' efforts) that black workers made a substantial structural advance in the economy. Demography, wartime full employment and labor shortages proved more important to the lot of black workers than their own efforts and those of their allies.

As after the First World War, so after the second, there came a repression to counter the growth of the Left. The Communist component of the trade union movement was wiped out, and in the general atmosphere of the early cold war black people, too, found themselves on the defensive. At the local level in Gary, the remaining trade union leaders made their peace with the corporation (as well as the local racketeers and Democratic party politicians), while various campaigns in the forties to racially integrate the schools and parks failed utterly.

Finally, in the early fifties, the inherently limited nature of the trade union when organized as a purely defensive institution of the working class—and one moreover that fully accepts capitalist property and legal norms—stood fully revealed. The Steelworkers Union gave up its right to strike over local grievances, which the Left had made a key part of its organizing policy, in return for binding arbitration, which better suited the needs and tempers of the emerging labor bureaucrats.

CORPORATE RACISM

The corporation thus regained effective full control over the work process. As a result, the corporation could increase the amount of profit realized per worker. It could also intensify the special oppression of the black workers; foremen could now assign them discriminately to the worst tasks without real union opposition. This corporate racism had the additional benefit of weakening the workers' solidarity. For its part, the union abolished shop stewards, replacing them with one full-time elected "griever." This of course further attenuated rank-and-file control over the union bureaucracy, aided in depoliticizing the workers and gave further rein to the union's inclination to mediate worker/employer differences at the point of production, rather than sharpen the lines of struggle in the political economy as a whole.

The corporate and union elites justified this process by substantial wage increases, together with other benefits such as improved pension and welfare plans. For these gains a price was paid. Higher product prices, inflation and a rising tax burden on the workers all ensued from the union's passive acceptance of corporate priorities.

There were extremely important racial consequences as well. For as the union leadership was drawn further and further into complicity with corporate goals, a large segment of the industrial working class found itself in the apparently contradictory position of opposing the needs of the poorest workers for increased social welfare services. A large part of the material basis for white working-class racism originates here. Gary steelworkers, struggling to meet their home mortgage payments, are loath to permit increased assessments for additional municipal services which they view as mostly benefitting black people.

UNITED STATES STEEL

Needless to say, the corporation helped to develop, promote and protect the Gary working class's new ways of viewing itself and its world.

In the mill, the corporation systematically gave the black workers the dirtiest jobs (in the coke plants, for example) and bypassed them for promotion—especially for the key skilled jobs and as foremen. Nor has that policy changed. Although about a third of the employees in the Gary Works are black, and many of them have high seniority, and although virtually all the foremen are promoted directly from the ranks without needing any special qualifications, there are almost no black (or Spanish-speaking) foremen. According to figures submitted by the United States Steel Corporation to the Gary Human Relations Commission, as of 31 March 1968, out of a total of 1,011 first-line supervisors (foremen) only 22 were black.

The corporation not only practices racism directly, it also encourages it indirectly by supporting other discriminatory institutions

540   in Gary. Except for some free professionals and small business, the entire business community is a de facto fief of the corporation. The Gary Chamber of Commerce has never to my knowledge differed from the corporation on any matter of substance, though it was often in its economic self-interest to do so. This has been true even with regard to raising the corporation's property assessment, which would directly benefit local business financially. And in its hiring and sales practices, as well as in its social roles, this group is a leading force for both institutional racism and racist attitudes in the community. For instance, it is well known that the local banks are very reluctant to advance mortgage money in black areas of town, thus assuring their physical decline. White workers then draw the reasonable conclusion that the movement of blacks into their neighborhoods will be at the expense of the value of their homes and react accordingly. The local media, completely dependent financially on the local business community, can fairly be described as overly racist. The story of the voting fraud conspiracy to prevent the election of the present mayor, Richard Hatcher, a black man, didn't get into the local paper until days after it made the front page of the *New York Times*.

The newspaper publisher is very close to the national Catholic hierarchy and the local bishop, who in turn is closely linked to the local banks. The church is rhetorically moderately liberal at the diocesan level, but among the ethnic parishes the clergy are often overly racist.

POLITICAL CONSIDERATIONS

While the United States Steel Corporation has an annual budget of $5 billion, the city of Gary operates on some $10 million annually. (This figure applies only to municipal government functions; it excludes expenditures by the schools, welfare authorities, the Sanitary Board and the Redevelopment Commission.)

And the power of the city government, as is usually the case in this country, is highly fragmented. Its legal and financial authority is inadequate to carry out the public functions for which it bears responsibility. The power of the mayor is particularly limited. State civil service laws insulate school, welfare, fire and police personnel from the control of City Hall. Administrative agencies control key functions such as urban renewal, the low income housing authority, sanitation, the park system and the board of health. Appointive boards with long and staggered terms of tenure, hire the administrators of these agencies; and although in the long run a skillful mayor can obtain substantial control over their operations, in the short run (especially if there are sharp policy differences) his power may well be marginal.

Two other structural factors set the context in which local government in Gary—and in America generally—is forced to operate. First, key municipal functions increasingly depend upon federal aid; such is the case with the poverty program, urban renewal, low income housing and, to a substantial degree, welfare, education and even police and sanitation. Thus, the priorities of the federal government increasingly shape the alternatives and options open to local officials, and their real independence is attenuated.

Second, the tax resources of local governments—resting for the most part on comparatively static real estate levies—are less and less able to meet the sharply rising costs of municipal services and operations. These costs reflect the increased social costs of production and welfare, costs that corporations are able to pass on to the general public.

This problem is particularly acute in Gary because of the ability of the corporation to remain grossly underassessed. As a result, there are implacable pressures to resist expansion of municipal services, even if the need for them is critical. In particular, since funds go to maintain existing services, it is virtually impossible for a local government to initiate any substantive innovations unless prior funding is assured. In this context, a sustained response to the urban crisis is prevented not only by a fragmentation of power but also by a lack of economic resources on a scale necessary to obtain significant results.

For the city of Gary, until the election of Mayor Hatcher, it was academic to talk about such considerations as the limits of local government as an instrument of social change and improvement of the general welfare. Before him, municipal government had been more or less content simply to mediate between the rackets on the one hand and the ethnic groups and business community on the other.

The Democratic party, structured through the Lake County machine, was the mechanism for accomplishing a division of spoils and for maintaining at least a formal legitimacy for a government that provided a minimum return to its citizenry. Left alone by the corporation, which subscribed to an inspired policy of live and let live where municipal politics were concerned, this political coalition governed Gary as it saw fit.

In return for the benevolent neutrality of the corporation toward its junior partner, the governing coalition refrained from attempting to raise the corporation's tax assessments or to otherwise insinuate itself into the absolute sovereignty of the corporation over the Gary Works. Air pollution activities were subjected only to token inspection and control, and in the entire history of the city the Building Department never sent an inspector into the mill. (These and other assertions about illegal or shady activities are based on reports from reliable informants and were usually verified by a second source. I served under Mayor Hatcher as director of the Office of Program Coordination until February 1969).

In this setting—particularly in the absence of a large middle class interested in "good government" reform—politics was little more than a racket, with the city government as the chief spoils. An informal custom grew up that representatives of different ethnic minorities would each hold the mayor's office for one term. The mayor then, in association with the county officials, would supervise the organized crime (mostly gambling, liquor and prostitution) within the community. In effect, the police force and the prosecutor's office were used to erect and centralize a protection racket with the mayor as its director and organized crime as its client. Very large sums of money were involved, as indicated by the fact that one recent mayor was described by Internal Revenue officials as having an estimated annual income while in office of $1.5 million.

Besides the racket of protecting criminal activity, other sources of funds contributed to the large illicit incomes of city officials. There were almost 1,000 patronage jobs to distribute to supporters or sell to friends. There were proceeds from a myriad of business transactions and contracts carried out under municipal authority. Every aspect of municipal activity was drawn into the cash nexus.

For instance, by local ordinance one had to pass an examination and pay a $150 fee for a contractor's license to do repair or construction work within city limits. The licensing statute was enacted to maintain reasonable standards of performance and thus protect the public. In reality, as late as 1967, passing the exam required few skills, except the ability to come up with $1,200 for the relevant officials, or $1,500 if the applicant was unfortunate enough to have black skin.

Gary municipal affairs also had a racist quality. The black population continued to rise until in the early sixties it composed an absolute majority. Yet the benefits of the system just outlined were restricted to the less scrupulous of the leaders of other ethnic groups, which constituted altogether only 40 percent of the population. The spoils came from all; they were distributed only among whites.

And this was true not only for illegal spoils and patronage but also for legitimate municipal services. As one example, after Hatcher became mayor, one of the major complaints of the white citizenry concerned the sharp decline in the frequency of garbage collection. This resulted, not from a drop in efficiency of the General Services division, as was often charged, but from the fact that the garbage routes were finally equalized between white and black areas.

In short, the city government was itself just another aspect of the institutionalized structure of racism in Gary. To assure the acquiescence of Gary's blacks to the system, traditional mechanisms of repression were used: bought black politicians and ward leaders, token jobs, the threat of violence against rebels and the spreading of a sense of impotence and despair. For instance, it was a Gary tradition for the Democratic machine to contribute $1,500 each week to a black ministers' alliance for them to distribute to needy parishioners—with the tacit understanding that when elections came around they would help deliver the vote.

HATCHER'S CAMPAIGN

The successful insurgency of Richard Gordon Hatcher destroyed the core of this entire relationship.

Hatcher developed what can best be described as a black united front, inasmuch as it embraced all sectors of the black community by social class, occupation, ideology and temperament. The basis of this united front was a commonly held view that black people as a racial group were discriminated against by the politically dominant forces. Creating it required that Hatcher bridge existing divisions in the black community, which he did by refusing to be drawn into a disavowal of any sector of the black movement either to his left or right—except for those local black politicians who were lackeys of the Democratic machine. Despite immense public pressure, for example, Hatcher refused to condemn Stokley Carmichael, even though scurrilous right-wing literature was widely circulated calling him a tool of Carmichael and Fidel Castro. Actually, the rumor that hurt Hatcher the most was the false assertion that he was secretly engaged to a white campaign worker—and it was so damaging in the black community that special pains had to be taken to overcome it.

Muhammad Ali was brought to the city to campaign for Hatcher, but Hubert Humphrey was not invited because of the bitter opposition of white antiwar elements within his campaign committee. It is worth noting that a substantial portion of Hatcher's financial and technical assistance came from a very small group of white liberals and radicals, who, while they played a role disproportionate to their numbers, suffered significant hostility from their white neighbors for involving themselves openly with Hatcher. Their support, however, made it possible for the campaign to appeal, at least rhetorically, to all the citizens on an interracial basis.

Of course, this support in the white community did not translate into votes. When the count was complete in the general election, only 13 percent of Gary's overwhelmingly Democratic white voters failed to bolt to the Republicans; and if one omits the Jewish professional and business section of town, that percentage falls to 6 percent (in blue-collar Glen Park)—a figure more explicable by polling booth error than goodwill.

Even in the Democratic primary against the incumbent mayor, Hatcher barely won, although he had the support of a large majority of the Spanish-speaking vote and overwhelming support (over 90 percent) of the black vote. His victory was possible, moreover, only because the white vote was split almost down the middle due to the entry of an insurgent and popular "backlash" candidate.

Hatcher's primary victory was particularly impressive given the obstacles he had to face. First, his entire primary campaign was run on less than $50,000, while the machine spent an estimated $500,000 in cash on buying black votes alone. Second, the media was openly hostile to Hatcher. And third, efforts were made to physically intimidate the candidate and his supporters. Death threats were common, and many beatings occurred. Without a doubt, the unprecedented action of the Hatcher organization in forming its own self-defense squads was essential in preventing mass intimidation. It was even necessary on primary day for armed groups to force open polls in black areas that would otherwise have remained inoperative.

These extraordinary methods demonstrated both how tenuous are the democratic rights of black people and what amazing organization and determination are necessary to enforce them when real shifts of power appear to be at stake. When the primary results came in, thousands of black citizens in Gary literally danced in the streets with joy; and everyone believed that the old Gary was gone forever.

544 HATCHER'S TEMPTATIONS

Immediately after the primary victory, the local alignment of forces was to some degree overshadowed by the rapid interposition of national ones. Until Hatcher won the primary, he was left to sink or swim by himself; after he established his own independent base of power, a new and more complex political process began: his reintegration into the national political system.

The county Democratic machine offered Hatcher a bargain: its support and $100,000 for the general election campaign in return for naming the chief of police, corporation counsel and controller. Naturally, Hatcher refused to accept a deal that would have made him a puppet of the corrupt elements he was determined to oust from power. Thereupon the county machine (and the subdistrict director of the Steelworkers Union) declared itself for, and campaigned for, the Republican.

But the question was not left there. To allow the Democratic party to desert a candidate solely because he was black would make a shambles of its appeal to black America. And dominant liberal forces within the Democratic party clearly had other positive interests in seeing Hatcher elected. Most dramatically, the Kennedy wing of the Democratic party moved rapidly to adopt Hatcher, offering him sorely needed political support, financial backing and technical assistance, without any strings attached. By doing this, it both solidified its already strong support from the black community and made it more reasonable for blacks to continue to place their faith in the Democratic party and in the political system as a whole.

As a necessary response to this development (although it might have happened anyway), the Johnson-Humphrey wing of the Democratic party also offered support. And this meant that the governor of Indiana and the Indiana State Democratic party endorsed Hatcher as well—despite the opposition of the powerful Lake County machine. Thus Hatcher achieved legitimacy within the political system—a legitimacy that he would need when it came to blocking a serious voting fraud plot to prevent his winning the election.

Despite clear evidence of what was happening, the Justice Department nevertheless refused to intervene against this plot until Hatcher's campaign committee sent telegrams to key federal officials warning them that failure to do so would result in a massive race riot for which the federal officials would be held publicly responsible. Only by this unorthodox maneuver, whose credibility rested on Hatcher's known independent appeal and constituency, was the federal executive branch persuaded to enforce the law. Its intervention, striking 5,000 phony names from the voters rolls, guaranteed a Hatcher victory instead of a Hatcher defeat.

The refusal of the Justice Department to move except under what amounted to blackmail indicated that the Johnson-Humphrey wing of the party was not enthusiastic about Hatcher, whose iconoclastic and often radical behavior did not assure that he would behave appropriately after he was in power. But its decision finally to act, together with the readiness of the Kennedy forces to fully back

Hatcher, suggests that there was a national strategy into which the Hatcher insurgency could perhaps be fitted.

My own view of that national strategy is that the federal government and the Democratic party were attempting to accommodate themselves to rising black insurgency, and especially electoral insurgency, so as to contain it within the two-party system. This strategy necessitated sacrificing, at least to a degree, vested parochial interests such as entrenched and corrupt machines.

Furthermore, black insurgency from below is potentially a force to rationalize obsolete local governments. The long-term crisis of the cities, itself reflecting a contradiction between public gain and private interest, has called forth the best reform efforts of the corporate liberal elite. Centered in the federal government, with its penumbra of foundations, law firms and universities, the political forces associated with this rationalizing process were most clearly predominant in the Kennedy wing of the Democratic party.

The economic forces whose interests are served by this process are first the banks, insurance companies and other sections of large capital heavily invested in urban property and, more generally, the interests of corporate capital as a whole—whose continued long-range profit and security rest on a stable, integrated and loyal population.

Thus the support given to Hatcher was rational to the system as a whole and not at all peculiar, even though it potentially implied economic and political loss for the corporation, United States Steel, whose operations on the spot might become more difficult. The interests of the governing class as a whole and of particular parts of it often diverge; this gap made it possible for Hatcher to achieve some power within the system. How these national factors would shape the amount and forms of power Hatcher actually obtained became quite evident within his first year of office.

MOSAIC OF BLACK POWER

When I arrived in the city five months after the inauguration, my first task was to aid in the process of bringing a semblance of order out of what can fairly be described as administrative chaos.

When the new administration took over City Hall in January 1968 it found itself without the keys to offices, with many vital records missing (for example, the file on the United States Steel Corporation in the controller's office) and with a large part of the city government's movable equipment stolen. The police force, for example, had so scavenged the patrol cars for tires and batteries that about 90 percent of them were inoperable. This sort of thing is hardly what one thinks of as a normal process of American government. It seems more appropriate to a bitter ex-colonial power. It is, in fact, exactly what happened as the French left Sekou Toure's Guinea.

There were no funds available. This was because the city council had sharply cut the municipal budget the previous summer in anticipation of a Hatcher victory. It intended, if he lost, to legislate a supplemental appropriation. But when he won without bringing in a council majority with him, its action assured that he would be espe-

546

cially badly crippled in his efforts to run the city government with a modicum of efficiency. Moreover, whenever something went wrong, the media could and did blame the mayor for his lack of concern or ability.

Not only did Richard Hatcher find his position sabotaged by the previous administration even before he arrived, but holdovers, until they were removed from their positions, continued to circumvent his authority by design or accident. And this comparatively unfavorable situation extended to every possible sphere of municipal activities.

Another problem was that the new administrators had to take over the management of a large, unwieldly and obsolete municipal system without the slightest prior executive experience. That there were no black people in Gary with such experience in spite of the high degree of education and intelligence in the black community is explicable only in terms of institutionalized racism—blacks in Gary were never permitted such experiences and occupational roles. Hatcher staffed his key positions with black men who had been schoolteachers, the professional role most closely analogous to running a government bureaucracy. Although several of these men were, in my view, of outstanding ability, they still had to learn everything by trial and error, an arduous and painful way to maintain a complex institution.

Furthermore, this learning process was not made any easier by the unusually heavy demands placed on the time of the mayor and his top aides by the national news media, maneuvering factions of the Democratic party, a multiplicity of civil rights organizations, universities and voluntary associations and others who viewed the mayor as a celebrity to be importuned, exploited or displayed. This outpouring of national interest in a small, parochial city came on top of and was almost equal to, the already heavy work load of the mayor.

Nor were there even clerical personnel to answer the mail and phone calls, let alone rationally respond to the deluge. The municipal budget provided the mayor with a single secretary; it took most of the first summer to make the necessary arrangements to pay for another two secretaries for the mayor's own needs. One result was that as late as June 1968 there was still a two-month backlog of personal mail, which was finally answered by much overtime work.

In addition to these problems there were others, not as common to American politics, such as the threat of violence, which had to be faced as an aspect of daily life. The problem of security was debilitating, especially after the King and Kennedy assassinations. In view of the mayor's aggressive drive against local organized crime, the race hatred whipped up during and after the campaign by the right wing and the history of violence in the steel town, this concern with security was not excessive, and maintaining it was a problem. Since the police were closely linked with the local Right, it was necessary to provide the mayor with private bodyguards. The presence of this armed and foreboding staff impaired efficiency without improving safety, especially since the mayor shrugged off the danger and refused to cooperate with these security efforts.

In addition, the tremendous amounts of aid we were offered by foundations, universities and federal officials proved to be a mixed blessing. The time needed to oversee existing processes was preempted by the complex negotiations surrounding the development and implementation of a panoply of new federal programs. There had never been a Concentrated Employment Program in Gary, nor a Model Cities Program, nor had the poverty program been locally controlled. Some of these programs weren't only new to Gary, they hadn't been implemented anywhere else either. The municipal bureaucracy, which under previous administrations had deliberately spared itself the embarrassment of federal audits, didn't have the slightest idea as to how to utilize or run these complex federal programs. Moreover, none of the experts who brought this largesse to Gary had a clear understanding of how it was to be integrated into the existing municipal system and social structure. These new federal programs sprang up overnight—new bureaucracies, ossified at birth—and their actual purposes and effects bore little relation to the legislative purposes of the congressional statutes that authorized them.

Needless to say, ordinary municipal employees experienced this outside assistance as a source of confusion and additional demoralization, and their efficiency declined further. Even the new leadership was often overwhelmed by, and defensive before, the sophisticated eastern federal bureaucrats and private consultants who clearly wanted only to help out America's first black mayor. The gifts, in other words, carried a fearful price.

BUREAUCRATIC ENEMIES

Except for the uniformed officials and the schools, which were largely outside the mayor's control, the standing city bureaucracy was a key dilemma for Mayor Hatcher.

The mayor had run on a reform program. His official campaign platform placed "good government" first, ahead of even tax reform and civil rights. Hatcher was deeply committed to eliminating graft and corruption, improving the efficiency of municipal government— especially the delivery of services to those sectors of the citizenry that had been most deprived—and he did not view his regime as merely the substitution of black faces for white ones in positions of power.

But he also had a particular historic injustice to rectify: the gross underrepresentation of blacks in the city government, and their complete exclusion from policy-making positions. Moreover, implicit in his campaign was a promise to reward his followers, who were mostly black. (At least most participants in the campaign assumed such a promise; Hatcher himself never spoke about the matter.)

Consequently, there was tremendous pressure from below to kick out everyone not covered by civil service protection and substitute all black personnel in their places. But to do so would have deepened the hostility of the white population and probably weakened Hatcher's potential leverage in the national Democratic party. He resisted this pressure, asserting that he believed in an interracial administration.

548   However, in addition to this belief (which, as far as I could determine, was genuine), there were other circumstances that dictated his course of action in this matter.

To begin with, it was always a premise of the administration that vital municipal services (police and fire protection, garbage collection, education, public health measures) had to be continued—both because the people of Gary absolutely needed them and because the failure to maintain them would represent a setback for black struggles throughout the country.

It also appeared that with a wholesale and abrupt transition to a totally new work force it would be impossible to continue these services, particularly because of a lack of the necessary skills and experiences among the black population—especially at the level of administration and skilled technical personnel. In this respect Hatcher faced the classic problem faced by all social revolutions and nationalist movements of recent times: after the seizure of power, how is it possible to run a complex society when those who traditionally ran it are now enemies?

The strategy Hatcher employed to meet this problem was the following. The bulk of the old personnel was retained. At the top level of the administration (personal staff, corporation counsel, chief of police, controller) new, trustworthy individuals were brought in. Then, gradually, new department heads were chosen, and new rank-and-file people included. If they had the skill already, they came at the beginning; if they didn't, they were brought in at a rate slow enough to provide for on-the-job training from the holdovers, without disrupting the ongoing functions of the particular department.

The main weakness of this gradualist strategy was that it permitted the old bureaucracy to survive—its institutional base was not destroyed.

The result was that the new political priorities of the administration could not be implemented with any degree of effectiveness in a new municipal political practice. City government remained remarkably like what it had been in the past, at least from the perspective of the average citizen in the community. While the political leadership was tied up with the kinds of problems I noted earlier, the bureaucracy proceeded on its own course, which was basically one of passive resistance. There were two aspects to this: bureaucratic inertia, a sullen rejection of any changes in established routine that might cause conflicts and difficulties for the employees; and active opposition based on politics and racism, to new methods and goals advocated by the mayor.

To cite just one example, the mayor decided to give a very high priority to enforcement of the housing codes, which had never been seriously implemented by preceding administrations. After much hard work, the Building Department was revamped to engage in aggressive inspection work. Cases stopped being "lost," and the number of inspections was increased by 4,000 percent while their quality was improved and standardized. Then it was discovered that cases pre-

pared for legal enforcement were being tabled by the Legal Department on grounds of technical defects.

I personally ascertained that the alleged legal defects were
simply untrue. I then assumed that the reason for the legal staff's behavior was that they were overburdened with work. Conferences were
held to explain to them the mayor's priorities so they could rearrange
their work schedule. Instead, a series of bitter personal fights resulted,
culminating in my removal from that area of work since the staff
attorneys threatened to resign if there were continued interference
with their professional responsibility. In the course of these disputes,
both black and white attorneys expressed the opinion that they did
not consider themselves a legal aid bureau for Gary's poor, and furthermore the root of the city's housing problem was the indolent and
malicious behavior of the tenants. In their view, it was therefore unjust
to vigorously enforce the existing statutes against the landlords. Thus,
despite the administration's pledge, black ghetto residents did not find
their lives ameliorated in this respect.

Gradually, then, the promise of vast change after the new
mayor took office came to be seen as illusory. Indeed, what actually
occured was much like an African neocolonial entity: new faces, new
rhetoric and people whose lives were scarcely affected except in their
feelings towards their government.

This outcome was not due to a failure of good faith on the
part of the Hatcher administration. Nor does it prove the fallacious
maximalist proposition that no amelioration of the people's conditions
of life is possible prior to a revolution. Instead, it was due to the decline of the local mass base of the Hatcher administration and the
array of national political forces confronting it.

Most black people in Gary were neither prepared nor able to
take upon themselves the functions performed for them by specialized
bureaucracies. They relied upon the government for education, welfare, public health, police and fire protection, enforcement of the
building codes and other standards, maintenance of the public roads
and the like. Unable to develop alternative popularly based community
institutions to carry on these functions by democratic self-government,
the new administration was forced to rely upon the city bureaucracy—
forced to pursue the option that could only result in minor changes.

ABORTED LIBERATION

The most significant consequence of the Hatcher administration's failure to transcend the structural terrain on which it functioned was
political, the erosion of popular support after the successful mobilization of energies involved in the campaign. The decline of mass participation in the political process contributed in turn to the tendency
of the new regime to solve its dilemmas by bureaucratic means or by
relying on outside support from the federal government.

The decline in mass support ought not to be confused with a
loss of votes in an election. Indeed, Hatcher is now probably as secure
politically as the average big city mayor. The point is that the mass

of the black population is not actively involved in helping to run the city. Thus, their political experiences are not enlarged, their understanding of the larger society and how it functions has not improved, and they are not being trained to better organize for their own interests. In short, the liberating process of the struggle for office was aborted after the initial goal was achieved—and before it could even begin to confront the profound problems faced by the mass of urban black Americans.

For example, after the inauguration, old supporters found themselves on the outside looking in. For the most part, since there was no organized effort to continue to involve them (and indeed to do so could not but conflict with the dominant strategy of the administration), they had to be content to remain passive onlookers. Moreover, the average citizen put a lot of faith in the mayor and wanted to give him an opportunity to do his job without intruding on the process.

Even among the most politicized rank-and-file elements there was a fear of interfering. Painfully conscious of their lack of training and experience, they were afraid of "blowing it." Instead they maintained a benevolent watchfulness, an attitude reinforced by the sense that Hatcher was unique, that his performance was some kind of test of black people as a race. (Whites were not the only people encouraged by the media to think in these terms.) There were of course some old supporters who were frankly disillusioned: they did not receive the patronage or other assistance they had expected; they were treated rudely by a bureaucratic holdover or were merely unable to reach the ear of a leader who was once accessible as a friend.

The ebbing away of popular participation could be seen most markedly in the Spanish-speaking community, which could not reassure itself with the symbolic satisfaction of having a member of its group in the national spotlight. With even less education and prior opportunity than the blacks, they found that the qualifications barrier to municipal government left them with even less patronage than they felt to be their due reward. This feeling of betrayal was actively supported by the former machine politicians and criminal elements, who consciously evoked ethnic prejudices to isolate the mayor and weaken his popular support.

What happened in the first year of the new administration, then, was a contradiction between efficiency and ethnic solidarity. At each point the mayor felt he had to rely upon the expert bureaucracy, even at the cost of increasing his distance from his mass base. And this conflict manifested itself in a series of inexorable political events (the appointment of outside advisors, for example), each of which further contributed to eroding the popular base of the still new leadership.

As Antonio Gramsci pointed out, beneath this contradiction lies a deeper one: a historic class deprivation—inflicted on the oppressed by the very structure of the existing society which barred the underclass from access to the skills necessary for it to run the society directly in its own interests and according to its own standard of civilization. Unless an oppressed social group is able to constitute itself as what Gramsci characterizes as a counterhegemonic social bloc, its conquest of state power cannot be much more than a change in leaders. Given the overall relation of forces in the country at large, such an undertaking was beyond the power of the black community in Gary in 1968. Therefore, dominant national political forces were able quickly to reconstitute their overall control.

NATIONAL POWER

What happened to Richard Hatcher in Gary in his first year as mayor raises important questions—questions that might be of only theoretical interest if he were indeed in a unique position. He is not. Carl Stokes, a black, is mayor of Cleveland. Charles Evers, a black, is mayor of Fayette, Mississippi. Thomas Bradley, a black, very nearly became mayor of Los Angeles. Kenneth Gibson, a black, is now mayor of Newark. The list will grow, and with it the question of how we are to understand the mass participation of blacks in electoral politics in this country and the future of their movement.

I believe that until new concepts are worked out, the best way of understanding this process is by analogy with certain national liberation movements in colonial or neocolonial countries. Of course, the participants—in Gary as in Newark—are Americans, and they aren't calling for a UN plebiscite. But they were clearly conscious of themselves as using elections as a tool, as a step toward a much larger (though admittedly ill-defined) ultimate goal—a goal whose key elements of economic change, political power, dignity, defense of a "new" culture and so forth are very close to those of colonial peoples. It is because Hatcher embraced these larger objectives (without, of course, using precisely the rhetoric) that his campaign can be thought of as part of a nationalist process that has a trajectory quite similar to that of anticolonial liberation movements.

In its weakened local posture, the Hatcher administration was unable to resist successfully a large degree of cooptation by the national political authorities. Despite a brave vote at the Democratic National Convention for Reverend Channing Philips, Hatcher was essentially forced to cooperate with the national government and Democratic party—even to the extent of calling on the sheriff of Cook County to send deputies to reinforce the local police when a "mini-riot" occurred in the black ghetto.

Without either a nationally coordinated movement or an autonomous base of local insurgency—one capable of carrying out on a mass scale government functions outside the official structure—Hatcher's insurgency was contained within the existing national political system. Or, to express it somewhat differently, the attempt by black forces to use the electoral process to further their national liberation was aborted by a countervailing process of neocolonialism carried out by the federal government. Bluntly speaking, the piecemeal achievement of power through parliamentary means is a fraud—at least as far as black Americans are concerned.

The process by which the national power maintained itself, and even forced the new administration to aid it in doing so, was relatively simple. As the gap between the popular constituency and the new government widened, like many another administration, Hatcher's found itself increasingly forced to rely upon its "accomplishments" to maintain its popularity and to fulfill its deeply held obligation to aid the community.

Lacking adequate autonomous financial resources—the mill remained in private hands, and it still proved impossible to assess it for tax purposes at its true value—accomplishments were necessarily dependent upon obtaining outside funds. In this case, the funds had to come from the federal government, preferably in the form of quick performance projects to maintain popular support and to enable everyone to appear to be doing something to improve matters.

These new programs injected a flow of cash into the community, and they created many new jobs. In his first year in office, the mayor obtained in cash or pledges more federal funds than his entire local budget. Hopes began to be engendered that these programs were the key to solving local problems, while the time spent on preparing them completed the isolation of the leadership from the people.

Then, too, the stress of this forced and artificial growth created endless opportunities for nepotism and even thievery. Men who had never earned a decent living before found themselves as high-paid executives under no requirement to produce any tangible results. Indeed, federal authorities seemed glad to dispense the funds without exercising adequate controls over their expenditures. A situation arose in which those who boasted of how they were hustling the system became prisoners of its largesse.

Even the most honest and courageous leader, such as Mayor Hatcher, could not help but be trapped by the aid offered him by the federal authorities. After all, how can any elected local executive turn down millions of dollars to dispense with as he sees fit to help precisely those people he was elected to aid: The acceptance of the help guaranteed the continuation of bonds of dependence. For without any real autonomous power base, and with new vested interests and expectations created by the flow of funds into the community, and with no available alternate path of development, the relation of power between the local leader and the national state was necessarily and decisively weighted toward the latter.

In Gary, Indiana, within one year after the most prodigious feat in the history of its black population—the conquest of local political power—their insurgency has been almost totally contained. It is indeed difficult to see how the existing administration can extricate itself from its comparative impasse in the absence of fresh national developments, or of a new, more politically coherent popular upsurge from below.

There is, however, no doubt that the struggle waged by the black people of Gary, Indiana, is a landmark on their road to freedom; for the experiences of life and struggle have become another part of their heritage—and thus a promise for us all.

ACTIVISM
Suppression
AVAILABILITY
Equality
MOBILIZATION
Dignity
Totalitarianism
DOMINANCE
ELITES
VIOLENCE
Tolerance
Pathos
Pluralism
MORALE
Injustice
Extremism
Control
Coercion
JUDGMENT
ACCESSIBILTY
MODERATION
MASSES
Insulation

Study Questions

1. Would it matter to you whether you lived in a mass, totalitarian, folk, or pluralistic society? Why? In which ways?
2. Which of the four kinds of societies listed in Kornhauser's typology comes closest to describing the United States today? Explain.
3. Do you believe that Harold Lasswell's garrison state is an inevitability for our country? What are some of the alternatives?
4. Which do you believe is a greater social ill, injustice or alienation? Is it possible to eliminate either one? How?

Mass and Totalitarian Society

14 The ever-increasing scale of social units, the absorption of individuals into bureaucratic settings, and the popular view that bureaucracy is everywhere have led to a conception of modern society as a mass society. This term, like bureaucracy, is much abused, and it is important that we try to define it clearly.

MODERN SOCIETY AS MASS SOCIETY

One popular misconception about mass society is that the assembly–line procedure of the automobile factory spills over into all spheres of social activity. Modern hospitals, clinics and other social services are seen as efficient but impersonal and routinized. Another misconception is that mass society comes about because as economic units become larger and larger, the small entrepreneur experiences increasing difficulty in operating and surviving. Another misconception is that life in modern society depends almost exclusively on organizational participation. As one sociologist has noted, we are born in an organization (the hospital), we are educated and work in organizations, we pray and play in organizations, and when we die, to be buried we need an official grant of permission from the government—the largest organization of all.[1] I see these situations as the consequences of industrial society and of urbanism rather than of mass society. To be more analytical, I want to identify the elements and the criteria of mass society. The following analysis is based on William Kornhauser's work, the *Politics of Mass Society*.[2]

KORNHAUSER'S TYPOLOGY

Two views or critiques of mass society are represented in modern thought: the aristocratic critique and the democratic critique. The aristocratic view is that the elites are not insulated against mass wishes, pressures, and participation. The democratic view is that in a mass society people are not integrated into broad social groupings. Individuals are atomized and have no political sociability. Each of

556

these views presents a different idea of the dangers in a mass society. One sees elites exposed to mass pressure from nonelites, the other sees the masses at the mercy of the elites. Both views have a common conception of society as naked and vulnerable: direct exposure to outside forces makes freedom precarious. In the aristocratic view, "the outside force" is the citizenry with its vulgar tastes, its irrationality, its spontaneous demands, and its inability to plan. The masses here have *too* much influence, for they control the elite. In the democratic view, on the other hand, the "outside force" is the elite's hunger for power, wealth, and domination. Both views imply loss of community in mass society as each group pursues its own short-term interests. Each group accusses the other of causing society's problems.

Kornhauser argued that more is needed than merely the presence of an elite and a mass to describe mass society. It is necessary, he said, to identify the *relationship* between the two. He did this with his theory of accessibility, and constructed a method of classifying different types of societies in order to clarify his ideas.

	Availability of Nonelites		
	High	Mass Society	Pluralistic Society
Accessibility of Elites			
	Low	Totalitarian Society	Folk Society

Kornhauser defined mass society as a societal unit in which elites are readily accessible to *influence* by nonelites and nonelites are available for *mobilization* by elites. Nonelites are available if they can be told what to do, when to do it, and how to do it. Elites are accessible if they can be influenced, if controls can be put on their decision—making powers, and if they can be made to move in different directions. When elites are accessible and nonelites are available there is a paucity of independent groups in the society. There are no coherent collective units between the state and the family or individual to protect the elites and nonelites from manipulation or mobilization by each other.

Folk society, described in chapter 12, requires inaccessible elites and unavailable masses. If folk society is to retain its traditional structure, the elites cannot be subjugated to the influence of the masses, and the masses, firmly bound by kinship and community, are unavailable to the elites.

Pluralistic society requires accessible elites and unavailable nonelites. To sustain freedom and diversity, the elites must be responsive to the opposition. Accessibility can come about through competition among independent groups that open channels of communication and power. The nonelites are unavailable because they are members of diverse groups that compete for their loyalties, energies, and resources.

In a totalitarian society, total control can be maintained only when the elites are not accessible and the mass is totally available. The

558   elites are inaccessible because they have a monopoly on the means of coercion, persuasion and scientific and artistic production. The populace is available, for the members lack all those independent social formations that could serve as a base of resistance to the elite.

The critics of mass society who adhere to the aristocratic view have fixed on popular access to elites as the distinguishing characteristic of mass society. Those who espouse the democratic view feel that mass society is predicated on the availability of nonelites. The salient factor here is that mass behavior occurs when both elites and nonelites lack social insulation. When elites are accessible to direct intervention by nonelites and when nonelites are available for direct mobilization, mass society emerges. To better understand this theory, the terms "mass behavior," "accessible elite," and "available nonelite" need to be clarified.

Mass behavior: In mass society the individual's attention is focused on issues which are remote from his personal experience and daily life. He is concerned for example, with national and international situations which he knows only through mass media. His concern for these remote issues, however, lacks definiteness and reality. In addition, responses are direct in mass society, and there is little reason to engage in discussion. The need to persuade or to talk with others who have different points of view does not exist, for there are no "others" with divergent views. Finally, mass behavior is highly unstable. It has a readily shifting focus, and the degree of response varies rapidly from mass apathy to intense concern. Mass behavior, then, is characterized by a focus of attention that is remote, and a style of response that is direct and unstable.

ACCESSIBLE ELITES

Elites have a special responsibility for forming and defending standards. In any large, complex system, protection of standards must be the work of a few. Thus, elites are essential for democratic society. It is important to attempt to ascertain who may gain entrance to the elites and who may influence them. These are distinct questions and should not be confused with one another. Influence is more important than entrance. Entrance is not a guarantee of influence. The mere fact of universal suffrage does not ensure accessible elites. There must be competition among the elites, alternative choices for the electorate, and channels of communication between the elites and nonelites.

Available Nonelites

People are available for mass behavior when they lack attachments to proximate objects, to their community, or to their work. They are then free to unite and respond to new issues or movements. The first selection in this chapter, written by Harold D. Lasswell, a political scientist, presents us with an excellent analysis of this phenomenon. Written some 30 years ago, it is a detailed examination of the organization of totalitarian control.

PLURALISM

The other two articles included in this chapter deal with extremism and protest. The article by Joseph Gusfield examines the possibilities of extremist behavior in a pluralistic society. Gusfield helps clarify the conditions under which pluralism encourages behavior that falls outside of the range of legitimate political processes.

The last selection, written by sociologist Ralph Turner, uses a value-measuring orientation to locate a decade of protest. Turner develops a scheme for analyzing the broad social movement of the 1960s and 1970s.

NOTES

1. Amitai Etzioni, *Modern Organizations* (Englewood Cliffs: Prentice-Hall Inc., New Jersey, 1964).

2. William Kornhauser, *The Politics of Mass Society* (New York: The Free Press, 1959).

HAROLD D. LASSWELL

The Garrison State

The purpose of this article is to consider the possibility that we are moving toward a world of "garrison states"—a world in which the specialists on violence are the most powerful group in society. From this point of view the trend of our time is away from the dominance of the specialist on bargaining, who is the businessman, and toward the supremacy of the soldier. We may distinguish transitional forms, such as the party propaganda state, where the dominant figure is the propagandist, and the party bureaucratic state, in which the organization men of the party make the vital decisions. There are mixed forms in which predominance is shared by the monopolists of party and market power.[1]

All men are deeply affected by their expectations as well as by their desires. We time our specific wants and efforts with some regard to what we reasonably hope to get. Hence, when we act rationally, we consider alternative versions of the future, making explicit those expectations about the future that are so often buried in the realm of hunch.

In the practice of social science, as of any skill in society, we

Reprinted by permission of *The American Journal of Sociology* 46 (January 1941). Copyright © 1941, The University of Chicago. Reprinted by permission of the author and the University of Chicago Press.

560   are bound to be affected in some degree by our conceptions of future development. There are problems of timing in the prosecution of scientific work, timing in regard to availability of data and considerations of policy. In a world where primitive societies are melting away it is rational to act promptly to gather data about primitive forms of social organization. In a world in which the scientist may also be a democratic citizen, sharing democratic respect for human personality, it is rational for the scientist to give priority to problems connected with the survival of democratic society. There is no question here of a scientist deriving his values from science; values are *acquired* chiefly from personal experience of a given culture, *derived* from that branch of culture that is philosophy and theology, *implemented* by science and practice.

The picture of the garrison state that is offered here is no dogmatic forecast. Rather it is a picture of the probable. It is not inevitable. It may not even have the same probability as some other descriptions of the future course of development. What, then, is the function of this picture for scientists? It is to stimulate the individual specialist to clarify for himself his expectations about the future, as a guide to the timing of scientific work. Side by side with this "construct" of a garrison state there may be other constructs; the rational person will assign exponents of probability to every alternative picture.[2]

Expectations about the future may rest upon the extrapolation of past trends into the future. We may choose a number of specific items—like population and production curves—and draw them into the future according to some stated rule. This is an "itemistic" procedure. In contrast, we may set up a construct that is frankly imaginative though disciplined by careful consideration of the past. Since trend curves summarize many features of the past, they must be carefully considered in the preparation of every construct. Correlation analysis of trend curves, coupled with the results of experiment, may provide us with partial confirmation of many propositions about social change; these results, too, must be reviewed. In addition to these disciplined battalions of data there is the total exposure of the individual to the immediate and the recorded past, and this total exposure may stimulate productive insight into the structure of the whole manifold of events which includes the future as well as the past. In the interest of correct orientation in the world of events, one does not wisely discard all save codified experience. (The pictures of the future that are set up on more than "item" basis may be termed "total.")

To speak of a garrison state is not to predict something wholly new under the sun. Certainly there is nothing novel to the student of political institutions about the idea that specialists on violence may run the state. On the contrary, some of the most influential discussions of political institutions have named the military state as one of the chief forms of organized society. Comte saw history as a succession (and a progression) that moved, as far as it concerned the state, through military, feudal, and industrial phases. Spencer divided all

human societies into the military type, based on force, and the indus- **561**
trial type, based on contract and free consent.

What is important for our purposes is to envisage the possible
emergence of the military state under present technical conditions.
There are no examples of the military state combined with modern
technology. During emergencies the great powers have given enormous
scope to military authority, but temporary acquisitions of authority
lack the elements of comparative permanence and acceptance that
complete the garrison state. Military dictators in states marginal to
the creative centers of Western civilization are not integrated with
modern technology; they merely use some of its specific elements.

The military men who dominate a modern technical society
will be very different from the officers of history and tradition. It is
probable that the specialists on violence will include in their training
a large degree of expertness in many of the skills that we have traditionally accepted as part of modern civilian management.

The distinctive frame of reference in a fighting society is fighting effectiveness. All social change is translated into battle potential.
Now there can be no realistic calculation of fighting effectiveness without knowledge of the technical and psychological characteristics of
modern production processes. The function of management in such a
society is already known to us; it includes the exercise of skill in
supervising technical operations, in administrative organization, in
personnel management, in public relations. These skills are needed to
translate the complicated operations of modern life into every relevant
frame of reference—the frame of fighting effectiveness as well as of
pecuniary profit.

This leads to the seeming paradox, that, as modern states are
militarized, specialists on violence are more preoccupied with the skills
and attitudes judged characteristic of nonviolence. We anticipate the
merging of skills, starting from the traditional accouterments of the
professional soldier, moving toward the manager and promoter of
large-scale civilian enterprise.

In the garrison state, at least in its introductory phases, problems of morale are destined to weigh heavily on the mind of management. It is easy to throw sand in the gears of the modern assembly
line; hence, there must be a deep and general sense of participation
in the total enterprise of the state if collective effort is to be sustained.
When we call attention to the importance of the "human factor" in
modern production, we sometimes fail to notice that it springs from
the multiplicity of special environments that have been created by
modern technology. Thousands of technical operations have sprung
into existence where a few hundred were found before. To complicate
the material environment in this way is to multiply the foci of attention of those who live in our society. Diversified foci of attention breed
differences in outlook, preference, and loyalty. The labyrinth of specialized "material" environments generates profound ideological divergencies that cannot be abolished, though they can be mitigated, by
the methods now available to leaders in our society. As long as modern

562   technology prevails, society is honeycombed with cells of separate experience, of individuality, of partial freedom. Concerted action under such conditions depends upon skillfully guiding the minds of men; hence the enormous importance of symbolic manipulation in modern society.

The importance of the morale factor is emphasized by the universal fear which it is possible to maintain in large populations through modern instruments of warfare. The growth of aerial warfare in particular has tended to abolish the distinction between civilian and military functions. It is no longer possible to affirm that those who enter the military service take the physical risk while those who remain at home stay safe and contribute to the equipment and the comfort of the courageous heroes at the front. Indeed, in some periods of modern warfare, casualties among civilians may outnumber the casualties of the armed forces. With the socialization of danger as a permanent characteristic of modern violence the nation becomes one unified technical enterprise. Those who direct the violence operations are compelled to consider the entire gamut of problems that arise in living together under modern conditions.

There will be an energetic struggle to incorporate young and old into the destiny and mission of the state. It is probable that one form of this symbolic adjustment will be the abolition of "the unemployed." This stigmatizing symbol will be obsolete in the garrison state. It insults the dignity of millions, for it implies uselessness. This is so, whether the "unemployed" are given a "dole" or put on "relief" projects. Always there is the damaging stigma of superfluity. No doubt the garrison state will be distinguished by the psychological abolition of unemployment—"psychological" because this is chiefly a matter of redefining symbols.

In the garrison state there must be work—and the duty to work—for all. Since all work becomes public work, all who do not accept employment flout military discipline. For those who do not fit within the structure of the state there is but one alternative—to obey or die. Compulsion, therefore, is to be expected as a potent instrument for internal control of the garrison state.

The use of coercion can have an important effect upon many more people than it reaches directly; this is the propaganda component of any "propaganda of the deed." The spectacle of compulsory labor gangs in prisons or concentration camps is a negative means of conserving morale—negative since it arouses fear and guilt. Compulsory labor groups are suitable popular scapegoats in a military state. The duty to obey, to serve the state, to work—these are cardinal virtues in the garrison state. Unceasing emphasis upon duty is certain to arouse opposing tendencies within the personality structure of all who live under a garrison regime. Everyone must struggle to hold in check any tendencies, conscious or unconscious, to defy authority, to violate the code of work, to flout the incessant demand for sacrifice in the collective interest. From the earliest years youth will be trained to subdue—to disavow, to struggle against—any specific opposition to the ruling code of collective exactions.

The conscience imposes feelings of guilt and anxiety upon the individual whenever his impulses are aroused, ever so slightly, to break the code. When the coercive threat that sanctions the code of the military state is internalized in the consciences of youth, the spectacle of labor gangs is profoundly disturbing. A characteristic response is self-righteousness—quick justification of coercive punishment, tacit acceptance of the inference that all who are subject to coercion are guilty of antisocial conduct. To maintain suspended judgment, to absolve others in particular instances, is to give at least partial toleration to countermores tendencies within the self. Hence, the quick substitute responses—the self-righteous attitude, the deflection of attention. Indeed, a characteristic psychic pattern of the military state is the "startle pattern," which is carried over to the internal as well as to the external threat of danger. This startle pattern is overcome and stylized as alert, prompt, commanding adjustment to reality. This is expressed in the authoritative manner that dominates military style—in gesture, intonation, and idiom.

The chief targets of compulsory labor service will be unskilled manual workers, together with counterelite elements who have come under suspicion. The position of the unskilled in our society has been deteriorating, since the machine society has less and less use for unskilled manual labor. The coming of the machine was a skill revolution, a broadening of the role of the skilled and semiskilled components of society.[3] As the value of labor declines in production, it also declines in warfare; hence, it will be treated with less consideration. (When unskilled workers are relied upon as fighters, they must, of course, share the ideological exultation of the community as a whole and receive a steady flow of respect from the social environment.) Still another factor darkens the forecast for the bottom layers of the population in the future garrison state. If recent advances in pharmacology continue, as we may anticipate, physical means of controlling response can replace symbolic methods. This refers to the use of drugs not only for temporary orgies of energy on the part of front-line fighters but in order to deaden the critical function of all who are not held in esteem by the ruling elite.

For the immediate future, however, ruling elites must continue to put their chief reliance upon propaganda as an instrument of morale. But the manipulation of symbols, even in conjunction with coercive instruments of violence, is not sufficient to accomplish all the purposes of a ruling group. We have already spoken of the socialization of danger, and this will bring about some equalitarian adjustments in the distribution of income for the purpose of conserving the will to fight and to produce.

In addition to the adjustment of symbols, goods, and violence, the political elite of the garrison state will find it necessary to make certain adaptations in the fundamental practices of the state. Decisions will be more dictatorial than democratic, and institutional practices long connected with modern democracy will disappear. Instead of elections to office or referendums on issues there will be government by plebiscite. Elections foster the formation and expression of public opinion, while plebiscites encourage only unanimous demonstrations of collective sentiment. Rival political parties will be suppressed, either by the monopolization of legality in one political party (more properly called a political "order") or by the abolition of all political parties. The ruling group will exercise a monopoly of opinion in public, thus abolishing the free communication of fact and interpretation. Legislatures will be done away with, and if a numerous consultative body is permitted at all it will operate as an assembly; that is, it will meet for a very short time each year and will be expected to ratify the decisions of the central leadership after speeches that are chiefly ceremonial in nature. Plebiscites and assemblies thus become part of the ceremonializing process in the military state.

As legislatures and elections go out of use, the practice of petition will play a more prominent role. Lawmaking will be in the hands of the supreme authority and his council; and, as long as the state survives, this agency will exert effective control ("authority" is the term for formal expectations, "control" is the actual distribution of effective power).

This means that instrumental democracy will be in abeyance, although the symbols of mystic "democracy" will doubtless continue. Instrumental democracy is found wherever authority and control are widely dispersed among the members of a state. Mystic "democracy" is not, strictly speaking, democracy at all, because it may be found where authority and control are highly concentrated yet where part of the established practice is to speak in the name of the people as a whole. Thus, any dictatorship may celebrate its "democracy" and speak with contempt of such "mechanical" devices as majority rule at elections or in legislatures.

What part of the social structure would be drawn upon in recruiting the political rulers of the garrison state? As we have seen, the process will not be by general election but by self-perpetuation through co-option. The foremost positions will be open to the officers corps, and the problem is to predict from what part of the social structure the officers will be recruited. Morale considerations justify a broad base of recruitment for ability rather than social standing. Although fighting effectiveness is a relatively impersonal test that favors ability over inherited status, the turnover in ruling families from generation to generation will probably be low. Any recurring crisis, however, will strengthen the tendency to favor ability. It seems clear that recruitment will be much more for bias and obedience than for objectivity and originality. Yet, as we shall presently see, modern machine society has introduced new factors in the military state—factors tending to strengthen objectivity and originality.

In the garrison state all organized social activity will be governmentalized; hence, the role of independent associations will disappear, with the exception of secret societies (specifically, there will be no organized economic, religious, or cultural life outside of the duly constituted agencies of government). Government will be highly centralized, though devolution may be practiced in order to mitigate "bureaucratism." There is so much outspoken resistance to bureaucratism in modern civilization that we may expect this attitude to carry over to the garrison state. Not only will the administrative structure be centralized, but at every level it will tend to integrate authority in a few hands. The leadership principle will be relied upon; responsibility as a rule will be focused upon individual "heads."

We have sketched some of the methods at the disposal of the ruling elites of the garrison state—the management of propaganda, violence, goods, practices. Let us consider the picture from a slightly different standpoint. How will various kinds of influence be distributed in the state?[4] Power will be highly concentrated, as in any dictatorial regime. We have already suggested that there will be a strong tendency toward equalizing the distribution of safety throughout the community (that is, negative safety, the socialization of threat in modern war). In the interest of morale there will be some moderation of huge differences in individual income, flattening the pyramid at the top, bulging it out in the upper-middle and middle zones. In the garrison state the respect pyramid will probably resemble the income pyramid. (Those who are the targets of compulsory labor restrictions will be the principal recipients of negative respect and hence will occupy the bottom levels.) So great is the multiplicity of functions in modern processes of production that a simple scheme of military rank is flagrantly out of harmony with the facts. Even though a small number of ranks are retained in the military state, it will be recognized that the diversity of functions exercised by each rank is so great that the meaning of a specific classification will be obscure. Summarizing, the distribution of safety will be most uniform throughout the community; distribution of power will show the largest inequalities. The patterns of income and respect will fall between these two, showing a pronounced bulge in the upper-middle and middle strata. The lower strata of the community will be composed of those subject to compulsory labor, tending to constitute a permanent pariah caste.

What about the capacity of the garrison state to produce a large volume of material values? The elites of the garrison state, like the elites of recent business states, will confront the problem of holding in check the stupendous productive potentialities of modern science and engineering. We know that the ruling elites of the modern business state have not known how to control productive capacity; they have been unwilling to adopt necessary measures for the purpose of regularizing the tempo of economic development. Hence, modern society has been characterized by periods of orgiastic expansion, succeeded by periods of flagrant underutilization of the instruments of production.[5]

The rulers of the garrison state will be able to regularize the rate of production, since they will be free from many of the conventions that have stood in the way of adopting measures suitable to this purpose in the business state. The business elite has been unwilling to revise institutional practices to the extent necessary to maintain a continually rising flow of investment. The institutional structure of the business state has called for flexible adjustment between governmental and private channels of activity and for strict measures to maintain

566　price flexibility. Wherever the business elite has not supported such necessary arrangements, the business state itself has begun to disintegrate.

Although the rulers of the garrison state will be free to regularize the rate of production, they will most assuredly prevent full utilization of modern productive capacity for nonmilitary consumption purposes. The elite of the garrison state will have a professional interest in multiplying gadgets specialized to acts of violence. The rulers of the garrison state will depend upon war scares as a means of maintaining popular willingness to forego immediate consumption. War scares that fail to culminate in violence eventually lose their value; this is the point at which ruling classes will feel that blood-letting is needed in order to preserve those virtues of sturdy acquiescence in the regime which they so much admire and from which they so greatly benefit. We may be sure that if ever there is a rise in the production of nonmilitary consumption goods, despite the amount of energy directed toward the production of military equipment, the ruling class will feel itself endangered by the growing "frivolousness" of the community.[6]

We need to consider the degree to which the volume of values produced in a garrison state will be affected by the tendency toward rigidity. Many factors in the garrison state justify the expectation that tendencies toward repetitiousness and ceremonialization will be prominent. To some extent this is a function of bureaucracy and dictatorship. But to some extent it springs also from the preoccupation of the military state with danger. Even where military operations are greatly respected, the fighter must steel himself against deep-lying tendencies to retreat from death and mutilation. One of the most rudimentary and potent means of relieving fear is some repetitive operation—some reiteration of the old and well-established. Hence the reliance on drill as a means of disciplining men to endure personal danger without giving in to fear of death. The tendency to repeat, as a means of diminishing timidity, is powerfully reinforced by successful repetition, since the individual is greatly attached to whatever has proved effective in maintaining self-control in previous trials. Even those who deny the fear of death to themselves may reveal the depth of their unconscious fear by their interest in ritual and ceremony. This is one of the subtlest ways by which the individual can keep his mind distracted from the discovery of his own timidity. It does not occur to the ceremonialist that in the spider web of ceremony he has found a moral equivalent of war—an unacknowledged substitute for personal danger.

The tendency to ceremonialize rather than to fight will be particularly prominent among the most influential elements in a garrison state. Those standing at the top of the military pyramid will doubtless occupy high positions in the income pyramid. During times of actual warfare it may be necessary to make concessions in the direction of moderating gross-income differences in the interest of preserving general morale. The prospect of such concessions may be expected to operate as a deterrent factor against war. A countervailing tendency, of course, is the threat to sluggish and well-established members of the upper crust from ambitious members of the lower officers' corps. This threat arises, too, when there are murmurs of disaffection with the established order of things on the part of broader components of the society.

It seems probable that the garrison state of the future will be far less rigid than the military states of antiquity. As long as modern technical society endures, there will be an enormous body of specialists whose focus of attention is entirely given over to the discovery of novel ways of utilizing nature. Above all, these are physical scientists and engineers. They are able to demonstrate by rather impersonal procedures the efficiency of many of their suggestions for the improvement of fighting effectiveness. We therefore anticipate further exploration of the technical potentialities of modern civilization within the general framework of the garrison state.

What are some of the implications of this picture for the research program of scientists who, in their capacity as citizens, desire to defend the dignity of human personality?

It is clear that the friend of democracy views the emergence of the garrison state with repugnance and apprehension. He will do whatever is within his power to defer it. Should the garrison state become unavoidable, however, the friend of democracy will seek to conserve as many values as possible within the general framework of the new society. What democratic values can be preserved, and how?

Our analysis has indicated that several elements in the pattern of the garrison state are compatible with democratic respect for human dignity. Thus, there will be some socialization of respect for all who participate in the garrison society (with the ever present exception of the lowest strata).

Will the human costs of a garrison state be reduced if we civilianize the ruling elite? Just how is it possible to promote the fusion of military and civilian skills? What are some of the devices capable of overcoming bureaucratism? To what extent is it possible to aid or to retard the ceremonializing tendencies of the garrison state?

It is plain that we need more adequate data from the past on each of these problems and that it is possible to plan to collect relevant data in the future. We need, for instance, to be better informed about the trends in the skill pattern of dominant elite groups in different parts of the world. In addition to trend data we need experimental and case data about successful and unsuccessful civilianizing of specialists on violence.[7]

Many interesting questions arise in connection with the present sketch about transition to the garrison state. What is the probable order of appearance—Japan, Germany, Russia, United States of America? What are the probable combinations of bargaining, propaganda, organization, and violence skills in elites? Is it probable that the garrison state will appear with or without violent revolution? Will the garrison state appear first in a small number of huge Continental states (Russian, Germany, Japan [in China], United States) or in a

568 single world-state dominated by one of these powers? With what symbol patterns will the transition to the garrison state be associated? At the present time there are four important ideological patterns.

FOUR WORLD-SYMBOL PATTERNS

In the Name of	Certain Demands and Expectations Are Affirmed
1. National democracy (Britain, United States)	Universalize a federation of democratic free nations
2. National antiplutocracy (also antiproletarians) (Germany, Russia, Japan, Italy)	Universalize the "axis" of National Socialistic powers
3. World-proletariat (Russia)	Universalize Soviet Union, Communist International
4. True world-proletariat (no state at present)	New elite seizes revolutionary crisis to liquidate "Russian betrayers," all "National Socialisms" and "plutocratic democracies"

The function of any developmental construct, such as the present one about the garrison state, is to clarify to the specialist the possible relevance of his research to impending events that concern the values of which he approves as a citizen. Although they are neither scientific laws nor dogmatic forecasts, developmental constructs aid in the timing of scientific work, stimulating both planned observation of the future and renewed interest in whatever past events are of greatest probable pertinence to the emerging future. Within the general structure of the science of society there is place for many special sciences devoted to the study of all factors that condition the survival of selected values. This is the sense in which there can be a science of democracy, or a science of political psychiatry, within the framework of social science. If the garrison state is probable, the timing of special research is urgent.[8]

NOTES

1. For a preliminary discussion of the garrison state see my "Sino-Japanese Crisis: The Garrison State versus the Civilian State." *China Quarterly* 11 (1937): 643–49.

2. We use the term "subjective probability" for the exponent assigned to a future event; "objective probability" refers to propositions about past events. The intellectual act of setting up a tentative picture of significant past-future relations is developmental thinking (see my *World Politics and Personal Insecurity* [New York and London, 1935], chap. i: "Configurative Analysis"; Karl Mannheim, *Man and Society in an Age of Reconstruction: Studies of Modern Social Structure* [New York, 1940]), Part IV: "Thought at the Level of Planning."

3. *See* T. M. Sogge, "Industrial Classes in the United States," *Journal of the American Statistical Association*, June, 1933; and Colin Clark, "National Income and Outlay," in A. C. Pigou, *Socialism versus Capitalism* (London: Macmillan

& Co., 1937), pp. 12–22. Sogge's paper is a continuation of an earlier investigation by Alvin H. Hansen.

4. Influence is measured by control over values (desired events). For purposes of analysis we have classified values as income, safety, and deference. To be deferred to is to be taken into consideration by the environment. Deference, in turn, is divided into power and respect. Power is measured by degree of participation in important decisions. A decision is a choice backed by the most severe deprivations at the disposal of the community (usually death). The making of these decisions in a community is the *function* of government. The *institution* of government is what is called government by those who live in a given community during a specified period of time; it is the most important secular decision-making institution. It is clear that the function of government may be exercised by other than governmental institutions, i.e., by "government" and by monopolistic "big business." (A state is one of the most influential communities in world-politics.) Respect is measured by reciprocal intimacy. Society can be divided into different classes on the basis of each value—or of value combinations. In the most inclusive sense politics studies conditions affecting the distribution of most values; in a narrower sense it studies power.

5. For the magnitude of these production losses *see*, e.g., Chart I, "Loss in Potential Real National Income Due to Depression, Unemployment of Men and Machines, 1930–1937," in National Resources Committee, *The Structure of the American Economy* (Washington, D.C., 1939), p. 2. The estimated loss of potential income was $200,000,000.

6. The perpetuation of the garrison state will be favored by some of the psychological consequences of self-indulgence. When people who have been disciplined against self-indulgence increase their enjoyments, they often suffer from twinges of conscience. Such self-imposed anxieties signify that the conscience is ever vigilant to enforce the orthodox code of human conduct. Hence, drifts away from the established order of disciplined acquiescence in the proclaimed values of the garrison state will be self-correcting. The guilt generated by self-indulgence can be relieved through the orgiastic reinstatement of the established mores of disciplined sacrifice.

7. For analysis of trends toward militarization in modern society consult Hans Speier, whose articles usually appear in *Social Research*.

8. Robert S. Lynd is concerned with the timing of knowledge in *Knowledge for What?* The book is full of valuable suggestions; it does not, however, specify the forms of thought most helpful to the end he has in view.

JOSEPH R. GUSFIELD

Mass Society and Extremist Politics

A dominant stream of thought in current political sociology explains many contemporary anti-democratic movements as products of a distinctive social organization—Mass Society. Writers who utilize this approach have maintained that modern, Western societies increasingly show characteristics of mass organization which sharply differ from the features of such societies in the nineteenth and earlier centuries. Mass societies, in this view, demonstrate a form of politics in which traditional sociological concepts, such as class or culture, are not relevant to an understanding of the sources, genesis, or careers of extremist, anti-democratic political movements. Mass politics is the form of political action unique to mass societies. As modern democratic societies become mass societies, we may then anticipate that political crises are likely to generate extremist, anti-democratic responses. Leading advocates of this theory of "mass politics," in whole or part, are Hannah Arendt, Erich Fromm, Karl Mannheim, William Kornhauser, Robert Nisbet, and Philip Selznick.[1] This paper is a critical analysis of this approach and a reformulation of some of the relations between mass societies and political action.

There are two major contentions in this paper. The first is a criticism of the assumptions about democratic politics underlying the theory of mass politics. The second is a reformulated theory of the relation between mass society and political extremism in contemporary, democratic societies.

It is our first contention that implicit in the theory of mass politics is an idealized conception of the pluralistic social and political system held necessary for the maintenance of democratic institutions. This conception is idealized in that it fails to give adequate weight to barriers which conflicts of interest offer to political harmony and compromise under any political structure.

Our second contention is that the elements of mass societies viewed with alarm by mass politics theorists in actuality contain positive connotations for the maintenance of democratic political institutions. Mass communications, bureaucratic institutions, and equalitarianism have implications which strengthen pluralistic political structures. Extremist politics may be expected in modern societies as a response of those adversely affected by the changes towards a mass society and most insulated from mass institutions. Contrary to the theory of mass politics traditional concepts of political sociology *are* adequate to the analysis of extremism.

It must be made clear that our major interest in this paper is

Reprinted from "Mass Society and Extremist Politics," *American Sociological Review* 27 (February 1962): 19–30, by permission of the author and The American Sociological Association.

in the explanation of anti-democratic movements as they develop within historically democratic societies. This excludes consideration of authoritarian regimes in traditional societies or the development of anti-democratic movements in developing economies under the impact of intensive social and economic change.[2] Our interest is confined to those writers who explain such modern extremist movements as Fascism, Communism, or McCarthyism by reference to characteristics of mass society. These represent one variant of mass society theory, but an influential one.[3]

MASS SOCIETY AND THE THEORY OF MASS POLITICS

Mass Society analysts view modern social systems as significantly different from non-industrial and earlier societies. Whatever the differences among individual writers, there is a common core of description in the term "mass society" which suggests the attenuation of primary and local associations and groups. Impersonal, bureaucratized relationships in large-scale organizations have replaced the informal systems of loyalty in small groups and local affiliations. Equalitarian conditions and ideologies have weakened systems of political and social authority characteristic of stratified communities. Technological innovations have made possible a high degree of standardization, both of products and ideas. The elongation of the chain of organizational command has enhanced the possibilities of oligarchic control as local groups are less viable, hence less resistant to control. The emphasis is upon the breakdown of immediate relationships and differentiations so that the population is now more homogeneous but also less sharply identified and affiliated with distinctive social groups. It is in this sense that the theorist of mass society views the traditional categories of sociological analysis—family, class, community, ethnic identity, etc. —as having lost significance in mass societies. The mass is masslike: shapeless, structureless, undifferentiated. Mass politics trace the implications of this loss of differentiation for the bonds of loyalty to democratic political institutions.

Exponents of mass politics viewpoints have described modern Western, industrial societies as ones in which persons lack attachment to primary and secondary associations. "The chief characteristic of the mass-man," Hannah Arendt has written, "is not brutality and backwardness, but his isolation and lack of normal social relationships."[4] Political extremism, manifested in anti-democratic movements, is seen as a result of the *structural* and *psychological* consequences for political loyalty or disattachment to democratic procedures and aims.

Supporters of this view hold that structural characteristics of bureaucratization and equality undermine the functions of secondary and primary associations in inculcating values and in transmitting political norms. In mass society, such theories maintain, secondary associations of school, church, community or union, operate in a large-scale fashion. Rank-and-file identification with the organizational elite is diminished as the member's associational life is peripheral and tangential. The high mobility rates and standardized life style destroy

572 economic class as an important source of motivation and interest in political events. Institutions functioning under conditions of mass society do not touch the character and the personal values of those exposed to them. Being solely instrumental means, the major associations and institutions of the society cannot act as agencies through which values are inculcated. Because of this, the political elites of the society cannot mediate political decisions to the acceptance of the rank-and-file. Such political "untouchables" are described by Selznick when he writes, "He has lost the meaning provided by the articulated social structure to which he belonged."[5]

In previous centuries the lack of integration of rank-and-file members of the society into political institutions was a matter of little political consequences. Mass societies, however, are politically equalitarian. The development of large aggregates of persons unattached to democratic political structures and norms is significant because such groups are capable of spontaneous development unguided by the norms of democratic society. The diminished role of intermediate structures—both institutions and specific political associations—leaves the person unattached and capable of being reunited into a new group. "A strong intermediate structure consists of stable and independent groups which represent diverse and frequently conflicting interests."[6] In mass society, however, the representative nature of these groups (classes, ethnic groups, regions, etc.) is undermined. Both because participation is peripheral and because political elites are limited in authority, mass societies are less able to control the values and political aspirations of citizens.

To the structural disintegration of society there is added the personal disorganization of the individual. The psychological consequences of mass society are described in terms of the feeling of detachment. The key word here is alienation, "a mode of experience in which the person experiences himself as an alien."[7] Whether the emphasis of the writer is on estrangement from work, the normlessness of contemporary culture or the powerless feeling of the individual in large-scale organizations, mass conditions are described as producing feelings of *malaise* and insecurity.

The alienation of the individual in modern societies is the psychological statement of detachment. It describes a condition in which the person is not involved in or committed to primary or secondary groups. It adds to this the description of the person as someone with positive, unfulfilled needs for identity, affection, and assurance.

In both its structural and psychological elements the theory of mass politics states that political alienation—the disattachment of the person from political institutions—is a function of the disintegrating influences of mass society on the ties of sentiment and loyalty to specific groups which characterized the social structure of democracies in an earlier historical period. Without attachment to primary or to intermediate structures, the individual has no bond to national political institutions which commands his loyalty to its political norms.

PLURALISTIC AND EXTREMIST POLITICS 573

In the emphasis on a transition from an earlier historical period to a modern, mass society the theories here considered have suggested that political democracy functioned relatively unimpeded under non-mass conditions. It is imperative then that we examine the type of political structure from which mass politics is seen as differing. Political extremism is so defined in contradistinction to pluralistic politics. The mass theorist sees pluralistic politics as impaired under current social conditions. As a corollary pluralistic structure is implicitly posited as an essential condition for democratic politics.

The theory of a balance of power among a plurality of groups has been the dominant analytical tool of American political scientists.[8] Its classic defense has been presented in Hamilton and Madison's *The Federalist Papers*. The theory presupposes a society of many and diverse social groups. The political institutions force each group to moderate and compromise their interests in the interplay of party, secondary association, and locality. In the pluralist conception of the citizens, each person is integrated into politics in his capacity as member of some segment of the society—worker, or manager, city or country dweller, Southerner or Northerner, immigrant or native, white or black. The units of politics are thus organized groups built upon the sentiments and interests of persons in their affiliations with specific primary associations which occupy positions and perform specific functions within the major institutions.

Pluralistic politics involves certain "rules of the game" by which political conflict is carried on. These "rules of the game," part of the definition of politics as an institution, are adhered to by the participants. Chief among tenets of democratic politics is acceptance of opposing forces into the political process on the same terms as those binding on one's own group. This acceptance supplies the necessity for political compromise and conciliation. If all groups possess some political power and are admitted into the political process, bargaining and negotiation are the chief modes of political conflict. Violence is ruled out as a possible way of solving social or economic conflicts.

It is essential to this process that each group be willing to accept the total or partial defeat of its aims and accept the total or partial achievement of the aims of its opponents. Compromise includes the ability to settle for less than full victory. This "realistic" orientation is achieved in an atmosphere governed by rational calculation of interests. It is most negated when objectives have become correlated with considerations of honor and when compromise, negotiation, and defeat are suffused with connotations of dishonor.

Political extremism occurs when movements advocate violation of the democratic, pluralist "rules of the game." Shils suggests a distinction between pluralistic and ideological politics which emphasizes the disattachment of the extremist from self-limiting and rationally calculative aspects of pluralism:

574   Extremism consists in going to an extreme in zealous attachment to
a particular value, e.g., private property, technic homogeneity, or status
equality. . . . The extremist must be deeply alienated from the complex of
rules which keep the strivings for various values in restraint and balance.
An extremist group is an alienated group. . . . Its hostility is incompatible with that freedom from intense emotion which pluralistic politics
needs for its prosperity. . . . The focus of the extremists attention on
one or a few completely fulfilled values and his impatience with compromise when a plurality of values, never internally consistent, have to be
reconciled with each other makes the extremist feel that he is worlds
apart from the compromising moderates.[9]

This distinction between pluralist and extremist politics differs,
as others have pointed out,[10] from traditional distinctions between
Right and Left, Conservative, Liberal and Radical, and reform and
revolution. It is a distinction between styles and not between contents.
It is in this sense that extremism is alienated from the institutions of
democratic politics. It denies the legitimacy of democratic political
institutions as devices for mediating conflict. Extremist style refuses
to accept the possible or probable outcomes of whole or partial defeat.
Total victory is too important in the hierarchy of values to permit of
compromise.

In several ways, then, the extremist breaks with the normative
patterns of pluralist political behavior: (1) *He attempts to close the
political process to opposing forces*: Politics is held to be the legitimate
area of conflict for some, but not for all groups. Both Fascism and
Communism have made this a cornerstone of the political structure
as well as a tenet of their movements.

(2) *He attempts to carry on social and economic conflicts outside of political institutions*: The confinement of conflict to politics
marks a cardinal principle of democratic politics. Violence, intimidation and fraud are excluded as means of achieving group ends.

(3) *He impairs the culture of democratic discussion*: An emphasis is placed on the value of uniform opinions and behaviors. The
criteria of rational calculation of interests is replaced by intensive
appeals to sentiment and symbolism. This strain in McCarthyism
captured the attention of those concerned with extremism in politics.
It is only in this sense that membership and participation in extremist
movements seems authoritarian. The extremist style has little appreciation of dissent and schism in the total society.

The extremist movement is marked by the low degree of commitment to the values of procedure in democratic institutions. Pluralist
norms enforce tolerance, barter, and the inclusion of opponents as joint
members of the same social system. Extremist resentment against democratic politics is not that of indifference but that of intensive conviction. It is the thoroughly moralistic attitude which marks the ex-
termist and distinguishes him from the slightly cynical pluralist.

As we have sketched it so far, political extremism is found in
one or both forms: an increased attachment to a single, over-riding
value or a weakened attachment to the norms of pluralist politics. In

either case, the extremist is alienated from the *existing* democratic order.[11]

The theorists of mass politics visualize extremist movements as consequences of weakened attachments to political institutions and persons resulting from the breakdown in functioning of primary and secondary associations in mass societies. Without a sense of affiliation to specific interest groups, the citizen has no way to develop a frame of reference for political events. Intermediate secondary associations cannot touch him sufficiently to act as forces limiting intensity of opposition and resentment of rival political claims. Political figures become distrusted and democratic institutions no longer legitimate sources of social control. In Kornhauser's words:

> ... intermediate groups help to protect elites by functioning as channels through which popular participation in the larger society (especially in the national elites) may be directed and restrained.[12]

The mass theorist goes a step further and suggests that such detachment from democratic political institutions leaves the individual susceptible to political participation in extremist channels. The socially alienated individual is not only politically alienated; he is also more likely to become the extremist activist than is the member of a structured interest group. He is no longer limited in his attack on rivals by the controls of a structured pluralistic society. His resentments against opposing groups and against the existing institutions themselves need not be confined to the calculative, instrumental style of democratic politics. The mass man is a passionate supporter of ideology.

Lack of control mechanisms regulating the political attitudes and behavior of mass citizenry furthers the extremist character of participation in politics. It enables the person to project destructive impulses into the political arena. Mannheim, for example, maintained that in traditional societies collective impulses and wishes are absorbed by smaller groups and directed toward group aims. The social disintegration of modern society, he felt, set such impulses free to seek integration around some new object, often a symbol or a leader.[13]

The attenuation of local and primary associations and mediating secondary interest groups and associations, is, in the theory of mass politics, the source of the extremism frequent in contemporary mass societies. As a system of analysis this view finds that traditional concepts of class and status aims are limited ways of characterizing political movements. As a philosophy of politics, the theory adds up to a defense of the virtues of a pluralistic political system. The transition from a pluralistic society to a mass society is implicitly and explicitly demoaned. For this reason, the analysis of pluralist assumptions is central to our discussion.

PLURALISTIC SOURCES OF POLITICAL EXTREMISM

The theory of mass politics assumes that a pluralistic social structure diminishes the possibilities that political action will take extremist directions. Conflicts and demands for change will occur but will be moderated by adherence to the style of democratic institutions. An analysis of this assumption, however, shows that extremism both *can* and often *does* occur within pluralistic structures. There are at least four situations in which pluralism either invites or fails to forestall behavior outside the range of democratic norms for the mediation of conflicts:

(1) *Disenfranchised classes*: Change often brings new groups into formation or increases the demands of old ones. In any case, at any given time, some groups are excluded from the political process. Often it is not in the interest of some or most of the included groups to accept new political forces. Excluded groups must either function outside of the political "game" or force their way into it. The militancy of the American Negro in the South today is of this nature. Compromise and legality are not relevant political alternatives unless a group is within the political structures in the first place.

(2) *Doomed and defeated classes*: The theory of democratic politics has never developed a satisfactory answer to the problem: When is compromise to be rejected? When is political defeat not an acceptable alternative to violence and other breaks with pluralist procedure? The facts of the American Civil War and of the Algerian crisis in contemporary France illustrate the thesis that well-structured groups, with channels of representation in parliamentary bodies, are far from willing to accept defeat of important aims through parliamentary procedures. Robert Dahl sees this as a serious impediment in democratic theory. Referring to the election of Abraham Lincoln in 1860, Dahl writes:

> Thus any election interpreted as a clear-cut victory for one side was almost certain to be so intolerable to the other that it would refuse to accept the outcome. . . . Where each side is large and regards the victory of the other as a fundamental threat to some very highly ranked values, it is reasonable to expect serious difficulties in the continued operation of a (pluralistic) system.[14]

This is apt to be the case under conditions of social or economic change which gravely threaten a previous position of power and supremacy. To such "doomed classes,"[15] the future looks far less inviting than the past. A radical reorganization of society, might be a solution to their problem but such a reorganization against politically ascendent forces is precisely what the moderating elements in the structure of political balance operate against. Recent discussions of the plight of the "old middle classes" in American life have stressed the indignation of these groups at their loss of power and status.[16] It is not a failure to "belong" that lies at the source of their alienation and possible "right-wing radicalism." Their response is touched off by the contents of the social changes to which they react.

(3) *Public opinion and the imbalance of competing interests*: The theory of democratic politics as a balance between competing interests often ignores the important role played by the neutral, non-

competing elements in the political process. A great many groups without specific interests in a particular issue nevertheless have power to effect governmental decisions. Such decisions are made with a concern for the general climate of opinion toward an issue. Whether the "public" is friendly or hostile is an important element in an interest group's decision to pursue its aims within or without the political process. As Murray Edelman has pointed out, labor will pursue its goals through economic processes (strikes, bargaining, etc.) when the political climate is hostile.[17] Recourse to non-political means is not ruled out by the existence of pluralistic machinery.

(4) *Development of periodic crisis*: Mass politics theory generally recognizes economic and military crisis as an essential "trigger" to extremist movements. Because pluralistic politics is oriented toward compromises between groups, it is less open to long-run considerations. This is especially the case in issues of foreign policy. Unless there is some consensual basis other than group interest, elites must "sell" policy in terms communicable to specific classes and interests. Even assuming a diffusion of power in the form of what Riesman calls "veto groups,"[18] a hiatus develops between long-run perspectives of governmental leaders and the short-run perspectives of intermediate associations and their constituencies. The result is often a stalemate and an immobilism which enables problems to develop into major crises. One instance of this is contained in LaPalombara's analysis of French and Italian politics in the post-war years.[19] He explains greater cohesion and agreement within the Italian moderate parties than among the French as a consequence of differences in the power of the Communist Party in each of the countries. Italian moderates were forced into agreement by fear.

> While there has not been any serious fear in France that PCF could come peacefully to power, this reassuring assessment has been denied the democratic party leaders in Italy. . . . They have not been able to permit themselves the capricious inaction in which the French Center Party Leaders have indulged over the last decade.[20]

Inability of political elites to deal with crisis is itself one strong source of mass alienation from a political institution. Third parties have fared better at the polls in the United States during periods of economic depression than during periods of prosperity.[21] As Lipset has pointed out, there is a direct correlation between levels of economic well-being and the existence of democratic political systems.[22] Prosperous countries may avoid problems which threaten political stability in less affluent nations.

In each of these four situations, extremist politics is developed and conducted by well-structured groups, representing discrete and organized parts of the social structure, acting to secure goals related to group needs. While such groups are alienated from the existing political institutions they are not socially disintegrated or unrelated to the society and its political system. They function within a pluralist framework in which their values receive short shrift. Failure to recog-

578   nize that pluralist assumptions cannot alone sustain political institutions is at the root of the implicit ideology of the theorist of mass politics.

THE PLURALIST IDEOLOGY

The sanguine view of political balance at the base of mass politics theory reveals a repetition of the ideological bias of nineteenth century liberalism—the assumption that there is a natural harmony of interests which sustains the social and political system. Occurrences of sharp conflict are therefore indicative of disruptions in the *form* of social arrangements. There is nothing in the *content* of interests and beliefs which makes compromise improbable. Mannheim reflects this ideology in a passage in *Man and Society* in which he suggests that experience in trade unions and in other associations trains participants for planning on a societal basis: "He is gradually realizing that by resigning partial advantages he helps to save the social and economic system and thereby also his own interests."[23]

The belief that participation in the primary and secondary associations of the society will moderate conflict arises from this ideological commitment to pluralist politics. It leads the mass politics theorist to identify political defeat with social alienation, to view extremist movements as actions of disattached persons, unrelated to specific social bases or pursuing interests of a discrete social base. Because of this tendency, the mass politics approach has felt traditional political analysis to be deficient.

It is *not* true that attachment to intermediate structures insures attachment to the larger national institutions and structures. As a society undergoes change, it is likely that specific groups will be adversely affected by economic or social change. Similarly, some groups may develop new aspirations and objectives. In both cases they may come to feel that the existent political order is insufficient to command their allegiance. A shifting balance of forces is, however, not the same phenomenon as the breakup of an associational structure, the shattering of a class, or the decline of primary group support. It is even reasonable to maintain that an external threat to a group promotes its sense of solidarity and aids in the development of group identity and organization.[24] Attachment to intermediate structures may indeed promote a shared sense of alienation of the group from the total political order. The more informal organization the group possesses the more likely it is that politically extremist sentiments can be communicated and legitimated. In playing the game of politics, it is not only important whether or not one is permitted to play, but also whether one is winning or not. This problem is not solved by the degree of access which the group has to political association.

The point can be made through an analysis of a frequently used study of McCarthyist attitudes, which mass politics theorists have used as support for their position. Trow's study of Bennington, Vermont found a disproportionate amount of support for Senator McCarthy among small businessmen, especially those holding the nineteenth century liberal hostility to both big business and labor unions.[25]

In explaining his findings, Trow maintains that not only are small businessmen "resentful of a world that continually offends their deepest values" but equally important is the fact that they have little voice or representation in political institutions, such as the major parties. Granting the rather dubious assumption that small business has little place in the current constellation of political and ideological forces in the United States, the picture of disaffection portrayed in Trow's study is a classic picture of a well-organized economic group losing out in the process of social and economic change. This type of disaffection is readily analyzed in terms of class and status conflict. If mass movements are not to be understood in traditional forms of political analysis, they must be shown to be unrelated to analysis in terms of group interests and discrete social bases. This would involve more than the traditional view that social change produces disaffection among groups adversely exposed to it.

The assumption of a natural harmony of interests gives rise to another failing of the mass politics approach. This is the lack of concern for the development of consensus around the norms of democratic politics. If it is assumed that representation of interests assures harmony, then the problem of achieving moral sentiments supportive of the political institution becomes meaningless. However, such moral sentiments *are* essential; otherwise, the source of moderate politics, of commitment to the political process *per se* is missing. When the values at stake are intensely held and the constellation of political forces is adverse to a group, there is nothing in pluralistic theory which suggests a source of loyalty to moderateness. Oscar Gass has expressed this in excellent fashion:

> I know that Democracy is a technique for reaching agreement, but it in turn rests upon a measure of agreement. It is, of course, formally true that, if only you agree on the technique of getting decisions, you don't have to agree on the outcome. But that is merely like saying that people can ride on the same bus even if they wish to get off at different places. The places must not be *too* different—or else they have to set a value on riding beyond that of getting to their destinations.[26]

A pluralistic system can be maintained only if the conflict of interest groups is balanced to some extent by cohesive elements in the cultural and social system which moderate the intensity of conflicts and which provide loyalties to maintenance of a defined area in which politics is conducted under pluralistic rules.[27] The ideology of pluralism has become a defense of moderateness, and an attack on political activism. Yet pluralist structure enhances activist sentiments.

MASS CULTURE AND POLITICAL COHESION

Contrary to mass politics theory, conditions of mass societies are not necessarily detrimental to sentiments supporting pluralistic politics. In fact the opposite appears to be the case. Certain conditions of modern, mass societies function to increase cohesion and consensus around norms of pluralist politics.

Mass politics approaches have emphasized bureaucratization, equalitarianism, and technological integration as forces weakening past mediating structures. It must also be pointed out that the same forces operate to incorporate persons into a larger national culture and social system. While mediating structures and local units may be weakened, direct attachment to the total society is enhanced. In Shils' phrase, "The new society is a mass society precisely in the sense that the mass of the population has become incorporated into *society*."[28]

Conditions of mass society develop a homogeneous set of cultural experiences for members. Technological forces have led to an economy and a means of communication which can absorb all the citizens in common. As this has occurred, the autonomy of the local community has given way to a national politics, a national economy and a national culture. In an era of high mass consumption, the equalization of incomes and the style-setting influence of a national market have promoted a more homogenous standard of living. In the use of commodities and of leisure, as well as in high rates of social mobility, class lines are becoming blurred. In this society, major social institutions operate in similar fashion upon all communities and within most classes. School, church, medicine, family and politics are increasingly open to the influence and control of centrally trained professionals and their organizations. The consequences of such homogenizing forces are the development of a national mass culture and a national society. In this society, common sentiments increasingly cut across the social segments of class, region, and other sub-cultural units. In this sense mass society is a new social system.

These features of mass society, of course, are recognized in the theories considered above. Where we differ, however, is in stressing these as positive agencies of social integration, rather than only as devices which weaken earlier units of social life. The theories of mass politics suggest only one possible relationship between mass societies and political extremism. In the remainder of this paper we wish to suggest another relationship, one in which the trend toward mass society provides opportunities for strengthening the attachments of the individuals to institutions which accept diversity and support political balance. The conditions of mass society, we suggest, mitigate against political extremism because they operate against the isolation of differentiated sub-cultures from which strong ideological attachments can develop. At the same time, they provide conditions which promote acceptance of innovations.

(1) *They provide sources of direct attachment to supra-local institutions.* It has become something of an axiom in electoral behavior studies that interest and participation is at its highest in national rather than local elections. In a mass society, the individual is oriented toward a national culture and stratification system. Mass culture is carried through national systems of communications and education which may be, and often are, in conflict with local groups. Lack of attachment to local agencies, kinship units and secondary associations by no means implies a lack of attachment to standards, tastes and values of the mass culture. The same is true in respect to political participation. As the

range of areas affected by local decisions grows smaller, the orientation of the individual to national political units grows more significant. Studies of cosmopolitan and local types indicate that the individual may be marginal within his local environment but very much committed to structures of occupational, educational and political organization at levels above that of the local community.[29]

(2) *Mass culture enhances the possibilities of substantive consensus.* We have argued above that although cultural and class diversity provides a resistant force against oligarchic controls, it may also develop intensive attachments to particular aims which prevent the compromise and toleration presupposed by political pluralism. Indeed, pluralistic politics is hard to reconcile with intensity of conviction and a moralistic approach to politics. Insofar as mass societies create homogeneous experience for a population, there is an increased possibility of consensus on substantive issues. Will Herberg's[30] thesis of a growing uniformity in American religions is a case in point. Similarity of education, consumer products, income and communications is also associated with similarity in morals and, to some extent, interests. The issues open to political conflict are then limited and less apt to arouse intense opposition. While this may mean a diminution in ideological commitments and controversy, it is hardly the same thing as production of extremist activism. Indeed, those who are critical of contemporary American society for its presumed conformist tendencies are often dismayed at the disappearance of activism, utopian thought and radical attitudes, all of which are also forms of extremism, alienation and discontent.

(3) *Mass culture can, and often does, shore up the support for consensus on procedural norms of pluralistic politics.* Because they include multiple sub-cultures, mass institutions are open to the influence of numerous social segments in ways in which local and class institutions are not. Further, mass culture is more apt to be influenced by norms of cosmopolitan and nationalized groups than local and sub-cultural units. Within American society today, the norms of pluralist styles in politics find more response at the national than at the local levels. Efforts to censor artistic and educational experiments and dissent are more frequent at the local than at the national levels of education and communications. The development of a mass educational system, with a high degree of equalitarian recruitment, has been a distinctive aid to the acceptance of civil liberties sentiment.[31]

(4) *Mass culture diminishes the intensity of social conflicts by evening out the impact of major social and cultural changes.* Major social changes are frequently disruptive and focus on dimensions which involve clashes between attackers and defenders of tradition. This is particularly true in areas of cultural conflict—religion, morality or race relations are examples. The appearance of mass communications and educational agencies diminishes the degree to which the population is differentially exposed to a new set of norms. This is seen in the current desegregation crisis in the South. Opposition to a national culture of race relations is found most intensively among those most localistic, least educated, least urban, least exposed to mass media, and least

582

integrated into the national economy.[32] Mass media, the extension of education and professionalization tend to equate the rates at which different classes and regions are exposed to changing standards.

(5) *Mass society increases the linkages between groups and minimizes the possibilities of "superimposition."* The concept of a pluralistic social system often fails to differentiate between two types of segmentation.[33] In one, which we will call "linked pluralism," there are multiple groups but membership in one often cuts across membership in others. A situation of linked pluralism, for example, would be one in which many Catholics are lower-class and many are middle-class while Protestants are similarly represented in each class. Both Catholics and Protestants are "linked" as members of the same social class. "Superimposed" segmentation occurs when membership in one group also implies membership in another. If most Catholics were lower-class and most Protestants were middle-class, then class and religion would be superimposed. It is fairly evident that intense social conflicts are maximized under conditions of superimposition and minimized under conditions of linked pluralism. In the example used, superimposition would mean that religious conflicts tended to be class conflicts as well.

The conditions of mass society tend to increase linked forms of pluralism and to minimize superimposed forms of pluralism. Perhaps the most salient aspects of this is a result of equalitarianism and mobility. When groups are not frozen by rigid stratification into a specific occupational and class position, such social categories as religion, race, residence, and community play less of a role as devices isolating one part of society from another.

It follows from this analysis that there are two major ways in which extremist movements may develop within the framework of contemporary mass societies. In one case, we are dealing with the general problem of reactions to social and economic change already discussed above in reference to "doomed classes" and to groups previously excluded from the political process. The transition from pluralistic structure to mass society is most keenly felt as loss and deprivation by those whose social and economic position is threatened by the development of bureaucratic organization, equalitarian social structure and mass culture. The attention given to the status loss and economic hardship of the "old middle classes" as the society becomes more consumption-oriented, more organizationally structured and more technically professionalized provides one strand of evidence in what Lipset has called the "extremism of the Center."[34] Riesman has expressed the same idea of reaction to change in characterological terms in saying:

> . . . his own life experience is often disappointing; he is deprived of a feeling of competence and place. Even this would not be so bad if the world made sense, if he could apply to what goes on his internalized standards of judgment, but as it is, neither his character nor his work is rewarded. In that situation he tends to turn both on himself . . . and on the world.[35]

The other case exists when groups are isolated from the major **583** institutions and cultural streams of mass society. Localized groups are less open to the impact of the mass agencies. The less educated, the lowest income levels, the least protected minorities, the most fundamentalist in religion are least oriented to the rhythm of modernity with which so much of mass influence is carried. In this case, it is those least "caught up" in the historical currents of transition that are most likely to be immune from the moderating influences of mass culture. To cite such groups as products *of* mass society is misleading.

Carried to a logical extreme, the mass society becomes a political community in which bland tolerance and uniform ideas are the rule. Carried to its logical extreme, pluralistic societies are likely to generate either disintegrating conflict or stalemate. It is fruitless, however, to push typologies to their logical extremes. An empirical sociology must be concerned with the interaction between mass and pluralistic conditions. Elements of one model interact with elements of the other, sometimes as figure, sometimes as ground. De Tocqueville pointed out that one of the characteristics of American political institutions was the moderation of popular government by a leaven of aristocratic rule. He viewed the Supreme Court power of review as one such instance of balance.[36]

Mass conditions are thus likely to present many features which are not only consistent with a pluralistic theory of politics but even enhance such features. Rather than providing a source of extremist movements they are just as likely to mitigate the development of opposition and to increase the degree of toleration for dissent. Whether variety and controversy are likely to develop under the dominance of mass conditions is another question. However, those who seek to understand the conditions of stable, democratic institutions are mistaken in dispensing with traditional concepts and in emphasizing mass society as a demonic villain.

NOTES

1. The following relevant writings embody the theory of mass politics: Hannah Arendt, *The Origins of Totalitarianism.* (New York: Harcourt, Brace and Co., 1954); Erich Fromm, *Escape from Freedom* (New York: Rinehart, 1945); Karl Mannheim, *Man and Society in an Age of Reconstruction* (London: Routledge and Kegan Paul, 1940); William Kornhauser, *The Politics of Mass Society* (Glencoe, Ill.: The Free Press, 1959); Robert Nisbet, *The Quest for Community* (New York: Oxford University Press, 1953); Philip Selznick, *The Organizational Weapon* (New York: McGraw-Hill, 1952).

2. *See* the discussion of the political effects of social and economic change in Western and non-Western societies in William Kornhauser, op. cit., chs. 7, 8.

3. We have confined our analysis here to theorists who find mass societies an explanatory tool in analyzing the rise of contemporary anti-democratic movements. Other writers have also described modern society as mass-like and have evaluated it in negative terms. This latter group, however, has not viewed political extremism as a likely consequence of mass conditions. Writers such as David Riesman, in *The Lonely Crowd*, and C. Wright Mills, in *The Power Elite*, have emphasized developing trends toward conformity and passivity rather than toward militance and activism. Still another stream in mass society writings is represented by E. A. Shils. He agrees that modern society is, by reason of mass conditions, best described as qualitatively different from earlier Western societies.

584

This stream of writings, however, denies the disorganizing and overconforming consequences stressed by the other views. See the positive acceptance of mass society in Edward A. Shils, "Mass Society and Its Culture," *Daedalus* 89 (Spring 1960) : 288–314.

4. Hannah Arendt, op. cit., p. 310.

5. Philip Selznick, op. cit., p. 283.

6. William Kornhauser, op. cit., p. 78.

7. Erich Fromm, *The Sane Society* (New York: Rinehart, 1955), p. 120.

8. The best descriptions of this process in contemporary political science are probably David Truman, *The Governmental Process* (New York: A. A. Knopf, 1951), and V. O. Key, *Parties, Politics and Pressure Groups* (New York: Thomas Y. Crowell, 1947).

9. Edward A. Shils, *The Torment of Secrecy* (Glencoe, Ill.: The Free Press, 1955), p. 231. In similar vein, Nathan Leites introduces his study of French politics by a statement exempting the Communists and the "extreme right" from his discussion. He reasons that their style in politics is distinctly different from the "national" groups of the Center. In the period of post-war politics which he studied, "the extremes entered but little in 'the game' so that the patterns of political calculation used in parliament had little reference to their behavior." Nathan Leites, *On the Game of Politics in France* (Stanford, Calif.: Stanford University Press, 1959), p. 1.

10. Milton Rokeach, *The Open and Closed Mind* (New York: Basic Books, 1960), ch. 3; Edward A. Shils, "Authoritarianism—Right and Left," in *Studies in the Scope and Method of 'The Authoritarian Personality,'* R. Christie and M. Jahoda, ed., (Glencoe, Ill.: The Free Press, 1954).

11. It should be emphasized that the degree of commitment of democratic populations to its political institutions is a relative matter. Many studies of attitudes toward civil liberties show a great gap between the acceptance of civil liberties among a minority of educated and participating citizens and the rank and file, especially among the lower-income and lesser educated. In this case, political extremism represents less an alienation *from* political institutions than it does the advent of increased political democracy. For studies of civil liberties see Samuel Stouffer, *Communism, Conformity and Civil Liberties* (Garden City, N.Y.: Doubleday, 1955); Seymour Lipset, "Democracy and Working-Class Authoritarianism," in *Political Man* (Garden City, N.Y.: Doubleday, 1960), pp. 97–130; and Raymond Mack, "De We Really Believe in the Bill of Rights?" *Social Problems* 3 (April 1956); 264–69.

12. William Kohnhauser, op. cit., p. 77.

13. Karl Mannheim, op. cit., p. 62.

14. Robert Dahl, *A Preface to Democratic Theory* (Chicago: The University of Chicago Press, 1956), pp. 97–98.

15. The term is used by Franz Neumann in "Notes on the Theory of Dictatorship," in *The Democratic and the Authoritarian State*, (Glencoe, Ill.: The Free Press, 1957), p. 251.

16. See the articles by Richard Hofstadter and by Seymour M. Lipset in Daniel Bell, editor, *The New American Right* (New York: Criterion Books, 1955). For a fuller treatment of this theme see Seymour M. Lipset, "Social Stratification and Right-Wing Extremism," *British Journal of Sociology*, 10 (December, 1959), pp. 1–32.

17. Murray Edelman, "Government's Balance of Power in Labor-Management Relations," *Labor Law Journal* 2 (January 1951) : 31–35. This point is also discussed in C. Wright Mills, *The Power Elite* (New York: Oxford University Press, 1957), pp. 246–48.

18. David Riesman, *The Lonely Crowd*, New Haven: Yale University Press, 1950, pp. 242–55.

19. Joseph LaPalombara, "Political Party Systems and Crisis Government: French and Italian Contrasts," *Midwest Journal of Political Science* 11 (May 1958) : 117–39.

20. Ibid., p. 133.

21. Murray and Susan Stedman, *Discontent at the Polls* (New York: Columbia University Prses, 1950), ch. 8.

22. Seymour M. Lipset, "Economic Development and Democracy," in *Political Man*, op. cit., pp. 45–76.

23. Karl Mannheim, op. cit., p. 70. For discussions of the assumption of a natural harmony of interests see the analysis of sociological thought in C. Wright Mills, op. cit., ch. 11; Werner Stark, "Christian Thought in Social Theory," in *Social Theory and Christian Thought* (London: Routledge and Kegan Paul, 1959); Ralf Dahrendorf, *Class and Class Conflict in Industrial Society* (Stanford, Calif.: Stanford University Press, 1958).

24. See the discussions of this factor in the history of labor movements in Sidney and Beatrice Webb, *History of Trade Unionism* (New York: Longmans, Green and Co., 1920), ch. 1, and in Selig Perlman, *Theory of the Labor Movement* (New York: Augustus M. Kelly, 1928), ch. 5.

25. Martin Trow, "Small Business, Political Tolerance, and Support for McCarthy," *American Journal of Sociology* 64 (November 1958); 270–81.

26. Oscar Gass, "Socialism and Democracy," *Commentary* 29 (June 1960): 574.

27. For an especially illuminating statement of this view, see Adolf Lowe, *The Price of Liberty*, Day-to-Day Pamphlets, No. 36, (London: Hogarth Press, 1937). Also see Edward A. Shils and M. Young, "The Meaning of the Coronation," *Sociological Review*, series 1 (1953), pp. 63–81. Political consensus as a focus of sociological study is a central theme in Seymour M. Lipset, "Political Sociology" (New York: Basic Books, 1959). Robret K. Merton, Leonard Broom, and Leonard S. Cottrell, Jr., ed., in *Sociology Today*.

28. Edward A. Shils, "Mass Society and Its Culture," op. cit., p. 288.

29. Robert K. Merton, "Patterns of Influence," in Paul Lazersfeld and Frank Stanton, editors, *Communications Research, 1948–49* (New York: Harper & Row, 1949), pp. 180–219; Alvin W. Gouldner, "Cosmopolitans and Locals," *Administrative Science Quarterly* 2 (December 1957 and March 1958): 281–306, 444–80.

30. Will Herberg, *Protestant, Catholic, Jew* (Garden City, N.Y.: Doubleday Anchor Books, 1955).

31. Studies of tolerance and authoritarianism have repeatedly shown a direct relation between amount of education and tolerance for political diversity. See Martin Trow, op. cit., and the summarization of many studies in Seymour M. Lipset, "Working-Class Authoritarianism," *Political Man*, op. cit.

32. Melvin Tumin, *Desegregation* (Princeton, N.J.: Princeton University Press, 1958).

33. This distinction and the terms "pluralistic" and "superimposed" are used in Ralf Dahrendorf, op. cit., pp. 213–18.

34. Seymour M. Lipset, *Political Man*, op. cit., pp. 131–34, 173–76.

35. David Riesman, op. cit., *see also* Joseph Gusfield, "Social Structure and Moral Reform," *American Journal of Sociology* 61 (November 1955): 221–32.

36. Alexis de Tocqueville, *Democracy in America* (New York and London: Oxford University Press, 1947), pp. 493–99.

RALPH H. TURNER

The Theme of Contemporary
Social Movements

The events of every era seem disorderly while they are happening. Only from the perspective of history do clear strands of meaning and pattern become evident. It is the aim of this brief statement to specu-late about the pattern underlying some of the events in the second half of the twentieth century thus far, and to suggest something of the direction that will be taken in the next decade or two.

The main question is just what contemporary social movements are all about and what they signal with respect to major changes in our social system. At present, movements dealing with the Vietnam war and ghetto protest are the most obvious and most on our minds. However, the Vietnam movements are excessively coloured by what we hope is a situation of limited duration, and it is necessary to look for the more lasting circumstances and more persistent themes in social movements. The civil rights movement has been tremendously impor-tant, but it has not been a major preoccupation of the American people. It has been more like a troublesome side-show, and the civil rights activists have constantly been forced to go to extremes in order even to get the population to give attention to their movement and its aims. Again, there is a good deal to be learned from examination of the civil rights movement, but this may well be secondary to the main preoccupations determining social change in the contemporary era.

MOVEMENTS AND INJUSTICE

Two main points are preliminary to the analysis that is to follow. First, any major social movement depends upon and promotes some norma-tive revision. In case of movements having the greatest significance for social change this normative innovation takes the form of a new sense of what is *just* and what is *unjust* in society.[1] This is quite dif-ferent from merely saying that the leaders and followers of a move-ment discover a problem and seek to do something about it. The prob-lem may have existed for a long time or it may be of relatively recent origin, and awareness of the problem may predate the movement by centuries. The change we are speaking of is represented in the dif-ference between conceiving of a problem as a *misfortune* and conceiv-ing of it as a state of *injustice*. Man has been intensely aware of misfortune throughout recorded history. He has established many institutional procedures to soften the impact of misfortune. He has always recognized the sympathy due to those who suffer misfortune, and he has always held a high opinion of charitable activities directed

From Ralph H. Turner, "The Theme of Contemporary Social Movements," *British Journal of Sociology* 20, no. 4 (December 1969). Reprinted by permission.

toward the relief of many types of misfortune. But misfortune is not **587**
the same thing as injustice. Death and illness are misfortunes. We are
deeply upset over the prospect of a young man dying of incurable
cancer, but we do not conceive it as a deep injustice which provokes
a sense of outrage against a system productive of such misfortunes.

The sense of misfortune and the sense of injustice can be distinguished by the difference between *petition* and *demand*. The victims
of misfortune petition whoever has the power to help them for some
kind of aid. The victims of injustice demand that their petitions be
granted. The poor man appealing for alms is displaying his misfortune. The Poor People's March on Washington to demand correction
of their situation expressed a sense of injustice.

Another way to indicate the distinction is by speaking of
charity as compared with *what people have a right to expect*. The
poor man asking for alms appeals to the good will of those who have
the resources to do something for him. The poor who marched on
Washington *demanded* what they claimed as their right. The labour
movement of the 1930's answered Henry Ford's declaration that he
already paid higher wages than his competitors by insisting that the
principle be established that a favourable wage structure was theirs
by right rather than because of an employer's generosity.

A significant social movement becomes possible when there is
a revision in the manner in which a substantial group of people look
at some misfortune, seeing it no longer as a misfortune warranting
charitable consideration but as an injustice which is intolerable in
society. A movement becomes possible when a group of people cease
to petition the good will of others for relief of their misery and demand
as their right that others ensure the correction of their condition.

INJUSTICE AND HISTORICAL ERAS

The second preliminary point is that major eras in history have
differed in the dominant sense of injustice which underlay the major
movements of the time and dictated the main direction of social change.
Karl Mannheim has offered one cogent characterization of the sequence of major movements during modern times.[2] He proposes that
there have been four major waves of movements beginning with
chiliastic developments expressed most dramatically in the peasant
revolts; continuing with the liberal humanitarian movements which
found their fullest expression in the French and American revolutions;
followed by a conservative movement; and culminating in the socialist
movements which were not only found in international communism
but gave the main colouring to the New Deal and the welfare state in
the United States and Britain.

In the analysis to follow we shall dwell primarily upon two of
these, namely, the *liberal humanitarian* and the *socialist* movements.
We believe that the chiliastic movement is a rather special case reflecting a preliminary stage of discontent, which is to some degree recapitu-
lated at the beginning of each new era. It lacks the relatively clear
image of the nature of reform to be brought about by the movement.
We shall also disregard the so-called conservative movement, feeling

588   that here Mannheim was misled in assigning to these reactions against
the liberal humanitarian movement the prominence of a major group
of movements in the reform of society. We shall speak of the era
dominated by the liberal humanitarian movements giving way to the
more recent era shaped by the socialist movements. We suggest that
the power of both the liberal humanitarian and the socialist conceptions of injustice has been largely exhausted.[3] We shall seek to identify
a 'utopia' or a new central theme which is capable of arousing the
enthusiasm and focusing the energies of discontent in the era that is
only now beginning to take shape.

Within each of these major eras there are one or two movements that colour the preoccupations and the social change effected
during the era. These are the movements that embody the main theme
most completely. Many other movements are lesser expressions of the
same goal, or movements seeking a more limited goal which is consistent with the principal movements. And there are also movements
directed toward other problems that do not seem at first to be directly
concerned with the era's central preoccupations. However, the emerging conception of injustice does colour all other important themes in
the same era. The main themes also persist from one era to the next
so that major movements in the next era retain much of the language
and much of the symbolism of the preceding era, but only insofar
as they can be incorporated into and subordinated to the newly emerging conception of injustice.

Two features of these eras must be observed. First, the sequence
may start later or proceed more slowly in some places than in others,
while the essential development order persists. For example, if 1848
marks the emergence of the socialist utopia as a leading factor in
European history, it is probably not until 1932 that socialist conceptions of justice became vital in the United States. Second subsidiary
issues—the troublesome side-problems in society from the point of view
of the large population—are especially likely to continue to be viewed
through the lens provided by the older sense of justice, at the same
time that central problems are being viewed with the new perspective.

If we look at the two eras specifically in terms of the major
new conception of injustice which dominated the movements, we see
first that in the American and French revolutions people asserted the
right to be ensured the opportunity to participate in ruling themselves.
Such specifics as freedom of speech, freedom of assembly, freedom of
the press, were all incident to and justified by insistence that people
should no longer merely petition to be heard, but that institutional
arrangements should be so revised as to ensure that all people could
be heard and participate in governing themselves in some tangible
and dependable way. It is characteristic that the fundamental injustice
of denying some people a full voice in determining their own destiny
was the touchstone which would supply solutions to all the other important problems of the era. Give people the right to vote and the
freedom to speak, to read and write and discuss their respective interests, and the problems of poverty and other avoidable misfortunes
would be well on the way to correction.

The socialist movements retain the symbolism of freedom and participation but subordinate them to a new sense of injustice. For the first time the fundamental right of people to demand that the essential material needs of life be provided for them was recognized. To the liberal humanitarians of the late eighteenth and early nineteenth centuries poverty was a misfortune and gross inequalities in material wealth and comfort might be regarded as unfortunate. But they were certainly not to be treated as injustices. The arguments of the New Deal era in American history incorporate the difference between the older liberal humanitarian philosophy and the newer socialist conception of fundamental injustice. The New Deal was essentially a victory, albeit a limited victory, for the view that freedom of the liberal humanitarian sort without an underpinning of material security is meaningless. The New Deal incorporated reforms reflecting the assumption that a society is obligated to provide for the material wants of its people, and that its people have a right to demand that these wants be met. The changed view of what is just and unjust is reflected in Franklin Roosevelt's Four Freedoms. By adding the *freedom from want* and the *freedom from fear*, Roosevelt departed drastically from the liberal humanitarian conception and acknowledged the right of people to demand that their society provide them with material needs.

Different movements in both eras varied in the extent to which they demanded total equality or the provision of some kind of minimum for all. The more extreme movements in each era held that any condition other than complete equality of representation or complete equality of material comforts and possession was unjust. The more moderate views usually won out in both eras, holding only that society must guarantee every citizen a minimum opportunity to participate in determining his own destiny and that every society must provide each citizen with the minimum necessities for a decent living.

It is easy to see how the main conceptions of injustice shaped the objectives of secondary movements. Two of the major secondary movements in the liberal humanitarian era in American society were the movement for women's suffrage and the abolition movement. The abolition movement was dominated by the conviction that freeing the slaves and granting them the same minimum political participation that was ensured for all other people would resolve the injustice of slavery. There was no recognition that it might be necessary to go further. Anything further that would be done for the slaves would be in the nature of charity rather than provision of what they could claim by right. Similarly, the problems of woman's role in modern society were viewed as soluble through the provision of political equality with men. Once women were given the vote and granted the same rights to speak and read and write, the injustice of woman's position would have been corrected.

The post-depression era in the United States has been dominated by the socialist's conception of injustice and our approach to a variety of problems has been coloured accordingly. Ever since the Second World War, one main approach to the problem of minority groups in our society has been to ensure the economic base for their existence. It is true that we have been involved in voter drives, and have been cleaning up the left-over business from the liberal humanitarian era in this respect. However, we have not been slow to recognize that the right to vote is not an end in itself, but merely a means, and we are not surprised that minority problems are not resolved merely by extending the franchise. Government commissions approaching the problem of urban riots consistently took the right of the population to demand provision for their minimum physical needs as the fundamental basis for recommendations regarding the prevention of rioting.

INJUSTICE IN THE CONTEMPORARY ERA

If we look at the contemporary era consisting of roughly the second half of the twentieth century, I think it has become quite clear that the liberal humanitarian ideology no longer has the vitality to rouse great populations to the active pursuit of reform or revolution. This is a discovery that seems to be coming last in our foreign policy. The contention that the socialist's conception of injustice, the demand for assurance of material wants or even for material equality is declining in its vitality, may be more difficult to substantiate. Nevertheless, a rather strong impression can be drawn from events in many spheres to suggest that as an accepted principle, the injustice of material want has become commonplace so that it draws ready assent without arousing excitement and enthusiasm for its implementation.

Neither aspect of the last observation should be overlooked. There is no contradiction in asserting that a principle that has become nearly consensual often fails to evoke enough enthusiasm to stimulate a drive toward alleviating the remaining injustices. The consensus is like that of many moral and religious doctrines, accepted as verbally unchallengeable truths that exercise declining influence over actual behaviour after they cease to be a feature of intergroup conflict.

The New Conception of Injustice

It is the central thesis of this paper that a new revision is in the making and is increasingly giving direction to the disturbances of our era. This new conception is reflected in a new object for indignation. Today, for the first time in history, it is common to see violent indignation expressed over the fact that people lack a sense of personal worth —that they lack an inner peace of mind which comes from a sense of personal dignity or a clear sense of identity. It is not, of course, a new thing that people have wondered who they are, nor that people have wondered whether man and man's life are worthwhile. The Old Testament contains poetic complaints about the meaninglessness of life, and the insignificance of man. Although this concern has been before us for millenia, the phenomenon of a man crying out with indignation because his society has not supplied him with a sense of personal worth and identity is the distinctive new feature of our era. The idea that a man does not feel worthy and who cannot find his proper place in life is to be pitied is an old one. The notion that he is indeed a victim of injustice is the new idea. The urgent demand that the institutions of our society be reformed, not primarily to grant man freedom of speech and thought, and not primarily to ensure him essential comforts, but to guarantee him a sense of personal worth is the new and recurrent theme in contemporary society.

Heretofore, the discovery of a purpose and a sense of worth in one's life was considered to be an individual problem. It was, of course, the concern of one's friends simply because any intimate is concerned with the well-being of a friend. But the idea that people have a right to demand that society provide them with a sense of personal worth still appears strange and incredible to most people. In the prevalent view, one who has not found his place in society, one who has no sense of personal worth, ought to conceal this deficiency from others, lest they think less of him for it. The picture of young people proclaiming to the world that they have not found themselves and expressing consequent indignation is simply incomprehensible in terms of traditional conceptions of justice.

These new views are perhaps most fully embodied in the doctrines of today's New Left. Well before the Vietnam war became the central preoccupation there were expressions of outrage against the depersonalizing and demoralizing effect of modern institutions, ranging from the family to the university and the state.

The main symbol of the new era is *alienation*. Here is a fine example of the way in which a term is borrowed from an earlier era but assigned new meaning. We know that the socialist movements borrowed the term democracy, but when we examine what they mean by a democratic government it is quite clear that it has little to do with the conception employed by the liberal humanitarians. Similarly, the concept of alienation is borrowed from Marx. It had original reference to the specific relationship of the labouring man to his work. In one way or another it meant simply that a man's work no longer mattered to him as it had in a handicraft era when he could take pride in his accomplishments, with various psychological overtones that made it more than simple job dissatisfaction. But the new meaning refers to a deeply psychological state. Man's alienation is now a divorcement of the individual from himself or the failure of the individual to find his real self, which he must employ as a base for organizing his life. Alienation has thus been transformed into the designation for a psychological or psychiatric condition which is quite different from the most important usage during the socialist era.

Each emergent conception of injustice has been associated with a major approach in philosophy. The philosophy provides the elaborated rationalization for the new sense of injustice and supplies the conceptual vehicles through which persons may reflect about the burning injustice which they must seek to correct. The liberal humanitarian era is clearly associated with rationalism in philosophy. The socialist era is associated with dialectical materialism and some of its more modern variations. American pragmatism might be considered a very watered down form, but one which clearly played a major part in setting the stage for the New Deal and the associated development of progressive education. The philosophy of the New Era is clearly *existentialism* in its many forms and variations. Existentialism focuses

592   on the problem of man's alienation, on the problem of man's existence and the dilemma of his efforts to uncover a viable sense of self.

In a sense each of these philosophies and each of these conceptions of injustice is focused in a different area of human concern. The liberal humanitarian movements with their rationalist philosophy focus in the realm of politics. The solution to man's problems are to be found in the political sphere and the reforms that are sought are primarily reforms in political institutions. The socialist sense of injustice, with dialectical materialism, concentrates upon the economic sphere. It is, of course, necessary to work through the political system; but the main aim is to achieve total reform in the economic system. The doctrine of the withering away of the state epitomizes the subordination of politics to economics in this view. The contemporary preoccupation falls initially in the psychological and the psychiatric spheres. But insofar as these internal problems are externalized, the attention is turned upon the social order which encompasses and transcends the merely economic and the merely political. The preoccupation then is with the social psychological and the social psychiatric and increasingly the sociological realm.

The Nature of the Constituency

In each major era the fundamental circumstance that has made possible the development of a revised sense of justice has been the rise in power and general standing of some major class. None of the great movements has been the product of groups who were moving downward nor of groups in abject powerlessness, poverty, or despair. There is a theory about earthquakes which says that there is a slow but imperceptible movement deep beneath the ground which continues for a period of time without compensating adjustments at the surface. Eventually so great a tension is built up that there is a sudden slippage at the surface, along an established fault line, releasing the accumulated tension in the violence of an earthquake. The important feature of this theory is that the underlying change has already occurred unnoticed and that the earthquake is merely a corrective adjustment. This is an apt model to describe what happens in our major social movements. The liberal humanitarian movements were movements of the rising industrial and business classes. They had been growing in economic power and in wealth, but their resources could not be fully converted into commensurate power and social status because of the traditional power of landowning and aristocratic classes. The liberal humanitarian movements may be regarded, first and foremost, as the readjustment through which industrial and business classes were able to throw off the traditional power of the aristocracy and the landed gentry and to assume the station in society toward which natural developments had been moving them. The specific way in which injustice was defined reflected the nature of impediments to realization of their full status by these rising classes. They already had the economic resources: all they needed was the freedom to capitalize on them. Hence, they had no occasion to think of economic deficiencies as a matter of injustice. The solution to their problem lay in undermining the monopoly of political power in the hands of the aristocracy. Hence, it appeared from their own perspective that the fundamental injustice in society was the failure to grant full participation by all the people in self-government. Of course 'all the people' initially had a rather limited meaning and was likely to be restricted to substantial citizens. Once the idea caught hold it had its own career and was extended from one group to another. But the basic notion that this was the fundamental injustice arose out of the peculiar set of conditions which at that time were preventing the rising business and industrial classes from realizing their full status in society.

The socialist movements seem to have been associated with the rising status of working classes in the societies where they prevailed. The conditions of industrial life had in fact improved the position of the labouring man. But at the same time by making him an employee of large concerns that might lay him off whenever it suited their concerns, the system had created a fundamental insecurity about economic conditions which prohibited the worker from exploiting to the full the relative wealth which he was in fact experiencing. The fact that the idea once established was then extended to the impoverished does not change the observation with regard to the source of this kind of thinking.

If my interpretation of what is happening in contemporary society is correct, we are seeing a new type of entity in society as the constituency for the dominant movements of our era. In the two previous eras the constituencies have been largely socio-economic classes, though this has been by no means clear-cut and exclusive, especially in the case of socialist movements. In the contemporary era, however, the major readjustments which are being made in society no longer concern socio-economic classes but concern *age groups*. The most striking phenomenon of the last quarter-century has been the increasing authority and independence and recognition accorded the youthful generation. There has been a reduction of parental authority and of institutional adult authority over adolescents and young adults in all spheres of life. There has been increasingly earlier introduction of children and adolescents to the major problems of our time. The rapid changes in society have meant that the technical expertise of the young is often superior to that of the more mature. Having gained considerable power and autonomy and comfort, young people now demand that the system be changed so as to remove the last restrictions to their assumption of an appropriate condition in society. In Herbert Marcuse they find a prophet who seems to declare that they are most fitted to bring about the needed transformation in society.

The problem of alienation and the sense of worth is most poignantly the problem of a youthful generation with unparalleled freedom and capability but without an institutional structure in which this capability can be appropriately realized. Adolescence is peculiarly a 'non-person' status in life. And yet this is just the period in which the technical skills and the new freedom are being markedly increased. The sense of alienation is distinctively the sense of a person who realizes great expectations for himself yet must live in a non-status.

For the movement to effect pervasive change in the institutions of society the new sense of justice must make substantial inroads outside of the movement's constituency. For this to happen, the problem at issue must not appertain exclusively to one class or age group. Political participation and economic justice had wide relevance in the eighteenth and nineteenth centuries. Today alienation is understandable to other groups than youth. The new sense of injustice can become the leaven for vast social changes because adults, the elderly, minority groups, and other organizable segments of society can see many of their own problems in the terms set forth by youthful activists.

From Chaos to Focused Movements

It is crucial to observe that the new movements have not yet discovered or formulated solutions to their problem. The liberal humanitarian movements formulated the solution to their problem as one of seeking political representation with related guarantees of freedom of speech, assembly, and press. The socialist movements defined their problem and identified the solution as either the dictatorship of the proletariat in the communist version or some form of welfare state in more moderate socialist versions. The contemporary movement is discovering the problem of alienation, is expressing indignation against society as the source of that alienation, but has not yet discovered or agreed upon a solution to the problem.

Solutions as Myths

It is important to recognize that all conceptions of rights are myths in the sense that they are practically unattainable. The idea of full participation by all the people in determining their destiny is surely a myth. We know that no system of representation can truly promise complete embodiment of the myth. Likewise we know that a doctrine such as 'from each man according to his ability, and to each man according to his need', is more effective as a slogan than it is as a measure of the working of a system. But what each of these prior movements has done is to go first through a period of 'crying out' about the problem of their era, and then gradually to reach an agreement with regard to the diagnosis and the procedures for correcting the condition. It would be most correct to say that the constituency of the movement comes to a tacit agreement that certain specific procedures and conditions shall be accepted as constituting achievement of the goal. Thus, the constituency of the liberal humanitarian movement agreed tacitly that the attainment of universal suffrage and a representative and free electoral system would be acceptable as constituting the achievement of the liberal aim. The critic can easily show that this is only partially the case. The important circumstance permitting a movement to develop and to focus its activities effectively so as to bring about reform was that people essentially agreed to believe in a falsehood. They agreed not to notice that the programme they had accepted would not actually be more than a limited step in the direction of the ideal of justice that formed the background for their movement.

Prior to the establishment and acceptance of the movement's fiction there can be little more than aimless protest, and the general pattern is one of disruption. There is characteristically a period of rather unpredictable and incomprehensible protest. The movement at this stage finds expression by going off in many different directions. The larger audience that has not yet accepted the new sense of injustice can see no rhyme or reason to the protest. Within each era, anarchy comes to be one conception, though a passing one, of the solution to the problem. Anarchy would bring an end to the restraints on the business and industrial classes. Anarchy would destroy the rule of the capitalist over the worker. Today, anarchy looms large as a theme in the new movements, promising a way to free youth from the restraints imposed by their elders. Students of contemporary protest have often interpreted the activities of youthful protesters and black power advocates as anarchistic. But if our inference from previous developments is correct, anarchy looms large during that preliminary stage after a new conception of injustice has taken hold within a core group, but when there has been no agreed-upon programme as yet for the reform of the injustice in question.

Within the next decade or two we look for the emergence of some widely accepted schemes for the elimination of alienation in society. These schemes will surely involve a somewhat more satisfying status for the young. The penetrating social critic will, of course, see that the schemes can never guarantee freedom from difficulty in attaining a personal sense of worth. But the important thing will be that members of the movement's constituency come to agree upon the fiction that the schemes proposed will actually do away with alienation. In fact, of course, the reforms, whatever they are, will have some such effect, since it will no longer be legitimate or expected that people should feel alienation when the reforms are achieved. Thus, in our own society, many people steeped in the liberal humanitarian ideology never doubt that they play a significant role in the control of their own destinies, because they see in operation the free electoral system which they take to be the guarantee of that participation. However, until such time as a programme does achieve agreement, we must expect a continuation of anarchistic themes, of apparently random disruptive protest, of apparent blatant power plays and increasingly widespread attacks upon modern society in all of its aspects. Once the myth has found its attendant fiction, we can expect a choosing up of sides and a clear differentiation which we do not yet have between those who seek change and those who resist it. The struggle will then be focused and will proceed in a fashion which begins to show the clear pattern which as yet is lacking.

Undoubtedly the new reforms will involve some manipulation of the political structure and the economy, reflecting the accumulated experience with earlier movements. The educational system is a prime object not only because youth are in it, but because we naturally look to education for clarifications and answers when the meanings of our lives and institutions are at issue,[4] and because the tentacles of education have been spreading rapidly into every sphere of life. The increasingly close connection between the educational product and bureaucratic institutions in both the public and private sectors will surely be seen as a source of alienation. Youth are unlikely to go so far as to dismantle what S. M. Miller calls the 'credential society',[5] since the movement leadership will be largely recruited from those who are earning credentials that entitle them to favoured positions in bureaucracies. But the passive, routinized, hierarchical, and continuous nature of the passage through schooling and bureaucratic employment will assuredly be a continuing target in the developing movements.

Associated Developments

It may seem strange to seize upon a problem that is expressed by only a rather small group of people and to place so much weight on the revolt of students in the face of all that is going on in modern society. However, I believe this step is justified and can be at least rendered plausible by calling attention to certain other developments.

First of all there have been developments in our society that have preceded the emergence of alienation as a household word, and given foundation to the general emphasis upon the problem of the individual's identity and his sense of worth and the responsibility of the society to ensure these. One of the contemporary issues is the extent to which the society is obligated to supply psychiatric care as an aspect of medical care programmes. Clinics to care for physical health have long been an accepted charity and with the rise of socialized medicine, which is one of the later phases of the socialist's concern with material well-being, there has been a growing view that society is obligated to provide medical care. However, even in some of the quarters that are most advanced in this respect, there is rejection of the notion that psychiatric care should be included. Perhaps this is one of the institutional areas in which the line of transition between the old and the new is the thinnest and the most easily traversed.

Another indication of the changes that are taking place can be found in the new way of viewing the concept of guilt. It is instructive to compare the earlier writings of Margaret Mead with the more recent writings of Helen Merrill Lynd. Margaret Mead distinguished guilt, as a highly internalized sense of right and wrong, from shame, that involved a more external sense.[6] In societies dominated by shame one does not feel upset about doing wrong, but only about being discovered or exposed in the act of doing wrong. In societies dominated by guilt one feels bad about the very idea of doing wrong, whether he is exposed or not. In this view of course, guilt represents a higher dedication to one's ideals and values, and under some circumstances it may be a good thing that people do experience guilt. Helen Lynd, on the other hand, seems to extend the implication of Freud's views more fully, and guilt becomes an unqualified evil thing.[7] It becomes the impediment to individual autonomy and to an individual sense of worth. Guilt is the invasion of the self by arbitrary and external standards. We have the impression that Lynd's usage has been gaining currency at the expense of Margaret Mead's.

The civil rights movement, as we have said, is partly a matter of winding up the unfinished business of the liberal humanitarian and the socialist movements. But there are at least two features which are striking about the contemporary civil rights movements that are not so apparent at an earlier period. First of all, the present activist movements among blacks are the movements of youth. They represent a rejection of the more mature leadership of a decade or two ago. The middle-aged Negroes are often caught in ambivalence, between hoping that some good may come from violent protest, yet fearing for their own total loss of control over Negro youth.

The second observation is that the theme of achieving human dignity and a sense of personal worth is beginning to play a larger and larger part in the ideology of Black protest. Carmichael and Hamilton's book on Black Power is predominantly the demand for an identity which can give the ordinary individual dignity and self respect.[8] The repudiation of integration is an assertion of personal worth, renouncing the idea that a black would demean himself to the extent of wanting to be accepted among whites. Insofar as many Negroes who are themselves perfectly capable of economic success and full participation in political process are brought into the movement in support of the more extreme factions, the emphasis again is upon the desire to make the identity 'Black' a matter of pride which can be the base for a sense of social worth. As Victor Palmeri remarked, "The name of the game now is status and identity, and only measures that reach those issues can be expected to have effect."[9]

Finally, there remains the question whether an age group can launch and carry a major movement for the reform of society in the way that an economic class can do so. Normally an economic class is one's life long membership group. The age group is intrinsically transitional, unless its span is artificially extended by the refusal to move on to a way of life appropriate to the next stage. It is very possible that youth movements are inherently abortive and can never be more than pawns in the service of other movements. Certainly most youth movements in history have been used by other groups rather than serving their own ends.[10] However, a change can well be under way. In recent times the period of youth has been starting earlier in life. High schools are beginning to show the same activism as colleges. And even junior high schools are no longer immune to organized youthful protest. Similarly the upper limits of youthfulness have been extended. The longer and longer period of college associated with graduate school have stretched the period of ambiguous status for many. If it is to be assumed that most movements cannot count on their activists remaining so for more than a decade, then there may well be an abundant supply of people who will spend from one to three years in high school and from six to ten years of college as minions of some youth movement.

The leaders of movements are often not truly members of the class in question. William Greene, of course, was not a labouring man, although he was President of the American Federation of Labor for an important period in the advancement of labour in our society. Similarly we are seeking the emergence of a new class of 'professional

598   youth'—men in their 30s, their 40s and even their 50s who identify
themselves with youth and who play the part of leaders in youthful
movements. David Riesman writes, 'For the last several years I have
been inquiring of every case of student protest in a university to discover whether it has proceeded without faculty legitimation or not.
There may be such cases, but I have not encountered them.'[11] Hence
youth may be for the first time an adequate constituency to carry the
major movements that shape the character of social change in our
society during the second half of the twentieth century.

The task of inferring the direction of long-term developments
while they are yet at an early stage is a prodigious one, demanding
more of intuition than of the conventional methods of social scientists.
Setting aside scientific caution, we have presented the fruits of such
intuitive reflection on the course of collective behaviour in the second
half of the twentieth century. Drawing upon one interpretation of the
earlier eras of liberal-humanitarian and socialist movements, we propose that a new era of social movements may be taking shape. The
emergent norm—the new sense of what is just and unjust—that is
central to these movements is the view that men have the right to demand assurance of a sense of personal worth from society. Alienation
in its more psychological meaning and the quest for identity become
the main complaints, and existentialism is the philosophy that serves
the ideologists of the new movements. The novel idea—not yet generally
accepted—that lack of a sense of personal worth is not private misfortune but public injustice is carried by youth, who are the main
constituency for the new movements in the same manner that a rising
industrial class and later a rising working class were constituencies
in the earlier eras. This theme colours to some degree all other important movements in the current era, such as 'Black Power' with its
greater emphasis on identity and self respect than on the traditional
goals of political participation or economic security. The myth that
defines the solution to injustice has not yet been formulated or disseminated, with the result that anarchy and unfocused disruptiveness
prevail. Not until such a myth has been generated and accepted as
sacred belief by a large part of the constituency will random disorder
and anarchy give way to relatively disciplined movements, with strategies geared to the promotion of identifiable reforms and transformations in society.

NOTES

1. This statement represents an extension of the *emergent norm* approach to
collective behaviour, applied earlier to crowd behaviour. Cf. 'Collective Behavior'
in R. E. L. Faris (ed.) *Handbook of Modern Sociology* (Chicago: Rand Mc-
Nally, 1964), pp. 382–425.

2. Karl Mannheim, *Ideology and Utopia*, trans. Louis Wirth and Edward
Shils (New York: Harcourt, Brace and Co., 1946).

3. Daniel Bell's classical study, *The End of Ideology* (Glencoe, Ill.: Free
Press, 1960), documents the exhaustion of these traditional ideas as spurs to
political action.

4. Suggested by Bernice Neugarten.

5. *Breaking the Credentials Barrier*, Ford Foundation reprint, 1967.

6. Margaret Mead, "Social Change and Cultural Surrogates," *J. Educational Sociol.* 14 (1940) : 92–110.

7. Helen Merrell Lynd, *On Shame and the Search for Identity* (New York: Harcourt, Brace and Co., 1958).

8. Stokely Carmichael and Charles V. Hamilton, *Black Power: The Politics of Liberation in America* (New York: Random House, 1967).

9. "Los Angeles and the Riot Report," *Los Angeles Times West Magazine,* 26 May, 1968, p. 17.

10. This is the point made by Karl Mannheim in his seminal essay, 'The Problem of Generations,' in *Essays on the Sociology of Knowledge* (London: Routledge & Kegan Paul, 1952), pp. 276–320; and amply documented by Lewis S. Feuer in *The Conflict of Generations* (New York: Basic Books, 1969).

11. Personal communication, 1968.

INTEGRATE

GHETTO

Stratification

Compromise

DYSFUNCTIONAL

REVOLUTION

Corporate   State

MERITOCRACY

EFFECTIVENESS

PROCESS-PRODUCT

TECHNOLOGY

EDUCATION   QUALITY OF LIFE

CULTURE

COUNTER

SKILL

Corporation

Group
Veto

ADAPTIVE

MOBILITY

Anomie   CHANGE   Status   SANITY   NORMS

PREJUDICE   Identification

Structural Fact   PREJUDICE

DOMINATION

Disorganization

Study Questions

1. What is your status? How mobile has your family been over the last three generations?
2. Which of the authors, Deloria, Carmichael and Hamilton, Morison, Domhoff, or Roszak appeals to you the most? In your opinion, who provides the best solutions to the problems of alienation and injustice in our society?
3. What does "quality of life" mean to you? How would you compare the "quality of life" for you with that of your family or parents?
4. Do you consider yourself a member of the counter culture? Why? Why not?
5. Present examples of limited identifications: are they dangerous?
6. What could be some unifying goals for all Americans? How could you communicate these to all Americans?
7. Do you agree with the Carmichael and Hamilton strategy? Would Domhoff or Morison agree with the strategy?

Social Mobility, Pluralism, and the Quality of Life

15

SOCIAL MOBILITY

Social mobility is the movement of individuals and categories of people from one position in society to another. It is movement in the stratification structure—a special application of the general problem of status placement.

There are two kinds of social mobility—vertical and horizontal. Vertical mobility is movement from one division or discrete category of social class up or down to another. Horizontal mobility is movement within a division or category and has to do with people improving their lot without changing their class positions.

Mobility can be looked at either in *inter*generational or *intra*generational terms. That is, it can take place either within the life of the individual or from one generation to another.

Mobility is a demographic and structural concept. It involves a rate of behavior and is a key to better understanding our society because it is a result of the way our society is organized. The story of the folk hero who rises from poverty to the presidency of a large corporation is exciting reading and is possible in our society, but the transmission of status from one generation to another is a social fact that has greater significance than the rags-to-riches story.

MOBILITY IN THE UNITED STATES

In 1955, Mabel Newcomber studied corporation executives to better understand the differences between the economic positions of members of various generations. She found that in 1900, 72 percent of board chairmen and corporation presidents were sons of high-ranking corporate officers; in 1925, the figure was 66 percent; in 1950, 69 percent. Those sons who were not chairmen of boards or corporation presidents tended to enter professions.[1] The transmission of status among business executives seems, therefore, to be a fairly stable phenomenon.

602

In 1955, a study conducted by W. Lloyd Warner and Paul S. **603**
Lunt sampled 5,000 high-status managers whose fathers had a variety
of occupations, in an attempt to establish a relationship between the
fathers' occupations and the probability of their sons becoming members of the managerial class. They determined that there was a high
probability that sons of business executives would become business
managers. With sons of salesmen, the probability was considerably
lower; with sons of manual laborers, the probability was lower still.
This study indicates that the transmission of status is fairly constant
and highly predictable.[2] How does this come about?

One of the obvious mechanisms by which status is transmitted
is direct influence. People with money and position have contacts they
can use to find positions for their children. Money is itself a direct
influence which allows people to expose their children to a first-rate
education; and education often determines social class.

Prejudice is another direct mechanism in the transmission of
status. Membership in organizations is sometimes based on religion
or other factors that have nothing to do with performance. Some fraternities and schools recruit only "their own kind."

A third mechanism, and perhaps the most important, is the
blind acceptance of some values or standards. This indirect mechanism
categorizes people by what are thought to be criteria of performance
or achievement. In reality, however, the judgments made are restricted
to a specific group and do not sample all possible candidates. People
who are tied together through either formal and informal ties that do
not give access to other, less familiar groups may not be aware of how
their classification systems limit them.

Despite the high probability of transmission of status, social
mobility does exist in this country, and is made possible by two basic
situations—the organizational requirement of flexibility, and the constant uncontrollable fluctuation in the supply of talent.

Flexibility is necessary because society is constantly undergoing change. As technology becomes more complex, new skills are
needed, and these skills create a demand for new positions and people.
Talent occurs at all levels of society, is not under the control of the
elites, and, therefore, talented people must be recruited from whatever
social strata they occupy.

STRUCTURAL FACTORS AFFECTING MOBILITY

One factor that affects social mobility is the constant change in the
number of available positions in a complex society. In the past, the
number of white collar positions greatly increased because of new
organizational needs. This increase changed the profile of occupational
distribution. The availability of different jobs mandated the acquisition of these skills by more people, and as an individual steps into
an available position, his social class may change. Another fact that
affects mobility is the birth rate for each social class. As long as the
poor have more children than the middle class they will supply talent
which is recruited into the middle class. This demographic fact is
fundamental to the amount and rate of mobility. Finally, there can be

a change in the social status of a position. Over a period of time society can change the value it places on certain types of work. Scientists are more valued today than they were 30 years ago. Prestige varies as occupations become more or less important to the society. People can thus be mobile without changing their occupation or their geographical location.

These factors point to an important trend in American life—a trend that has been called the development of meritocracy.[3] In a meritocracy, status is conferred not by transmission through families, but by education, which becomes the key to mobility. There is ample and recent evidence for this in a work by Peter Blau and Otis D. Duncan. According to their study, a person's social class and the amount of money he will earn can be best determined by the kind of education he has had.[4] This is the meaning of meritocracy; men of power and influence are educated for their positions, and are not selected because they come from certain families or are chosen by God.

In summary, changes in the occupational structure greatly influence social mobility. This is especially true for industrial societies which are remaking the world of work and leisure. The rate of mobility in complex industrial societies such as the United States, Germany, and Sweden, is about the same—4 percent.

REVIEW AND RECONCILIATION: PLURALISM AND MOBILITY

Modern industrial society can be characterized by bureaucracy, stratification and mobility that stresses merit, the industrial organization of work, and by elements that force some social critics to call it a mass society. We have seen how mass society leads to the destructive impact of the breakup of traditional groupings and its resultant disorganization. We have seen how bureaucracy increases the scale of society and the size of organizations. We have seen how markets lead to a rationalistic, utilitarian society and the growth of organizations based on hierarchy and segmentation rather than fellowship and communality. On the one hand we have mass organization and industrialization which lead to the breakup of society, and on the other the concepts of bureaucracy and stratification which stress over-organization. Thus, there are two critical views of modern society: the first, that it is unorganized and segmented, the second that it is overorganized, that every aspect of our lives is controlled. Are these opposite views based on conflicting data? Can they be reconciled? Both views seem to have validity.

A look at modern society reveals that the instruments of control and productive organization are over-organized, and that the instruments of representation are under-organized. Groups and organizations that represent us, that act as protective devices, that furnish our identity, are lacking. And these groups are the salient features of a pluralistic society.

For a pluralistic social organization to exist, there must be heterogeneity of power. There must also be diverse interests. There must be plural centers of organization—effective groups that serve as bases of political socialization, communication, and power. These groups must vie in the political arena for their own interests. They must be neither completely independent nor fractionated, but broadly based with cross-cutting memberships. If these factors exist, the competing interests of the groups will lead to complicated networks of compromise, and social order will evolve. Each group will have a stake in the society and a commitment to abide by the society's rules.

There have been several critiques of the pluralistic scheme. David Riesman supplies one which supports the pluralistic view, yet examines its flaws. According to Riesman, who sees American society as pluralistic, veto groups prevent domination by any one group. The moment one group with a particular goal develops, another group arises to oppose that goal. Riesman argues that integration and compromise—inherent in true pluralism—which prevent domination, also destroy effectiveness. Political goals cannot be achieved with veto groups in a pluralistic society, because there is not enough power to accomplish overall societal goals, but only enough to thwart the goals of the opposition.[5]

The critique presented by C. Wright Mills examines pluralism in a very different way. Mills denies that the society of the United States is pluralistic. He says that while there may be elites in different sectors of society, these elite groups do not all have the same degree of power or effectiveness. However, different elite groups may converge because of similar interests or because of the interlocking of formal or informal organizations.[6] Both Mills and Fred J. Cook take the position that politicians, military and business leaders all cooperate to make big government, big profits, and a big arms race.[7] They counter the notion that elite groups may make concessions by arguing that the concessions they make are neither important nor do they have impact. The power of such a group is not an abstraction, but is very much an issue in your lives.

It is difficult to determine which one of the foregoing theories is closer to social reality. An individual's point of view regarding the existence of a pluralistic society depends, at least in part, upon his social position and power. Distance from the sources of power appear to create perceptual difference in the evaluation of social reality. People who are close to the center of power seem to accept the notion of pluralism much more readily than those who are not. If a group is not represented in the pluralistic structure, its members generally reject the theory of pluralism as a mediating force between individuals and their government.

In a system like ours, which stresses stratification and mobility, pure pluralism is impossible. There is an important conceptual relation between the possibility of pluralism and the fact of social class. The procedural norms that tell us how to get to the top take account of ability. But even though these procedural norms are specified, other variables such as family influence and prejudice are free to operate. Procedural norms may stress the notion of merit and ability but they do not prevent manipulation by groups with power. Ideally, all groups are equally represented in a pluralistic society that emphasizes mobility based on merit. In reality, however, the notion of organizational effectiveness prevents the representation of certain interests. That is why we have class domination in the political scene and why we have more and more protest, such as sit-ins and strikes, from the unrepresented of our society. It would seem then that the wealthy and the established have little to protest about; that only the disaffected, the uneducated, the insulted and the injured have many grievances. This is however not true, for the quality of life affects all members of society. While equal opportunity is an ideological value in our country, that value position is not closely related to the way social organization actually operates.

SOCIAL ORGANIZATION AND THE QUALITY OF LIFE

The selections in this book are all based on the assumption, implicit and explicit, that to be human is to participate in group life, in organization, in concert with others. I have stressed the theme of social organizations as something apart from an individual actor's intentions, motivations, and dispositions.

Social organization is something beyond the mere intentions and motivations of men. Social organization has a reality of its own and is intimately connected with the notion of quality of life. I explain the phrase "quality of life" by referring to four levels of reality that occur at each level of analysis described in chapter 2. At the organic level I think of the material things that nurture the organism; good food, fresh air, clean water, decent housing, and good medical care. At the psychological level I speculate about the educational system that teaches and nurtures the child, the mental health services available, and the sense of security, trust, and well-being that the community and society provide the person. At the social level I am concerned with adequate organization of the instruments of production and the decentralization of the instruments of control. I am also concerned with the role of ethnic minorities, the poor and the young in our political processes. At the cultural level, I am concerned with facts such as governmental and public support for a national and local theatres, educational television, individual musicians, dancers, sculptors, and painters being minimal. The summary phrase "quality of life" implies all of the above and I believe that most of us will agree that the quality of life, as we move into the 1970s, is bleak and going down. The relationship between social organization and the quality of life is implied throughout this book.

Whether you read about communication networks or bureaucracy, these group facts reveal the importance of this relationship. Moreover, you have seen how the quality of life was transformed by the development of a market economy. In modern society, with increasing specialization and interdependence, imperative order becomes critical, and there is emphasis on universalism and performance. Some social critics believe that impersonal, segmented participation is desirable because, by giving only parts of ourselves in specific situations, we can experience life in more varied ways. This is the view expressed by Harry Morton:

The fact that we approach life today without feeling the need for a big key that fits everything together as one great whole, and are able to concentrate instead on isolating particular issues, and dealing with them as they come up, shows that we have a basic confidence that the world is held together, is strong, is self consistent, has regularity in it, and can be put to the test without everything in life going to pieces."[8]

Other social critics argue that people in modern society lack solidarity, anchorage, and identity. They feel that each man wants to find his niche but does not know where the niches are. Anomie, a condition described by Emile Durkheim, occurs when traditional norms have broken down; when meanings are unclear; when positions and niches can no longer be located. Anomie can be considered the antithesis of order. There is the expectation that one's own behavior cannot determine the outcome he seeks. There is also an inability to interpret events in the environment as right or wrong.

One important issue is whether there is a place for you. Are there cohesive organizations with which you are actively involved that protect your interests? Do you see the possibility of improving the quality of life for yourself and others? Each of the authors in this final chapter proposes a vision of what is possible for America and Americans.

The first article in this chapter is an excerpt from lawyer Vine Deloria, Jr's book, *Custer Died for Your Sins*. Deloria is a Sioux and writes savagely and passionately about the experiences and misperceptions of Indians by whites. He describes some of the parallels between Indian tribes and modern corporate structure and believes that a truce will be established between industrial America and American Indians. Deloria argues that nationalism rather than militancy will help bring a better future for all Americans.

The second article is by Theodore Roszak, an historian who writes about the development of a new value scheme and a new culture among young people. In his book *The Making of a Counter Culture*, Roszak describes the reason for the creation of the counter culture and the intellectual sources of the movement. The excerpt you will be reading describes the main thrust of the counter culture.

The third article, "The Search for New Forms," is written by the former head of SNCC, Stokely Carmichael, and the political scientist, Charles V. Hamilton, and is taken from their book, *Black Power: The Politics of Liberation in America*. Their concern is with an independent politics for blacks as a beginning step towards liberation.

The fourth article is also written by an historian, Elting E. Morison, who discusses the introduction of a single technological change in the United States Navy—continuous-aim firing. He describes and analyzes how this change was introduced, how it was opposed, and how the change was finally accepted by the navy. From this case study Morison goes on to develop some tentative conclusions about change in social life. He points to the importance of having identifications that are beyond one's personal interest and to a concern for process rather than product. Whether American society will develop some unifying goal for its diverse elements is an important question. The last article, by psychologist G. William Dumhoff, discusses in detail the possibilities and problems involved in nonmilitary revolution.

All six authors pose significant and pertinent questions about the present social organization of American society. Each one offers possible solutions to problems of our future as citizens and members of the human race.

NOTES

1. Mabel Newcomber, *The Big Business Executive* (New York: Columbia University Press, 1955).

2. W. Lloyd Warner and Paul S. Lunt, *The Social Life of a Modern Community* (New Haven: Yale University Press, 1941).

3. Michael Donlop Young, *The Rise of Meritocracy* (London: Thames & Hudson, 1958).

4. Peter Blau and Dudley Duncan, *The American Occupational Structure* (New York: John Wiley, 1967), p. 403.

5. David Riesman, "Who Has the Power?" from *The Lonely Crowd* (New Haven: Yale University Press, 1951).

6. C. Wright Mills, *The Power Elite* (New York: Oxford University Press, 1956).

7. Fred J. Cook, *The F. B. I. Nobody Knows* (New York: Macmillan Co., 1964).

8. Harry O. Morton, *The Mastery of Technological Civilization*, cited in Harvey Cox, *The Secular City* (New York: Macmillan Co., 1965), p. 66.

VINE DELORIA, JR.

Indians and Modern Society

One of the intriguing little puzzles which anthropologists, Congressmen, missionaries, educators, and others often pose for themselves is whether an Indian tribe can survive in a modern setting. For the most part the question is posed as if the Indians were just coming out of the woods with their flint-tipped arrows and were demonstrating an unusual amount of curiosity about the printing press, the choochoo train, the pop machine, and other marvels of civilized man.

Black militants overbearingly tell Indians to "revolt, confront, destroy," the "powerstructure" that oppresses them. Confusing notori-

INDIANS AND MODERN SOCIETY

ety with success, they equate confusion with progress, draw on their vast storehouses of knowledge of the modern world, and advise Indians to become militant.

Everywhere an Indian turns he is deluged with offers of assistance, with good, bad, and irrelevant advice, and with proposals designed to cure everything from poverty to dandruff. Rarely does anyone ask an Indian what he thinks about the modern world. So assured is modern man that he has absolute control of himself and his society that there is never any question but what Indians are moving, albeit slowly and inefficiently, toward that great and blessed land of suburban America, the mecca for all people.

When an Indian considers the modern world, however, he sees being inevitably drawn into social structures in which tribalism appears to be the only valid form of supra-individual participation. The humor becomes apparent when the Indian realizes that if he simply steps to the sidelines and watches the rat race go past him, soon people will be coming to him to advise him to return to tribalism. It appears to many Indians that someday soon the modern world will be ready to understand itself and, perhaps, the Indian people.

In March of 1968 the Southern Christian Leadership Conference began plans to have a massive march on Washington. The march was to be comparable, SCLC hoped, to the great marches of the past which had been instrumental in producing Civil Rights legislation. The purpose of the Poor People's Campaign was to bring attention to the plight of the poor with the hopes that Congress, which was then considering a six-billion-dollar cut in social welfare programs, would respond with a gigantic outpouring of funds to eradicate poverty. As the Poor People's Campaign gained momentum the purpose narrowed to the proposition of guaranteed jobs or a guaranteed annual income.

Notably absent from the list of supporting organizations in the campaign was the Congress of Racial Equality. CORE had been a leader in the Civil Rights struggles of the past. It was headed by black nationalists who endorsed black power. It was regarded as one of the militant left-leaning organizations of blacks in the nation. But CORE refused to fall into line with the campaign because it was busy taking another approach to the problems of black poverty.

The CORE solution was unveiled in July of 1968 at a joint news conference which featured Roy Innis, Acting Director of CORE, and four Republican Congressmen, Charles Goodell of New York, Robert Taft, Jr., of Ohio, Thomas Curtis of Missouri, and William Widnall of New Jersey. CORE proposed the Community Self Determination Act, which was designed to promote black capitalism of which CORE and Richard Nixon had both cooed approvingly earlier in the year.

The basic thrust of the Community Self-Determination Act of 1969 (which was not passed in the Ninetieth Congress but which has now been introduced again) was the Community Development Corporation. The Community Development Corporation, called affectionately CDC in the news conference, was to operate in six categories of activity:

1. Provider of neighborhood services and community improvement: basic education, child welfare, day care, pre-school training, health, consumer education, home ownership counseling, college placement, job finding, recreation, legal aid, and other services now available from federal sources.
2. Owner of stock of business enterprises.
3. Sponsor, owner, or manager of housing in the community.
4. Planning agency for neighborhood renewal.
5. Representative of community interests in areas of public policy.
6. Encourager of outside financial sources to assist self-help efforts of the community.

In short, the CDC was to be the all-purpose corporation by which black poverty was to be eliminated from the black ghettos and self-determination given to ghetto areas. The CDC was hailed as an important new step in the development of black pride and initiative in the private area.

If the CDC was brand-new for blacks it had a mighty familiar ring to the Indian people. The tribal council, as set up under the Indian Reorganization Act, had precisely the same powers, functions, and intents. Indians have been using the tribal council as organized under IRA for nearly a generation. As Indians viewed the "new" CDC, the blacks were finally ready to tribalize. One young Indian waggishly suggested that if they made up enrollments they might call them blacklists.

In the corporate structure, formal and informal, Indian tribalism has its greatest parallels and it is through this means that Indians believe that modern society and Indian tribes will finally reach a cultural truce. The corporation forms the closest attempt of the white man to socialize his individualism and become a tribal man. And certainly when one thinks back to what has been written over the last decade about corporate existence, one can see the startling parallels.

The devastating books of Vance Packard and William H. White outlined in detail how the corporation impinges upon individual man in his private life and reorients him toward non-indivdual goals. In the 1950s no existence was hated by the undergraduate as much as that of the organization man. The early beatnik and his descendant, the hippie, both abhorred the organization man. Many a career was nipped in the bud rather than let it develop in the insidious ways of corporate existence.

But in the corporation, man was offered a tribal existence of security and ease. The corporation provided everything a man might need if he were to maintain an affluent life over and above that of non-corporate man and befitting a person of vast educational achievement. The higher the degree, the more privileges bestowed upon corporate man. With untold fringe benefits covering all conceivable circumstances which might arise, organization man dwelt in an economic tribe to which he needed only give his allegiance and daylight hours.

In return he had social and economic security rarely equalled since the days of feudalism.

Post-war developments of the corporation created the phenomenon of the merger. As corporations were piled together to form conglomrates, it became possible for a man to work for a great many corporations which were enclosed within one monstrous holding corporation so diversified that it rarely knew how far its tentacles extended.

The corporation became comparable to the great Indian coalitions such as the Iroquois and the Creek confederacies which stretched for thousands of square miles and in which a member was entirely safe and at home. And like the Indian tribes, success was measured against those outside the corporations, by prestige and honors. Where eagle feathers measured an Indian's successes, thickness of carpets measured executive success. Where a war chief might be given his choice of the loot of a war, the annual bonus and stock option became a regular means of rewarding the successful executive, home fresh from the competitive wars.

In short, corporate life since the last world war has structured itself along the lines taken a couple of centuries earlier by Indian tribes as they developed their customs and traditions of social existence. Totems have been replaced by trade marks, powwows by conventions, and beads by gray flannels. War songs have been replaced by advertising slogans. As in the tribe, so in the corporation the "chief" reigns supreme.

The life of the rugged individualist, beloved hero of Republican hymns, has now disappeared. The little family grocery or drug store, such as spawned the two chief contestants of the 1968 Presidential campaign, has now become the outpost, the frontier settlement, of the corporate conglomerate giant. Small businesses have all but vanished over the past two decades as the "chain" has driven them out of existence. Opportunity now exists within the corporate giant as a member of the tribe. The individual seeks fame only in bringing home the honors for his company.

Classifying the corporation as the tribe takes a little reorientation for most Americans because they are so quick to judge by outward appearances. Rarely do they meditate on how something really operates. Instead they want to believe that because something is shiny and appears new, it is new.

But in understanding the corporation as a form of tribalism, a number of new paths of understanding are made possible. The life of organization man is not simply one of allegiance to a cold unfeeling machine. Rather it becomes a path by which he can fulfill himself within certain limits. But going outside of the limits is taboo. It negates the existence by which organization man has defined himself and allowed himself to be defined. Just as a Cherokee or Sioux would have never done anything to eliminate himself from the tribe and accepted the limits by which the tribe governed itself, so the organization man must remain within the limits of his corporate existence.

The primary purpose of the tribe, then and now, was to ensure as beneficial a life as possible for members of the tribe. The hunting grounds of the tribe had to be defended at all costs. Outside of that, individual freedom ran rampant. Certainly the CDC proposed by CORE, which will cover all aspects of social existence, purports to do the same.

It would appear then that we are witnessing the gradual tribalizing of the white man as his economic tribes become more and more oriented toward social services for their members. What is now needed is the frank admittance by the white man that he is tribalizing and the acknowledgment that his tribalism will gradually replace government as we now know it, submerging the differentiated society into a number of related economic social units.

When executives can admit what they are doing, then it will be possible to form programs around those left out of corporate existence—the poor—and organize them as tribes also, completing the circuit from Pilgrimish individualism to corporate tribalism. Preliminary treaty-making—price fixing—has been declared wrong because it infringed upon non-corporate victims. The government decreed that until these victims became sufficiently strong to embark on corporate warfare, it would protect them. Government thus stands as arbitrator between corporate and non-corporate man, a role previously occupied by the Onondagas in the Iroquois League.

It is not only in economic terms that America is tribalizing. Scholars and students of the modern family bemoan the fact that the family unit is disappearing and members of the family now have their primary interests outside the home. The old picture of the clan gathered around the fireplace or trooping through the snow to grandmother's house is fast fading into the historical mists.

In place of the traditional family has come the activist family in which each member spends the majority of his time outside the home "participating." Clubs, committees, and leagues devour the time of the individual so that family activity is extremely limited. Competition among clubs is keenly predicated upon the proposition that each member should bring his family into its sphere. Thus Boy Scouts is made a family affair. PTA, the YMCA, the country club, every activity, competes for total family participation although it demands entry of only one member of the family.

Clubs as social tribes wage fantastic warfare for the loyalties of the individuals of a community. Their selling point is that only by participating in their activity can a family partake of the snowy trips to grandmother's house in modern terms. The numena of American mythology is plastered indiscriminately over activities in order to catch unsuspecting participants and offer a substitute existence.

The American family is thus split into a number of individuals each claiming his blood relationship as a commitment on other members of the same biological source to support his tribe as against theirs. At best it is a standoff, with each member giving half-hearted recognition of the multitude of tribes to which the family as a conglomerate belongs.

The best example in intellectual circles of a tribal phenomenon is the magazine. *Playboy* early capitalized on tribal existence, although exemplified in the hutch instead of the tipi, and turned a magazine into a way of life. If ever there was a tribal cult oozing with contemporary mythology and tribal rites it is the Playboy club. Identity is the last concern of the Playboy, yet it is what his tribe offers him— and with a key.

Perhaps the only segment of American society to face tribalism head on has been the long-haired hippie and his cousins, yippies, zippies, and others. In 1966 strange beings began to appear on Indian land, proclaiming their kinship with the redskins in no uncertain terms. Some Indians thought that the earlier VISTA program had spoiled things for the hippies by their inept performance on the reservations, but no one had seen anything until the summer of 1966.

I used to sit in my office and suddenly find it invaded by a number of strange beings in gaudy costumes who would inform me of their blood-intellectual relationship with Indians. When one is used to the strange smells of legislation written by the Interior Department and is suddenly confronted by an even more exotic perfume, it is unsettling indeed.

Yet many hippies whom I met had some basic humanistic beliefs not unlike those of Indian people. Concern for the person and abhorrence for confining rules, regulations, and traditions seemed to characterize the early hippie movement. When the hippies began to call for a gathering of the tribes, to create free stores, to share goods, and to gather all of the lost into communities, it appeared as if they were on the threshold of tribal existence.

I remember spending a whole afternoon talking with a number of hippies who had stopped in Denver on the way west. They were tribally oriented but refused to consider customs as anything more than regulations in disguise. Yet it was by rejecting customs that the hippies failed to tribalize and became comical shadows rather than modern incarnations of tribes.

Indian tribes have always had two basic internal strengths, which can also be seen in corporations: customs and clans. Tribes are not simply composed of Indians. They are highly organized as clans, within which variations of tribal traditions and customs govern. While the tribe makes decisions on general affairs, clans handle specific problems. Trivia is thus kept out of tribal affairs by referring it to clan solutions.

Customs rise as clans meet specific problems and solve them. They overflow from the clan into general tribal usage as their capability and validity are recognized. Thus a custom can spread from a minor clan to the tribe as a whole and prove to be a significant basis for tribal behavior. In the same manner, methods and techniques found useful in one phase of corporate existence can become standard operating procedure for an entire corporation.

Hippies, at least as I came to understand them, had few stable clan structures. They lived too much on the experiential plane and refused to acknowledge that there really was a world outside of their own experiences. Experience thus became the primary criteria by which the movement was understood. Social and economic stability were never allowed to take root.

It seemed ridiculous to Indian people that hippies would refuse to incorporate prestige and social status into their tribalizing attempts. Indian society is founded on status and social prestige. This largely reduces competition to inter-personal relationships instead of allowing it to run rampant in economic circles. Were competition to be confined to economic concerns, the white conception of a person as a part of the production machine would take hold, destroying the necessary value of man in his social sense.

With competition confined within social events, each man must be judged according to his real self, not according to his wealth or educational prowess. Hence a holder of great wealth is merely selfish unless he has other redeeming qualities besides his material goods. Having a number of degrees and an impressive educational background is prerequisite to prestige in the white world. It is detrimental in the Indian world unless the person has the necessary wisdom to say meaningful things also.

Hippies, at least initially, appeared to throw off the white man's prestige symbols while refusing to accept the Indian prestige symbols. Hence there was no way in which tribalism, in its most lasting form, could take root in the hippie movement. What prestige they had, came with publicity. Quickly the media turned them into a fad and the hippie with something to say became no more than Batman or the Hoola Hoop.

Additional to hippie failure to tribalize was their inability to recognize the existence of tribal capital, particularly land. Tribal existence has always been predicated upon a land base, a homeland, within which tribal existences could take place. The primary concern of Indian tribes has been the protection of the land to which they are related. Once landless, a people must fall back upon religion, social values, or political power. But with a land base, nationalism in a tribal setting is more possible.

Only a very few hippies made an effort to develop a land base. A few communes are beginning to spring up around the country. But most of the flowers, unfortunately, have yet to be planted.

Inter-corporate competition has revealed the necessity of banding together for political purposes to defend hunting grounds, be it oil import quotas, tariffs, or subsidies. In this respect white corporations are more aware of the inevitability of conflict than are Indian tribes. Whites know how to best use the corporate structure in an infinite variety of ways. And they know how to manipulate the governmental structure to obtain the goals of their corporations.

Some corporations, particularly social corporations such as those listed annually in the various United Fund appeals, have already mastered the technique of taxing the rest of society to support their ventures. They are thus one step beyond even the profit-making corporations which offer a substantial number of fringe benefits to their employees.

The United Fund agencies have achieved a status comparable to the Magi of yesteryear. The Magi, conquered by the Persians, promptly set themselves up as religious experts and soon exercised incredible control over Persian society. They burrowed right into the fabric of Persian life and dominated it. In the same way, United Fund agencies have captured the priesthood of social activity and now exact their pound of flesh as necessary organizations upon which the life-blood of the community depends.

Examine, if you will, the agencies listed in the United Fund appeal the next time you are called upon to give. By and large they all do what everyone else is doing. Only, they appear to be doing it somehow differently. Had they been active in a meaningful pro-grammatic manner, it would have been unnecessary for the govern-ment to conduct a War on Poverty. But should the government win its War on Poverty tomorrow, United Fund agencies would continue on their merry way.

What then is the genius of the United Fund agency? We called them above, the priesthood of our society and they *are* priests in the mediating sense. Where fraternities, sororities, and service clubs have the same basic clientele, United Fund agencies have developed a me-diating role between diverse segments of society. They collect from one set of clientele and distribute to another set. Thus, as interme-diaries they cannot be eliminated because they would leave two diverse sets of clients with peculiar needs—those who need to give and those who need to receive.

As the fortunes of agencies and foundations like the United Fund rise and fall, so do tribalism and tribal existence. These agencies are the weathervane of our society. We can tell at a glance how our society is responding to the expansion of tribal corporations by their progress and setbacks. As tribal corporations meet the challenges of modern life, there will be less use for United Fund agencies and their revenues and programs will decline. But if the tendency is away from tribalized existence on the corporate level, these agencies will expand and their revenues will increase. People will need to become more meaningfully involved and will seek out both services and recipients for their funds. Thus such agencies are an accurate indicator of giving and receiving in our society. From them we can take one cue as to what the future holds.

There is another aspect of modern society to which Indian society relates and that is law. The evolution of law is as fascinating as it is complex. The manner in which Indians and law can combine in the modern world depends upon an understanding of the nuances of law.

We first came across law in its original cradle of tribalism in the Old Testament. Torah, law, comes from a root word meaning to extend one's hand as if pointing the way. A careful reading of the Old Testament and its concern for law can reveal—as it does for the jews—

a standard of behavior by which a person can be fulfilled. Thus originally law was not confining or regulating but indicating the way to a better life.

In feudal days law once again rose from the ruins of Roman codification as customs gradually became the laws of England and western European civilization. Only in certain aspects were early laws regulatory or confining. In most cases they were indicative of interpersonal relationships.

The history of America has shown the gradual replacement of custom and common law with regulatory statutes and programs so that law today is more a case of legalizing certain types of behavior and penalizing other types of behavior. We are just passing through the most radical period of law as a confining instrument of social control.

The programs initiated by President Johnson are sometimes looked at as the logical extension of the New Deal concept of government as development agent for social welfare programs. It has been said that the War on Poverty was simply a rehash of the WPA projects and the CCC camps. But close examination of the Economic Opportunity Act, the Economic Development Act, the Model Cities programs, Urban Renewal, and other Great Society programs will reveal a basic foundation completely foreign to New Deal concepts. All of these programs are founded upon the premise that the federal government must help local efforts to accomplish certain things, but that government itself cannot do those things for local people. Law has thus begun a new cycle of existence as a means to social fulfillment.

Programs of the Great Society point the way toward experimentation by local people in various ways and means of creating a more meaningful existence. They therefore become vehicles for change and fulfillment of potential, rather than payoffs in modern economic ventures. While there is no doubt that Great Society programs have political overtones, within certain limits most American citizens can participate in them.

The great fear of minority groups in the 1968 elections was that law and order meant a return to the conception of law as an instrument of confinement and away from the idea of law as an expansion of opportunities. Regulated existence has rarely been able to provide the stability and potential which societies need to survive. When codification has been emphasized, societies have tended to decline because law has traditionally been a means of confinement and oppression.

When law takes on its most creative aspect, customs develop to operate internally within the social structure. The vacuum created by expanding and developing programs and laws gives rise to the need for internal controls by which men can govern themselves. Customs naturally arise to fill this need and custom depends upon participation by all members of society.

A good example of custom is the American system of two political parties as an undefined adjunct to the Constitution. Nowhere does the Constitution outline the need or the structure for political participation. No parties are mentioned. They have arisen through customs which filled in the missing pieces of the Constitution. No one had to follow one path or another. But over the years a significant number of citizens adopted the same customs and the great political processes of our nation took shape.

As the political parties became structured with rules and regulations, additional customs arose which by their solution gave meaning to the unarticulated problems of the process. Thus, for example, for a while the candidate remained at home awaiting the demand of the people that he become a candidate. This custom was overcome by Roosevelt's daring visit to the convention in 1932 and the rise of primaries in the various states.

As we become aware of our customs we will become more able to live in a tribalizing world. Tribal society does not depend upon legislative enactment. It depends heavily in most areas upon customs which fill in the superstructure of society with meaningful forms of behavior and which are constantly changing because of the demands made upon them by people.

One of the chief customs in Indian life is the idea of compensation instead of retribution in criminal law. Arbitrary punishment, no matter how apparently suitable to the crime, has had little place in Indian society. These customs have by and large endured and many tribes still feel that if the culprit makes a suitable restitution to his victim no further punishment need be meted out by the tribe.

Contrast this outlook with the highly emotional appeals to "lawnorder" over the last year and it is easy to see that the white man's conception of criminal law has changed little from the harsh code of the ancient eastern despots. America's prison population continues to climb as society attempts to punish those guilty of violating its mores. Little is done to restore the victim to his original state. The emphasis is on "getting even" on the victim's behalf by imposing a term of imprisonment on the offender.

With the passage of the 1968 Civil Rights Act, Indian tribes fell victim to the Bill of Rights. The stage is now set for total erosion of traditional customs by sterile codes devised by the white man. Some tribes are now fighting to get the law amended because the law allows reliance on traditional Indian solutions only to the extent that they do not conflict with state and federal laws.

Although the Bill of Rights is not popular with some tribes, the Pueblos in particular, I do not believe that it should be amended. With the strengthening of tribal courts Indian tribes now have a golden opportunity to create an Indian common law comparable to the early English common law.

Many national leaders have encouraged Indian judges to write lengthy opinions on their cases incorporating tribal customs and beliefs with state and federal codes and thus redirecting tribal ordinances toward a new goal. Over the next decade the response by Indian judges in tribal court may well prove influential in the field of law. Perhaps the kindest thing that could be said of non-Indian law at present is

618

that it combines punishment and rehabilitation in most instances. With a additional push for compensatory solutions Indian people could contribute much to the solution of the problem of crime in the larger society.

The stage is now being set, with the increasing number of Indian college students graduating from the universities, for a total assault on the non-human elements of white society. Ideologically the young Indians are refusing to accept white values as eternal truths. Such anomalies as starvation in the midst of plenty indicate to them that the older Indian ways are probably best for them.

Movements to re-educate Indians along liberal lines only serve to increase the visibility of the differences between their own backgrounds and the backgrounds of the non-Indians. Yet the bicultural trap, conceptually laid for Indians by scholars, does not appear to be ensnaring the most astute young Indian people. Accommodation to white society is primarily in terms of gaining additional techniques by which they can give a deeper root to existing Indian traditions.

The corporaton serves as the technical weapon by which Indian revivalism can be accomplished. At the same time it is that element of white culture closest to the tribe and can thereby enable it to understand both white and Indian ways of doing business. As programs become available, tribal councils should simply form themselves as housing authorities, development corporations, and training program supervisors, continuing to do business according to Indian ways. The tribe is thus absorbing the corporation as a handy tool for its own purposes.

Of all the schemes advocated today for the solution of poverty, the guaranteed annual income appears to be the most threatening to ultimate tribal progress. Guaranteed annual income would merely accelerate the inertia which continues to nip at the heels of reservation development. Yet the humanistic basis of the guaranteed annual income is solidly within Indian traditions.

In the old days a tribe suffered and prospered as a unity. When hunting was good everyone ate, when it was bad everyone suffered. Never was the tribe overbalanced economically so that half would always starve and half would thrive. In this sense all tribal members had a guaranteed annual income.

With the basic necessities guaranteed by tribal membership, means had to be devised to grade the tribe into a social ladder. Exploits in hunting, warfare, and religious leadership effectively created status necessary to structure the interpersonal relationships within the tribe. A man was judged by what he was, not by what he owned.

Society today has largely drifted away from accomplishments. Concern is focused instead on "image"—what a man appears to be, not what he is. Thus the 1968 elections saw Richard Nixon cautiously refuse to face any issues which might have taken votes away from him. In previous years the Kennedys made even greater use of image and it will probably never be known exactly what the Kennedys accomplished on behalf of their constituency. People will rather remember Jack and Bobby as they appeared on television.

As Indians continue to appear in modern society other issues will come to be drawn in certain areas. Some tribes have zoned their reservations so that the land is used primarily for the benefit of reservation people. Gradually planners in the white society will come to recognize the necessity of reserving land for specific use rather than allow helter-skelter development to continue unchecked.

Education must also be revamped; not to make Indians more acceptable to white society, but to allow non-Indians a greater chance to develop their talents. Education as it is designed today works to destroy communities by creating supermen who spend their lives climbing the economic ladder. America is thus always on the move and neighborhoods rarely have a stable lasting residency. In the future, minority groups must emphasize what they share with the white society, not what keeps them apart. Black may be beautiful but such a slogan hardly contributes to the understanding of non-blacks. Intensity turns easily to violence when it has no traditions and customs to channel it into constructive paths of behavior. The powwow serves as more than a historical re-enactment of ancient ways. In a larger sense it provides an emotional release heavily charged with psychological and identity-absorbing tensions. This is perhaps one reason why "red is beautiful" has not become a necessary slogan.

Non-Indians must understand the differences, at least as seen in Indian country, between nationalism and militancy. Most Indians are nationalists. That is, they are primarily concerned with development and continuance of the tribe. As nationalists, Indians could not, for the most part, care less what the rest of society does. They are interested in the progress of the tribe.

Militants, on the other hand, are reactionists. They understand the white society and they progress by reacting against it. First in their ideas is the necessity for forcing a decision from those in decision-making positions. Few militants would be sophisticated enough to plan a strategy of undermining the ideological and philosophical positions of the establishment and capturing its programs for their own use.

Nationalists always have the option of resorting to violence and demonstrations. Militants shoot their arsenal merely to attract attention and are left without any visible means to accomplish their goals. Hence militancy must inevitably lead on to more militancy. This is apparent in the dilemma in which the SCLC found itself after the 1966 Civil Rights Bill. Demonstrations had proved successful and so SCLC found itself led on and on down that path, never satisfied. Even after King's death, when SCLC could have changed its goals and techniques, it continued to the disaster of Resurrection City.

But Indian tribes riding the crest of tribal and nationalistic waves will be able to accomplish a great many things previously thought impossible by Indian and non-Indian alike. There is every indication that as Indians articulate values they wish to transmit to the rest of society, they will be able to exert a definite influence on social developments.

At present the visible poverty of Indian tribes veils the great potential of the Indian people from modern society. But in many ways

620   the veil is lifting and a brighter future is being seen. Night is giving way to day. The Indian will soon stand tall and strong once more.

THEODORE ROSZAK

The Making of a Counter Culture

In the "today," in every "today," various generations coexist and the relations which are established between them, according to the different conditions of their ages, represent the dynamic system of attractions and repulsions, of agreement and controversy which at any given moment makes up the reality of historic life.[1]

If we agree with Ortega that the fitful transition of the generations is a significant element in historical change, we must also recognize that the young may do little more than remodel the inherited culture in minor or marginal ways. They may settle for alterations that amount to a change of superficial fashion, undertaken out of mere pique or caprice. What is special about the generational transition we are in is the scale on which it is taking place and the depth of antagonism it reveals. Indeed, it would hardly seem an exaggeration to call what we see arising among the young a "counter culture." Meaning: a culture so radically disaffiliated from the mainstream assumptions of our society that it scarcely looks to many as a culture at all, but takes on the alarming appearance of a barbaric intrusion.

An image comes at once to mind: the invasion of centaurs that is recorded on the pediment of the Temple of Zeus at Olympia. Drunken and incensed, the centaurs burst in upon the civilized festivities that are in progress. But a stern Apollo, the guardian of the orthodox culture, steps forward to admonish the gate-crashers and drive them back. The image is a potent one, for it recalls what must always be a fearful experience in the life of any civilization: the experience of radical cultural disjuncture, the clash of irreconcilable conceptions of life. And the encounter is not always won by Apollo.

*   *   *

Perhaps the young of this generation haven't the stamina to launch the epochal transformation they seek; but there should be no mistaking the fact that they want nothing less. "Total rejection" is a phrase that comes readily to their lips, often before the mind provides even a blurred picture of the new culture that is to displace the old. If there is anything about the ethos of Black Power that proves particularly attractive even to young white disaffiliates who cannot gain access to the movement, it is the sense that Black Power somehow implies an entirely new way of life: a black culture, a black consciousness . . . a black soul which is totally incompatible with white society and aggressively proud of the fact. Black Power may build any number of barriers between white and Negro youth, but across the barriers a common language can still be heard. Here, for example, is Bobby Seale of the Oakland Black Panthers speaking to a meeting of the Center for Participative Education held at the University of California at Berkeley in September 1968. The crisis at hand stemmed from a decision of the UC regents to deny a Black Panther spokesman access to the campus. But for Seale, as for the students, the issue had deeper cultural implications. Everything—the meaning of authority, of personal identity, of Judeo-Christian ethics, of sexual freedom—was somehow involved in this single act of administrative censorship.

Archie and Jughead never kissed Veronica and Betty. Superman never kissed Lois Lane. We are tired of relating to comic book conceptions. Adam should have defended the Garden of Eden against the omnipotent administrator. Life, liberty, and the pursuit of happiness don't mean nothing to me if I can't go home and feel safe with my wife in bed replenishing the earth.[2]

At first glance, it may not be apparent what sentiments of this kind (and they were the substance of the address) have to do with an issue of academic freedom. But Seale's audience had no trouble understanding. They readily recognized that authoritarianism in our society operates overtly or subtly at every level of life, from comic strip imagery to Christian theology, from the college classroom to the privacy of the bedroom—and they were prepared to discard the culture that relied on such sleazy coercion, root and branch. . . . I believe that, despite their follies, these young centaurs deserve to win their encounter with the defending Apollos of our society. For the orthodox culture they confront is fatally and contagiously diseased. The prime symptom of that disease is the shadow of thermonuclear annihilation beneath which we cower. The counter culture takes its stand against the background of this absolute evil, an evil which is not defined by the sheer *fact* of the bomb, but by the total *ethos* of the bomb, in which our politics, our public morality, our economic life, our intellectual endeavor are now embedded with a wealth of ingenious rationalization. . . .

If the counter culture is, as I will contend here, that healthy instinct which refuses both at the personal and political level to practice such a cold-blooded rape of our human sensibilities, then it should be clear why the conflict between young and adult in our time reaches so peculiarly and painfully deep. In an historical emergency of absolutely unprecedented proportions, we are that strange, culture-bound animal whose biological drive for survival expresses itself *generationally*. It is the young, arriving with eyes that can see the obvious, who must remake the lethal culture of their elders, and who must remake it in desperate haste.

* * *

To take the position I assume here is undeniably risky. For once a cultural disjuncture opens out in society, nothing can be guaranteed. What happens among the minority that finds itself isolated by the rift is as apt to be ugly or pathetic as it is to be noble. . . .

And our alienated young: how shall we characterize the counter culture they are in the way of haphazardly assembling? Clearly one cannot answer the question by producing a manifesto unanimously endorsed by the malcontented younger generation: the counter culture is scarcely so disciplined a movement. It is something in the nature of a medieval crusade: a variegated procession constantly in flux, acquiring and losing members all along the route of march. Often enough it finds its own identity in a nebulous symbol or song that seems to proclaim little more than "we are special . . . we are different . . . we are outward-bound from the old corruptions of the world." Some join the troop only for a brief while, long enough to enter an obvious and immediate struggle: a campus rebellion, an act of war-resistance, a demonstration against racial injustice. Some may do no more than flourish a tiny banner against the inhumanities of the technocracy; perhaps they pin on a button declaring "I am a human being: do not mutilate, spindle, or tear." Others, having cut themselves off hopelessly from social acceptance, have no option but to follow the road until they reach the Holy City. No piecemeal reforms or minor adjustments of what they leave behind would make turning back possible for them.

But where is this Holy City that lies beyond the technocracy— and what will it be like? Along the way, there is much talk about that, some of it foolish, some of it wise. Many in the procession may only be certain of what it must *not* be like. A discerning few—and among them, the figures I will be discussing in the chapters that follow—have a shrewd sense of where the technocracy leaves off and the New Jerusalem begins: not at the level of class, party, or institution, but rather at the non-intellective level of the personality from which these political and social forms issue. They see, and many who follow them find the vision attractive, that building the good society is not primarily a social, but a psychic task. What makes the youthful disaffiliation of our time a cultural phenomenon, rather than merely a political movement, is the fact that it strikes beyond ideology to the level of consciousness, seeking to transform our deepest sense of the self, the other, the environment.

The psychiatrist R. D. Laing captures the spirit of the matter when he observes: "We do not need theories so much as the experience that is the source of the theory." Such a distinction between theory and experience, challenging as it does the validity of mere analytical clarity as a basis for knowledge or conviction, cannot help but carry an anti-intellectual tone. The tone becomes even more pronounced when Laing goes on to define the goal of "true sanity" as being in one way or another, the dissolution of the normal ego, that false self competently adjusted to our alienated social reality: the emergence of the "inner" archetypal mediators of divine power, and through this death a rebirth, and the eventual re-establishment of a new kind of ego-functioning, the ego now being the servant of the divine, no longer its betrayer.[3]

When psychiatry begins to speak this language, it moves well beyond the boundaries of conventional scientific respectability. But if the dissenting young give their attention to figures like Laing (he is one of the leading mentors of Britain's burgeoning counter culture), it is surely because they have seen too many men of indisputable intelligence and enlightened intention become the apologists of a dehumanized social order. What is it that has allowed so many of our men of science, our scholars, our most sophisticated political leaders, even our boldest would-be revolutionaries to make their peace with the technocracy—or indeed to enter its service so cheerfully? Not lack of intellect or ignorance of humane values. It is rather that technocratic assumptions about the nature of man, society, and nature have warped their experience at the source, and so have become the buried premises from which intellect and ethical judgment proceed.

In order, then, to root out those distortive assumptions, nothing less is required than the subversion of the scientific world view, with its entrenched commitment to an egocentric and cerebral mode of consciousness. In its place, there must be a new culture in which the non-intellective capacities of the personality—those capacities that take fire from visionary splendor and the experience of human communion—become the arbiters of the good, the true, and the beautiful. I think the cultural disjuncture that generational dissent is opening out between itself and the technocracy is just this great, as great in its implications (though obviously not as yet in historical import) as the cleavage that once ran between Greco-Roman rationality and Christian mystery. To be sure, Western society has, over the past two centuries, incorporated a number of minorities whose antagonism toward the scientific world view has been irreconcilable, and who have held out against the easy assimilation to which the major religious congregations have yielded in their growing desire to seem progressive. . . . What *is* new is that a radical rejection of science and technological values should appear so close to the center of our society, rather than on the negligible margins. It is the middle-class young who are conducting this politics of consciousness, and they are doing it boisterously, persistently, and aggressively—to the extent that they are invading the technocracy's citadels of academic learning and bidding fair to take them over.

The task of characterizing the non-intellective powers of the personality in which our young have become so deeply involved is far from easy. Until the advent of psychoanalysis, the vocabulary of our society was woefully impoverished when it came to discussion of the non-intellective aspects of life.

*   *   *

624   Even psychoanalysis has been of little help in the discussion of the
nonintellective, mainly becauses its approach has been burdened with
a mechanistic vocabulary and an objective standoffishness: a prying
examination from the "outside," rather than a warm experiencing
from the "inside." In reviewing the intellectual history of the generation that saw the appearance of Freud, Sorel, Weber, and Durkheim—
the first generation to undertake what it hoped would be respectably
scientific research into man's irrational motivations—H. Stuart Hughes
observes:

> The social thinkers of the 1890s were concerned with the irrational only
> to exorcize it. By probing into it, they sought ways to tame it, to canalize
> it for constructive human purposes.[4]

As the spell of scientific or quasi-scientific thought has spread
in our culture from the physical to the so-called behavioral sciences,
and finally to scholarship in the arts and letters, the marked tendency
has been to consign whatever is not fully and articulately available
in the waking consciousness for empirical or mathematical manipulation, to a purely negative cath-all category (in effect, the cultural garbage can) called the "unconscious" . . . or the "irrational" . . . or the
"mystical" . . . or the "purely subjective. . . ." The more sophisticated
may admit the legitmacy of allowing artists to moon and daydream.
But the world, as every practical man knows, can do without poems
and paintings; it can scarcely do without dams and roads and bombs
and sound policy. Art is for the leisure hours: the time left over from
dealing with realities and necessities.[5]

*   *   *

To assert that the essence of human sociability is, simply and beautifully, the communal opening-up of man to man, rather than the
achievment of prodigious technical and economic feats—what is this
but to assert an absurdity?

Further, what is it to assert the primacy of the non-intellective
powers but to call into question all that our culture values as "reason"
and "reality"? To deny that the true self is this small, hard atom of
intense objectivity we pilot about each day as we build bridges and
careers is surely to play fast and loose with psychopathology. It is
to attack men at the very core of their security by denying the validity
of everything they mean when they utter the most precious word in
their vocabulary: the word "I." And yet this is what the counter culture undertakes when, by way of its mystical tendencies or the drug
experience, it assaults the reality of the ego as an isolable, purely
cerebral unit of identity. In doing so, it once again transcends the
consciousness of the dominant culture and runs the risk of appearing
to be a brazen exercise in perverse nonsense.

Yet what else but such a brave (and hopefully humane) per-
versity can pose a radical challenge to the technocracy? . . .

When one first casts an eye over the varieties of youthful dissent, it may seem that there is considerably less coherence to this coun-

ter culture than I have suggested. To one side, there is the mind-blown bohemianism of the beats and hippies; to the other, the hard-headed political activism of the student New Left. . . . But I think there exists, at a deeper level, a theme that unites these variations and which accounts for the fact that hippy and student activist continue to recognize each other as allies. Certainly there is the common enemy against whom they combine forces; but there is also a positive similarity of sensibility.

The underlying unity of these differing styles of dissent is revealed by the extraordinary personalism that his characterized New Left activism since its beginnings. . . . For most of the New Left, there has ultimately been no more worth or cogency in any ideology than a person lends it by virtue of his own action: personal commitments, not abstract ideas, are the stuff of politics. Such is the burden of the observation Staughton Lynd offered to the 1968 New University Conference when he lamented the fact that even radically inclined academics too often fail to "provide models of off-campus radical vocation." They teach Marxism or socialism; but they do not "pay their dues."

The intellectual's first responsibility is, as Noam Chomsky says, "to insist upon the truth. . . ." But what truth we discover will be affected by the lives we lead. . . . to hope that we can understandingly interpret matters of which we have no first-hand knowledge, things utterly unproved upon the pulses . . . is intellectual hubris. . . . I think the times no longer permit this indulgence, and ask us, at the very least, to venture into the arena where political parties and workingmen, and young people do their things, seeking to clarify that experience which becomes ours as well, speaking truth to power from the vantage-point of that process of struggle.[6]

The remarks return us to R. D. Laing's distinction between "theory" and "experience." For the radical intellectual as much as for anyone else, Lynd contends, truth must have a biographical, not merely an ideological, context.

It is this personalist style that has led the New Left to identify alienation as the central political problem of the day. Not alienation, however, in the sheerly institutional sense, in which capitalism (or for that matter any advanced industrial economy) tends to alienate the worker from the means and fruits of production; but rather, alienation as the deadening of man's sensitivity to man, a deadening that can creep into even those revolutionary efforts that seek with every humanitarian intention to eliminate the external symptoms of alienation. Whereever non-human elements—whether revolutionary doctrine or material goods—assume greater importance than human life and well-being, we have the alienation of man from man, and the way is open to the self-righteous use of others as mere objects. In this respect revolutionary terrorism is only the mirror image of capitalist exploitation. As the French students put it in one of their incisive May 1968 slogans: *"Une revolution qui demande que l'on se sacrifice pour elle*

626   *est une revolution a la papa.*" ("A revolution that expects you to sacrifice yourself for it is one of daddy's revolutions.")

* * *

The issue the students are addressing themselves to here, with
their sentimental regard for "love," "loneliness," "depersonalization,"
makes for a vivid contrast to the more doctrinaire style of many of
their radical predecessors. A generation ago at the time of the Spanish
Civil War, Harry Pollitt, the leader of the British Communist Party,
could with a clear conscience tell the poet Stephen Spender that he
ought to go to Spain and get himself killed: the party needed more
martyred artists to bolster its public image. *That* is ideological politics
—the total subordination of the person to party and doctrine. . . . Now
this is precisely the sort of corrupted human relations that has been
largely absent from New Left politics. Instead, there has been a pre-
cociously wise fear of wielding power over others and of unleashing
violence in behalf of any ideal, no matter how rhetorically appealing.
In the New Left, you pay your *own* dues; nobody pays them for you;
and you, in turn, don't enforce payment on anybody else. As Kenneth
Keniston of the Yale Medical School observes in a recent study: ". . .
in manner and style, these young radicals are extremely 'personalistic,'
focused on face-to-face, direct and open relationships with other people;
hostile to formally structured roles and traditional bureaucratic patterns of power and authority"—a characteristic Keniston traces to the
child-rearing habits of the contemporary middle-class family. The trait
is so well developed that Keniston wonders if "it is possible to retain
an open, personalistic, unmanipulative and extremely trusting style,
and yet mount an effective program on a national scale."[7] The worry
is real enough; organizational slackness is bound to be the price one
pays for pursuing the ideal of participative democracy. But then it is
perhaps a measure of our corruption as a society that we should believe democracy can ever be anything other than "participative."

As I write this, however, I am bleakly aware that an ideological
drift toward righteous violence is on the increase among the young,
primarily under the influence of the extremist Black Powerites and a
romanticized conception of guerrila warfare. . . .

It would be my own estimate that those who give way to the vice
of doctrinaire violence and its manipulative ways are still a strict minority among the dissenting youth—though an obstreperous minority
which, for obvious reasons, attracts much attention from the press. . . .
Nevertheless, the prevailing spirit of New Left politics remains that
reflected in the SDS motto "One man, one soul." The meaning of the
phrase is clear enough: at whatever cost to the cause of the doctrine,
one must care for the uniqueness and the dignity of each individual
and yield to what his conscience demands in the existential moment.

* * *

We grasp the underlying unity of the counter cultural variety,
then, if we see beat-hip bohemianism as an effort to work out the personality structure and total life style that follow from New Left social

criticism. At their best, these young bohemians are the would-be utopian pioneers of the world that lies beyond intellectual rejection of the Great Society. They seek to invent a cultural base for New Left politics, to discover new types of community, new family patterns, new sexual mores, new kinds of livelihood, new esthetic forms, new personal identities on the far side of power politics, the bourgeois home, and the consumer society. When the New Left calls for peace and gives us heavy analysis of what's what in Vietnam, the hippy quickly translates the word into *shantih*, the peace that passes all understanding, and fills in the psychic dimensions of the ideal. If investigating the life of *shantih* has little to do with achieving peace in Vietnam, perhaps it is the best way of preventing the next several Vietnams from happening. Perhaps the experiments we find at the hip fringe of the counter culture are still raw and often abortive. But we must remember that the experimenters have only been with us for a dozen or so years now; and they are picking their way through customs and institutions that have had more than a few centuries to entrench themselves. To criticize the experiments is legitimate and necessary; to despair of what are no more than beginnings is surely premature.

* * *

It is precisely because New Left politics is related to an entire culture of disaffiliation that the possibility of any enduring alliance with even the most outcast elements of the adult generation is severely diminished. As long as the young in their politics emphasize the further integration of the poor and disadvantaged into technocratic affluence, they can expect to enjoy ad hoc liaisons with workers and their unions, or with the exploited minorities. But such alliances are not apt to outlast successful integration. When the lid blows off the black ghettos of our cities, the ensuing rebellion may look like the prologue to revolution. The dissenting young then give their sympathy and support to the insurrection—insofar as Black Power will permit the participation of white allies.[8] But soon enough, whatever the black guerrillas may intend, the main activity of the day becomes wholesale looting—which is the poor man's way of cutting himself in on the consumer society. And at that point, the angry agitation that fills the ghetto begins to sound like a clamor at the gates of the technocracy—*demanding in.*

* * *

What, after all, does social justice mean to the outcast and dispossessed? Most obviously, it means gaining admission to everything from which middleclass selfishness excludes them. But how does one achieve such admission without simultaneously becoming an integral and supportive element of the technocracy? How do Black Power, black culture, black consciousness stop short of becoming steppingstones to black consumption, black conformity, black affluence: finally, to a middle-class America of another color? The dilemma requires the most painstaking tact and sensitivity—qualities that are apt to be in short supply among the deprived in the heat and turmoil of political struggle.

* * *

Once the relations of the counter cultural young and the wretched of the earth get beyond the problem of integration, a grave uneasiness is bound to set in. The long-range cultural values of the discontented young must surely seem bizarre to those whose attention is understandably riveted on sharing the glamorous good things of middle-class life.[9] How baffling it must seem to the long-suffering and long-deprived to discover the children of our new affluence dressing themselves in rags and tatters, turning their "pads" into something barely distinguishable from slum housing, and taking to the streets as panhandlers. Similarly, what can the Beatles' latest surrealist LP mean to an unemployed miner or a migrant farm laborer? . . .

But the bind in which the counter culture finds itself in dealing with disadvantaged social elements is doubled at another level with a painful irony. As has been mentioned, it is the cultural experimentation of the young that often runs the worst risk of commercial verminization—and so of having the force of its dissent dissipated. It is the cultural experiments that draw the giddy interest of just those middle-class swingers who are the bastion of the technocratic order. . . .

There is no diminishing the tendency of counter cultural dissent to fall prey to the neutralization that can come of such false attention. Those who dissent have to be supremely resourceful to avoid getting exhibited in somebody's commercial showcase—rather like bizarre fauna brought back alive from the jungle wilds . . . by *Time*, by *Esquire*, by David Susskind. On such treacherous terrain, the chances of miscalculation are immense. Bob Dylan, who laments the nightmarish corruptions of the age, nevertheless wears his material thin grinding out a million-dollar album a year for Columbia—which is more apt to find its way to the shelf beside a polished mahogany stereophonic radio-phono console in suburbia than to any bohemian garret. Vanessa Redgrave, a veteran of Committee of 100 sit-downs in Whitehall who will don *fidelista* fatigues to sing Cuban revolutionary ballads in Trafalgar Square, also lends her talents to the glossy *Playboy* pornography of films like *Blow-Up*. . . .

From such obfuscation of genuine dissenting talent, it isn't far to go before the counter culture finds itself swamped with cynical or self-deceived opportunists who become, or conveniently let themselves be turned into, spokesmen for youthful disaffiliation. Accordingly, we now have clothing designers, hairdressers, fashion magazine editors, and a veritable phalanx of pop stars who, without a thought in their heads their PR man did not put there, are suddenly expounding "the philosophy of today's rebellious youth" for the benefit of the Sunday supplements . . . the feature to be sandwiched between a report on luxury underwear and a full-color spread on the latest undiscovered skin-diving paradise at which to spend that summer of a lifetime. And then, for good reason, the counter culture begins to look like nothing so much as a world-wide publicity stunt. One can easily despair of the possibility that it will survive these twin perils: on the one hand, the weakness of its cultural rapport with the disadvantaged; on the other, its vulnerability to exploitation as an amusing side show of the swinging society.

*   *   *

. . . To overcome the commercializing and trivializing tactics of the technocratic society will require outlasting the atmosphere of novelty that now surrounds our youth culture and which easily assigns it the character of a transient fad. In the process, there will have to be a maturation of what are often for the young no more than shrewd insights and bright instincts, so that these can become the thoughtful stuff on an adult life. If the counter culture should bog down in a colorful morass of unexamined symbols, gestures, fashions of dress, and slogans, then it will provide little that can be turned into a life-long commitment—except, and then pathetically, for those who can reconcile themselves to becoming superannuated hangers-on of the campus, the love-in, the rock club. It will finish as a temporary style, continually sloughed off and left behind for the next wave of adolescents: a hopeful beginning that never becomes more than a beginning. As for the task of introducing the oppressed minorities into the counter culture: I suspect that this may have to wait until the black revolution has run its course in America. At which point the new black middle class will produce its own ungrateful young, who, as the heirs of everything their parents thought worth struggling for, will begin, like their white counterparts, to fight their way free of technocratic entrapment.

But beyond the problems raised by such social maneuvering, there lies an even more critical project: that of defining the ethical dignity of a cultural movement which takes radical issue with the scientific world view. The project is vitally important because there must be a reply to the challenge raised by the many uneasy intellectuals who fear that the counter culture arrives, not trailing clouds of glory, but bearing the mark of the beast. No sooner does one speak of liberating the non-intellective powers of the personality than, for many, a prospect of the starkest character arises: a vision of rampant, antinomian mania, which in the name of permissiveness threatens to plunge us into a dark and savage age.

*   *   *

The problem at hand confronts us with a familiar, but much misunderstood, dichotomy: the opposition of reason and passion, intellect and feeling, the head and the heart. . . . Again and again in moral discourse this troublesome polarity intrudes itself upon us, pretending to be a real ethical choice.

*   *   *

And simply to bring the catalogue up to date: what are we to identify as the basic deficiency of all the technical experts who now administer the world-wide balance of terror? Is it intellect our scientists and strategists and operations analysts lack? These men who preside with an impersonal eye over a system of mass murder capable of greater destruction than all the lynch mobs and witch-hunters in

630   history: is it their capacity to *reason* that is flawed? Surely Lewis
Mumford goes to the heart of the matter when he insists that the situation confronts us with something that can only be called "mad rationality"; and he reminds us of Captain Ahab's chilling confession: "All
my means are sane: my motives and object mad.[10]

We are correct in feeling that serious ethical discussion must
get beyond ad hoc evaluations of specific actions—which is essentially
the area of life we leave to the law. But we are mistaken, I think, in
believing that the dichotomy between rational and impulsive, deliberate and passionate styles of action is a more meaningful level of discourse. Indeed, I would contend that this dichotomy confronts us with
inherently non-moral considerations. Neither rationality nor passionate impulse, as they characterize styles of behavior, guarantees anything about the ethical quality of action. . . .

We enter a searching discussion of moral action only when we
press beyond the surface style of conduct in which men express their
ethical sensibilities and seek the hidden source from which their action
flows. If, again, we think of conduct as a vocabulary, then we can see
that our use of that vocabulary will depend wholly upon what we try
to "say" through what we do. Our action gives voice to our total vision
of life—of the self and its proper place in the nature of things—as we
experience it most movingly. For many men this vision may be pathetically narrow, bounded on all sides by socially prescribed rules and
sanctions; they may have only the dimmest awareness of a good or
evil which is not the product of social inculcation and enforcement. In
that case, a man behaves as he does out of fear or ingrained subordination and with little personal authority. Perhaps the conduct of most
men is shaped in this way—and too often it is just such automatized
dutifulness that we take to be rational and responsible. Yet, even so,
there lurks behind our socially certified morality some primordial
world view which dictates what reality is, and what, within that reality,
is to be held sacred.

* * *

We have no serviceable language in our culture to talk about
the level of the personality at which this underlying vision of reality
resides. But it seems indisputable that it exerts its influence at a point
that lies deeper than our intellective consciousness. The world view we
hold is nothing we learn in the same conscious way in which we learn
an intellectual subject matter. It is, rather, something we absorb from
the spirit of the times or are converted into, or seduced into by un-
accountable experiences. It is, indeed, this guiding vision that determines what we finally regard as sanity itself. We can, therefore, see
why two men like Bertrand Russell and Herman Kahn—neither of
whom can be fairly accused of despising reason, logic, or intellectual
precision—can emerge as such implacable antagonists on so many great
issues. Russell himself, in grasping the primacy of vision over the superficial style of thought, speech, and conduct, has said, "I would
rather be mad with the truth than sane with lies." "Mad," to be sure,

from the viewpoint of others; for what brings a man close to the truth will become his own standard of sanity.

When I say that the counter culture delves into the nonintellective aspects of the personality, it is with respect to its interest at this level—at the level of vision—that I believe its project is significant. Undeniably, this project often gets obscured, especially among the more desperate young who quickly conclude that the antidote to our society's "mad rationality" lies in flinging oneself into an assortment of mad passions. Like too many of our severely self-disciplined solid citizens and "responsible" leaders, they allow their understanding to stop at the level of surface conduct, accepting as final the dichotomy between "spontaneous" and "deliberate" styles of behavior. They also believe

. . . that the unsought and inspired belongs to special individuals in peculiar emotional states; or again to people at parties under the influence of alcohol or hasheesh; rather than being a quality of all experience. And correspondingly, calculated behavior aims at goods that are not uniquely appropriated according to one's fancy, but are in turn only good for something else (so that pleasure itself is endured as a means to health and efficiency). "Being oneself" means acting imprudently, as if desire could not make sense; and "acting sensibly" means holding back and being bored.[11]

But while a good deal of our contemporary youth culture takes off in the direction of strenuous frenzy and simulated mindlessness, there also moves through the scene a very different and much more mature conception of what it means to investigate the nonintellective consciousness. This emerges primarily from the strong influence upon the young of Eastern religion, with its heritage of gentle, tranquil, and thoroughly civilized contemplativeness. Here we have a tradition that calls radically into question the validity of the scientific world view, the supremacy of cerebral cognition, the value of technological prowess; but does so in the most quiet and measured of tones, with humor, with tenderness, even with a deal of cunning argumentation. If there is anything off-putting to the scientific mind about this tradition, it does not result from any unwillingness on the part of the Eastern religions to indulge in analysis and debate. It results, rather, from their assertion of the intellectual value of paradox and from their conviction that analysis and debate must finally yield to the claims of ineffable experience. Oriental mysticism comprehends argumentation; but it also provides a generous place for silence, out of wise recognition of the fact that it is with silence that men confront the great moments of life. Unhappily, the Western intellect is inclined to treat silence as if it were a mere zero: a loss for words indicating the absence of meaning.

However sternly one may wish to reject the world view of Lao-tzu, of the Buddha, of the Zen masters, one cannot fairly accuse such figures of lacking intellect, wit, or humane cultivation. Though their minds lay at the service of a vision that is incompatible with our conventional science, such men are the prospective participants of neither a lynch mob nor a group-grope party. Fortunately, their ex-

632   ample has not been lost on our dissenting young; indeed, it has become one of the strongest strains of the counter culture.

 . . . It will be sufficient to say at this point that the exploration of the non-intellective powers assumes its greatest importance, not when the project becomes a free-for-all of pixilated dynamism, but when it becomes a critique of the scientific world view upon which too many of the brightest splendors of our experience lie hidden.

NOTES

1. Jose Ortega y Gasset, *Man and Crisis,* trans. Mildred Adams (London: Allen & Unwin, 1959), p. 45.

2. From a recording of the address presented over KPFA (Berkeley) on September 24, 1968.

3. R. D. Laing, *The Politics of Experience and The Bird of Paradise* (London: Penguin Books, 1967), p. 119.

4. H. Stuart Hughes, *Consciousness and Society* (New York: Vintage Books, 1958), pp. 35–36. Only Bergson and Jung, among major thinkers of the period outside the arts, treated the non-rational side of human nature with an intuitive sympathy. But who, in the scientific community or the academy, any longer regards them as "major thinkers"?

5. One might expect some softening of this compulsively utilitarian rationality to stem from the new and now lavishly subsidized field of sleep research, which tells us of the absolute necessity of nonintellective experience. For a fascinating survey of this work, see Gay G. Luce and J. Segal, *Sleep* (London: Heinemann, 1967). Whatever else the sleep researchers may prove, however, they have already revealed the pathos of a society that must have it demonstrated by way of encephalographs and computers that the relaxation of rational consciousness and the experience of dreaming are vital to healthy life. But they do so seemingly without any awareness of the part science, with its militant intellectuality, has played in obscuring this fact. It is this blind spot which will probably lead to their research, like all science worth its subsidies these days, being used for idiotic ends. For example, Herman Kahn and Anthony Wiener, in their book *The Year 2000* (New York: Macmillan, 1967) give us a prognosis of "programmed dreams." Another instance of the technocratic principle: never let happen naturally and enjoyably what can be counterfeited by the technicians.

6. Lynd's address appears in *The New University Conference Newsletter,* Chicago, May 24, 1968, pp. 5–6.

7. See Kenneth Keniston, *Young Radicals* (New York: Harcourt, Brace & World, 1968). The study is based on the National Steering Committee of the 1967 Vietnam Summer.

8. Cf. Daniel and Gabriel Cohn-Bendit: "The differences between the revolutionary students and the workers spring directly from their distinct social positions. Thus few students have had real experience of grinding poverty—their struggle is about the hierarchical structure of socitey, about oppression in comfort. They do not so much have to contend with a lack of material goods as with unfulfilled desires and aspirations. The workers, on the other hand, suffer from direct economic oppression and misery—earning wages of less than 500 francs per month, in poorly ventilated, dirty and noisy factories, where the foreman, the chief engineer and the manager all throw their weight about and conspire to keep those under them in their place." *Obsolete Communism: The Left-Wing Alternative,* p. 107. Yet despite these radically different political horizons, Cohn-Bendit argues that there can be a common cause between the two groups, based on his tactic of "spontaneous resistance" in the streets.

9. Lewis Mumford, *The Transformations of Man* (New York: Collier Books, 1956), p. 122.

10. From Paul Goodman's contribution to Frederick Perls, Ralph Hefferline, and Paul Goodman, *Gestalt Therapy* (New York: Delta, 1965), p. 242.

STOKELY CARMICHAEL AND CHARLES V. HAMILTON   **633**

The Search for New Forms

We are aware that it has become commonplace to pinpoint and describe the ills of our urban ghettos. The social, political and economic problems are so acute that even a casual observer cannot fail to see that something is wrong. While description is plentiful, however, there remains a blatant timidity about what to *do* to solve the problems.

Neither rain nor endless "definitive," costly reports nor stop-gap measures will even approach a solution to the explosive situation in the nation's ghettos. This country cannot begin to solve the problems of the ghettos as long as it continues to hang on to outmoded structures and institutions. A political party system that seeks only to "manage conflict" and hope for the best will not be able to serve a growing body of alienated black people. An educational system which, year after year, continues to cripple hundreds of thousands of black children must be replaced by wholly new mechanisms of control and management. We must begin to think and operate in terms of entirely new and substantially different forms of expression.

It is crystal clear that the initiative for such changes will have to come from the black community. We cannot expect white America to begin to move forcefully on these problems unless and until black America begins to move. This means that black people must organize themselves without regard for what is traditionally acceptable, precisely because the traditional approaches have failed. It means that black people must make demands without regard to their initial "respectability," precisely because "respectable" demands have not been sufficient.

The northern urban ghettos are in many ways different from the black-belt South, but in neither area will substantial change come about until black people organize independently to exert power. As noted in earlier chapters, black people already have the voting potential to control the politics of entire southern counties. Given maximum registration of blacks, there are more than 110 counties where black people could outvote the white racists. These people should concentrate on forming independent political parties and not waste time trying to reform or convert the racist parties. In the North, it is no less important that independent groups be formed. It has been clearly shown that when black people attempt to get within one of the two major parties in the cities, they become co-opted and their interests are shunted to the background. They become expendable.

We must begin to think of the black community as a base of

organization to control institutions in that community. Control of the ghetto schools must be taken out of the hands of "professionals," most of whom have long since demonstrated their insensitivity to the needs and problems of the black child. These "experts" bring with them middle-class biases, unsuitable techniques and materials; these are, at best, dysfunctional and at worst destructive. A recent study of New York schools reveals that the New York school system is run by thirty people—school supervisors, deputy and assistant superintendents and examiners. The study concluded: "Public education policy has become the province of the professional bureaucrat, with the tragic result that the status quo, suffering from many difficulties, is the order of the day."[1] Virtually no attention is paid to the wishes and demands of the parents, especially the black parents. This is totally unacceptable.

Black parents should seek as their goal the actual control of the public schools in their community: hiring and firing of teachers, selection of teaching materials, determination of standards, etc. This can be done with a committee of teachers. The traditional, irrelevant "See Dick, See Jane, Run Dick, Run Jane, White House, Nice Farm" nonsense must be ended. The principals and as many teachers as possible of the ghetto schools should be black. The children will be able to see their kind in positions of leadership and authority. It should never occur to anyone that a brand new school can be built in the heart of the black community and then given a white person to head it. The fact is that in this day and time, it is crucial that race be taken into account in determining policy of this sort. Some people will, again, view this as "reverse segregation" or as "racism." It is not. It is emphasizing race in a positive way: not to subordinate or rule over others but to overcome the effects of centuries in which race has been used to the detriment of the black man.

The story of I.S. 201 in New York City is a case in point. In 1958, the city's Board of Education announced that it would build a special $5-million school in District 4, whose pupils are 90 percent black, 8 percent Puerto Rican, with the remaining 2 percent white. The concept was that students from elementary schools in that district would feed into the new school at the fifth grade and after the eighth grade would move on to high school. This concept, at least according to official policy, was supposed to speed integration.

The parents of children who might be attending the school mobilized in an attempt, once and for all, to have a school adequate for the needs of Harlem. The Board had picked the site for I.S. 201: between 127th and 128th Streets, from Madison Avenue to Park Avenue—in the heart of Central Harlem. The parents argued against this location because they wanted an integrated school, which would be impossible unless it was located on the fringes, not in the heart, of Central Harlem. Their desire clearly points up the colonial relationship of blacks and whites in the city; they knew the only way to get quality education was to have white pupils in the school.

The Board of Education indicated that the school would be integrated, but the parents knew it could not be done and they demonstrated against the site during construction. When they saw that the school would have no windows, they also raised the question of whether this was merely a stylistic or practical innovation, or a means of closing out the reality of the community from the pupils for the hours they would be inside.

During the spring and summer of 1966, some six hundred pupils registered at I.S. 201—all of them black or Puerto Rican. Their parents then threatened that if the school wasn't integrated by fall, they would boycott it. The Board of Education, giving lip service to the parents, passed out and mailed 10,000 leaflets to the white community—in June!

Needless to say, few people go to a school on the basis of a leaflet received while getting off the subway or wherever, and even fewer (white) people want to send their children to school in Harlem. the request for "volunteers" had no effect, and on September 7, the Board of Education finally admitted its "apparent inability to integrate the school." It was the inability of that class . . . "whose primary interest is to secure objects for service, management, and control," the objects in this case being the mothers of I.S. 201. Threatened by a boycott, the school was not opened as scheduled on September 12, 1966.

At this point, the parents—who were picketing—moved in the only way they could: to demand some form of control which would enable them to break out of the old colonial pattern. In view of the fact that whites would not send their children to the school, one parent stated, "we decided we would have to have a voice to ensure that we got quality education segregated-style. We wanted built-in assurances." The parents knew that within a few years, given that pattern, this new school would be like all others which started with fine facilities and deteriorated under an indifferent bureaucracy. The parents' demands thus shifted from integration to control.

On September 16, Superintendent Bernard E. Donovan offered them a voice in screening and recommending candidates for supervisory and teaching positions at the school. An East Harlem community council would be set up with a strong voice in school affairs. The parents also wanted some control over the curriculum, the career guidance system, and financial matters, which the Board deemed legally impossible. Shortly afterward, the white principal—Stanley Lisser— voluntarily requested transfer. A black principal had been one of the parents' key demands. With these two developments, the parents announced that they would send their children to school.

At this point (September 19), however, the United Federation of Teachers bolted. The teachers at I.S. 201 threatened to boycott if Lisser did not stay. Within twenty-four hours, the Board had rescinded its agreement and restored Lisser. (It is contended by many that this was the result of planned collusion between the Board and the U.F.T.) Nine days late, the school opened. The parents became divided; some gladly began sending their children to school while others did the same because they were unaware that the agreement had been rescinded.

The parents' negotiating committee had moved to get outside help, while the city's top administrators, including Mayor Lindsay,

636 entered the picture. A Harlem committee representing parents and community leaders proposed on September 29 that I.S. 201 be put under a special "operations board" composed of four parents and four university educators with another member selected by those eight. This board would pass on the selection of teachers and supervisors, and evaluate the curriculum at I.S. 201 as well as three elementary or "feeder" schools. But the U.F.T. attacked this proposal. As the struggle dragged on, it became clear that once again efforts by the community to deal with its problems had been laid waste.

Later, in October, the Board of Education offered the parents a take-it-or-leave-it proposal. It proposed a council of parents and teachers that would be purely advisory. The parents flatly rejected this. Father Vincent Resta, a Catholic priest and chairman of the local school board which covered I.S. 201, stated, "In theory the Board's proposal is something that could work. But an advisory role implies trust. And the community has absolutely no reason to trust the Board of Education." The local board later resigned en masse.

But the issue of community control did not end there. It had become clear to the parents that their problems were not restricted to School District 4. When the Board of Education met to discuss its proposed budget in December, 1966, I.S. 201 parents and other came to protest the allocation of resources. Unable to get any response, at the end of one session they simply moved from the gallery into the chairs of those meeting and elected a People's Board of Education. After forty-eight hours, they were arrested and removed but continued to meet in another location, with the Rev. Milton A. Galamison—who had led school boycotts previously in New York City—as President.

At one of its executive sessions on January 8, 1967, the People's Board adopted a motion which stated its goals as:

1. To seek to alter the structure of the school system . . . so it is responsible to our individual community needs, in order to achieve real community control. This may require legislative or state constitutional convention action. This means, of course, decentralization, accountability, meaningful citizen participation, etc.
2. To develop a program which will get grassroots awareness for, understanding of, and support for the goal stated above. It is suggested that we give up top priority to organizing and educating parents and citizens in the poverty areas (approximately 14).
3. That we recognize that power should not rest in any central board, including our own, and that by every means possible we should encourage the development and initiative of local people's groups.

The parents at I.S. 201 failed because they are still powerless. But they succeeded in heating up the situation to the point where the dominant society will have to make certain choices. It is clear that black people are concerned about the type of education their children **637** receive; many more people can be activated by a demonstrated ability to achieve results. One result has already been achieved by the I.S. 201 struggle: the concept of community control has now rooted itself in the consciousness of many black people. Such control has long been accepted in smaller communities, particularly white suburban areas. No longer is it "white folks' business" only. Ultimately, community-controlled schools could organize an independent school board (like the "People's Board of Education") for the total black community. Such an innovation would permit the parents and the school to develop a much closer relationship and to begin attacking the problems of the ghetto in a communal, realistic way.

The tenements of the ghetto represent another target of high priority. Tenants in buildings should form cohesive organizations—unions—to act in their common interest vis-a-vis the absentee slumlord. Obviously, rents should be withheld if the owner does not provide adequate services and decent facilities. But more importantly, the black community should set as a prime goal the policy of having the owner's rights forfeited if he does not make repairs: forfeited and turned over to the black organization, which would not only manage the property but own it outright. The absentee slumlord is perpetuating a socially detrimental condition, and he should not be allowed to hide behind the rubric of property rights. The black community must insist that the goal of human rights take precedent over property rights, and back up that insistence in ways which will make it in the self-interest of the white society to act morally. Behavior—in this case, the misuse of property—can be regulated to any extent the power structure wishes. No one should be naive enough to think that an owner will give up his property easily, but the black community, properly organized and mobilized, could apply pressure that would make him choose between the alternatives of forfeiture or compliance. Thousands of black people refusing to pay rents month after month in the ghettos could have more than salutary effect on public policy.

As pointed out in Chapter I, virtually all of the money earned by merchants and exploiters of the black ghetto leaves those communities. Properly organized black groups should seek to establish a community rebate plan. The black people in a given community would organize and refuse to do business with any merchant who did not agree to "reinvest," say, forty to fifty percent of his net profit in the indigenous community. This contribution could take many forms: providing additional jobs for black people, donating scholarship funds for students, supporting certain types of community organizations. An agreement would be reached between the merchants and the black consumers. If a merchant wants customers from a black community, he must be made to understand that he has to contribute to that community. If he chooses not to do so, he will not be patronized, and the end result will be *no* profits from that community. Contractors who

638

seek to do business in the black community would also be made to understand that they face a boycott if they do not donate to the black community.

Such a community rebate plan will require careful organization and tight discipline on the part of the black people. But it is possible, and has in fact already been put into effect by some ethnic communities. White America realizes the market in the black community; black America must begin to realize the potential of that market.

Under the present institutional arrangements, no one should think that the mere election of a few black people to local or national office will solve the problem of political representation. There are now ten black people on the City Council in Chicago, but there are not more than two or three (out of the total of fifty) who will speak out forcefully. The fact is that the present political institutions are not geared to giving the black minority an effective voice. Two needs arise from this.

First, it is important that the black communities in these northern ghettos form independent party groups to elect their own choices to office when and where they can. It should not be assumed that "you cannot beat City Hall." It has been done, as evidenced by the 1967 aldermanic elections in one of the tightest machine cities in the country: Chicago. In the Sixth Ward, an independent black candidate, Sammy Rayner, defeated an incumbent, machine-backed black alderman. Rayner first ran in 1963 and missed a run-off by a mere 177 votes. He then challenged Congressman William L. Dawson in 1964 and lost, but he was building an image in the black community as one who could and would speak out. The black people were getting the message. In 1967, when he ran against the machine incumbent for the City Council, he won handily. Precincts in the East Woodlawn area that he had failed to carry in 1963 (23 out of 26), he now carried (19 out of 26). The difference was continuous, hard, day-to-day, door-to-door campaigning. His campaign manager, Philip Smith, stated: "Another key to Sammy's victory was the fact that he began to methodically get himself around the Sixth Ward. Making the black club functions, attending youth meetings and all the functions that were dear to the hearts of Sixth Ward people became the order of the day."[2]

The cynics will say that Rayner will be just one voice, unable to accomplish anything unless he buckles under to the Daley machine. Let us be very clear: we do not endorse Rayner nor are we blind to the problems he faces. It is the job of the machine to crush such men or to co-opt them before they grow in numbers and power. At the same time, men like Rayner are useful only so long as they speak to the community's broad needs; as we said . . . black visibility is not Black Power. If Rayner does not remain true to his constituents, then they should dislodge him as decisively as they did his predecessor. This establishes the principle that the black politician must first be reponsive to his constituents, not to the white machine. The problem then is to resist the forces which would crush or co-opt while building community strength so that more of such men can be elected and compelled to act in the community's interest.

(It should be noted that Rayner is one of numerous black leaders who have rejected the term Black Power although their own statements, attitudes and programs suggest that they endorse what we mean by Black Power. The reason for this, by and large, is a fear of offending the powers-that-be which may go by the name of "tactics." This again exemplifies the need to raise the level of consciousness, to create a new consciousness among black people.)

The very least which Sammy Rayner can give the black community is a new political dignity. His victory will begin to establish the *habit* of saying "No" to the downtown bosses. In the same way that the black Southerner had to assert himself and say "No" to those who did not want him to register to vote, now the Northern black voter must begin to defy those who would control his vote. This very act of defiance threatens the status quo, because there is no predicting its ultimate outcome. Those black voters, then *accustomed* to acting independently, could eventually swing their votes one way or the other —but always for *their* benefit. Smith signaled this when he said: "The disbelievers who felt that you could not beat City Hall are now whistling a different tune. The victory of Sammy Rayner in the Sixth Ward should serve as a beacon light for all who believe in independent politics in this city. . . . Rayner is going to be responsible for the aldermanic position taking on a new line of dignity. Black people are going to be able to point with pride to this man, who firmly believes that we need statesmanlike leadership instead of the goatsmanship we have been exposed to."[3]

Let no one protest that this type of politics is naive or childish or fails to understand the "rules of the game." The price of going along with the "regulars" is too high to pay for the so-called benefits received. The rewards of independence can be considerable. It is too soon to say precisely where this new spirit of independence could take us. New forms may lead to a new political force. Hopefully, this force might move to create new national and local political parties—or, more accurately, the first *legitimate* political parties. Some have spoken of a "third party" or "third political force." But from the viewpoint of community needs and popular participation, no existing force or party in this country has ever been relevant. A force which is relevant would therefore be a first—something truly new.

The second implication of the political dilemma facing black people is that ultimately they may have to spearhead a drive to revamp completely the present institutions of representation. If the Rayners are continually outvoted, if the grievances of the black community continue to be overlooked, then it will become necessary to devise wholly new forms of local political representation. There is nothing sacred about the system of electing candidates to serve as aldermen, councilmen, etc., by wards or districts. Geographical representation is not inherently right. Perhaps political interests have to be represented in some entirely different manner—such as community-parent control

640 of schools, unions of tenants, unions of welfare recipients actually taking an official role in running the welfare departments. If political institutions do not meet the needs of the people, if the people finally believe that those institutions do not express their own values, then this institutions must be discarded. It is wasteful and inefficient, not to mention unjust, to continue imposing old forms and ways of doing things on a people who no longer view those forms and ways as functional.

We see independent politics (after the fashion of a Rayner candidacy) as the first step toward implementing something new. Voting year after year for the traditional party and its silent representatives gets the black community nowhere; voters then get their own candidates, but these may become frustrated by the power and organization of the machines. The next logical step is to demand more meaningful structures, forms and ways of dealing with long-standing problems.

We see this as the potential power of the ghettos. In a real sense, it is similar to what is taking place in the South: the move in the direction of independent politics—and from there, the move toward the development of wholly new political institutions. If these proposals also sound impractical, utopian, then we ask: what other real alternatives exist? There are none; the choice lies between a genuinely new approach and maintaining the brutalizing, destructive, violence-breeding life of the ghettos as they exist today. From the viewpoint of black people, that is no choice.

NOTES

1. Marilyn Gittell, "Participants and Participation: A Study of School Policy in New York City," New York: The Center for Urban Education. As quoted in the *New York Times*, April 30, 1967, p. E90.

2. Philip Smith, "Politics as I See It," *The Citizen*, Chicago (March 22, 1967).

3. Ibid.

ELTING E. MORISON   **641**

A Case Study of Innovation

In the early days of the last war, when armaments of all kinds were in short supply, the British, I am told, made use of a venerable field piece that had come down to them from previous generations. The honorable past of this light artillery stretched back, in fact, to the Boer War. In the days of uncertainty after the fall of France, these guns, hitched to trucks, served as useful mobile units in the coast defense. But it was felt that the rapidity of fire could be increased. A time-motion expert was, therefore, called in to suggest ways to simplify the firing procedures. He watched one of the gun crews of five men at practice in the field for some time. Puzzled by certain aspects of the procedures, he took slow-motion pictures of the soldiers performing the loading, aiming, and firing routines.

When he ran these pictures over once or twice, he noticed something that appeared odd to him. A moment before the firing two members of the gun crew ceased all activity and came to attention for a three-second interval extending throughout the discharge of the gun. He summoned an old colonel of artillery, showed him the pictures, and pointed out this strange behavior. What, he asked the colonel, did it mean? The colonel, too, was puzzled. He asked to see the pictures again. "Ah," he said when the performance was over, "I have it. They are holding the horses."

This story, true or not, and I am told it is true, suggests nicely the pain with which the human being accommodates himself to changing conditions. The tendency is apparently involuntary and immediate to protect oneself against the shock of change by continuing in the presence of altered situations the familiar habits, however incongruous, of the past.

Yet, if human beings are attached to the known, to the realm of things as they are, they also, regrettably for their peace of mind, are incessantly attracted to the unknown and to things as they might be. As Ecclesiastes glumly pointed out, men persist in disordering their settled ways and beliefs by seeking out many inventions.

The point is obvious. Change has always been a constant in human affairs; today, indeed, it is one of the determining characteristics of our civilization. In our relatively shapeless social organization, the shifts from station to station are fast and easy. More important for our immediate purpose, America is fundamentally an industrial society in a time of tremendous technological development. We are thus constantly presented with new devices or new forms of power that, in their refinement and extension, continually bombard the fixed structure of our habits of mind and behavior. Under conditions such as these, our

Reprinted from *Engineering and Science*, April 1950 and *The California Institute of Technology Quarterly*, Spring 1960 by permission of the publisher and the author.

salvation—or at least our peace of mind—appears to depend upon how successfully we can, in the future, become what has been called in an excellent phrase a completely "adaptive society."

It is interesting, in view of all this, that so little investigation, relatively, has been made of the process of change and human responses to it. Recently psychologists, sociologists, and cultural anthropologists have addressed themselves to the subject with suggestive results. But we are still far from a full understanding of the process, and still farther from knowing how we can set about simplifying and assisting an individual's or a group's accommodation to new machines or new ideas.

CONTINUOUS-AIM FIRING

With these things in mind, I thought it might be interesting and perhaps useful to examine historically a changing situation within a society; to see if from this examination we can discover how the new machines or ideas that introduced the changing situation developed; to see who introduces them, who resists them, what points of friction or tension in the social structure are produced by the innovation, and perhaps why they are produced and what, if anything, may be done about it. For this case study, the introduction of continuous-aim firing in the United States Navy has been selected. The system, first devised by an English officer in 1898, was introduced into our Navy in the years 1900-1902.

I have chosen to study this episode for two reasons. First, a navy is not unlike a society that has been placed under laboratory conditions. Its dimensions are severely limited; it is beautifully ordered and articulated; it is relatively isolated from random influences. For these reasons the impact of change can be clearly discerned, the resulting dislocations in the structure easily discovered and marked out. In the second place, the development of continuous-aim firing rests upon mechanical devices. It, therefore, presents for study a concrete, durable situation. It is not like many other innovating reagents—a Manichean heresy, or Marxism, or the views of Sigmund Freud—that can be shoved and hauled out of shape by contending forces or conflicting prejudices. At all times we know exactly what continuous-aim firing really is. It will be well now to describe, as briefly as possible, *what* it is.

The governing fact in gunfire at sea is that the gun is mounted on an unstable platform—a rolling ship. This constant motion obviously complicates the problem of holding a steady aim. Before 1898 this problem was solved in the following elementary fashion. A gun pointer estimated the range of the target—ordinarily about 2800 yards. He then raised the gun barrel to give the gun the elevation to carry the shell to the target at the estimated range. This was accomplished by turning a small wheel on the gun mount that operated the elevating gears. With the gun thus fixed for range, the gun pointer peered through open sights, not unlike those on a small rifle, and waited until the roll of the ship brought the sights on the target. He then pressed the firing button that discharged the gun. There were, by 1898, on some naval guns, telescope sights which naturally enlarged the image of the target for the gun pointer. But these sights were rarely used by gun pointers. They were lashed securely to the gun barrel and, recoiling with the barrel, jammed back against the unwary pointer's eye. Therefore, when used at all, they were used only to take an initial sight for purposes of estimating the range before the gun was fired.

Notice now two things about the process. First of all, the rapidity of the fire was controlled by the rolling period of the ship. Pointers had to wait for the one moment in the roll when the sights were brought on the target. Notice also this: There is in every pointer what is called a "firing interval"—the time lag between his impulse to fire the gun and the translation of this impulse into the act of pressing the firing button. A pointer, because of this reaction time, could not wait to fire the gun until the exact moment when the roll of the ship brought the sights onto the target; he had to will to fire a little before, while the sights were off the target. Since the firing interval was an individual matter, varying, obviously, from man to man, each pointer had to estimate, from long practice, his own interval and compensate for it accordingly.

These things, together with others we need not here investigate, conspired to make gunfire at sea relatively uncertain and ineffective. The pointer, on a moving platform, estimating range and firing interval, shooting while his sight was off the target, became in a sense an individual artist.

ELIMINATING SOME UNCERTAINTIES

In 1898, many of the uncertainties were removed from the process, and the position of the gun pointer radically altered by the introduction of continuous-aim firing. The major change was that which enabled the gun pointer to keep his sight and gun barrel on the target throughout the roll of the ship. This was accomplished by altering the gear ratio in the elevating gear to permit a pointer to compensate for the roll of the vessel by rapidly elevating and depressing the gun. From this change another followed. With the possibility of maintaining the gun always on the target, the desirability of improved sights became immediately apparent. The advantages of the telescope sight, as apposed to the open sight, were for the first time fully realized. But the existing telescope sight, it will be recalled, moved with the recoil of the gun and jammed back against the eye of the gunner. To correct this, the sight was mounted on a sleeve that permitted the gun barrel to recoil through it without moving the telescope.

These two improvements—in elevating gear and sighting—eliminated the major uncertainties in gunfire at sea and greatly increased the possibilities of both accurate and rapid fire.

You must take my word for it that this changed naval gunnery from an art to a science, and that gunnery accuracy in the British and our Navy increased about 3,000 percent in six years. This doesn't mean much except to suggest a great increase in accuracy. The following comparative figures may mean a little more. In 1899 five ships of the North Atlantic Squadron fired five minutes each at a lightship

644 hulk at the conventional range of 1,600 yards. After twenty-five minutes of banging away, two hits had been made on the sails of the elderly vessel. Six years later one naval gunner made 15 hits in one minute at a target 75 x 25 feet at the same range; half of them hit in a bull's-eye 50 inches square.

Now, with the instruments (the gun, elevating gear, and telescope), the method, and the results of continuous-aim firing in mind, let us turn to the subject of major interest: How was the idea, obviously so simple an idea, of continuous-aim firing developed; who introduced it; and what was its reception?

INTRODUCTION OF AN IDEA

The idea was the product of the fertile mind of the English officer, Admiral Sir Percy Scott. He arrived at it in this way, while, in 1898, he was the captain of H.M.S. *Scylla*. For the previous two or three years he had given much thought, independently and almost alone in the British Navy, to means of improving gunnery. One rough day, when the ship, at target practice, was pitching and rolling violently, he walked up and down the gun deck watching his gun crews. Because of the heavy weather they were making very bad scores. Scott noticed, however, that one pointer was appreciably more accurate than the rest. He watched this man with care and saw, after a time, that he was unconsciously working his elevating gear back and forth in a partially successful effort to compensate for the roll of the vessel. It flashed through Scott's mind at that moment that here was the sovereign remedy for the problems of inaccurate fire. What one man could do partially and unconsciously, perhaps all men could be trained to do consciously and completely.

Acting on this assumption, he did three things. First, in all the guns of the *Scylla*, he changed the gear ratio in the elevating gear, previously used only to set the gun in fixed position for range, so that a gunner could easily elevate and depress the gun to follow a target throughout the roll. Second, he rerigged his telescopes so that they would not be influenced by the recoil of the gun. Third, he rigged a small target at the mouth of the gun, which was moved up and down by a crank to simulate a moving target. By following this target as it moved, and firing at it with a subcalibre rifle rigged in the breech of the gun, the pointer could practice every day. Thus equipped, the ship became a training ground for gunners. Where before the good pointer was an individual artist, pointers now became trained technicians, fairly uniform in their capacity to shoot. The effect was immediately felt. Within a year the *Scylla* established records that were remarkable.

THE PERSONALITY OF THE INNOVATOR

At this point I should like to stop a minute to notice several things directly related to, and involved in, the process of innovation. First, the personality of the innovator. I wish there were space to say a good deal about Admiral Sir Percy Scott. He was a wonderful man. Three small bits of evidence must suffice, however. First, he had a certain mechanical ingenuity. Second, his personal life was shot through with frustration and bitterness. There was a divorce, and a quarrel with the ambitious Lord Charles Beresford—the sounds of which, Scott liked to recall, penetrated to the last outpost of empire. Finally, he possessed, like Swift, a savage indignation directed ordinarily at the inelastic intelligence of all constituted authority—especially the British Admiralty.

There are other points worth mention here. Notice first that Scott was not responsible for the invention of the basic instruments that made the reform in gunnery possible. This reform rested upon the gun itself, which as a rifle had been in existence on ships for at least forty years; the elevating gear, which had been, in the form Scott found it, a part of the rifled gun from the beginning; and the telescope sight, which had been on shipboard at least eight years. Scott's contribution was to bring these three elements, appropriately modified, into a combination that made continuous-aim firing possible for the first time. Notice also that he was allowed to bring these elements into combination by accident, by watching the unconscious action of a gun pointer endeavoring through the operation of his elevating gear to correct partially for the roll of his vessel.

THE PREPARED MIND IS NOT ENOUGH

Scott, as we have seen, had been interested in gunnery; he had thought about ways to increase accuracy by practice and improvement of existing machinery; but able as he was, he had not been able to produce on his own initiative and by his own thinking the essential idea and modify instruments to fit his purpose. Notice here, finally, the intricate interaction of chance, the intellectual climate, and Scott's mind. Fortune (in this case the unaware gun pointer) indeed favors the prepared mind, but even fortune and the prepared mind need a favorable environment before they can conspire to produce sudden change. No intelligence can proceed very far above the threshold of existing data or the binding combinations of existing data.

All these elements that enter into what may be called "original thinking" interest me as a teacher. Deeply rooted in the pedagogical mind often enough is a sterile infatuation with "inert ideas"; there is thus always present in the profession the tendency to be diverted from the *process* by which these ideas, or indeed any ideas, are really produced. I well remember with what contempt a class of mine, which was reading Leonardo da Vinci's *Notebooks*, dismissed the author because he appeared to know no more mechanics than, as one wit in the class observed, a Vermont Republican farmer of the present day. This is perhaps the result to be expected from a method of instruction that too frequently implies that the great generalizations were the result, on the one hand, of chance—an apple falling in an orchard or a teapot boiling on the hearth—or, on the other hand, of some towering intelligence proceeding in isolation inexorably toward some prefigured idea, like evolution, for example.

This process by which new concepts appear, the interaction of fortune, intellectual climate, and the prepared imaginative mind, is an interesting subject for examination offered by any case study of

646

innovation. It was a subject that momentarily engaged the attention of Horace Walpole, whose lissome intelligence glided over the surface of so many ideas. In reflecting upon the part played by chance in the development of new concepts, he recalled the story of the three princes of Serendip who set out to find some interesting object on a journey through their realm. They did not find the particular object of their search, but along the way they discovered many new things simply because they were looking for *something*. Walpole believed this intellectual method ought to be given a name—in honor of the founders—Serendipity; and Serendipity certainly exerts a considerable influence in what we call original thinking. There is an element of Serendipity, for example, in Scott's chance discovery of continuous-aim firing in that he was, and had been, looking for some means to improve his target practice and stumbled upon a solution, by observation, that had never entered his head.

EDUCATING THE NAVY

It was in 1900 that Percy Scott went out to the China Station as commanding officer of H.M.S. *Terrible*. In that ship he continued his training methods and his spectacular successes in naval gunnery. On the China Station he met up with an American junior officer, William S. Sims. Sims had little of the mechanical ingenuity of Percy Scott, but the two were drawn together by temperamental similarities that are worth noticing here. Sims had the same intolerance for what is called spit-and-polish and the same contempt for bureaucratic inertia as his British brother officer. He had for some years been concerned, as had Scott, with what he took to be the inefficiency of his own Navy. Just before he met Scott, for example, he had shipped out to China in the brand new pride of the fleet, the battleship *Kentucky*. After careful investigation and reflection he had informed his superiors in Washington she was not a battleship at all—"but a crime against the white race."

The spirit with which he pushed forward his efforts to reform the naval service can best be stated in his own words to a brother officer: "I am perfectly willing that those holding views different from mine should continue to live, but with every fibre of my being I loathe indirection and shiftiness, and where it occurs in high place, and is used to save face at the expense of the vital interests of our great service (in which silly people place such a childlike trust), I want that man's blood and I will have it no matter what it costs me personally."

From Scott in 1900 Sims learned all there was to know about continuous-aim firing. He modified, with the Englishman's active assistance, the gear on his own ship and tried out the new system. After a few months' training, his experimental batteries began making remarkable records at target practice. Sure of the usefulness of his gunnery methods, Sims then turned to the task of educating the Navy at large. In 13 great official reports he documented the case for continuous-aim firing, supporting his arguments at every turn with a mass of factual data. Over a period of two years, he reiterated three principal points: First, he continually cited the records established by Scott's ships, the *Scylla* and the *Terrible*, and supported these with the accumulating data from his own tests on an American ship; second, he described the mechanisms used and the training procedures instituted by Scott and himself to obtain these records; third, he explained that our own mechanisms were not generally adequate without modification to meet the demands placed on them by continuous-aim firing. Our elevating gear, useful to raise or lower a gun slowly to fix it in position for the proper range, did not always work easily and rapidly enough to enable a gunner to follow a target with his gun throughout the roll of the ship. Sims also explained that such few telescope sights as there were on board our ships were useless. Their cross wires were so thick or coarse that they obscured the target, and the sights had been attached to the gun in such a way that the recoil system of the gun plunged the eyepiece against the eye of the gun pointer.

RESPONSE FROM WASHINGTON

This was the substance not only of the first but of all the succeeding reports written on the subject of gunnery from the China Station. It will be interesting to see what response these met with in Washington. The response falls roughly into three easily identifiable stages.

First stage: no response. Sims had directed his comments to the Bureau of Ordnance and the Bureau of Navigation; in both bureaus there was dead silence. The thing—claims and records of continuous-aim firing—was not credible. The reports were simply filed away and forgotten. Some, indeed, it was later discovered to Sims' delight, were half eaten away by cockroaches.

Second stage: rebuttal. It is never pleasant for any man to have his best work left unnoticed by his superiors, and it was an unpleasantness that Sims suffered extremely ill. In his later reports, he not only used accumulating data to clinch his argument, but he changed his tone. He used deliberately shocking language because, as he said, "They were furious at my first papers and stowed them away. I therefore made up my mind I would give these later papers such a form that they would be dangerous documents to leave neglected in the files." To another friend he added, "I want scalps or nothing and if I can't have 'em I won't play."

SIMS GETS ATTENTION

Besides altering his tone, he took another step to be sure his views would receive attention. He sent copies of his reports to other officers in the fleet. Aware, as a result, that Sims' gunnery claims were being circulated and talked about, the men in Washington were then stirred to action. They responded—notably through the Chief of the Bureau of Ordnance, who had general charge of the equipment used in gunnery practice—as follows:

1. Our equipment was in general as good as the british;
2. since our equipment was as good, the trouble must be with the men, but the gun pointer and the training of gun pointers were the responsibility of the officers on the ships;

648   3. and most significant—continuous-aim firing was impossible.

Experiments had revealed that five men at work on the elevating gear of a six-inch gun could not produce the power necessary to compensate for a roll of five degrees in ten seconds. These experiments and calculations demonstrated beyond peradventure or doubt that Scott's system of gunfire was not possible.

Only one difficulty is discoverable in these arguments; they were wrong at important points. To begin with, while there was little difference between the standard British equipment and the standard U.S. equipment, the instruments on Scott's two ships, the *Scylla* and the *Terrible*, were far better than the standard equipment on our ships. Second, all the men could not be trained in continuous-aim firing until equipment was improved throughout the fleet. Third, the experiments with the elevating gear had been ingeniously contrived at the Washington Navy Yard—on solid ground. It had, therefore, been possible, in the Bureau of Ordnance calculation, to dispense with Newton's first law of motion, which naturally operated at sea to assist the gunner in elevating or depressing a gun mounted on a moving ship. Another difficulty was of course that continuous-aim firing was in use on Scott's and some of our own ships at the time the Chief of the Bureau of Ordnance was writing that it was a mathematical impossibility. In every way I find this second stage, the apparent resort to reason, the most entertaining and instructive in our investigation of the responses to innovation.

Third stage: name calling. Sims, of course, by the high temperature he was running and by his calculated overstatement, invited this. He was told in official endorsements on his reports that there were others quite as sincere and loyal as he and far less difficult; he was called a deliberate falsifier of evidence.

SIMS GETS ACTION

The rising opposition and the character of the opposition was not calculated to discourage further efforts by Sims. It convinced him that he was being attacked by shifty, dishonest men who were the victims, as he said, of insufferable conceit and ignorance. He made up his mind, therefore, that he was prepared to go to any extent to obtain the "scalps" and the "blood" he was after. Accordingly he, a lieutenant, took the extraordinary step of writing to the President of the United States, Theodore Roosevelt, to inform him of the remarkable records of Scott's ships, of the inadequacy of our own gunnery routines and records, and of the refusal of the Navy Department to act. Roosevelt, who always liked to respond to such appeals when he conveniently could, brought Sims back from China late in 1902 and installed him as Inspector of Target Practice, a post the naval officer held throughout the remaining six years of the Administration.

With this sequence of events (the chronological account of the innovation of continuous-aim firing) in mind, it is possible now to examine the evidence to see what light it may throw on our present interest—the origins of and responses to change in a society.

First, the origins. We have already analyzed briefly the origins **649** of the idea. We have seen how Scott arrived at his notion. We must now ask ourselves, I think, why Sims so actively sought, almost alone among his brother officers, to introduce the idea into his service. It is particularly interesting here to notice again that neither Scott nor Sims invented the instruments on which the innovation rested. They did not urge their proposals because of pride in the instruments of their own design.

THE ENGINEER AND THE ENTREPRENEUR

The telescope sight had first been placed on shipboard in 1892 by Bradley Fiske, an officer of great inventive capacity. In that year Fiske had even sketched out on paper the vague possibility of continuous-aim firing, but his sight was condemned by his commanding officer, Robley D. Evans, as of no use. Instead of fighting for his telescope Fiske turned his attention to a range finder. But six years later Sims took over and became the engineer of the revolution.

I would suggest, with some reservations, this explanation: Fiske, as an inventor, took his pleasure in great part from the design of the device. He lacked not so much the energy as the overiding sense of social necessity that would have enabled him to *force* revolutionary ideas on the service. Sims possessed this sense. In Fiske we may here find the familiar plight of the engineer who often enough must watch the products of his ingenuity being organized and promoted by other men. These other promotional men, when they appear in the world of commerce, are called entrepreneurs. In the world of ideas they are still entrepreneurs.

Sims was one, a middle-aged man caught in the periphery (as a lieutenant) of the intricate webbing of a precisely organized society. Rank, the exact definition and limitation of a man's capacity at any given moment in his own career, prevented Sims from discharging all his exploding energies into the purely routine channels of the peace-time Navy. At the height of his powers he was a junior officer standing watches on a ship cruising aimlessly in friendly foreign waters. The remarkable changes in systems of gunfire to which Scott introduced him gave him the opportunity to expend his energies quite legitimately against the encrusted hierarchy of his society. He was moved, it seems to me, in part by his genuine desire to improve his own profession, but also in part by rebellion against tedium, against inefficiency from on high, and against the artificial limitations placed on his actions by the social structure, in his case junior rank.

Now having briefly investigated the origins of the change, let us examine the reasons for what must be considered the weird response we have observed to this proposed change. Here was a reform that greatly and demonstrably increased the fighting effectiveness of a service that maintains itself almost exclusively to fight. Why then this refusal to accept so carefully documented a case; a case proved incontestably by records and experience? Why should virtually all the rulers of a society so resolutely seek to reject a change that so markedly

650   improved its chances for survival in any contest with competing societies?

There are the obvious reasons that will occur to everyone—the
source of the proposed reform was an obscure junior officer 8,000 miles
away; he was, and this is a significant factor, criticizing gear and
machinery designed by the very men in the bureaus to whom he was
sending his criticisms. And furthermore, Sims was seeking to introduce
what he claimed were improvements in a field where improvements
appeared unnecessary. Superiority in war, as in other things, is a
relative matter, and the Spanish-American War had been won by the
old system of gunnery. Therefore, it was superior even though of the
9,500 shots fired, at varying but close ranges, only 121 had found
their mark.

A less obvious cause appears by far the most important one.
It has to do with the fact that the Navy is not only an armed force;
it is a society. In the forty years following the Civil War, this society
had been forced to accommodate itself to a series of technological
changes—the steam turbine, the electric motor, the rifled shell of great
explosive power, case-hardened steel armor, and all the rest of it. These
changes wrought extraordinary changes in ship design, and, therefore,
in the concepts of how ships were to be used; that is, in fleet tactics,
and even in naval strategy. The Navy of this period is a paradise for
the historian or sociologist in search of evidence of a society's responses to change.

A SPREADING DISORDER

To these numerous innovations, producing as they did a spreading
disorder throughout a service with heavy commitments to formal organization, the Navy responded with grudging pain. It is wrong to
assume, as civilians frequently do, that this blind reaction to technological change springs exclusively from some causeless Bourbon dis-
temper that invades the military mind. There is a sounder and more
attractive base. The opposition, where it occurs, of the soldier and the
sailor to such change springs from the normal human instinct to protect oneself and more especially one's way of life. Military organizations are societies built around and upon the prevailing weapon systems. Intuitively and quite correctly the military man feels that a
change in weapon portends a change in the arrangements of his society.

Think of it this way. Since the time that the memory of man
runneth not to the contrary, the naval society has been built upon the
surface vessel. Daily routines, habits of mind, social organization,
physical accommodations, convenions, rituals, spiritual allegiances
have been conditioned by the essential fact of the ship. What then
happens to your society if the ship is displaced as the principal element by such a radically different weapon as the plane? The mores
and structure of the society are immediately placed in jeopardy. They
may, in fact, be wholly destroyed. It was the witty cliche of the 20's
that those naval officers who persisted in defending the battleship
against the apparently superior claims of the carrier did so because

the battleship was a more comfortable home. What, from one point of view, is a better argument?

A DISLOCATION IN NAVAL SOCIETY

This sentiment would appear to account in large part for the opposition to Sims; it was the product of an instinctive protective feeling, even if the reasons for this feeling were not overt or recognized. The years after 1902 proved how right, in their terms, the opposition was. From changes in gunnery flowed an extraordinary complex of changes in shipboard routines, ship design, and fleet tactics. There was, too, a social change. In the days when gunnery was taken lightly, the gunnery officer was taken lightly. After 1903, he became one of the most significant and powerful members of a ship's company, and this shift of emphasis naturally was shortly reflected in promotion lists. Each one of these changes provoked a dislocation in the naval society, and with man's troubled foresight and natural indisposition to break up classic forms, the men in Washington withstood the Sims onslaught as long as they could. It is very significant that they withstood it until an agent from outside—outside and above—who was not clearly identified with the naval society, entered to force change.

This agent, the President of the United States, might reasonably and legitimately claim the credit for restoring our gunnery efficiency. But this restoration by *force majeure* was brought about at great cost to the service and men involved. Bitterness, suspicions, wounds were caused that it was impossible to conceal or heal.

Now this entire episode may be summed up in five separate points:

1. The essential idea for change occurred in part by chance, but in an environment that contained all the essential elements for change, and to a mind prepared to recognize the possibility of change.

2. The basic elements—the gun, gear, and sight—were put in the environment by other men; men interested in designing machinery to serve different purposes, or simply interested in the instruments themselves.

3. These elements were brought into successful combination by minds not interested in the instruments for themselves, but in what they could do with them. These minds were, to be sure, interested in good gunnery, overtly and consciously. They may also, not so consciously, have been interested in the implied revolt that is present in the support of all change. Their temperaments and careers indeed support this view. From gunnery, Sims went on to attack ship designs, existing fleet tactics, and methods of promotion. He lived and died, as the service said, a stormy petrel, a man always on the attack against higher authority, a rebellious spirit.

4. He and his colleagues were opposed on this occasion by men who were apparently moved by three considerations: honest disbelief in the dramatic but substantiated claims of the new process; protection of the existing devices and instruments with which they identified themselves; and maintenance of the existing society with which they were identified.

652

5. The deadlock between those who sought change and those who sought to retain things as they were was broken only by an appeal to superior force; a force removed from and unidentified with the mores, conventions, devices of the society. This seems to me a very important point. The naval society in 1900 broke down in its effort to accommodate itself to a new situation. The appeal to Roosevelt is documentation for Mahan's great generalization that no military service should or can undertake to reform itself. It must seek assistance from outside.

Now, with these five summary points in mind, it may be possible to seek, as suggested at the outset, a few larger implications from this story. What, if anything, may it suggest about the general process by which any society attempts to meet changing conditions?

NO SOCIETY CAN REFORM ITSELF?

There is, to begin with, a disturbing inference half concealed in Mahan's statement that no military organization can reform itself. Certainly civilians would agree with this. We all know now that war and the preparation of war is too important, as Clemenceau said, to be left to the generals. But military organizations are really societies—more rigidly structured, more highly integrated than most communities, but still societies. What then if we make this phrase to read, "No society can reform itself"? Is the process of adaptation to change, for example, too important to be left to human beings? This is a discouraging thought, and historically there is some cause to be discouraged.

This is a subject to which we may well address ourselves. Our society, especially, is built, as I have said, just as surely upon a changing technology as the Navy of the 90's was built upon changing weapon systems. How then can we find the means to accept with less pain to ourselves and less damage to our social organization the dislocations in our society that are produced by innovation? I cannot, of course, give any satisfying answer to these difficult questions. But in thinking about the case study before us, an idea occurred to me that at least might warrant further investigation by men far more qualified than I.

A primary source of conflict and tension in our case study appears to lie in this great word I have used so often in the summary—the word *identification*. It cannot have escaped notice that some men identified themselves with their creations—sights, gun, gear, and so forth—and thus obtained a presumed satisfaction from the thing itself, a satisfaction that prevented them from thinking too closely on either the use or the defects of the thing; that others identified themselves with a settled way of life they had inherited or accepted with minor modification and thus found their satisfaction in attempting to maintain that way of life unchanged; and that still others identified themselves as rebellious spirits, men of the insurgent cast of mind, and thus obtained a satisfaction from the act of revolt itself.

PERSONAL IDENTIFICATION

This purely personal identification with a concept, a convention, or an attitude would appear to be a powerful barrier in the way of easily acceptable change. Here is an interesting primitive example. In the **653** years from 1864–1871 ten steel companies in the country began making steel by the new Bessemer process. All but one of them at the outset imported from Great Britain English workmen familiar with the process. One, the Cambria Company, did not. In the first few years those companies with British labor established an initial superiority. But, by the end of the 70's, Cambria had obtained a commanding lead over all competitors.

The Bessemer process, like any new technique, had been constantly improved and refined in this period from 1864–1871. The British laborers of Cambria's competitors, secure in the performance of their own original techniques, resisted and resented all change. The Pennsylvania farm boys, untrammeled by the rituals and traditions of their craft, happily and rapidly adapted themselves to the constantly changing process. They ended by creating an unassailable competitive position for their company.

How then can we modify the dangerous effects of this word *identification?* And how much can we tamper with this identifying process? Our security, much of it, after all, comes from giving our allegiance to something greater than ourselves. These are difficult questions to which only the most tentative and provisional answers may here be proposed for consideration.

THE DANGER OF LIMITED IDENTIFICATIONS

If one looks closely at this little case history, one discovers that the men involved were the victims of *severely limited* identifications. They were presumably all part of a society dedicated to the process of national defense, yet they persisted in aligning themselves with separate parts of that process—with the existing instruments of defense, with the existing customs of the society, or with the act of rebellion against the customs of the society. Of them all, the insurgents had the best of it. They could, and did, say that the process of defense was improved by a gun that shot straighter and faster, and since they wanted such guns, they were unique among their fellows—patriots who sought only the larger object of improved defense. But this beguiling statement— even when coupled with the recognition that these men were right, and extremely valuable and deserving of respect and admiration— cannot conceal the fact that they were interested too in scalps and blood. They were so interested, in fact, that they made their case a militant one and thus created an atmosphere in which self-respecting men could not capitulate without appearing either weak or wrong or both. So these limited identifications brought men into conflict with each other, and the conflict prevented them from arriving at a common acceptance of a change that presumably, as men interested in our total national defense, they could all find desirable.

It appears, therefore, if I am correct in my assessment, that we might spend some time and thought on the possibility of enlarging the sphere of our identifications from the part to the whole. For example, those Pennsylvania farm boys at the Cambria Steel Company were, apparently, much more interested in the manufacture of steel than in

654

the preservation of any particular way of making steel. So I would suggest that in studying innovation we look further into this possibility: the possibility that any group that exists for any purpose—the family, the factory, the educational institution—might begin by defining for itself its grand object, and see to it that that grand object is communicated to every member of the group. Thus defined and communicated, it might serve as a unifying agent against the disruptive local allegiances of the inevitable smaller elements that compose any group. It may also serve as a means to increase the acceptability of any change that would assist in the more efficient achievement of the grand object.

There appears also a second possible way to combat the untoward influence of limited identifications. We are, I may repeat, a society based on technology in a time of prodigious technological advance, and a civilization committed irrevocably to the theory of evolution. These things mean that we believe in change; they suggest that if we are to survive in good health we must become an "adaptive society." By the word "adaptive" is meant the ability to extract the fullest possible returns from the opportunities at hand; the ability of Sir Percy Scott to select judiciously from the ideas and material presented both by the past and present and to throw them into a new combination. "Adaptive," as here used, also means the kind of resilience that will enable us to accept fully and easily the best promises of changing circumstances without losing our sense of continuity or our essential integrity.

INADEQUATE SOLUTIONS

We are not yet emotionally an adaptive society, though we try systematically to develop forces that tend to make us one. We encourage the search for new inventions; we keep the mind stimulated, bright, and free to seek out fresh means of transport, communication, and energy; yet we remain, in part, appalled by the consequences of our ingenuity and, too frequently, try to find security through the shoring up of ancient and irrelevant conventions, the extension of purely physical safeguards, or the delivery of decisions we ourselves should make into the keeping of superior authority like the state. These solutions are not necessarily unnatural or wrong, but historically they have not been enough, and I suspect they never will be enough to give us the serenity and competence we seek.

A NEW VIEW OF OURSELVES

If the preceding statements are correct, they suggest that we might give some attention to the construction of a new view of ourselves as a society which in time of great change identified itself with and obtained security and satisfaction from the wise and creative accommodation to change itself. Such a view rests, I think, upon a relatively greater reverence for the mere *process* of living in a society than we possess today, and a relatively smaller respect for and attachment to any special *product* of a society—a product either as finite as a bathroom fixture or as conceptual as a fixed and final definition of our **655** Constitution or our democracy.

Historically, such an identification with *process* as opposed to *product*, with adventurous selection and adaptation as opposed to simple retention and possessiveness, has been difficult to achieve collectively. The Roman of the early republic, the Italian of the late fifteenth and early sixteenth century, or the Englishman of Elizabeth's time appear to have been most successful in seizing the new opportunities while conserving as much of the heritage of the past as they found relevant and useful to their purpose.

We seem to have fallen on times similar to theirs, when many of the existing forms and schemes have lost meaning in the face of dramatically altering circumstances. Like them we may find at least part of our salvation in identifying ourselves with the adaptive process and thus share with them some of the joy, exuberance, satisfaction, and security with which they went out to meet their changing times.

G. WILLIAM DOMHOFF

How to Commit Revolution in Corporate America

I appear here today by courtesy of the Legal Staff of the Regents of the University of California. Now I know that they didn't invite me, that the Student Mobilization Committee invited me, but I also know that the Regents put out a ruling that faculty members will be fired for participating in any strike. Thus, being a good and faithful employee, and much enjoying the sunshine and redwoods of Santa Cruz, I thought I'd better get clearance from university experts on the matter of this student strike before I did anything rash and compromising. And, thank goodness, these legal men assured me that I wouldn't be fired for appearing here today—just so long as I didn't advocate anything illegal.

Since the title of my little talk is "How to Commit Revolution in Corporate America," and since committing revolution might be construed by some people as being somewhat illegal, I certainly

This is the slightly revised and extended text of a speech given to the Student Strike Rally at the University of California, Santa Cruz, on April 26, 1968. The footnotes were added in May, 1971. Several sentences in the text were added in 1970. Reprinted by permission of the author and the publisher from Peninsula Observer, pp. 1–8.

wouldn't want to appear to be advocating it. No, I don't advocate anything. I consider myself as acting in one of the many capacities of a well-rounded professor in the modern multi-versity—as a consultant, just a consultant, to some group of citizens within the community that feels a need to call upon its tax-supported knowledge factory to give advice on a particular activity or undertaking. As a consultant, then, I'm not being illegal. In fact, I am doing what every good professor does, although for a tremendously reduced fee, and I expect to get credit for it when I am considered for promotion and tenure.

I am well aware that most of you aren't revolutionaries—that you are mostly upper-middle-class people cutting loose from home by temporarily growing beards or indulging in exotic potions or getting all caught up in doing good things for your less fortunate brethren from the other side of the tracks. I know that most of you think it is just a matter of a little more time, a little more education, and a little more good will before most of this country's social and economic problems are straightened out, and I suspect that many of you who are currently among the earnest and concerned are going to be somewhere else in a few years, as is that idealistic student group of past years, your parents. But maybe someday some of you will be looking around for a revolutionary consulting service. Maybe someday you will wise up to the Square Deals, New Deals, Fair Deals, New Frontiers, and other quasi-liberal gimmicks used to shore up and justify an over-developed, inhuman, and wasteful corporation capitalism as it gradually rose to power in the 20th century. Maybe someday some significant number of people, Left and Right, will really learn that courage, integrity, and a casual style aren't enough to bring about meaningful, substantial changes, that moral anguish has to be translated into changes in the social structure to do more than make you feel all warm and good and guilt-free inside. Maybe some day others of you, who are already on the right road, will learn that no matter how militant or violent or critical you may be, you are still not your own person and a revolutionary as long as you merely try to get your leaders to pay attention and better understand, whether it be through letters or sit-ins or time bombs. Maybe you will learn to ignore the leaders you are harassing and decide to replace them and their system —with yourselves and your own system, and on that day you will become revolutionaries instead of militant supplicants appealing to the stuffy Father Figures for a little more welfare and social justice, and a little less war.

At any rate, if and when you give up on these little attempts at minor social improvements, and turn to the really exhilarating experience of freeing your own self by committing revolution, then perhaps these observations may be of some use. I offer them in a tentative fashion, fully expecting them to be reworked, challenged, developed. Since I am only a consultant, no hard feelings if you reject them. We academics are very philosophical about such matters. It's part of being professional, of being a good consultant.

There are three aspects, I think, to any good revolutionary

program for corporate America. These aspects are closely intertwined, **657**
and all three must be developed alongside each other, but there is
nonetheless a certain logic, a certain order of priorities, in the manner
I present them. First, you need a comprehensive, overall analysis of
the present-day American system. You've got to realize that the corporation capitalism of today is not the 19th-century individual capitalism that conservatives yearn for. Nor is it the pluralistic paradise that
liberals rave about and try to patch up. Nor is it the finance capitalism
of the American Communists who are frozen in their analyses of
another day.

Second, you need relatively detailed blueprints for a post-
industrial America. You've got to show people concrete plans that
improve their lot either spiritually or materially. There's no use scaring
them with shouts of socialism, which used to be enough of a plan
however general, but which today only calls to mind images of Russia,
deadening bureaucracy, and 1984. And there's no use boring them
with vague slogans about participation and vague abstractions about
dehumanization. You've got to get down to where people live, and
you've got to get them thinking in terms of a better America without
the spectre of Russia, rightly or wrongly, driving any thought of risking social change out of their heads.

Third, and finally, you need a plan of attack, a program for
taking power. For make no mistake about it—before most people get
involved in revolutionary activity they take a mental look way down
the road. Maybe not all the way down the road, but a long way down.
They want to know what they are getting into, and what the chances
are, and whether there is really anything positive in sight that is worth
the gamble. In short, I suspect that most people just don't fit the
formula that seems to be prevalent in America: get people involved
in anything—rent strikes, anti-nuclear testing demonstrations, rat
strikes, draft demonstrations, whatever, and gradually they will develop a revolutionary mentality. According to this theory, apparently,
people will realize their power and want more if they win the rat
strike, or they will wise up if they are hit on the head by a peace officer
at the draft demonstration. Well, maybe that works for some people,
but I wouldn't count on it, and I wouldn't rely on it to the exclusion
of all else. Actually, most people seem to sink back into lethargy when
the rats are gone; or nuclear testing in the atmosphere is abandoned.
And I know of no convincing evidence that getting people hit on the
head or thrown in jail makes them into revolutionaries—certainly
many of those who believe this didn't become revolutionaries by this
route. So, ponder carefully about this activity for activity's sake. You
need a plan of attack, not just some issues like peace or rats. And one
thing more on this point: that plan has to come out of your analysis
of the present socioeconomic system and out of your own life experience, that is, out of the American experience, and not out of the experiences of Russia, or China, or Cuba, all of which have been different
from each other, and are different from the U.S.A. The world moves,
even in America, and as it moves new realities arise and old theories
become irrelevant. New methods become necessary. If you expect to

658 be listened to, you will have to look around you afresh and build your own plan, abandoning all the sacred texts on What Is To Be Done.

An analysis of the system, a set of blueprints, and a program for gaining power. That is the general framework. Let me now say something more concrete about each, admitting in advance that some points will be touched on only lightly and that others, which should be read as friendly criticisms of past and present efforts of American revolutionaries, may be too cryptic for those who have not observed these movements or read about their beliefs and strategies.

As to the analysis, here I will be the most cryptic. The name of the system is corporation capitalism. Huge corporations have come to dominate the economy, reaping fabulous, unheard-of profits and avoiding their share of the taxes, and their owners and managers—the corporate rich—are more and more coming to dominate all aspects of American life, including government. Corporate rich foundations like Ford, Rockefeller, and Carnegie finance and direct cultural and intellectual innovations, corporate rich institutes and associations like the Council on Foreign Relations, the Committee for Economic Development, and the Rand Corporation do most of the economic, political, and military research and provide most of the necessary government experts and consultants. As for the future, well, Bell Telephone is undertaking a pilot project in which it will run a high school in the Detroit ghetto, and Larry Rockefeller has suggested that every corporation in New York "adopt" a city block and help make sure that its residents are healthy, happy, and nonriotous. Adopt-a-block may never happen, and corporations may not run many high schools any time soon, but such instances are symbolic of where we are probably headed—corporation feudalism, cradle-to-the-grave dependency on some aspect or another of a corporate structure run by a privileged few who use its enormous rewards to finance their own private schools, maintain their own exclusive clubs, and ride to hounds on their vast farm lands. Even agriculture is being corporatized at an amazing rate. Many family farmers are in a state of panic as the corporate rich and their corporations use tax loopholes to gobble up this last remaining bastion of 19th-century America.

Much work on this necessary analysis of corporation capitalism, or feudalism, has been done, but much more needs to be done. It is a scandal, or, rather, a sign of corporate rich dominance of the universities, that so little social stratification research concerns the social upper class of big businessmen, that so little political sociology research concerns the power elite that is the operating arm of the corporate rich, indeed, that so much of the social sciences in general concern themselves with the workers, the poor, and other countries—that is, with things that are of interest to the corporate rich. If you want to know anything interesting about the American power structure you have to piece together the hints of journalists, read the few books by a handful of Leftists who are academic outcasts, follow the research reports of two excellent student groups, and listen to and read Dan Smoot. Dan Smoot? Yes, Dan Smoot. Properly translated, he has a better view of the American power structure than most American political scientists, who of course merely laugh at him. He may not use the same labels I would for the men in charge (he thinks David Rockefeller & Co. are communists or dupes!), but at least he knows who's running the show, It is truly a commentary on American academia that he and one journalist—Establishment journalist Joseph Kraft—have done the only work on the all-important Council on Foreign Relations, one of the most influential policy-forming associations of the corporate rich. While the professors are laughing at Dan Smoot and equating the business community with the National Association of Manufacturers and the U.S. Chamber of Commerce, Smoot is keeping up with the activities of the richest, most powerful, the vanguard of corporation feudalism.

This really brings you to your first revolutionary act, more research on the American power structure. Just turning the spotlight on the power elite is a revolutionary act, although only Act One. Ideas and analyses are powerful, and they shake people up. The problem of would-be American revolutionaries has not been an overemphasis on ideas, but the use of old ones, wrong ones, and transplanted ones. That is why C. Wright Mills grabbed American students and parts of American academia. He had new, relevant ideas and facts about the here and now—he exploded old cliches and slogans, and, I think he created more radicals with his work than any hundred Oakland and Los Angeles policemen with their billy clubs.*

But analysis is not only important so you can better criticize the system. It is also necessary in developing blueprints and plans of attack. As to the developing of blueprints, to go beyond mere devastating criticism of the system you have to understand it so you can figure out what kind of a better system you can build on it. The most important and obvious point here is that you will be building on a fully industrialized, non-farming system. This means that your post-industrial society can look very different from systems built on pre-industrial, agricultural bases such as was the case in Russia, China, and Cuba.

As to the importance of a good analysis in developing a program for taking power, this is essential because it tells you what you can and cannot expect, what you can and cannot do, and what you should and should not advocate. Let me give four examples: 1. Corporation capitalism, if it can continue to corporatize the "underdeveloped" world and displace small businessmen and realtors in the cities, may have a lot more room for reforms. In fact, if creature comfort is enough, it may come to satisfy most of its members. Be that as it may, and I doubt if it can solve its problems in a humanly tolerable way, the important point is that no American revolutionary should find himself shocked or irrelevant because the corporate rich agree to nationwide health insurance or guaranteed annual incomes, or pull out of one of their military adventures. And don't get your hopes up for any imminent collapse. Better to be surprised by a sudden turn that hastens your time schedule than to be disappointed once again by the flexibility of the corporate rich. This means that you should rely on

*The Vietnam War, the draft, and the civil rights struggle are another matter. They created more revolutionaries than C. Wright Mills.

your own program, not depression or war, to challenge the system and bring about change, and that you should have a flexible, hang-loose attitude toward the future. Predictions of the inevitability of anything, whether collapse or socialism, fall a little flat and leave us a little jaded after comparing earlier predictions with the experience of the 20th century. We need a political philosophy that is a little more humble and open than those which currently encompass American leftists. 2. Corporation capitalism seems to be very much dependent on overseas sales and investments, probably much more so than it is on the military spending necessary to defend and extend that Free World empire. And even if some economists would dispute that, I think it is 100 percent safe to say that most members of the corporate rich are convinced that this overseas economic empire is essential—and that is what affects their political and economic and military behavior. Thus, the corporate rich fear, nay, more than that, have utter horror of isolationism, and that suggests that you revolutionaries should agree with conservatives about the need for isolationism. 3. The American corporate rich have at their command unprecedented, almost unbelievable firepower and snooping power. This makes it questionable whether or not a violent revolutionary movement has a chance of getting off the ground. It also makes it doubtful whether or not a secret little Leninist-type party can remain secret and unpenetrated very long. In short, a non-violent and open party may be dictated to you as your only choice by the given fact of the corporate leaders' military and surveillance capability, just as a violent and closed party was dictated by the Russian situation. 4. The differences between present-day corporation capitalism and 19-century individual capitalism must be emphasized again and again if you are to reach or neutralize those currently making up the New Right. Those people protest corporation capitalism and its need for big government and overseas spending in the name of small business, small government, competition, the market place—all those things destroyed or distorted by the corporate system. You must agree with the New Right that these things have happened and then be able to explain to them how and why they have happened, not due to the communists or labor, or liberal professors, but due to the growing corporatization of the society and the needs of these corporations. You can't give up on these New Rightists—they know the Rockefellers, the J. J. McCloys, the Averell Harrimans, the Paul Hoffmans, the Adlai Stevensons, and the John V. Lindsays run American society. (Here I am just naming some of the relatively few multimillionaire businessmen and corporation lawyers known to the American public.) And, like the New Left, they don't like it. It is your job to teach them that the new corporate system is the problem, not the motives and good faith of the corporate rich they call communists and dupes of liberal academics.

Now, as to your second general need, blueprints for a post-industrial America. Blueprints are first of all necessary to go beyond mere criticism. Any half-way moral idiot can criticize corporation capitalism, anyone can point to slums, unemployment, waste, phony advertising, inflation, shoddy goods, and on and on. To be revolutionary, you have got to go beyond the militantly liberal act of offering some criticism and then asking people to write their congressman or to sit in somewhere so that the authorities will do something about the problem. And it is necessary for you to self-consciously begin to develop this plan because it is not going to miraculously appear after a holocaust or emanate mystically from the collective mind of that heterogeneous generalization called The Movement. Individuals are going to have to develop aspects of these blueprints, wild, yea-saying blueprints that you can present with excitement and glee to Mr. and Mrs. Fed-up America. It is not enough to be for peace and freedom, which is really only to be against war and racism. It is not positive enough. As a smug little man from the Rand Corporation—a consultant for the other side—once reminded me, everyone, even him, is for peace and justice—the differences begin when you get to specifics.

Blueprints are also necessary to break the Russian logjam in everyone's thinking, revolutionary and non-revolutionary alike. Only by talking about concrete plans, thus getting people reacting to them and thereby developing their own plans, will people forget about Russia, a centralized, bureaucratic, industrializing country that is neither here nor there as far as you are concerned, and has no relevance to either your criticisms or plans. In short, you have got to show people that your concern is America, that you love America, and that your moral concern is based upon what America could be, as compared with what it is. No one should out-American you. You, as revolutionaries, have a right to that flag. And if you don't feel like grabbing the present American flag right at this juncture, then reach back into American revolutionary history, to the unfinished revolution, for your flags. Like that great snake flag, that great phallic message, of the Gadsden Rebellion, with its prideful warning hissing out across the centuries: DON'T TREAD ON ME.*

The point is that you are Americans and that you want to build a better, a post-industrial America, that you want to use the base your forefathers gave you to realize the American dream. Forget all this internationalism talk. The foreign revolutions some of you often hope to copy were fought by men who were fervent nationalists, not bigoted ethnocentrics who believed that no other nationalism was as good or moral as theirs, but nationalists who were of their people, who loved their country and its culture, and who really lived and developed their own heritage. They talked internationalism, they read widely, they were appreciative and tolerant of many other culture ways, but they were heart and soul products of their land and its traditions. To throw away the potent psychological force of nationalism because it has been identified in this country with an Americanism that is often parochial and ethnocentric, and especially anti-Semitic, is to ignore, ironically enough, one of the few things you can learn from studying other 20th-century revolutions: a feeling for your country and its little nuances is an intimate and potent part of Western man. If that sounds too

---

*It is a great flag even though the Gadsden Rebellion leaves something to be desired as a model for present day activities.

narrow and unfeeling for some of you, I would add that it is probably wrong anyhow to think your internationalism somehow supports foreign revolutionaries. Do you really think the Viet Cong derive any strength from telegrams of support or demonstrations by little New York-based committees on This and That? That's Dean Rusk's mentality. Don't you think the Cong and the Russians and the Chinese are big enough to take care of themselves? Isn't it perhaps a little bit paternalistic to think you are in any way helping those indigenous movements? Your task is here at home, and the way to get to this task is to develop a set of blueprints to go with your critique.

Now, I don't make these statements, and this distinction between nationalism and ethnocentrism, as one who has not considered the problem long and hard. As a Freudian-oriented psychologist, I believe more than anyone, certainly more than you who subscribe to one or other of the environmentalisms (liberalism and Marxism in their various guises) that predominate in American social science, that people everywhere have the same basic psyche, the same wishes and fears. I believe that the transition rites, myths, and rituals from tribes all over the world show that all men and women suffer from fears of separation from mother and group, that all men come to feel rivalry toward father and brother, that all men must go to the desert or the mountain to sruggle for independence from their parents, and that all people have a strange sweet ambivalence toward death. In short, I know that all people have the same problems, but I also know that there are such things as personality and culture, that is, that we all have slightly different ways of handling our wishes and fears. And since I know that these personality and cultural differences are in good part, if not totally, defenses against anxiety and wishes that cause anxiety, I recognize that to attack them, or to ask people to discard them without offering them to a new set of defenses, is to invite resistance, is to invite fear and distrust. We are faced with the seeming paradox that men who share the same problems can easily come to mistrust or hate each other if one person's defenses threaten those of the other. So I am saying that you should bypass these resistances, that as theoretical psychologists you should of course recognize the psychic universality of mankind, but that as revolutionaries you should also recognize that such a general truism is of no use to you in your day-to-day dealings with people if you are not sensitive to and sympathetic toward those individual and group defenses called personality and culture. In short, you have got to recognize that we are all nationalists in the sense of our identity, and work with this fact, trying to bring out the best in your own national tradition. If this sounds risky to you somehow, as something that might lead to outcomes you don't advocate, or to a narrow parochialism, then you have underestimated the importance of blueprints in your revolutionary program. For it is the blueprints that are the key to transcending narrow outlooks and ensuring that only the best in the American national character is more fully manifested. It is the explicitly stated blueprints which ensure that some implicit retrogressive program does not come to tacitly guide your actions as a revolutionary movement.

What could this post-industrial society look like? Naturally, as **663** you might suspect of someone trying to be a respectable consultant, I have a few suggestions, all tentative, and I will mention some of them to give you an idea of what I mean, but I want to emphasize that it is on this project that so many more people could become totally in-volved in the revolutionary process. If it would be by and large in-tellectuals, academics, and students who would work on the analysis and critique of the growing corporation feudalism, it would be people from all walks of life who would be essential to this second necessity. You need men and women with years of experience in farming, small business, teaching, city planning, recreation, medicine, and on and on, to start discussing and writing about ways to organize that part of society they know best for a post-corporate America. You need to pro-vide outlets via forums, discussions, papers, and magazines for the pent-up plans and ideals of literally millions of well-trained, experi-enced, frustrated Americans who see stupidity and greed all around them but can't do a thing about it. You need to say, for example, "Look Mr. and Mrs. City Planning Expert trapped in this deadly bureaucracy controlled by big businessmen, draw up a sensible plan for street de-velopment, or park development, in your town of 30,000 people." "Look, Mr. Blue Collar Worker, working for this big corporation, how should this particular plant be run in a sensible society?"

And, you need not only to discuss and to develop these pro-grams, you need to make them clear to every American, not only to the ones you might win to your side because the present systems dis-gusts them morally, or exploits them, or ignores them, or rejects them. No, even more, you need to reach the many millions more who, once they did not fear you or distrust you, would be willing to live under either the new or old system. And make no mistake about their im-portance. When people talk about the small percentage of Bolsheviks who took over Russia, they often forget the overwhelming numbers who passively accepted them, in that case out of disgust with war, despair, and the lack of a plan of their own that they really believed in.

Let me repeat to make its importance clear: the neutralization of large masses should be a prime goal for a program to develop and present blueprints for a post-corporate America. To this end it should be personally handed by some one revolutionary to every person in America. Each person should receive a short, simple, one-page handbill especially relevant to his situation or occupation. It would begin, for example, "Policeman, standing here protecting us from Evil at this demonstration, Where Will You Be After The Revolution?" And then, in a few short sentences you will tell this bewildered soul, whom you embraced after handing him his message, that there will still be a great need for policemen after the revolution, but that policemen will tend to do more of the things that they like to do—helping, assisting, guiding—rather than the things that get them a bad name, that is, faithfully carrying out the repressive dictates of their power elite mas-ters. You will tell him that you know that some policemen are preju-diced or authoritarian, but that you know that is neither here nor there because orders on whether to shoot ("to do whatever is necessary to keep 'law and order' in this ghetto'') or not to shoot come from officials higher up who are intimately intertwined in the corporate system.

Similar handbills should be prepared for every person. Some would hear good things, like more money and better health. Some would hear things that would surprise them or make them wonder, like "You won't be socialized, Mr. Small Businessman producing a novelty or retailing pets on a local level, because the socialized corporations can produce more than enough; and furthermore, keep in mind that government in a post-corporate America couldn't possibly harass you as much as the big bankers who won't lend you money, the big corporations who undercut you, and the corporate-oriented politicians who overtax you." Others, for whom there is no good news, would get such cheery messages as "Insurance Man—we hope you have other skills, like gardening or typing; "Corporate Manager—we hope you like working for the anonymous public good as much as you liked working for anonymous millionaire coupon clippers;" "CIA man—we hope you are as good at hiding as you are supposed to be at seeking."

Perhaps most of all, there has to be a consideration of the role of Mr. John Bircher, Mr. Physician, Mr. Dentist, and others now on the New Right. They who are put off or ignored by the increasing corporatization have to be shown that their major values—individuality, freedom, local determination—are also the values of a post-corporate America. This does not mean they will suddenly become revolutionaries, but it is important to start them wondering as to whether or not they would find things as bad in the new social system as they do in this system which increasingly annoys them, exasperates them, and ignores them. They must be weaned from the handful of large corporations and multimillionaires who use them for their own ends by talking competition while practicing monopoly, by screaming about taxes while paying very little, and by talking individuality while practicing collectivism.

What would a post-industrial America look like? First of all, it would be certain American institutions writ large—like the Berkeley food co-op that is locally controlled by consumers, like the Pasadena water and electric systems that are publically owned, like the Tennessee Valley Authority which has allowed the beginnings of the sane, productive, and beautiful development of at least one river region in our country. In short, the system would start from local controls and work up, like it used to before all power and taxes were swept to the national level, mostly by war and the big corporations. And, as you can see, it would be a mixed system, sometimes with control by regional authorities, and sometimes, as should be made clear in the handbill to certain small businessmen, with control in private hands. For many retail franchises, for many novelty productions, and, I suspect, for many types of farms and farmers, depending on region, crop involved, and other considerations, private enterprise may be the best method of control.

The question will be raised—is this promise of some private ownership pandering to a voting bloc? Is it like the old communist trick of the united front? The answer is a resounding NO. Any post-corporate society that does not maximize chances for freedom, flexibility, and individuality is not worth fighting for. Given the enormous capabilities of corporate production, the economic and cultural insignificance of most small businessmen, and the very small number of family farmers, there is simply no economic or political or cultural reason to socialize everything. Some pre-industrial societies may have had to socialize everything to defend their revolutions against hostile forces, but that is only another way in which your situation differs from theirs.

I have left the most obvious for last. Of course the corporations would be socialized. Their profits would go to all people in lower prices (and thus higher real wages) and/or repair to local, state, and national treasuries in the amounts necessary to have a park on every corner (replacing one of the four gas stations), and medical, dental, educational, recreational, or arts facilities on the other corners (replacing the other three gas stations—there being no need for any but a few gas stations due to the ease of introducing electric cars when a few hundred thousand rich people are not in a position to interfere). But how to man this huge corporate enterprise? First, with blue collar workers, who would be with you all the way in any showdown no matter how nice some members of the corporate rich have been to them lately. Second, with men from lower-level management positions who have long ago given up the rat race, wised up, and tacitly awaited your revolution. Fantasy? Perhaps, but don't underestimate the cynicism at minor levels of the technostructure. I have spoken with and to these groups, and there is hope. They are not all taken in, any more than most Americans are fooled by the mass media about domestic matters. They are just trapped, with no place to go but out if they think too much or make a wave. Now, "out" is easy enough if you're young and single, but it's a little sticky if you didn't wake up to the whole corporate absurdity until you were long out of college and had a wife and two kids. Cultivate these well-educated men and women whose talents are wasted and ill-used. Remind them that the most revolutionary thing they can do—aside from feeding you information and money so you can further expose the system and aside from helping to plan the post-corporate society—is to be in a key position in the technostructure when the revolution comes. You may not win many of them percentagewise, but then it wouldn't take many to help you through a transition.

Then too, part of the corporate system would disappear—one computerized system of banking and insurance would eliminate the incredible duplication, paperwork, and nonsense now existent in those two "highly profitable" but worthless areas of the corporate economy. Corporate retails would be broken up and given to local consumer co-ops, or integrated into nationalized producer-retailer units in some cases. Corporate transports (air, rails, buses) would be given in different cases to state, local, and national government, as well as to, on occasion, the retailers or producers they primarily serve. The public utilities, as earlier hinted, would finally be given to the public, mostly on the local and regional level, probably on the national level in the case of telephones. The only real problem, I think, is manufacturing, where you have to hold the loyalty of technicians and workers to survive a transition. Blue collar control may be the answer in some cases, regional or national government control in others. Here, obviously, is one of those questions that needs much study, with blue collar and white collar workers in the various industries being the key informants and idea men.

I have not here presented a final, detailed set of blueprints for a post-corporate America, but I hope I have suggested how important the development of such blueprints is, that I have tossed out a few ideas that might have merit or start you thinking, and that I have made you wonder as to how much energy and enthusiasm might possibly be released by taking such a project to Americans in all walks of life. The so-called "false consciousness" of Americans is not primarily in their misperceptions of "the power structure." Many are already wise to liberal baloney on this score, especially blue collar workers. The "false consciousness" is in a lack of vision, a resigned cynicism, a hopeless despair. "Struggle" without vision will never achieve success in America.

I come, then, finally to the third necessity, a program for taking the reins of government from the power elite in order to carry out the plan developed by revolutionary visionaires. It is on this point that there is likely to be found the most disagreement, the most confusion, the most uncertainty, and the most fear. But I think you do have something very important to go on—the ideas and experiences and successes of the civil rights and new left and hippie movements of the past several years. If they have not given you an analysis of corporation capitalism or a set of blueprints, which is their weakness, they have given you the incredibly precious gift of new forms of struggle and new methods of reaching people, and these gifts must be generalized, articulated, and more fully developed.*

I have a general term, borrowed from a radical hippy, that I like to use because I think it so beautifully encompasses what these movements have given to you—psychic guerrilla warfare—the "psychic" part appealing to my psychologist instincts and summarizing all hard-hitting non-violent methods, the "guerrilla warfare" part hopefully giving to those who want to take to the hills enough measure of satisfaction to allow them to stick around and participate in the only type of guerrilla warfare likely to work in corporate America. For make no mistake about it, psychic guerrilla warfare is a powerful weapon in a well-educated, highly industrialized country that has a tradition of liberal values and democratic political processes. And it is the kind of guerrilla warfare that America's great new acting-out girls can indulge in on an equal basis with any male anywhere. It is the confrontation politics of the New Left—teach-ins, marches, walk-ins,

---

*Events since this speech was written show that the spirit and approach of the New Left have been lost. This makes me even more uncomfortable with what follows than I was when I wrote it.

sit-ins, push-ins, love-ins, folk rocks, and be-ins. It is the non-violent, religiously based, democratically inspired, confrontation morality of Martin Luther King, and it is the unfailing good humor, psychological analysis, and flower power of the hippie. Together they are dynamite— what politician or labor leader can fault confrontation, what true Christian or Jew can react violently to non-violence, and what disgruntled middle-classer can fail to smile or admit begrudging admiration for the best in American hippiedom?

Before I suggest how and where to lay this psychological dynamite, I know I must force myself to say a few words concerning what you are wondering about the most, the role of violence. The words aren't easy for me to say, a look at history makes the ground shaky under me, and many will secretly or openly assume that this is cowardly rationalization by an academic. Despite all this, I reject the lesson of history by claiming that the situation is different in this over-industrialized country: I don't think violence will work in corporate America, 1968. I don't believe in non-violence as a way of life as some people do, so I don't argue from any philosophic base. Nor do I deny the necessity for violence in most revolutionary efforts. No, I'm just afraid violence is not a winning strategy in corporate America, and a winning strategy is the primary concern of the revolutionary consultant. There is first of all the brute fact of this country's incredible military hardware. But there is more than that. This democracy is far from perfect, and the corporate rich have buggered its functioning at a zillion different junctures, but it has never been tested to its limits either. You've got to see just how much there is to the claim that values and political institutions would win out in a showdown. There are even liberals who might be willing to die for such a cause.

Is this doubt about the usefulness of violence in corporate America only the opinion of an academic type? I think not. It was also the opinion of Che Guevara, and my reference to him will be my first and only appeal to authority, to sacred text. Indeed, it is almost a tragedy that those who love and admire Che, and at the same time dream of physical guerrilla warfare in the U.S.A., should overlook his very first premise for it—people take to physical guerrilla warfare only when they have lost all hope of non-violent solutions. El Che is said to have laughed long and hard when asked about the possibility of guerrilla warfare in this country. In short, he too apparently believed that what works in the maldeveloped, exploited hinterland of the corporation capitalist empire does not necessarily apply in the overdeveloped, affluent center.

Americans have not lost their hope. Furthermore, they are not likely to lose it by any of the means currently being used to escalate physical confrontations, for such confrontations do not "expose" the most fundamental aspects of the political system. The only way people would lose their faith in the political system, if they are capable of losing it at all, is in a full and open and honest test of its promise. The political system has got to be tested totally by completely unarmed men and women, and if that doesn't sound courageous enough for you, then you have need for a more hairy-chested proof of masculinity and

668   integrity than I do. And if you argue that people won't listen, that
they haven't listened in the past few years, then I say it's because you
haven't yet brought to them an analysis that rings true enough, that
you haven't yet hit them with a program that is exciting enough, and
that you haven't yet provided them with a plan of attack that is be-
lievable enough to be worth trying. I say you really haven't turned on
with all your intellectual and libidinal resources, that you haven't
given them your best shot. What you have done so far is great, but it
is only a prelude. You've got to escalate your incredibleness, your
audacity, your cleverness, and your playfulness, not your physical
encounters, if you are to break through the American malaise.

Enough of such moralizing. Back to the more manic matter
of psychic guerrilla warfare. How do you direct this dynamite to its
task of destroying the ideological cover of the corporate rich? First,
you start a new political party, a wide-open, locally based political
party dedicated to the development of blueprints for a post-corporate
America and to the implementation of them through psychic guerrilla
warfare.* It should be a party with a minimal, low-key ideology which
does not find it necessary to have a position on every age-old question
in ontology, epistomology, and Russian and Chinese history. It should
be a party open to anyone prepared to abandon all other political affiliations and beliefs—in other words, it would not be an Anti-This-Or-
That coalition of liberal Democrats, Communists, Trotskyists, and
Maoists. In fact, ignore those groups. The best members will drop out
and join yours. For the rest, they have no constituencies and would
soon fall to fighting the old fights among themselves anyway—Communist and Anti-Communist, Pro-Soviet and Anti-Soviet, and on and
on ad tedium. No, you don't need that—it would destroy you like it
destroyed them. In fact, they need you, for if you got something
going the party would be big enough for all of them to work in without
seeing each other or having to defend the Old Faiths. You've got to
show them how to do it here so they can transcend their ties to the
ideas of other countries and other ages.

In addition to declining offers of coalition, and instead seeking
converts, such a party should reject as inappropriate the Leninist
"democratic centralism" for an American revolutionary party. Not
that all the old lefties would give it up—some would probably join your
party and try to "caucus" or "bore from within," but the open give
and take of ideas and the local autonomy of chapters could handle
the little organizational games they have become so good at while
organizing and reorganizing each other over the past thirty or forty
years.

Before I go on, let me pause to make some things clear. For
all my despair over certain Old Left ideas, I think many of the Old
Leftists I have met are well-meaning people—it's when they start plan-

---

*I have come to question this judgment. A political party may be the last
phase of a new plan for taking power. It may even be that the analysis and
blueprints should be presented in non-partisan elections and Democratic Party
primaries!

ning that their minds lock into the old patterns. Further, I respect their admiration for their heroes. Lenin was great. So was Trotsky. So were Eugene Debs and Thomas Paine, and so are Mao and Fidel, but they have nothing to teach you except guts and perseverance because your situation is different. Honor them for their courage and their example, but most of all, for their ability to let go of sacred texts and do what was necessary in their given society even when it contradicted received doctrine (as it always did) : to take power in a pre-industrial state on a very small base, to march to the countryside instead of waiting for the workers, to rely on peasants. If they could forget the sacred texts of their masters, why can't you go beyond theirs? You need your own Lenins, not theirs, your own Ches, not theirs, and I suggest they will be as different as the first is from the second. Begin this self-reliance by starting your own kind of American revolutionary party, one not open to FBI subversion because an open party depends on ideas, and FBI men, having no ideas, would be unable to maintain their cover.*

So what does this party do besides present a constant withering critique of corporation capitalism and build blueprints for a post-industrial America? It practices all forms of psychic guerrilla warfare whenever and wherever there is a possible convert. Eventually, and on the right occasions, it even enters elections, not to win votes at first, but to win converts. In making its pitch, it doesn't ask men and women to quit their jobs or take to the hills, but rather it asks them to commit their allegiances to new socioeconomic arrangements, to help develop new social and intellectual institutions, to financially support the growth of the party, to read party-oriented newspapers, to convert and neutralize friends and neighbors, and to stand firm if the corporate rich try something funny.

After building chapters in every town or city district in the country by word of mouth and small group contact, you would gradually begin to participate in local elections to gain further attention. Then you would enter legislative elections, both to gain converts and to win seats, for the more legislative seats you hold, state and national, the better for the sudden takeover that will come later. You avoid like the plague winning any executive offices, for to be a mayor or governor when you don't control the whole system is meaningless and a waste of energy. You couldn't do anything liberals won't eventually do until you control the Presidency. In other words, I'm not suggesting a gradual takeover, which would wear you down, compromise your program, and perhaps allow you to develop an ameliorist mentality as you got used to a little bit of influence and status. Indeed, the British Labor Party should be as sad a lesson to you as any other recent experience, and you should not repeat their failure to force a total and complete change the minute you take power. If they couldn't do it, well, you can, because once you take over the presidency in a one-election shot,

*Here I followed sacred text in calling for a new party. I did not try to figure out whether or not the two-party system could be cracked by taking over the Democratic Party.

670   or general uprising a la France (almost) in 1968, there is enough power concentrated there to accomplish drastic changes overnight. In short, the corporate rich are dependent upon the executive branch to keep their economic system from depression and collapse.

I don't mean to imply that you would only control the presidency, that you would only move on the national level. Actually, you should move on the whole system at once, for each local chapter would have developed parallel governments that would also enter elections for the first time when you decided you had the popular support to win the Presidency. All members of a given chapter would train themselves to fill some government job at local levels—they would be like the shadow cabinets of British politics only more so. The transition would be sudden—one election, and it would be total in the sense of taking money, power, and status from the corporate rich.

But what about the military, you ask? Everyone knows that any serious revolution must not only isolate the ruling social class and eliminate its economic base, but it must do away with the army that is its ultimate instrument. How is that possible in America? By keeping it a civilian, draftee army and by infiltrating its officer ranks. As long as the American army is not a standing, professional army, as long as it is made up mostly of civilian recruits serving short terms, then you have control of that army to the degree that you have the loyalty of the majority of citizens.* However, to ensure leadership, at a certain point it would become necessary for party members to sacrifice themselves, not by avoiding the draft, but by joining the ranks of military officers. If that sounds like a very great sacrifice, I agree, but perhaps it will appeal to those among you who like undercover games. Infiltration is an old trick, but the amazing thing is that most American radicals of the past have been concerned with infiltrating labor unions, the Democratic Party, everything but what needs infiltrating, which is the army.

Let me be sure I am being clear. Now is not the time to begin infiltrating the army, but at some point along the line that would become a prime task. Such infiltrators, at least perhaps in some cases, could be secret members of the party, its only secret members. Their only task would be to make sure that the corporate rich could never turn military firepower on the non-violent revolution. They would do this by advocating one thing and one thing only—the subservience of the military to civilian government, the refusal to take sides in an internal political controversy. In so doing they would be indistinguishable from non-party members within the military who truly accepted this tradition. It may be that there are many of those, but that should no be counted on.

O.K., that's action, even if it doesn't prove to unfold exactly as outlined, but who does this party address itself to as its agitators and organizers drive around on open-air trucks, complete with folk rock bands, shouting their message and distributing their handbills in every

---

*In 1970-71 the Army began to have problems with draftees in Vietnam. Some refused orders, a few killed officers.

town, county fair, ghetto, and shopping center in the country? What is its potential constituency? The answer is first of all a very general one, but this very generality frees American revolutionaries from trying to duplicate the past or fit into theoretical molds. You should direct yourself to anyone disgusted with the present system and assume that your potential constituency is everyone not wrapped up in the power elite. This even includes sons and daughters of the corporate rich who have seen enough and want out—they've always been there in small numbers on the American Left anyhow, so why pretend differently?* In other words, I'm suggesting that you not immediately begin to pander to blue collar workers because some theory says they are the key to revolution. They may be necessary or they may not, but do they have to be with the party from day one? I don't think so. Kick the Cult of the Proletariat, accept your origins and those of any converts, and look, for openers, to where the rumble is. I suggest as follows: the initial base is, as C. Wright Mills said, radical intellectuals and students. The intellectuals have got to start talking like Gene Debs and Malcolm X. They have got to blast out of the classroom and clinic like Mills and Ben Spock, carrying their revolutionary consultation services to every group in the country that will send them an airplane fare or bus ticket. What with the protection of tenure and the right of academic freedom, and with lots of universities opening up in Canada, Australia, and New Zealand, professors are the least vulnerable group in American society.** They ought to be ashamed of themselves for not raising 100 times more ruckus than they are now—just so they don't advocate anything illegal, of course. These professors and their students also have to continue work on the analysis, and begin involving people in their local community in work on the blueprints. They should form small study-action groups in every university, college, and junior college town in the country, off the campus, of course, because the revolution will not be won by cowing harmless administrators and liberal professors.

These small study-action groups have to prepare themselves for a psychic blitz of their most important constituency. That constituency is simply called youth—blue collar, white collar, blue skin, black skin, who cares? They are pouring out of schools like crazy, affluence has made them somewhat independent and hang-loose, many of them don't communicate with their parents, and people under age 25 are going to be a majority in a very few years. Catch them in those years when they are sociologically part of a unique subculture and psychologically looking for something moral and true meaningful for their lives, and sock it to them with analyses and programs that will make them as wise to the slick McCarthys, Kennedys, and Rockefellers as they are to

*Unfortunately, most try to pretend they are poor instead of figuring out how to use their position to expose the class and to speak to American underclasses in a way that impresses them and gives them confidence.

**This sentence was spoken with some little sarcasm. I recognize that professors, particularly untenured ones, are subject to considerable pressure and harrassment.

672   the Rusks, Johnsons, and Nixons. If you don't get them the first time around, don't start cursing at them; at least they have something to chew over when they get out there in the boring jobs corporate America has to offer them. I know that right now (April, 1968) an amazing number of the young are enamored of the long hair and sing-song voice of a Bobby Kennedy or the integrity and professorial cool of a Eugene McCarthy, but that's all those two birds have got—with no program but a little more of the same, wedded to corporation capitalism, and committed to a party with a reactionary Southern wing and a fistful of New York investment bankers—their time is going to run out if they can't produce. Young people react to the put-on, they hate to be fooled or talked down to or pandered to, and someday they will have had enough—they will remember Humphrey's sell-out, if you are there to remind them; they will remember Johnson's campaign fibs about his plans for Vietnam, if you never let them forget it; and they will start looking around again.

After youth, the early appeals or the party must be to the disaffected teachers, librarians, nurses, and bureaucrats of the white collar class. They are the ones hit by inflation and hurt by the limitations on government spending, not the unionized blue collar workers who often can strike for higher wages.* And besides, you've got something immediate for them—thanks to the Hippies, you can teach them how to be Happy. Happy? Yes, Happy. Get your Hippy friends out of the woods, put a light trim on their beards and hairdo's, and start them to work on the poor, wasted paper pushers and people manipulators. I'm serious. They can be had. They're going no where, they're restless, and their rage shows how jealous they really are. Their kids—using flower power and psychic guerrilla warfare, can cajole them over the line. After all, these people raised the turned-on kids. Their emptiness and searching is reflected in their children, who have to resort to modern-day ambrosias and Eastern mystical religions to overcome their boredom. If the kids can be had, the parents can be had—if you handle them with psychological bribery and good-humored taunts rather than threats and insults.**

As I've implied throughout, an effort has to be made toward those on the Right. I'm under no illusions about the difficulties of this, but I insist that it is necessary to dismiss talk about racism and fascism on the Right as if racism and authoritarianism are exclusive to this group: all white Americans are racists, and parts of the blue collar world are probably worse than the Right. As to fascism, if we get a European-style dictatorship in this country, it will probably be more like France anyway, and it will be instituted by the corporate rich presently in power in order to get around their difficulties with Congress and local governments. So forget all this talk about fascism, which has scared American revolutionaries into the laps of the liberals almost as well as the cry of communism has scared the Right into the

*This contrast can be exaggerated. I am probably guilty of that here.

**These last few sentences read almost like a fairy tale in 1971. In the spring of 1968 they didn't seem too fanciful.

arms of the corporate rich. Old Left and liberal talk about fascism amounts to their fear of angering the corporate masters to the point where they call on their supposed Right-wing shock troops. See if you can make contact with those people on the New Right, who really have no place to go because there is no turning back now that the huge corporations have destroyed individual capitalism. Of course they don't share your program, but they do share your view of the power structure and your desire for more individuality and local autonomy.

I suggest two important points in talking with this potential constituency about your blueprints. First, religion is not an issue in the U.S.A. Revolutionaries of recent times have thought it was, and that is a great tragedy. The fact is that religion was here before capitalism, it will probably be here long after capitalism, it is not a trick of the ruling class, and it is not necessarily opposed to all change in the socioeconomic sphere. True, certain organized, institutionalized aspects of religion may resist, but these aspects are not determinative in any case. They can be safely ignored, and religion can be fully respected by those who prefer transcendentalist, mystic, and humanistic expressions of their life-serving impulses. Even more, as Martin Luther King's example has reminded us once again, the New Testament has a Social Gospel that can be social dynamite; it can be a force for change as well as standpatism, and I predict that a lot of clergymen will be with you.

This point about religion is closely related to my next point in dealing with the New Right—respect for individuality and personality. Neither Left nor Right really does this despite their rhetoric. They are both in part personality cults. The fact that personality types who find different styles appealing tend to concentrate in the two different camps attests to this exclusionary bias. (Here I am relying on my own research as well as that of others who have actually studied the problem.) A revolution must transcend personality and respect individuality if it is to get to its task of reaching large masses of people. In fact, personal diversity will be an asset in getting the attention of all types of people. Different religions, different styles, and different hair arrangements must be de-emphasized (not changed), and consciously subordinated by self-analysis and devotion to common goals through the mechanism of the blueprints. The enemy is corporation capitalism, not religion, personality structure, or type of oral indulgent—pot on the Left, alcohol on the Right—used to lessen anxiety and dispel depression.

Why haven't I mentioned black people till now? Aren't they important? Am I just another Whitey who doesn't care about the black man? Not at all. I suggest that you do what the black man told you to: let him do his own thing and you get to work building a party that can unite with him someday far off down the road after you've overcome your racism and he's made up his mind about where he's going and with whom. Maybe someday your party will have a black wing and a white wing instead of a left wing and a right wing, but for now the black man is right—you've got nothing to tell him, and he's got to go it on his own with himself and "The Man" in order to win his

674   manhood. Nobody has ever been given anything worth having. Finally some black men are learning that freeing fact, and the sooner the brown man and the red man learn it, all the sooner are they going to split on that paternalistic pap and unctuous benevolence called the Democratic Party. Leave the black man alone to find out for himself— there are already plenty of would-be white revolutionaries bugging him to tears, trying to take the seemingly easy way to a small, quick success in terms of lots of militants.

Of course black people should be welcome in your party, as is anyone who shares your beliefs, but I suspect it will be awhile before many will be along. One group is going to go a separate and/or violent route. They've had enough and they will have to see some fine action from a revolutionary party before they are going to buy any dreams and hopes again. I don't blame them. I for one will never get uppity or moralistic, as so many of the liberals do, black and white, if some blacks decide to wreck the system. I understand their rage, I feel their rage, and I've always wondered why they didn't bring the whole mess to the ground. But despite my sympathy I don't mistake the catharsis of wrecking the system for changing it. Revolutionary movements grow more slowly and have positive goals. But I hope you can show these black radicals something—the one's I've watched have the juice to turn on masses like nothing I've ever seen. Malcolm X was the finest American agitator since Eugene Debs, and a revolutionary party would need a hundred more like him.

Then there's another group of blacks who are committed to non-violence but who think John F. Kennedy freed them! Imagine. Like the Socialists of the Old Left, their hang-up is a faith in the Democratic Party that knows no bounds, through thick and thin, Raw Deal and Screw Deal. Pictures of JFK abound in their homes. The tragic thing about this group is that they don't know they freed themselves— they pushed that smooth-talking young conservative to the wall before he would make a move. These people don't know their own power— they haven't quite achieved the assertiveness and pride of the black separatists. Nor do they understand the limitations of the present socioeconomic system—they are still hoping it will assimilate them economically. Apparently their faith in God and American democracy even includes corporation capitalism. Many even refuse to talk about the Vietnam war, hoping that their white masters will give them a little more if they keep their traps shut about the repression of other colored peoples.

So, one black group—the separatists—has revolutionary instincts but unlikely methods, while the other black group has great methods but the mentality of everyday members of the Democratic Party (and you can't get much more mundane than that). Perhaps by the time these two groups are done exploring their respective paths they will want to help build a revolutionary party. Your job is to have the semblance of one for them to react to if they run up against the limits of the present system.

What about blue collar workers? Well, what about them? Don't wait till they're ready to swing. If you can't make it without them, you can't make it without them, but at least have a party they have to react to. And don't waste any time trying to control or shape labor unions, which are conservative bureaucratic institutions these days, rightfully looking out for the working man in day-to-day battles with the corporate leaders. Confront these people at home, at school, and at play and get them involved in the party and its activities. In short, don't get caught in Old Left fixations.

Now I know there are many thousands of dedicated and far-seeing blue collar workers who would be with you from the start, heart and soul, sweat and tears, but don't get the idea that any great percentage of organized labor will be willing to risk leaving the Democratic Party. Right now they have it relatively good—as long as they're working, or are insulated against automation, or have cost-of-living raises built into their contracts as chcecks against inflation. But no matter how nicely some of the corporate rich treat blue collar in wartime, don't worry, because there is no question about where blue collar masses would be in a showdown if you have done your homework carefully.*

I have said what I think must be done and who will be the most likely to initially respond. Now I want to speculate on what would happen in the shortrun. When the revolutionary party started, one of three things could happen—it might be snuffed out, it might be left alone to grow very rapidly, or, forbid, it might flop. Flopping I won't consider here, because all it means is that is was the wrong time and place for your ideas; nothing ventured, nothing gained. As to being snuffed out by the corporate rich at the start, I find that highly unlikely—they are more liable to find the whole thing laughable and unbelievable, giving the new revolutionists as much free mass media coverage as they have given any other good human interest story. Then too, they are not likely to want to react violently to a non-violent party, at least not until they found it a serious threat.

Some of you may ask—wouldn't the snuffing out come from the ultra-right? Aren't they the classical perpetrators of violence against revolutionaries? Well, maybe, but I think not in corporate America. They would find it hard to bring themselves to move against a movement that shares their enemies and general values, if not their specific programs; that was in no way involved in or interested in or tied to a foreign power as most recent American radical groups have been; and that in no way attacks the American political structure or the precious right of religious freedom. Each step of the way, as I hope you realize, I've tried to take account of, react to, neutralize this New Right, this Right which is really different in its situation from all previous Rights. But if I am wrong, if they become violent, that is a job

---

*By homework I mean showing them something better and how to achieve it. They already understand what capitalism does to them . . . their problem is they've resigned themselves to it because they can't see risking a struggle they don't believe will succeed. They don't love the present economic system, but a lot of them have more to lose than they can see gaining in a vaguely defined "struggle" for abstractions like "freedom" and "justice."

676 for the police, for you too should support your local police. In fact, place all party headquarters as near as possible to police stations and FBI offices so they can better protect you, and maybe take a few stray hits themselves. In short, if violence comes early on from the Right, you must count on the power elite and the liberals to deal with them physically, thus setting the stage for the later showdown between you and the real enemy. The power elite and the liberals don't like the ultra-right one little bit anyway, and they would, I think, rather defend liberties against the Right than allow the slaughter of a minute revolution party which could be dealt with later if things got out of hand.*

But I just don't assume violence from the Right or anywhere else. To assume violence is to invite violence in the manner of the "defensive," paranoic aggression that has been the rationalization and cause of much of the violence of history. Break that vicious circle, drop your defenses, and thereby free your opponents to break out of the cycle with you. The first move is yours, and it takes a lot of guts. It requires getting close to your opponents, embracing them, and de-mythologizing their image of the "dangerous revolutionary," not to mention their image of the "Greedy Jew" and the "sexy Negro." In other words, more psychic guerrilla warfare, this time using motivational analyses borrowed from the study of unconscious and not-so-unconscious fantasies. Disarm your opponents by psyching them, by embracing them, and by constantly reminding them of their democratic, non-violent values.

So let's assume that the party is not snuffed out in its early stages and that it grows. Then the power elite is in a bind—they will have to compete with it, which means a move towards the Welfare State, or, failing that, they would have to repress it, which would be the great watershed for American liberals, liberalism, and democracy. If you are non-violent, open, of all religions, and not tied to a foreign power, they would be destroying America to move on you. Liberals would have no course but to join the fight on your side or admit that socioeconomic privileges are more basic than political institutions and values; some might even be annoyed enough to join you in the air-conditioned, music-equipped prison cells that the corporate rich are likely to provide. More generally, at that point the masses of people in America would have to draw their own conclusions about what is to be done. All bets would be off; it would be a new game. Your job is to force them to make that choice between democracy and corporation feudalism by taking the system on its promise and testing it to its limits. Either way, you win—a democratic, non-violent takeover or proof to all that when it gets down to the nitty-gritty, even in America, the only way to power is to complement the analysis and the vision of a new society with the barrel of the gun. But, I repeat, you have to assume good faith and remain non-violent—to secretly arm, or to try to

---

*The question of violence from the Right seems basic to me. I don't think most people give it enough thought, especially in a country where the ultra-Right is much larger than the Left. I fear my suggestions fall far short of dealing adequately with this problem.

goad the corporate rich into violence, is to destroy the power of your movement. In short, psychic guerrilla warfare requires as much courage and risk as the physical kind. It is no place for the fainthearted who are unwilling to die for a great cause.

To conclude, let me outline what you should do today and tomorrow if you are revolutionaries (if you are in California, wait until after the November elections so as not to undercut your many friends who are working hard in the Peace and Freedom Party). First, start a chapter of a future revolutionary party. Call it, say, the American Revolutionary Party or the 1776 Party so as to make your intention clear from the start. Then, to set the sort of tone you want for the thing, print up a membership card, something like, "I, the undersigned, am a card-carrying member of the American Revolutionary Party, dedicated to replacing corporation capitalism with a post-corporate America through psychic guerrilla warfare." Then start a chapter newsletter in which you invite people to discuss and develop blueprints for your local area—for running its schools, its beaches, its universities, its utilities, and its factories. Send particularly good ideas and articles, especially those relevant to the national level or other cities, to the editorial staff of the nationwide party journal.

At the same time, begin to hold classes in which you teach about the nature of corporation capitalism and discuss blueprints for a post-corporate America. Such educational efforts are a must, one of the few lessons to be learned from the Old Left, and they are the start of the parallel educational structure that each local chapter should strive to develop.

As soon as you have enough people in the chapter who are dedicated and know what it's all about, then you look for opportunities to reach larger numbers of people through confrontation politics— marches, rallies, sit-ins, whatever, but always including explicit mention of the party and its goals. If there is a local bond issue asking for higher property taxes to support the schools, then that's the time to show in detail how the corporate rich distort the tax structure and force the burden on the middle levels, even to the point of bribing the tax assessors in some cities. Agree with the New Right that taxes are killing them and tell them why, agree with the liberals on the need for better schools and show them how they would be in a post-corporate America. If the issue is an increase in the gasoline tax, then maybe that's the time to shock conservatives about the price manipulations and tax dodges by the pious oil companies who help finance the New Right. In short, armed with a real understanding of the present system and the beginnings of plans for a better one, you use every occasion possible to get people's attention and gain converts.

If you bother to go on campus for other than speeches to interested student groups, use picketing not to stop recruiters or Dow Chemical agents but to educate and convert more students and professors. Aside from exposing the complicity of leading universities and research institutes in the machinations of the corporate rich (which ranges from CIA involvement at MIT and Michigan State to overseas economic front men at Stanford Research Institute), your

678   main concern is elsewhere. The university is not the key structure in the system, and just exposing its uglier aspects is enough to get you a careful hearing from most students, and even some professors. In short, this advice about dealing with the universities is part of a larger strategy—ignore the corporate rich and their tag-alongs. You have no criticisms or suggestions to offer them. There is nothing they can do to satisfy you, short of joining your party. Don't try to change them and their policies. Leave that for liberals. Talk to people, don't debate with the power structure.

Now, once the party exists and has a distinct identity, you can of course support just causes. You are for anything that makes people's lives better. Making things worse is not going to speed up any "dialectic." The important thing is to show that you are for these causes without getting so caught up in them that you can't see the forest for the trees. Don't get sidetracked. Support "liberal" causes and speak kindly to and of the liberals who fight for them, but do not become the errand boys for these single-issue and short-run causes.

Once you have a good-sized local chapter, then add "politics" to your other activities. This consists of developing parallel governments and councils ready to step in if and when, and of running for legislative offices in the hopes of winning and thus gaining a better platform from which to reach people.

But action would not take place only on the local level. All the while, the many locals would be in contact through social (not, ugh, business) meetings at regional and national levels. Then too, they would contribute representatives and ideas and money to a loose national party structure which would consist mostly, at the outset, of the editorial staff of the nationwide journal and the organizers, agitators, and revolutionary consultants who would travel around the country helping to organize and strengthen locals. Every chapter would contribute a few members to this national-level effort each year, thus ensuring that a great many members from all over the country get national-level experience and perspective. This not only cross-fertilizes the locals and helps maintain an overall outlook, but it provides some basis for developing a shadow government for the national level and for the selection of candidates for national offices. During the summer the national organization would also coordinate the Student Organizing Teams who would in groups of 20 to 30 spend several weeks in every hamlet in the country carrying the message of the party to the hinterlands. The groups would be made up of those with an empathy for and knowledge of rural America, including return-to-the-land type of hippies. Their goal would be to develop a chapter, however small, in any settlement or town where people would listen, and listen they might, for the descendants of those people who became populists in the 1890s and took potshots at local bankers and judges in the 1930s are being had once again by the corporate oligarchy.

What do you do next? What do you do if the infiltration of the army is not very far along and the corporate rich attempt to suppress your fast-growing movement? Well, how should I know? And who cares? You can't expect to anticipate everything. If your analysis

is sound, if your blueprints are appealing, and if your psychic guerrilla warfare has blown the minds and ideological cover of the power
elite, then you are part of the most exciting, inspiring, and creative
thing in human history: an unstoppable mass movement *that can take
care of itself*. Power grows not out of a gun, but out of underclasses
united in a common action, underclasses armed with ideas, a vision,
and moral fervor. So armed they cannot be beaten. They will suddenly
surge ahead of their "leaders," deciding on the spot the tactical questions of how to seize state power.

The real problem for you, then, is not how to end, but how to
begin, how to get goal-oriented masses into action in such a way that
it is impossible (or too late) for the corporate rich to destroy the
revolutionary movement by violent means. And good luck, for the
enormity of the task is staggering even in contemplation.*

If I were writing the paper today (May 1971), I would suggest
a different "plan of attack" to go with the analysis and the blueprints.
I would suggest the formation of Real Democrat clubs which would
run on the blueprints in every Democratic primary from precinct
captain to president. I would by-pass all the problems of third parties
and seek to get a hearing for the most radical goals I could imagine
via the platforms of the Democratic Party. The party ideology—human
rights over property rights, etc.—is vague enough to allow anyone
under its tent, and the specific goals of the Democratic Party are
determined by victors in primaries and by the planks drawn up at
party conventions. Thus, there is no reason why Real Democrats would
be expelled for their views. Being a Democrat is easy—you just have
to register and (to have any standing) support the party's candidates.
This seems no problem to me, for if the Real Democrats lost the
primary, it would make more sense to support the moderate Democrats
than to help a neanderthal Republican by running a third-party candidate and splitting the vote (and in the process, the Democratic Party).
I feel very hesitant in making this suggestion; after all, it doesn't
sound very "radical." I confess to arriving at it by a process of elimination; all the other routes seem even more futile. But I don't think
anyone advocating "working within the Democratic Party" has tried
this particular approach in any systematic way. (My thanks to Pete
MacDowell for the idea of implementing this approach through Real
Democratic clubs.) I wouldn't want to try to defend this new suggestion very seriously, but I think it is worth discussion.

---

*It may be that there is no way to begin such a movement in a corporation-
dominated America which will make small bread-and-butter concessions and
which commands enormous technology for fighting and spying. I never thought
such a movement had much hope, but I would be less honest if I did not
admit to being even more skeptical and dubious in 1971. Old Left ideas once
again dominate radical thought, and the corporate rich are prepared to deal
harshly with any movement (violent or nonviolent) which seeks large-scale
economic changes.

Appendix:
Bringing It All Back Home

ELLEN NEIMAN AND PATRICIA STRAUSS

The first day of class in an introductory sociology course usually brings together, in a large lecture hall, a great many students with widely divergent backgrounds, interests, motivations, and abilities. Most of them are not sociology majors; they have enrolled in the course to fulfill the social science requirement of their college or department. But, discounting the effect of schedule conflicts and the inevitable problem of first-choice classes already filled, sociology is more appealing than other available social science subjects or the students would not be seated where they are. Some arrive with enthusiasm; some with vague notions of what sociology is and a vague interest in discovering more; some are just putting in their time. The instructor has an opportunity and a responsibility to allow student interest to broaden and deepen on many levels by presenting introductory sociology as more than a lecture-examination survey course. The challenge lies in the diversity of the students' goals and needs and in the nature of the subject matter itself. The material presented can be useful and contribute to a student's major interest, whether it be sociology as he now perceives it, or economics, or art, and to his life as it is and can be. The manner of coming together of student and subject matter can make the difference between a rich and a poor learning experience for teacher and learner alike.

Although most introductory sociology courses are taught by the traditional lecture-examination format, there are alternatives which can facilitate the expansion of the student's personal and academic world to include theoretical sociological concepts. If students have an opportunity in the classroom for exploration and discussion, and can directly relate themselves to the course content, learning can take place which is significant for them and which can be retained after the final examination is over. We have found that lectures and examinations can be supplemented in a way that enhances and enlivens teaching and learning and helps students become more involved in their own learning process.

The method presented here was developed and revised during three consecutive quarters of an introductory sociology course taught by Jerome Rabow and a group of undergraduate teaching assistants at the University of California in Los Angeles. The course framework consisted of one lecture a week by the instructor and small discussion groups, composed of one teaching assistant and approximately ten students, held twice weekly. In the discussion group meetings, the students, aided by their teaching assistant, began to understand and apply sociological theory to the articles and books they had read, to other learning situations, and to their own lives outside the classroom. The theories and concepts of sociology dealt with in the lectures will not be discussed in detail here. However, the lecture material formed a basis for discussion in the group meetings, and the connection between lectures, reading, and discussion must be perceived by the students if the course content is to cohere for them. When theory becomes practice in this way, when it can be argued about, when it is seen as viable in real life, it is more likely to become part of the student's own body of knowledge. Once it is understood, it can be accepted or rejected, used or discarded by the individual.

A number of steps were taken to ensure the smooth organization and operation of the discussion group meetings so they would provide the optimum medium for learning. First, the instructor decided on the number of lectures and discussion meetings per week which would be best for the presentation of the material and for the students. At the time of enrollment, each student was required to register for both the lecture *and* a discussion group at one of the various times it was offered. We found that partial registration in either the lecture or the discussion group alone created management and evaluation problems for everyone involved in conducting the course.

The next step was to make sure the groups were small, with a limit of ten to twelve students in each. (Ten or fewer students are preferable, but because sociology is a popular course, the limit may have to be raised. If the size of the group expands beyond twelve, quiet students will find nonparticipation relatively easy, and the more verbal members will dominate the sessions. An imbalance of this kind damages the group interaction process and inhibits learning for all students. Even in an ideally small group of eight to ten, interaction problems as well as problems with the course material itself, can arise. Therefore, the teaching assistants must not only have a grasp of the course content, but also some awareness of the rudiments of group dynamics, so that they can function as facilitators and as contributors of vital information during the discussion sections.)

After the number of discussion groups was determined on the basis of probable enrollment in the course, an equal number of teaching assistants was carefully chosen. Recruitment was most difficult the first time the lecture-discussion format was used. (After the initial experience with discussion groups and undergraduate teaching assistants, those students with outstanding ability in the role of facilitator and resource person can recommend others. Initially, the course instructor may know students he would like to work with, or the instructors of their sociology courses may be acquainted with students whom they can recommend. These students may in turn, be able to recommend others. Or all interested students with a predetermined grade point average or other qualifications may be invited to apply for teaching assistantships. Generally, juniors and seniors are more adequately prepared for the task, both academically and socially, than are freshmen and sophomores, but occasionally an exceptional lower classman does an outstanding job. In any event, all prospective teaching assistants should be interviewed, both to help the instructor evaluate their capabilities and to inform them of their responsibilities. If sufficient funds are not available to pay a salary to all the teaching assistants, they may be offered course credit equal to the credit received by their students. The credit can be given in the form of a selected studies course or its equivalent, if the mechanics of enrollment and credit are set up prior to registration time. In such a case, the instructor would usually determine grades for the teaching assistants on the basis of consultation with them. Grading and evaluation of the students can be the joint responsibility of the instructor and the teaching assistants. In the discussion section, evaluation should be a continuous process, but the teaching assistants can provide the instructor with a participation grade for each student two or three times during the quarter or semester. Essay examinations, consisting of questions chosen from a longer list offered earlier for study and review can be given during the course. These examinations can be graded by the teaching assistants, with supervision by the instructor.)

We found that the undergraduate teaching assistants at the University of California played a key role in the processes of social organization and learning within their discussion groups. The manner in which the students assimilated the assigned material was greatly influenced by the knowledge, preparedness, and enthusiasm of their teaching assistant. The students and their teaching assistant were responsible to each other for coming to the discussion group prepared to dig into the material and bring it to life. To do this, the teaching assistants themselves—most of whom were assuming the role for the first time—needed supervision, standards, an opportunity to discuss problems, and some group interaction of their own.

As part of the course for which they received credit, the teaching assistants met as a group for three hours once a week with Professor Rabow. Since the group was large and therefore unwieldy, it was divided into small groups of the same size as the discussion groups. The meetings served a twofold purpose. First, the teaching assistants were able to discuss problems that arose during the week and to develop possible solutions. The problems were sometimes unique and sometimes universal, but in all cases a forum for airing them was extremely helpful. Second, the articles and books to be discussed by the group during the following week were analyzed, debated, and applied to life and other learning experiences by the same method as that used with students in the groups themselves. The opportunity to compare thoughts with other highly capable students helped the teaching assisants to gain a clearer and deeper understanding of the material. During these work sessions, Professor Rabow assumed the role of the teaching assistant at a group meeting. He encouraged discussion, interpreted the material, and provided needed information, but was not a major contributor or dominant member of the group. The discussion was carried by all group members. All arrived prepared, and all were responsible to themselves and to the other group members for participating in the session.

The atmosphere in the small discussion groups led by teaching assistants for students or by the instructor for his group of teaching assistants, was one of informality and amity. The discussions were thus fruitful, the learning experiences happy and meaningful. We found that an all-day meeting of instructor and teaching assistants about a week before the course started helped the teaching assistants to know one another and started them working together in a personal, mutually interested fashion. The meeting lasted for about ten hours and included relaxing and working time. Some student teachers met each other for the first time. Some were introduced to the discussion group format for the first time. Some had already studied by the method and were able to help the novices.

The student teacher can begin to encourage and facilitate the learning of others through his role of leader in discussion group meetings in a variety of ways. He can have an unusual and exciting learning experience of his own, through preparation for his teaching assistant's tasks in group and through discussions about the course materials with his peers.

Each teaching assistant should have some basic knowledge in sociology and a readiness for learning more. Each should try to be open and caring about every group member, to help the group begin to learn together, and each should be equipped with a discussion procedure, a framework upon which the group can build its knowledge of concepts and theory, applied to and integrated with reading materials and daily life. At UCLA, two discussion methods have been used for introductory sociology. Both have been successful, dependent on student goals and needs. Both are presented here.

DISCUSSION METHOD I

An important step in implementing a successful discussion is the discussion technique itself. The technique presented here has been adapted from William Fawcett Hill's manual, *Learning Through Discussion*.[1] It is an effective method for group analysis and discussion of printed material. The terms used in outlining the major steps of the discussion method have been taken from Hill's "Group Cognitive Map," "a procedural tool which outlines an orderly sequence that a group should follow in order to learn from discussion."[2] The Group Cognitive Map consists of the following:

    1. definition of terms and concepts,

2. general statement of author's message,
3. identification of major themes or subtopics,
4. allocation of time,
5. discussion of major themes and subtopics,
6. integration of material with other knowledge,
7. application of the material,
8. evaluation of author's presentation, and
9. evaluation of group and individual performances.[3]

At the outset, there are two basic principles that the teaching assistant and the students must understand and practice. First, it is essential that each member of the group come prepared to be active in the discussion. Every individual must read the assigned material and try to understand it as fully as possible. It will often be necessary for students to read the material several times. Questions about the sections of the readings that particularly confuse or particularly interest the students can then be brought to the discussion and will be helpful to the whole group.

Second, the students must realize that they are ultimately responsible for carrying on the discussion. The teaching assistant should not lecture on the material to be covered. His major role is that of resource person, active only if the students are unable to clarify or comprehend a concept. He can augment the discussion by posing challenging questions, but the weight of the discussion should be carried by the students themselves. This requires a certain amount of patience, trust, and belief in the students' capabilities. Students should be encouraged to rely on their own resources and those of the other members of the group. The group can be as informative and interesting, and as concerned about the subject matter and each other, as the members wish to make it.

During the first discussion group meeting, before the course lectures and reading assignments are actually under way, the teaching assistant usually has an opportunity to discuss class business with his students. At that time, in addition to answering questions, he can explain the *Learning Through Discussion* procedure, the criteria for evaluation of student participation, and his expectations for the group. He should stress the importance of attending group meetings and arriving prepared for discussion. He can suggest that the students use notes or outlines of the assigned readings to help them organize and understand the author's ideas. When the discussion begins, however, books and notes should be put away, so that students can learn by speaking and listening, unencumbered by piles of paper.

Once the procedural matters are understood, the group is ready to begin the discussion. Until the students arrive at step seven of the Group Cognitive Map—application of the material—they should discuss the readings without offering their own views or opinions. They are not required to reproduce the material verbatim, but rather are asked to put the author's thoughts into their own words. The discussion at this point should not be shaped by the students' personal feelings toward either author or subject matter. During the application and evaluation, they will have an opportunity to voice their own opinions. Although this pattern may seem rigidly structured, it becomes logical and easy to handle after being practiced a few times.

The first step in the discussion is to define any terms or concepts the students may find confusing or unclear. Since basic terms and concepts are vital to the further understanding of the material, students should be encouraged to ask for definitions of even the most seemingly simple terms if they need them. Students who think that they have understood such terms may gain an even fuller comprehension of them, and those who feel they do not understand may discover they have some degree of understanding after all. It is important, however, to deal with definitions and clarifications as quickly and concisely as possible, because this step is only the first building block of the entire *Learning Through Discussion* structure, with many more to follow. If there are no requests from the students for clarification or definition, the teaching assistant may ask the group to explain a concept or word which he believes is significant, especially if the students need to understand it for continuing discussion. Sometimes, particularly at the start of the course, students have difficulty isolating troublesome or meaningful concepts, and the teaching assistant can help them develop this skill. Concept clarification is very critical for the development of a productive discussion.

The next step is the formulation of a general statement. In formulating this statement, the students should incorporate the author's major reason or reasons for writing the book or article and the basic theme of his work into one or two sentences, which should be as precise as possible. After one student has proposed a general statement, others may wish to revise and expand it. Or a student may totally disagree with the statement that was made and propose an alternative. If at all possible, the group should try to agree before proceeding to the next step. It is often necessary to incorporate several of the statements made by students into one mutually acceptable general statement.

The third step is the statement of the author's major subtopics. Sometimes the subheadings of his article may be useful for this purpose. If the subheadings are too numerous or totally absent, however, the major subtopics must be gleaned from the body of the work. There is a tendency for students to become involved in lengthy discussion of the material while they are trying to isolate the subtopics. The teaching assistant should help them state the subtopics simply at this point, so that the material can be seen as a whole before it is pulled apart in discussion. Again, the group should be in agreement before they move on to the next step.

The allocation of time is a simple process usually handled by the teaching assistant or a volunteer or appointed group leader. The purpose of this step is to ensure that there will be enough time to cover each of the remaining steps. If there is an hour remaining for the group meeting after the first three steps are completed, one practical arrangement would be to allot fifteen minutes each for the discussion of the themes, the integration, and the application, ten minutes for the evaluation of the author, and five minutes for the evaluation of the group. This scheme may vary from meeting to meeting, and need not be strictly adhered to even within one discussion session, as long as all steps of the Group Cognitive Map are covered.

During the discussion of the subtopics, the students should restate, in their own words, the author's views on a specific subtopic. It is important to remember that at this stage only the author's views are to be presented. The group members should build upon statements the other participants make and at all times feel free to ask questions about anything that is unclear. They may either question the *meaning* of another student's statement of the *validity* of it in relation to the author's actual statements. Once the discussion of the subtopics is exhausted, or when the allotted time is over, the group can move on to integration.

Integration involves the comparison of other written materials with the work that is being discussed. In presenting the supplementary materials, the students must show a plausible connection between them and the main article. The supplementary readings may either support or negate the theories, concepts, or empirical evidence that was presented in the discussion article. After several meetings, the students may compare previous course readings with the current assignment. They may also present material that they have read outside of the course. This time should also be used for connecting the broad sociological theories and concepts presented in lecture with the assigned reading. Here, again, the student should deal with the theories and viewpoints of the various authors rather than with his own opinions. He will then be in a better position to discover contradictions in the readings and to begin to develop his own hypotheses.

During the time set aside for application, group members are encouraged to offer their personal feelings and opinions. The students' responses to the reading material in relation to their own areas of concern or life experiences may involve any part of society at any point in time. Any member of the group should feel free to question, challenge, or support another student's opinion.

The evaluation of the author should encompass both positive and negative reactions. This step enables students to use and develop their critical faculties. At first, the students may find it difficult to evaluate the readings, and the teaching assistant should offer examples. One reason for postponing the evaluation of the author until the end of the discussion is to allow the students to decide whether or not their evaluations are valid after gaining a more thorough understanding of the material. A student may find that his initial reaction arose out of confusion.

The final step, evaluation of group and individual performance, is essential for continual growth of the group process. At this time, individual and group problems relating to learning sociology by the discussion method should be explored. Without prior experience in self-evaluation, group members often feel very uncomfortable in negatively evaluating other members or in being evaluated by their peers. The teaching assistant can help in the beginning by making observations and evaluations of the group, offering advice that will help the discussion move smoothly, and demonstrating that criticism, whether positive or negative, can effectively move the group members toward greater awareness of one another, mutual concern, and increased knowledge.

Student groups sometimes are better able to begin criticism and evaluation when they have a set of standards. Hill lists several criteria for efficient operation of the *Learning Through Discussion* method:[4]

1. prevalence of a warm, accepting, nonthreatening group climate
2. learning approached as a cooperative enterprise
3. learning accepted as the raison d'etre of the group
4. participation and interaction by everyone
5. leadership functions distributed
6. group sessions and the learning task enjoyable
7. material adequately and efficiently covered
8. evaluation accepted as an integral part of the group operation
9. regular attendance by members who come prepared[4]

As time goes on, group members can add to or subtract from this list, and they can even discontinue the practice of evaluating performance at every session. The evaluation procedure can then be used as needed, and group problems can often be dealt with as they occur, rather than at the end of the session. Both of these evaluation methods can be successful; the important point is that all group members try to make evaluation continuous, with an eye toward improving the learning process and increasing the store of knowledge for each student.

DISCUSSION METHOD II

A different approach to the learning of sociological theory in the discussion groups is based on the connection between the substance of sociology as the study of social organization and the students' search for relevance and for a connection between the world and themselves. The method uses *Learning Through Discussion* techniques, but is primarily related to the student's potential desire and need to read and discuss scholarly material so that he can better understand and relate to organized, scientific theories and concepts which are applicable to his own life.

The steps of the *Learning Through Discussion* Group Cognitive Map are designed to help the student focus, throughout most of the discussion, on the expressed thoughts and ideas of the author of the material, and not on his own. It is felt that ". . . groups never discover what the author has to say if they begin by giving their personal opinions."[5] However, if learning is most significant when it is directly related to the learner's own motives and purposes, then the students must be able to make a connection between the printed words and their individual and collective concerns.

At the introductory level, many sociology students have great difficulty making the connection between theory and practice when they are assigned certain readings and told to come back next time prepared to discuss the contents of an article or book. The time spent reading the material may seem wasted if the words have not spoken to anything approaching an interest or experience of the student. Often, students are unable to discuss the material adequately because it meant nothing to them when they read it, or they did not understand it and therefore were not motivated to finish it. The problem is to find a way for a student to approach his reading with enough enthusiasm and interest to sustain him through study and analysis of the material, so that he can actively participate in his group discussions and begin to make sociology part of his working body of knowledge. Examining his own social world is often a road into formal theory.

By starting the study of a major sociological area of thought with some exploration of practical applications, students can be helped to see that we all live in a world full of sociology, and they can begin to focus on the central ideas of the readings. The value of this approach can be lost, however, if there is no control over time or content in the discussion section, for participation can be reduced to conversation or disputation if there are no safeguards.

Therefore, at the end of each discussion section, a period of time is set aside for introduction of a new concept to be analyzed during the next meeting. For fifteen or twenty minutes, the group members can share their thoughts about the meaning of the concept in their lives; how it affects them and others in their world; how it manifests itself in a myriad of ways at home, at the university, and in the community. During the time allotted, the teaching assistant can give guidance to the students if they begin to wander away from the central issue, or if they need assistance in crystallizing their thought about the theory and its applications, or if they argue too much and participate too little. For a time, constraints of what the textual material *ought* to mean in their lives are removed, and students can explore the causes and effects of accepted concepts without being unduly influenced by the experts.

At the end of the first full class meeting, after discussion of chapter 1, the uses and purposes of sociology and the role of the sociologist, a short time can be given to exploring the properties of groups, which is the subject of chapter 2. The teaching assistant can start the discussion with some questions which will help the students grope their way toward some beginnings of understanding about groups: What is a group? What do groups do? Do groups have any impact on our lives? As the students answer these questions in their own way, and without using the correct terminology, they may be talking about group properties, the systematic relationships between group properties, and the impact of group properties upon individuals, which is the main thrust of the Leavitt article. The student who then reads about this can make an intimate connection between his experiences with the concept and the conceptualization of his experience. The group members will vary in their experiences and in their interest in conceptualizations of them, but these differences aid, rather than hinder, the teaching and learning process.

When the concept of power is introduced, students can make their unique contributions about resources for power, kinds of power, effects of power on those who have it and those who do not. They can express divergent views and disagreement in an open an encouraging atmosphere. They will not, at that time, be acquainted with definitions or accepted theories, but they will have ideas about the uses and abuses of power and know that they feel it and use it in some ways every day.

When the discussion sessions end, the students can go home and begin working with the assigned reading materials. They take with them ideas and shared experiences that will bring to life the concepts and theories they will read about. At the time of the next discussion section meeting, the nine steps of the Group Cognitive Map of *Learning Through Discussion* can be efficiently used by the students. During the time for application, group members can compare their early efforts to applications based on newly acquired knowledge. Again, time should be set aside at the end of the discussion to introduce the next chapter or subject and to discuss its implications.

This method encourages the student to pursue knowledge that is related to his own goals and needs as he perceives them. The growing ability to see life in a sociological way validates the material for the student. Subject matter and life's social experiences are thus unified, and the student quite naturally becomes a responsible participant in his own learning process and that of his group. Sociology, more than any other discipline, appropriately lends itself to this approach.

NOTES

1. Hill, William Fawcett, *Learning Through Discussion* (Beverly Hills, Calif.: Sage Publications, Inc., c. 1969).

2. Ibid., p. 22.

3. Ibid., p. 23.

4. Ibid., p. 41.

5. Ibid., p. 27.

DATE DUE

DATE DUE

DEC 15 '74

RETURNED 90